Win-Win Discipline

Strategies for All Discipline Problems

Dr. Spencer Kagan
Dr. Patricia Kyle
Sally Scott, M.A.

Kagan

Kagan Publishing
981 Calle Amanecer
San Clemente, CA 92673
1 (800) 933-2667
Fax: (949) 545-6301
www.KaganOnline.com

ISBN: 978-1-879097-81-0

Win-Win Discipline
Strategies for All Discipline Problems

Table of Contents

THE BUILDING BLOCKS

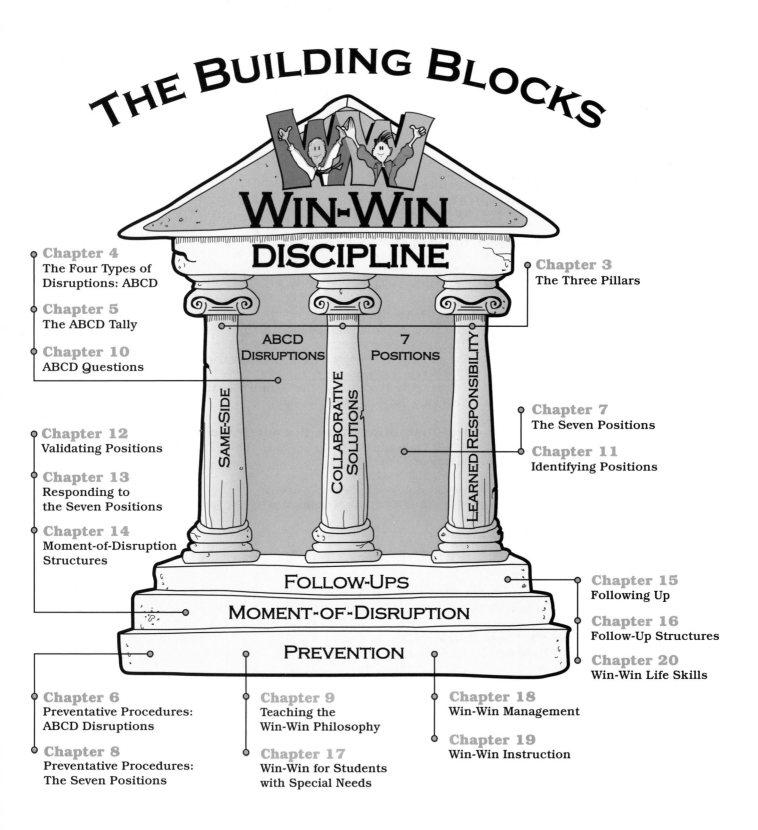

WIN-WIN DISCIPLINE

ABCD DISRUPTIONS · 7 POSITIONS

SAME-SIDE · COLLABORATIVE SOLUTIONS · LEARNED RESPONSIBILITY

FOLLOW-UPS

MOMENT-OF-DISRUPTION

PREVENTION

Win-Win Discipline. Kagan Publishing • 1 (800) 933-2667 • www.KaganOnline.com

Preventative Procedures: ABCD Disruptions

A Is for Aggression

B Is for Breaking Rules

Win-Win Discipline. Kagan Publishing • 1 (800) 933-2667 • www.KaganOnline.com

v

Preventative Procedures: ABCD Disruptions (Continued)

C Is for Confrontation

D Is for Disengagement

Preventative Procedures: The Seven Positions

Attention-Seeking

Avoiding Failure

Preventative Procedures: The Seven Positions (Continued)

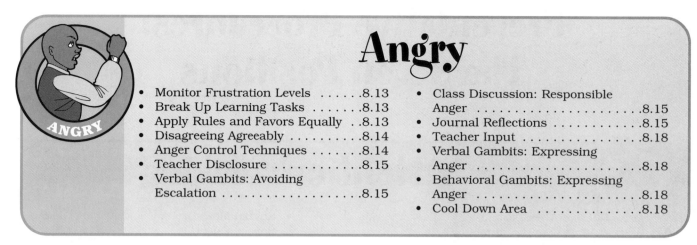

Angry

Control-Seeking

Energetic

Preventative Procedures: The Seven Positions (Continued)

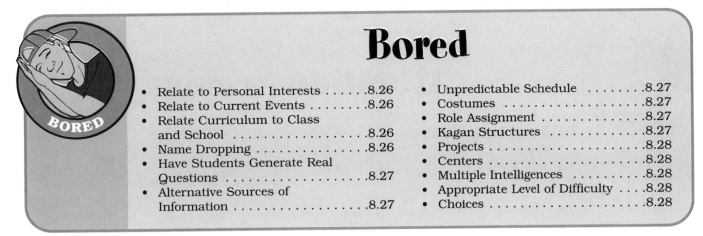

Bored

Uninformed

Moment-of-Disruption Strategies

Attention-Seeking

Avoiding Failure

Angry

Moment-of-Disruption Strategies (Continued)

Control-Seeking

Energetic

Bored

Uninformed

Moment-of-Disruption Structures

Structure	Page	Disruption Type A	B	C	D	Attention-Seeking	Avoiding Failure	Angry	Control-Seeking	Energetic	Bored	Uninformed
Acknowledge Student Power	14.12			●					●			
Consequences* • Establishing Consequences • Consequences Reminder • Implementing Consequences	14.14	●	●	●	●	○		●	●	○		
Cool Down* • Establish Cool Down Procedures • Cool Down Reminder • Implement Cool Down	14.27	●		○				●				
Coupons* • Establish Coupons • Implement Coupons	14.35		●			●				○		
Cues: Verbal & Non-verbal*	14.39	○	●	○	○	●		○	○	○		●
Expectation Reminder*	14.42	○	●	○	○	●		○		○		●
Grandma's Rule	14.45			○	●	○	○		○	○	●	○
I-Messages Plus	14.47	●	○	●	○	○		●	●	○	○	○
Language of Choice	14.50	●	○	●	○	○		●	●	○	○	○
Make a Better Choice	14.53	●	○		○	●	●	●		●	●	
Model It!	14.56	○	●	○	○	●		○		○		●

Moment-of-Disruption Structures (Continued)

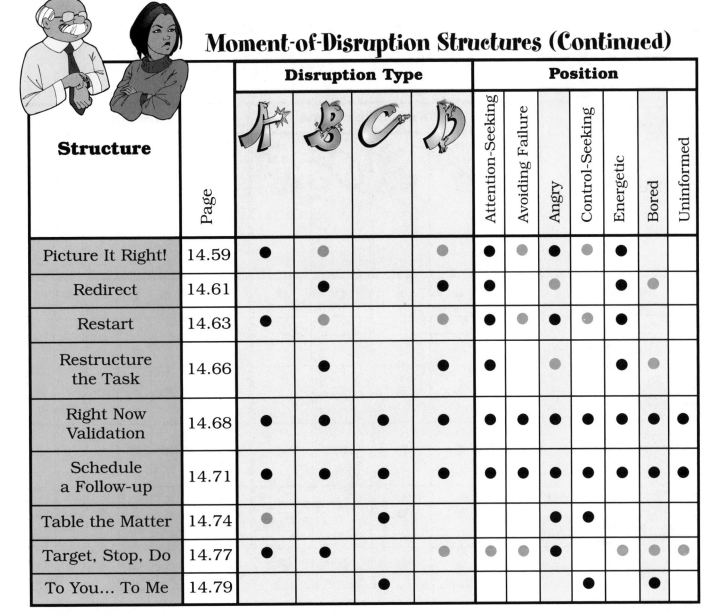

Structure	Page	Disruption Type				Position						
		A	B	C	D	Attention-Seeking	Avoiding Failure	Angry	Control-Seeking	Energetic	Bored	Uninformed
Picture It Right!	14.59	●	○		○	●	○	●	○	●		
Redirect	14.61		●		●	●		○		●	○	
Restart	14.63	●	○		○	●	○	●	○	●		
Restructure the Task	14.66		●		●	●		○		●	○	
Right Now Validation	14.68	●	●	●	●	●	●	●	●	●	●	●
Schedule a Follow-up	14.71	●	●	●	●	●	●	●	●	●	●	●
Table the Matter	14.74	○		●					●	●		
Target, Stop, Do	14.77	●	●		○	○	○	●		○	○	○
To You... To Me	14.79			●					●		●	

* = These structures need pre-established procedures.
● = Most useful functions
○ = Recommended

Follow-Up Structures

Structure	Page	Disruption Type				Position						
		A	B	C	D	Attention-Seeking	Avoiding Failure	Angry	Control-Seeking	Energetic	Bored	Uninformed
Contracts	16.5	●	○	●	○	○	○	●	●	●	○	○
Parent Conference	16.9											
Re-establish Expectations	16.12	●	●	○		○	○	●	○	○		●
Replacement Behavior	16.17	●	○	○	○	●	○	●	○	○	○	○
Responsible Thinking	16.22	○	●	○	○	○	○	●	○	○	○	○
Same-Side Chat	16.26	○	○	○	○	●	○	○	●	○	○	○

● = Most useful functions
○ = Recommended

Win-Win Discipline. Kagan Publishing • 1 (800) 933-2667 • www.KaganOnline.com

Index of Win-Win Structures and Strategies

Index of Win-Win Structures and Strategies (Continued)

Index of Win-Win Structures and Strategies (Continued)

Preface: History and Appreciations

History. Over five years ago I began work on Win-Win Discipline. The concept sprang from my experience with cooperative learning. We had discovered that when teachers, schools, or districts implemented cooperative learning, the incidence of discipline problems decreased. "What is your new discipline program?" the vice principal would ask. "We have not instituted a new discipline program," I would respond. "Oh yes, the vice principal would insist, you must have, the number of referrals has decreased dramatically."

As I analyzed this, I realized cooperative learning was preventing disruptive classroom behaviors by going "with" rather than "against" students. In the traditional classroom teachers work hard to keep students from moving, seeking attention, and talking. Students who pursue those needs by getting out of their seats, calling out an answer, or whispering or passing notes, are seen as discipline problems. Teachers using our cooperative learning structures include plenty of movement, peer attention, and social interaction as part of every lesson. So the needs of students are met on a regular basis; they do not have to become disruptive to meet their needs. It is a win-win: Students get their needs met, are more engaged, and learn more; teachers win too, they are free to teach with fewer disruptions.

As my thinking about this progressed, the need for a comprehensive Win-Win Discipline program crystallized. I realized that if we systematically analyzed the needs of students and the types of disruptions they engaged in, we could systematically create and implement preventative procedures and strategies for the moment-of-disruption that meet students' needs, or better yet, teach students to meet their own needs responsibly.

It was at that point that I invited Patti Kyle and Sally Scott to collaborate with me on a book, Win-Win Discipline. Patti and Sally both had spent a good part of their professional careers specializing in creating and implementing discipline solutions. When we first met, I had us brainstorm all the types of disruptive classroom behaviors. Little colored Post-its® covered the table. Then we categorized the behaviors. The ABCD category system eventually emerged. Next, we turned to brainstorming all the reasons students might engage in those disruptive behaviors. The positions, named and renamed, defined and redefined, final-

Win-Win Discipline. Kagan Publishing • 1 (800) 933-2667 • www.KaganOnline.com

xviii

ly took their final form. (For some time we worked with six positions; it was Sally who kept asking, "What about the kid who simply acts in school the way he acts at home, not knowing the rules of the game at school are different?" — The uninformed position emerged, to complete the set of seven.)

Next, we turned to solutions. As a former clinical psychologist, I was very comfortable leading our discussions about the need to look beyond behavior to the places from which behavior springs, and the nature of positions. When we turned to classroom discipline solutions, however, I felt inadequate. I kept asking Patti and Sally, "What would you do with the kid who...?" They gave me their responses. Some were well-established discipline procedures; others were creative inventions — honed through years of experience.

Eventually the basic framework was created and we began training teachers in Win-Win Discipline. Sally was the lead trainer and trainer of trainers. It was the night before her first one-week Win-Win Institute at our annual Summer Academy that one of the biggest breakthroughs occurred. Sally approached me in near panic! Having been for years a cooperative learning trainer, she knew the power of Kagan Structures. They were step-by-step sequences that made training and implementation easy. Sally said, "We can't train discipline the way others train it; we need Win-Win Discipline Structures!" It was at that moment, frantically, that we began a process that took years to perfect: Developing what the teacher does and says at each step of implementing each discipline structure. We were doing for discipline what we had done for cooperative learning — giving teachers concrete, repeatable, step-by-step sequences tailored to produce specific types of learning. The Win-Win Structures proved to be easy to learn, easy to implement, and tremendously powerful.

Over the years additional structures were designed. The first structures were traditional discipline approaches like **Acknowledge Student Power, I Messages,** and **To You... To Me.** As the program progressed traditional structures were tweaked to better align with the Win-Win philosophy (**I Messages,** for example, became **I Messages Plus**) and many novel structures were invented to implement Win-Win. Rather than imposing discipline solutions on students, we had students **Make a Better Choice** or **Picture It Right. Same-Side Chat** emerged as the most powerful of all discipline structures.

In the process of seeking Win-Win solutions, we were redefining discipline. Discipline was no longer something a teacher did to a student; it was something a student acquired. Never satisfied with ending disruptions, we aimed at teaching students autonomous responsibility. Ending a disruption helped for a moment; teaching students to meet their own needs responsibly

Win-Win Discipline. Kagan Publishing • 1 (800) 933-2667 • www.KaganOnline.com

xix

was a skill for a lifetime, ending future disruptions. Consistently successful Win-Win solutions can be created only if we respond to the unique needs of each student. Any one-size-fits-all discipline program is hit-and-miss because students are in different positions and a strategy that works well with one fails miserably with another. Win-Win Discipline does for discipline what differentiated instruction does for instruction — it shows us how to tailor our responses to the position of the student. In the process, the role of the teacher is transformed: The teacher is not a disciplinarian, but rather a facilitator. The teacher helps the student acquire skills for a lifetime.

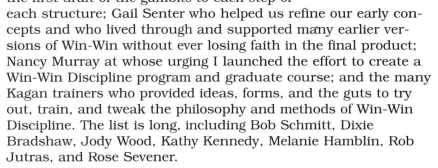

Appreciations. Many people have contributed to Win-Win Discipline. I want to express my appreciation to Sally Scott who has taken the lead in translating the philosophy and strategies into exciting workshops; Patti Kyle who brought many traditional approaches to discipline to our initial discussions and who wrote a partial, very rough draft of a number of the chapters; Liz Warner who worked with Sally to write the first draft of the gambits to each step of each structure; Gail Senter who helped us refine our early concepts and who lived through and supported many earlier versions of Win-Win without ever losing faith in the final product; Nancy Murray at whose urging I launched the effort to create a Win-Win Discipline program and graduate course; and the many Kagan trainers who provided ideas, forms, and the guts to try out, train, and tweak the philosophy and methods of Win-Win Discipline. The list is long, including Bob Schmitt, Dixie Bradshaw, Jody Wood, Kathy Kennedy, Melanie Hamblin, Rob Jutras, and Rose Sevener.

Miguel Kagan made substantive suggestions on many chapters and contributed text to the Special Needs chapter. Miguel also designed the layout for the book and guided its progress from manuscript to finished product. JoAnne Putnam, one of the nation's leading experts on inclusion, made many formative comments on my first draft of the Special Needs chapter. Thomas Lickona, one of the nation's leading experts on character education, made many formative comments on my first draft of the character education section of the Life Skills chapter.

Dave Sanders, my faithful assistant, took many burdens off my back. Dave in his magical way located obscure references and resources; created tables, forms, and the index; deciphered my handwritten corrections and inserts; checked and re-checked tables, put the footnotes into style, and acted as liaison with teachers, trainers, Patti Kyle, and the publications department at Kagan. Dave, thank you for allowing me to focus on what I do best.

Miles Richey did the page layout for the book and surprised and delighted me with his creative input. Tony Swagler made the pages come along with his talented illustrations; Tony tells the Win-Win story through his artistic intelligence. Celso Rodriguez designed the Win-Win logo that adorns the cover and the ABCD icons that give voice to letters. Jackie Jacobs read the entire manuscript and made innumerable editing and wording suggestions on the first draft. Kim Fields provided final editing, polishing this final draft.

I have left until next to last expressing my appreciation to the person who has most supported me as I struggled for years to create this book — my wife. Laurie Kagan put up with my moods — my highs, my lows, and my occasional tantrums when I realized there were years of work in front of me. She carved out space for me to work on the seemingly never-ending project, running interference when other things threatened to distract. Laurie, like always, put her needs aside, focusing on the goal of improving life for students and teachers. Laurie made many substantive contributions as well. Not only did she invent and co-invent with me and Sally Win-Win Structures (**Restart, Picture It Right, Make A Better Choice**), she was the one who sent me back to my computer time and again to come back with a better draft as she and Sally struggled to create user-friendly Win-Win training materials. Without Laurie, Win-Win Discipline would have remained mere ruminations.

Finally, I would like to express my appreciation to the hundreds of teachers who have now gone through our Win-Win workshops and institutes. First, thank you for your patience as you waited for this long-promised book. Second, thank you for your support. So many of you have told me how the Win-Win Discipline training has given you a new set of lenses and that now you see your students and others in a whole new light. When you tell me that Win-Win has changed you as a teacher and as a person, I am rewarded beyond words.

Spencer Kagan
Reno, Nevada
March 1, 2004

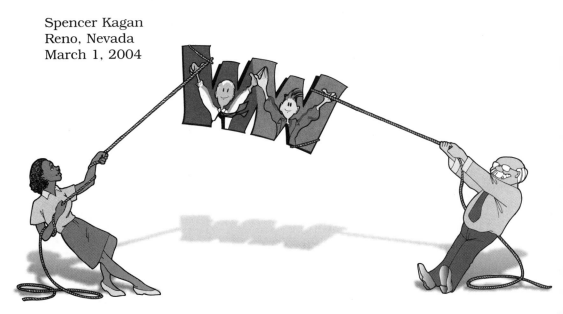

Chapter 1

Welcome to Win-Win Discipline

Welcome to Win-Win Discipline. In this book, you will find a philosophy for dealing with classroom disruptions and concrete, step-by-step strategies to make that philosophy a reality in any classroom.

The philosophy is transformative. Participants in our Win-Win Discipline Institutes regularly report that Win-Win has changed their lives. Not only has it given them new lenses through which to view their students and their role as educators; it has actually revolutionized their relations with their own children and spouses. Participants report their interactions in supermarkets and at the bank are transformed! Things appear very different when viewed through the Win-Win lenses, and when we put on those lenses, we become someone different. Win-Win looks beyond behavior to the place from which the behavior springs, and with that perspective, suddenly we understand others and relate to them in a very different way. Win-Win changes who we are.

The Three Types of Win-Win Strategies

1 **Preventative Procedures:** What to do before disruptions occur to prevent them.

2 **Structures for the Moment-of-Disruption:** What to do in the moment-of-disruption to end the disruption and to make future disruptions less likely.

3 **Follow-Ups:** What to do following disruptions to convert them into learning opportunities for students.

The strategies are carefully crafted and classroom proven. They eliminate and end disruptions, but that is not the ultimate goal of Win-Win Discipline. Win-Win looks beyond the disruptions and converts disruptions into opportunities to teach the disruptive student more responsible behaviors for the classroom and for life.

Win-Win Discipline. Kagan Publishing • 1 (800) 933-2667 • www.KaganOnline.com

When you adopt Win-Win Discipline, discipline itself becomes something fresh, positive: **Discipline is not something you do to a student; it is something you help a student acquire.**

Win-Win Premises

There are some very simple ideas in this book:

- Almost all disruptions can be categorized into four types, ABCD.

- Almost all disruptions spring from one of seven student positions.

- Positions are part of the universal human condition.

- We never accept disruptive behaviors, but we always accept and validate positions.

- In attempts to meet the needs of their positions, students sometimes engage in disruptive behaviors.

- Our job as Win-Win teachers is to teach students responsible alternatives to disruptive behaviors, how to meet their needs in responsible ways, so they win and we win.

- The ultimate goal of a discipline program is not ending disruptions, but teaching autonomous responsibility.

As simple as these ideas are, they are transformative. We welcome you to try them — to discover a simple way to convert discipline problems into learning opportunities — to be the teacher you were meant to be.

Win-Win Discipline puts us back into the role for which we entered our profession — to teach, to help students become all they can be.

Welcome to Win-Win.

Chapter 2

The Building Blocks of Win-Win Discipline

Win-Win Discipline is a fresh approach to classroom discipline. It treats discipline the way the dictionary defines discipline. It is designed to help students acquire discipline — responsible behavior patterns to meet their needs. Once this happens, their need for disruptive behavior drops away.

Dis-ci-pline
Training expected to produce a specific character or pattern of behavior, especially training that produces moral or mental improvement.
—American Heritage Dictionary

In Win-Win Discipline, every disruption is viewed by the teacher as a learning opportunity — a teachable moment. Disruptions are guideposts. They tell us what kinds of responsible behaviors students need to learn — what needs to be taught. Disruptions by students are often immature, undisciplined, self-defeating attempts to meet a need. When the student learns mature, responsible ways to meet those needs, *the student wins:* the student gets his/her needs met without becoming a discipline problem. The *teacher and class win:* They become part of a productive learning environment, without disruptions. Thus the name, "Win-Win."

The essence of Win-Win Discipline is symbolized by the building blocks illustrated at right:

The Three Pillars

The most important building blocks are the three pillars that support Win-Win Discipline. The pillars are essential; they support all we do in Win-Win. If the pillars are not in place, our attempt to build a Win-Win Discipline program collapses.

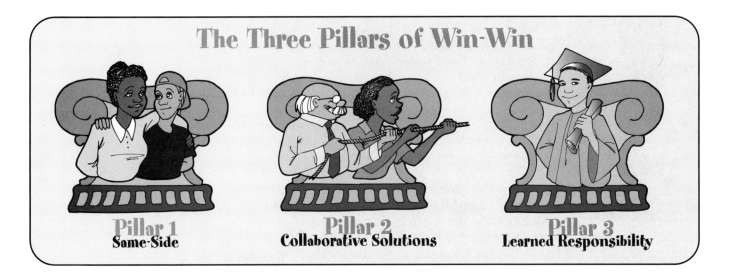

The Three Pillars of Win-Win

Pillar 1
Same-Side

Pillar 2
Collaborative Solutions

Pillar 3
Learned Responsibility

The pillars embody the philosophy of Win-Win Discipline, both the vision and how to realize the vision. The ultimate goal is learned responsibility. The way to reach that goal is to adopt a same-side orientation with students and share with them responsibility for creating discipline solutions.

Same-Side: The teacher feels and communicates to the disruptive student that the teacher is on the same-side with the student, wants to team up with the student, identifies with the student, and understands where the student is coming from.

Collaborative Solutions: The student and teacher share the responsibility of co-creating discipline solutions. The discipline solution is not imposed on the student. It is something the student helps create.

Learned Responsibility: The discipline solution leads to critical new learning for the student. The student learns more responsible behaviors to meet his/her needs, so disruptions are less likely in the future. This third pillar, Learned Responsibility, is the ultimate goal of Win-Win Discipline. Win-Win aims not at merely ending disruptions; it aims at teaching positive, responsible behaviors. Win-Win is a positive educational program.

Although the three pillars of Win-Win are simple, they are powerful and transformative. The three pillars allow us to view our students and ourselves through a new set of lenses. Through the lenses of Win-Win, discipline methods that previously appeared adequate appear inadequate. For example, discipline strategies and approaches that aim at ending disruptions, even when they work, are viewed as inadequate if they do not result in students learning more responsible behavior.

A common discipline trick is to use proximity; that is, to stand close by a student who is off task or disruptive. Although proximity might work well to end a disruption, it does not teach a student autonomous responsibility. If we stop at ending disruptions, we need to pin a note on the student at the end of the school year that reads: "This student needs proximity!" Win-Win goes beyond the stopgap approach of ending disruptions – it teaches autonomous responsibility. At the end of the school year students emerging from a Win-Win classroom need no notes pinned on them. They are not just *behaving* responsibly; they have *become* responsible.

When the focus is on ending disruptions, paradoxically, we fail to end disruptions. In schools that adopt disruption-ending discipline programs, many of the same students are discipline problems throughout the course of their entire schooling experience. When the same students are disruptive each year, it is a signal that our discipline program is short-sighted. Too often we have ignored that signal, failing to refocus on the true aim of a successful discipline program — fostering autonomous responsible thinking and behavior.

The Same-Side and Collaborative Solutions pillars support the goal of Win-Win: acquisition of learned responsibility. Adopting a same-side orientation and sharing the responsibility for creating discipline solutions support learning because students do not resist the suggestions by someone they perceive to be genuinely on their side. Students identify with and own solutions they have helped create. If they do not perceive the teacher to be "on their side," they will resist the discipline solution and are likely to resist as well the academic learnings the teacher offers. Discipline solutions that are imposed on a student without the student's input may work in the moment to end a disruption. In the long run, though, they are self-defeating. They fail to teach responsibility and almost always generate resentment, which will surface at a later time in a different way as one more disruption. No one wants to be manipulated, treated as an object. When the Win-Win teacher communicates that he/she understands and accepts where the student is coming from, it elevates the discipline process. The teacher's understanding helps the student accept his/her own needs. Students are then more willing to seek responsible ways of meeting their needs rather than acting them out in disruptive ways.

- For an in-depth presentation of the three pillars, see
Chapter 3. The Three Pillars.

2.4

Win-Win Discipline. Kagan Publishing • 1 (800) 933-2667 • www.KaganOnline.com

The ABCD Disruptions

One of the important discoveries of Win-Win Discipline is that almost all disruptive behavior can be classified into one of four types: ABCD. Almost all disruptive behavior is either Aggression, Breaking the Rules, Confronting the Teacher, or Disengagement.

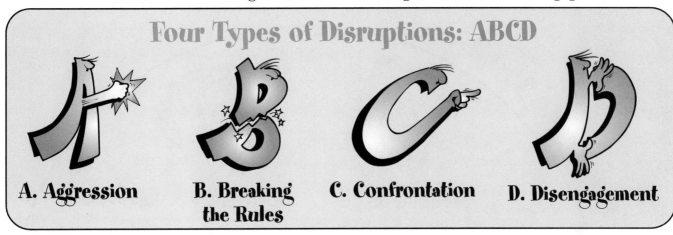

Four Types of Disruptions: ABCD

A. Aggression **B. Breaking the Rules** **C. Confrontation** **D. Disengagement**

Why is it important to understand the ABCD's of disruptive behavior? We need to respond to each type of disruptive behavior very differently. If a student or class is aggressive, the student or class probably needs to learn cool down procedures, conflict resolution strategies and/or how to disagree politely. If they are often breaking the rules, we need to re-teach the rules or go back to basics and help students see how rules help us reach our goals as a class. If confrontation is the issue, acknowledging student power or a same-side chat may be in order. If students are frequently disengaged, we need to re-examine our curriculum and instruction: Is our curriculum developmentally appropriate? Are we using proven, engaging instructional strategies?

Understanding the ABCD's of Disruptions are signposts directing us to effective responses in the moment-of-disruption as well as appropriate preventative procedures.

- For an in-depth presentation of the ABCD Disruptions, see Chapter 4. The Four Types of Disruptions: ABCD.

The Seven Positions

How do we get to Win-Win outcomes? Outcomes that meet the needs of disruptive students while meeting the teacher's need to teach and for all students to learn? At essence it is simple: Win-Win Discipline is based on the concept of "Positions." Almost every disruption springs from an attempt to meet needs associated with one of seven positions. Positions are "the place a student is at." For example, the student who is constantly asking questions, clowning around, has something to add to everyone else's comment, makes strange noises, blurts out, and dresses loudly, is almost certainly in a position of seeking attention. Attention-

Seeking is one the seven positions identified in Win-Win Discipline.

Once we see disruptive behavior as merely an attempt to meet the needs associated with a position, our job becomes clear. The student needs to learn non-disruptive ways to meet those needs.

The Seven Positions

1. Attention-Seeking

2. Avoiding Failure

3. Angry

4. Control-Seeking

5. Energetic

6. Bored

7. Uninformed

When that happens, the student wins: he/she gets needs met without becoming a discipline problem and learns responsible behavior for life. We win also, and so does the rest of the class: we become part of a smooth-running, productive learning community.

As Win-Win teachers, we always accept a student's position. Positions are part of the universal human condition. All of us, one time or another, have been in each of the seven positions:

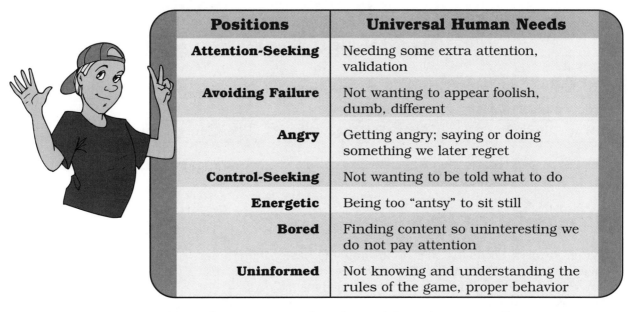

Positions	Universal Human Needs
Attention-Seeking	Needing some extra attention, validation
Avoiding Failure	Not wanting to appear foolish, dumb, different
Angry	Getting angry; saying or doing something we later regret
Control-Seeking	Not wanting to be told what to do
Energetic	Being too "antsy" to sit still
Bored	Finding content so uninteresting we do not pay attention
Uninformed	Not knowing and understanding the rules of the game, proper behavior

Discipline programs that do not take into account the seven positions are bound to have a hit-or-miss outcome. Why? Because a preventative strategy or response to a disruption that works perfectly for a student seeking attention may not work at all for the student who is too energetic to sit still or for a student who simply does not understand the class rules or procedures. We can only reach win-win solutions if the student is part of the formula. We need to understand the student's position if we are to formulate effective discipline solutions.

There is nothing wrong with being angry, bored, or in any of the other positions. The positions are part of the universal human condition. The question is: What do we do when we are in a position? Do we have mature, responsible ways of dealing with the needs of the position, or are we disruptive to others? If we do not have mature ways to deal with our needs, we resort to disruptive behaviors in primitive attempts to meet our needs. When, as teachers, we understand the position of the disruptive student, we can work with the student to help him/her learn more responsible ways to meet his/her needs. Win-Win Discipline transforms the discipline process. Rather than punishing or controlling students, the goal of Win-Win is to empower students with important new learnings. Win-Win Discipline makes discipline synonymous with what we as teachers do best — teach.

- For ways to recognize The Seven Positions see **Chapter 7. The Seven Positions.**

Disruptive Behaviors vs. Positions

	Disruptive Behaviors	Positions
What is it?	What Students Do	Why They Do It
Where does it come from?	Attempt to Meet Needs	Rooted in Human Condition
How do we recognize it?	Observable	Inferred
Win-Win Philosophy	Disruption Not Accepted	Position Validated

Preventative Procedures

When student needs are met on an ongoing basis, there is less need to become disruptive. Win-Win Preventative Procedures are everyday ways of meeting student needs — creating a more responsive classroom. We all need attention. If the classroom is structured so every student gets positive attention on a regular basis, there is less need for students to act out. We all have energy. If there are positive ways to express that energy, there will be fewer disruptions.

So Win-Win Preventative Procedures are put in place even before students enter class, and are maintained on an ongoing basis every day. Win-Win Procedures are simple, but make a huge difference. They are the many ounces of prevention of Win-Win Discipline. A teacher who greets students by name as they enter class each day has gone a long way to ensure students will not need to act out to get attention. A teacher who uses instructional strategies that include movement has a more energized class and is less likely to experience disturbances that spring from the need to express energy. A teacher who provides students choices allows students to fill their need for control so they don't need to become disruptive to assert their ability to control. When Win-Win Preventative Procedures are in place, most discipline problems disappear.

Win-Win provides eleven sets of Preventative Procedures, one set for each of the four disruptive behaviors, and one set for each of the seven positions.

- For procedures to prevent each of the four types of disruptive behaviors, see **Chapter 6. Preventative Procedures: ABCD Disruptions.**
- For procedures to prevent disruptions springing from each of the seven student positions, see **Chapter 8. Preventative Procedures: The Seven Positions.**

Strategies and Structures for the Moment-of-Disruption

In the moment-of-disruption, it is a life-saver to have ready-made strategies and structures. Moment-of-disruption strategies are simple responses any teacher can easily use; structures are step-by-step proven response sequences that structure the interaction of the student with the teacher and/or curriculum. For example, a simple often-used **strategy** to meet the need of the student seeking attention or to get a disengaged student to focus is to use the student's name in an example. A powerful **structure** is Make a Better Choice. Make a Better Choice is a four-step structure. The teacher tells the student to: 1) Stop the disruptive behavior; 2) Think of a better choice; 3) Verbalize the better choice; and 4) Act on the better choice. Once a teacher has practiced the Make a Better Choice structure a few times, it becomes automatic in the face of certain kinds of disruptions.

Win-Win Discipline offers scores of strategies and twenty-one carefully crafted structures for the moment-of-disruption. Win-Win provides guidelines as to which structures to use for each of the ABCD Disruptions and for each of the Seven Positions. Win-Win offers the most comprehensive collection of discipline strategies and structures of any discipline program. Why so many strategies and structures? Because Win-Win is based on the premise that discipline responses must match student disruptions and position. A strategy that is perfect for one student is a total failure for another. Why? Students are in different positions and have different needs. Intelligent selection of appropriate strategies for the moment-of-disruption and beyond are the most important skills of a Win-Win teacher.

> **When the only tool you have is a hammer, every problem begins to resemble a nail.**
> —*Abraham Maslow*

- For ways to respond to ABCD disruptions, see **Chapter 10. ABCD Questions.**
- For ways to respond to disruptions springing from each of the seven positions, see **Chapter 13. Responding to the Seven Positions.**
- For a step-by-step presentation of Moment-of-disruption Structures, see **Chapter 14. Moment-of-Disruption Structures.**

Follow-Ups

Follow-Ups are meetings or chats with individual students or the whole class following a disruption. Often in the moment-of-disruption, it is clear that one or more of the three pillars have not been put in place. For example, if a student is being aggressive, the teacher might respond with a Target, Stop, Do. That is, the teacher might simply say, "Jake! Stop shoving! What you need to do right now is keep your hands to yourself!" Although a Target, Stop, Do ended the disruption, there was no indication the teacher was on the same-side with the student and there was no shared responsibility and probably no learned responsibility. Ending a disruption is fine. But if, over time, a Win-Win teacher finds the three pillars are not in place with a student, the teacher will have a follow-up with the student. A follow-up is not called for after each disruption, even if the pillars are not in place. But if, over time, it is clear we are not making progress in putting the pillars in place, a follow-up is in order. For example: a Same-Side Chat is helpful to put the Same-Side Pillar in place; a Replacement Behavior follow-up might be used to put the Shared Responsibility pillar in place; a Responsible Thinking follow-up may be what is needed to foster Learned Responsibility.

- For when and how to follow up, see **Chapter 15. Following Up.**
- For a step-by-step presentation of follow-up structures, see **Chapter 16. Follow-Up Structures.**

Special Needs

Students with special needs at different times are in any of the seven positions, just like all students. There are, however, connections between special needs and student positions as well as types of disruptive behavior. For example, students classified as ADHD more often than other students are disengaged, coming from a position of being energetic. Like with all students the Win-Win teacher accepts the position of students classified as having special needs, but does not accept disruptive behavior. The Win-Win teacher works with students with special needs so they can learn non-disruptive ways to meet their needs. Win-Win offers unique ways to meet the legal requirements of special education legislation and is especially powerful in meeting special needs.

- For an exploration of Win-Win approaches to special needs, and special needs legislation, see **Chapter 17. Win-Win for Students with Special Needs.**

Win-Win Management, Instruction, and Life Skills

Management. Teachers who manage their classrooms efficiently and with a Win-Win approach have far fewer discipline problems because there is less down-time to breed disruptions and the management helps students meet their needs without being disruptive. For example, a teacher who takes role by calling students' names one-at-a-time creates boredom and opportunity for disruptions; the teacher that uses an attendance board to automatically take role eliminates both the boredom and the temptation for disruptions. To take another example, as a Win-Win teacher uses class meetings to make important decisions, students see a model of treating one another with respect, and fill their need for control.

- For a presentation of a host of Win-Win Management techniques, see **Chapter 18. Win-Win Management.**

Instruction. Instructional strategies, too, can be more or less efficient and can meet or fail to meet students needs. For example, a teacher who uses classbuilding structures to practice academic content meets the needs of energetic students to move without losing time off academics. A teacher who has students learn and use the Sum-the-Ranks decision-making structure avoids conflicts and resentments, and meets the students' needs for control.

- For Win-Win approaches to Instruction, see **Chapter 19. Win-Win Instruction.**

Life Skills. There are many life skills that are responsible ways to meet needs. Once learned, they reduce classroom discipline problems, but more importantly, they empower students for life. Students need to learn to disagree politely, create challenges for themselves when bored, break difficult tasks into bite-sized pieces, make optimistic attributions, control anger, acquire character virtues, and develop emotional intelligences, to name just a few of the important Win-Win life skills.

- For a presentation of Life Skills, see **Chapter 20. Win-Win Life Skills.**

Win-Win = New Lenses

Win-Win Discipline provides step-by-step methods for preventing disruptions, categorizing disruptive behaviors, identifying the student positions, and selecting the appropriate response to convert disruptions into learning opportunities. A preview of Win-Win, though, would not be complete without conveying the transformative power of Win-Win Discipline. When Win-Win Discipline is fully understood and mastered, it changes how we view discipline, disruptive students, and even our role as educators. Win-Win is a new set of lenses. It provides us with a vision. Once we put on the Win-Win lenses, everything looks different:

The Disruptive Student. Through the lenses of Win-Win Discipline, the disruptive student no longer looks like a bad kid but, rather, a kid struggling in ineffective ways to meet needs associated with the universal human condition.

The Disruptive Act. When we put on the Win-Win Discipline lenses, the disruptive act no longer appears like an obstacle to the teaching-learning process but, rather, a clue as to what needs to be taught. We actually see the disruptive act as a teaching-learning opportunity. Through the lenses of Win-Win, every disruption is a learning opportunity.

Discipline Strategies. The three pillars of Win-Win Discipline help us view discipline strategies quite differently, more critically. With those lenses in place, we look for discipline strategies that really serve to teach students long-term responsibility. Some apparently effective strategies appear ineffective when viewed through Win-Win lenses because they do not place the teacher and student on the same-side, do not engage the student in producing solutions, and/or do not result in learned responsibility. Although giving students a stern look may serve well in the moment-of-disruption to get them to stop disruptive behaviors, the stern look does nothing to teach the students more appropriate ways to meet their needs. As Win-Win Discipline teachers, we strive for far more than a bag of tricks to end disruptions. We strive to achieve the ultimate goal of being a teacher — to bring forth from each student his/her very best.

Discipline. Win-Win Discipline does not view discipline as an attempt by the teacher to punish or control disruptive behavior. Rather, discipline is an attempt by the teacher to help students acquire discipline — to add to their repertoire of skills for a lifetime to deal with the needs associated with the human condition. Win-Win Discipline goes back to the root meaning of discipline: training that produces moral or mental improvement.

Win-Win = New Opportunities

Win-Win Discipline offers new opportunities to teachers. It frees teachers from most discipline problems through preventative procedures (see **Chapters 6. Preventative Procedures: ABCD Disruptions,** and **8. Preventative Procedures: The Seven Positions**), and it provides concrete, step-by-step structures to deal with those discipline problems that are not prevented. It frees teachers to do what teachers do best — teach!

Win-Win Discipline offers new opportunities to students. In important ways, the disruptive student is a victim of his/her disruptive behavior. The disruptive student does poorly in school. More importantly yet, the disruptive student is a slave to his/her losing behavior pattern. Win-Win actually liberates disruptive students.

The Win-Win Process transforms disruptions, discipline problems, into learning opportunities. For the disruptive students, it offers the most important learning they can master. Many disruptive students are unhappy, struggling in immature, irresponsible ways to meet needs. As long as the student is engaged in that struggle, the student is unhappy. Once the student has learned responsible, mature ways to meet those needs, he/she is free to enjoy academic learning, and take his/her place as a responsible citizen. Learning responsible ways to meet our needs liberates us. The Win-Win teacher frees the disruptive student from the need to be disruptive and in the process gives the student an opportunity to be happy.

Throughout our lifetimes, we will have moments when we need attention, become angry, or need to gain control of our lives. Each of the seven positions has associated needs. There is nothing wrong with having those needs. Whether or not we will be successful in life, however, hinges to a large extent on our acquiring a repertoire of mature, responsible, effective, non-disruptive behaviors to meet those needs. Win-Win Discipline is designed to provide disruptive students skills for a lifetime.

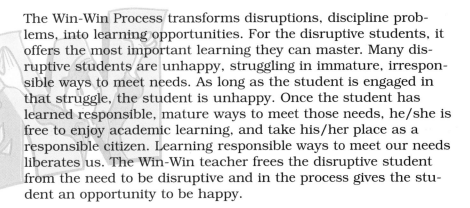

Win-Win Building Blocks: Why So Many Blocks?

Win-Win Discipline is a very comprehensive program, dealing with four types of disruptive behaviors, seven student positions, cues and indicators to identify the seven positions, and strategies and structures to use before, during, and after a disruption. In addition it provides links to instruction, management, and life skills. It is reasonable to ask: *Why so many building blocks? Is all this necessary?*

The answer: Yes. The starting point for most beginning teachers in discipline is *What do I do when the student does X?* Although having effective responses for the moment-of-disruption is essential, the experienced teacher knows the student is much less likely to do X if there had been engaging instruction, efficient management, life skill instruction, and/or any number of preventative procedures. Each of the building blocks to effective discipline contributes to reducing the incidence of disruptions, so a comprehensive discipline program must consider them all. We present the strategies and structures of Win-Win Discipline here with full knowledge that even the very best and most experienced teacher will not use them all. They are resources to draw from, to come back to repeatedly over the course of a teaching career. Win-Win Discipline is not a program we put in place and then are finished; it is an approach we continually build. The perfect discipline program has never been implemented. The skills of crafting successful discipline responses is always a work in

Win-Win Discipline. Kagan Publishing • 1 (800) 933-2667 • www.KaganOnline.com

2.13

progress. Win-Win Discipline is a philosophy and set of strategies from which we draw as we continually improve our skills.

For teachers plagued with discipline problems, the most empowering building blocks of the Win-Win approach to discipline are its concrete, step-by-step strategies and structures. Win-Win Discipline offers concrete *before, during, and after* discipline strategies. It emphasizes the before part of the formula; that is, Win-Win Discipline is based on the premise that students are disruptive primarily in attempts to meet unfulfilled needs, and that if we structure our classrooms so those needs are satisfied on a regular basis, the students do not need to be disruptive. This proposition is simple, yet it is transformative. Students who otherwise would be disruptive are near model students when we implement the proactive, preventative Win-Win procedures. Win-Win recognizes, though, that in spite of our best efforts to prevent discipline problems, disruptions will occur. That is where the *during* part of the formula comes in. Win-Win provides a process to respond successfully in the moment-of-disruption. Whereas one-size-fits-all discipline programs have hit-and-miss outcomes, Win-Win is successful with all discipline problems because it tailors the intervention to the behavior and position of the disruptive student. A strategy that works well with one student fails with another because the students are in different positions. Recognizing this, Win-Win tailors the response in the moment-of-disruption to the position of the student. Finally, Win-Win follows up. *After* the disruption, Win-Win Discipline implements follow-up procedures as well as life skills programs to ensure that the disruptive student learns autonomous, responsible behavior, so the need for a discipline program disappears. Idealistic? Pie-in-the-sky? Yes. But realistic and down-to-earth? YES!

2.14

Win-Win Discipline. Kagan Publishing • 1 (800) 933-2667 • www.KaganOnline.com

Win-Lose vs. Win-Win Discipline

Win-Lose Discipline	Win-Win Discipline
Only one side wins	Everybody wins – students, teachers, parents, and administrators
"Me versus you" approach; student and teacher are adversaries	"We" approach; teachers and students are allies
Discipline done to students, imposed	Discipline is collaborative, acquired
Discipline is controlling behavior	Discipline is teaching responsible behavior
Disruptive behavior viewed as misbehavior, bad	Disruptive behavior is viewed as attempt to meet needs, a learning opportunity
Mainly short-term solutions	Long-term solutions as well as structures for the moment-of-disruption
Strategies without a how, when, and with whom	Differentiated structures geared to the type of disruptive behavior and the position of the student
Limited options	Comprehensive: many strategies to match teacher style and student position
Lack of connection between discipline choices and teaching	Emphasis on discipline link with curriculum, instruction, and management
Parent and community not emphasized	Parent and community alliances emphasized

The Building Blocks

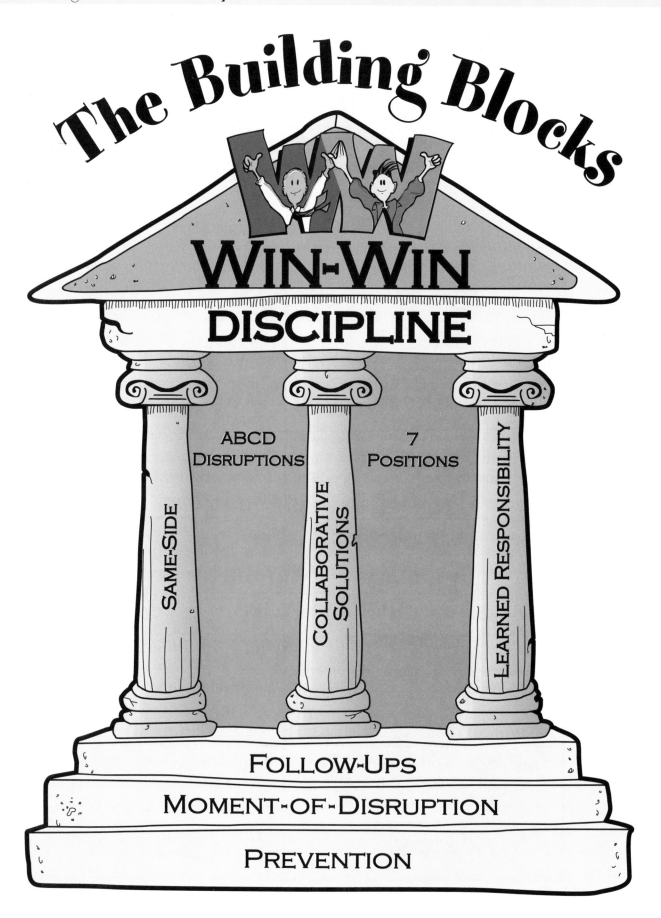

The Three Pillars

Win-Win Discipline is built on three pillars. The pillars are the philosophy of Win-Win. The tools of Win-Win — the procedures and structures — are just an expression of this philosophy. When we understand the three pillars of Win-Win, the necessity of identifying and responding to student behaviors and positions with a range of carefully crafted Win-Win procedures and structures becomes clear. The three pillars are:

- **Same-Side**
- **Collaborative Solutions**
- **Learned Responsibility**

Pillar I. Same-Side

The Win-Win teacher accepts the position of the disruptive student while rejecting the disruptive behavior. A Win-Win teacher understands that all of us at one time or another:

Pillar 1
Same-Side

- need some extra attention
- try to avoid embarrassment
- get so angry we do things we later regret
- need to feel we are in control of our lives
- have so much energy we can't sit quietly
- get bored
- simply do not know the rules of the game

The Win-Win teacher understands that the seven student positions are part of the universal human condition. We have all been there. There is nothing wrong with being in a position; often we do not have a choice as to the position in which we find ourselves in a given moment. We can, however, choose what we do about the position we are in, and we can learn to take care of the needs associated with our positions without being disruptive to others.

3.2

Win-Win Discipline. Kagan Publishing • 1 (800) 933-2667 • www.KaganOnline.com

Thus, the Win-Win teacher is empathetic and feels himself/herself to be on the same-side with the disruptive student. The position of the Win-Win teacher is

> **"I understand where you are."**
> **"I've been there too."**
> **"We've all been there."**

The Win-Win teacher communicates an understanding for positions in a variety of ways. As preventative procedures, the teacher might give a bit of extra attention to a student, do a five-minute energizer with the whole class to burn off excess energy, take an extra moment to make sure a student understands rules or procedures, or use any number of the dozens of Win-Win Preventative Procedures. In the moment-of-disruption and afterwards, the Win-Win teacher uses structures like Right Now Validation, To You... To Me, and Same-Side Chat to communicate an understanding and acceptance of student positions. In these ways, the Win-Win teacher creates a "We" environment. The Win-Win philosophy is *"We are in this together to create a win-win leaning environment for all."* The essence of the first pillar of Win-Win Discipline, Same-Side, is that the teacher and students are in a cooperative rather than adversarial relationship.

The Win-Win teacher looks beyond the disruptive behavior, seeing and validating the position from which it springs. From this perspective, disruptive behavior is usually an immature or irresponsible attempt to meet the needs associated with a position. The Win-Win teacher, while not accepting the disruptive behavior, identifies with the disruptive student and wants to help the student meet his/her needs in a more mature, responsible way.

Disruptive ways of meeting needs may work in the short-run, as when the class clown is able to grab everyone's attention. If anger has built up sufficiently, it may feel great in the moment to hit someone, but in the long run, impulsive and aggressive behaviors are self-defeating; they lead to poor school performance and inability to maintain satisfying long-term relationships. The Win-Win teacher wants disruptive students to learn ways of relating which are adaptive in the long run — which will serve students well for life. Win-Win Discipline is in part a program to develop skills for life.

> *A really great teacher is someone who...* **tries to look at it from your point of view every time you do something crazy.**
> —*Wan Ling, 14, Surabaya, Indonesia*[1]

Benefits of the Same-Side Pillar

- The teacher communicates and models respect and understanding.

- The teacher creates a "We" feeling so students are less likely to be confrontational.

- The teacher fills the student's need for recognition and attention.

- The teacher opens student/teacher communication and more fully understands the position of the student.

- The teacher is in a position to team up with the student to co-create discipline solutions.

Pillar II. Collaborative Solutions

The essence of the second pillar is to actively involve students in creating discipline solutions: Collaborative Solutions.

Students participate in generating discipline solutions. Discipline is done *"with,"* not *"to"* the students.

Pillar 2
Collaborative Solutions

Sharing responsibility for the discipline solution is fundamental to Win-Win and occurs at many levels. As part of prevention, students participate in creating class rules and expectations. In the moment-of-disruption, they are asked to help envision solutions through Win-Win structures like Picture It Right and Make a Better Choice.

Often in the moment-of-disruption there is not time to work together with a student to create a solution to the discipline problem. If over time a sense of shared responsibility is not established, then the Win-Win teacher can follow up with the student. Many of the Win-Win Follow-up Structures engage students in generating discipline solutions: Together with the teacher students co-create contracts and consequences. Follow-ups are designed to foster responsible behavior and thinking.

Although the Collaborative Solutions Pillar is very important, it is important to note that the ultimate authority for discipline rests with the teacher. The Win-Win teacher does not abdicate responsibility for creating a discipline solution. The teacher knows, however, that the best solutions to discipline problems result from collaborative involvement with students.

> *A really great teacher is someone who...* **will listen and talk to you and will help you no matter what.**
> —*Christina, 12, Medora, Indiana*[2]

Benefits of the Collaborative Solutions Pillar

- Students are much more willing to adhere to a rule or norm they have helped create.

- During collaborative involvement in solving the problem, students focus on the need for the solution and can more fully identify with and embrace the solution.

- Co-creation of solutions is especially helpful in meeting the needs of students seeking a sense of control. When students seek control, they are predisposed to oppose any solution they did not participate in creating because it feels imposed upon them.

- The true needs of students emerge in the process of collaborating to solve discipline problems.

- A positive atmosphere in the class is created as teacher and students work together, reinforcing the Same-Side pillar.

- The teacher is viewed not as an adversary, but as a friend.

- Democracy, caring, and mutual respect are modeled.

Pillar III. Learned Responsibility

**Pillar 3
Learned Responsibility**

Effective discipline results in long-term learned responsible behavior. The third pillar, Learned Responsibility, emphasizes the ultimate goal of Win-Win Discipline: self-management and autonomous, proactive life skills. Many discipline programs are satisfied if disruptive behavior is controlled or eliminated in the moment-of-disruption. Not so with Win-Win Discipline.

There are many discipline tricks that will control behavior in the moment-of-disruption, but do nothing to help students learn responsible ways of meeting the needs associated with their positions. For example, a student makes silly noises to get the attention of the teacher or class. In that moment the teacher can do any number of things to make sure the student will stop making silly noises.

The teacher could:

- Put the student on the spot: *"Sue, how would you answer the question of...."*
- Put the student down: *"Sue, you really sound grown-up when you make those noises."*
- Use the student as an example in the content: *"Now let's say Sue was faced with the problem of...."*
- Stand next to the student.

These tricks might work well to end the disruption in the moment, either through intimidation, embarrassment, or by meeting the needs of the student in the moment. Nevertheless, these discipline strategies in isolation are not Win-Win solutions. They do not meet the standards of the third pillar of Win-Win: Learned Responsibility. While ending the disruption in the moment, these stopgap measures have done nothing to teach the student more responsible ways to meet his/her needs in the future. In fact, these discipline tricks may well result in more disruptions later because they have served to reinforce the disruptive behavior — the student has learned that he/she can get extra attention or help by being disruptive.

Discipline tricks that do not help the student learn responsible ways to meet his/her needs are stopgap solutions that leave the disruptive student likely to be disruptive the next time a need arises. In contrast, Win-Win solutions emphasize learning new, more responsible ways to meet one's needs, so disruptive behaviors are less likely to arise in the future.

To determine if the pillar of Learned Responsibility has been respected, the teacher need only ask the Pin-A-Note Question: "When I send him off to next year's teacher, do I need to pin a note on him saying which discipline tricks work best?" For example, a student has been making silly noises and the teacher rightly assesses that the student is seeking attention. To end the disruptions the teacher uses proximity (stands by the student) and/or name-dropping (uses the student's name while continuing with the instruction). These methods work and the student stops making silly noises. The teacher then asks himself/herself the "Pin-A-Note Question."

In our example, the answer is Yes! The note would read, *"When Johnny makes silly noises, just use proximity or name-dropping!"* The teacher must "Pin-A-Note" because there has been no learned responsibility. When the third pillar of Win-Win Discipline is respected, the student learns autonomous, non-disruptive ways of meeting the needs associated with his/her position and the answer to the Pin-A-Note Question is a resounding No!

Pin-a-Note Question.

"When I send Johnny off to next year's teacher, do I need to pin a note on him?"

Learned Responsibility and Academic Success

When students learn responsible behavior, they learn the academic content more readily. The skills of learning responsibility and learning content cannot be separated. As a student learns more responsible behavior, the student has more skills to apply to content learning. We are not detracting from our primary mission of teaching content when we focus on teaching responsible behavior; rather, we are facilitating the learning of the content areas.

Think for a moment of the skills that students need to master: math, reading, social studies, and science. Among others, they need to be able to:

- Listen
- Pay attention
- Follow directions
- Persevere
- Finish tasks
- Work independently
- Ask appropriate questions

These are the skills of responsible behaviors! Responsible behaviors and responsible learning are intertwined. Neither stands alone. As we teach students the skills of responsible behavior, we are teaching them the skills of being a good student. The Win-Win Discipline process improves academic achievement not only because it eliminates disruptions, but also because responsibility skills transfer.

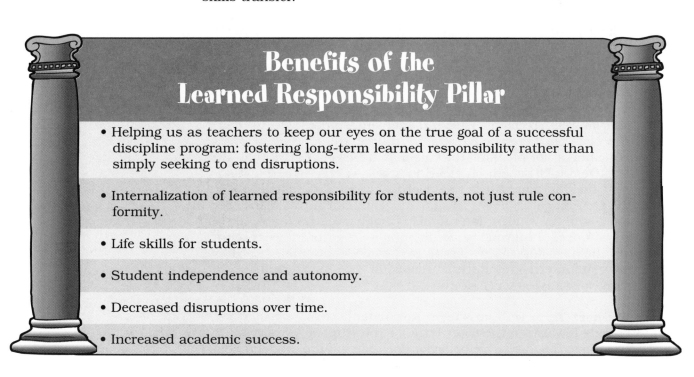

Benefits of the Learned Responsibility Pillar

- Helping us as teachers to keep our eyes on the true goal of a successful discipline program: fostering long-term learned responsibility rather than simply seeking to end disruptions.

- Internalization of learned responsibility for students, not just rule conformity.

- Life skills for students.

- Student independence and autonomy.

- Decreased disruptions over time.

- Increased academic success.

Learned Responsibility Is a Process

Learned Responsibility does not happen over night. Disruptive students face the most difficult types of learning. Why is it so difficult to learn responsible behavior?

1. Unlearning. Unlearning is far more difficult than learning something for the first time. Not long ago my daughter changed her name. She was "Monica" for 26 years and then decided to become "Kamala." I am having a devil of a time respecting her desire to be called Kamala because every time I see her, "Hi Mona" pops out of my mouth. It is at that point that I realize my error and correct myself. How much easier it would have been if only we had named her Kamala from the start! Disruptive students are in the same tough position: They don't have the luxury of turning back time to learn responsible ways to meet their needs during their initial years of social interaction; they have to do the tough job of unlearning disruptive behavior patterns. To become responsible every disruptive student has to struggle with unlearning old habits. This is a process, and so we must be patient.

2. External Reinforcement. Most disruptive students have a powerful history of reinforcement driving their disruptive behavior. For example, let's say a student has a need for attention and then engages in some attention-getting antic. This works to get them attention from both teacher and peers. Even if it is negative attention, in the moment his/her need for attention has been filled and the student has been reinforced for the disruptive behavior. To become responsible, the student has to resist this reinforcement history and learn not to repeat it. It is only human nature to continually repeat behavior that has been reinforced.

3. Internal Reinforcement. Disruptive students have received a second type of reinforcement for their disruptive behavior — internal reinforcement. When an energetic student gets up and sharpens his/her pencil for the third time, the reprimand or punishment for breaking the rule may be less powerful than the positive reinforcement of releasing excess energy. When a student seeking control tells the teacher "I won't do the homework," the student gets a powerful rush of feeling in control. When we work with the student later to help him/her learn more adaptive ways to feel in control, we are fighting a powerful internal reinforcement history. Many disruptive behaviors are maintained by powerful internal reinforcers because in the short-term the behavior satisfies basic needs.

4. Short-Term vs. Long-Term Rewards. Disruptive behaviors provide rewards in the short-term for the student, even if in the long-term the disruptive behavior does not get the student what he/she wants. Turning down short-term rewards in favor of long-term gains is very difficult, as anyone trying to lose weight

3.8

Win-Win Discipline. Kagan Publishing • 1 (800) 933-2667 • www.KaganOnline.com

can tell you. It is hard to delay gratification — turn down that piece of candy in the moment in hopes of eventually shedding unwanted pounds. It is the same for disruptive behavior patterns. In the short-term it is difficult not to make the jesting comment or to jab a peer, knowing it will provide immediate attention or establish a feeling of control. We have the difficult task of helping students see that in the long run doing well academically will garner more positive attention and feeling of control.

5. Procedural Memory. Procedural memories are routines we can carry out without conscious effort. Think about how you can carry on a conversation or listen to a radio program while driving — you can do so because driving has become a procedural memory. Procedural memories are maintained in deep structures in the brain and are very resistant to modification. Unfortunately, some students have engaged in certain kinds of disruptive behaviors often enough for those behavior sequences to become procedural memories. Without conscious forethought, the student needing attention makes a clown-like comment or gesture; without thinking, the student seeking control gives a peer a put-down. These well-established behavior sequences take great effort to modify. So again, in working with disruptive students we must be patient and understanding. Even if the student consciously wants to change, he/she may exhibit a disruptive behavior sequence without realizing it.

6. Emotion-Driven Impulses. Powerful emotions drive most disruptive behavior. For example, the release of energy or anger is associated with powerful physiological processes. Brain research tells us that emotional learning is especially potent. When a student has learned ways to deal with the emotional impulses, even disruptive ways, that learning is especially difficult to unlearn.

7. Identity Shifts. Students adopt styles to meet the needs associated with their positions. The student who is often in an angry position develops an aggressive style; the student who is often seeking control develops a dominant, controlling style. Styles become part of who we are. Thus, learning non-disruptive behaviors for some students is a task no less than redefining themselves. Identity shifts are very difficult and usually occur only over time and only with plenty of support.

Given all these difficulties, we must realize from the outset that learned responsibility is a process, and we must be patient and supportive with the disruptive student. Learning to validate oneself rather than seeking attention from others is a lifelong process, but as Win-Win teachers, we can help all students learn, no matter where they are in this process.

Our role in fostering learned responsibility is to mediate a transition from disruptive to responsible ways of meeting needs. Our orientation toward the student is a critical element in this transition. A student who is seeking attention from others needs to learn to validate himself/herself. If through Win-Win procedures and structures we can create an environment rich in validation from peers and teacher, the student eventually internalizes that orientation. The student moves from dependence on external validation to internal validation, adopting the orientation toward self that is modeled by teacher and peers. This transition, though, is a long-term process and we cannot demand or expect immediate change in orientation toward self. Although we can and often must demand immediate change in disruptive behavior, we are patient in fostering change in self-orientation.

The process occurs for each position. A student who is seeking control is given many choices. Only over time does the student internalize the feeling of control and then does not have to prove he/she has control by controlling others or refusing to accept assignments. Again, although our ultimate goal is an autonomous sense of internal control, we help the student get there through teacher-mediated behaviors, including providing students with an environment rich in choices.

The rest of this book provides procedures, structures, follow-ups, and programs to help students along the path from irresponsible behaviors to autonomous responsible behaviors. Discipline is not what a teacher does to a student — it is the responsibility skills the teacher helps a student acquire.

> *A really great teacher is someone who...* **believes in you and understands you.**
> —*Lisa Ann, 12, Perth, Western Australia*[5]

The Learned Responsibility Process

Disruptive Orientation	Teacher-Mediation	Responsible Orientation
Student Attempts to Fulfill Needs Through Disruptive Behaviors	*Student Needs Fulfilled Through Teacher-Initiated Procedures and Structures*	*Student Needs Fulfilled Through Autonomous Responsible Behaviors*
Attention-Seeking	Teacher provides attention and helps student gain attention through responsible behaviors.	**Self-Validation**
Avoiding Embarrassment	Teacher structures tasks for success and helps student transform "I can't" messages into "I can."	**Self-Confidence**
Anger-Venting	Teacher helps student deal with angry feelings in responsible ways.	**Self-Control**
Control-Seeking	Teacher provides choices and helps students internalize a sense of choice.	**Self-Determination**
Energetic	Teacher helps student channel energy into learning tasks.	**Self-Directing**
Bored	Teacher provides engaging, developmentally appropriate curriculum and instruction linked to student interest.	**Self-Motivated**
Uninformed	Teacher informs student of appropriate behaviors.	**Self-Informing**

Three Approaches to Discipline

The three pillars are a philosophy. They are an orientation. When we assume a same-side orientation toward students and collaboratively seek solutions that will meet their needs and the needs of others, they learn responsibility for a lifetime. The Win-Win philosophy is a balanced approach. It is not Win-Lose (teacher wins at expense of students) and also not Lose-Win (teacher loses while students get their way). The Win-Lose teacher imposes a rigid disciple code, ignoring the positions of the students. In the long run this Win-Lose approach results in a lose-lose as students disrespect a teacher not sensitive to their needs. They may sabotage the lesson and/or rebel. In contrast, the Lose-Win teacher is so permissive in attempting to meet the needs of students that the teacher loses control of the class-room. This too becomes a lose-lose as the teacher is unable to teach, and students fail to learn. In the Win-Win classroom stu-dents' needs are considered, but so too are the teacher's needs to teach and maintain control of the classroom. A Win-Win solu-tion considers everyone's position.

• For a summary of the difference in the three approaches, see Three Approaches to Discipline on the following page.

Three Approaches to Discipline		
1	**2**	**3**
Win-Lose Discipline	**Lose-Win Discipline**	**Win-Win Discipline**

Three Approaches to Discipline

	Win-Lose	Lose-Win	Win-Win
Attitudes & Feelings	Teacher: "I'm in control!" Students: "Let's get out of here." Student position discounted Teacher disrespects students	Teacher: "Students can do what they want," or "Kids will be kids." Students: "We are in control." Teacher's needs are discounted	Teacher: "I'm able to teach. Power is not an issue. Teaching is rewarding." Students: "We get to learn. Class is enjoyable. We are respected and cared for." Needs of teacher and student respected
Teacher/Student Relationship	Student vs. teacher No positive relationship with student Negativity Formal: no sharing or caring Students shut down	Teacher permissive, may try to befriend students Teacher begs and pleads Students ignore teacher Students disrespect teacher	Mutual respect, understanding Cooperative Caring Validating
Class Climate	Cold　　　　　Negative Stale　　　　　Impersonal Isolating　　　　Restrictive Harsh Revolt brewing	Wild Out of control Students as loud as they want Students play, have fun, eat, throw airplanes, listen to music, leave room	Happy　　　　　Positive Motivated　　　　Active Productive　　　　Collaborative Safe　　　　　Focused but fun Teachers and students working toward a common goal
Management & Discipline	Structured, rigid management Students to office Frequent write-ups No conferencing Public humiliation	Unstructured, loose management Lack of consequences Students not on task, not following rules Students make rules; students in control	Proactive, preventative Students become self-monitoring, learn self-control Respectful – no public humiliation Positive peer pressure
Curriculum	Textbook driven Worksheets Lack of differentiation Lack of links to student interests or needs	Students in control — get teacher off track Content not relevant to students or standards Standards not clearly articulated, not being reached	Relevant to students' interests and needs Standards driven Engaging Accessible to all students; differentiated
Instruction & Assessment	Lecture Students bored Note taking No multiple intelligences No cooperative learning Rigid right/wrong testing	Students not listening Students engaged, talking, having fun, but not listening and not learning Lack of objective assessment	Lively interaction; variety of teaching methods Frequent processing Differentiated instruction Cooperative learning Checking for understanding Multiple intelligences; multiple approaches to assessment
Three Pillars	No Same-Side No Collaborative Solutions No Learned Responsibility	No Same-Side No Collaborative Solutions No Learned Responsibility	Same-Side Collaborative Solutions Learned Responsibility
Outcome	Students may learn, but hate school Students may rebel Students feel punished Teacher tired, isolated	Students act out, fail to learn Students feel abandoned Teacher is depressed, helpless, frustrated, disempowered, burned-out, in denial	Students learn and love learning Increased achievement, self-esteem Inclusion; mutual respect Teacher enjoys students and teaching

The Pillars Support Win-Win

All of Win-Win Discipline is based on three pillars. The three pillars provide a powerful new way of supporting the transition among students to autonomous responsible behavior. Students are seldom disruptive when they know the teacher is on their side, working with them to solve problems, helping them learn valuable skills to serve them for a lifetime. The three pillars communicate caring, love, and foster development of responsible thinking and behavior. The pillars help us as teachers keep focused on our true mission: to provide students with learning opportunities which will serve them well when we are no longer part of their lives. When the three pillars are firmly in place, good discipline is synonymous with good teaching. Our job is to foster learning. And what more important life skill can students acquire than learning responsibility? With the pillars in mind we are not satisfied with getting a disruptive student to stop being disruptive. We go way beyond that, obtaining a deep understanding of where our students are coming from to help them learn skills to responsibly meet their needs, not just in the moment, but for a lifetime.

References

[1-5] Bluestein, J. (Ed.) *Mentors, Masters, and Mrs MacGregor: Stories of Teachers Making a Difference.* Deerfield Beach, FL: Health Communications, Inc., 1995, pp. 114, 315, 115, 215, 269.

Chapter 4

The Four Types of Disruptions: ABCD

- **Johnny punches José.**
- **Susie comes into class chewing gum.**
- **Maria shouts at the teacher, "You don't know everything!"**
- **Leon is doodling during lecture.**

Each of these students is engaged in disruptive behavior — behavior that keeps them and/or others from learning. A discipline problem is any behavior that disrupts the learning process — a sign that discipline needs to be learned. Johnny, Susie, Maria, and Leon are engaging in the kinds of behaviors any discipline program must address.

But each of the four students is engaged in a different type of disruption, calling for a different response. Obviously, when a student is doodling, it does little good to remind him/her of the rule prohibiting chewing gum in class. Similarly, more efficient management methods are not the indicated discipline response when a student is confronting the teacher. Rule reminders do help prevent rule breaking; effective management methods do help prevent disengagement. A differentiated disciple program is not "one response fits all." A Win-Win teacher responds to different types of disruptive behaviors with different discipline strategies, strategies which address the need expressed by the disruptive behavior.

The Four Types of Disruptions

A Is for Aggression

B Is for Breaking Rules

So, a starting point of any good discipline program has to be distinguishing different types of disruptive behaviors. An extremely useful way to differentiate disruptive behaviors is a simple ABCD category system:

Once we know the type of disruption, we can select appropriate discipline responses. More importantly, we can put in place procedures and programs that prevent those disruptions. The ABCD system is easy to remember and easy to work with. The ABCD system works for categorizing discipline problems for both individuals and for the class as a whole. It is a guide, pointing to appropriate responses in the moment-of-disruption, as well as appropriate preventative procedures and programs.

Classifying Disruptions: Two Rules

The ABCD classification system is very simple. There are only two rules to remember:

- **Three Before B**
- **Teacher-Directed Aggression = Confrontation**

Rule 1: Three Before B. Use the Breaking the Rules category only as a last resort. We use the Breaking the Rules category only if a disruptive behavior does not fit one of the other three categories.

ABCD categories are not mutually exclusive. When a student hits another student, the student is breaking a rule *and* is aggressive. When a student goes to sleep during class, the student is breaking a rule *and* is disengaged. How then do we classify the behavior? Follow this rule: **Three Before B.**

*Use the **Breaking the Rules** category only if the behavior does not fit any of the other three categories.*

C Is for **Confrontation**

D Is for **Disengagement**

The reason we try first to classify the behavior as Aggression, Confrontation, or Disengagement is that those categories are more specific. Breaking the Rules covers many things, so it gives us the least amount of information. Knowing a student is Aggressive gives us much more information about how to respond in the moment-of-disruption than does knowing the student is Breaking a Rule.

Rule 2: Teacher-Directed Aggression = Confrontation. A teacher says, "Your assignment tonight is the problems on pages 10 through 12." A student calls out, "You B----!"

Swearing at someone is always aggression, but refusing to accept an assignment from the teacher is also a confrontation. How shall we classify this disruption? The rule is: ***Classify aggression toward the teacher as confrontation.***

Aggression toward the teacher is usually a form of protest. We have very different strategies for preventing and dealing with confrontation than preventing and dealing with aggression. When there is aggression toward the teacher, more often than not we will be more successful responding to the confrontation than the aggression (unless of course there is a threat to someone's safety). Why? Learning to control one's aggression does not deal with the problem. It controls only the symptom. If the student is in conflict with the teacher, the most fundamental issue is preventing and dealing with the confrontation. If we are successful in that, the aggression disappears.

*Use the **Aggression** category for all aggression except Teacher-Directed Aggression. Teacher-Directed Aggression = Confrontation.*

Why Classify?

Responding Appropriately. The most important reason to classify behavior, of course, is that it indicates the best ways to respond. We need to respond to a confrontation differently than disengagement or aggression. Once we have classified the disruptive behavior, we can ask behavior-specific questions that direct us to appropriate ways to respond. For example, when a student is aggressive, our first concern is for safety — safety of other students, as well as the safety of the disruptive student and ourselves. When a student is not engaged, our first concern is making the curriculum and instruction developmentally appropriate, relevant, and engaging. As we will see, asking and responding to those questions is fundamental to Win-Win Discipline.

Being Specific. Because the ABCD system focuses on behavior, it provides specific information. To say a student is disrespectful does not give us enough information about what the student is actually doing. The student could have intentionally broken school property (aggressive behavior), interrupted the

Reasons to Classify Disruptions

1. **Responding Appropriately**
2. **Being Specific**
3. **Being Objective**
4. **Communicating**
5. **Making It Manageable**

lesson by repeatedly sharpening his/her pencil (breaking a rule), argued with the teacher (confrontation), or put his/her head on the desk during a learning task (disengaged). ABCD pushes us to go beyond labels like "disrespectful," "disobedient," "rude," and "undisciplined." Instead, in Win-Win we look at actual behavior, which in turn helps us seek differentiated solutions.

Being Objective. Classifying disruptive behavior into the four types helps us be more objective. In the heated moment-of-disruption we want to keep a cool head. If in the moment-of-disruption, we think objectively about the type of behavior the student is choosing, we are less likely to get hijacked by our own emotional reactions. The ABCD system focuses on behavior, not subjective reactions to behavior. To say a student is disengaged leads us to think about ways to make curriculum and instruction more engaging; to say a student is disrespectful leads us to have an adverse reaction toward the student.

Communicating. Identifying the Disruptive Behavior: ABCD is useful also as a communication tool. Teachers do not operate in isolation. When there are disruptive behavior problems, the classroom teacher communicates with many individuals. When communicating with colleagues for problem-solving purposes, either informally or on a Multi-Disciplinary Team, being able to communicate specifically what is going on in the situation can facilitate finding Win-Win solutions. Educators also communicate with the student and with parents or guardians. Focusing specifically on what is happening is crucial to creating Win-Win solutions. Calling a behavior "disruptive" or "irresponsible" is vague, referring to any number of possible behaviors. Using specific terminology is more solution-oriented.

Making It Manageable. Finally, it is comforting to realize there are only four types of disruptive behaviors. Rather than thinking in terms of numerous categories of possible disruptions, we have to deal with just four types.

Identifying Behaviors: ABCD

A. Aggression

Aggression comes in many forms. The essence of aggression is an attempt to hurt another. The aggressive act can aim to harm the other physically (hitting, biting, punching) or psychologically (put-downs, intimidation). It can take the form of verbal abuse (yelling, swearing) or gestures (giving "the finger", disdainful looks). It can be direct (hurting the person) or indirect (breaking someone's possession, putting down their family or friends). It can take subtle forms as well, as in the passive aggressive student who is an expert at frustrating others by not giving them what they want. Whatever form it takes, the essence of aggression is action aimed at harming others.

Examples of Aggressive Behaviors

Direct Physical	Indirect Physical	Direct Verbal	Signs & Gestures	Indirect
Hitting	Destroying things	Put-downs	Disrespectful hand/finger displays	Insulting family, friends
Kicking	Throwing things	Swearing at	Making faces	Tattling on
Slapping	Taking possessions	Calling names, teasing	Body language of disdain	Insinuating poor taste
Biting	Hiding others' possessions	Insulting dress or possessions	Rolling eyes	Ignoring

See page 4.9 for additional Aggressive behaviors.

B. Breaking Rules

Teachers, schools, and districts have different rules. Most rules can be derived from two basic principles: 1) show respect for others and 2) do not disrupt learning. Rules which flow from those principles include not interfering with the teacher's ability to teach and not interfering with other students' ability to learn. Some schools, however, have many specific rules involving a variety of behaviors including the exact length of permissible apparel of different kinds.

Examples of Breaking the Rules

Timeliness	Materials	Dress	Behavior
Absences	Not covering books	Length, type of clothes	Chewing gum
Being on time	Not bringing materials to class	Drug and alcohol logos	Leaning back on a chair
Turning in assignments on time	Writing in text	Make-up, hair style	Sharpening pencils
Returning permission slips	Purchasing materials	Gang-related colors, insignias	Passing notes

See page 4.9 for additional Breaking the Rules behaviors.

C. Confrontation

When we hear a "You can't make me," we know we are dealing with a confrontation. A confrontation is a power play. The student verbally or non-verbally asserts that the teacher is not in charge, shows disrespect for the teacher, or attempts to undermine the teacher's authority. There are many forms of confrontation including: aggression and disrespect toward the teacher, refusing to obey or do assignments, and instigating other class members toward disobedience or disrespect for the teacher.

Examples of Confrontational Behaviors

Aggression Toward Teacher	Disrespect	Refusing	Instigating
Hitting	Talking back	Refusing to do assignments	Repeated complaining
Profanity	Flirting with teacher, sexual innuendo	Refusing to sit, move, obey: "You can't make me"	Taking charge, telling others what to do
Arguing with teachers	Contradicting, interrupting	Doing the opposite	Modeling disobedience
Putting down the teacher	Disdainful facial expressions toward teacher	Refusing to participate	Initiating rebellion; putting down the task

See page 4.9 for additional Confrontrational behaviors.

Some students have made a fine art form of confronting the teacher. They are ready with a justification as to why things should be done the way they want, rather than the way the teacher prefers. Defiance can come in the shape of *"I don't see why I should have to do this"* or *"Why are you picking on me? All the others kids are doing it too."* Defiance also can be displayed non-verbally. By doing the opposite of what is asked or expected, a student can confront the teacher without uttering a single word.

D. Disengagement

The fourth type of disruptive behavior is disengagement. The other three types of disruptive behaviors usually disrupt the teacher and/or the rest of the class. Disengagement can be a solo disruption, involving only the disengaged student. It is tempting to ignore the student who is disengaged, as the student may not be disrupting anyone else. But in Win-Win Discipline, we define a discipline problem as anything that disrupts the teaching/learning process, even if only one student is disrupted. We take disengagement seriously — it goes to the heart of what we define as a discipline problem. Disengagement can take many forms, including off-task behaviors, tuning out, or random activity.

Examples of Disengagement

Off Task - Behavior	Off Task - Verbal	Tuning Out	Hyperactivity
Writing notes	Asking off-subject questions	Sleeping	Horseplay
Wandering	Blurting out	Daydreaming	Carelessly rushing through work
Performing wrong task	Playing dumb	Head on desk	Laughing, giggling
Grooming	Socializing	Doodling	Fidgeting with materials

See page 4.9 for additional Disengaged behaviors.

The Four Types of Disruptions: ABCD

Aggression	Breaking Rules	Confrontation	Disengagement
Accusing, blaming others	Absent without excuse	Argumentative with teacher	Asking for assistance before trying
Arguing	Bringing forbidden things to school	Asking pseudo questions	Asking off-subject questions
Banging on desk	Cheating	Attempting to take charge	Breaking pencils to get out of seat
Biting	Chewing gum: smacking, blowing, popping bubbles	Blaming others	Clowning around
Breaking, destroying things	Chewing tobacco	Calling teacher names	Daydreaming
Bullying	Drugs, smoking, alcohol	Complaining	Doodling
Displaying weapons	Eating in class	Contradicting the teacher	Excessive absences
Fighting	Giggling	Denying misbehavior	Excessive restroom breaks
Head banging	Graffiti	Doing the opposite of what is requested	Fidgeting
Hitting	Humming	Flirting with teacher	Grooming
Invasion of personal space	Inappropriate language	Gesturing disgust toward teacher or assignment	Horseplay
Kicking	Inappropriate noises	Hitting teacher	Hyperactivity
Making fun of others	Intentionally falling out of chair	Ignoring directions	Inattentiveness
Nagging	Interrupting learning	Inappropriate answers	Incomplete work or homework
Name calling	Late or missing homework	Inciting others to disobey	Laughing out loud
Obscene gestures	Leaving without permission	Insolent facial expressions	Not doing the work
Playing rough	Making noise in the hall	Interrupting teacher	Not having books or materials for class
Poking others	Messing up the classroom	Lying	Not listening
Profanity	Misusing equipment	Making excuses	Not participating
Pulling hair	Non-stop talking	Mumbling	Off task
Pushing	Passing notes	Pointing fingers at teacher	Off-task behavior
Self-mutilation	Possessing weapons	Questioning teacher's ability or knowledge	Passing notes
Sexual innuendoes	Running in classroom	Refusing to cooperate	Playing with materials
Shoving	Screaming	Refusing to obey	Pretending to work
Spitting at others	Sharpening pencils at inappropriate times	Slamming books	Rolling pencils on desk
Stealing	Shuffling	Swearing at teacher	Rushing work to get to free time
Swearing at others	Singing out	Talking back	Skipping class
Teasing	Socializing inappropriately	Telling others what to do	Sleeping
Temper tantrums	Spitting	Whining about assignments	Socializing during instruction
Threatening, intimidating	Standing on furniture		Wandering around the room
Throwing things	Stealing		
Touching others (unwanted)	Sticking feet out		
Tripping others	Talking, blurting out		
Vandalism	Tapping, drumming on things		
Verbal abuse, cursing	Tapping feet		
Violating property of others	Tardiness		
Violent outbursts	Tipping chair		
	Unnecessary movement		
	Whispering at inappropriate times		
	Whistling		
	Yelling		

Only Four!

When faced with myriad forms of classroom disruptions, it is a relief to see them as one of only four types. But the real relief comes when we find that most all of the disruptions can be prevented when we adopt procedures to prevent the ABCD disruptions. See **Chapter 6. Preventative Procedures: ABCD.** At this point, though, you may find it useful to cement your learning by taking the following quiz.

Quiz Yourself
– Identify Disruptions: ABCD!

Below are descriptions of disruptive behaviors. Your job: Identify the disruption, ABCD.

Remember the Rules:
1) **Three Before B.** Only use Breaking the Rules if the disruption does not fit Aggression, Confrontation, or Disengagement.
2) **Teacher-Directed Aggression = Confrontation.**

Self Quiz: Identify that Disruption: ABCD

Disruption	A	B	C	D
Banging on desk				
Cheating				
Doodling				
Eating in class				
Making fun of others				
Lying to the teacher				
Ignoring directions				
Late or missing homework				
Insolent facial expressions				
Not doing the work				
Stealing				
Singing out				
Swearing at the teacher				
Skipping class				
Sleeping				
Displaying weapons				

For Answers, see Part VII, Resources D.1.

4.10

Win-Win Discipline. Kagan Publishing • 1 (800) 933-2667 • www.KaganOnline.com

Chapter 5

The ABCD Tally

If we are to have an effective discipline program, it must be a differentiated program. That is, we need to respond differently to different types of disruptions. A response that works well to deal with disengagement may be totally ineffective in responding to aggression or confrontation.

To determine which of the four types of disruptions are most common for an individual or class, we do a simple ABCD Tally. The tally records each disruption as A, B, C, or D. Notice, we use the same tally form if we are charting the disruptive behaviors of the whole class or those of a single student.

The Four Types of Disruptions

A Is for
Aggression

B Is for
Breaking Rules

C Is for
Confrontation

D Is for
Disengagement

Sample **Class** ABCD Tally

	Monday	Tuesday	Wednesday	Thursday	Friday	Total
Aggression	I I	I I	I I I	I	I I	10
Breaking the Rules	I I I I I I	I I I I I	I I I I I I	I I I I	I I I I	25
Confrontation	I I	I		I	I	5
Disengagement	I		I I	I	I	5

Use the **Class ABCD Tally** to record and classify all **class** disruptions.

Sample **Individual** ABCD Tally

	Monday	Tuesday	Wednesday	Thursday	Friday	Total
Aggression	I		I			2
Breaking the Rules	I I I		I		I	5
Confrontation		I				1
Disengagement		I				1

Use the **Individual ABCD Tally** to identify the type of disruptive behaviors displayed by an **individual student.**

Class ABCD Tally

Instructions: Each time a disruptive behavior occurs in your class, put a check in the appropriate box. Your class pattern will emerge.

Class Period_____

Observation Period:

Beginning Date _____ Ending Date _____

	Monday	Tuesday	Wednesday	Thursday	Friday	Total
Aggression						
Breaking the Rules						
Confrontation						
Disengagement						

Win-Win Discipline. Kagan Publishing • 1 (800) 933-2667 • www.KaganOnline.com

Individual ABCD Tally

Instructions: Each time a student is disruptive, put a check in the appropriate box. That student's pattern will emerge.

Class Period_____ **Student Name**_____
Observation Period:
   Beginning Date _____ **Ending Date** _____

	Monday	Tuesday	Wednesday	Thursday	Friday	Total
Aggression						
Breaking the Rules						
Confrontation						
Disengagement						

How to Use the ABCD Tally

You can do an ABCD Tally for an individual student and/or for the class as a whole. A decision is made to observe the class or a specific individual for a predetermined length of time. During that observation period, tallies are made to record each disruptive behavior observed. At the end of the observation period, the number of each type of disruption is totaled. The totals indicate the type of disruptive behavior most frequent for the individual or class.

The ABCD Graph

To create a graphic picture of disruption type, use the ABCD Graph. To use the graph, simply fill in the number of boxes corresponding to the number of disruptions for the individual student or for the class.

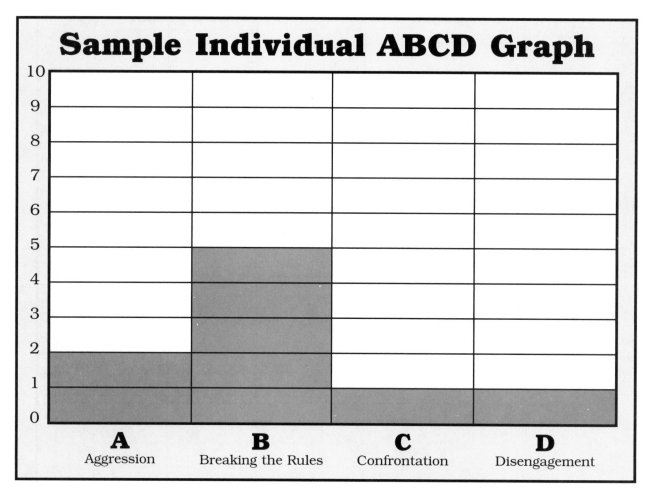

The ABCD Graph shows us at a glance which disruptive behaviors are most frequent, pointing us to the appropriate preventative procedures.

Class ABCD Graph

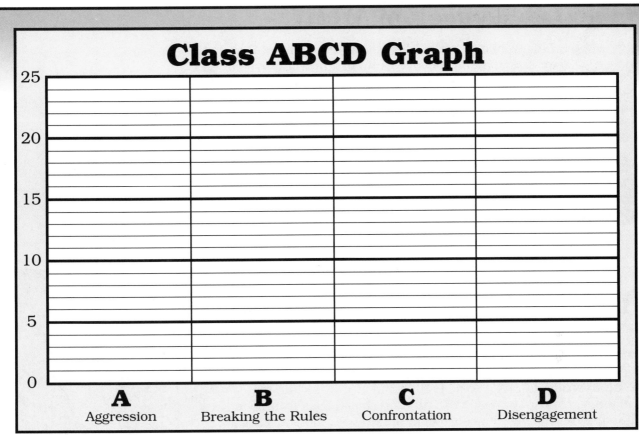

Individual ABCD Graph

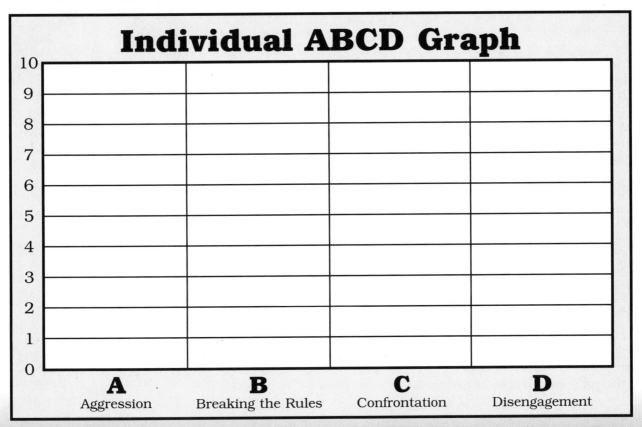

Tally Done? Now What?

Once we know which disruption type is most frequent, we know where to concentrate our preventative efforts. For example, if rule breaking is common, we want to review and implement preventative procedures that address rule breaking. If disengagement is frequent, very different preventative procedures are needed. The preventative procedures most effective for each of the four ABCD disruption types are presented in **Chapter 6**.

Dealing with the Disruptive Group

Sometimes a group of students play off one another to be disruptive. This group disruption may take different forms: A group of students may decide to all come into class late the same day, they may conspire to all drop their books in unison at a chosen time, or they may begin making odd noises, each playing off the other. Usually the students are seeking positive attention from one another or a group leader. Sometimes they are expressing resentment or are staging a confrontation. If the group disruption is a one-time event, it may be tolerated or even treated with humor. If however, it is a repeated event, group disruptions must be dealt with head-on because they threaten to undermine the teacher's authority.

Some teachers become extremely threatened and frustrated by a group of students who repeatedly gang up to create disruptions. *"My classroom is impossible; there is a gang of students dedicated to making teaching and learning impossible."*

Often there is one student who is a leader, and the other students are vying for his/her attention. Their disruption is an attempt to win the favor of the leader and to be included in the group. Interestingly, the leader may not be who the teacher thinks it is. Some students are very skilled in getting others to be disruptive without themselves being detected.

Sally Scott, school principal and a major contributor to Win-Win Discipline, has designed a step-by-step procedure for classroom teachers that is very effective in ending this type of group disruption:

Step 1: Make a List. Make a list of the students involved, from most to least likely to comply with the teacher. If, for example, there are five students involved, number one on the list is the student who would most likely agree to stop going along with the disruptive group; number five is the presumed leader of the group.

Step 2: Obtain Support. Meet with the principal and, if possible, obtain support for this plan. Show your principal this plan. Tell the principal there is a group of students playing off one another to create disruptions and explain that you will attempt to establish a relationship with the students one-at-a-time, and that following that when you believe the student will agree to end being disruptive, you want to be able to give the student a choice to end being disruptive or to be reassigned to a different class. Explain to the principal that it is not your desire to reassign the student, but rather to get the student to agree to follow the established class rules. (If the principal will not agree to this plan, explore alternative plans that involve the student spending time-out in another class or time-out within your own class.)

Step 3: Same-Side Chat with Most Compliant Student. Meet with the least disruptive student several times, using the Same-Side Chat structure. Establish a positive relationship. Do not talk about homework or disruptive behavior. Rather get to know the student as a person. *What are his/her likes and dislikes? How does he/she spend time after school and over the summer break? What does he/she hope to do after graduating from high school?* (See Same-Side Chat, Chapter 16.26.) The Same-Side Chat does not have to be a formal meeting. It can take the form of what Sally calls the Win-Win Miracle Minute. Every once in a while spend a minute with the student in the hall or right before or after class asking about how he/she did in his/her last game, how his/her sister is doing, whether he/she enjoyed the family trip, etc.

Step 4: Give the Student a Choice. When a Same-Side Orientation has been achieved, give the student a choice. Explain how the group disruptions are interfering with your ability to teach and other student's ability to learn and that you cannot allow them to continue. Give the student a choice: Either he/she agrees not to participate in the group disruptions or you will have a meeting with him/her, his/her parents, and the principal and will have him/her reassigned to another class. If you have established a Same-Side Orientation, bonding with the student, and have chosen the most compliant member of the group, it is extremely likely the student will comply. If not, you have to follow through with the reassignment.

> *I know it feels good to be included in the group and one way to do that is to join in when they start a disruption. But your behavior is inappropriate. It is disruptive to me personally and it distracts other students from enjoying and learning from the lesson. I know you can agree not to participate in any more group disruptions. You have to make a choice by tomorrow. You have to agree not to join in again in any more of the disruptions or else you and I will have a meeting with your parents and the principal to explain why it is necessary for you to be reassigned to another class.*

Step 5: Repeat with Next Most Compliant. Repeat steps three and four with the second most compliant student, then the third most compliant and so on, working up the list. By the time all students have complied except the leader, the leader has lost his/her support and is likely to comply as well.

Preventative Procedures: ABCD Disruptions

"An ounce of prevention is worth a pound of cure."
— *Benjamin Franklin,*
Old Richard's Almanac

Think for a moment about polio.

Doctors struggled for years treating that dreaded disease. For years their well-intended treatment efforts made little difference. People continued to die or be crippled for life. Then, a new approach was tried. Rather than treatment, the medical profession adopted a preventative approach. When a preventative vaccine was perfected, the disease was eliminated!

Teachers crippled by discipline problems in their classrooms need to take to heart this lesson from the medical profession: *responding to a disruption is of little worth compared to preventing it.*

In first period, a student is a serious discipline problem every day, frequently disengaged. In second period, every day the same student is happily engaged in learning. What is the difference? The student has not changed. The difference is in the approach to curriculum, instruction, and management. The period two teacher has curriculum and instructional methods that are engaging for the student. The teacher has efficient management techniques that leave little downtime – little time for disruptive behaviors.

Notice, the critical difference in the number of discipline problems in first and second period is not the discipline program the teachers use. It is not whether or not the teacher puts the students' names on the board, uses tokens to catch them being good, nor the effective use of "the look." *Eliminating discipline problems for the most part does not come about by adopting a discipline program!* Solving discipline problems for the most part springs from creating engaging curriculum and instruction, adopting effective management techniques, and using myriad everyday procedures that prevent the occurrence of disruptive behaviors.

In this chapter we will present simple preventative procedures that eliminate a huge percent of disruptive behaviors. The procedures are oriented to each of the four types of disruptions, ABCD. To determine which procedures are most needed for an individual or class, first we need to determine the type of disruption most often occurring by that individual or in that class. As we have seen, this is accomplished with the ABCD Tally (Chapter 5).

Once we have determined which disruption is most frequent, we implement preventative procedures tailored to that disruption type. In this chapter the prevention strategies are organized by type of disruptions, ABCD. If an ABCD Tally on an individual student reveals he/she is often aggressive or confrontational, you will want to try some of the procedures that reduce or eliminate aggression or confrontation. The ABCD Tally tells us which preventative strategies we most need to use — it is our road map to success in preventing disruptive behavior. You will not want to read all the ABCD procedures now but, rather, turn to them as you need them or as you want to stretch your repertoire of good teaching and management techniques. The preventative procedures are presented as resources, not as bedside reading.

Ounces of Prevention. Don't think of the Win-Win Procedures as medicine for a cold. Rather, they are good nutrition and exercise which, when used on a regular basis, prevent colds. The procedures are designed for regular use with the whole class and can be instituted the first day of class, before a single disruption occurs. Although the Win-Win Procedures are a powerful set of tools for preventing specific behaviors, more importantly, they are simply good procedures any teacher can adopt to create a more responsive, productive, smoother running classroom.

The procedures listed in this chapter are ounces of prevention. They will not prevent all disciple problems. Even with all of the procedures to prevent Aggression in place, some aggression almost certainly will occur. When it does, there are many Win-Win strategies for the moment-of-disruption and beyond. But the preventative procedures in this chapter are the place to start. With Win-Win preventative procedures in place, the incidence of disruptions is reduced dramatically.

Preventative Procedures for ABCD Disruptions

Many Win-Win procedures are effective for more than one type of disruptive behavior. For ease, most are presented in this chapter only once, under the disruption type for which they are most useful. Often though, a preventative procedure serves to prevent more than one type of disruption.

A Is for Aggression

Aggression will occur. Aggression occurs in a classroom for many reasons. When we see aggression, we usually think it is motivated by anger. That is often the case, but many other things may motivate a student toward aggression, including:

- Seeking attention from peers or the teacher
- Wishing to distract attention from potential failure at a learning task
- Trying to control another student or the teacher
- Attempting to secure a position in the status hierarchy
- Wanting to burn off excess energy
- Being bored and wanting to "get something going"
- Simply not knowing aggression is not permitted, using "home" or "street" behaviors at school

The prefrontal lobes of students are not fully developed until their early twenties. And it is this part of the brain which helps inhibit inevitable impulses to hit, shove, bite, scratch, kick, or verbally assault with profanity and criticism. Knowing the impulse toward aggression is inevitable and that it will sometimes be acted upon, the Win-Win teacher puts in place procedures which make aggression less likely.

Peer Mediators. Train students to be effective mediators of peer conflicts. Students have legitimate power in the classroom and can be a force for creating solutions rather than creating problems.

Anger Management. Teach your students practical steps to deal with their anger. The school counselor can help in this instruction. Display controlled anger yourself.

Conflict Resolution. There are many excellent conflict resolution programs. Especially powerful are programs that train students to be peer mediators.[1] It is helpful for students to learn the eight modes of conflict resolution symbolized by the saying **STOP HAAC:**

8 Modes of Conflict Resolution

S	**= Share**
T	**= Take Turns**
O	**= Outside**
P	**= Postpone**
H	**= Humor**
A	**= Avoid**
C	**= Compromise**
C	**= Chance**

See *Cooperative Learning.*[2]

Disagreeing Agreeably: Modeling. Use polite disagreement gambits to express your own disagreement with students, authors, historical characters, and contemporary political figures.

Disagreeing Agreeably: Practice. Have students practice the gambits for disagreeing agreeably. Gambits are functional phrases such as:

- *I beg to differ...*
- *I understand your point of view; in my opinion...*
- *Let's agree to disagree on that.*

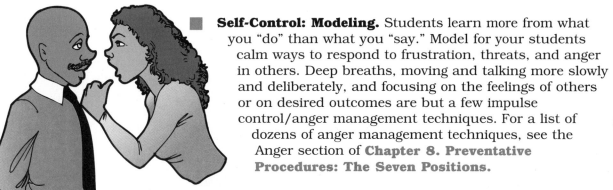

Self-Control: Modeling. Students learn more from what you "do" than what you "say." Model for your students calm ways to respond to frustration, threats, and anger in others. Deep breaths, moving and talking more slowly and deliberately, and focusing on the feelings of others or on desired outcomes are but a few impulse control/anger management techniques. For a list of dozens of anger management techniques, see the Anger section of **Chapter 8. Preventative Procedures: The Seven Positions.**

Social Skills. Teach students the skills they need to work effectively in groups and to interact with each other, for example, taking turns, sharing materials, listening to each other, and disagreeing without arguing.

Teambuilding. Teambuilding goes a long way toward preventing aggression. Teambuilding activities help students know and like each other as well as understand and respect individual differences. When students have bonded as a team, they are far less likely to be aggressive toward each other. See *Teambuilding.*[3]

Classbuilding. Create a sense of community in the class by using classbuilding activities. These activities allow students to get acquainted, identify with the class and others, and value differences. See *Classbuilding.*[4]

Silly Sports and Goofy Games. Aggression often occurs on the playground due to the intense competitiveness of many traditional playground activities. Aggression is reduced when we put more play on the playground. A collection of over 200 silly sports and goofy games provides enough non-competitive playground activities so students can play a new non-competitive game each day of the school year.[5]

Regular Exercise. Regular exercise releases endorphins, the "feel good" hormones. Students who get regular, aerobic exercise are far less likely to react to frustration or threat with aggression. They are generally calmer and learn better as well.

■ **60 Beats per Minute Music.** Music at 60 beats per minute or slower is calming, especially music with no words played at a relatively low level. If tensions are rising, the Win-Win teacher may soothe the classroom with calm music, preventing aggression that might otherwise occur.

■ **Prepare Responses.** It is hard to think rationally in the face of aggression, so both teachers and students benefit when procedures for responding to aggression are established and practiced before any aggressive outburst occurs. Response procedures include "Think Time" and "Take a Walk."

■ **Think Time.** Teach students the power of think time — to take time to think before they react. Teach them they don't always need to come up with a solution on the spot. Teach them the gambits:

- *I'm going to respond to you, but not right now.*
- *Let me think about that and get back to you.*
- *It would be good if we both took some time to think over what to do.*

■ **Take a Walk.** Allow students to take a cool down walk.

- Additional ways to prevent aggression are presented in the section on the Angry position in **Chapter 8. Preventative Procedures: The Seven Positions.**

B Is for Breaking Rules

Rules will be broken. To minimize this, the Win-Win teacher will do the following:

Rule Guidelines

- **Have students participate in rule creation**
- **Keep rules simple**
- **Make sure all students understand the rules and procedures**
- **Make sure all students understand and identify with the reason for the rules and reinforce the rules**
- **Have students practice behaviors consistent with the rules**
- **Repeatedly refer to the rules**
- **Repeatedly appreciate students for their rule compliance**

Win-Win Discipline. Kagan Publishing • 1 (800) 933-2667 • www.KaganOnline.com

6.6

The Win-Win teacher is liberal with praise, often letting students know how much he/she appreciates how their behavior is contributing to a harmonious class.

Making Sure Students Remember and Understand the Rules

■ **Keep Rules Simple.** Limit the number of rules to five. For example, Liz Warner used these five rules in her class:

> 1. Come to class ready to learn.
> 2. Respect the rights and property of others.
> 3. Ask for help when needed.
> 4. Offer help to others.
> 5. Strive to act responsibly at all times.

■ **One Rule.** Some teachers prefer to run their class with only one rule or agreement that covers everything: *In our class we agree to foster our own learning, the learning of others, and the ability of the teacher to teach.* With this agreement in place, the students can self-evaluate and see how all disruptive behavior violates the basic agreement.

■ **T-Chart Rules.** Create a T-chart with the class for each of the class rules. On one side of the giant T brainstorm "What It Will Look Like" in this class if we are all following that rule. On the other side of the giant T brainstorm "What It Will Sound Like" in this class if we are all following this rule.

■ **Rule Poster.** Have students design a rule poster.

> ## 3 Rules About Rules
> 1. Keep Them Simple & Realistic
> 2. Use Positive Language
> 3. The Fewer Rules the Better

■ **Personal Rule Sheet.** Photocopy the rules on color card stock and three-hole punch. Give a copy to each student to put in the front of his/her binder.

■ **Letter to Parents.** Explain the class rules and procedures in a letter that parents are to read and discuss with the student, sign, and return. This may be a stand-alone letter or may be included in a student orientation packet.

■ **Clarify the Rule.** Make sure that the students know what the rule means. Clarify with concrete examples of what it looks like and sounds like. Have students act out what rule adherence does and does not look like.

■ **Model the Rule.** Modeling of the rule is crucial to create understanding. Model the rule in different ways. Model rule adherence and non-adherence for the students, have them model rule adherence in skits, hold up as an example, and praise good rule adherence.

■ **Pantomime the Rule.** Have students play a guessing game. A team acts out rule adherence or rule non-adherence and the other teams have to guess the rule and determine if there was adherence or non-adherence.

■ **Students Name Each Rule.** Have students give a name for each rule. For example:

> *A really great teacher is someone who...* **explains and doesn't tell.** *—Sammy, Houston, Texas[6]*

Name That Rule

Ready Rule:	Come to class ready to learn.
Respect Rule:	Respect the rights and property of others.
Request Rule:	Ask for help when needed.
Offer Rule:	Offer help to others.
Responsibility Rule:	Strive to act responsibly at all times.

■ **Rule Mnemonics.** The five rules above might become Oh! 4R's.

■ **Multiple Intelligences Rule Reminders.** Include a variety of ways for students to remember the rules: songs, kinesthetic symbols, posters, pictures, skits.

■ **Illustrate the Rules.** Read stories and show pictures that illustrate the importance of the rules. Have students write stories that convey the moral messages embodied in each of the rules.

■ **Check for Understanding.** Check to see if students understand the rules; check to see if they can apply the rules. Have students write their understanding of the rules. Have students explain to a partner or explain in writing why each rule is important. Use checking for understanding gambits:

Check for Understanding

> *"Does that make sense?"*
> *"Let's explain it in our own words."*
> *"Do you need me to explain that again for you?"*
> *"Were the directions clear to everyone?"*
> *"Did you need some help?"*
> *"Did you get it?"*
> *"Do we all know what to do now?"*
> *"Are we sure we understand it all?"*
> *"Let's see if we got that right."*

■ **Teach and Re-teach Rules.** Many effective teachers spend the first week of school spending most of the time teaching procedures and only about a third of the time teaching content![7] They more than make up for the lost time because of the increased efficacy and lack of lost time all school year. Teaching the rules and procedures once is not enough. Have a rule or procedure of the week that you re-teach on a rotating basis.

Focus on Purpose

■ **Collaboratively Create Rules.** Students who have input into the process of creating the rules remember the rules better. Have students help create the rules. Use Thinkpad Brainstorming followed by Categorizing and a Team Statement to have students generate, categorize, and state their team's rules. For descriptions of these structures see *Cooperative Learning*.[8] From these, synthesize a class set. If an important rule is neglected, you can draw the students' attention to that area, and they will fill the gap, feeling they created the rules rather than having them imposed on them.

At Sparks High School in Sparks, Nevada, Leslie Doukas teaches computer science and works with freshmen in the AVID program (Advancement Via Individual Determination). The program is designed to help under-represented children go to college, and help open doors for students with a low GPA, whose low-income parents have not attended college. Leslie describes her process of generating class rules as follows:

Generating Class Rules by Leslie Doukas

1. First, we brainstorm, using the Inspiration® software program, all the things good students do to learn. Students make a list, then share with a partner. They get to do "consecutive blurting." They don't raise their hands, but rather look around and find a time to speak, and I type like mad.
2. Then I ask students which things seem to belong together and I move the icons into groups. Together we come up with names for each group.
3. Students, working in small groups, combine the bubble stems into lists of phrases. I then combine the lists.
4. We look at the list one last time, and I ask them if they think a "good teacher" list would be different. We talk about how, in my classes, ALL students are co-teachers, helping each other. I remind them of the "ask 3 before you ask me" rule they learned in elementary school, and tell them I am likely to ask them who else they asked when they ask me a question.
5. I ask them if they could accept this list as class rules – by then they always do.
6. I send the list home for students to explain to their parents, and for both to sign.
7. I post the lists in the classroom, and we use them as a reference when we need to.

For an example of the uncategorized web and subsequent categorized list of good student attributes generated by Leslie's students, see pages 6.10 and 6.11.

Attributes of Good Student

Sample uncategorized web

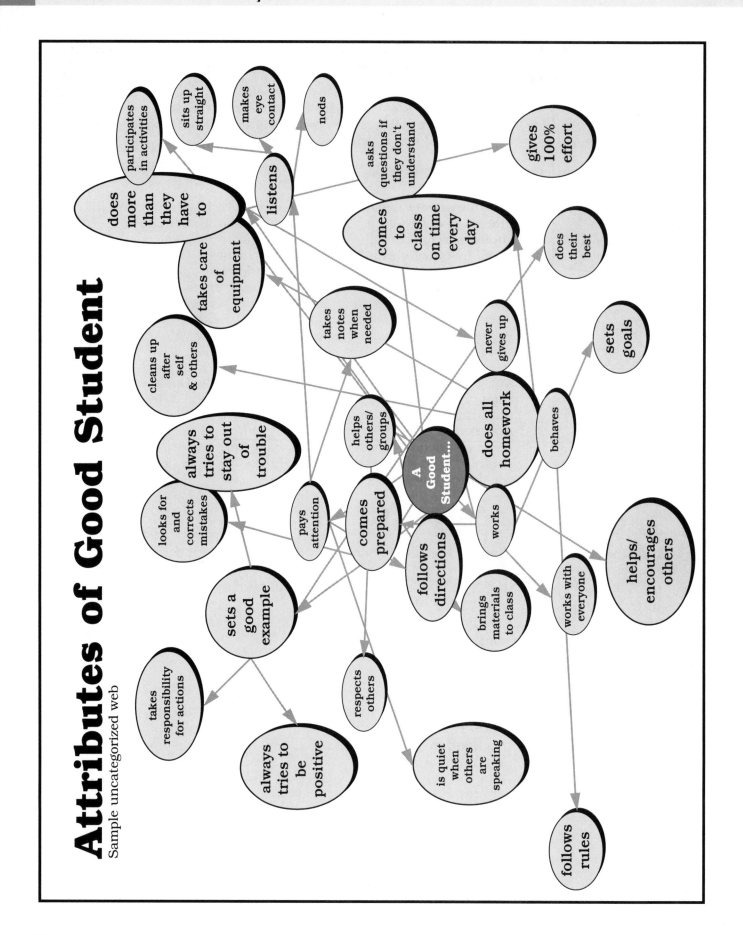

Good Student Attributes
Class Rules

Students developed this list Friday in class from their homework last week. We've agreed that they will conform to these rules while in school. Consequences were listed in the AVID freshman house handout I gave them the first day of school.

1. Work
    a. comes prepared
        i. does all their homework
        ii. brings materials to class
    b. sets goals
    c. does more than they have to
        i. never gives up
        ii. gives 100% effort
    d. participates in activities

2. Others/Groups
    a. respects others
    b. works with everyone
    c. helps/encourages others

3. Behavior
    a. comes to class on time everyday
    b. follows rules
    c. sets a good example
        i. takes responsibility for actions
        ii. always tries to stay out of trouble
        iii. always tries to be positive
        iv. does their best
    d. cleans up after themselves and others
    e. takes care of equipment

4. Attention
    a. listens
        i. eye contact
        ii. nods
        iii. sits up straight
    b. is quiet when others are speaking
    c. takes notes when needed
    d. follows directions
        i. asks questions if they don't understand
        ii. looks for and corrects mistakes

_____   _____
    Parent's Signature   Student's Signature

■ **Rename Rules.** If the term "rules" feels harsh or externally imposed, call them "Procedures," "Guidelines," "Agreements," "Class Constitution," "Code of Conduct," or "Code of Responsible Behavior." Have students create the alternative name for the rules.

■ **Students Teach Rules.** Form student teams and have each team teach one rule or procedure to the class.

■ **Share Rule Purpose.** Help your students understand the rationale behind the rule. When students understand the purpose of the rule, they are more apt to comply. One way to have students focus on the rules is to ask what would happen if there were no rules. Begin with:

> *What if there were no rule about which side of the street to drive on?*

Have students write or talk about the chaos that would result. Once that is firmly planted, go on to ask the "what if" questions associated with the other rules or procedures:

> *What if everyone took things that did not belong to them? What if we allowed everyone to hit anyone anytime he/she was angry?*

Foster Rule Adherence

■ **Practice Rules.** Have students practice the rules. For example, when you see someone offering help to a study buddy, stop the class. Let everyone see what you saw. Then say, *"Now everyone turn to your partner and say, 'Would you like some help with the next problem?'"*

■ **Eliminate Temptations.** Anticipate which rules are likely to be broken and proactively eliminate temptations. To eliminate the temptation to cheat:

> *"I know it is tempting to peek at a neighbor's paper during this test, so we are going to use our test-taking seating arrangement."*

To eliminate the temptation to play with materials:

> *"Please put all of your materials in your desks so you will not be tempted to play with them while I read this to you. I want your full attention."*

Non-verbal Rule Cues. Establish and use non-verbal cues with the whole class to prompt rule adherence. Common signals:

- A no talking signal to be used during silent study
- A signal to focus on the teacher to be used before giving input
- A signal to clean up desks to be used in preparation for a transition

Reinforce Rule Adherence. Catch students being good and let them know you appreciate it.

"Thank you all for coming to class today with no gum. Our class has a perfect record on that this week."

"I appreciate how you were all in your seats doing your Ready, Set, Go Work before the bell rang. We have a great class."

"You know, I never have to remind the class about.... You guys are great!"

Verbalize Responsible Behavior. Comment on good adherence to the rules. This reinforces rule adherence but also serves as a reminder.

"I appreciate how quickly and quietly everyone moved their desks in preparation for the test. Thank you."

- Additional ways to prevent students from Breaking the Rules are presented in the section on the Uninformed Position in **Chapter 8. Preventative Procedures: The Seven Positions.**

Involve Parents. Long Hill Elementary School in Cumberland County, North Carolina, has every teacher, student, and parent sign a Behavior Goals Pledge to clarify expectations. See page 6.14. At the high school level, the behavior contract can take a more formal tone. See for example the contract signed by students and parents at Horseheads High School, New York, on page 6.15.

C Is for Confrontation

Students will sometimes confront a teacher, refusing to do what the teacher has requested. Many confrontations are a form of aggression — aggression directed at the teacher. Some can be a very calm refusal to go along with whatever the teacher has proposed for the class or the student.

Like aggression, confrontations occur for many reasons. Most often a confrontation is a power play in which a student is asserting control: *"You can't tell me what to do, I'm in charge of me."*

Long Hill Elementary School Behavior Goals

 We pledge to respect our school family, their belongings, and school property (be kind, ask to borrow materials and return them, treat school property with care).

 We pledge to practice self control in everything we do (listen and follow directions, wait out turn to speak, keep hands/feet/objects to ourselves, remain seated).

 We pledge to be responsible by coming to school prepared to learn and participate in the learning process (have assignments completed, have needed supplies, eat breakfast, be on time, get plenty of rest, share ideas with classmates when appropriate, ask questions when we don't understand).

 We pledge to always walk in a quiet and orderly manner (walk on the right-hand side in a single-file line).

 We pledge to be good team members at Long Hill Elementary School (be cooperative, supportive of schoolmates, display a positive attitude).

_____
Student's Signature

_____
Parent's Signature

_____
Teacher's Signature

_____
Date

Behavior/Attendance Contract

Student Name _____

Date _____

The student listed above agrees to the following terms and conditions. He/she understands that any violation of this contract could result in a review of educational placement.

- You must report to school on time and ready to work everyday.

- You must report to class on time and be prepared.

- All homework must be completed on time.

- You cannot leave school grounds without the permission of your administrator.

- You cannot have any illegal absences; if you are going to be absent, you must notify Mrs. Jones at 123-4567, extension 1234 by 7:15 am.

- You must follow all of the rules listed in the student handbook.

None of these conditions are meant to put any additional burden on the student. These expectations are held for all students attending Horseheads High School.

Student _____

Parent _____

Administrator _____

Guidance Counselor _____

Date _____

The need to feel in charge of oneself is positive. But students trying to establish a sense of control may assert control in inappropriate ways or at inappropriate times. Other reasons for confrontations include:

- Revenge for feeling ignored or feeling mistreated
- Attempting to gain attention or respect from peers
- Expressing displaced anger (taking it out on the teacher)
- Generalized resentment toward authority
- Attempt to assert independence or status
- Avoiding embarrassment associated with doing poorly on an assignment

Sidestep the Power Play. One of the most important rules for dealing with confrontations is to never get involved in a power play. Seldom is it our job as teachers to make a student do or not do anything. We can provide consequences for doing or not doing things, but it is almost always the student's choice as to what he/she will do. An important exception, of course, is when a student is a threat to himself/herself or others. The more students perceive themselves to be in charge, making choices not controlled by the teacher, the less they will feel a need to confront the teacher.

Adopt a "We" Approach, not "You vs. Me." Have a positive attitude toward students. Project that we are all in this together, and if we work together, we can create an environment where we can all enjoy teaching and learning. Let students know that you are on their side.

Student Involvement in the Decision-Making. Actively involve students in the classroom decision-making process; promote a positive sense of control. Have students involved in creating rules, procedures, consequences, and appropriate curriculum decisions.

Student Focus Groups. Use focus groups of students to generate solutions for classroom problems. When class behaviors are confrontational, they need to be heard.

Suggestion Box. Have a box in the classroom where students can deposit suggestions for classroom improvements. Act on suggestions when possible. Tally and chart suggestions acted on.

Class Contract. Create contracts based on solutions negotiated with students. When agreements are written down, signed, and formalized, it makes them more real and more likely to be followed. Contracts can be formalized or very informal. See contracts, **Chapter 15. Following Up**.

Give Choices. Give students choices in the classroom. The more legitimate choices the students have, the less they will be battling you for power in disruptive ways. Give students some choices about how they complete their assignments. Having control over how they do their assignments motivates students to do their schoolwork. Being given a few options, rather than one, gives students a positive sense of control and matches their intelligence more effectively. Engage students in the learning process by giving them options about selection and direction of assignments.

Decision-Making Structures. Employ cooperative learning structures that teach students effective decision-making, such as Consensus Seeking, Spend a Buck, Proactive Prioritizing, Fist to Five. See *Cooperative Learning.*[9] Engaging in frequent decision making enhances students' sense of power and reduces the need for confrontation.

Class Chat Time. Conduct regular Class Chat Times to actively involve students in the decision-making process. Class Chat Times are an excellent venue to solve problems, improve the class, plan events, give support, and make announcements.

Phrase Assignments as Choices.
>*It is your choice to work on the fraction problems or the topic sentences first.*
>*If you choose to do the extra credit, you can earn up to X points.*
>*If you finish early, you can choose from among these three sponge activities.*

Provide Choices.
>*Tonight for homework you can choose among three alternatives....*
>*Your team can choose the format for your presentation. You might choose a skit, an interview, a quiz show, a video production....*
>*There are two algorithms for columnar addition. After you have learned both, you will be able to choose the one you like best.*

Programs and Procedures. Students who feel important have a sense of pride and esteem, have a sense of power, and have their needs filled are far less likely to be confrontational. Among the programs and procedures that give students a sense of importance or power:

- Self-esteem builders
- Student of the week
- Seek, act on student suggestions
- Democracy – let students vote
- Relate content to personal experiences
- Student awards
- Celebrate accomplishments
- Birthday celebrations
- Positive peer comments, praise

• For additional ways to prevent confrontations, see control-seeking in **Chapter 8. Preventative Procedures: The Seven Positions**.

■ **Gambits for When a Student Challenges:**
Student Challenges
"I can tell you don't like me."
"I think you are harassing me."
"My parents said you blame me for everything. They said I don't need to listen to you."

Possible Teacher Responses
"I'm sorry you feel that way."
"I'm sorry I've given you that impression."
"Obviously you're angry and I'm angry, too. Let's talk about this tomorrow."
– Give plenty of wait time.
"I can see why you feel that way."
"I can understand you're feeling defensive right now…"
"Perhaps he/she (your lawyer, dad, etc.) would have some good suggestions."

D Is for Disengagement

Students become disengaged when:

• The learning task is too difficult or too easy (not developmentally appropriate)
• Instructional strategies are repetitive and isolating (boring worksheet work)
• Work is meaningless, lacks relevance to the student
• Management procedures create long wait times

For example, if a teacher passes out papers one at a time, it leaves plenty of time for students to become disengaged. If instead, the teacher says, "Materials Monitors in each team quickly and quietly come up and get supplies for your teams," the papers are distributed quickly and there is little time for disengagement.

To prevent disengagement, the Win-Win teacher focuses on what we call the Big 3: Curriculum, Instruction, and Management. When there is engaging curriculum, delivered in an engaging way, with crisp management techniques, students seldom become disengaged. See **Chapter 18, Win-Win Management** and **Chapter 19, Win-Win Instruction.** Also see Cooperative Learning, Multiple Intelligences, and Differentiated Instruction in **Chapter 17. Win-Win for Students with Special Needs.**

Brain research reveals we are biologically prepared to attend to novel stimuli. To keep attention focused, use developmentally appropriate curriculum and instruction that includes:

- Novelty
- Variety
- Choices
- Individualization

Engaging Curriculum

▪ **Relevant Curriculum.** The more students can see the connection between the academic content and their lives, the more engaging the curriculum. Use examples and problems related to student interest. Students are more motivated to find out how many ice cream cones there are in four rows of six than how many dots there are in four rows of six. Show students how they will use the curriculum skills and content in their own lives. Disengagement is reduced if curriculum is relevant to the students' lives and experiences.

▪ **Developmentally Appropriate Curriculum.** Students become disruptive if curriculum is too easy or too difficult. In the face of curriculum that is too difficult, some students "cover up" with a disruption to avoid frustration and embarrassment. Adjust curriculum to ability. See Differentiated Instruction in **Chapter 17. Win-Win for Students with Special Needs.**

▪ **Restructure the Learning Task.** Monitor student progress, restructuring the learning task for individuals if the task is too easy or too difficult.

▪ **Centers.** *"When you finish your individual work you can go to one of the centers in the back of the room. There you will find Spin-N-Think games with higher-level thinking questions. You can play with others who finish early."*

▪ **Individualized Instruction.** Each student takes a pretest and works on problems which are aligned with ability as revealed by the pretest score.

▪ **Flash Card Game.** Students have their own set of flash cards and play with a partner, setting aside those they get correct so they are always working at a challenge level.

▪ **Progressive Sponges.** For students who finish early, use a progressive sponge. Have a series of problems, each more difficult than the prior problem, and say, *"For those of you who finish early, your sponge problems are..."*

Engaging Instruction

▪ **Variety.** Variety is the spice of life. Exclusive use of any one instructional strategy is a prescription for disengagement. The brain has evolved to attend to novelty and to social stimuli. The single most powerful way to create engagement, therefore, is to use a range of cooperative learning instructional strategies.

Any one instructional strategy used too long creates boredom and disengagement. Hold students' attention by brief learning sessions, changing the instructional strategy on a regular basis.

The most engaging instructional strategies are those that use cooperative learning because they include choices, variety, novelty, and social stimuli. All of these elements of effective instruction are "built-in" to Kagan Structures. Kagan Structures can be used as part of any lesson, in any content area, at any grade.

"Students, you have been working with your shoulder partner for ten minutes. Now pair up for the next five minutes to do problems with your face partner."

"Now that you have used RoundRobin to generate ideas, turn to your shoulder partner and do a RallyRobin to recall what was generated. If you have extra time, come up with some new ideas."

"Yesterday we did our review with Numbered Heads Together. Today let's try Boss/Secretary."

"Let me share a new variation on Numbered Heads Together — it's called Traveling Heads."

"Class, yesterday we had sustained silent reading of portions of Chapter 5. Today we will use Partner Expert Group Jigsaw."

"Yesterday we did Numbered Heads Together using AnswerBoards to respond. Today we will try some variations on Numbered Heads Together: Traveling Heads Together and Kinesthetic Responses."

"Class, we have a choice: We can review yesterday's lesson using Showdown or Numbered Heads Together. Let's use Fist to Five to make our decision."

"Johnny, you have a choice: You can study for the test using a worksheet of review questions, or review the same questions playing Spin-N-Think."

"Class, today you are going to make some choices as to where you stand on an Agree-Disagree Line-up."

"Class, today we will experiment with a brand new structure — one we have never tried. It's called Sharing Secrets."

For over one hundred cooperative learning structures, see *Cooperative Learning*.[10]

Visuals. Use drawings, pictures, symbols, posters, charts, graphs, graphic organizers, films, videos, and other visuals to depict the content.

Catchy Phrase. Use catchy phrases to focus the class when it is too noisy.

"We'd better push the escape button on this noise."
"I need to use the 'Silence Spray' in this class right now."

Energizers. When energy is fading in the classroom, get students up and actively involved in an activity that replenishes their waning energy. Silly Sports and Goofy Games are great energizers. For over 200 energizing games, see *Silly Sports and Goofy Games.*[11]

Relaxers. When energy is too high, have students use a relaxation technique such as relaxation breathing or progressive relaxation. For the details of Relaxation Breathing and Progressive Relaxation, see **Chapter 14. Moment-of-Disruption Structures**.

Multiple Intelligences. Multiple intelligences structures, used on a regular basis in the classroom, provide variety, novelty, and allow students to receive and express learning using their preferred intelligence. Students who are not very engaged listening to a lecture become very engaged when Draw It! or Lyrical Lessons are the mode of instruction. For instructional strategies to engage the range of intelligences, see *Multiple Intelligences.*[12]

Student Input. Let students generate ways to make instruction more fun and interesting. Let them choose structures.

Student-Directed Learning. After Kagan Structures have been used for some time in the classroom, it becomes natural to have students direct the class using the structures. Student-Directed Numbered Heads Together can create greater engagement than Teacher-Directed Numbered Heads Together.

The Brain Is a Social Organ

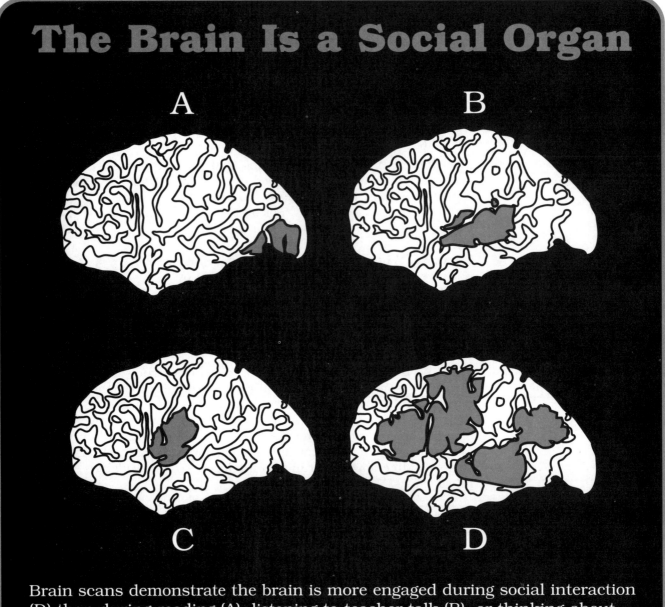

A

B

C

D

Brain scans demonstrate the brain is more engaged during social interaction (D) than during reading (A), listening to teacher talk (B), or thinking about what one will say (C).[13]

Sample Kagan Structure: Talking Chips

Use Talking Chips to regulate student communication and bring about equal participation. Students each have a chip they put in the center when they have shared in the group. They cannot share again until everyone has put his/her chip in and the chips are retrieved for more rounds of sharing. See *Cooperative Learning*.[14]

Engaging Management

Prescriptions for *disengagement*:

- Pass out papers slowly, one at a time, keeping the whole class waiting.
- Have quick students sit with nothing to do, waiting for slower students to finish.
- Take role by calling out students' names one at a time, slowly.
- Give a long string of complex directions so students are confused, ask for clarification, and force you to repeat the directions.

Poor Management = Disengagement

Some management tips which reduce down-time and disengagement:

Learning Tasks

Ready, Set, Go Work. An assignment is posted on the board for students to begin as soon as they take their seats. Board work or "Bell Work" as it is sometimes called, allows the teacher to greet students at the door and/or finish administrative work while students are actively engaged in a learning task.

Staged Projects. Giving a huge project all at once is a prescription for off-task behavior, disengagement, and failure. The classic examples are the fifth grade state report or the sixth grade country report given all at once, due in two weeks. Teachers who want all students engaged will break the projects into stages: picking a state, deciding on references, taking notes from references, first draft…. There are checks and celebrations at the completion of each stage.

Clear Expectations/Goals. Let students know what is expected of them. Show students what finished products look like. Tell the class exactly how they will be graded.

Signals and Signs

Hand Signals. A variety of hand signals improve management. Hand Signals include a Quiet Signal, Over My Head, and Too Fast.

- For details on these and other management signals, see: **Chapter 18. Win-Win Management.**

Direction Giving

Trigger Instructions. Don't have students start performing while you are still delivering your instructions. Use a trigger.

> **Triggered Instructions:** *"Class, just listen until I say, 'Go.' When I say, 'Go,' you will take out your paper and pencil, put your name on the top, and draw your diagram. Be sure to label all the parts. Go."*
>
> **Non-Triggered Instructions:** *"Class, take out your paper and pencil, put your name on the top, and draw your diagram. Be sure to label all the parts."*

With non-triggered instructions, students begin working before the instructions are finished, and many miss the last part of the instructions, needing to ask for clarification later. A trigger is easy to put in place. Just begin your instructions with phrases like:

- *When I say, "Go"…*
- *Don't begin until I say, "Start."*
- *When I clap my hands…*
- *I want everyone just listening until…*

Bite-Sized Instructions. Break instructions into bite-sized pieces. The rule of thumb: Give as many instructions at a time as the slowest students can follow without needing clarification. Whenever we give directions and the students then have to ask for clarification and/or are confused, we have probably broken the bite-sized rule.

Rather than saying, *"You are going to put your things away and line up,"* break the instructions into bite-sized pieces. Say, *"When I say, 'Go,' you will quickly and quietly put your things in your desk."* [Pause. Wait until students are ready for the starting gun]. *"Go!"* [They put their things away.] Then say, *"When I clap my hands, you will all stand up, quietly push your chairs under your desks, and stand behind your chairs."* [Pause. Wait until students are ready]. Clap! *"Good job! Now, when I put my hand on my desk, take your places in line, remembering the line-up procedure."* [Pause. Put your hand on your chair. Catch anyone who jumped the gun. Then put your hand on your desk.]

Concrete, Modeled Instructions. Directions that model what will be said or done are easier to follow.

> **Modeled:** *"You will take the red cardstock paper like this (modeling) and tear jagged pieces like these (modeling) which you will place on the blue cardstock like this (modeling)."*
>
> **Abstract:** *"You will tear jagged pieces from the first colored cardstock and place them on the second colored piece."*

■ **Whisper.** Lower your voice to get students' attention. Students quiet down to hear what you are saying. Any time you are raising your voice to get attention, you are probably working too hard and not modeling the kind of respectful class you would like.

Simultaneous Management Techniques

Avoid one-at-a-time management procedures. Whenever possible, have more than one student at a time engaged.

■ **Simultaneous Response Modes.** One teacher calls on students one at a time to answer questions. The teacher next-door uses:

- AnswerBoards
- Thumbs up or down
- Finger responses

He/She may simply say, *"Turn to your shoulder partner (the student right next to them). A's in each pair give your best answer."* There are numerous advantages to this simultaneous approach:

- Half the class can be engaged in answering, not just one student.
- The teacher can listen in to several respondents, not just one, checking for understanding.
- Students who otherwise would not respond become engaged.
- The teacher is able to hear responses from a more authentic sample of the class, not just from the high achievers.

■ **Simultaneous Distribution of Materials.** One teacher walks around handing back quiz materials one at a time. The other says, *"Material Monitors in each team come get your teams quizzes."* To avoid public embarrassment, the quizzes are folded so only the name is showing. The one-at-a-time teacher takes over five minutes to pass out the papers for a class of thirty. The teacher who does it simultaneously takes about a minute. A few minutes of savings does not seem like much, but when multiplied by all the times papers are passed out or materials are distributed, by the end of the school year the simultaneous management approach has saved days of instructional time!

■ **Simultaneous Team Formation.** One teacher calls out the names of students one at a time to tell them which team they will be on. The teacher using the simultaneous management approach has the names of the students on cards. The cards are taped to the team desk before students enter the room. They are to find their name and sit at that team when they enter. The one-at-a-time teacher creates about ten minutes of disengagement from learning.

Procedures

Model, practice, and reinforce routines and procedures. Have procedures in place for all the little things which otherwise would disturb the class.

> • A detailed description of procedures and routines is provided in **Chapter 18. Win-Win Management.**

Label Supplies. Make it easy for students to find materials; show the students where the materials are kept and label them so they're easy to find.

Crisp Transitions. Model transitions; practice and reinforce quick, quiet transitions. *"Students, when I clap my hands, you will all quickly and quietly move your chairs to the test-taking positions we have practiced. Let's see how quickly we can all get in position."* [Clap]

Sponge Activities. Post sponges: *"If you finish early, your choices are..."*

Team Questions: Three Before Me. Rather than allowing individual students to interrupt the lesson with questions which concern only them, put in place the "Team Questions Only" rule: If a student has a question, he/she does not interrupt the teacher. When the teacher is finished talking, the student asks a teammate. If no teammates can answer the question, then all students on the team raise their hands. It is a team question and the teacher comes over to the group and consults with them. Some teachers call this the Three Before Me rule because students have to ask three others before they ask the teacher.

Perks and Fun

The Win-Win teacher also creates an ongoing upbeat, positive, engaging classroom by managing energy levels, balancing learning tasks with perks, and incorporating fun activities. Among the many fun activities a Win-Win teacher may use are:

- Art activity
- Bingo!
- Center time
- Computer time
- Cooking project
- Couch potato reading
- Hat day
- Ice breaker
- Ice cubes
- Individual games
- Picnic
- Reading time
- Sing silly songs

- Talk time
- Video
- Visualizations: Mental Trips
- Water break
- Water games with water balloons
- Work with a partner

■ **Celebration Gambits.** Make celebration gambits a regular part of your class:

Have students lead the class in celebrations, team handshakes, team pats on the back, cheers:

"Hip Hip Hooray!"
"YES!"
"WAY TO GO!"
"We are awesome!"
"We are SOOOOOOO good!"
"Yea TEAM!"
"WE ROCK!"
"Hallelujah!"

A detailed description of celebration and Praise Gambits is available as a handy desk SmartCard.[15]

■ **Class Incentives.** Have class-created incentives that the class can work toward. Let the class generate a list of incentives.

- For additional ways to prevent disengagement, see the section on the Bored Position in **Chapter 8. Preventative Procedures: The Seven Positions.**
- For additional management tips and procedures, see **Chapter 18. Win-Win Management.**

Ounces of Prevention = Tons Fewer Disruptions

In this chapter we have overviewed some of the most important ways to prevent disruptive behaviors. Many teachers are amazed how disruptions disappear when these ounces of prevention are put in place. But procedures for preventing the four types of disruptive behaviors are but half the prevention story. The other half involves procedures that meet the needs associated with the seven student positions. If a student has an unmet need, he/she may become disruptive to meet that need. Let's turn, then, to the seven student positions to get a better understanding of student needs so we can help students meet their needs in responsible, rather than disruptive, ways.

References

[1]Kreidler, W. *Creative Conflict Resolution.* Glenview, IL: Scott, Foresman and Company, 1984.

Kreidler, W., Furlong, L. *Adventures in Peacemaking.* Cambridge, MA: Educators for Social Responsibility, 1995.

Johnson, D., Johnson, R. *Teaching Students to Be Peacemakers.* Edina, MN: Interaction Book Company, 1987.

[2]Kagan, S. *Cooperative Learning.* San Clemente, CA: Kagan Publishing, 1994, p. 14:28.

[3]Kagan, S., Kagan, L., & Kagan, M. *Teambuilding.* San Clemente, CA: Kagan Publishing, 1997.

[4]Kagan, S., Kagan, L., & Kagan, M. *Classbuilding.* San Clemente, CA: Kagan Publishing, 1995.

[5]Kagan, S. *Silly Sports and Goofy Games.* San Clemente, CA: Kagan Publishing, 2000.

[6]J. Bluestein, (Ed.) *Mentors, Masters, and Mrs. MacGregor: Stories of Teachers Making a Difference.* Deerfield Beach, FL: Health Communications, Inc., 1995, p. 213.

[7]Everston, C., Emmer, E. and Worsham, M. *Classroom Management for Elementary Teachers 6th Ed.* Boston, MA: Allyn & Bacon, 2003.

[8]Kagan, S. *Cooperative Learning.* San Clemente, CA: Kagan Publishing, 1994.

[9]Kagan, S. *Cooperative Learning.* San Clemente, CA: Kagan Publishing, 1994.

[10]Kagan, S. *Cooperative Learning.* San Clemente, CA: Kagan Publishing, 1994.

[11]Kagan, S. *Silly Sports and Goofy Games.* San Clemente, CA: Kagan Publishing, 2000.

[12]Kagan S., & Kagan, M. *Multiple Intelligences: The Complete MI Book.* San Clemente, CA: Kagan Publishing, 1998.

[13]Carter, R. *Mapping the Mind.* Berkeley, CA: University of California Press, 1998, p. 150.

[14]Kagan, S. *Cooperative Learning.* San Clemente, CA: Kagan Publishing, 1994.

[15]Kagan, S. Communications Booster Smart Card. San Clemente, CA: Kagan Publishing, 2003.

Chapter 7

The Seven Positions

In the last two chapters, we saw how identifying and anticipating the four types of disruptive behavior allows us to prevent disruptions. But ABCD is only half the prevention story. The rest of the story involves student positions. Once we can identify and understand student positions, we have an even more powerful set of prevention tools. If we anticipate student positions, we can prevent most discipline problems because most discipline problems are attempts by students to meet needs associated with their positions. Most disruptions are position-based. In this chapter, we will learn to identify the seven student positions which most often lead to disruptions. And in the chapter that follows, **Chapter 8. Preventative Procedures: The Seven Positions**, we will explore preventative procedures for each of the seven student positions.

ABCD tells us what students do; positions tell us why. A reminder:

Disruptive Behaviors vs. Positions

	Disruptive Behaviors	**Positions**
What is it?	What Students Do	Why They Do It
Where does it come from?	Attempt to Meet Needs	Rooted in Human Condition
How do we recognize it?	Observable	Inferred
Win-Win Philosophy	Disruption Not Accepted	Position Validated

Disruptions spring from positions: the student who needs attention, clowns around in class, or in some other irresponsible way attempts to meet the need for attention. The disruptive behavior occurs because the student is in the position of needing attention and does not know how to meet that need in responsible, non-disruptive ways. The student who is in a position of seeking control might refuse to do an assignment just to prove that no one can make him/her do anything. The need for control is a legitimate need — we all need to feel in control of our lives —

but the disruptive student attempts to meet that need in a way that interferes with his/her learning and/or the learning of fellow students. Positions have related needs, and students sometimes seek disruptive ways to meet those needs.

When the needs associated with student positions are met in responsible ways, students do not need to be disruptive.

In Win-Win, we recognize and validate the student's position and its associated needs. To prevent position-based disruptions, we structure our classroom so the needs of each position are met on an ongoing basis. If we can structure our classrooms so that the needs of students are met, we have gone a long way toward preventing disruptions. For example, if we meet and greet students at the door each day and adopt some other procedures that meet the need for attention, students in the position of needing attention will not need to clown around to meet their need for attention. When their needs are met, students do not have to resort to disruptive behaviors to meet those needs.

Students are wildly disruptive in Classroom A, but not at all disruptive in Classroom B. Students are wildly disruptive with Substitute Teacher A, but not at all disruptive with Substitute Teacher B. Why? Classroom B is structured so student needs are met on an ongoing basis — they do not have to be disruptive to meet their needs. Substitute Teacher B prevents disruptive behavior by understanding and relating to the needs associated with the seven student positions.

The ultimate, long-term goal of Win-Win Discipline is to have each student learn responsible, non-disruptive ways to meet his/her needs. In the short run, however, the most powerful thing we can do to prevent discipline problems is to implement preventative procedures which meet the needs associated with the positions.

What then are the most important student positions? What are their associated needs? How can we recognize student positions? What happens to us and our classroom when we recognize and identify with student positions?

What Is a Student Position?

A Student Position Is:

- An interaction of attitudes, emotions, perceptions, cognitions, and physiology, which influences the behaviors the student chooses.

- A psychological state with associated needs. The need is often unconscious, so students act out their needs without being able to verbalize them. Attempts to fill unconscious needs are often disruptive and not understood by the student.

- A state which may be true of a student one moment but not another. A student may be in an angry position after being hit, but may not be in that position an hour later. A student may be in the position of needing attention after feeling ignored, but may not be in that position after feeling recognized. Positions are states, not traits.

- Where the student is coming from at a given time.

What Are the Seven Positions?

There are seven student positions that most often drive disruptions:

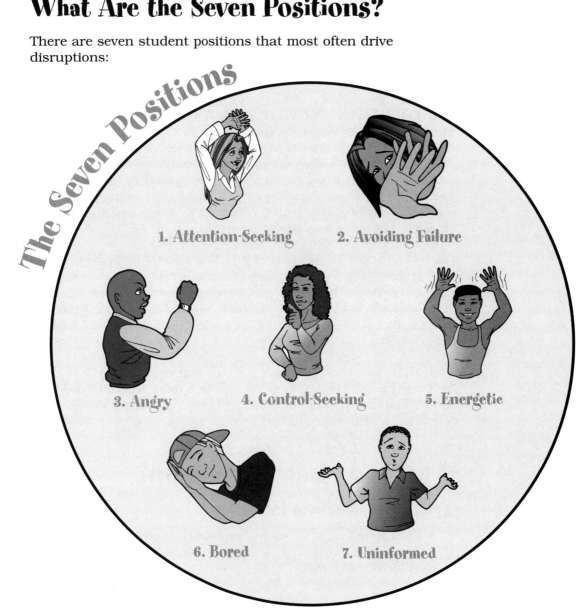

The Seven Positions

1. Attention-Seeking
2. Avoiding Failure
3. Angry
4. Control-Seeking
5. Energetic
6. Bored
7. Uninformed

Win-Win Discipline. Kagan Publishing • 1 (800) 933-2667 • www.KaganOnline.com

Attention-Seeking

We all need attention. It is rooted in our biology. Infants who did not cry when too long abandoned had a lower probability of survival. Humans, given their initial extreme dependency (a horse walks at birth; humans take a year), need the attention of others, especially adult others.

Attention-seeking is a universal need and we all have many ways of seeking positive attention. Some students, however, at times attempt to fill their need for attention in inappropriate ways, such as clowning around, talking back, or wearing forbidden or almost-forbidden hairstyles or clothes. The need for attention can at times be so strong that students will strive even for negative attention as in the case of the student who bragged, "The teacher screamed louder at me than at you." Inappropriate ways of seeking attention, of course, can be very disruptive. If we satisfy the need for attention among students on a regular basis, they have less need to act disruptively.

Avoiding Failure

No one likes to fail. And we strive especially hard not to fail if the failure will result in public embarrassment. Some kinds of failures are much worse than other failures. Picture this: The teacher hands back the graded tests. You receive a failing mark. You look up and find everyone else in the class has gotten a perfect score. How do you feel? If, instead, you receive the failing mark and when you look up, see that everyone else in the class has failed too, how do you feel? Most of us would feel a sense of relief. In the first case, we make an internal attribution: "I must be dumb" or "I'm really not good in this subject." In the second case, we make an external attribution to the teacher or the test: "The teacher did not teach that well" or "The test was too hard." We try especially hard to avoid failures which will result in a negative internal attribution. No one wants to feel dumb, weak, unpopular — a failure.

Students will become disruptive if it is the only way to avoid failure, especially a failure that will lead to public embarrassment or a negative internal attribution. A student may refuse to do an assignment if it is less painful to say to himself and others, "I just didn't feel like doing it," than to risk the possibility of failure.

How we structure our classrooms will determine to a large extent how many students need to be disruptive to avoid failure. Contrast two scenarios:

■ **Classroom A:** *"Your homework is the problems on pages 10 to 11. Tomorrow we will grade your homework by trading papers with* *someone in the class. The grades will be posted this week. You should find these problems easy. If you do miss any of the problems, you will be assigned to a tutoring group, depending on the type of problem you miss the most."*

Classroom B: *"Your homework is the problems on pages 10 to 11. Tomorrow you will be able to grade your own homework in class. No one will be allowed to see anyone else's homework; you are not to share grades. After we grade the homework, all students will choose one tutoring group to join, depending on the type of problem they would like to work on."*

The student who fears public embarrassment associated with failure is much more likely to do the homework assignment in Classroom B than in Classroom A because the chance for public failure is reduced.

Angry

Anger is a natural reaction in many situations, including but not limited to:

- **Aggression**
- **Defeat**
- **Fear**
- **Frustration**
- **Humiliation**
- **Inhibition of impulses**
- **Jealousy**
- **Loss**
- **Moral outrage**
- **Pain**
- **Threat**

An angry outburst can be the result of several of these situations in combination, like the straw that broke the camel's back. For example, students coming in after losing at a sporting activity on the playground are much more predisposed toward an angry outburst in the face of a frustrating learning experience than those who won on the playground. Students may not be aware of what has predisposed them toward a display of anger; when asked why they got angry, they probably would not mention the playground defeat even if it were a factor.

Many factors can create anger. Frustration – trying hard repeatedly and not succeeding at the task – eventually makes most of us want to break whatever we are working on. Feeling that we have been treated unfairly, whether or not the treatment was actually unfair, leads to a sense of moral outrage that can trigger an angry outburst. The attribution process plays an important role in anger as well. Interesting experiments show that a person being treated rudely is far less likely to feel angry toward the tormentor if he/she finds out that this individual has been suffering in his/her personal life. Generalizing from this experiment,

Win-Win Discipline. Kagan Publishing • 1 (800) 933-2667 • www.KaganOnline.com

we might predict that students will display less anger toward each other if the norm is to share about personal upsets, and that a teacher might do well to model sharing when things are not going well, rather than putting on a face.

Anger is part of life, including life in a classroom. Classrooms are about learning, and learning new material is often associated with frustration, inhibition of impulses, persistence in the face of difficulties, threat to one's ego, and jealousy of those for whom the learning comes more easily. Thus, the potential for anger is always present, and as teachers we need to look at the many ways we can lower that potential, as well as putting in smooth practiced procedures for occasions when angry outbursts occur.

Control-Seeking

None of us wants to feel like a pawn, moved about by forces beyond our control. Who wants to be told what to do, how to do it, and when to have it done? We relish the experience of personal choice; we want to feel in charge of ourselves. The experience of choosing, while difficult for some and at times fraught with anxiety, gives us our sense of freedom. We all strive to seek control of our lives in various ways.

There is a great deal of research on learned helplessness showing that all organisms become depressed when they cannot control their outcomes.[1] In extreme cases, when we cannot control our outcomes, "feel good" neurotransmitters become depleted and there is clinical depression. The need to feel a sense of control is rooted in our biology.

The need for control can take many forms. The student who asks if he/she can do an essay rather than take a test is attempting to take control. The student in a cooperative learning team who tries to tell everyone else what to do is attempting to take control. The student who refuses to do an assignment may be trying to prove, "No one tells me what to do." Obviously, control seeking can lead to disruptive behaviors.

By recognizing and validating students' need for control by, for example, allowing students many choices, we prevent disruptions because students do not have to be disruptive to fill their need for control.

Energetic

In an interesting experiment years ago, normal people were admitted to mental hospitals as patients as a test of how normal people act and are treated in abnormal environments. One of the things these pseudopatients noted is that they found themselves pacing the halls. In the logbook of one of the patients it was noted that the patient engaged in "abnormal pacing behavior."

When asked about this later, the man, who in his real life was an active person, simply explained that he was accustomed to exercise and that the only way he could get the exercise he needed in the mental hospital was to pace.

The need to move, to touch and manipulate things, is basic. Primary teachers spend a great deal of time socializing students to sit in one place. If the need to move is strong enough, it overrides that socialization. By including plenty of opportunities for movement, including work with hands-on manipulatives and classbuilding structures in which students get up from their seats and move in the room, teachers can prevent disruptive expressions of energy. When the need to move and express oneself physically is met on a regular basis, energetic students do not have to disrupt the class to fill their need.

Bored

Boredom is the opposite of peak experience. Mihaly Csikszentmihalyi, a Harvard psychologist, explains both boredom and peak experience in his classic book, *Flow*.[2] Flow occurs when there is an optimal relationship between ability and task difficulty. Most all of us have experienced moments of flow — when we are totally engaged in an activity, time seems to disappear, we are tremendously productive, and there is a sense of effortlessness in our work. Csikszentmihalyi explains that this optimal experience occurs when the task we are working on matches our ability. If we work on a task that is too difficult for our ability level, we feel anxiety and have the impulse to stop the work. If we work on a task that is too easy for our ability, we feel boredom and lose interest. Everyone has the need to avoid boredom and avoid anxiety — we are happy when we are in a state of flow.

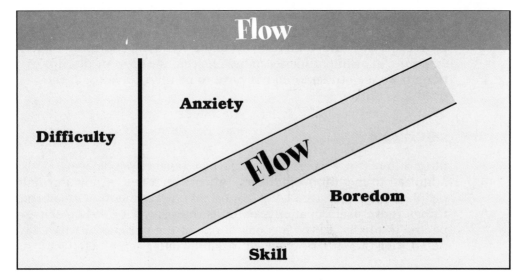

A student who is not engaged in a learning task because it is too easy or because it is not of interest may seek stimulation in alternative ways — some of which can be disruptive to others. In the extreme case, a student punches another student, not out of anger, but simply to "get something going." The student is seeking stimulation in a disruptive way. When as teachers we provide learning tasks that match student ability level, make the tasks intrinsically interesting, and provide rationale for doing the tasks, we avoid boredom and reduce or eliminate the need for students to seek stimulation in disruptive ways.

> *If teaching were the same as telling, we'd all be so smart we could hardly stand it.*
> — Mark Twain

Uninformed

Alex punches Pete in the shoulder. Alex is not angry, he is not bored, he is not seeking control, nor is he seeking attention. At home and in Alex's neighborhood a punch in the shoulder is simply a way of relating. Alex does not know that the rules of appropriate behavior at school are different. He is uninformed. Sandy uses a curse word. She hears profanity at home and in her neighborhood all the time and simply hasn't realized yet that the rules of appropriate behavior at school are different.

Being uninformed is not knowing the rules of the game. A teacher tells Alex there is no punching allowed in school and tells Sandy that profanity is forbidden. Alex still punches and Sandy still uses profanity. To paraphrase Mark Twain, "Telling ain't teaching," and Alex and Sandy are still uninformed. It will take time for them to learn the rules of appropriate behaviors. We don't learn all the rules overnight, especially if we have spent a lifetime playing by different rules.

Modern brain research has distinguished different types of memory systems, located in different parts of the brain. It turns out that the way we remember what we ate for dinner last night (episodic memory), the way we remember the names of the ten amendments (semantic memory), and the way we remember how to drive a car (procedural memory) are very different, involving whole different brain systems. The way we remember "the rules of the game," which behaviors are right and wrong in which environments, is a type of procedural memory, and procedural memory is produced by repetition. Thus, for students to be informed, the Win-Win teacher must explain the rules many times, in many ways, and provide rehearsal and practice opportunities. Even if a student has been told the rules several times, the student may remain in the uninformed position. In Win-Win we use the term "uninformed" to describe a student who has not yet obtained procedural memory of a responsible behavior. Becoming informed is a process, not a one time event.

Positions and Associated Needs

Each of the seven student positions is associated with basic needs. If these needs are met on a regular basis within the class-room, students are unlikely to be disruptive. If, however, the only way a student can meet those needs is to be disruptive, dis-ruptions will be frequent. Understanding the simple reality that disruptions are attempts to meet needs gives us great power in preventing them. All we have to do is know, recognize, accept, and relate to these seven basic needs as we structure what goes on in our classroom. Specific ways to do that are presented in **Chapter 8. Preventative Procedures: The Seven Positions.**

Positions = Basic Human Needs

Position	Need
Attention-Seeking	To feel cared about by others
Avoiding Failure	To feel successful
Angry	To express displeasure
Control-Seeking	To feel able to influence people and events
Energetic	To move, touch, be expressive
Bored	To be motivated, to have interesting stimuli
Uninformed	To know how to interact responsibly

Remembering the Seven Positions

There are many ways to remember the seven student positions, and because we each have a different pattern of intelligences, each of us will prefer to remember them in different ways. One of the most popular ways to remember the seven positions is to use kinesthetic symbols. When I teach the positions, I teach them as three pairs plus one, with a kinesthetic symbol associated with each position.

Attention-Seeking — Avoiding Failure. To remember this pair, first wave a hand wildly as if you are trying to get the teacher's attention. Then place your hands in front of your face, palms out as if you are hiding behind your hands. The attention-seeking student wants everyone to see what he or she can do; the student who is avoid-ing failure does not want anyone to see what he/she can't do; that student is hiding his/her fear of failure.

Anger — Control. To remember this pair, first make a fist and shake it at an imaginary opponent. Then keep a fist but extend and point your index finger, while shaking your hand as if you are telling someone what to do. The angry student wants to hit; the control-seeking student wants to tell others what to do (and not be told what to do).

Energetic — Bored. To remember this pair, first raise your open hands about head height, palms forward, fingers extended, and shake both hands as if they are letting off electrical current. Then take both hands and bring the palms together and rest your head on the back of your right palm, as if you are going to sleep. The energetic student has so much energy he/she just can't stop moving; nothing is stimulating the bored student who feels like going to sleep.

Uninformed. To remember this position, just open your eyes and mouth wide and raise a hand as if in surprise. The uninformed student is surprised by rules of appropriate behavior. He/she is simply unaware.

Understanding the Positions

We can try to understand the seven positions objectively, seeing how the positions spring from the human condition and understanding their origin in evolution, biology, and brain structure and function. But there is another, even more important way to understand the seven positions — subjectively.

Unless we can identify with the positions, feel what it is like to be in each position, walk in the shoes of those in each position, know the position from the inside, we will never realize the highest potential of a Win-Win teacher. We will never be as sharp as we can at recognizing the positions or taking the "same-side" with disruptive students.

The position you most need to work on is the one you least recognize in yourself. It will be the position you will have the most difficulty with in your classroom. Sometimes we have a tendency to react negatively to traits in others that we will not readily accept in ourselves. Since we all have all the positions, if you find yourself reacting strongly to a trait evident in a student's behavior, try to determine which of the seven positions that student is exhibiting and work toward recognizing that same position in yourself.

How can we understand the positions from within? On the next pages are some discussion questions and suggested activities. Think, journal, discuss, and interact over them with a partner or small group. They are designed to help you own each position in yourself and to help you identify with students in each position.

Can You Admit?

Attention-Seeking

Describe a time when...
- You have basked in positive attention.
- You have sought attention and were rejected.

Have your ever wanted...?
- To be the star?
- To feel you are really special to someone?
- To catch someone's eye?

Can you admit...?
- That there are secret ways you dress, act, perform, or flirt in order to get attention in your life now?
- That there is someone you would like to give you more positive attention?

Take a moment to feel...
- What it is like to really want approval, attention, to stand out, to be noticed.
- The emotions you experienced when you received plenty of positive attention. Bask in the feeling. What is it like?

Assume the body position and facial expression of...
- Pretend you really want attention and are not getting it. What do your face and body look like?
- Now you are getting attention you crave. Show it with your facial expression and body language.

Tap out a rhythm for...
- Attention-seeking

Describe the color of...
- Attention-seeking

Discuss this statement or question...
- What are ways you seek attention now in your life? Are there alternative ways you might try?
- If you had a great need for attention, what are some things you might do which would disturb others?

7.12

Win-Win Discipline. Kagan Publishing • 1 (800) 933-2667 • www.KaganOnline.com

Can You Admit?

Avoiding Failure

Describe a time when...
- You were really afraid of failing. Was the fear more of the public embarrassment, or was the fear of what the failure would bring?
- What failure do you fear most: fear of public speaking, a fear of having your work displayed, or...?

Have your ever wanted...?
- To succeed at something but not admit it to others — a sort of secret ambition?
- To keep your performance a secret so you would not be embarrassed if you did not succeed?

Can you admit...?
- Saying you had not studied for a test when in fact you really studied hard, so that if you did poorly, you would have an excuse?
- Feigning confidence — being worried but not showing it?
- Hesitating before calling to ask for a date, for fear of rejection?
- Having "butterflies in your stomach" before a performance? Describe where and when.

Can you imagine...?
- Describe the worst public embarrassment you can imagine.

Take a moment to feel...
- What it is like to be afraid of failure but not really admit that to yourself or others.
- How you felt before taking your first driver's test.
- How you felt going on your first job interview.
- How you felt going to work on your first day of teaching.

Assume the body position and facial expression of...
- Pretending to be confident when secretly you fear failure.

Tap out a rhythm for...
- Avoiding embarrassment

Describe the color of...
- Avoiding failure

Discuss this statement or question...
- Fear of failure is never the problem; it is pretending that one is not afraid, or it is attempting to cover it up — that is the real problem.
- We all fear failure and it is ok to keep our fears a secret. What is not OK is when we pretend to ourselves or others.

Win-Win Discipline. Kagan Publishing • 1 (800) 933-2667 • www.KaganOnline.com

7.13

Can You Admit?

Being Angry

ANGRY

Describe a time when...
- You said something out of anger you later regretted.
- You did something out of anger you later regretted.

Have your ever wanted...?
- To put someone down out of anger?
- To hit someone out of anger?

Can you admit...?
- Have you ever been in a rage? Can you remember seething over something?
- Has there ever been a time when you felt angry but only later found out what was bugging you?

Take a moment to feel...
- What it is like to be a student in a classroom who is so angry the instruction and content just seem like a blur in the background. What might have set that off?

Assume the body position and facial expression of...
- Anger. Make an angry face. What exactly happens with your eyebrows? Your jaw?
- Assume an angry body position. What happens with your arms and hands? How are you standing?

Tap out a rhythm for...
- Anger

Describe the color of...
- Anger

Discuss this statement or question...
- What are some of your little "pet peeves"?
- What is the mildest form of anger you have ever experienced? Is an irritation a mild form of anger?
- What is the most intense form of anger you have ever experienced?
- When you are angry, what are some of the ways you vent?
- What are some of the ways you calm yourself down?
- Discuss this statement: Anger is never right or wrong, it just is.
- Discuss this statement: Anger is a healthy emotion.

Can You Admit?

Control-Seeking

Describe a time when...
- You had the rush of a strong sense of control. Was it:
    - The first time you were behind the wheel driving?
    - When you could attract someone's interest?
    - When you first left home to live on your own?
    - When you got your first paycheck?
    - When you found you could support yourself?

Have your ever wanted...?
- To just get your own way when you knew it really did not matter?
- To spend time arranging things when you knew your time might be used more wisely another way?

Can you admit...?
- Some little things in your life now that give you a sense of control?
- Knowing where things are?
- Being able to control your computer?
- Keeping a daybook?

Take a moment to feel...
- Some little things in your life now that give you a sense of control.

Assume the body position and facial expression of...
- What it is like to seek control.

Tap out a rhythm for...
- Control-Seeking

Describe the color of...
- Control-Seeking

Discuss this statement or question...
- Control-seeking is not just seeking control over others; it is seeking control of your own life. Do you like things that are predictable? What do you do to make your world more predictable?
- Is there a time you can remember when you tried to control others just to give yourself that little comfortable feeling of control?
- How do you resist being controlled by others?
- Do you have a place you can go where you feel most in control? Imagine yourself in that place. How exactly do you feel?
- Imagine a situation in which you are totally out of control. What is going on? How do you feel? What do you do to regain a sense of control?

Win-Win Discipline. Kagan Publishing • 1 (800) 933-2667 • www.KaganOnline.com

7.15

Can You Admit?

Being Energetic

Describe a time when...
- You were too antsy to sit still.
- You felt restless enough that it interfered with your ability to concentrate.

Have your ever wanted...?
- To just "jump out of your skin"?
- To get up and take a walk even if you knew you needed to finish a task?

Can you admit...?
- Ever being fidgety?
- Ever having failed to finish a task because you were just too on edge?

Take a moment to feel...
- Restless

Assume the body position and facial expression of...
- Excess energy

Tap out a rhythm for...
- High energy

Describe the color of...
- Being Energetic

Discuss this statement or question...
- Remember a time when you felt restless. How did your restlessness express itself in your body?
- Think about a time you had a lot of energy and then "worked it off" swimming, running, dancing, or in some other way. What is your favorite way to work off energy?
- Do you get a calm feeling after a workout? Is you mind clearer? Can you concentrate more? Now imagine the opposite. How must it feel to have so much energy you cannot concentrate? You just HAVE TO do something.
- Have you ever been so restless you fidgeted in your chair? Or could not stay seated?
- What are some positive ways you now get the exercise you need?
- Was there a time in your life when you needed more exercise to feel good?
- Imagine having five times that much energy. What would your life be like? How would your energy disturb others?
- Imagine yourself tied down in a chair, unable to move. Now imagine a fly walking slowly on your face, tickling you. You want to slap it but cannot. Get into that feeling. Does this help you identify with what it must be like to be the most energetic student in your class during quiet seat time?

Can You Admit?

Being Bored

Describe a time when...
- You were bored.

Have your ever wanted...?
- To think about other things during a lecture because it was not interesting to you?

Can you admit?
- Finding yourself daydreaming during a lecture?

Take a moment to feel...
- Bored

Assume the body position and facial expression of...
- Boredom

Tap out a rhythm for...
- Boredom

Describe the color of...
- Boredom

Discuss this statement or question...
- Imagine going to an opera. You cannot understand the language. You do not have the synopsis and do not know what is happening on stage. The actors seem to just stand and sing forever. You wish they would move, but they just stand and sing. How are you feeling?
- What is the most boring lecture you ever sat through? What made it boring for you? Was it boring for everyone, or did some find it interesting?
- What is the most boring situation you can imagine being in?
- When was the last time you were really bored?
- What are situations in which you feel bored?
- Has there ever been a time in your life when nothing seemed very exciting?
- Think about the most interesting thing you have ever observed or studied. What made it so interesting? Think about the least interesting thing. What made it so boring?
- How does your body feel when you are bored?
- Assume the body position and facial expression of being really bored.
- Have you ever picked a fight just to alleviate boredom?
- Have you ever done anything else you later regretted just to escape boredom?

Can You Admit?

Being Uninformed

Describe a time when...
- You just did not know that appropriate way to behave.

Have your ever wanted...?
- To hide with shame because you broke a social norm?

Can you admit?
- Trying to "fake it" rather than admit you did not know something?

Take a moment to feel...
- Uninformed

Assume the body position and facial expression of...
- Being Uninformed

Tap out a rhythm for...
- Being Uninformed

Describe the color of...
- Being Uninformed

Discuss this statement or question...
- Have you ever gone to a social event and found yourself either over-dressed or under-dressed?
- What are some other times you did not know the rules of appropriate dress or behavior?
- Are there some unspoken rules of behavior at faculty meetings? What are they?
- Have you ever learned the unspoken rules the hard way?
- Have you ever been in a foreign country and felt out of place?
- Imagine yourself going to a foreign country where the custom is to bow a different depth each time you greet someone. They follow some rule about how deeply to bow, but you don't know what it is. You are about to greet someone and don't know how low to bow. How do you feel?
- How about manners? Have you ever found yourself at a fancy restaurant not sure which fork to use first, or whether your water glass is the one on the left or the right?
- Name a time in a social situation you commited a faux pas. Describe your worst social blunder. What did you say or do or fail to say or do?
- Have you ever been with a group of strangers and felt unsure if you were doing the right thing? Describe the feeling you had.

The Next Step

Now that we have a sense of the seven student positions and how relating to the positions can prevent disruptions, let's take the next step. Let's identify specific preventative strategies that respond to the needs associated with each position. The strategies are presented in **Chapter 8. Preventative Procedures: The Seven Positions.** Many teachers are amazed by how simple preventative procedures eliminate most discipline problems. But really it should not be amazing — when student needs are met on a regular basis as part of the ongoing classroom procedures, students do not need to be disruptive to meet their needs.

Quiz Yourself –
Identify the Seven Positions

As a check for understanding, take a moment to identify the position of each student in the scenarios below.

1. Stephanie
In Mrs. Gordon's class, Stephanie wants everything her way. She comes to the front of the room and says, "I don't see why I should have to do this assignment. You can't make me."

2. Steve
Another student in Mrs. Gordon's class, named Steve, hit a classmate in the stomach in the hallway. When asked why, Steve said, "He was looking at me funny." When Mrs. Gordon talks to Steve, he lashes out at her, "Why are you always picking on me? You are not fair."

3. Todd
Todd is another student in Mrs. Gordon's class. He just said for the tenth time today, "Why do we have to do this?" Nothing seems to grab his interest.

4. Karen
Karen practically hides in the back of Mrs. Gordon's class. She is hoping no one (not even the teacher) will notice her. School is very frustrating for her because she does not believe she can do the work.

5. Alice
Alice is always waving her hand to be called on; she always has something to add. She wears outlandish outfits. Today as she walked to her seat, she poked a student and then glanced up to see if the teacher noticed.

6. Austin

Austin is bouncing off the walls again. It seems to Mrs. Gordon that he is constantly in motion. She wishes he would put all that activity to good use. She gets tired just looking at him.

7. Frank

Frank is exasperating Mrs. Gordon for the twentieth time this week. No matter how many times she explains to Frank the class rules, he always seems as if he is in a blue fog. Mrs. Gordon just wants him to "get it" so she doesn't have to tell him over and over how to treat the other students in this class.

For Quiz Answers, see Part VII, Resources D.1.

References

[1] Seligman, M. *Helplessness: On Depression, Development, and Death.* San Francisco, CA: W.H. Freeman and Company, 1975.

[2] Csikszentmihalyi, M. *Flow: The Psychology of Optimal Experience.* New York, NY: HarperCollins Publishers, 1990.

Preventative Procedures: The Seven Positions

A student in period three is always striving for attention, asking questions and doing disruptive things just to get the teacher's attention. That same student leaves period three, goes to period four, and never asks the teacher a question, is never disruptive, and seems to be a model student. What is the difference? The period four teacher always greets students at the door and uses cooperative learning. As soon as the student enters the room, he/she receives attention from the teacher and then sits down to interact with peers. A student who feels recognized and appreciated by teacher and peers does not strive for attention.

If a baby is well fed, it does not cry for food. A wise parent adopts a regular feeding schedule in order to avoid the crying. A wise teacher adopts procedures so that positive attention is a regular part of the diet in his/her classroom, avoiding many disruptions. A Win-Win teacher prevents most disruptions by recognizing, accepting, and responding to the student positions.

In this chapter we overview ongoing procedures that meet students' needs and teach responsible ways for them to meet their own needs, preventing discipline problems. All of us, at one time or another, have found ourselves in each of the seven positions, sometimes needing extra attention, needing to assert our sense of control, needing to vent our anger.... The Win-Win teacher accepts that being in the various positions is part of the human condition, so on a regular basis he/she practices procedures that respond to the needs of each position. In the Win-Win classroom all students regularly have their needs met, so they seldom feel the need to resort to disruptive behaviors to meet their needs. Ongoing procedures that meet student needs are the most important tool we have for preventing discipline problems and creating a smooth running, productive learning community.

How are the preventative procedures in this chapter different from those in **Chapter 6. Preventative Procedures: ABCD Disruptions**? The procedures in Chapter 6 are behavior oriented. Almost all disruptions can be categorized into the ABCD categories. By using the ABCD Tally, a teacher can assess which types of disruptions occur most frequently and then turn to the procedures in Chapter 6 to determine which types of procedures to emphasize. The procedures presented in the present chapter are position oriented. They are procedures to prevent position-based disruptions. When the position-based needs of students are met, they are far less disruptive because they do not need to be disruptive to meet their needs.

The position-based procedures in this chapter are practiced with the class as a whole, without regard to the specific dynamics of the class or the needs of individual students. The assumption is that at one time or another we are all in each of the positions, so by practicing all of the position-based procedures, the Win-Win teacher goes a long way toward preventing disruptions. With basic needs met, students do not need to be disruptive to meet their needs.

Some students have extreme needs. They will act out even when ABCD and Position-Based Procedures are in place. They are the exception, but we need to know what to do in the moment of their disruption. For those exceptional students, the Win-Win preventative procedures are not enough. For those students we have Win-Win structures for the moment-of-disruption and follow-ups.

Most teachers are surprised. When the ABCD Procedures and Position-Based Procedures are in place — and no teacher is expected to implement all the procedures — most students who would be disruptive become engaged, responsible learners. So Win-Win procedures are the place to start. Only when Win-Win procedures are firmly in place do we know if a student is truly a discipline problem. Most are not.

Procedures for the Seven Positions

Attention-Seeking

We all need attention. We seek positive attention in many ways, including buying the pretty new outfit or sporty car, styling our hair, doing well on a test, and making the clever remark — all in hopes of earning a bit of attention. If we cannot obtain positive attention, the need for attention is great enough that we will work even for negative attention. The class clown bids for attention from the class even though he/she knows it will result in negative attention from the teacher. A student wearing outlandish outfits, hair styles, or jewelry knows it will be met with negative attention from his/her parents, but negative attention is better than no attention at all.

The Win-Win teacher accepts that the need for attention is part of the human condition and provides students with ample positive attention, knowing attention fills a need and that if students receive positive attention on an ongoing basis, they will be far less likely to seek attention in disruptive ways.

A really great teacher is someone who... **says hi to me when I come in.** *—Hannah, 5 3/4, Cherry Hill, New Jersey[1]*

Greet 'Em. Greet all students at the door by name. Greet them in the hall by name. While passing Pete in the hall, in front of his peers, say, "Nice job on the homework assignment, Pete."

Smile. A smile goes a long way in your classroom in giving positive attention. Smile often. Make all students recipients. A special smile from the teacher can make the day of a student needing attention.

Express Appreciation. Say "Thank you for…" or "I appreciate…." Appreciate specific student responsible behaviors, even if the responsible behavior is something the students are supposed to be doing. "Thank you all for coming in and getting started right away on the bell work. We are off to a great start."

Affirmations. Point out students' positive characteristics. Comment when students are helpful, honest, hard working, friendly, compassionate, empathetic. Affirmations can be delivered verbally or written.

Acknowledge Student Feelings. One of the surest ways to fill a need for attention is to acknowledge feelings. Relate to the feelings of individual students with gambits like:

- "You must be feeling…"
- "It is frustrating for all of us when we work hard and still haven't got it."
- "That would make anyone really proud."
- "I see you really like…"
- "At first, I was the same way. I had trouble with…"
- "That would get me really angry too…"
- "Sometimes when I get really frustrated, I just take a break and come back to it later."

Relate also to the feelings of the whole class with gambits like:

- "I understand how you are feeling. It is frightening to know a lot depends on one test. But all any of us can do is take a deep breath, relax, and do the best we can."
- "Everyone is excited about vacation tomorrow. Turn to the person next to you, and in pairs take one minute each to tell your partner what you plan to do."

Morning Announcements. Recognize at least one or two students each morning in the morning announcements. Pass around the recognition.

Student's Name in an Example. Use student's name in instructional examples, as in, "Now let's say Sue had 10 apples and she sold each one for 35 cents …."

> "A really great teacher is someone who… **appreciates that what one thinks and says is more important than what one uses to fill in the blanks.**"
> —*Krista, 17, Mays Landing, New Jersey*[2]

◼ **Positive Phone Calls Home.** Place positive phone calls home to parents. Positive phone calls are a great strategy to use with all of your students, but it is particularly useful with your students seeking attention. It gives students some positive attention and makes it less likely that they will be disruptive to get attention.

◼ **Letter Home to Students.** Mail a letter to students before school starts welcoming them to your class. Mail or e-mail a complimentary letter to students mid-semester or midyear.

◼ **Chat Time.** Schedule time for a "getting to know you better" chat. Ask about family, friends, hobbies, or after school interests. Leave the door open for the student to ask for another chat. See Same-Side Chat, **Chapter 16. Follow-Up Structures.**

◼ **Hang Time with Teacher.** Engage one-on-one with a student in an activity of his/her choosing. Relate to the student's strongest intelligence by drawing together, writing a poem together, solving a logic game, playing chess together, planting a flowering plant, singing together, discussing feelings or dreams, or playing a physical game such as two-square or tetherball.

◼ **Special Meals.** Eat lunch with a small group of students each Friday, rotating groups so each student feels special.

◼ **Special Guest.** Allow the student to invite a favorite person to class. Make this a birthday tradition so students can invite a guest on their birthday.

◼ **Buddies.** Having classroom buddies can help a student seeking attention to feel that others care for him/her. Students can support each other in making responsible behavior choices when each student has a buddy and makes the people-to-people connection so important for students seeking attention.

◼ **Foster Grandparent.** You can involve the community and meet important attention needs of your students through using older individuals as foster grandparents. Some students that choose disruptive behavior need a positive connection with an adult. Teaming them with an older individual in the community is win-win for all.

◼ **Rotate Roles.** Rotate roles so students get turns to:

- Be first in the lunch line.
- Be exercise leader.
- Be teacher assistant.
- Have a special seat.
- Sit at the teacher's desk.
- Sit in the teacher's chair.
- Spend positive time with the principal.

Assign classroom roles of the week, requiring students to fill out a "job application." Allow students the privilege of being responsible for classroom pets over weekends or on holidays, making sure everyone in the class expresses their appreciation to that student afterwards.

■ **Special Recognition.** Notice and comment on students' clothes, hair, special effort, and successes. Use names often. Ask about family and friends.

■ **Recognition Ceremonies.** Establish birthday ceremonies. Include an interview of the birthday person in front of the whole class. Have recognition ceremonies for accomplishments.

■ **Bulletin Boards.** Have a "Student of the Week" bulletin board, celebrating that student with baby pictures and a coat of arms (have four sections to the shield: hobbies, family, friends, favorites). Display student work on a "We're Proud" bulletin board, making sure everyone's work gets celebrated.

■ **Praising Gambits.** Teach, model, and have students practice praising gambits to use with each other. Students who receive frequent positive peer attention are far less likely to disrupt the class seeking positive teacher attention. During pair or group work have students stop and tell their partner or teammates:

- "You are very intelligent!"
- "That is so insightful!"
- "Brilliant!"
- "You always make me think!"
- "Great ideas (words, pictures, explanation, etc)!"
- "You are an incredibly brilliant person!"
- "I found your response to be thoughtful!"
- "Your responses are always so well thought out!"
- "You are awesome!"
- "I am impressed by your brilliance!"
- "Your idea is outstanding!"
- "TIGHT!"

■ **Co-op Role: Praiser.** Classmates can satisfy much of the need for attention if the classroom is structured to include peer praise. Assign a rotating role of Praiser. Have students develop praising gambits to put on the back of the Praiser Role Card. On Monday Student 1 is the Praiser, on Tuesday Student 2, and so on. The Praiser Role can be assigned for special projects as well.

- A pre-made set of pop-up role cards with gambits, including the Praiser Role Card, is available through Kagan Publishing. See **Part VII, Resources F.**

■ **Kagan Structures.** Many Kagan Structures provide undivided peer attention. For example, during a Team Interview the three teammates give special attention to the interviewee, and each in

> *A really great teacher is someone who...*
> *...takes time for each student.*
> —*Tiffini, 16, Medora, Indiana*[4]

turn gets to be the interviewee. During Timed Pair Share, each student gets the undivided attention of his/her partner. Cooperative Learning[5] describes dozens of structures that meet the need for attention among peers, as well as how to set up and manage cooperative learning teams. Cooperative Structures for Classbuilding[6] describes structures like Find Someone Who to make sure everyone in the class is recognized for his/her special qualities and abilities. Cooperative Structures for Teambuilding[7] provides structures and activities so each student on a team knows and respects his/her teammates.

> • For ways to respond in the moment-of-disruption when a student is seeking attention see **Chapter 13. Responding to the Seven Positions.**

Avoiding Failure

We all attempt to avoid embarrassment. We rush to clean it up when we have a spill on our blouse or tie. One student, fearing failure, doesn't study just so he/she can have an excuse when he/she does poorly on the test: "Oh, I didn't study for that test." It is far more painful (embarrassing) to have studied and failed than to have not studied and failed. If I studied and failed, I must not be very smart. If I did not study and failed, I can pretend to myself and to others that I am smart; I would have done just fine on the test had I studied. Another student doesn't turn in a report, saying, "I wasn't interested in that topic." Fearing failure, it was less painful to say, "I didn't care," than to say, "I was afraid of trying but failing." These students don't try in order to have an excuse when they fail.

There are many other ways students act to avoid embarrassment. A student on the playground is about to lose in a competitive game. Rather than experience the embarrassment of the loss, the student starts a fight. The fight is not motivated by anger, but, rather, by the desire to avoid public embarrassment. The fight diverts attention from the loss. Another student would really like to serve on the student council but does not run, fearing the embarrassment of a loss. A third student avoids embarrassment by not taking challenging classes. Yet another student avoids embarrassment by not going out for an athletics team. Students go to great lengths to have the "in" clothes, ways of speech, and behavior patterns — all in attempts to the avoid embarrassment of not being part of the "in group."

Whenever possible the Win-Win teacher avoids putting students in situations which could result in public embarrassment.

■ **Avoid Putting Students "On the Spot."** A Win-Win teacher does not call on students individually until they have had ample guided practice and support, including a chance to ask for more time to consult with peers.

> ❝A really great teacher is someone who... **gives individualized help before or after school or during lunch so that nobody feels embarrassed about getting special attention.**❞ **—Aaron, 15, Aurora, Colorado[8]**

■ **Private Feedback.** Following tests or projects, grades are given out privately. This means graded work is not handed to the person in the front of the row to pass back and is not given to a materials monitor to distribute. When a student's behavior needs correction, whenever possible the Win-Win teacher attempts to give feedback in private.

■ **Class Norms.** The teacher sets the class norm so mistakes are not a source of embarrassment, but rather viewed as a learning opportunity, saying things like:

- "It is never wrong to not know, only to not ask for help when you do not know."
- "Mistakes are our guides: they tell us the direction for learning."
- "The biggest mistake is not being willing to make a mistake."
- "The biggest risk for a learner is not being willing to take a risk."
- "It takes far more courage to try and fail than not to try."
- "All of us make mistakes. It is part of the learning process. If you never make mistakes, you are working on problems far too easy for you."

■ **Posters.** Have students create posters illustrating the power of persistence in the face of setbacks. They might illustrate quotes such as:

- We learn wisdom from failure much more than from success. We often discover what will do by finding out what will not do; and probably he who never made a mistake, never made a discovery.
  —Samuel Smiles (1816–1904)

- Genius is one per cent inspiration and ninety-nine per cent perspiration. As a result, a genius is often a talented person who has simply done all of his homework.
  —Thomas Alba Edison (1847–1931)

- Success is going from failure to failure without a loss of enthusiasm.
  —Sir Winston Spencer Churchill (1874–1965)

- Always bear in mind that your own resolution to succeed is more important than any one thing.
  —Abraham Lincoln (1809–1865)

- Results? Why, man, I have gotten lots of results! If I find 10,000 ways something won't work, I haven't failed. I am not discouraged, because every wrong attempt discarded is just one more step forward....
  —Thomas Alba Edison (1847–1931)

- It is nobler to try and fail, than fail to try.
  —Spencer Kagan (1944–)

> **"A** *really great teacher is someone who...* **tells you it's ok to make mistakes (and how to correct them)."**
> —**Karli, 11, Farmington, New Mexico**[9]

> **"A** *really great teacher is someone who...* **is always nice about wrong answers."**
> —**Lauren, 9, York, Pennsylvania**[10]

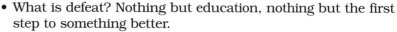

- What is defeat? Nothing but education, nothing but the first step to something better.
  —Wendell Phillips (1811–1884)

- Our greatest weakness lies in giving up. The most certain way to succeed is to always try just one more time.
  —Thomas Alba Edison (1847–1931)

- Failure is the path of least persistence.
  —Author unknown

- Persistence melts resistance.
  —Spencer Kagan (1944–)

■ **Class and Team Discussions.** Have students discuss the persistence quotes and find examples in their own life and in the lives of their parents when persistence paid off. Have students examine round river rocks and discuss how, over time, water shapes rocks. Have them create a class book titled "Persistence Melts Resistance." Each student adds a page of personal anecdotes to the book.

■ **Interviews.** Have students interview adults and discuss times when persistence paid off.

■ **Focus on the Student's Strengths.** It is vital that you comment on the strengths of your students. It is by building on their strengths that students coming from a position of avoiding failure can make positive changes in their lives.

■ **Gambits: Asking for Help.** Students can learn, practice, and celebrate gambits that make it acceptable to ask for help. In the Win-Win class, asking for help is seen as a virtue, far better than pretending to know when one does not.

- "Please help me with _____."
- "I don't understand _____. Who can explain?"
- "I'm having trouble with this problem. Can someone on the team help me?"

■ **Gambits: Checking for Own Understanding.**
- "Let me be sure I have this. Please watch me as I work this problem."
- "Let me put that in my own words to see if I got it all."
- "If I understand..."

■ **Gambits: Checking for Understanding of Others.** Teachers and peers practice checking for understanding in others to make sure they know how to perform a problem or understand the directions before performing on their own.

- "Could you repeat that back?"
- "Let me see if you got all my main points…"
- "Let me hear you say that in your own words…"

Gambits: Asking for Clarification.
- "I'm not sure I understood; could you explain it another way?"
- "I think I have it; could you do one more sample problem?"
- "Let me see if Susan (a different teammate) can explain that to me with a drawing."

Signal: Checking for Understanding. Before having students work on an assignment, the teacher has them signal with thumbs up, down, or wavering horizontally to indicate: "I got it," "I don't understand," or "I'm shaky on that."

Signal: Confusion. The teacher sets up a signal system so that at any time a student can signal that they do not understand. A common signal requesting clarification is a hand with palm flat waved above one's head.

Signal: Slow Down. A common signal requesting that the instructor slow down is to begin by placing two hands together, palms flat, and then slowly pulling them apart. This signal gives the speeding teacher the message to slow down.

- For a comprehensive treatment of classroom management signals, see **Chapter 18. Win-Win Management.**

Celebrate Accomplishments. Students who are avoiding failure need to stop and take stock of their accomplishments. In the Win-Win class, we frequently stop to celebrate the accomplishments of the class and individuals. Look for all types of accomplishments: improvement, straight desk, persistence, special skills, outside activities.

Affirmations. When students know they are a success in some areas, they are more willing to risk failure in other areas. The Win-Win teacher provides plenty of positive feedback to students on an ongoing basis, pointing out their

- **Virtues:** "I appreciate how helpful you were when…"
- **Management of emotions:** "You did a good job of controlling your anger."
- **Effort:** "I really like how you hung in there."
- **Choices of clothes:** "What a cool outfit."
- **Successes in extra-curricular activities:**
  Athletics: "Great play in the game yesterday."
  Music: "I really enjoyed your performance."
  Chess: "That last gambit was brilliant."

The teacher makes the affirmative comments verbally, with a nod, and/or in a note.

Self-Confidence Building. Students avoiding failure lack confidence in their ability to succeed. One way to build self-confidence among students is to organize tasks into bite-sized mini-tasks with feedback and celebrations after completion of each mini-task. A second way is to provide plenty of guided practice before individual practice. A third approach is to have students reflect on past successes. Teaching students encouragement gambits for peer support ("You can do it!") and self talk ("I can do it.") are helpful as well. "I can't" messages are hard to overcome, so use self-confidence builders frequently and over time.

Self-Concept Building. Help students obtain a more positive image or perception of themselves. Among the approaches are having students visualize themselves as successful, have peers share positive attributes they find in each other, and comment on positive attributes like:

- "You are clever."
- "You really look sharp."
- "You are a great leader."
- "You are kind."

When students have self-confidence, they are more willing to admit their areas of weakness rather than masking them through avoidance of failure.

Encouragement. We all need encouragement. Encouragement is particularly important for those who otherwise might give up in the face of frustration and those who might avoid a task for fear of failure. Encouragement helps students adopt a sense of "I can do it." Couple encouragement with reflection so that students take time to internalize the feeling of support. The ultimate goal of encouragement is self-support. Notice how in the following statement the Win-Win teacher couples encouragement with self-reflection.

- "You are doing great sticking in there even though this is a tough assignment. You must feel proud of yourself."

Positive Expectations. Expectations are a self-fulfilling prophecy. Imagining something helps bring it about. Approach all students as if they have the ability to choose responsible behavior. Positive expectations lead to positive outcomes. By visualizing a successful outcome, you help bring it about. Students coming from an avoidance of failure position are sometimes frustrating to work with because their progress is slow and they do not respond quickly to strategies to build up their "I can," but by holding onto the view that they can succeed, eventually you actually help them succeed. They internalize your attitude toward them.

Mistakes Are Part of the Learning Process. Build your class around the concept that mistakes are part of the learning process. For students avoiding failure, fearing making a mistake keeps them from trying. When students make an effort to learn, a natural part of the process is to make mistakes. You can cut through their fear-avoidance cycle by helping them look at mistakes as part of the learning process — discovering what we know and don't know. Students need to learn from their mistakes. Model this attitude as well when you make a mistake.

Role Assignment: Encourager. Peers can provide encouragement which helps students persist in the face of difficulties. To structure for encouragement, assign a rotating role of Encourager. Have students develop encouragement gambits to put on the back of the Encourager Role Card. On Monday Student 1 is the Encourager, on Tuesday Student 2, and so on. The Encourager role can be assigned for special projects as well.

- A pre-made set of pop-up role cards with gambits, including the Encourager Role Card, is available through Kagan Publishing. See **Part VII, Resources F.**

Kagan Structures. The Kagan Structures minimize potential for public failure by including peer tutoring and support prior to individual accountability. For example, in Numbered Heads Together students consult with teammates and signal they are all ready before being called on as individuals. In Team Pair Solo students work first as a team and then as pairs before being called on as individuals.[13]

Some structures do have students perform as individuals first, as in Showdown. But these structures have students perform on their own only in front of supportive teammates, with the understanding that it is OK to miss a problem — the norm in a good cooperative learning classroom: What we miss guides us as to what to work on as a group.

- For ways to respond in the moment-of-disruption when a student is avoiding failure see **Chapter 13. Responding to the Seven Positions.**

Angry

When students are truly angry, a series of centrally mediated autonomic nervous system reactions occur preparing them for flight or fight. With extreme anger, as during a fight, reactions become automatic. Reason is short-circuited. This has two implications for the Win-Win teacher: We want to structure so students do not become angry, and once they do, we want to help them calm down so reason can again prevail. It does little good to attempt to reason with a student while he/she is very angry. It does even

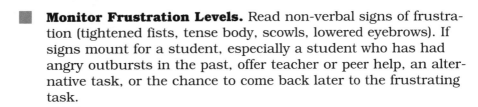

less good for us to become angry because we elicit cues that intensify and prolong the angry episode.

A great deal of research has been done about anger. It turns out that many of us grew up with a common misconception. We believed that it is always good to "get one's anger out." The belief in the benefits of catharsis or venting one's anger sprang from the psychoanalytic notion that repressed emotions had to become conscious for rational decision making to prevail. It turns out, however, that venting one's anger often re-ignites the flames that need to die down before rational thought can take over. As teachers it is usually best that we leave the catharsis and venting approaches to the psychologists and instead concentrate on preventing arousal of anger and helping students calm down once they have become angry.

We go a long way to preventing anger by preventing the major causes of anger among students: frustration, physical or psychological threats, pain, and a sense of being treated unfairly.

The pillars of Win-Win provide some excellent guidelines. If students have a hand in co-creating consequences, they are much less likely to feel they have been treated unfairly. Further, as we communicate we are on their side and there to help them, we create a less threatening environment. The same preventative measures we take to avoid embarrassment also go a long way to reducing anger because failure is a form of frustration and frustration triggers anger. Following are procedures that can be used to prevent overt displays of anger.

Preventing Angry Outbursts

■ **Monitor Frustration Levels.** Read non-verbal signs of frustration (tightened fists, tense body, scowls, lowered eyebrows). If signs mount for a student, especially a student who has had angry outbursts in the past, offer teacher or peer help, an alternative task, or the chance to come back later to the frustrating task.

■ **Break Up Learning Tasks.** Three 15 minute sessions on a topic will lead to dramatically more learning than will one 45 minute session, for a number of reasons related to learning theory. But breaking up difficult learning sessions also greatly reduces the probability of frustration, reducing the probability of angry outbursts. Breaking up learning tasks is helpful as well for students in other positions, as it reduces the probability of boredom and provides an outlet for excess energy.

■ **Apply Rules and Favors Equally.** Make it obvious that the rules apply equally to all. If a student feels singled out, he/she will feel unfairly treated and will be angry. The feeling of unfairness will result if the student feels the teacher is playing favorites. As difficult as it is, make sure all students know you care equally about their learning and about them as a person. The alternative is to invite anger.

Disagreeing Agreeably. Teach students gambits (verbal phrases) they can use to disagree without inviting resentment or retaliation:

- "I see it differently."
- "I would say that a little differently."
- "I have a different opinion about that."
- "I understand and respect your opinion. In my opinion..."
- "I see how you could see it that way. From my perspective..."

Anger Control Techniques. There are a host of self-control techniques to help students manage anger. Among the things we can do to reduce mounting anger are the following:

- Breathe deeply
- Concentrate on one's breath
- Concentrate on a puzzle or game
- Count to ten
- Commune with nature; garden
- Distraction: watch a movie, read a book
- Drink a glass of water
- Eat a treat
- Exercise
- Focus on desired outcomes
- Get adult help
- Go to a cool down center
- Journal
- Listen to music
- Meditate
- Play a game
- Play with a pet
- Recall a pleasant experience
- Reflect on the feelings of others
- Self talk: This too will pass; next year I won't even remember this
- Think time
- Talk it over with a friend
- Tense and relax a muscle group
- Think about something pleasant
- Walk away
- Write about the problem

Following an angry outburst the Win-Win teacher says, "We all get angry sometimes. Let's look at some responsible ways to deal with our anger." Teach students the power of counting to ten, of imagining the consequences of their actions before acting out, of seeking help, of postponing action. Have students suggest anger management techniques. A Win-Win teacher encourages students to experiment with different anger reduction strategies and to identify those strategies that work for them. The teacher lets students know each of us has to develop our own preferred style of dealing with anger and that a strategy which works well for one may not work for another. Have students create, discuss, and "try on" new anger management strategies.

■ **Teacher Disclosure.** Experiment with your own anger management techniques; share with your students what works best for you. Let students know that what works best for you may not be what works best for them.

■ **Verbal Gambits: Avoiding Escalation.** When students are not angry, work with them to learn what to do and what to say when they are angry. Have students try on and practice gambits to avoid anger escalation. Gambit development can include learning ways to disagree without invalidating another person and leaving room for the other person to calm down.

- "Right now we are too worked up to talk it over. Let's do that later."
- "I just need to go sit down before I do or say something I will regret."
- "We both are angry right now. Let's get a drink of water and calm down."

■ **Class Discussions: Responsible Anger.** Have students discuss times when it is natural to feel anger. Talk about times anger motivates us to solve social problems. Let students discover anger is neither right nor wrong — what we do about our anger, though, can be responsible or irresponsible. Have the class talk about things they can do to express anger responsibly. Use sample scenarios as a basis for class discussions. Have student teams make sample scenarios to trade with other teams for discussion. Use worksheets to facilitate discussion. (See Samples.)

■ **Journal Reflections.** Use Journaling to have the class reflect on responsible alternatives to aggression.

Acting Responsibly

For each item decide which is the most responsible way to act, and why.

1. You are on the playground in line at the drinking fountain. Someone shoves you from behind.

    a. You politely tell them not to shove.

    b. You tell them in a stern voice not to shove.

    c. You tell them that if they shove you again you will tell on them.

    d. You turn around and shove them back.

Write the letter of your choice. Explain your thinking.

_____

_____

_____

_____

_____

2. You are in class and someone trips you.

    a. You kick them.

    b. You do nothing to them and tell the teacher.

    c. You make a joke of it.

    d. You say "You will get yours later."

Write the letter of your choice. Explain your thinking.

_____

_____

_____

_____

When Is It OK to Feel Anger?

Is it OK or NOT OK to feel anger? Mark the line indicating where you stand, then discuss answers with a partner.

1. Someone calls you a name.

OK _____ Not OK

2. Someone hits you for no reason.

OK _____ Not OK

3. Someone hits you because you have hit them.

OK _____ Not OK

4. You see someone trip a best friend.

OK _____ Not OK

5. You see someone trip a person you do not know.

OK _____ Not OK

6. A person dressed in tattered clothes is standing in a shop next to a person dressed in fine clothes. The shop owner calls the police because someone has stolen something. The policeman immediately begins questioning the poorly dressed person, but does not question the well dressed person.

OK _____ Not OK

Expressing Anger Appropriately

■ **Teacher Input.** Students need to know that we all get angry sometimes. It is always okay to feel anger. The difference between a responsible and irresponsible person is not whether they get angry or not, but what they do if they get angry. Students need to learn there are responsible ways to deal with one's anger.

■ **Verbal Gambits: Expressing Anger.** Teach students verbal phrases they can use to express anger appropriately:

- "I felt angry when you..."
- "I really don't like it when..."
- "It doesn't help me when you..."

■ **Behavioral Gambits: Expressing Anger.** Teach students responsible behaviors to practice when they have the impulse to hit, fight, scream, or put down another student. Have them practice via role-plays, tabling the matter, taking a walk, discussing the issue with authority, and paraphrasing the other person's feelings.

Responding to Anger

■ **Cool Down Area.** Have a place where students can go to calm down following an outburst or if they feel they are getting angry. A "Quiet Zone" or "Cool Down Center" is designated as a non-punitive proactive place for students to regain composure. The area should be a low stimulation area. Ideally there are dim lights, no interaction with others, and quiet individual tasks like drawing, writing, or reading. Avoid tasks that have right-wrong answers. The heat of anger is not the time to have students reflect on the causes or consequences of their anger — reflection on what got them angry is likely to get them even more angry. You can come back to discussing causes and alternative behaviors later, after the student has completely calmed down.

- For ways to respond in the moment-of-disruption when a student is angry see **Chapter 13. Responding to the Seven Positions.**

Control-Seeking

None of us want to feel like a leaf in the wind, at the mercy of powers beyond our control. At certain ages students go through a stage of separating themselves from adult authority and are especially concerned with developing autonomy. The impulse

8.18

Win-Win Discipline. Kagan Publishing • 1 (800) 933-2667 • www.KaganOnline.com

toward independence is healthy. But if it takes the form of rejecting all adult authority or testing adult authority at every opportunity, it can be quite disruptive in the classroom. The best way to prevent disruptions rooted in the student's need for control is to sidestep any power plays and to give students as much autonomy, independence, choice, and control as is consistent with good instruction and good classroom management.

A really great teacher is someone who... **gives me a choice of who I want to be.** *—Laura, 11, Clarkson, Western Australia[14]*

Give Students Choices. Many things that we commonly choose for students are things we can, at least part of the time, let them choose. Among the choices we sometimes can offer students are as follows:

- Where their team will sit
- Where each of them will sit within the team
- How they will decorate the student bulletin board
- Choice of music (among reasonable alternatives)
- Choice of centers
- Decisions about what to study
- How to study
- When to study
- With whom to do buddy practice
- How to show what they have learned (presentation, essay, quiz, video, display board...)

Responsibilities. To the extent possible, consistent with good instruction, let students take control rather than controlling things yourself.

- "Today we will move our desks for the test. Before you leave class, I want you to return your desks to the position they are in now. I don't want to have to remind you. Take a moment and decide how you are going to remind yourselves."

- "It is your responsibility to get the permission slip signed. I won't be giving reminders. I want everyone in their teams to decide how you are going to take responsibility to make sure all your teammates get in their slips. Make a plan and record it."

Ask for Help. Ask your students on a regular basis to help you. Ask them to tell how the lesson could have been improved. In the middle or end of the lesson have students list two things the teacher did that helped them learn, one thing they did that helped them learn, and any suggestions they have for the teacher or themselves — What could have helped them learn more?

What Helped Me Learn?

Two things the teacher did that helped me learn.

1 _____

_____

_____

_____

2 _____

_____

_____

_____

One thing I did that helped me learn.

_____

_____

_____

_____

_____

What could help me learn more?

_____

_____

_____

_____

_____

■ **Validate the Need for Choices.** When it is appropriate, let students know that you understand their need to establish control. When you see a student struggling to establish independence or control, you might make statements like:

- "Everyone needs to know their opinion counts."
- "Everyone needs to feel they have some control over his/her life."
- "No one wants to feel bossed around."
- "Freedom means being able to choose for yourself."
- "Part of growing up is making responsible choices on your own."

■ **Class Meetings.** One of the most powerful tools for giving students choices and a sense of control is the class meeting. Class meetings are described in **Chapter 18. Win-Win Management.**

■ **Focus Groups.** Focus groups involve students in generating solutions for classroom problems. Students meet in small groups to generate ways to solve classroom problems or to make instruction or curriculum more meaningful. By empowering students to have a say in what or how they study, or how they are to interact in the classroom, the teacher satisfies the need for control and gives students a genuine opportunity to develop autonomy.

■ **Gambits:** Students learn and practice gambits to request a choice. Gambits that engender a sense of choice include:

- "I would prefer…"
- "If it is OK with you, let's…"
- "If I could chose, I would…"
- "My favorite is … because…"
- "How about…?"

■ **Class Roles.** Class roles help students satisfy their need for control.

- "Susie will read the announcements today. Everyone listen to Susie. Susie, you are in charge."

- "John will be the bell captain for this assignment. John, you will ring the 5-minute and 1-minute warning. You are responsible to make sure everyone knows how much time they have left."

■ **Team Roles.** Team roles have the advantage of allowing many students to assume positions of responsibility and control. Everyone can have a role, as when the teacher announces:

- Person 1: You are the ***Task Master***. Your job is to keep the group on task and follow the RoundTable rule of each one in turn being a recorder.

- Person 2: You are the **Checker**. When the group finishes a problem, you check with your partner team to be sure you have the same answer.
- Person 3: You are the **Cheerleader**. Your job is to have the group celebrate after finishing each problem.
- Person 4: You are the **Materials Monitor**. Your job is to gather the materials for the team, distribute them, and make sure they are all repackaged and returned to their place when your team has finished.

- The 12 most common team roles and associated gambits can be found in Cooperative Learning.[15] A colorful pop-up social role card kit provides the role cards and gambits for each role. See **Part VII, Resources F.**

Role Assignment: Task Master. To meet the need for control, assign roles to students in their groups. Having any role gives students a sense of control. A role which is particularly helpful for those seeking a sense of control is the Task Master. When the group gets off task, the Task Master brings the group back on task with gambits like:

- "Have we finished problem three yet?"
- "That is really interesting. What we need to be working on is…"
- "Let's see if we can finish before the bell rings."

Have students develop Task Master gambits to put on the back of the Task Master Role Card. Rotate the roles. On Monday Student 1 is the Task Master, on Tuesday Student 2, and so on. The Task Master role can be assigned for special projects as well. A pre-made set of pop-up role cards with gambits for each role, including the Task Master role, is available through Kagan Publishing. See **Part VII, Resources F.**

Student-Led Conferences. A great way to provide a legitimate sense of control is to put students in charge of conducting parent/teacher/student conferences. Student led conferences empower students to take responsibility for their own actions.

Kagan Structures. A number of Kagan Structures are designed to facilitate student decision making.[16] Voting is the worst structure to use because it always creates winners and losers, polarizing the class and creating resistance among the losers to the majority decision. Alternatives to voting include:

- Consensus Seeking
- Dot Wall
- Fist to Five
- Placemat Consensus
- Proactive Prioritizing
- Rotation Rank
- Spend-a-Buck
- Sum-the-Ranks

> • For ways to respond in the moment-of-disruption when a student is seeking control, see **Chapter 13. Responding to the Seven Positions.**

Energetic

We all have energy and all need to use it. The experience of being "antsy" after sitting through a long lecture is common to most of us. We are built to move. When the need to move is unsatisfied long enough, it interferes with clear thinking and learning. The Win-Win teacher recognizes and accepts the need for movement and so in many ways incorporates movement into classroom activities.

Energizers and Brain Breaks. Silly Sports and Goofy Games[20] is a collection of over 200 activities which work well to burn off excess energy and refocus students on learning. A few of the most popular Silly Sports and Goofy Games to help students "get their energy out" in fun, non-disruptive ways:

- Blind Caterpillar
- Everyone's It!
- Hagoo!
- Pair Balances
- Quick Tag
- Target Walk

> • Sample Silly Sports are provided at the end of this book. **See Part VII, Resources E.**

Extra-Curricular Activities. When we think of encouraging students to express their energy in responsible ways, playground sports and games come to mind. In addition to Silly Sports, we can encourage any number of positive energy releases:

- Campus Clean-Up Crew
- Dance Club
- Drama Club
- Hiking Club
- Walking Club
- Yoga Club

Special Roles. Special roles also help students release their energy in positive ways:

- Chalkboard Cleaner
- Eraser Cleaner
- Exercise Leader
- Fish Tank Cleaner
- Materials Monitor
- Office Messenger
- Special Errand Captain

"A really great teacher is someone who... **allows the children to joke around by having a few minutes of telling jokes but doesn't let the class get out of control.***"*
—*Rebecca, 12, Perth, Western Australia*[17]

■ **Calming Music.** Music at 60 or fewer beats a minute has a calming effect. With this kind of music playing in the background, students who otherwise might be too energetic to learn calm down and focus.

■ **Reduce Stimulation.** Anything that cuts down external stimulation is likely to calm a student — unless, of course, they are in a state of rage, in which case you want to distract them from internal stimulation. One of the easiest ways to reduce external stimulation is to have students work alone or to have them shut their eyes while listening to music or nature sounds.

■ **Stress Apples.** Hands-on manipulatives, such as a squeezable Stress Apple and Hand Candy, release energy, allowing students to calm down and focus. See **Part VII, Resources F.**

■ **Gambits.** Help students learn responsible gambits to use when they feel restless.

- "I'm feeling restless.... Would it be OK if I...?"
- "Can I be the next one to clean the board?"
- "I'm ready for an exercise break."

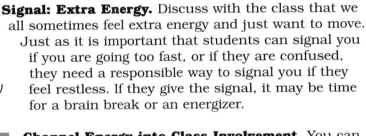

■ **Signal: Extra Energy.** Discuss with the class that we all sometimes feel extra energy and just want to move. Just as it is important that students can signal you if you are going too fast, or if they are confused, they need a responsible way to signal you if they feel restless. If they give the signal, it may be time for a brain break or an energizer.

■ **Channel Energy into Class Involvement.** You can change the activities in the classroom when students have excess energy. Active teaching strategies engage students, allowing them to channel energy into learning. Incorporating movement into learning activities helps students release excess energy.

■ **Managing Energy Level.** Teach students what to do when their energy is overflowing. Arrange a signal the student can give you when he/she needs to work off energy. You might allow the student to stand up and do a simple exercise that does not disrupt the teaching. Provide energetic students concrete strategies to deal with their energy so they won't need to resort to disrupting.

■ **Role Assignment: Materials Monitor.** The energetic student enjoys a chance to move. A role which is particularly helpful for those seeking movement is Materials Monitor or Materials Manager. When the group needs to get or return materials, the Materials Manager gets a chance to move. All students need the opportunity to move, so rotate roles. On Monday Student 1 is the Materials Monitor, on Tuesday Student 2, and so on. The Materials Monitor Role can be assigned for

> *A really great teacher is someone who...* **lets us play games in the classroom like "Duck, Duck, Goose."** —*Luke, 6, Cogan Station, Pennsylvania*[18]

> *A really great teacher is someone who...* **lets you move around a lot.** —*Andrew, 9, Mishawaka, Indiana*[19]

special projects as well. A pre-made set of pop-up role cards with gambits, including the Materials Manager, is available through Kagan Publishing. See **Part VII, Resources F.**

> • Roles are described in more detail in **Chapter 18. Win-Win Management.**

■ **Kagan Structures.** Many of the Kagan instructional strategies include movement. Classbuilding structures all include getting up and interacting with others in the class.[21] Among the many classbuilding structures are:

- Corners
- Find Someone Who
- Formations
- Give One, Get One
- Inside-Outside Circle
- Similarity Groups

A number of the review structures and thinking skill structures also include movement. Some of the many learning structures which include movement are:

- Carousel Review
- Carousel Feedback
- Circle-the-Sage
- Logic Line-Ups
- Roam-the-Room
- Roving Reporter
- Stir-the-Class
- Stroll-Pair-Share
- Traveling Heads Together

These structures are described in detail in Cooperative Learning[22] and Multiple Intelligences.[23]

> • For ways to respond in the moment-of-disruption when a student is energetic, see **Chapter 13. Responding to the Seven Positions.**

"A really great teacher is someone who... *gets your interest and keeps it.*"
—Eric, 21, Ithica, New York[24]

"A really great teacher is someone who... *will challenge you but not overwhelm you.*"
—Daniel, 13, Mishawaka, Indiana[25]

Bored

True boredom, mental listlessness, as the dictionary defines it, occurs when there is a lack of interest or motivation. The antidote, of course, is to generate motivation and interest. As teachers, we must be careful to distinguish true boredom from feigned boredom. Pseudo-boredom may occur for a number of reasons, but the most common is an attempt to avoid the embarrassment associated with a public failure. Fearing failure, the student says, "Oh, I don't care about that." The student is feigning boredom to mask a fear of failure: It is much less embarrassing to say "I don't care" than "I'm afraid." We treat pseudo-boredom, which is really just disguised fear of failure, in the same way we treat any fear of failure — we make sure the student knows he/she can succeed.

We treat true boredom by generating motivation and interest. Motivating and interesting curriculum and instruction is nothing short of good teaching. Good teachers do not experience disruptions based on boredom.

Creating, Sustaining Interest

■ **Relate to Personal Interests.** If we have students generate a list of things they would like to learn on a topic and structure the lesson so they see that it will satisfy their genuine interest, we have gone a long way toward eliminating boredom.

■ **Relate to Current Events.** Don't wait until current events are in the history books. Study them with your class now, or at least link your curriculum to current events.

- If the topic is World War II, ask how our most recent (or current) war was like or unlike World War II.
- If the topic is percentages, have the students do percentage problems based on data from the latest Gallup poll.
- If the topic is Macbeth, have students compare and contrast the characters to contemporary movie or rock stars.
- If the topic is geology and the students are studying the various types of rocks, have them bring in rocks from their neighborhoods to classify.

■ **Relate Curriculum to Class and School.** Use incidents that come up in class to illustrate curriculum.

- How does the law of supply and demand relate to interruptions during our limited review time?
- How does this story relate to what happened on the playground yesterday?
- Can we express class time vs. lunch and break times as a ratio? As a fraction? As a percent? In a pie graph?
- The industrial revolution was based in part on division of labor. What are examples of division of labor in our classroom as we do team projects? How does division of labor apply to the jobs in our school?

■ **Name Dropping.** While teaching a lesson, occasionally slip in student names.

- "Now to illustrate my point, Susan, lets say…"
- "When calculating the area of a circle, Bob, we…"
- "One of the literary techniques used in the passage, Joe, is…"

> " *A really great teacher is someone who…* **makes learning interesting rather than just reading things out of a book.** "
> —*Erica, 11, Beardstown, Illinois* [26]

8.26

Win-Win Discipline. Kagan Publishing • 1 (800) 933-2667 • www.KaganOnline.com

■ **Have Students Generate Real Questions.** Create a student question bank. Have students work in teams to make deposits to the question bank. Draw questions from the bank to discuss or research. See Cooperative Learning and Higher-Level Thinking[27] for many excellent examples of ways to have students generate and answer real questions.

■ **Alternative Sources of Information.** Make the textbook but one of many sources of information. Encourage interviews, Internet, newspaper archives, experiments.

■ **Unpredictable Schedule.** "Class, today we are going to turn our class schedule upside down and begin the day with reading and end the day with math."

■ **Costumes.** Wear a costume related to the class content. Have students wear costumes related to the class content.

■ **Role Assignment.** Students become more engaged when they have a special role. Class becomes more interesting when roles are rotated, so Monday a student might be the Cheerleader, Tuesday the Recorder, Wednesday the Quiet Captain, and so on. The most frequently assigned roles are:

> 1. Checker
> 2. Cheerleader
> 3. Coach
> 4. Encourager
> 5. Gatekeeper
> 6. Materials Monitor
> 7. Praiser
> 8. Question Commander
> 9. Quiet Captain
> 10. Recorder
> 11. Reflector
> 12. Task Master

A pre-made set of the twelve pop-up role cards with gambits for each role is available through Kagan Publishing.[28]

■ **Kagan Structures.** Rita Carter, in her wonderful book, Mapping the Mind,[29] provides active brain imaging scans which demonstrate tremendously greater brain activity when people are in interaction, explaining something to a partner compared to when they are just reading, or listening to a lecture. See Brain Scans, **Chapter 6. Preventative Procedures: ABCD Disruptions, Page 6.22.** The royal road to brain engagement is social interaction. For dozens of engaging cooperative learning structures which can be used as part of any lesson to increase engagement, see Cooperative Learning.[30]

Quiet Captain

> *A really great teacher is someone who...* **comes and sits next to me and helps me with words that I cannot read or understand.** *—Thi Huyen, 12, Perth, Western Australia*[33]

Sparking Motivation

Projects. Allow students alone or in teams to acquire and/or demonstrate their learning via projects. Presentations to the rest of the class spark greater motivation than any other approach. Students are most fully engaged when doing cooperative projects, especially if they are given choice of what to study and how to present their findings. Co-op Co-op and Co-op Jigsaw are structures for successful cooperative projects, ensuring student choice, mutual support, as well as equal participation and individual accountability. See *Cooperative Learning*.[31]

Centers. Motivation increases when students can rotate through learning centers, especially if the centers are self-directed and have a clear task to accomplish in a limited time.

Multiple Intelligences. Students who are not at all motivated to listen when the teacher talks become very attentive when the teacher draws or acts. Present material in each of the eight intelligences. See *Multiple Intelligences*.[32]

Appropriate Level of Difficulty. Motivation peaks when there is a match between student ability and task difficulty. When the match occurs, students are in flow. See Flow Diagram page 7.8. When the task is too easy, boredom results; when the task is too hard, anxiety or giving up results. There are a number of things we can do to adjust task difficulty to student ability:

• Monitor and adjust task difficulty by observing levels of boredom and anxiety — both of which lead to off-task behavior.
• Have students rate tasks on a scale from too easy to too difficult.
• Allow students graduated tasks: *"If you get 80% or better, you move up to…"*
• Include challenging extra credit problems for those who finish early.
• Give challenge options: *"If you want more difficult problems, you can work on…"*
• Give support options: *"If you are having difficulty with these problems, turn to…"*

Choices. Allow students choices:

• What part to study first
• How to study
• How to demonstrate knowledge
• When to work on projects
• How much time to allot for presentations
• How to set up the room during presentations
• Whom to invite to class as guest lecturer
• Which of two films to watch on an historical event
• Which of two literature books to read

> *A really great teacher is someone who…*
> *…**will reach out to help a student, even if the student doesn't ask for help.***
> —Anthony, 18, Mays Landing, New Jersey[34]

> *A really great teacher is someone who…*
> *…**doesn't make you scared to ask a question.***
> —Dorothy, 10, Edmonds, Washington[35]

- For ways to respond in the moment-of-disruption when a student is bored see **Chapter 13, Responding to the Seven Positions.**

Uninformed

On the first day of class Johnny punches Peter, who sits in the row next to him, and uses a colorful curse word to describe him. It turns out that Johnny is not trying to make trouble at all and would like to be a good student. He is simply treating Peter the way kids in his home and neighborhood treat each other. He has not learned that there are different norms for behavior at school. He is uninformed. The Win-Win response to a student who is uninformed is to find ways to get the student to know and identify with school and classroom norms.

Much of what has been described as ways to prevent rule breaking responds to the needs of the uninformed student. (See **Chapter 6. Preventative Procedures: ABCD Disruptions**.) Often private meetings or coaching sessions are useful to avoid embarrassing the uninformed student. Classroom norms, procedures, and rules can be conveyed in many ways; a student who does not understand the rules one way may grasp them immediately when they are taught in a different way. And of course, as much as possible we want to empower the uninformed student to obtain information and help on his/her own. All students need to know that the only dumb question is the one that isn't asked.

- **Heterogeneous Cooperative Learning Teams.** The most effective cooperative learning teams consist of four students, one high achieving, two middle achieving, and one low achieving student. This configuration, of course, is a powerful solution to communicating rules and procedures in a non-threatening way, and the uninformed student has three teammates to help him/her.

- **Tutors.** Peer tutors, teacher aides, cross-age tutors, as well as parent and community volunteers all can help students "get" the norms, rules, and procedures. Tap into the tutoring resources within your own classroom and school. On an occasional basis, operating as a classroom tutor is beneficial for all students. We learn as we teach. This creates a Win-Win situation for both tutor and tutee.

- **Adult Mentor.** Use parents and other adults in the community to mentor students. Students that disrupt often have a strong need for a positive connection with an adult. Knowing someone cares can make the big difference. The mentor also serves as a positive role model.

- **Foster Grandparent.** A foster grandparent program is a great way to involve the community. As stated previously, students that disrupt often have a strong need for a positive connection with an adult. Teaming them with an older individual in the community is a Win-Win situation: the foster grandparent has added meaning and purpose and the student has added support and guidance.

Skills for Independence. Generate a list of skills your students need in order to be independent learners in your class, teach those skills, and provide practice. Autonomy is the goal, but students need instruction and support to move in that direction.

Schedule on Board. Writing the daily schedule on the board, including what the students are working on, helps all students stay informed.

Multiple Intelligences. Teach rules and norms in many ways:

Multiple Intelligences Approaches to Rules

• **Verbal/Linguistic**	Have students write a poem about the rule(s).
• **Logical/Mathematical**	Have students derive reasons for the rule(s).
• **Visual/Spatial**	Have students make a poster to support the rule(s).
• **Musical/Rhythmic**	Have students write a rule rap, chant, or song.
• **Bodily/Kinesthetic**	Have students act out the rule(s).
• **Naturalist**	Have students create an analogy from nature.
• **Interpersonal**	Have students teach the rule(s) to a partner.
• **Intrapersonal**	Have students keep a journal about the rule(s).

Gambit Development: Requesting Help. Work with students so they have gambits to clarify procedures:

- "What is the procedure for...?"
- "Can you please explain how...?
- "Could you please help me with...?

Gambit Development: Offering Help. Ask the class the following question: What do you do or say if you see someone breaking a rule? Have the class develop polite gambits to help other students know and understand the rules. Develop class norms. Do they think written help notes are best? Or is it better to offer help verbally? Help students develop gambits that will not belittle the person they are trying to help:

- "Can I offer you some help on...?"
- "Would you like some help with...?"
- "Let me help you. The way to..."
- "Our procedure for turning in late homework is..."

■ **Role Assignment: Question Commander.** One of the cooperative learning roles which most helps students be informed is the Question Commander. It is the job of the Question Commander to check to see if anyone has questions or needs help. Legitimizing this role in the group makes it easier for the uninformed student to acknowledge his/her questions and get them answered. Have the students generate gambits for the Question Commander, like:

- "Let's see, does anyone have any questions?"
- "Let's all do a practice problem to see if we have any questions."
- "Let's take turns asking a question of the person on our right to see if we all really know this."

Have students develop Question Commander gambits to put on the back of the Question Commander Role Card. Rotate the roles. On Monday Student 1 is the Question Commander, on Tuesday Student 2, and so on. The Question Commander role can be assigned for special projects as well.

A pre-made set of pop-up role cards with gambits for each role, including the Question Commander, is available through Kagan Publishing.[36]

The New Student

■ **Buddy.** Assign new students a buddy — someone who knows the class norms well and can explain them. Prepare the buddy. Have them identify with the difficulty of being a new student. Reinforce their efforts at taking the new student under their wing. If the buddy is a high status student, you have probably provided a model the new student will emulate.

■ **Conference.** Meet privately with the new student in a special orientation session. Let the student share. Become someone they can talk to. See Same-Side Chat, **Chapter 16. Follow-Up Structures.**

The Student Just Can't Remember

■ **Verbal and Non-verbal Cues.** For students who need special help remembering a rule, one option is to develop individual verbal or nonverbal cues as reminders. See Cues: Verbal and Non-verbal, **Chapter 16. Follow-Up Structures.**

- For ways to respond in the moment-of-disruption when a student is uninformed, see **Chapter 13. Responding to the Seven Positions.**

Procedures = Prevention

When the Win-Win preventative procedures are in place, a host of powerful forces act in concert to prevent classroom disruptions:

- Students know, identify with, and have practiced the rules.
- Students experience choices and do not feel controlled.
- Students find the curriculum and instruction are interesting and motivating.
- Students can de-escalate conflicts and diffuse anger.
- Student needs are met on a regular basis.
- Students feel themselves to be members of a caring community of learners.
- Students receive plenty of attention and affirmations.
- Students enjoy plenty of academic support and success due to supportive instructional strategies and from peer support and tutoring.
- Students know they can be successful.
- Students are secure, knowing they will not be put on the spot.
- Students have many positive outlets for excess energy.
- Students know what to do when they don't know what to do: they have ways to signal the teacher to slow down and have gambits for asking for help from peers and teacher.

Perhaps most important of all, students feel themselves to be on the same-side with the teacher. The teacher knows their position, where they are coming from, meets their needs and helps them meet their own needs. The teacher sidesteps power plays, looking beyond the behavior to their position, his/her needs. The student knows the teacher may not always accept his/her behavior, but always accepts him/her as a person. The teacher is someone who supports the students, someone they want to please, not someone they want to confront. When the Win-Win procedures are in place, most discipline problems disappear.

References

[1, 2, 3, 4, 8, 9, 10, 11, 12, 14, 17, 18, 19, 24, 25, 26, 33, 34, 35] Bluestein, J. (Ed.) Mentors, Masters, and Mrs MacGregor: Stories of Teachers Making a Difference. Deerfield Beach, FL: Health Communications, Inc., 1995, p. 72, 163, 314, 215, 73, 114, 75, 214, 213, 270, 159, 39, 316, 38, 317, 38, 117, 272, 36.

[5] Kagan, S. Cooperative Learning. San Clemente, CA: Kagan Publishing, 1994.

[6] Kagan, S., Kagan, L., & Kagan, M. Classbuilding. San Clemente, CA: Kagan Publishing, 1995.

[7] Kagan, S., Kagan, L., & Kagan, M. Teambuilding. San Clemente, CA: Kagan Publishing, 1997.

[13] Kagan, S. Cooperative Learning. San Clemente, CA: Kagan Publishing, 1994.

[15] Kagan, S. Cooperative Learning. San Clemente, CA: Kagan Publishing, 1994.

[16] Kagan, S. Cooperative Learning. San Clemente, CA: Kagan Publishing, 1994. p. 13:5–9.

[20] Kagan, S. Silly Sports and Goofy Games. San Clemente, CA: Kagan Publishing, 2000.

[21] Kagan, S., Kagan, L., & Kagan, M. Classbuilding. San Clemente, CA: Kagan Publishing, 1995.

[22] Kagan, S. Cooperative Learning. San Clemente, CA: Kagan Publishing, 1994.

[23] Kagan S., & Kagan, M. Multiple Intelligences: The Complete MI Book. San Clemente, CA: Kagan Publishing, 1998.

[27] Wiederhold, C. Cooperative Learning and Higher-level Thinking. San Clemente, CA: Kagan Publishing, 1995.

[28] Kagan, S. Pop-Up Social Role Card Kit. San Clemente, CA: Kagan Publishing, 1997.

[29] Carter, R. Mapping the Mind. Berkeley, CA: University of California Press, 1998.

[30] Kagan, S. Cooperative Learning. San Clemente, CA: Kagan Publishing, 1994.

[31] Kagan, S. Cooperative Learning. San Clemente, CA: Kagan Publishing, 1994.

[32] Kagan S., & Kagan, M. Multiple Intelligences: The Complete MI Book. San Clemente, CA: Kagan Publishing, 1998.

[36] Kagan, S. Pop-Up Social Role Card Kit. San Clemente, CA: Kagan Publishing, 1997.

Chapter 9

Teaching the Win-Win Philosophy

*Win/Win is not a technique;
it's a total philosophy of
human interaction.*[1]
—*Stephen R. Covey*

When students grasp the Win-Win philosophy and begin to seek solutions that are positive for all concerned, their classroom and school are transformed. Many or most discipline problems disappear because students consider the impact of their behavior on others and refrain from disruptive and irresponsible behaviors.

Learning the Win-Win philosophy goes beyond reducing discipline problems — when internalized, Win-Win transforms a student's life. As described by Stephen Covey:

> *Win/Win is a frame of mind and heart that constantly seeks mutual benefit in all human interactions. Win/Win means that agreements or solutions are mutually beneficial, mutually satisfying. With a Win/Win solution, all parties feel good about the decision and feel committed to the action plan. Win/Win sees life as a cooperative, not a competitive arena. Most people think in terms of dichotomies: strong or weak, hardball or softball, win or lose. But that kind of thinking is fundamentally flawed. It's based on power and position rather than on principle. Win/Win is based on the paradigm that there is plenty for everybody, that one person's success is not achieved at the expense or exclusion of the success of others.*
>
> *Win/Win is a belief in the Third Alternative. It's not your way or my way; it's a better way, a higher way.*[2]

How is this philosophy best conveyed? Implicitly, we teach the philosophy on a daily basis as we model it for our students. We teach the philosophy as we repeatedly ask students to reflect on and generate Win-Win solutions. We teach it also by labeling actions as Win-Win, win-lose, or lose-win.

Explicit instruction in the Win-Win philosophy can take many forms as we draw from examples from literature, history, and applied science. The most powerful approach we have found, however, is what we have come to call The Win-Win Lesson.

The Win-Win Lesson

Goal: Students reflect on the impact of responsible versus disruptive behavior for themselves and others and make a commitment to an ongoing process of seeking responsible, Win-Win solutions.

Time: Several one hour sessions, usually spread out during the first week of school.

Steps:

Step 1. Teacher Write: Teacher creates the Win-Win Lesson Frame. At the top of the frame might be the following: "The Way We Want Our Class to Be..." At the left are the seven positions with a space following each to write disruptive and responsible things to say and do (see graphic). If the lesson is to be broken up, the teacher might deal with only one or two positions in each segment of the lesson.

The way we want our class to be...				
	Disruptive		Responsible	
	Say	Do	Say	Do
Attention-Seeking	• Blurt out • Brag •	• Wear crazy clothes • Poke others on way to seat •	• Contribute good ideas • Give a clever compliment	• Raise hand • Perform in school play • Get good grades
Avoiding Failure				

Step 2. Teacher Talk: Teacher validates first position: Attention-Seeking.
"We all seek attention. It is a basic need. Some of the ways I hope to get positive attention are..."

Step 3. Teacher Talk: "We all can seek attention in ways that are responsible or ways that are disruptive. For example, a responsible way to seek attention is to raise your hand when you want to be called on. A disruptive way to seek attention is to blurt out. Another responsible way to seek attention is to study hard to try for a good grade so we will get positive attention from our parents, peers, and teacher. Some disruptive ways to seek attention are to come into class talking very loudly, wearing outlandish clothes, knocking over chairs."

Step 4. RallyRobin: "Turn to your shoulder partner and name irresponsible ways to seek attention."

Step 5. Students Share: "Person One on each team, please stand. When I say 'go', please come to the board, take some chalk, and write in your answers."

Step 6. RallyRobin: "Now turn to your face partner and take turns naming responsible ways to seek attention."

Step 7. Students Share: "Person Two on each team, please stand. All the Twos please come to the board to write in your answers."

Step 8. Teacher Question w/ Team Discussion: "How would you like our class to be? Would you like bragging, poking, blurting out, and the other disruptive ways of seeking attention, or would you prefer these responsible behaviors? Think about it. [Pause]. Discuss it in your groups."

9. Teacher Comment: "As I listen in, I hear you prefer the more responsible behaviors."

Step 10. Teacher Question w/ Team Discussion: "Why? Please continue discussing in your groups."

Step 11. Repeat: The sequence or some variation of it is continued for the seven positions, usually broken up and delivered in separate sessions over several days or weeks.

Step 12. Teacher Talk: *"If this is the way we want our class to be, what are some of the things you can do to make it more that way. Look at the chart. Take out paper. Write a commitment letter: In order to make our class the way we want it to be, I agree to…"*

Step 13. The Chart as a Posted Reference. When disruptive behavior occurs, the teacher goes to the chart, points out the behavior, and asks, "Is this the way we want our class to be? What would be the responsible alternative?" The Disruptive vs. Responsible Behaviors Chart is a continual point of reference in the Win-Win classroom.

Comment: The power of the Win-Win Lesson is that students derive responsible norms for their classroom. The norms are not imposed on the students, but rather emerge from the way the students themselves want the class to be.

The process can be extremely powerful. When asked why they would rather choose the responsible alternatives, with no suggestions from the teacher the students say things like: *"I would feel safer"; "The class would be fair"; "We would all be on the same side"; "Everyone would win."*

During Step 12 one boy said, *"I don't want to brag anymore to get attention. I would rather get attention by being a good friend."* A girl said, *"I see it is not as important the clothes you wear as how well you are a good listener."*

Win-Win Philosophy

When we view discipline through Win-Win lenses, our view of disruptive students and our role as educators is transformed. A disruption is merely an uneducated attempt to meet basic needs we all share. Our role as teachers then is to convert the disruption into a learning opportunity so students learn responsible, non-disruptive ways to meet their needs.

We Win: Our class has fewer disruptions and we fulfill our roles as educator.

The Student Wins: The student learns to replace disruptive, self-defeating behaviors with responsible, fulfilling ways to satisfy basic needs.

The Class Wins: Students have the opportunity to be part of a productive and caring learning community.

Teaching the Win-Win Philosophy: Transforming the World!

Who we are and how we approach our students conveys a philosophy. We have no choice as teachers: We cannot choose not to teach a philosophy. The philosophy we model in our daily interaction with our students, like it or not, becomes a lesson for our students. If we manipulate students, we teach them to be manipulative. If we use sarcasm, we teach them to put down others. If we blindly respond to each student's disruptive behavior without looking for the needs from which the disruption sprang, we teach blind insensitivity. If we look beyond the disruptive behavior to see and relate to the student's position, we teach sensitivity, caring, and model the Win-Win philosophy.

As we model the Win-Win philosophy and teach it to our students, we all become more rooted in a Win-Win way of seeing situations and solving problems. As this happens, as we live Win-Win, we view our mission as educators in an expanded way. Yes, teaching our academic content is important. Yes, efficiently ending disruptions so all students can learn is important. But, if our students leave our class able to look beyond themselves, able to approach each new situation asking not just what they can get, but asking also what is in the best interests of others, then we have given them a gift that goes beyond academics. As students adopt a Win-Win philosophy in their interactions with others, they lead a richer life and make life more fulfilling for others. Ultimately, teaching the Win-Win philosophy transforms the world.

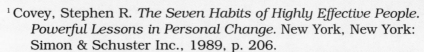

References

[1] Covey, Stephen R. *The Seven Habits of Highly Effective People. Powerful Lessons in Personal Change.* New York, New York: Simon & Schuster Inc., 1989, p. 206.

[2] Covey, Stephen R. *The Seven Habits of Highly Effective People. Powerful Lessons in Personal Change.* New York, New York: Simon & Schuster Inc., 1989, p. 207.

ABCD Questions

> • **Manuel pinches Carlos.**
> • **Krista brings her books to class uncovered.**
> • **Sandy yells at the teacher, "You can't make me do that!"**
> • **Mike falls asleep while working on his worksheet.**

The Win-Win teacher does not see all these disruptions as simply disruptive behavior. The Win-Win teacher sees them as ABCD; that is, with practice, categorizing disruptions become automatic. We read each scenario above and think:

A Is for Aggression
B Is for Breaking the Rules
C Is for Confrontation
D Is for Disengagement

Once we see the disruption as A, B, C, or D, we are more likely to choose a discipline response that fits the behavior. The Win-Win teacher responds differentially to each of the four types of behavior, knowing aggression is best met with a very different response than disengagement.

Prevention Is Preferable. Often, when possible, the very best response to a disruption is to give minimum attention to the disruption in the moment and to check over the preventative procedures described in Chapters 6 and 8. The Win-Win teacher views the disruption as a cue. It tells the teacher which preventative procedures might best be instituted or reinstated.

Thus, although we will look at three different questions for each type of disruption, when faced with a disruption, the first question a Win-Win teacher always asks is: *"Do I have procedures in place that could prevent this type of disruption in the future?"* ***Prevention is always preferable.***

When Prevention Fails. If the problem is not lack of preventative measures with the class, then we must look at the behavior and position of the individual disruptive student to select our best response. Again, often a very minimal response in the moment with an individual follow-up is preferable to trying to deal with the disruptive student at any length while the rest of the class is losing time from academics. Simply telling the student his/her behavior is disruptive and that you need to meet with him individually in a follow-up is preferable to trying to teach the student responsible behavior while the rest of the class is waiting and watching. The student will be more open to learn in the privacy of an individual meeting and you will have time to formulate your response.

■ **Informed Discipline: Respond to Disruption + Position.** In this chapter, we will focus narrowly on the four ABCD disruptions and suggest critical questions and some options in response to each. The discipline response, however, is formulated based on the type of ABCD disruption *and* the student's position. With practice, the Win-Win teacher creates a discipline response considering both the type of disruption and position of the student. Before we can make a fully informed discipline response, we need to know not just the type of disruption we are dealing with, but also the position from which it springs. A Win-Win teacher responds to a student breaking the rules very differently if the student is uninformed about the rules than if the student is informed about the rules but in a position of confrontation!

In subsequent chapters, we will determine how to identify and respond to student positions in the moment-of-disruption. In this chapter, we will describe three disruption-specific questions to ask of each of the ABCD disruptions and some responses a teacher might consider depending on the answers to those questions.

■ **Three Disruption-Specific Questions.** In the moment-of-disruption we have mentally categorized the behavior ABCD, we ask ourselves three disruption-specific questions to help formulate our most appropriate response. There are different questions for each of the four types of disruptions. The answers to the three disruption-specific questions are important guides to help us create an effective discipline response. For example, if the disruption is Aggression, we must know in the moment-of-disruption if there is a threat to anyone. If so, we must take immediate action to ensure the safety of everyone in the classroom. If there is no immediate threat, we might choose a different course of action. This chapter identifies three critical questions for each type of disruptive behavior — these are helpful guides to responding effectively in the moment-of-disruption.

Behavior-Specific Questions: ABCD

A. Aggression
1. Is the student a threat to self or others?
2. Have I controlled my reaction?
3. Does this student have strategies to control aggression?

B. Breaking the Rules
1. Does the student recall the rule?
2. Does the student understand the rule?
3. Can the student apply the rule?

C. Confrontation
1. Have I controlled my reaction?
2. Have I given the student choices?
3. Am I using a Win-Win leadership style?

D. Disengagement
1. Is the learning relevant and developmentally appropriate?
2. Have I used a variety of teaching strategies?
3. Have I used efficient management techniques?

A. Aggression

- Is the student a **threat** to self or others?
- Have I **controlled** my reaction?
- Does this student have **strategies** to control aggression?

A1. Is the Student a Threat to Self or Others?

Aggressive behavior can be dangerous to others physically and psychologically. As teachers, our first concern is for the safety of everyone in our classroom. We need to prevent or terminate threatening or aggressive behavior quickly, not only because aggressive behavior is unsafe, but also because it can trigger more aggressive behavior via retaliation or contagion.

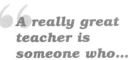

> *A really great teacher is someone who...* **helps people so they won't hurt each other.**
> —*A. J., 8, Mishawaka, Indiana*[1]

Structures that are helpful if a student is a threat to self or others include:

Cool Down Reminder: *"Are we getting close to needing cool down?"*
Cool Down: *"Please take some time in the cool down area now."*
Target, Stop, Do: *"Susie, right now you are poking Sarah; you need to keep your hands to yourself and open your book to page 112."*

- For step-by-step details of these structures, see **Chapter 14. Moment-of-Disruption Structures.**

A2. Have I Controlled My Reaction?

In the heat of aggression, even when aggression is not directed toward us, the teacher, it is important for us to monitor our own reaction. Aggression begets aggression. If we are calm, we can defuse emotions and model a more rational approach.

The importance of our remaining calm in the face of aggression is underscored by recent brain research revealing the existence of mirror neurons. When we read the faces of those around us, mirror neurons fire to produce the emotions in us that mirror the emotions projected by the faces around us. We are genetically wired to be copy-cats! This is why infants will stick out their tongues in response to adults sticking out theirs. Until the discovery of mirror neurons, it was a total mystery how the infant would "know" that his tongue corresponds to the tongue of the adult. Although we can understand the adaptive purpose of this hard wiring (there is a survival advantage in feeling fear when those around us do), the contagion of emotions in a classroom can be disastrous in the moment-of-disruption. The most powerful tool we have in countering a negative contagion of emotions is controlling our own emotional reaction.

■ **Teacher Think Time.** If there is not an emergency, the Win-Win teacher pauses for a moment before reacting. This not only models self-control, it allows for a more thoughtful response. The teacher simply says, "This is serious. Before deciding what to do, I need to think about the best solution." By carving out some think time, the teacher avoids overreacting and is more likely to settle on a better solution.

■ **Calm Voice.** By using a calm voice even in the face of aggression, the Win-Win teacher models a response which will counter aggression.

Structures that are helpful for teacher self-control include:

I-Messages Plus: *"When you stick out your leg and try to trip a classmate, I feel frustrated. I want our class to be safe and friendly and I want to be able to teach, not police the class. Your classmates are distracted from learning — our real mission here. Can you think of a better choice"?*
Model It: *"I get angry too."*
Schedule Follow-Up: *"We need to talk this through. Let's meet after...."*

> • For step-by-step details of these structures, see **Chapter 14. Moment-of-Disruption Structures.**

A3. Does This Student Have Strategies to Control Aggression?

In the face of aggression, safety is our first concern. Our second concern is being a positive model of self-control. Next, we help the aggressive student learn self-control.

Students who exhibit aggressive behaviors need support in controlling their aggression. First we turn to preventative procedures. As you will recall, there are a number of strategies that can be implemented by the teacher to prevent outbursts of anger.

> • For a list of twenty-six Anger Control Techniques that can be employed by students to manage their own behavior and prevent aggressive displays of anger, see **Chapter 8,** page 8.14.

Structures that are helpful for student self-control include:

Consequences Reminder: *"Remember the consequences we agreed on."*
Consequences: *"We need to implement the consequences we agreed on now."*
Language of Choice: *"You need to work quietly on your project, or we will have a meeting after class to discuss this. It's your choice."*

Make a Better Choice: *"I want you to think of a better choice you could make right now."*

Picture It Right: *"If we were at our very best right now, how would it look?*

Right Now Validation: *"Right now you are feeling angry. That's OK, but what you need to do is take a few slow, calm, deep breaths and then return to your work on your project."*

> • For step-by-step details of these structures, see **Chapter 14. Moment-of-Disruption Structures.**

B. Breaking the Rules

- • Does the student **recall** the rule?
- • Does the student **understand** the rule?
- • Can the student **apply** the rule?

The three critical questions for Breaking the Rules address three levels of Bloom's Taxonomy. We start with checking for Knowledge, move to Understanding, and then to Application. Does the student know what the rule is? If so, does the student comprehend the rule? And if so, can the student apply the rule to new situations? If the answer to any of these questions is no, we go into teaching mode, teaching for recall, comprehension, or application. Actively involving students in the formulation of rules and in discussion of their purpose helps ensure yes answers to the three questions and helps create buy-in as well.

> • For ways to create buy-in, see **Chapter 9. Teaching the Win-Win Philosophy.** For ways to establish expectations, procedures, and routines, see **Chapter 18. Win-Win Management.**

If the student actually knows, understands, and can apply the rule, but consciously chooses not to, the disruptive behavior is almost certainly a choice springing from one of the seven positions, and our response will depend on the student's position. For example, we respond differently to a student breaking the rules in order to establish a sense of control than a student breaking the rules for attention or out of anger toward the teacher.

B1. Does the Student Recall the Rule?

There are many ways to improve rule recall, including:

- **Keep Rules Simple**
- **T-Chart Rules**
- **Rule Poster**
- **Personal Rule Poster**
- **Letter to Parents**
- **Clarify the Rule**
- **Model the Rule**
- **Pantomime the Rule**
- **Use Mnemonics**
- **Multiple Intelligences Rule Reminders**
- **Illustrate the Rules**
- **Check for Understanding**
- **Teach and Re-teach the Rules**

- For details on these rule procedures, see **Chapter 6. Preventative Procedures: ABCD Disruptions.**

Once the rule procedures are in place, they serve as a foundation on which the teacher can build to control unacceptable behavior in the moment-of-disruption. One strategy that can be quite effective is "Point to Chart."

Point to Chart. When students are disruptive, use the non-verbal signal of pointing to the rule chart or the "The Way We Want Our Class to Be" chart to make students aware of their behavior and to get them back on track.

Structures that are helpful for reminding students include:

Cues; Verbal: *"Class, please take a moment now and look over the class rules chart."*
Cues; Non-Verbal: *"Teacher walks to, and looks intently at the class rules chart."*
Expectation Reminder: *"Remember the expectations we agreed on, the way we want out class to be. Let's take some time now to re-establish our class expectations."*
Target, Stop, Do: *"Susie, right now you are answering out without being called on; you need to raise your hand and be called on before answering."*

- For step-by-step details of these structures, see **Chapter 14. Moment-of-Disruption Structures.**

B2. Does the Student Understand the Rule?

Understanding fosters rule adherence. As a new driver in my teen years, I broke the speed limit. When I was brought to the police station, I expected punishment. Instead, the officer simply asked me why there was a speed limit. I did not give a very coherent response. He then calmly talked about breaking distance and how easily a child could run into the street unexpectedly, directly into the path of my car. If I did not have sufficient breaking distance at that point, I would kill or cripple the child. Following that, I was much more cautious. The "discipline for understanding" approach of the officer transformed the speed limit rule for me. Instead of something externally imposed, it became something that made sense to me. Understanding fosters compliance.

Among the ways to foster understanding are the following:

- Collaboratively Create Rules or Expectations
- Students Name Each Rule
- Rename Rules
- Students Teach Rules
- Share Rule Purpose
- Ask the "What if" Questions

- For details on these procedures, see **Chapter 9. Teaching the Win-Win Philosophy** and **Chapter 6. Preventative Procedures: ABCD Disruptions.**

In the moment-of-disruption, we need to determine if the student not only can name the rule, but also can explain it. Can the student provide the rationale? If not, we have a teachable moment.

Structures that are helpful for student understanding include:

Consequences Reminder: *"Remember the consequences we agreed on. Can you tell me why we agreed on those consequences"?*
Consequences: *"We need to implement the consequences we agreed on now, because...."*
I-Messages Plus: *"I feel frustrated when you drop your books and make noises, it keeps me from my job, teaching. And it distracts your classmates from their job, learning. Can you think of a better choice"?*
Schedule Follow-Up: *"We need to talk this through. Let's meet after...."*

- For step-by-step details of these structures, see **Chapter 14. Moment-of-Disruption Structures.**

B3. Can the Student Apply the Rule?

Understanding results from interactions of neurons in the cortex and neocortex, the most recently evolved outer layers of the brain. *Understanding* the necessity of driving a car carefully in icy conditions, however, is very different than *being able* to skillfully drive in icy conditions. Even if we memorize the department of motor vehicles rule book perfectly, we may not be able to follow those rules while actually driving a car. Following rules involves procedural knowledge. Procedural knowledge occurs in deeper, older areas of the brain. There is only one road to procedural knowledge: practice. And some students need more practice than others.

Let's offer an example. Laurie can tell you there is a rule that prohibits chewing gum in class. She can even expound at length on why it is a good rule; she has no objection to the rule. Nevertheless, on Tuesday Laurie enters class chewing gum! Her cognitive understanding of the rule is not the same as a procedural application. Laurie needs to make it a habit to toss her gum in the wastebasket before entering class. Once we have established buy-in, to help students establish a procedural application of rules, we have students practice what to do. It does nothing for procedural memory to remind Laurie of the rule or even to post a "No Gum Chewing" sign. Laurie needs to check herself for gum chewing as she enters class every day. Through practice, Laurie builds procedural memory – ability to apply cognitive understanding.

Some of the ways to build ability to apply rules:

- Practice Rules
- Eliminate Temptations
- Non-verbal Rule Cues
- Appreciate Rule Adherence
- Verbalize Responsible Behavior

- For ways to have students practice the rules and gain a procedural knowledge of the rules, see **Chapter 6. Preventative Procedures: ABCD Disruptions.**

If there has been a great deal of practice and a student still cannot apply the rules, there are various options for individual follow-ups. In a one-to-one meeting with the student, the teacher can teach Replacement Behavior and/or Re-establish Expectations in a way tailored to individual abilities.

- For ways to teach Replacement Behavior and Re-establish Expectations, see **Chapter 16. Follow-up Structures.**

Structures that help students apply rules include:

Coupons: *"Thank you for using your coupon wisely."*
Redirect: *"Have you done problem four yet?"*
Restart: *"Stop! Look! Listen!"*
Right Now Validation: *"Right now you are feeling sleepy. That's OK, but what you need to do is sit up and focus on the questions."*

• For step-by-step details of these structures, see
  Chapter 14. Moment-of-Disruption Structures.

C. Confrontation

- **Have I controlled my reaction?**
- **Have I given the student choices?**
- **Am I using a Win-Win leadership style?**

When a student confronts the teacher, either through active hostility or passive non-compliance, the first question for the teacher to ask is, Have I controlled my reaction? If the teacher gets hooked (angry, sucked into a power play), then a Win-Win solution is impossible. To structure for a Win-Win solution, the teacher controls his/her own understandable frustration and anger, sidestepping the power play. Instead, the teacher gives the student choices and adopts a Win-Win leadership style.

C1. Have I Controlled My Reaction?

Controlling Teacher Response. Students that confront the teacher are often quite skilled at pushing the teacher's buttons. Getting the teacher to lose it could be the pay-off they seek. We need to keep our own reaction under control, so we resist the temptation to push back when students push our buttons. This can be very difficult because a confrontation releases a whole set of integrated biological responses called the fight or flight defense alarm reaction.

Each of us needs to develop our own strategies for controlling our reactions to confrontational behavior. Teachers adopt different techniques:

- Deep breaths
- Moving
- Talking more slowly
- Identifying students' needs

When faced with confrontation, we need to maintain emotional control and remember that the primary way for students to learn self-control is for us to model our own self-control. In preparing for those moments, recall times when you were able to control your reaction in the moment of a confrontation. Identify what you did that helped you maintain self-control. Prepare those responses for the next time you will need them. Visualize yourself using them.

Preparing your responses beforehand makes it far easier to obtain control than if you are attempting to come up with a strategy in the moment of the confrontation.

Experienced teachers have developed their own strategies; consult with them. Planning ahead and having your own strategies ready is key to being successful. The goal is to avoid the confrontation and get the disruptive student and the rest of the class back on task. Later, work with the disruptive student to identify the source of the confrontation and explore alternative, more responsible ways to meet his/her needs.

Structures that are helpful for controlling teacher reactions include:

Model It: *"I get angry (sad, upset, hurt), too."*
Schedule Follow-Up: *"We need to talk this through. Let's meet after...."*
Table the Matter: *"Let's give this a rest for now. We can talk about it later when we have both calmed down."*
To You... To Me: *"To you, this lesson may be boring; to me, it is important because..."*

> • For step-by-step details of these structures, see
> **Chapter 14. Moment-of-Disruption Structures.**

C2. Have I Given the Student Choices?

Students are less likely to oppose something they have chosen, so, confrontations are reduced dramatically if we provide choices. Although we cannot allow students the choice of whether or not we will study math, we can allow choices about when it will be studied, which strategies we will use, and, to some extent, how they will demonstrate their understanding of the material.

"Students, today we can choose to study math in the morning or in the afternoon. What would you prefer?"

"Today we can review using RallyCoach or Showdown. Each team will get to choose."

"To demonstrate that you have mastered the fraction concepts, you have a choice: would you rather make up and solve your own pizza fraction problems, or would you rather I give you a list of fraction problems to solve?"

"Tomorrow we will conclude our study of the poems of Milton. To demonstrate your mastery of the unit, you have a choice: you can submit your own poem using stylistic elements we have studied, you can write an essay about the stylistic elements we have studied, or you can create a Mind Map of the stylistic elements with examples."

"For our unit on colonial times, each of you will choose to study one figure of the times. You can then choose to write a dialogue between that figure and a modern figure, portray that figure in a

monologue, or create an illustrated time line of the most important events of your figure's life."

Class Meeting. Another way to give students choices is to hold a class meeting and allow them to have input in class decisions. Students who are involved in creating rules, procedures, consequences, and appropriate curriculum decisions are far less likely to confront the teacher regarding those rules and procedures. When students feel ownership of the class, they are motivated to make responsible behavior choices. Voice and choice elicit student cooperation and create an "our class" atmosphere.

> • For details on how to run class meetings and allowing student decision making, see **Chapter 18. Win-Win Management.**

Structures that are helpful providing choices include:

Acknowledge Student Power: *"I can't make you do that assignment. If you choose to do it you can raise your grade, if you chose not to do it you will not earn any points. It is your choice."*
Language of Choice: *"You need to... or..."*

> • For step-by-step details of these structures, see **Chapter 14. Moment-of-Disruption Structures.**

C3. Am I Using a Win-Win Leadership Style?

A Win-Win leadership style is a democratic leadership style. The Win-Win teacher solicits and respects student input. The students feel part of the decision making process, but they know that the teacher has final authority.

Some elements of a Win-Win leadership style include the following:

> • The teacher shows respect for the needs and wishes of students.
> • The teacher asks for student input on how to better run the class.
> • Students and teacher co-create discipline solutions.
> • The teacher carves out areas of choice for students in curriculum and instruction.
> • Minority opinions are respected.
> • The dignity of each individual is maintained.
> • Individual differences are celebrated.
> • The feeling is same-side: "we" rather than "teacher vs. students."

When a teacher assumes a Win-Win leadership style, students are far more likely to return the respect they are given.

A structure that supports the Win-Win leadership style is:

Right Now Validation: *"Right now you are feeling antsy. That's OK, we all get restless sometimes. What we need to do is a quick round of 'Everyone's It'.[2] [See* **Resources E** *at end of this book.] We can all release our energy and then get back to work refreshed."*

> • For step-by-step details of Right Now Validation, see **Chapter 14. Moment-of-Disruption Structures.**

D. Disengagement

> • Is the learning relevant and **developmentally appropriate**?
> • Have I used a variety of **teaching strategies**?
> • Have I used efficient **management techniques**?

When students are not engaged in the learning process, we need to ask first about the Big 3: Curriculum, Instruction, and Management. With relevant, developmentally appropriate curriculum, engaging instruction, and efficient management, disengagement is highly unlikely.

D1. Is the Learning Relevant and Developmentally Appropriate?

Disengagement is reduced if curriculum is relevant and developmentally appropriate.

> • For ways to make curriculum relevant and developmentally appropriate, see **Chapter 6. Preventative Procedures: ABCD Disruptions** and the Differentiated Instruction section of **Chapter 17. Win-Win for Students with Special Needs.**

A structure that is helpful making the curriculum developmentally appropriate is:

Restructure the Task: *"Let's take this part a step at a time."*

> • For step-by-step details of Restructure the Task, see **Chapter 14. Moment-of-Disruption Structures.**

D2. Have I Used a Variety of Teaching Strategies?

Disengagement is unlikely when engaging instructional strategies are used on a consistent basis. Students become more engaged when instruction includes:

- Choices
- Cooperative Learning

- Energizers
- Multiple Intelligences
- Novelty
- Relaxers
- Student Input
- Variety
- Visuals

- For details on these ways to make instruction more engaging, see **Chapter 6. Preventative Procedures: ABCD Disruptions** and **Chapter 19. Win-Win Instruction.**

D3. Have I Used Efficient Management Techniques?

Disengagement is reduced when management is efficient. Among the ways to tighten management are:

Learning Tasks
- Ready, Set, Go Work
- Staged Projects
- Clear Expectations/Goals

Signals and Signs
- Hand Signals
- Varied Signals
- Teach Timer

Direction Giving
- Trigger Instructions
- Bite-sized Instructions
- Concrete, Modeled Instructions
- Whisper

Simultaneous Management Techniques
- Simultaneous Response Modes
- Simultaneous Distribution of Materials
- Simultaneous Team Formation

Procedures
- Label Supplies
- Crisp Transitions
- Sponge Activities
- Team Questions: Three Before Me

Perks and Fun
- Celebrations
- Class Incentives

- For details on these management techniques, see **Chapter 6. Preventative Procedures: ABCD Disruptions** and **Chapter 18. Win-Win Management.**

Structures that are helpful management techniques include:

Grandma's Rule: *"When you finish your math practice sheet, you can go to the choice tables to pick a favorite learning game."*
Model It!: *"I get angry (sad, upset, hurt), too."*
Redirect: *"Have you done problem four yet?"*
Restart: *"Stop! Everyone stop whatever you are doing. I need everyone to look at me – all eyes on me. Good. Now listen carefully as I give the directions."*
Right Now Validation: *"Right now you are feeling bored. That's OK, we all get bored sometimes. What we need to do is find a way to make this more exciting."*
Schedule Follow-up: *"We need to talk this through. Let's meet after..."*

- For step-by-step details of these structures, see **Chapter 14. Moment-of-Disruption Structures.**

ABCD Questions – Faithful Guides

For each of the four types of disruptions, there are three critical questions. The questions are faithful guideposts, pointing toward responses appropriate to the disruption at hand. The questions compel us to look back: Have we emphasized enough the preventative procedures that might have eliminated the disruption? The questions also compel us to look at the moment-of-disruption: Do we need to address an immediate threat or to control our own reaction?

The questions, however, are only general direction posts; they are not full maps to a discipline solution. We cannot consistently formulate a successful Win-Win Discipline response by looking at behavior alone. The disruptive behavior is half the picture. The other half is the reason for the disruptive behavior, the position of the student. To ensure a successful Win-Win Discipline response, we must consider both behavior and position. It is to that second half of the equation, identifying the position of the student, which we turn in our next chapter.

References

[1]Bluestein, J. (Ed.) *Mentors, Masters, and Mrs MacGregor: Stories of Teachers Making a Difference.* Deerfield Beach, FL: Health Communications, Inc., 1995, p. 316.
[2]Kagan, S. *Silly Sports and Goofy Games.* San Clemente, CA: Kagan Publishing, 2000.

Chapter 11

Identifying Positions

- **Ben punches Simon.**
- **Kamala enters class chewing gum.**
- **Mike puts a thumbtack on the teacher's chair.**
- **Laurie puts her head down on the desk and closes her eyes.**

Did Ben punch Simon because he is angry with Simon, or is it a friendly punch? Did he want to get some attention from Simon or the teacher? Is it really not out of anger or attention at all, but to establish dominance or control? Or perhaps the punch was to release some energy. But is it possible that Ben just doesn't know that school rules forbid punching, even a friendly punch?

Did Kamala come into class chewing gum because she enjoys being reminded by the teacher (she enjoys that little bit of special attention, even though it is negative)? Or did she simply forget the rule or forget that she was chewing gum? Or is it that she wants to establish control, prove that no one tells her what to do?

Did Mike set the tack on the teacher's chair because he is seeking attention from the rest of the class? Is it to get even for some offense the teacher never intended, but which Mike felt? Or is he just full of energy and engages in outrageous behavior without thinking of consequences and without any real anger?

Did Laurie get disengaged because she wants to give the teacher the message that worksheet tasks are boring? Is she hoping the teacher will come over and ask her what's wrong? Or is she sleepy and does not know that naps in class are against the rules?

We can never infer a position with certainty from just observing behavior. But if we use all the tools available to us, we can know with a fair degree of certainty the position driving the disruptive behavior of a student. We will not be 100% accurate 100% of the time, but the more accurate we are, the better our chance of selecting a successful response to the disruptive behavior. If we pay no attention to student position, our discipline program will have random, hit-or-miss consequences. In the box (see opposite page) is an example of how misreading student position leads to an ineffective discipline strategy.

Misreading Student Position:
Ticket to Ineffective Discipline

Mrs. Johnson has just announced the homework assignment: textbook problems 1 through 20. As soon as the assignment is announced, Jack in the back of the class stands up, slams his book on the desk, and yells, "I'm not going to do those stupid problems, and you can't make me!"

A discipline problem has occurred. Any student behavior that disrupts the learning process is a discipline problem.

Mrs. Johnson assumes Jack is in the position of seeking control. She responds accordingly, helping Jack see that doing the problems in no way limits Jack's control. Mrs. Johnson says, *"Jack, it is your choice. I cannot make you do those problems. Doing the problems or not doing the problems is entirely up to you. I can't follow you home and force you to do your homework. Homework is always under your control. If you do the problems, you will earn the homework points; if not, you won't. It is always your choice. You are in control."*

Now, if Mrs. Johnson is correct in her assumption that Jack is disruptive because he is seeking control, her discipline response is perfectly appropriate and in the long run will be effective. Mrs. Johnson has helped Jack meet his need for control and to see that he does not have to be disruptive to feel in control. Jack will probably test some, but over time, with the help of Mrs. Johnson's approach, he will realize that he does not have to refuse to do the homework to have a sense of control.

Let's assume, however, that Mrs. Johnson is wrong about Jack's position. Let's assume that Jack was not seeking control at all, but, rather, was avoiding failure. Jack feels that if he does the homework, he is likely to fail, and he does not want to feel the pain of public embarrassment associated with failure. So Jack is refusing to do the assignment, masking his fear with a "you can't make me." But even Jack does not fully understand his own motivation; he is acting out of fear, but could not verbalize his position. Unconsciously, Jack knows it is far less painful to say, *"I won't do the assignment"* than to say, *"I'm afraid to do the assignment."* Jack does not admit the fear to himself. He is convinced he simply does not want to do the assignment. He is not just fooling others; he his fooling himself.

Now, if Mrs. Johnson does not understand Jack's position, her discipline response will be ineffective. If she thinks his position is one of seeking control rather than avoiding failure, she will emphasize that the choice is up to Jack to do or not to do the assignment. Not having related to the need to avoid failure, that need goes unmet, and Jack simply chooses not to do the assignment. Telling a student who fears failure that he/she can choose not to do the problems will almost certainly lead to the student simply choosing not to do the problems! Mrs. Johnson's discipline response fails because it does not respond to the position of the student. Efficient discipline responses occur when they respond to the position of the disruptive student.

If Mrs. Johnson correctly identifies Jack's position as Avoiding Failure, she will respond accordingly, saying something like, *"Jack, I would like to meet with you privately."* When they meet, Mrs. Johnson would provide some coaching on the problems, reassure Jack that performance feedback will be private, and ensure that Jack sees that he can do the assignment successfully before attempting it alone. Mrs. Johnson might provide more guided practice before moving to independent practice, perhaps using a cooperative learning structure like Team-Pair-Solo in which students practice first as a team, then as a pair, before taking on the problems on their own. Having related to the needs associated with Jack's position, Mrs. Johnson's discipline response has a high probability of success.

The same disruptive behavior (refusing to do an assignment) can spring from different student positions (the need for control vs. the need to avoid failure). Knowing the student position is critical because, as the example shows, a discipline strategy that is highly effective with a student seeking control (choices) is ineffective with a student avoiding failure (ensure success). To be effective on more than a random basis, we need to identify student positions.

> **A discipline program that responds only to the disruptive behavior and not the underlying student position will have a hit-and-miss success rate. To have consistent success, a discipline program must identify and respond to the position of disruptive students.**

This chapter is designed to help us identify the seven positions while rejecting the disruptive behavior.

Recognizing Student Positions

■ **You Already Have the Most Important Skill.** We will never be perfect in identifying student positions, but we can hone highly effective skills in this area. If you have agreed with the argument we have laid out so far in this chapter, you have acquired the most important skill of all — trying. Following their training in Win-Win Discipline, a remarkable number of teachers have commented that the program gives them "new eyes." They see each disruption differently, focusing not on the behavior itself but, rather, on the place from which it springs. A beginning teacher reports, *"By just looking for their position, it was easy to end disruptions. A bit of attention here, a choice there, a rule reminder over here, and my class was running more smoothly than ever."* When we look beyond behavior and see the disruptions are only reflections of unmet needs, the change in our approach to discipline is phenomenal. When we hone our skills of perception to see below the surface, positions begin to become remarkably clear. An experienced teacher reported, *"Win-Win Discipline is much bigger than a set of classroom strategies. It has changed the way I see friends, acquaintances, my family, and even myself!"*

Simply looking for student positions will carry you a long way. To determine a student's position, you have five clues in the moment-of-disruption and six strong indicators to use following the disruption.

> *A really great teacher is someone who...* **knows how you feel by the way you are acting.** *—Lauren, 12, Mishawaka, Indiana[1]*

Identifying Student Positions
5 Clues & 6 Indicators

Clues in the Moment-of-Disruption

In the moment-of-disruption we have five clues to help us know a student's position.

1. **Your gut reaction**
2. **Your impulses**
3. **Disruptive student's reaction to intervention**
4. **Classmates' reactions to the disruption**
5. **Facial expressions and body language**

Indicators Following the Moment-of-Disruption

Following the Moment-of-Disruption, if we are uncertain of the student's position, we can gather further evidence, using six indicators.

1. **Interviews with disruptive student**
2. **Disruptive student's reaction to different interventions**
3. **Interviews with classmates**
4. **Interviews with prior teachers**
5. **Interviews with parents**
6. **Cumulative charts**

Clues to Student Positions
(In the Moment-of-Disruption)

Student Position	Teacher Gut Reaction	Teacher Impulsive Reaction	Disruptive Student Reaction To Intervention	Classmate Reactions	Facial Expression; Body Language
Attention-Seeking	Drained, Irritated, Annoyed	Nag, Scold	Temporary Compliance	Amused, Irritated	Catching an eye; Looking up
Avoiding Failure	Sympathetic, Protective, Challenged, Helpless	Tutor; Give up, Write off	Feigns lack of interest; "I can't." Half-hearted effort	Resentment, Pity	Avoiding eye contact; Low muscle tone
Angry	Threatened, Fearful, Protective, Indignant, Outraged	Remove, Punish, Retaliate	Anger, Revenge-Seeking, Sulking	Fearful, Angry	Jaw protrudes; Eyebrows lowered and drawn; Lips pressed; Fist clenched
Control-Seeking	Challenged, Angry, Threatened, Frustrated	Force compliance, Put down, Overpower, Fight	Get in the "last word"; Power-plays; Argue/Justify	Defiance, Deference	Crossed arms; Tightly closed lips; Pointing; Staring; Puffed up; Loud
Bored	Invalidated	Discount, Engage	Off-task	Reject, Ignore	Low muscle tone; Droopy eyes
Energetic	Overwhelmed, Exhausted, Drained	Suppress	Continues, Increases, Modifies activity; Playful smile	Distraction, Annoyance, Envy	High muscle tone; Animated movement
Uninformed	Pity, Helpful, Exasperated, Impatient	Help, Inform, Ignore	Grateful; Lack of understanding; Obedient	Annoyance, Pity, Impatience	Surprise: Wide eyed; Lowered head

Win-Win Discipline. Kagan Publishing • 1 (800) 933-2667 • www.KaganOnline.com

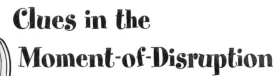

Clues in the Moment-of-Disruption

In the emergency presented by the disruption, we cannot stop everything and gather all possible evidence as to student position. But in the moment-of-disruption, we do have five powerful clues available to us at a glance. With time, we become practiced in tuning into those clues to help us infer the disruptive student's position. As we get better at relating to student positions, our discipline becomes more effective.

◼ **Clue 1: Your Gut Reaction.** Our gut reaction is our first clue. For example, if we look inside, we find we feel very different when a student is confronting us than when a student is seeking attention. When a student is confronting us, we feel challenged. We are likely to become defensive. We don't want someone taking over our class; we don't want a loss of control in front of the whole class. If the student is strong or is being successful in his/her play for power or control, we might feel threatened.

In contrast, our reaction is quite different toward the student who is seeking attention. In some ways it is almost the opposite. Whereas our gut tells us the control-seeking student wants to *take something* from us (our power, our control), attention-seeking students want *us to give them something* (our attention, ultimately, our love). We feel drained. If the attention seeking continues, we become irritated, annoyed.

It turns out we have a different gut reaction to each of the seven positions. Not every teacher responds in the same way to each position. It is your job to tune in to your own reactions. Each of us carries with us a great internal position detector — our gut reactions. Some people call this intuition; others call it instinct. In fact, we actually have very different physiological responses when we are attacked than when someone tries for our attention. Most people experience these responses as "gut reactions." Although we don't all react in the same way to each position, we each have different reactions to each position, so with practice, in the moment-of-disruption we can tune in to a little voice giving us clues to help determine student position. All we have to do is tune in.

Some common teacher gut reactions to each of the seven positions are presented in the second column of the chart, Clues to Student Positions, p. 11.6.

◼ **Clue 2: Your Impulses.** Whereas your gut reactions are feelings, your impulses are impetus toward actions. When I watch Peter hit Hal for no apparent reason, I feel protective toward Hal and angry toward Peter. Those are feelings. My impulses are to hug or in some other way comfort Hal and to punish or in some other way let Peter know he cannot hurt other students without consequences.

My impulses toward action are my second clue for determining position. It turns out that each of us has different impulses toward students coming from different positions. When Matt gets out of his chair for the fourth time this hour, I have the impulse to pick him up and tape him down to his chair! Jennifer's incessant tapping of her pencil makes me want to grab the pencil away! These impulses to suppress behavior are a clue that I am reacting to students coming from a position of energy. When their energy disrupts the class, I have the impulse to suppress it.

My impulsive reaction to an energetic student is quite in contrast to my impulsive reaction to a student in a position of boredom. When a student is bored, I feel invalidated (my lesson is not working) and have the impulse to engage the student in some way or to focus on other students who are engaged, discounting or ignoring the bored student.

When a student is uninformed, my impulse is to help or inform him/her, but if I have done that many times to no avail, I might have the impulse to ignore the student.

Tuning in to our impulses is the second internal barometer we have for detecting student position. The remaining clues and indicators are external. They involve observing others or soliciting their input.

Reminder:

Clue 1: *How do I feel*?
Clue 2: *What do I feel like doing*?

■ **Clue 3: Disruptive Student's Reaction to Intervention.** If we watch the disruptive student carefully as we intervene, the student reveals his/her position. The student seeking attention gets more relaxed when attention is given, but if the student is ignored, he/she tries harder for attention or tries in a different way. Ignoring students seeking attention is a sure way to drive them to new heights in their search for what they need. A slight smile appears when the need is met, and pouting, frowning, or intensified action appears when the need goes unmet.

Positions have associated needs, and needs are drives. The needs drive us to act. When the need is satisfied, it subsides and drive level goes down. When the need goes unmet, drive increases and we call forth greater or different efforts in an attempt to meet the pressing need.

The uninformed student is often grateful in response to a rule reminder. He/she has a need to know. With the same rule reminder, the student coming from a position of control reacts in the opposite way. Rather than grateful, the control-seeking student is oppositional (no one can tell me what to do!). The position of control demands even greater assertion of defiance, so the student is likely to challenge the validity of the rule, point out how the rule is not always being applied in an equitable way, or in some other way protest.

When a task is assigned, the student who is bored responds well to making the task more challenging or interesting; the student who is avoiding failure backs off even more in the face of greater challenge, finding additional excuses not to do the task.

The student who punches a classmate out of anger responds to intervention quite differently than the student who punches because of excess energy or playfulness. When the teacher prohibits the behavior, the angry student might sulk; the playful student might smile. In one case, satisfaction of the need has been interrupted; in the other case, the need has been satisfied.

Carol trips Mary. The teacher intervenes. If Carol is coming from a position of anger, she may comply with the intervention, but she does so with a smirk. Her non-verbal communication yells back at Mary, communicating, "Mary, it doesn't matter what the teacher does to me; I GOT YOU!" If on the other hand Carol tripped Mary out of boredom or excess energy (let's get something really exciting happening in this room), her reaction to the teacher's intervention will be quite different, perhaps feeling genuine remorse. Hurting Mary was not the need; the need was to get stimulation. In the moment-of-disruption, Carol did not think about the potential harm to Mary. Upon reflection she feels sorry. The angry student and the energetic student have very different needs, even if their behavior in this case was the same. For the angry student, harm to Mary was not an unintentional by-product; it was the very aim of the disruptive behavior. For the energetic student, there was no harm intended.

Students cannot be put into a box, and no two students play out their positions in the same way or react in the same way to an intervention, even if their disruptions are triggered by the same position. But if we watch disruptive students carefully as we intervene, we have another powerful set of clues to know what position they are coming from.

■ **Clue 4: Classmates' Reactions to the Disruption.** Classmates react quite differently to disruptions springing from different positions. Carlos catches the teacher in an error and points it out in front of the whole class. If Carlos is coming from a position of Attention-Seeking (look at me; aren't I clever?), the class is likely to be amused. If Carlos is constantly contradicting the teacher in an attempt to get attention, the class will become irritated with him (there goes Carlos, AGAIN).

If however, Carlos is coming form a position of seeking control (I'm smarter than you. I can teach the class.), the class is not amused or irritated. They back off. They sense a power play in progress. There will be a struggle for control. They become very watchful, wondering who will come out on top. This watchful orientation during a struggle is quite in contrast to the amused or irritated response that says, "There goes Carlos trying to be cute again."

Mary pinches Carol. Classmates have their antennae out. They sense the meaning of the pinch. If it is playful, an invitation to a mock fight, they smile, anticipating some fun. If it is out of anger, they become wary. A real fight might erupt.

Mario fails to turn in his homework. The class responds with pity if they sense he is avoiding failure, but they respond with deference if they sense he is setting up a confrontation to establish control.

Like all clues, classmate reactions are only clues. But if we watch our class carefully, the powerful messages they emit in the moment-of-disruption are important clues as to which position is driving the disruptive student's behavior.

■ **Clue 5. Facial Expressions and Body Language.** Each of the positions is associated with needs that are expressed in the face and body. The angry face is universally recognized, even among primitive people who have had no contact with written words or Western ways. Darwin was the first to systematically record what the eyes, eyebrows, nose, lips, jaw, and facial muscles do when one experiences different emotions, and his observations have held true and extend even to non-human primates.

For example, during anger the eyebrows are lowered and drawn together and vertical lines appear between the brows. The upper eyelids are often lowered, pushed down by the lowered brows, contributing to the look of a stare. Eyes often have a bulging appearance. Nostrils may be dilated. Lips are either pressed firmly together or, of course, may be open as when shouting. The body, too, communicates the message.

Anger is associated with high muscle tension — and a fist. Breathing rate and heart rate usually increase and sometimes a person turns markedly red due to the increased flow of oxygenated blood.

Not all the positions have such clear-cut facial expressions and body language, and mild forms of anger may not reveal themselves in the dramatic ways described. Nevertheless, tuning into facial expressions and body language in the moment-of-disruption is yet another important clue as to student position.

Some of the most noteworthy expressions are noted in the chart, including the following:

Position	Body Language
Attention-Seeking:	Furtive glances to see if the student has caught your eye. Smile when caught striving for attention.
Avoiding Failure:	Look down, away. Slumping. Protects work from the view of others. Dejected facial expression. Flaccid muscle tone.
Angry:	Angry facial expressions. Tense muscle tone. Rapid breathing. Red face.
Control-Seeking:	Stands tall. May use proximity — In-your-face stance. Often associated with anger.
Bored:	Faraway look. Sleepiness. Flaccid muscle tone. Lack of focus.
Energetic:	Movement of hands, body, face. Often associated with fleeting attention. Animated facial expressions.
Uninformed:	Puzzled, confused look. Failure to attend to or engage in assigned tasks or appropriate behaviors.

Indicators Following the Moment-of-Disruption

When the emergency of the disruption has passed, we have time to go beyond the clues available in the moment-of-disruption. There are additional indicators we can use to determine student position. For most students, we don't need to use additional indicators. But if a student is not responding to our discipline, or if we are having a hard time reading his/her position, we might employ additional indicators to determine the student's position. With a really difficult discipline problem, we want all the help we can get. When we consider all available clues and indicators, we end up with an excellent batting average.

■ **Indicator 1: Interviews with Disruptive Student.** One of the best ways to find out a student's position is to ask. Asking, though, will only get you reliable information if you have established rapport. Asking about position in the absence of established rapport will usually elicit defensiveness. After all, we are talking about a sensitive area — basic unmet needs. Asking has a second pitfall: students do not always know.

Students who frequently strive for attention may not be aware that they are attention-seeking. They act out their need without really understanding it. In fact, if they really understood their position, they would seek more responsible ways to meet their needs on their own. The most important goal of Win-Win Discipline is to enable students to recognize their needs and learn responsible, rather than disruptive, ways to meet their needs. Asking a student who does not really know he/she is striving for attention almost always evokes a defensive reaction.

But asking does reveal position — if it is done right. We start by establishing trust with the student, by talking about safe things. When students feel that we are on their side, we can begin talking with them about things that make them feel good, secret ambitions, great moments in their lives, fears, and so on. With time they will reveal their unmet needs, their positions.

For students who are reluctant to talk, try manipulatives. Students who are reticent often talk fluently about a picture they have drawn or a clay model they have built. Let them talk about those things, not themselves. In the process, they will reveal themselves. For younger students, doll play is very revealing. Have students draw a picture of a really happy time in their life and write or tell you about it. What makes them happy often reveals position.

■ **Indicator 2: Disruptive Student's Reaction to Different Interventions.** Over time, a difficult student will create more than one disruption. While this is not pleasant, it does give us an opportunity to experiment and learn more about the student's dominant position. If I give special attention to a student and it has no impact on rate or type of disruption, I might revise my hypothesis about his/her position and try choices or other ways of helping the student establish a sense of control. If those strategies work, I have support for the conclusion that the dominant position is control-seeking. If they don't work, I might select from yet a different set of strategies. Over time, I find what works and what does not and, in the process, better understand the student's position.

█ **Indicator 3: Interviews with Classmates.** Over time, students get to know their classmates well. Students each assume certain positions in the class dynamics. Pete is the class clown. Anthony is always challenging the teacher, trying to be boss. Terry never seems to know what is going on. Bob is always bursting with energy. Natalie always seems bored, half asleep.

Many students are very astute observers. They have four advantages over the teacher:

1. Classmates get to see the student outside of class.
2. Classmates have a long personal history with the student.
3. Classmates are not always busy delivering the lesson and, therefore, can devote attention to observing other students.
4. Classmates observe the disruptive student from a different perspective — they get to see the student when the teacher is not looking.

Further, if your class is involved in cooperative learning, teammates get to know each other very well.

If we are trying to understand a student's position as well as we can, we would be foolish not to take advantage of these additional eyes and ears.

During informal chats with classmates of the disruptive student we can lead the conversation around to a particular disruption, soliciting in direct and indirect ways:

- What do you think Johnny really felt when he said the lesson was stupid?

- Does Anthony argue with his other teachers, or just with me?

- What do you think would really interest Natalie? What does she get most excited about?

- Pete is always clowning around. Do you think he does it to get everyone to laugh, or is it that he just wants to make the class more exciting?

█ **Indicator 4: Interviews with Prior Teachers.** Talking with last year's teacher is a rich source of information, especially at the beginning of the school year. Even if the teacher is not versed in Win-Win Discipline and has never heard of "positions," he/she has had a year to gather information. Prior teachers know:

1. When the student is disruptive
2. Ways the student is disruptive
3. Which kinds of discipline strategies seem to work best with that student
4. Relevant personal history of the student

All are important indicators of student position.

Indicator 5: Interviews with Parents. If last year's teacher has had a year to gather data, how long have the parents had? Although, interestingly, many students are a Dr. Jekyll and Mr. Hyde (a model of good behavior at home and a terror on wheels at school, or vice-versa), parents are a rich source of information to help us understand student position. Is the student the youngest in a large family, always trying to be noticed? Does the student have control issues at home? What sets off an angry outburst? Has the student always been prone to angry outbursts, or is it a reaction to a recent event? What works well at home when the student is too high-energy to sit still? And so on. Establishing rapport with a parent and just letting him/her talk can be a royal road to understanding student position.

Indicator 6: Cumulative Charts. If last year's teacher has not figured out the position of the student, perhaps a prior teacher or counselor has. Cumulative charts are an additional indicator.

Putting It All Together:
Identifying the Seven Positions

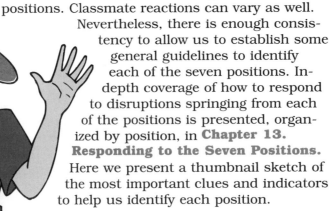

Each of us will have different gut reactions and impulses when confronted with disruptions coming from the seven positions. Classmate reactions can vary as well. Nevertheless, there is enough consistency to allow us to establish some general guidelines to identify each of the seven positions. In-depth coverage of how to respond to disruptions springing from each of the positions is presented, organized by position, in **Chapter 13. Responding to the Seven Positions.** Here we present a thumbnail sketch of the most important clues and indicators to help us identify each position.

Attention-Seeking

When students are seeking attention, a traditional teacher is usually annoyed or irritated. The teacher's impulsive reaction is to get the student to stop being a pest. The teacher may nag, scold, and remind — or reprimand the student verbally. Often the student's reaction to intervention is temporary compliance: "Oh, I'm sorry; I forgot" or "I won't do it again." The student has gotten a bit of attention from the teacher in the moment-of-disruption and so has his/her need for attention satisfied, at least temporarily. The disruption has served its purpose. Because the student has not learned responsible ways to meet his/her needs, the disruptive behavior will occur again. The other students' reaction is generally amusement or irritation. They have the student labeled as the "class clown."

The Win-Win teacher uses as few words as possible to deal with a disruption springing from attention-seeking. When teachers give in to their impulse to scold or in some other way reprimand the attention-seeking student, they fall into the trap of inadvertently reinforcing the disruptive behavior. What attention-seeking students really need is not a moment of attention, but a lifetime of being able to meet their need for attention through responsible behavior choices rather than through disruptions. Ultimately, Win-Win strategies help the students learn self-validation so they are not as dependent on attention from others.

Avoiding Failure

Our gut reaction to a student avoiding failure depends in part on the way the student attempts to avoid doing difficult work. Some students may seek to appear helpless, saying "I can't." Initially, at least, they may elicit sympathy or a protective feeling. Others may mask their fear of failure by a hostile confrontation, saying, "You can't make me do this stupid work." In response to the disrespect of our lesson, most of us feel challenged.

Although we may feel protective and helpful at first, when our efforts to get the student to do the work fail, the helpfulness transforms itself into a feeling of frustration or helplessness. We have tried numerous approaches and nothing seems to work. We all know students who have elevated helplessness to an artform. For them, playing dumb or helpless is a safe place, and they are not going to be dragged from that position. Eventually the teacher's impulsive reaction is to just give up. It is simply too frustrating to continue trying while repeatedly failing to get much of a response.

The student response to intervention may well be to dig in. Students can be quite clever about proving their lack of ability.

They may mask their fear of failure by feigning lack of interest, saying, "I could do this if I wanted, but I just don't care." Or the student may retreat to a persistent passive and non-responsive position, saying, "I don't know" or "I can't."

Classmates' reaction is to feel sorry for the student or to feel resentment toward the student avoiding failure, as he/she usually takes up a lot of teacher time. Sometimes they see through the feigned lack of interest and feel pity or irritation. The negative stereotype is the "turtle" — in the face of threat the turtle pulls in its head, stubbornly refusing to come out.

The Win-Win teacher recognizes the fear behind the façade and works to convert the fear into confidence, the "I Can't" into "I Can." The Win-Win reaction encourages students to participate, not by what is said, but by making it safe. Tutoring, private feedback, and breaking tasks into smaller chunks are powerful tools. The Win-Win teacher focuses and builds on the student's strengths. Over time, the student develops self-confidence.

Angry

Angry students trigger a strong reaction. Anger may be directed at classmates or at the teacher. When directed at classmates, the primary gut reaction of the teacher is protectiveness. When directed at the teacher, he/she may feel hurt, outraged, fearful, or indignant. The teacher feels under attack.

When anger is directed at classmates, our impulsive reaction is to remove the student from the class or in some other way isolate the angry student and protect the classmates. When the anger is directed at us, our first impulsive reaction is to punish or retaliate.

The student's angry feelings may have nothing to do with the teacher personally; the teacher may simply be a convenient scapegoat: the feelings vented by the student may have been generated elsewhere. In the process of venting their anger, students may hurt others physically, threaten or insult others verbally, or destroy something that others care about.

Attempts to reason with a student in the moment of an angry outburst usually fail. In the moment of an angry outburst the student is not thinking rationally; he/she wants to vent. Attempts to restrain the angry student often will be met with resistance — his/her need to vent is being frustrated, adding fuel to the fire. The student may lash out at the teacher or at other students.

When anger is directed toward the teacher, other students are angry or fearful. (But if they harbor their own resentments toward the teacher, they may be envious). When the anger is directed at peers, other students usually react with fear. The negative stereotype: "classroom bully."

The Win-Win teacher avoids inappropriate retaliation, modeling what the angry student most needs to learn — self-control. After assuring that the class is safe, the first reaction in response to an angry outburst is to structure so the student can cool down. It is only after the student has regained his/her composure and is thinking rationally that it makes sense to attempt to reason with him/her. Over time, Win-Win strategies help angry students acquire self-control.

Control-Seeking

Control-seeking may take the form of a quiet refusal to do what one is told, or a very active confrontation with the teacher. Some students seek control in a passive way, refusing to do what is requested or even doing the opposite. Their noncompliance is a way of saying, "You can't make me; I can do what I want." With quiet noncompliance, often our gut reaction is a feeling of frustration. In contrast, if there is an active confrontation, in the moment-of-disruption our gut reaction is high arousal — we feel challenged, threatened. We feel our position as the leader in the classroom is being challenged: Who is in charge here anyway? Quiet noncompliance produces a much subtler feeling of being challenged. The teacher's impulsive reaction may be to make the student comply. An extreme reaction is the impulse to overpower or fight with the control-seeking student. At root, this is an impulse to reassert control, to establish who is boss.

Many students seeking control know just how to push the teacher's buttons. If teachers allow their buttons to be pushed, they are likely to lose in the ensuing confrontation. In the moment of confrontation, the student is choosing the time, the place, the issue, and the audience. Further, the student has a great deal invested in "looking good" in front of his/her peers. Thus if the teacher approaches a power struggle with a win-lose orientation, an orientation that would put the student in his/her place, the odds of success are slim. The student has stacked the odds in his/her own favor.

The student's reaction to intervention may be to try to get in the last word, pull power plays, argue, and justify. The students want to be in control, in charge. A student seeking control wants to do things according to his/her own choosing, not that of the teacher. Challenging the teacher in front of the whole class is exciting; it may feel like an opportunity to emerge from the underdog position.

Classmates' reactions can be deference to the control-seeking student or to feel rebellious toward the student, resisting being controlled. If they have control issues they may be envious of the student with the guts to confront the teacher. The negative stereotype: "the boss."

The Win-Win teacher avoids the power play. The Win-Win reaction is to provide legitimate choices and to give control-seeking students decisions to make and responsibilities so they can meet their need for control through responsible behavior. With time, the control-seeking student internalizes the feeling of choice and does not have to prove his/her power, moving to a position of internal locus of control.

Energetic

In reaction to an extremely energetic student, we feel overwhelmed, exhausted, and/or drained. The impulsive reaction of the traditional teacher is to suppress this "energizer bunny." When feeling suppressed, the energetic student's reaction may be to continue or even increase the activity level. The disruptive student is full of energy but has not learned how to channel that energy productively. Other students tend to be distracted or annoyed, or they may become envious, wishing they too could express so much uninhibited energy.

The Win-Win teacher avoids suppressing energy. Rather, the Win-Win teacher channels it. Energy, when properly channeled, increases learning, so the Win-Win teacher provides plenty of ways to include movement and manipulatives in learning tasks. As a consequence, the energetic student does not have to be disruptive to express his/her energy. Eventually, the student bursting with energy learns how to harness and redirect the energy in positive ways on his/her own. He/she moves to a position of self-directed energy.

Bored

When a student is in a bored position, the teacher's position is to feel invalidated. The reaction of the teacher is something like, *"After all the trouble I have put into planning this lesson, this student has the gall to be bored."* Since the teacher's efforts on the behalf of this student are not paying off, the teacher's reaction is to discount the information that the student's behavior is giving and to disregard it. This allows the teacher to avoid looking at what is at the root of the boredom or lack of motivation.

The bored student has not been engaged by the instruction. It could be that the school work is not appropriately geared for the student, not challenging enough or too challenging. It could be that the instruction is lacking in relevance for the student or that no connection has been made with students' interests and experience. It could be that the student is a passive recipient of the learning and has not been actively involved. The student's reaction is to be off-task. Other students' reaction is to reject this student. The negative stereotype is that of the "couch potato."

The Win-Win reaction is to vary teaching strategies, make learning relevant for the student, and actively involve the student in the learning process. Ideally, the student that is coming from a bored position is led toward a position of self-motivation.

Uninformed

In Win-Win, we use the term "uninformed" in a special way. We do not mean "never been told." We mean "not yet acquired that knowledge." Imagine a student coming from a home and neighborhood in which profanity is common among adults and children. The student comes to school and uses profanity. The teacher tells the student that such language is forbidden in school. The next hour or the next day that student again reverts to this inappropriate language. Although the student has been told that profanity is forbidden, he/she is still uninformed. The student has not acquired procedural knowledge — it is not yet part of him/her.

Whereas episodic learning (remembering what you had for dinner last night) is one trial learning, procedural learning (remembering how to ride a bike) occurs over trials. We practice a procedure over and over until it becomes automatic, part of who we are. Episodic and procedural memory are actually processed in very different ways in our brains, and in different places. Many disruptive behaviors (profanity, failing to ask permission before acting, getting off task) involve procedural rather than episodic memory and, therefore, telling, even telling repeatedly, does not inform the student. Practice is the royal road to procedural memory, to moving from uninformed to informed.

A teacher who does not understand this, who confuses telling with teaching, initially may feel helpful toward the uninformed student, but the helpfulness turns to impatience and exasperation. *"How many times have I told you? Why can't you remember? Why can't you just do what I ask?"*

The teacher's impulse is to exasperatedly tell the student "one more time," or to just give up on the student. The student just doesn't seem to get it, reacting with a lack of understanding. Uninformed students may be obedient in the moment, but will be disruptive again later. They have not acquired the responsible skills. The other students are often annoyed, rolling their eyes at the uninformed student. They may even feel pity. The negative stereotype: "clueless."

The Win-Win reaction is to understand that procedural knowledge is a process, and so the Win-Win teacher provides plenty of practice opportunities. Rules are taught many times in many ways, until rule and procedure compliance becomes automatic. The Win-Win teacher relies more on practice than telling. Telling the rule one more time to a student who is not complying with the rule has little added value. Having the student act it out is far more memorable. The long-range goal is to help uninformed students become more responsible, to acquire the rules of the game, and ultimately to become self-informing, actively seeking and practicing responsible behavior.

Student Positions in Action

Let's peek into Mr. Blake's class to see some positions in action.

Jonathan

Jonathan is a master at making annoying noises in class. When he isn't using his underarms to make sounds, he is busy elevating burping to an art form. He has just let out his fourth loud belch. The other students in the class laugh and laugh. Mr. Blake turns and gives him a very annoyed look and scolds him by saying, *"Jonathan, how many times have I told you not to interrupt the lesson with your loud burps? Nobody can learn with your constant interruptions. Don't you want everyone to be able to learn? What is your problem?"* *"I'm sorry,"* Jonathan says for the fourth time today, *"I really don't mean to. I'll try harder; really I will."* Mr. Blake sighs as he turns back to the lesson and thinks to himself, *"Well, I've certainly heard that before. We'll see how long that lasts."*

Jonathan is coming from an attention-seeking position. Mr. Blake's position is one of irritation and he responds impulsively by nagging Jonathan again. In the process, Mr. Blake gives Jonathan a lot of attention for his inappropriate noises and actually makes it more likely that Jonathan will continue these disturbances. Jonathan goes along with Mr. Blake temporarily; he doesn't argue with him but will probably be repeating his actions again shortly, particularly with the other students finding him so amusing. Being the "class clown" satisfies his need to be cared for by others, unfortunately at the price of disrupting the lesson.

Tony

Tony feels as if he is a complete failure. He just doesn't understand these math problems that Mr. Blake is trying to teach him and feels that he never will. Mr. Blake is frustrated because it feels as if he has tried everything to motivate Tony, but nothing ever seems to get a response from him. Tony just says, "I can't" over and over. Mr. Blake feels so helpless he just wants to give up, but instead, he says to Tony, *"I know you can do it. If you just put some more effort into it, I am sure you will be able to fig-ure it out."* Tony picks up his pencil and starts to work on a problem, but as soon as Mr. Blake walks away, Tony sighs and puts his head on the desk. The other kids are get-ting bugged by Tony because the teacher spends so much time trying to help him.

Tony is coming from an avoiding failure position. He honestly believes that he can't do it, even though in the past he has been able to after Mr. Blake has given him lots of help. It all seems so overwhelming to him; he doesn't even want to try. He is like an "ostrich" with his head stuck in the sand. Mr. Blake wants to help him but doesn't know how to reach this student. He knows that a teacher can't give up on a student, but it is so frustrating to keep trying and trying and to get so little result. The other students resent the fact that Tony takes up so much teacher time every day. Tony's need to feel successful is buried under a mountain of "I can't" messages.

Allison

Allison snuck into the classroom and ripped up two textbooks yesterday. Today she called Jennifer a pig and a witch and slapped her on the way to class. Mr. Blake is outraged by her behavior and doesn't know how to deal with the nasty things that she does day after day. He lashes out at her and tells her, *"You are the worst student I've ever had. How can you be so mean to the other students? They are all afraid of you. If you don't stop, you are going to be removed from this class. Do you understand me?" "I don't care what you think and I hope I am removed from this class,"* retorts Allison. *"It is the worst class I've ever been in. I don't like any of the kids and they deserve what they get."*

Allison is coming from an angry position. Her anger stems from a troubled home environment – her father physically abus-es her mother on a regular basis. Needing an outlet, Allison vents her anger on her teacher and the other students in class. The things that Allison does incense her teacher who would like to strike back at her or at least have her removed from class. He feels that it is not fair to the other students to have her there. Allison is hurtful and destructive on a daily basis. The other students want nothing to do with this "bully." Unfortunately, Allison's need to express displeasure in an appro-priate way is never met because no one is helping her learn to deal with her feelings in a responsible manner.

Charlie

"You can't make me," Charlie says belligerently to his teacher, Mr. Blake. *"I don't want to do it and you can't make me."* Mr. Blake wrings his hands and angrily says, *"We'll see whether I can make you or not. I'm the one in charge around here, not you."*

"I shouldn't have to do this," counters Charlie. *"I did something just like it in Mrs. Bailey's class last year and it is not fair for you to expect me to do it again. I won't do it no matter what you do."* Charlie then stomps off to his desk. The other students move out of his way. They know that Charlie is the real "boss" in this classroom. Mr. Blake is clenching his fist as he walks away.

Charlie is coming from a control-seeking position. It has to be his way or nothing. Mr. Blake feels as if his authority is challenged by Charlie and wants to overpower him, but he doesn't really know what to do to get him to cooperate. Charlie argues with the teacher at the least provocation and needs to make sure that he gets the last word in. His need to feel that he can influence people and events is being met through constant disruptions and power plays rather than through fulfilling worthwhile responsibilities.

Michael

Michael is bouncing off the walls again in Mr. Blake's class. Mr. Blake gets tired just looking at him. *"If he would only sit still for two seconds, he would probably learn something in this class,"* thinks Mr. Blake. *"I just want to get him to settle down for a few minutes."* Michael continues to move about the classroom, stopping to look at anything that catches his eye on the way. He is oblivious to Mr. Blake's reaction, and he doesn't notice how much his "energizer bunny" activity keeps the other students from doing their work.

Michael is coming from an energetic position. He is full of energy all the time and finds it hard to sit still or focus his energy. Mr. Blake is overwhelmed by all of his activity, but his attempts to suppress it meet with little success. Michael has a need to move, touch, and be expressive, but he has not learned how to channel that energy into productive tasks.

Carol

Carol doesn't think that she can stand being in class one more second. Everything is so incredibly boring. She just wants out. She starts fidgeting with some things in her desk just to occupy herself. Mr. Blake notices her preoccupation and tells her, *"Pay* attention Carol. You are going to need to do this on your own shortly and if you don't listen, you won't be able to." Mr. Blake can't believe how uninvolved Carol is in the lesson day after day. *"I put a lot of time and energy into preparing for class. How dare she act as if she doesn't have the time of day for it! I guess if she doesn't pass, it will be her own fault. I'm doing my part, but she isn't."* The other students don't want to deal with Carol because she is a "couch potato" that doesn't contribute much.

Carol is coming from a bored position. Mr. Blake lectures a lot of the time and Carol feels like she can't listen to one more word. *"Why can't he be more like Mrs. Gardner,"* Carol thinks. *"She has us doing some really neat projects."* Carol has not been engaged by the instruction. She thinks the learning has nothing to do with her, so she finds other things to occupy her time. Mr. Blake feels invalidated by Carol. He puts effort into planning and resents Carol's attitude toward the lesson. He discounts her actions as Carol's problem, not his. Carol's need to experience fun and stimulation is not being satisfied by the instruction in Mr. Blake's class.

Joanne

Joanne has a blank look on her face again as Mr. Blake tells her, *"You need to ask the other students before you help yourself to their paper. They would probably be glad to give you some, but just saying 'give me' or just taking the paper gets them very upset. Why can't you just ask nicely? I've told you this several times,"* adds an exasperated Mr. Blake. Joanne continues to look at him blankly. *"I don't know what I'm going to do with you,"* mutters Mr. Blake as he moves on to help the next student.

Joanne does not know how to exhibit the responsible behavior. She has grown up in a family of twelve, where it is common to grab what you need, when you need it. Unfortunately, Mr. Blake's impatience with her is interfering with her learning more acceptable ways to interact with her peers. She really doesn't understand what Mr. Blake is trying to get her to do because he doesn't take the time to actually teach her what needs to be done in the situation. Joanne's need to know how to act and interact responsibly with others is not being met.

Frequent Questions about Student Positions

Can the Student Be in More than One Position?

Sometimes it can feel like a student is coming from all or many of the positions at the same time. We are all in each of the positions at one time or another — the positions are rooted in the human condition. So it is not surprising that a student may be trying to meet the needs of more than one position with the same disruption. A student motivated by a control-seeking position may want everyone to notice his/her power plays. A student who is avoiding failure may enjoy the special attention gained by not doing his/her work. An angry student may be gratified by the sense of control he/she has during the angry outburst.

How Should I Respond if a Student Is in More than One Position?

The purpose of determining the student position is not to stick one more label on the student but, rather, to get at the heart of the need that is being met by disruptive behavior. If a student is motivated by more than one position, that is important for us to know. The Win-Win teacher wants to understand students. But with regard to selecting a discipline response, focus on the position that seems most dominant. We are always making our "best guess" and always have the chance to regroup. Often when a student is in two or more positions, and we relate to one, another will emerge. Think of the positions as a hierarchy of needs. Once the most salient need is satisfied, the student will begin to focus on the next most important need.

Can One Position Lead to Many Different Disruptive Behaviors?

Often a student exhibiting many disruptive behaviors is motivated by one dominant position. The disruptive behaviors are all part of the student's struggle to seek attention, avoid failure, or fulfill the needs associated with one of the other positions. This is actually good news. A teacher can focus on strategies that respond to the student's dominant position and may be able to prevent many disruptive behaviors.

11.24

Win-Win Discipline. Kagan Publishing • 1 (800) 933-2667 • www.KaganOnline.com

Are Positions Linked to ABCD Behaviors?

> • *When we see a student hit another student, it is natural to assume the aggressive student is angry.*
>
> • *When we see a student confront the teacher, it is natural to assume that the student is seeking control.*
>
> • *When we see a student disengaged, it is natural to assume the student is bored.*

Although it is natural to assume a one-to-one relationship between position and behavior, we can never with any certainty infer position from behavior alone.

In fact, all these assumptions are quite likely false! Although it is natural to assume a one-to-one relationship between position and behavior, *we can never with any certainty infer position from behavior alone.* The aggressive student may be angry, but a student may hit another to:

- Become the center of attention
- Try to assert dominance or control
- Release energy
- Create such a disturbance that no one will focus on the fact that he/she is failing at the learning task; that is, to avoid failure

Aggression may spring from any of the positions. In fact, any behavior may spring from any of the seven positions!

Confronting the teacher may spring from:

- Attention-Seeking (I will get attention by arguing.)
- Avoiding Failure (I refuse to do these problems so no one will see me fail.)
- Anger (The teacher treated me unfairly.)
- Control-Seeking (I'll do it my way.)
- Energy (The teacher wants me to sit quietly and I just can't.)
- Boredom (Let's get something going.)
- Uninformed (I don't know how not to talk back.)

This lack of one-to-one relation between behavior and position is true for all the behaviors and positions. One of the most frequent errors in interpersonal communication is to infer position from behavior alone. Looking beyond behavior is a sign of maturity. It is a cornerstone of Win-Win Discipline to distinguish behaviors and positions, always taking care to look for and identify the position that underlies disruptive behavior, never assuming that behavior alone is an indicator of position.

Quiz Yourself – Identify that Position!

What Does Your Reaction Tell You?

Instructions: Draw a line connecting the student position with the teacher reaction.

Student Position	Teacher Reaction

 **1**

a **Gut Reaction:** Threatened, Fearful, Protective, Indignant, Outraged
Impulsive Reaction: Remove, Punish, Retaliate

 **2**

b **Gut Reaction:** Overwhelmed, Exhausted, Drained
Impulsive Reaction: Suppress

 **3**

c **Gut Reaction:** Sympathetic, Protective, Challenged, Helpless
Impulsive Reaction: Tutor, Give up, Write off

 **4**

d **Gut Reaction:** Pity, Helpful, Exasperated, Impatient
Impulsive Reaction: Help, Inform, Ignore

 **5**

e **Gut Reaction:** Drained, Irritated, Annoyed
Impulsive Reaction: Nag, Scold

 **6**

f **Gut Reaction:** Challenged, Angry, Threatened, Frustrated
Impulsive Reaction: Force compliance, Put down, Overpower, Fight

 **7**

g **Gut Reaction:** Invalidated
Impulsive Reaction: Discount, Engage

For Answers, See Part VII, Resources D.2.

Quiz Yourself – Identify that Position!
What Does Facial Expression & Body Language Tell You?

Instructions: Write the student position in the box next to the appropriate facial expression and body language.

Facial Expression & Body Language	Student Position
1 High muscle tone; Animated movement	
2 Crossed arms; Tightly closed lips; Pointing; Staring; Puffed up; Loud	
3 Surprise: Wide eyed; Lowered head	
4 Low muscle tone; Droopy eyes	
5 Jaw protrudes; Eyebrows lowered and drawn; Lips pressed; Fist clenched	
6 Catching an eye; Looking up	
7 Avoiding eye contact; Low muscle tone	

For Answers, See Part VII, Resources D.2.

Quiz Yourself – Identify that Position!

What Does Classmate Reaction Tell You?

Instructions: Fill in the blank with the appropriate student position.

1 When classmates react with **fear** and/or **anger**, the student's position is likely to be _____.

2 When classmates react with **resentment** and/or **pity**, the students' position is likely to be _____.

3 When classmates are **distracted, annoyed,** and/or **envious**, the student's position is likely to be _____.

4 When classmates react with **defiance** and/or **deference**, the student's position is likely to be _____.

5 When classmates react with **amusement** and/or are **irritated**, the student's position is likely to be _____.

6 When classmates react with **annoyance, impatience,** and/or **pity**, the student's position is likely to be _____.

7 When classmates **reject** and/or **ignore** the student, the student's position is likely to be _____.

For Answers, See Part VII, Resources D.2.

Quiz Yourself – Identify that Position!

What Does Disruptive Student Reaction Tell You?

Instructions: Fill in the student position.

1 When the student reacts with **anger, revenge-seeking,** and/or **sulking**, the student's position is likely to be _____.

2 When the student reacts with **gratitude, lack of under-standing,** and/or **obedience**, the students' position is likely to be _____.

3 When the student reacts with **playfulness**, the student's position is likely to be _____.

4 When the student reacts with **defiance**, the student's position is likely to be _____.

5 When the student reacts with **temporary compliance**, the student's position is likely to be _____.

6 When the student reacts with **half-hearted effort**, the student's position is likely to be _____.

7 When the student reacts with **off-task behavior**, the student's position is likely to be _____.

For Answers, See Part VII, Resources D.2.

Identifying Student Positions: Differentiated Discipline in Action

If we ignore student positions, our discipline responses will be hit or miss because the same discipline solution that helps one student know and meet her/his needs fails to respond to the needs of another. Not all students learn well from the same instructional strategies, so we need differentiated instruction. Similarly, not all students respond well to the same discipline strategies, so we need differentiated discipline. We can never consistently create Win-Win solutions by ignoring student positions. Identifying student positions, thus, is the royal road to consistently successful discipline solutions. Win-Win is differentiated discipline; it is discipline tailored to the needs and position of each student. As we become more skilled at identifying student positions and practiced in using the simple cues and indicators, we are on the path to creating a consistently successful, differentiated discipline program.

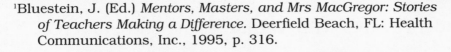

References

[1]Bluestein, J. (Ed.) *Mentors, Masters, and Mrs MacGregor: Stories of Teachers Making a Difference.* Deerfield Beach, FL: Health Communications, Inc., 1995, p. 316.

Chapter 12

Validating Positions

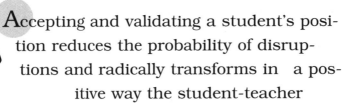

Accepting and validating a student's position reduces the probability of disruptions and radically transforms in a positive way the student-teacher relationship. The power of validating a student's position is illustrated by the famous New York entertainer and network radio show host, David Brenner. David provides this account of his experience in Dr. Jacobs' high school physics class:

I was a disruptive student, as I said before. I upset every class because I was always thinking funny. So Dr. Jacobs and I made a deal: He would give me five minutes at the beginning of the class to tell my jokes, to joke around, to do anything I wanted for exactly five minutes, then I had to shut my mouth for the rest of the period.

He would get up there as soon as the bell rang and everyone was in their seats. He would say, "Ladies and gentlemen, Physics 101 is proud to present the comedy styling and antics of David Brenner." And then I would do five minutes. He'd sometimes cut me off right in the middle of a joke! But I could use those five minutes however I wanted. I could make fun of him or do anything I wanted to do.

He knew how to harness that energy. He would have spent a lot more than five minutes getting me under control. All my other teachers tried for years with a lot less success.

— David Brenner[1]

We do not have to restructure our whole class to validate student positions, but successful long-term discipline solutions depend on validation. It is not enough to know student positions; we need to communicate to the student that we know and accept where he/she is coming from. To a large extent the art of Win-Win is to communicate an acceptance of student position while refusing to accept disruptive behavior. This chapter shows how.

Need to Validate Student Positions

Having identified a student position, the Win-Win teacher finds a variety of ways to communicate to the student the following message:

Although I find your disruptive behavior unacceptable, I understand and fully accept your position.

The Win-Win teacher validates student positions for a number of reasons:

1. When a student feels validated, a basic need is met and he/she relaxes, becoming less likely to be disruptive.

2. When a student feels validated, then he/she likes the teacher more and is more open to input, more compliant.

3. Feeling validated by the teacher, the student wants to please him/her.

4. Feeling validated for who he/she is, an otherwise disruptive student no longer needs to be disruptive because his/her disruptive behavior was merely a misguided attempt to win acceptance for who he/she is.

5. If the student does not feel accepted by the teacher, he/she is likely to become more disruptive out of anger. *If you reject me, I will reject you.*

6. When we validate a student's position, we create a bridge for him/her — a bridge toward self-knowledge and self-acceptance. Feeling his/her position is known and accepted by the teacher, the student can better know and accept it. The teacher actually models an orientation toward the student that the student can internalize. And until the student knows and accepts his/her own position, the student will continue to act out the needs of the position rather than consider responsible alternatives.

All of us come from each of the different positions at one time or another. It is part of the human condition. At one time or another we all have needed some extra attention, been angry, wanted to avoid failure and embarrassment, and been bored. Everyone wants to have the feeling of being in control rather than being controlled by others, and we all have areas in which we do not know the appropriate ways to act. Most all of us at some time have had so much energy that we become "antsy" or couldn't sit still any longer.

Win-Win Discipline. Kagan Publishing • 1 (800) 933-2667 • www.KaganOnline.com

12.3

When we see a student in one of the seven positions, and we are insightful and have been honest with ourselves, we know the student is in a place we have been. The student is just a mirror of ourselves at some time in our life. The needs of each position are rooted in what it is to be human. As a reminder, we present for a second time the box that shows that each position is associated with an important, basic need:

Positions and Basic Needs

Position	Need
Attention-Seeking	To feel cared about by others
Avoiding Failure	To feel successful
Angry	To express displeasure
Control-Seeking	To feel able to influence people and events
Energetic	To move, touch, be expressive
Bored	To be motivated, to have interesting stimuli
Uninformed	To know how to interact responsibly

There is never anything wrong with being in a position or having the needs associated with that position. What can be disruptive, though, is what we sometimes do to meet those needs.

One student meets the need for attention by being a model student and gaining praise from teacher and parents. Another meets the same need by becoming the class clown. The problem is never the position; the problem is the behavior. If we can get the class clown to learn responsible rather than disruptive ways to meet the need for attention, we have created a Win-Win Discipline solution. The student gets his/her needs met, and the teacher and class are freed from the disruptive behavior.

Paradox 1: Win-Lose = Lose-Lose

The starting point toward a Win-Win solution, therefore, is to accept and validate student positions. If we reject student positions, we are headed for a Win-Lose solution. In a Win-Lose discipline solution, the teacher suppresses the disruptive behavior, but the student does not get his/her needs met. A Win-Lose solution is a prescription for another disruption down the road. Following a Win-Lose solution, unmet needs simmer, eventually boiling over into another disruption. Thus, paradoxically, in the long run there is never a Win-Lose: short-run Win-Lose solutions become long run Lose-Lose outcomes.

Paradox 2: Self-Acceptance = Change

Validating the student position helps communicate that we are on the same-side as the student. Through validation we let students know we accept and care about them. Feeling this, the student is more likely to accept himself/herself. Change is possible only when we recognize where we are; if we expend our energy in denial, we are stuck, and change is unlikely. Here we have a second paradox: self-acceptance leads to change.

As Win-Win teachers, we validate student positions, taking a step toward helping students know and accept the needs associated with their positions. Once students know their needs, there is less need to act them out. A student who knows his/her needs is better positioned to seek and accept ways to meet those needs through responsible behavior rather than through disruptive behavior.

Validate Student Positions, Not Disruptive Behaviors

Validating student position does not mean accepting the disruptive behaviors that spring from that position. Win-Win teachers do not fall into the Lose-Win trap, in which disruptive students can do what they want even though the teacher and the rest of the class suffer. As teachers, we want to communicate acceptance of our students, but it is always an error to communicate acceptance by accepting unacceptable behavior. On the contrary, we clearly reject disruptive behaviors. But by validating the positions from which disruptive behavior springs, we open students to discovering and adopting more responsible behaviors.

Ways to Validate Student Positions

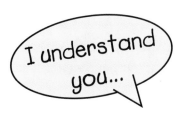

If possible, the Win-Win teacher validates the student positions before disruptions ever occur. Communicating acceptance goes a long way toward preventing disruptions. When possible, even in the moment-of-disruption the teacher in some way communicates acceptance for the student position, while firmly rejecting the disruptive behavior. Students who sense the teacher is really on their side are much more likely to end their disruptive behaviors. If the emergency of the disruption does not allow validation of student position, the Win-Win teacher has the fall-back option of including position validation as part of the follow-up.

■ **Validation Gambits:** A few validating words can make a dramatic difference:

"We all need approval sometimes. It felt really good to me yesterday when a student told me she enjoyed the lesson. I bet you would feel great if you aced this test."

"None of us wants to fail. Let's practice these problems in our teams now so when we do this type of problem on the homework alone tonight, we will be sure to get them all right."

"All of us feel angry when we feel we have been treated unfairly. Certainly I did not want to treat you unfairly. Let's review what happened."

"None of us want to be told what to do all the time. For that reason tonight you will have a choice between two types of homework. You get to decide."

"Well, all of us sometimes get bored. How can we make this more interesting for you?"

"You are just busting with energy today! Let's see if we can work together to channel that energy into some productive learning."

"I can see how you did not remember the rules. That happens to all of us sometimes. Let's work together to figure a way to make them easier for you to remember."

> It happens to all of us...

■ **Validation Notes.** Students love a positive, validating note from the teacher. A validation note not only fills the need for special recognition or attention, it helps a student accept his/her position.

"Jan, I could see you really grabbed the class's attention today with your presentation. That must have felt great! Keep up the terrific work."

"Sue, it's really hard to stick in there and keep trying when the work is difficult and you are not sure you are going to understand it. You really persevered in the face of tough problems today. I'm proud of you."

"Joe, all of us get angry when someone insults us. I appreciate how well you controlled your anger today."

"Pam, we all want the feeling of being in control – of being able to choose. I thought you were really mature when you asked if you could do an art project instead of an essay to show what you have learned from the team project."

"Sam, today when you came into the room after lunch, I could see you were full of energy. I was afraid you might disrupt others. Instead, you channeled all your great energy into the project. Thanks. Remember, having energy, even lots of energy, is never a problem. We just have to be careful we don't disrupt others. Today you used your energy wisely."

"Dan, I could tell you were not really interested in the science content today until you started to build that model. What a great way to turn something that was boring for you into something interesting. You have my respect."

"Bob, Wow! Today you asked me about the rotation rules for group roles. What a good job of informing yourself!"

■ **Non-verbal Validation.** We can validate positions non-verbally. A gesture, a smile, or a nod can communicate worlds.

1. Darren is bored. With a look you let him know that you understand and accept that he is bored. Your look tells him it is OK to be bored sometimes; we all get bored occasionally.

2. Phillip is about to give up rather than risk failure. With a hand on his shoulder, you let him know that you understand how difficult it is to hang in there.

3. Janna walks in wearing a new dress. With a smile, you communicate you notice and that it is just fine to want to show off and be noticed.

4. Corrie walks in angry. With a glance, you communicate that it is OK to be angry but that you expect her to control her actions.

How is this possible? Are we talking mysticism here? Not at all. There is a simple technique that allows us to communicate to students that we accept their position without saying a word!

What is the trick? Experts estimate that about 80% of human communication is non-verbal. Our face, body position, muscle tensions, breathing rate and volume, and even our heart field communicate worlds to those around us. That is why young children and animals have correct instinctive positive or negative reactions toward a stranger, even before the person says a word.

How then can we use this unconscious communication to transmit to our students a message of acceptance of their basic position? Remember this: **WE ALMOST ALWAYS COMMUNCIATE WHAT WE FEEL, WHETHER WE INTEND TO OR NOT.** So the trick is simple. ***To communicate acceptance of positions, all we have to do is feel acceptance of positions.***

Have you ever met someone for the first time and immediately you felt accepted — truly accepted? You could not understand why, but without a word being spoken, you knew that it was OK to be you.

How did that happen? The person truly accepted you and so you felt that. Feelings are communicated non-verbally. The more fully you accept a student, the more fully the student feels accepted.

Have you ever had the opposite reaction? You were around someone for the first time and without a word being spoken, within a few minutes you knew with certainty that person did not like you? How did that happen? Simple: the person's emotions were communicated non-verbally.

So it is not difficult to use non-verbal communication to let students know that we understand and accept their position. All we have to do is truly accept their position. There is no fooling the brain. It is a very sophisticated decoder of non-verbal messages.

This is part of the reason the Same-Side Pillar is so critical for Win-Win Discipline. Unless we are truly on the same-side with a student, it does not matter what we say; we will communicate non-acceptance, and when that happens, we hinder the change process and often elicit disruptive behavior.

How then do we get on the same-side with our students? How do we become empathetic with their position? To our knowledge there is but one way. We have to put ourselves in their position, to feel what it is like to be them. We walk a mile in *their* moccasins. At one time or another, we have all needed extra attention, so when we see a student seeking attention, we remember what that feels like. We *identify* with them. In a sense, for a moment we become them emotionally. All of us have felt the need to vent our anger. When we see a student venting anger in a disruptive way, we don't accept the disruptive behavior, but we identify with and accept the student's position. When this happens, we communicate acceptance — not with our words but with our being. When we can assume a Same-Side position, much of the battle for a Win-Win outcome is won. When a student truly feels received, feels we identify with him/her and that we are on the same-side, resistance melts. The student is then willing to team up to find non-disruptive alternatives.

Two Approaches to Discipline: Same-Side vs. Opposite-Side

Successful implementation of Win-Win depends on putting on a new set of lenses — looking beyond the disruptive behavior, seeing the place from which the disruptive behavior springs. When we put on the Win-Win lenses, we approach discipline in a fresh way: we position ourselves on the same-side with students.

While refusing to accept the disruptive behavior, the Win-Win teacher sees disruptions as merely uneducated attempts to meet basic needs we all share. Once we see the disruptive student as striving for attention or approval, trying to avoid public embarrassment, or merely trying to fulfill some other basic need, it is easy to team up with the student — to enter a process to help the student acquire responsible, non-disruptive ways to meet his/her needs. Our role as teacher is transformed: Rather than disciplining disruptive students, we help them *acquire* discipline. It becomes our job to convert the disruption into a learning opportunity. When we put on the Win-Win lenses, we transform both our view of disruptive students and our view of our role as an educator. Our approach to discipline is transformed; we move to a Same-Side position with disruptive students.

Win-Win's Same-Side orientation is in stark contrast to the Opposite-Side orientation that has traditionally characterized discipline approaches. Let's explore the Win-Win difference.

The Opposite-Side Approach. The Opposite-Side approach focuses on the behavior of the disruptive student. There are two paths that lead to an Opposite-Side position. Traditionally teachers approached discipline from a **moralistic perspective**: behavior was good or bad, right or wrong. From this perspective the disruptive student is a bad student, choosing the wrong type of behavior. The moralistic teacher views only the behavior, judging it as bad or wrong, not looking beyond the behavior to the position from which the behavior springs. Often, the disciplinary action that arises from this position is punishment — bad behavior needs to be met with negative consequences. As well-intended as this orientation may be, it almost always backfires because judgment and punishment breed anger, which usually leads to direct or indirect retaliation.

A second path that leads to an Opposite-Side position is to focus narrowly on the effects of disruption on the teacher and/or classmates. The disruptive student is seen as a nuisance, preventing efficient teaching and learning. This **pragmatic perspective** views the disruptive student as an obstacle to efficient teaching and learning. To end the disruption, the pragmatic teacher is tempted to ignore the disruptive student and/or use rewards and punishments. These behavioral techniques, though, often backfire and in the long-run seldom lead to learning autonomous responsible behavior. The hope that lack of attention will extinguish the disruptive behavior is usually dashed: The last thing a student looking for attention wants is to be ignored — usually he/she will resort to even greater disruptions, seeking to fill the unfulfilled need. In the long run using various rewards and/or punishments to bribe or threaten the student into conformity also usually fails. Punishment is a form of attention; by punishing a student seeking attention we are likely to inadvertently reinforce the very behavior we are hoping to eliminate. The reward/punishment approach at very best temporarily placates or suppresses the need; it does not relate to the student. The disruptive student is not searching for a reward or a punishment; the student seeks someone to relate to his/her needs, to be accepted, cared about. A token is no substitute for genuine caring. A token approach may breed a desire for additional tokens, but it does not fill the student's need and it does not teach the student how to meet his/her own needs.

The Opposite-Side orientation, with its emphasis on punishing, suppressing, and controlling behavior, does not help students learn responsible ways to deal with their needs. At best it may end a disruption, but it leaves the student no better prepared to deal with his/her needs in the future, making future disruptions almost inevitable.

The Same-Side Approach. The Win-Win teacher puts on a different set of lenses, looking beyond the disruptive behavior to the position of the student. The teacher *relates to the student*: *Where is the student coming from? How can I help the student learn to meet his/her needs in non-disruptive ways?* From this Same-Side position the teacher views disruptive behavior as merely an immature or uneducated attempt to meet basic needs. The teacher responds by doing what teachers do best — structuring learning opportunities — helping the student learn responsible ways to satisfy his/her needs. While the Opposite-Side approach views the student from the outside, as an object, the Same-Side approach views the student from the inside, as a person craving what we all crave — positive attention, success, and an opportunity to express oneself and meet one's needs. Once on the Same-Side with the student, the Win-Win teacher goes with, rather than against, the student. Win-Win teachers do not judge students and do not try to manipulate them; rather they establish a genuine relationship with the students. (It is for this reason, as we will see, that the Same-Side Chat is the single most important of all Win-Win Structures). At first the disruptive student may test to see if the teacher really is on his/her side. *Is this teacher really reaching positive outcomes for me?* When the testing is over, when the student believes the teacher will consistently maintain a Same-Side approach, the student is no longer motivated to disrupt the teacher or class — the teacher becomes an ally, a friend. In some cases the Win-Win teacher becomes the very first adult ally the student has ever had.

Win-Win teachers have faith in their students. They believe all students can become respectful, productive students. They approach the student as a person not as a disruption, with care rather than manipulation. They know students need someone who can see and relate to them, not just react to their behavior. They know that by being genuinely on the same-side with the student, they provide essential conditions for learning and growth.

Same-Side vs. Opposite-Side Approaches to Discipline

	Opposite-Side	Same-Side
Focus On	Disruptive Behavior	Student Position
View of Student	Student Is Bad; Student Is Nuisance	Student Is Striving to Meet Basic Needs
Discipline Approach	Punish; Reward; Ignore	Relate to Student

Validating Student Positions: Building Bridges

Student validation is the Same-Side Pillar in action. We take the side of our students and communicate that we understand and accept them. We couple this acceptance of their position, however, with a clear message that we do not accept their disruptive behavior. By communicating an acceptance of the student's position and a rejection of the student's behavior, we build two kinds of bridges:

First, validation builds a bridge between the student and ourselves: *I am no different from you: I, too, sometimes get angry, antsy, or bored.* When the student feels his/her position is accepted (even if the teacher will not accept the disruptive behavior), when the student knows the teacher identifies with him/her, the student reciprocates, identifying with the teacher. Care becomes mutual and the student is less motivated to disrupt the teacher's class and more motivated to want to help the teacher. When the student feels rejected, the student is more likely to strike back with disruptive behavior; when the student feels accepted, the student is more likely to reciprocate with positive behavior.

The second bridge is harder to see: it is within the student. Validation of student position builds a bridge to student self-knowledge. The disruptive student often is out of touch with his/her own position. The student acts out his anger or boredom or energy without understanding it or even experiencing it. Until the student knows his/her position, he/she is destined to act it out. Validation from the teacher is like holding up a mirror — the student begins to understand and accept himself/herself.

Receiving consistent validation from the teacher, the student internalizes the validation and begins to adopt a new attitude toward himself/herself: *I am OK. There is nothing wrong with me. My behavior has not been acceptable, but I am liked, cared for, and accepted.* From this attitude of self-acceptance and self-liking flows a number of benefits: the student experiences improved self-esteem, confidence, and acceptance of others. The student distinguishes himself/herself from his/her behavior and realizes it is possible to maintain his/her identity while changing his/her behavior.

Good therapists know about the paradoxical nature of change: When a therapist communicates that he/she wants to change a patient, he/she meets resistance and the patient does not change. Paradoxically, when the therapist communicates acceptance of the patient, the patient begins to change. Until we feel accepted, in contact with ourselves, we do not have the knowledge or courage to change. Validation builds the self-knowledge and self-acceptance necessary for change.

References

[1]Bluestein, J. *Mentors, Masters and Mrs. MacGregor: Stories of Teachers Making a Difference.* Deerfield Beach, Florida: Heath Communications, Inc. 1995, p. 5.

Quiz Yourself — Validate that Position!

Below are vignettes of students engaged in disruptive behavior.

Your job:

1) Identify the behavior, ABCD.
2) Identify the position or positions from which the behavior springs.
3) State how you would validate the position of the student. (For now, don't worry about responding to the disruption or communicating that the disruptive behavior is unacceptable. We will get to that later!)

Reminders:

1. Three Before B — Only use Breaking the Rules if the behavior does not fit Aggression, Confrontation, or Disengagement.
2. Aggression toward a teacher is classified as Confrontation.

---

1. Fran
Unlike the other students, as she enters the class, Fran walks to her desk without putting her homework in the homework basket. Later she interrupts the teacher while he is talking with a student, innocently asking, "What are we supposed to do with our homework"?

Type of Disruption _____

Dominant Position _____

Validate the Student Position _____

_____

_____

2. Allison

Allison kicked another student as she moved to her seat and slammed her books on her desk as she sat down. When her teacher began the lesson, Allison just glared at him.

Type of Disruption _____

Dominant Position _____

Validate the Student Position _____
_____
_____

3. Anthony

Anthony feels as if he can't understand the math problems that Mr. Blake is trying to teach him. He doesn't admit he is afraid to do the problems, instead, when the worksheet is passed out, Anthony says, "These problems are dumb!" and opens a reading book.

Type of Disruption _____

Dominant Position _____

Validate the Student Position _____
_____
_____

4. Enrique

Enrique is bouncing off the walls again in Mr. Blake's class. Mr. Blake gets tired just looking at him. Today as Enrique worked his way through the aisle to take his seat, he poked every student he passed on the way! *If he would only sit still for two seconds*, thinks Mr. Blake. *I just want him to settle down for a few minutes.*

Type of Disruption _____

Dominant Position _____

Validate the Student Position _____
_____
_____

For Answers, See Part VII, Resources D.2.

5. Charlie

"You can't make me!" Charlie says belligerently to his teacher, Mr. Blake. "I don't want to do it and you can't make me!"

Type of Disruption _____

Dominant Position _____

Validate the Student Position _____

_____

_____

6. Betty

Betty doesn't think she can stand being in class one more second. Nothing seems interesting. Her mind is wandering. Betty wishes the bell would ring, but it seems to be taking forever. The clock seems to be moving in slow motion.

Type of Disruption _____

Dominant Position _____

Validate the Student Position _____

_____

_____

7. Abe

Abe does his assignments but finds time to disrupt the class in various ways. He is a master at making strange noises. When he isn't using his underarms to make sounds, he is busy elevating burping to an art form. While writing his essay, he has just let out his fourth loud belch. The other students in the class laugh and laugh.

Type of Disruption _____

Dominant Position _____

Validate the Student Position _____

_____

_____

For Answers, See Part VII, Resources D.2.

Win-Win Discipline. Kagan Publishing • 1 (800) 933-2667 • www.KaganOnline.com

12.15

Chapter 13

Responding to the Seven Positions

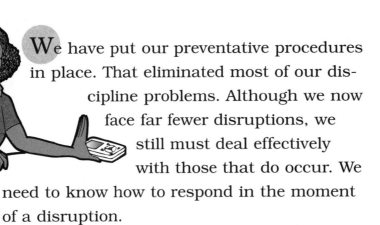

We have put our preventative procedures in place. That eliminated most of our discipline problems. Although we now face far fewer disruptions, we still must deal effectively with those that do occur. We need to know how to respond in the moment of a disruption.

Ideally, in the moment-of-disruption we would achieve five goals:

1. **Quickly end the disruption and minimize the missed instructional time for all students.**
2. **Communicate that the disruptive behavior is unacceptable.**
3. **Communicate validation of student position.**
4. **Communicate a Win-Win orientation, a willingness to team up and seek mutually beneficial solutions.**
5. **Foster long-term learning of autonomous responsible behaviors.**

Accomplishing all five of these goals, of course, is the dream scenario.

The ideal, to convert a disruption into an important learning opportunity, often is not realized in the moment-of-disruption. Often, in the emergency of a disruption there is not enough time to create a learning opportunity; in the heat of a disruption we may not be able to understand a student's position, let alone validate the position.

Although we will not formulate the perfect response to most disruptions, we do have many tools already in place. First we know to categorize the type of disruption, ABCD, and to ask the three disruption-specific questions. They are powerful guides toward an effective response. Aggression means we must check for safety; Disengagement means we need to check our curriculum, instruction, and management, and so on. So in the moment-of-disruption, we can categorize the disruption and ask the three corresponding questions. With practice, this becomes automatic.

Further, we have tools to identify a student's position and understand the need to respond differently depending on position. We respond to a wisecrack intended to get a laugh (breaking the rules springing from attention-seeking) very differently than we respond to one designed to undermine the teacher's authority

Win-Win Discipline. Kagan Publishing • 1 (800) 933-2667 • www.KaganOnline.com

13.2

(confrontation springing from control-seeking). We respond differently to the angry student who trips another with intent to hurt (aggression springing from anger) than to a playful student who trips another for a laugh (aggression springing from energy). With practice, using the position clues becomes almost automatic and we see beyond each disruption to the position from which it springs. Often we are not certain about a student's position and so need to make our best guess, trying a response, noting how the student responds. With time, we are able to correctly categorize the student's position.

Thus in the moment-of-disruption, we respond as well as we can to both the type of disruption and the position of the student. In the moment-of-disruption, we communicate that the disruptive behavior is not acceptable, but that we understand and accept the position of the student. The essence of Win-Win is to accept student positions while rejecting disruptive behaviors, helping students learn non-disruptive alternatives — responsible ways to meet the needs of their positions.

There is no question — it takes great skill to formulate an artful response in the moment-of-disruption. Often it is a very difficult task, indeed. No teacher always makes the perfect discipline response. This chapter, however, provides strategies and structures to make that task easier. With proven discipline responses at our disposal, we are more likely to make the wise response.

Discipline Responses: An Art. Responding effectively in the moment-of-disruption is an art. It is an art that we are all in the process of perfecting. Part of the reason it is difficult to respond in the most efficient way to a disruption is that we have different goals in the moment-of-disruption, depending on the following factors:

- Position of the student in the moment-of-disruption
- History of disruptions by the disruptive student (amount, type)
- History of disruptions in the class (amount, type)
- The point in the lesson at which the disruption occurs

Further, each disruption has unique, unpredictable elements; therefore, our goals during any one disruption may vary. Our many goals may include:

- Ending the disruption
- Getting the class refocused on academic content
- Creating a safe classroom
- Allowing the disruptive student to cool down
- Helping a disruptive student see that he/she can be successful with the content
- Helping a disruptive student consider more responsible alternatives

- Helping a disruptive student become aware of what he/she is doing
- Helping a disruptive student see the effect of his/her behavior on others
- Meeting the needs of the disruptive student
- Helping a disruptive student learn to meet his/her own needs
- Moving toward self-validation instead of attention-seeking, self-control instead of aggression, self-confidence instead of fear of failure...

Given the complexity of responding to disruptions, the art of discipline will always remain an art, not a science. Nevertheless, having at our disposal proven discipline responses makes us more likely to create successful responses.

There is another reason formulating a successful response in the moment-of-disruption is difficult: often the disruptive student is disrupting in response to deep emotional needs that he/she does not understand. The student trying to grab our attention does not really understand that underlying the bid for attention is a bid for love and acceptance. Many students act out their needs without even knowing what they are seeking. In the short run, the attention-seeking student gets a payoff, a bit of attention, but in the long run, all those payoffs don't add up to what the student really craves. Any completely self-aware and rational student would realize that constantly interrupting the teacher for attention will not serve him/her as well as putting that energy into creating an outstanding report which will earn attention in a far more adaptive way. Ultimately, the student craves self-validation, something that can never be obtained by those mini bids for attention.

The student fighting our every move has no idea his/her issue is control and that opposing the teacher will never really add up to obtaining a sense of internal control. The student who refuses to do the work in order to avoid failure doesn't realize that he/she is caught in a self-defeating cycle in which the avoidance leads to less learning which, in turn, leads to more need to avoid. We are aware of the negative results of the cycle, but telling it to the student will do little good in the moment that he/she is causing a disturbance to mask the fear of failure.

Yes, if the disruptive student were completely self-aware and rational in the moment-of-disruption, our job would be easy. We would simply explain that in the long run, disruptive behavior is self-defeating. We would simply ask the student to choose a non-disruptive alternative and he/she would comply.

But, of course, in the moment of an angry confrontation, the disruptive student is not open to rational discourse. At the moment the class clown has the whole class in hysterics, it will do no good to inform him/her that the need for attention could be met in more adaptive ways! In the heat of a fight, instructing the angry student about the long-term positive payoffs of anger management will have no impact!

No, we need strategies and structures that will quickly end the disruption in the moment, but which will direct the student toward learning non-disruptive alternatives in the long run. Behavior change precedes insight. After students have adopted responsible behaviors, they will see that the disruptive behaviors were self-defeating.

Structures vs. Strategies. The bulk of this chapter is a summary of structures and strategies that respond to each position. In Win-Win, we use the term "structure" to describe a well-defined, proven, step-by-step teacher–student interaction sequence. Moment-of-disruption structures are designed to quickly end a disruption, dignify the student, and/or set the stage for the student to learn non-disruptive alternative behaviors. Many, but not all, of the structures validate the student's position and open the door to learning more responsible behaviors. Some simply end the disruption, and require a follow-up for the student to learn more responsible alternatives. Moment-of-disruption structures are discipline responses. Each Win-Win structure responds well to at least one type of disruption and one student position; many respond well to many types of disruptions springing from many positions.

There are many strategies a teacher may use in the moment-of-disruption, such as sparking engagement in a disengaged student by using the student's name as part of a content example. For example:

"If Susie had two pizzas and wanted to divide them equally so that she and her two best friends get an equal share, how would Susie divide the pizzas?"

Proximity, a hand on a shoulder, catching the eye of a student, and pointing to a rule chart, are but a few of the many strategies effective teachers use. They are not, however, structures. They are not step-by-step sequences of interaction between the teacher and student, and many cannot be used with a range of disruption types and positions. Win-Win structures are a special type of strategy. They are a step-by-step interaction sequences, which can be used repeatedly with a range of disruption types and with students coming from various positions.

A Word of Reassurance. It is not expected that any teacher beginning the Win-Win approach will use or even know all the strategies and structures. The structures are powerful tools, but they are best learned gradually. We recommend you try one, experiment with it, modify it, and make it your own. Once you have mastered a Win-Win structure, you will probably want to begin experimenting with another. Aim for success by attempting to learn only one structure at a time. Choose one which feels comfortable and which responds to a discipline problem in your classroom. With time, you will master a number of Win-Win structures and in the moment-of-disruption will be able to select among them to implement the best one for a given discipline problem at hand.

In the long run slow and sure is far faster to the goal. If you try to learn and implement too many Win-Win structures at once, you run the risk of overwhelming and confusing yourself and your students.

What's Ahead. The remainder of this chapter is a summary of strategies and structures to use in the moment-of-disruption, organized by position. A detailed step-by-step description of the structures is presented in **Chapter 14. Moment-of-Disruption Structures.**

Attention-Seeking

We all need attention. Infants throughout the animal kingdom that do not cry out for attention have less chance of survival. Human infants who are not touched wither, fail to mature, and often die. The need for attention is so great that if we cannot obtain positive attention, we will work for negative attention. Being scolded can be better than being ignored. Because of this, students and teachers can fall into a trap: the student does something annoying and the teacher reprimands the student. The reprimand is a form of attention, so it is reinforcing, actually increasing, the probability the student will again do something annoying!

An interesting experiment proved this point with young students.[1] The target disruption was "out of seat behavior." That is, teachers were struggling with a fairly common discipline problem among very young students: Students getting out of their seats without permission. In a tightly controlled experiment, teachers were randomly assigned to respond in one of two different ways. One group was told to respond with a rule reminder each time a student got out of his/her seat without permission. The other group was told to ignore the behavior and compliment someone who was sitting in his/her seat. Within weeks, there were very few students getting out of their seats without permission in the classrooms where teachers ignored the out of seat behavior. In the classrooms where teachers responded with rule reminders, out of seat behavior increased dramatically! To prove the point, the experimenters reversed the conditions. Those teachers who were previously told to ignore the out of seat behavior were told to respond

> *The greatest gift you can give another is the purity of your attention.*
> —*Richard Moss*

instead with rule reminders. Those who had previously responded with rule reminders were told to ignore the out of seat behavior. Within a few weeks, the behavior of the students completely reversed itself. Students who had previously been getting out of their seats without permission were now remaining seated — that had become the ticket to attention in those classes. And in the room where students had been sitting, students were now frequently popping out of their seats without permission — that had become their ticket to attention, even if the attention was in the form of a rule reminder.

The experimenters had proven the power of two learning principles: reinforcement and extinction. Reinforcement: When behavior is followed by a reward, the probability of that behavior increases. Extinction: When there is no reward for behavior, the probability decreases. The experiment proved something else: a rule reminder can be rewarding and actually increase the probability of future rule infractions!

Reinforcement: Whatever we attend to, we get more of.
Extinction: What we ignore, we get less of.

Given this process, we want to attend to responsible behavior and ignore irresponsible behavior to the greatest extent possible. In other words: Catch them being good!

Seeking attention may be an unconscious motivation within the student. The student cannot verbalize that he/she is performing the annoying behavior to seek attention. Nevertheless, receiving attention for a behavior reinforces it and increases the probability of its repeated occurrence, even if the student and teacher are not aware of the process.

> *Attention of any kind can be reinforcing, and a student may misbehave for attention even if the he/she is unaware he/she is seeking attention.*

> *The only thing worse than being talked about is not being talked about.*
> — *Oscar Wilde*

Thus in the moment-of-disruption, we must be careful not to inadvertently reinforce disruptive ways of getting attention. Using as few words as possible at the moment-of-disruption helps avoid the trap of unintentionally reinforcing the disruptive behavior. The best course to chart in navigating the tricky seas of attention-seeking is to: 1) ignore or at least minimize the attention we give to disruptive attention-seeking and 2) as much as possible, pay attention to responsible behaviors. Whether the student is aware of this process or not, if they are truly seeking attention, they will begin to act more responsibly and less disruptively. The older the student is, the more we may want to make our reinforcement of responsible behaviors low key and private.

Attention-Seeking

Eventually, we would like for students to learn self-validation so they are not continually seeking attention from others. Initially, though, we want to support them in getting attention for responsible behavior rather than through disruptions.

Strategies for When Students Are Attention-Seeking

Moment-of-disruption strategies for attention-seeking fall into two opposite categories: those designed to communicate that disruptive behavior is not a way to get attention and those designed to fill the need for attention. It is only when the student is not being disruptive that we attempt to reinforce responsible ways of seeking attention.

■ **Hand Signals.** You meet with students seeking attention and arrange a hand signal that you will give them when they are disrupting. You are giving them a non-verbal reminder to get their behavior back on track. The brief non-verbal cue keeps you from inadvertently reinforcing the disruptive behavior. The meeting with the students to plan the signal gives them a little dose of attention from you as you two seek to solve the problem together, but it would still be important to seek out responsible behaviors of these students to highlight. As previously mentioned, with older students, the focus on their responsible behavior needs to be low key and private.

■ **Ignore It.** If the student is disruptive in an attempt to get attention, in the long run the disruptive student, the class, and we as teachers are better off not giving that behavior immediate attention. When possible, in the moment-of-disruption we ignore attention-seeking behavior, or at least delay our response to it. The alternative is to inadvertently reinforce the disruptive behavior. It varies from teacher to teacher which attention-seeking behaviors can be ignored. We cannot ignore behavior if doing so takes us beyond our comfort level.

Ignoring is actually a much more complex strategy than it appears on the surface. Often teachers think that they are using this strategy, but their body language is shouting at the student to stop and, therefore, the teacher is not really ignoring at all. In order for ignoring to work, it needs to be a whole body commitment.

Ignoring a behavior is not the same as not being aware of the behavior. In fact, it helps to tell the student ahead of time that his/her disruptive attention seeking will be ignored.

> ## Strategies for Responding When Students Are Attention-Seeking
>
> - **Hand Signals**
> - **Ignore It**
> - **Physical Touch**
> - **Private Written Note**
> - **Proximity**
> - **Student's Name in an Example**
> - **Gambits for When Students Make Silly Comments**

"Mike, if you make annoying sounds again in class (substitute shouting out, dropping books, pretending to fall from a chair...), I plan to ignore it, so as not to steal valuable time from the rest of the class. Instead, we will look for a solution in a follow-up after class. I just don't want you to rob the other students of valuable time on academics."

Essentially, you are letting the student know his/her disruptive behavior will not earn attention in the moment-of-disruption. Granted, it will get attention in the form of a follow-up, but when reinforcement is delayed in time, it loses most, if not all, of its reinforcing properties.

Class cooperation is also necessary for this strategy to work. If you ignore the attention-seeking disruption but all the students give it attention, then the Ignore It strategy will not work. Peer attention is a powerful reinforcer. If you use the Ignore It strategy, if possible, have students ignore it also but then give plenty of attention when the attention-seeking student is behaving appropriately.

Physical Touch. A caring touch on the shoulder can redirect the student seeking attention with minimal disruption to the lesson. You need to be sensitive, though, to the fact that some students do not like any touch and some schools and districts prohibit physical contact of any kind between teachers and students.

Private Written Note. A private written note can stop disruptive behaviors springing from attention-seeking, without interrupting teaching. The note can communicate positive feedback or a need to stop disruptive behavior. Some teachers have notes made up ahead of time:

- Thank you for staying on task.
- I appreciate your positive attitude.
- Please stop!

If you use notes, share with the students the nature and purpose of the procedure:

"Class, our learning time is valuable. I don't want to steal time from that to deal with disruptions or even to let you know when I appreciate your behavior. So, sometimes I will just give you a note of appreciation or a request to stop disruptive behavior. If you get a note, there is no need to interrupt the class. Please just attend to my request."

Proximity. A simple way to meet the need for attention while ending many disruptions is to continue with a lesson but simply move close to the disruptive student. Without a word spoken or a moment lost from the lesson, proximity can end many disruptions.

Attention-Seeking

■ **Student's Name in an Example.** Another way to meet the need for attention without losing a moment from the lesson is to include the student's name in an example. It communicates that you are attending to the student and can re-orient a student toward the content without losing instructional time.

■ **Gambits for When Students Make Silly Comments**

Examples of Silly Student Comments:
- *"If you give me $1,000.00 I'll get my homework in."*
- *"I'll do it if you don't give me any more homework this week."*

Possible Teacher Gambits:
- *"Interesting thought, but it won't work in this class."*
- *"You're pulling my leg, right?"*
- *"If I do it for you, I'll have to do it for everybody!"*
- *"When I win the lottery, then we'll discuss that."*
- *"You have a great sense of humor, but let's get serious."*
- *"Interesting thought, but in reality…"*
- *"Explain exactly how that would solve this problem."*
- *"That isn't the picture I had in mind."*
- *"It would be nice if you didn't have to come to school, but I'd miss you."*

Moment-of-Disruption Structures for
Attention-Seeking

Recommended Structures

- **Coupons**
- **Cues: Verbal and Non-verbal**
- **Expectation Reminder**
- **I-Messages Plus**
- **Make a Better Choice**

- **Picture It Right!**
- **Redirect**
- **Restart**
- **Right Now Validation**
- **Schedule Follow-Up**

Also Useful

- **Consequences**
- **Grandma's Rule**
- **Language of Choice**

- **Model It!**
- **Target, Stop, Do**

For details of these structures, see **Chapter 14. Moment-of-Disruption Structures.**

Structures for When Students Are Attention-Seeking:

Coupons

Students are reminded to trade one of their limited supply of coupons for "too frequent" behavior. The coupon approach helps the student monitor and limit disruptive behavior, fostering self-control. *"Thank you for using your coupon wisely."*

Cues: Verbal and Non-verbal

The teacher uses pre-established verbal or non-verbal cues to elicit appropriate behavior. Class cues are established; specific cues may be established for individual students. **Verbal:** *"Class, please take a moment now and look over the class rules chart."* **Non-verbal:** *Teacher walks to and looks intently at the class rules chart.*

Expectation Reminder

Prior to a possible disruption or at the outset of a disruption, students are reminded of pre-established expectations, procedures, or rules. When a number of students are violating the rules, the teacher may stop the lesson to re-teach the rules. *"Remember the expectations (rules, procedures) we agreed on. Let's take some time now to review how we want out class to be."*

I-Message Plus

Calmly informing students of your own feelings is an I-Message designed to make students aware of their stimulus value (effect on others). An I-Message Plus adds encouragement to adopt non-disruptive alternatives. *"I feel X when you do Y, and your class-mates feel Z. Can you think of a better choice?"*

Make a Better Choice

Through Make a Better Choice, the teacher calls for reflection rather than obedience, leaving it to the student to create a more responsible alternative. *"I want you to think of a better choice to make right now."*

Picture It Right!

The class or an individual takes responsibility for imagining responsible alternatives as they pause, close their eyes, and picture it right. *"If we were at our very best right now, how would it look?"*

Redirect

Redirect diverts attention and behavior away from a disruptive episode and toward a responsible learning activity. *"Have you done problem four yet?"*

Avoiding Failure

■ Restart

When the class is out of control, like a computer that has crashed, it is time to Restart. We stop talking, stop doing, pause, see a positive and negative model by the teacher, see a positive model by a classmate, and then restart. *"Stop! Look! Listen!"*

■ Right Now Validation

The teacher acknowledges and validates the student or class position and then directs the student to more responsible behavior. *"Right now you are feeling _____. That's OK, but what you need to do is _____."*

■ Schedule Follow-Up

In order not to disrupt the class while implementing the three pillars, a follow-up meeting with the student is scheduled. *"We need to talk this through. Let's meet after...."*

Avoiding Failure

We all need to feel successful and want to avoid failures, especially public failures that can lead to embarrassment. Avoiding failure helps us preserve our self-respect and our status within the group. It is much less painful to say to one-self and others, "I didn't care and so I didn't try," than to say, "I really cared a lot and tried my hardest but failed anyway." So avoiding failure is protection for our ego.

Some students have many areas of success in their lives and, therefore, can easily admit a failure or difficulty in one area. Others do not. We all know the student who can easily say, "Those problems were really hard for me," and others who would not admit that publicly. Paradoxically, those who can admit that an area is difficult get better at it; those who cannot admit their weaknesses avoid that area and, so, do not improve.

Students have many ways of masking their fear of failure. Faced with a difficult worksheet and potential failure, Alex starts poking the student in the seat in front of him. If he makes enough of a distraction, no one will focus on the fact that he cannot solve the problems. He is being aggressive, but not out of anger. His aggression springs from avoiding failure. Another student can feign boredom, but the real position is avoiding failure.

When we sense a student is avoiding failure, we have several options. We can restructure the learning task so the student sees he/she can succeed. Cooperative learning and peer tutoring

> *An excuse is worse and more terrible than a lie, for an excuse is a lie guarded.*
> **—Pope John Paul II**

can give students the encouragement and support they need. We can make feedback private, so there will be no potential for public embarrassment associated with performance. Teacher and parental encouragement and support help. But probably the most important thing we can do is to restructure the task breaking it into small pieces so the student feels each can be accomplished, leading to eventual success at the task as a whole.

If we structure for success often enough, students who otherwise would avoid failure by not doing the learning task become self-confident and persist or ask for help in the face of difficulty rather than giving up and masking their failure.

Strategies for When Students Are Avoiding Failure

■ **Appreciation.** Any progress made by the student can be appreciated. Appreciation focuses on growth and improvement. Appreciation ultimately aims at having students look within themselves for their validation, eliminating the need for excessive external attention. Appreciation helps students develop self-validation skills by modeling an attitude toward the student which he/she eventually internalizes. The teacher can directly foster internalization by having the student make self-statements:

"Tell yourself you are proud of yourself for sticking in there."

"Give yourself a pat on the back for all the hard work."

"Don't be shy. Say, 'I'm brilliant.'"

■ **Bite-Sized Instructions.** Students avoiding a task for fear of failure find the task more approachable if it is broken into small chunks. A rule of thumb is to give only the amount and complexity of instructions you are sure all students can follow without asking for clarification. Requests for clarification or avoidance of the task are clues that we may need to make the instructional bits more bite-sized. Celebrations following completion of each chunk help motivate students to persist in the face of difficulty.

■ **Cooperative Structures.** Probably the single most powerful set of tools we have for students when they are avoiding failure is to use a number of cooperative learning structures. Many structures can be used at the drop of a hat with no special planning or preparation. When avoiding failure is at the root of student disruptions, we can shift to a cooperative structure

Strategies for Responding When Students Are Avoiding Failure

- Appreciation
- Bite-sized Instructions
- Cooperative Structures
- RallyCoach
- Team-Pair-Solo
- Numbered Heads Together
- Encouragement
- MI Instruction
- MI Encourager
- Monitor and Adjust
- Peer Tutoring
- Private Feedback Reminder
- Practice Reattribution
- Teacher Tutoring
- Share Fears
- Gambits for When Students Blame Others

Avoiding Failure

which makes it clear to them that they will have plenty of encouragement, support, and tutoring to avoid failure. Essentially, they can avoid failure without being disruptive and without avoiding the learning task.

A few of the many examples of cooperative learning structures are RallyCoach, Team-Pair-Solo, and Numbered Heads Together.

■ **RallyCoach.** With any existing worksheet or set of problems, students take turns. One does a problem while the other checks, coaches, and praises. The students cannot practice incorrectly because each problem is checked. They know they cannot fail because they have peer support. The emphasis shifts from evaluation to learning and so fear of failure literally evaporates.

■ **Team-Pair-Solo.** Seated in teams of four, students work on a specific type of problem as a team. Only when they are sure they can do the problems as a pair do they break up into pairs, alternating doing another set of the same type of problems. Finally, when they are certain everyone can do the problems on their own, they work solo. There is no fear of failure because the students do not move to the solo work until everyone is ready.

■ **Numbered Heads Together.** Seated as a team of four, each student has a number. The teacher asks a question or poses a problem. Each student performs alone. It is made clear that it is not expected that everyone will get all the problems right. After the students perform alone, they share their answers with teammates and receive coaching and help if they need it. Only when they signal that they are certain that they can perform correctly on their own does the teacher call a number, and the student with that number performs on his/her own. As with the other cooperative structures, students do not fear failure because they have plenty of peer support and tutoring prior to performing on their own.

■ **Encouragement.** If students bog down or show signs of giving up, encouragement can tip the balance and help get them through without giving up. Discouragement is the early warning sign for avoiding failure. It is the discouraged student who becomes disruptive, masking his/her fear of failure by muttering *"This assignment is stupid."* The antidote to discouragement, of course, is encouragement. The Win-Win teacher makes plenty of encouraging statements and has peers make encouraging statements to each other.

> *"You are putting a lot of time into writing your story. I'll bet you will feel really good about all that effort when you share your story."*

"You are working hard with your team on that project. I know it is tough at times. Hang in there and you will come out with a great project."

"Students, turn to your partners and tell them, "This looks really tough now, but with practice it is going to get easy!"

"When the going gets tough, the tough get going."

■ **MI Instruction.** When a student is avoiding failure, it is because the work is not easy for him/her. The student may pretend disinterest or create some other diversion, but the reality is that if the work were easy, the student would do it and would not need to create a disruption of some sort to avoid doing the work.

Different students have different intelligences, and for any given student, some ways of learning are difficult while others are easy. Don Campbell tells the story of a student in his class who simply was not able to remember the multiplication facts in spite of hours of practice. Don knew the student was good at art. He asked her to simply decorate her most difficult multiplication flash cards with pictures. When she finished, she knew all those multiplication facts. He had the opportunity to test her years later, and she still knew the facts and could still remember what picture was on each card! Because she was strong in the visual/spatial intelligence, learning the multiplication facts by associating them with a visual image was easy for her.

The multiple intelligences literature is replete with similar stories. Students who are failing become excellent students when allowed to learn through their strongest intelligence. One of the most dramatic stories is of a boy who was doing poorly in school until he learned to mind map. He went on to do what his teachers proclaimed would be impossible for him.[2]

Another case history is of Paula, who was in special education classes until she was encouraged to act out the letters and words using kinesthetic symbols. She went on to be an above-average student.[3]

So, one of the strongest sets of tools we have for students who are avoiding failure is to provide alternative ways of learning — learning through a different intelligence.

• For many ways to teach any content through each of the eight intelligences, see *Multiple Intelligences: The Complete MI Book*.[4] See also page 19.5 and pages 17.29–34.

■ **MI Encourager.** When we see a student becoming disruptive out of the desire to avoid failure, we can give the student an MI encourager:

"You know, all of us have areas of strength and areas of weakness. In school, an area of strength for me was…. It was easy for me. But I was terrible in…. I really had to struggle with that. If you are having a difficult time with…, don't let that get you down. We all have areas that don't come easily, but it pays to hang in there. With time you'll get it."

■ **Monitor and Adjust.** If we constantly monitor the progress of students, we can pick out those for whom the content is difficult. If we see them floundering, we can adjust the curriculum difficulty or pace of instruction. In this way, we can catch students at the moment they otherwise would avoid failure by feigning disinterest or by creating some other distraction.

■ **Peer Tutoring.** The research on peer tutoring reveals that the tutors show academic and non-academic gains, which are almost as strong as those of their tutee. A great win-win! When a student is struggling to avoid failure, you can offer him/her a tutor, either from within the class or from an upper grade level. As a twist on this, you can have the struggling student become a tutor for a younger student. The literature has many examples of poor students becoming excellent students after having the opportunity to tutor. See below, The Power of Peer Tutoring.

■ **Private Feedback Reminder.** Private performance feedback is a general preventative procedure in the Win-Win classroom. It can be helpful in the moment-of-disruption to remind students that only the teacher will see the student's grade on a worksheet, essay, test, quiz, or project.

The Power of Peer Tutoring

Fighting negative attitudes, low expectations, and frequent truancies on the part of his 8th and 9th grade remedial reading students, Hanoch McCarty also faced the challenge of finding reading materials his students could read and yet would find even slightly engaging. Finally, an idea occurred to Mr. McCarty: He "hired" his students to be reading tutors of elementary school children. The idea worked beyond expectations: The elementary students were grateful for the extra help and attention, and, more importantly, the remedial reading students began to change. They began to dress better, their attendance improved immensely, and their negative attitudes began to disappear, replaced with feelings of responsibility towards their own "students." The remedial students increased their reading level by one to three grade levels that year.

When one of the remedial reading students showed up for school even though he was sick, Mr. McCarty asked why he had come to school, his reply was, *"Oh, man, I couldn't miss today; I'm a **teacher**! My students would miss me, wouldn't they?"*[5]

■ **Practice Reattribution.** At the moment-of-disruption, if it is determined that a student is avoiding failure, you can redirect his/her attributions. Research shows that optimists tell themselves that the setback is only temporary and specific. (*"It will get better. There are other things I do well."*) Pessimists say that the setback is permanent and pervasive. (*"This ruins everything forever."*) Optimists persist in the face of difficulties. Pessimists give up. But pessimists can learn optimism.[6] Have students reflect on the things they can do well and times when things came easily to them. This counters the defeatist mindset of "I never succeed at anything."

■ **Teacher Tutoring.** Many students who are disruptive to avoid failing become model students when they can confidently perform the work. One of the most powerful techniques for producing academic gains and boosting confidence is one-to-one tutoring by the teacher, a parent, older student, or a competent adult.

■ **Share Fears.** All of us have fears of failing. If we create a norm in which it is OK to admit the fear of failing, students will be more likely to get the help they need rather than "faking it" or masking the fear via a disruption. Have students in pairs, teams, or as a class, discuss areas in which they fear failure — areas in which they are afraid to do or try. Admit your own areas of fear. Create a norm in which it is OK to have fears, but not OK to pretend. Once students can admit their fear of failure, they will stick with difficult content longer; it is not something they have to hide.

■ **Gambits for When Students Blame Others**
One way to attempt to avoid responsibility for disruptive behavior is to blame others. A Win-Win teacher artfully redirects the student to take responsibility for his/her behavior.

Examples of Students Blaming Others:
- *"Why are you always picking on me? Roger and Spencer are the real problems. Why aren't they here?"*
- *"Laurie told me to do it. She won't like me if I don't do what she says."*

Possible Teacher Gambits:
- *"Since we're the only two here, let's take care of this now."*
- *"They're on my list too."*
- *"My concern is for you. Let me tell you why."*
- *"You always have at least two choices, to act or not act."*
- *"It shows you're 'grown up' (more mature) when you accept responsibility."*
- *"Taking ownership for actions takes a lot of courage."*
- *"Let me worry about them, let's take care of you now."*
- *"I can tell by your body language, you're angry. Why don't you sit down, and we'll continue."*

My Most Embarrassing Moment

Describe your most embarrassing moment. Be sure to include all the details including when it happened, where it happened, who was involved, what you did, how you felt.

_____

_____

_____

_____

_____

_____

_____

_____

_____

_____

_____

_____

_____

_____

_____

_____

Illustrate your most embarrassing moment here.

The Worst Failure
I Can Imagine

What is the worst failure you can possibly imagine? Describe the failure in detail including what the failure is, why it is such a failure, and what you could do to recover.

_____

_____

_____

_____

_____

_____

_____

_____

_____

_____

_____

_____

_____

_____

_____

Illustrate the failure here.

Avoiding Failure

Structures for When Students Are Avoiding Failure

■ **Make a Better Choice**

Through Make a Better Choice, the teacher calls for reflection rather than obedience, leaving it to the student to create a more responsible alternative. "I want you to think of a better choice to make right now."

■ **Restructure Task**

The teacher restructures the learning task to stimulate greater engagement. "Let's take this part a step at a time."

■ **Right Now Validation**

The teacher acknowledges and validates the student or class position and then directs the student to more responsible behavior. "Right now you are feeling _____. That's OK, but what you need to do is _____."

■ **Schedule Follow-Up**

In order not to disrupt the class while implementing the three pillars, a follow-up meeting with the student is scheduled. "We need to talk this through. Let's meet after...."

Moment-of-Disruption Structures for
Avoiding Failure

Recommended Structures

- **Make a Better Choice**
- **Restructure Task**

- **Right Now Validation**
- **Schedule Follow-Up**

Also Useful

- **Grandma's Rule**
- **I-Messages Plus**
- **Model It!**

- **Picture It Right!**
- **Target, Stop, Do**

For details of these structures, see **Chapter 14. Moment-of-Disruption Structures.**

Angry

> *No man can think clearly when his fists are clenched.*
> —*George Jean Nathan*

We all get angry at times. That is a natural biological response to frustration and threat. Anger helps us survive: it prepares us to avoid threats and signals others not to threaten us. We all know the student who is picked on mercilessly until he/she displays anger, and then the others back off. Students need to learn that their anger is never the problem, but what they do when angry can be a problem. There are different ways of "handling" anger — some responsible and others disruptive.

In the moment of an anger-based disruption, sometimes it is all we can do to get the angry student to calm down. Sometimes, though, the angry outburst is not so prolonged or severe, in which case we can guide the student to explore non-disruptive ways of handling anger.

To get students to calm down, we can help them express their anger either directly (catharsis) or indirectly (transfer), or do something which sets off responses that inhibit the anger (reciprocal inhibition). If the anger is strong enough, we may need to have the student leave the situation that produced the anger.

In the classic western movie, two cowboys get into a knock-down, drag-out brawl. When they are completely exhausted, their anger drained, they dust themselves off, put their arms around each other's shoulder and head off for a drink together. Sometimes we can help students most if we allow them to "get their anger out" — but without the brawl. There are various safe ways to have students express their anger, and some work better than others, depending on the student. Other times, disruptive students and everyone around them are much better off if we do the opposite of "getting the anger out," distracting them from the anger rather than re-igniting the flames by having them talk about what has made them angry.

The rule of thumb: Use catharsis if you feel the student will be able to get through the anger. If, however, talking about it or expressing it is likely to upset the student even more, take the opposite course — get the student involved in something else and reserve dealing with the anger until a calmer moment.

We are likely to respond with anger ourselves when anger is directed at our students or at us. Controlling our own reaction is critical because students learn from the model we provide. Only if we have a controlled reaction are we likely to formulate a Win-Win Discipline response.

Eventually, we would like students who are angry to be able to exhibit self-control on their own. Initially, though, we want to support them in dealing with their feelings in a responsible way.

Strategies for When Students Are Angry:

Catharsis

Catharsis according to the American Heritage Dictionary, is "a release of emotional tension, as after an overwhelming experience, that restores or refreshes the spirit." We have all had the experience of being so angry we could not think of anything else. To have a very angry student try to concentrate on studies can be like telling him/her to ignore someone poking pins in his/her back. Sometimes it is best to let the student express the anger (or any other emotion) before trying to return to studies. A caution: if the student is so angry that expressing it will only get him/her more angry, avoid the catharsis strategies in the moment-of-disruption. There are a number of safe forms of catharsis:

> *Holding on to anger is like grasping a hot coal with the intent of throwing it at someone else; you are the one who gets burned.*
> —*Buddha*

■ **Catharsis: Draw It Out.** Some students express themselves more naturally with pictures than words. If a student is very angry, you can have him/her draw a picture expressing his/her anger.

> *"I know you are really angry. We all get angry at times. It is good to express our anger, but without hurting others. One safe way is to draw a picture. Will you draw a picture showing me what made you angry or what your anger makes you want to do."*

■ **Catharsis: Mold It.** Other students work best with their hands. Give them some molding clay and let them express their anger through the clay or putty with instructions like those for drawing. See Hand Candy, **Part VII, Resources F.**

■ **Catharsis: Talk It Out.** For some, an opportunity to talk through what made them angry helps them calm down. Sometimes the best thing we can do is simply listen.

■ **Catharsis: Write It Out.** For yet others, writing is the natural medium. Recently something angered me. I left work in a puff. At home my wife approached me to talk it through. I was in the middle of writing a letter to the person who had angered me. I told my wife I would talk with her after I had finished writing the letter. I was amazed: by the time I had finished the letter, I was rather calm. It appears that writing, for me, is the natural catharsis.

■ **Catharsis: Choice.** Give students a choice as to how to express their anger. They will gravitate to their natural medium.

■ **Catharsis: Exercise.** The impulse to fight when angry is part of the fight or flight defense alarm reaction. When faced with a threat, biological reactions prepare us to either fight or flee. One way to deal with those impulses is find non-disruptive ways to act them out. If an angry student runs a lap, the student has

13.22

Win-Win Discipline. Kagan Publishing • 1 (800) 933-2667 • www.KaganOnline.com

actually carried out something he/she is biologically prepared to do (flee) and afterwards feels better. The same kind of release of the fight or flight defense alarm reaction can be obtained in many ways, including jumping rope, lifting weights, or hitting a ball. One advantage of having students release their anger through exercise is that they are learning socially acceptable ways to deal with those feelings.

Exercise in itself is not catharsis, because the purely physical activity does not connect to the source of the anger. Nevertheless, it is an important tool for us to use in helping students deal with their anger. Students who get regular strenuous exercise are less likely to have angry outbursts in class and are less likely to be too energetic to concentrate on studies.

Catharsis: The Tetherball. The time-honored tetherball is little more than a punching bag on a string designed for two pairs of fists. Beating up the tetherball or hitting the tackle dummy is a lot better than beating up a peer. I have witnessed students who were so angry they could not speak. After playing tetherball for about ten minutes, they walked away completely calm, their anger spent.

Distraction

The mind can only fully focus on one thing at a time. As I concentrate on writing this, the sound of traffic outside my window disappears. If a student is very angry, rather than catharsis, distraction is the strategy of choice. When a student is very angry, getting him/her to express that anger only gets him/her more worked up. At that point, we want to get the student to think about other things. Parents use distraction all the time with infants. The infant wants to grab something which is dangerous and the parent whisks the infant away, orienting him/her toward some other object, saying, "Oh, look at this!" With young students, we can get away with something quite similar. A student is angry and we say, *"You know, something really amazing happened to me this morning...."* If we are good at story telling, the anger is left in the wake.

With older students, distraction usually will not work without their compliance, unless we are very artful. It is much easier to be honest with them, engaging them in the distraction process with comments like:

"Right now we are all too worked up to think about this. Let's read another episode from our book."

"If we talk about this now, we might say something we will regret later. Instead, let's...."

Strategies for Responding When Students Are Angry

Catharsis
- Draw It Out
- Mold It
- Talk It Out
- Write It Out
- Choice
- Exercise
- The Tetherball

Distraction
- Guided Imagery
- Leave the Field
- Perspective Shift
- Induction

Reciprocal Inhibition
- Concentration
- Think Time: Student
- Food
- Humor

Transfer
- Academic Content

Teach, Model Positive Alternatives
- Reminder: STOP HACC
- Replacement Reminder
- Think Time: Teacher
- Class Meeting
- Peer Mediation

Angry

Angry

The advantage of honesty is that students can fully grasp the distraction process and are more likely to use it on their own when they are too angry to react rationally.

Guided Imagery. Have students close their eyes and imagine going to a calm, peaceful place, perhaps by the edge of a tranquil lake. Once they have traveled to that place in their mind's eye, help them focus on the sound of the birds, the lapping water, the warm day, the shade of the tree they are sitting under, and so on. They can practice going to that place, and later go to that place on their own to calm down.

Leave the Field. When the sight of an opponent after a fight makes a student lunge forward, determined to continue the fight, it is best to have the student "leave the field." Sometimes it is best to simply separate the angry person from the stimuli that precipitated the anger. Leaving the field can be a physical act (see the Cool Down structure on 13.28) or a psychological act, as when the student becomes completely absorbed in a story or an intriguing puzzle, while not physically leaving the area of the fight.

Perspective Shift. One way of shifting an angry student out of his/her anger for the moment is to get him/her to engage in a perspective shift. There are different kinds of perspective shifts. One is to ask him/her to role play the other person and tell why he/she is angry. Another is to shift the perspective so the angry incident is literally put in another perspective:

> *"Right now we are taking this really seriously. When you are both 80 years old, do you think you will remember it?"*

> *"If the president were to show up right now, what do you think he would say about this fight?"*

> *"Pretend you both were me (the teacher). What do you think I most want the solution to be? What do you think I most want you to learn from this fight?"*

Induction. When students are aggressive, they do not become less aggressive by being punished. In fact, punishing aggression generally leads to more aggression due to the modeling and to the frustration punishment provides. Telling students their behavior is bad also does not serve to reduce future aggression. What does serve to make them less aggressive is induction — inducing in them the feelings they created in others. Research on moral development has revealed that induction is one of the most powerful ways of fostering the development of a conscience. Some statements which help students know their effect on others are:

> *"I want you to think about how Johnny felt when you did that."*

" *For every minute you remain angry, you give up sixty seconds of peace of mind.* "
—*Ralph Waldo Emerson*

"If you were Johnny, how would you feel if someone...."

"How could you have acted so that Johnny would not have felt hurt?"

Reciprocal Inhibition

There are important biological "on-off" switches. Just as a fist cannot be both clenched and open at the same time, we cannot be angry and loving at the same time. Opposing nervous systems are involved. These systems are reciprocally inhibiting — that is, one inhibits the other. This gives us some power over anger: if we can turn on the system that is incompatible with anger, we turn off the anger. Anger is associated with sympathetic nervous system arousal. The parasympathetic nervous system is antagonistic to the sympathetic nervous system and, when sufficiently aroused, turns it off. Thus anything that sets off a parasympathetic nervous system reaction turns off anger. Pleasurable stimuli such as love, food, humor, beautiful scenery, calm music, and even the endorphin high following strenuous exercise can shift students from anger. So at times we can use these stimuli to help students control their anger in the moment-of-disruption.

Reciprocal Inhibition: Concentration. When we concentrate intensely on something, our mind is in control rather than our feelings. Therapists work hard to get some people to stop thinking so they can discover what they feel. When we want to help students control their anger, we do the opposite. We shift the focus from their feelings by having them concentrate on something, such as solving a problem, locating the hidden figure in a puzzle, or even finding the solution to a rope trick. When our minds are occupied, the opportunity for our feelings to dominate is eliminated — and vice versa.

Think Time: Student. Having students think about their behavior when they are angry has a number of positive effects:

- Thinking is antagonistic to feeling, so anger is reduced.
- Thinking about what is best to do inserts thought between stimulus and response and helps in impulse control.
- Students may come up with better solutions.
- Think time slows the process and allows everyone to cool down.
- Having students think when they are angry is practice of a behavior we hope they will internalize and do on their own later.

Some think time prompts are:

"We are all worked up right now, so let's take a few minutes to quietly think about what we could have done to avoid this."

"I want each of you to sit down and quietly think about how your behavior affected the other person."

Angry

"Until I decide otherwise, there will be no talking. We are all going to just think about what we can say to the other person to let him/her know we are sorry."

■ **Reciprocal Inhibition: Food.** Food is pleasurable. Just the thought of a delicious meal releases "feel good" hormones and a parasympathetic reaction which counters anger. Having students think about, talk about, or draw favorite desserts can allow release from anger. Actually eating food is a more powerful anti-anger device. When hungry, students are more likely to snap at one another.

■ **Reciprocal Inhibition: Humor.** If we can laugh at the situation or ourselves, anger loses its grip. Humor can help us not take the situation or ourselves too seriously.

"How about if we all go out and buy some anvils so we can drop them on each other's heads like the roadrunner and the coyote?"

"When I count to three, I want you both to make the most terrible, disgusting face you can toward each other. Try to make the other person throw up."

Transfer

Contrary to what some pop psychology would have us think, transfer is not always a bad thing. If a student is angry and he/she can vent that anger toward another target, that can serve as a calming release which will direct him/her toward more rational thought. There are many possible ways to facilitate transfer.

■ **Transfer: Academic Content.**
"Who are you most angry toward in the story? Tell why. What would you say or do to that person if you were in the story?"

"We are halfway through this history chapter. With which historical character do you disagree most? Why? Pretend you are debating that person. What would you say?"

"We have been studying forms of pollution. Which kind of pollution angers you the most? What would you say to the person responsible for that kind of pollution? What would you do, if you could?"

Teach, Model Positive Alternatives

The Win-Win teacher models and teaches many positive alternatives to anger, using STOP HACC, the Replacement Behavior structure, Teacher Think Timer, Class Meetings, and Peer Mediation.

Speak when you are angry and you will make the best speech you will ever regret.
—Ambrose Bierce

■ **Reminder: STOP HACC.** If we have put the STOP HACC mnemonic in place (See Chapter 6.4), when students are in a conflict, we can remind them of the eight modes of conflict resolution and have them choose the one that would be best to use in the moment-of-disruption. There are three advantages to this: 1) students start thinking instead of feeling, 2) students are likely to hit on a better solution, and 3) students may internalize the process and become better at conflict resolution.

■ **Replacement Reminder.** One structure to use as a follow-up to an angry outburst is to teach a student replacement behaviors. Replacement behaviors are things to do when anger builds up. Rather than hitting someone, the student can take a walk. If replacement behaviors have been established and practiced, in the moment-of-disruption, we can give students a quick reminder to practice their replacement behavior.

- For a description of the Replacement Behavior structure, see **Chapter 16. Follow-Up Structures**.

  "Remember, Jack, when you feel as if you are going to lose your temper, you have practiced thinking about your favorite Nintendo game instead. Make sure you think about that now."

■ **Think Time: Teacher.** Allow yourself Think Time models, a positive approach to anger. In dealing with anger, it is important to remember that you don't always need to come up with a solution on the spot. You can indicate at the moment-of-disruption that you are going to deal with a situation, but then allow yourself some think time. This avoids overreacting.

Combining teacher think time with the student having a cool down time can be a very positive combination.

  "Tom, I am very frustrated by what you just did. You need to go to the cool down area to get yourself together, and I need to think about what would be appropriate in the situation. We will discuss it together later."

■ **Class Meeting.** A teacher may call a class meeting to deal with feelings of anger or to decide on how best to respond to angry or destructive acts. See procedures for Class meetings, **Chapter 18. Win-Win Management.**

■ **Peer Mediation.** If you have a peer mediation program in place, a peer mediator often can handle an angry outburst. Peer mediators are trained in a specific step-by-step process for dealing with fights. There are several advantages: students can internalize the process, angry students can model the calm reaction of a

Angry

peer, and the teacher is freed to focus on other things. Students who are often angry can be trained to be peer mediators, which accelerates their internalization of the rational approach to frustration and resolution of conflicts.

Structures for When Students Are Angry:

■ Consequences

Prior to disruptions the teacher establishes just consequences. To avoid an impending disruption the teacher may remind students of the consequences. If the disruption continues the teacher implements the consequences. Thus there are three phases of Consequences: 1. Establishing Consequences; 2. Consequences Reminder; and 3. Implementing Consequences. "Remember the consequences we agreed on." "We need to implement the consequences we agreed on now."

■ Cool Down

Prior to the moment-of-disruption the teacher establishes cool down procedures. When emotions begin to escalate, the teacher gives a cool down reminder. "Are we getting close to needing cool down?" If emotions continue to escalate, the teacher implements pre-established cool down procedures. Implementing pre-established cool down procedures allows everyone to regain his/her composure, minimizes loss of instructional time, and helps students internalize self-monitoring and self-control. "Please take some time in the cool down area now." Thus there are three phases of cool down: 1. Establish cool down procedures; 2. Cool down reminder; and 3. Implement cool down. "Are we getting close to needing cool down?" "Please take some time in the cool down area now."

■ I-Messages Plus

Calmly informing students of your own feelings is an I-Message, designed to make students aware of their stimulus value (effect on others). An I-Message Plus adds encouragement to adopt non-disruptive alternatives. "I feel X when you do Y, and your classmates feel Z. Can you think of a better choice?"

■ Language of Choice

Language of choice provides immediate consequences, allowing the disruptive student to make a more responsible choice. "You need to _____ or _____."

■ Make a Better Choice

Through Make a Better Choice, the teacher calls for reflection rather than obedience, leaving it to the student to create a more responsible alternative. "I want you to think of a better choice to make right now."

13.28

Win-Win Discipline. Kagan Publishing • 1 (800) 933-2667 • www.KaganOnline.com

Moment-of-Disruption Structures for
Angry

ANGRY

Recommended Structures

- Consequences
- Cool Down
- I-Messages Plus
- Language of Choice
- Make a Better Choice
- Model It!

- Picture It Right!
- Right Now Validation
- Schedule Follow-Up
- Table the Matter
- Target, Stop, Do

Also Useful

- Cues: Verbal & Non-verbal
- Expectation Reminder

- Redirect
- Restart

For details of these structures, see Chapter 14. Moment-of-Disruption Structures.

Model It!

Modeling and disclosing one's own responsible behavior (self-control, persistence in the face of difficulty, politeness) helps students identify with the teacher and acquire responsible behaviors. "Right now, I feel stuck. But I know if I keep trying, I will figure it out."

Picture It Right!

The class or an individual takes responsibility for imagining responsible alternatives as they pause, close their eyes, and picture it right. "If we were at our very best right now, how would it look?"

Right Now Validation

The teacher acknowledges and validates the student or class position and then directs the student to more responsible behavior. "Right now you are feeling _____. That's OK, but what you need to do is _____."

Schedule Follow-Up

In order not to disrupt the class while implementing the three pillars, a follow up meeting with the student is scheduled. "We need to talk this through. Let's meet after...."

■ **Table the Matter**

The teacher uses Table the Matter to acknowledge the need to meet and discuss, while allowing time for emotions to settle down and for student and teacher reflection before meeting. "Let's give this a rest for now. We can talk about it later when we are both calm."

■ **Target, Stop, Do**

Target, Stop, Do is a very brief, focused, forceful sequence, designed to get the disruptive student's attention, inform the student what he/she needs to stop doing, and redirect the student to what he/she needs to do. "Susie, Right now you are doing _____. You need to be doing _____."

Control-Seeking

To feel that what we do makes a difference, that we are in control of the things around us and ourselves, is a basic need. Those who lose their sense of control fall into depression. With complete loss of the sense of control, people actually give up and die, with no physical ailments.[7] Therefore, we want to support the striving for control among our students. Obtaining and maintaining a sense of control is part of what it is to be healthy.

Like all needs, however, the drive for a sense of control can play out in disruptive behaviors. When that happens, we want to make sure the student knows the disruption is not acceptable, but that the drive for control is healthy.

This position, seeking control, is a search for a *sense of control.* A student may actually be in control but not have a sense of control. For example, even if a student chooses to do a project the student may feel that he/she was forced to do the project. If so, there is no sense of control. Making choices does not in itself satisfy the need for control. Rather, the need is satisfied by owning the choices one makes, feeling in charge.

A student who daily makes many choices will not have a sense of control if he/she does not own them — experience the choices as his/her own. Students attempt to meet their need for control via various disruptive behaviors:

- You can't make me.
- I'll show the class who is boss.
- I'll do nothing and prove you can't make me.
- I won't follow the rules or directions — I'll do it my way.
- I'll raise my hand every few minutes and force the teacher to talk about what I want — I'm not really interested in the questions I'm asking, but I'm proving I can direct the class.

Those disruptive attempts, however, miss the point and will not lead to a sense of control. What the student really seeks is not to control others or even the situation, but rather to have an internal feeling of controlling himself/herself.

How can we help students achieve a sense of control? Choices and responsibilities are key. We can acknowledge the students' ability to choose, give them responsible alternatives from which to choose, and have them reflect on the fact that they are choosing. We can let students perform roles in their teams and in the class and assume responsibilities that provide a sense of control. We avoid confrontations. Power plays are often misguided attempts by the student to obtain an internal sense of control by controlling others. A stable internal sense of control comes from controlling oneself.

Strategies for When Students Are Control-Seeking

Calm Consequences. A student heatedly says, *"I won't do that assignment, and you can't make me."* We might calmly respond with something like, *"If you choose to do the assignment, you have a chance to earn X points; if not, you won't."*

We calmly state consequences, rather than picking up the challenge to make the student do something. *We control consequences, but calmly allow the student to control choices.* When we use Calm Consequences we remain centered. We remain proactive rather than reactive — controlling what it is our job to control and allowing the student to control his/her own choices.

Choices. Providing plenty of choices is good preventative medicine, avoiding disruptions for students seeking to establish a sense of control. But choices can help in the moment-of-disruption as well. A student says, *"I won't do that stupid assignment."* We might respond with, *"That is your choice. But what would make it a worthwhile assignment for you? How would you choose to set up the assignment?"* It is quite possible this approach will lead to deciding on an assignment which will meet the learning objectives while also meeting the need for control. Students tailor-making their own assignments often leads to learning experiences that are more difficult, more sophisticated, and more developmentally appropriate.

Humor. In the moment of a potential power struggle, you can use humor to redirect the situation, placing you and the student on the same-side, laughing at what is going on.

"Oh my! I almost forgot. For a moment I thought I was the teacher and I was supposed to give the assignments."

Strategies for Responding When Students Are Control-Seeking

- **Calm Consequences**
- **Choices**
- **Humor**
- **Owning Choices**
- **Sidestep the Power Play**
- **Plus/Minus T-Chart**

Control-Seeking

"Let's flip a coin. Heads you design the assignment for the class, tails I do."

■ **Owning Choices.** Have students stop and reflect on the fact that they are choosing.

> *"Class, I am about to give you your homework assignment. Before I announce the homework assignment, I want everyone to take a moment and reflect on something. It is always your choice whether to do any assignment or not. If you chose to do it or not, it is your choice. You are always making choices. You are in charge. I want you to own your choices. Owning our choices is what gives us a sense of control, of freedom. Think for a moment, own your choice. Are you going to choose to do the assignment or not? Why? Own your choice."*

Forms can help students own their choices. See Choices I Make, Plus/Minus Choice Matrix, and When I Feel "In Control."

■ **Plus/Minus Choice Matrix.** When a student makes a confrontational choice springing from seeking control, have him/her make a Plus/Minus Choice Matrix. Every choice has advantages and disadvantages. Have the student fill out the form as completely as possible before making a decision. Even if after filling in the Choice Matrix the student still refuses to do the work, we will have had him/her engage in a rational decision-making process which models a cognitive process that he/she might use mentally in the future. The student has owned the choice and will have a greater sense of internal control. As this process is internalized, the student will be weaned from reactive control-seeking behaviors (reacting against others) and adopt a more proactive approach (consciously owning choices).

Choices I Make

Some choices we make lead to positive consequences like when we study hard and then earn a good grade. Some choices lead to negative consequences like when we stay up too late and then feel sleepy the whole next day. On the form below, list positive and negative choices and their consequences.

Positive Choices	
Choice	**Consequence**

Negative Choices	
Choice	**Consequence**

Plus/Minus Choice Matrix

Use this form to make a wise choice. First, identify the choice you are considering, (like going to the movies) and write it under, "Do It." Then, write the alternative under, "Or…" (like doing homework). List as many positives and negatives as you can think of for each choice in the matrix. Finally, make a decision and write it on the line below.

Do It

Or…

	positives +	negatives −

My decision is to _____

13.34

Win-Win Discipline. Kagan Publishing • 1 (800) 933-2667 • www.KaganOnline.com

When I Feel "In Control"

Making a good decision and taking action often makes us feel "In Control." Failing to make a decision or failing to take action often makes us feel "Out of Control." First, list decisions and actions from your life that have made you feel "In Control." Second, list other times you failed to decide or act on and then felt "Out of Control." Finally, write how you can be more "In Control."

In Control	Out of Control
Examples of When I Have Felt "In Control"	Examples of When I Have Felt "Out of Control"
Decisions I've Made	**Decisions I Failed to Make**
Actions I've Taken	**Actions I Failed to Take**

How I Can Be More "In Control"

_____

_____

_____

_____

_____

_____

■ **Sidestep the Power Play.** In the moment-of-disruption, with a student seeking control, we sidestep the power play. The power play is an attempt by the student to set up a way of proving that no one can make him/her do something. We respond by helping the student make the case! *"I can't force you to do that. It is entirely your choice."* This stance helps the student own his sense of control while avoiding a win-lose disruption.

It is easy to get trapped into responding to a confrontation by becoming confrontational:

> *You'll do what I say.*
> *No I won't!*
> *Oh YES you will!*

In a teacher-student power play, no one wins because the more energy the teacher expends trying to force a student to do something, the more energy the student expends resisting. For every action there is a reaction of equal or greater force. Plus, of course, a power play goes against the basic pillars of Win-Win. Our goal is not to force good behavior, but to have students learn autonomous responsible behavior.

When we take our two-year-old visiting and we go to a house that is not "child-proof," confrontations are inevitable. We have to take away things the child might otherwise break. The child will struggle to touch or hold those things. In this mini-confrontation, we are patient. We know the child does not see the big picture, the need to keep expensive things from getting broken. In the moment of a classroom confrontation, the student does not see the big picture, the need to keep the class running harmoniously. The student is driven only by his/her own needs. When we see the student in that light, it is much easier to see our role as teacher and avoid getting involved in a power play.

Structures for When Students Are Control-Seeking

■ Acknowledge Student Power

The teacher calmly acknowledges the student's power, *"I can't make you."* The teacher then clarifies the consequences of alternatives from which the student can choose. This structure is designed to help students obtain a sense of control and to take responsibility for their choices.

Moment-of-Disruption Structures for
Control-Seeking

Recommended Structures

- Acknowledge Student Power
- Consequences
- Language of Choice
- Right Now Validation

- Schedule a Follow-Up
- Table the Matter
- To You... To Me

Also Useful

- Cool Down
- Cues: Verbal and Non-verbal
- Grandma's Rule
- I-Messages Plus

- Make a Better Choice
- Model It!
- Picture It Right!
- Restart

For details of these structures, see Chapter 14. Moment-of-Disruption Structures.

■ Consequences

Prior to disruptions the teacher establishes just consequences. To avoid an impending disruption the teacher may remind students of the consequences. If the disruption continues the teacher implements the consequences. Thus there are three phases of Consequences: 1. Establishing Consequences; 2. Consequences Reminder; and 3. Implementing Consequences. *"Remember the consequences we agreed on." "We need to implement the consequences we agreed on now."*

■ Language of Choice

Language of Choice provides immediate consequences, allowing the disruptive student to make a more responsible choice. *"You need to _____ or _____."*

■ Right Now Validation

The teacher acknowledges and validates the student or class position and then directs the student to more responsible behavior. *"Right now you are feeling _____. That's OK, but what you need to do is _____."*

■ Schedule a Follow-Up

In order not to disrupt the class while implementing the three pillars, a follow-up meeting with the student is scheduled. *"We need to talk this through. Let's meet after...."*

Control-Seeking

■ **Table the Matter**

The teacher uses Table the Matter to acknowledge the need to meet and discuss while allowing time for emotions to settle down and for student and teacher reflection before meeting. *"Let's give this a rest for now. We can talk about it later when we are both calm."*

■ **To You... To Me**

To You... To Me acknowledges the student's perspective and informs him/her of the teacher's perspective. In this way the teacher communicates understanding and facilitates a perspective shift in the student. *"To you, this lesson may be boring; to me, it is important because..."*

Energetic

Energy is a gift. Many of the great contributors to mankind have had what seems like boundless energy. We want students to realize that having a high level of energy doesn't make someone abnormal; it is to be desired. The basic need to move, touch, manipulate things, interact, and be expressive is a gift which prompts us to know and understand, create and invent, relate and care. The energy of students is never the problem.

Of course, like any gift, energy can be used in responsible or disruptive ways. We are all too familiar with the student who just can't seem to sit still, who cannot keep his/her hands off everything and everyone, and who has to be restrained from non-stop talking. The challenge for the Win-Win teacher is to accept the energy of the student, reject disruptive behavior, and to help him/her learn to channel the energy in positive directions. Unchanneled energy detracts from learning — of both the energetic student and those around him/her. In the extreme, students with a great deal of unchanneled energy receive the label of ADHD, Attention Deficit Hyperactivity Disorder. See Discussion of ADD, pages 17.13–15.

How do we help students with boundless energy to channel it in productive, rather than disruptive, directions? How can they learn to focus their energy on learning rather than dissipating it in so many directions that it does not lead to a positive outcome? Among the strategies in the moment-of-disruption for energetic students are to provide energy releases, use strategies to calm students down as needed, and to channel their energy in productive ways. Ultimately, of course, the goal is to teach students to self-monitor and adjust their own energy levels and find non-disruptive, productive outlets for their gift.

Strategies for When Students Are Energetic:

Energy Releases

■ **Energizers.** Students low in energy and those high in energy both benefit from frequent energy breaks or energizers. Movement creates greater blood flow to the brain, and the blood carries oxygen and glucose, nutrients necessary to make the neural connections we call learning. Students high in energy benefit by the chance to release that energy; students low in energy are energized by the movement. An energizer can be as simple as standing up and pretending to swim in place, first doing the freestyle, next the backstroke, and finally the breaststroke. Another quick energizer is to run in place for just one minute.

■ **Exercise.** The whole class benefits from a regular exercise program. Energetic students release excess energy and so can concentrate more. In the moment-of-disruption, an individual student can be allowed to run a lap around the building, jump rope for three minutes, or do any number of simple exercises. The five minutes of time lost from academics is well compensated for by the more focused concentration when the student returns, and from the lack of disruption of the rest of the class.

■ **Roles and Responsibilities.** If an individual student is becoming restless, he or she might be assigned a special role or responsibility that involves movement, such as being the team or class materials monitor, or the courier to take something to or retrieve something from the office.

■ **Silly Sports and Goofy Games.** All interactive games serve to release energy for those with excess energy and to energize those who have too little energy. The most comprehensive collection of energizing games is Silly Sports and Goofy Games.[8] It contains over 200 energizing activities. If students are becoming disruptive because they need to move, the Win-Win teacher goes with the need, providing a quick energizer. Often within two or three minutes of an energizer such as Quick Tag or the Balloon Bounce, students are ready to concentrate again. See sample **Silly Sports and Goofy Games, Part VII, Resources E.**

Calming Strategies

■ **Calm Curriculum.** A Win-Win teacher is always managing energy levels. If students are too energetic, the

---

Strategies for Responding When Students Are Energetic

Energy Releases
- **Energizers**
- **Exercise**
- **Roles and Responsibilities**
- **Sports and Goofy Games**

Calming Strategies
- **Calm Curriculum**
- **Music at 60**
- **Progressive Relaxation**
- **Relaxation Breathing**
- **Remove Distractions**
- **Visualization**
- **Guided Imagery**
- **Mental Retreats**

Channeling Energy Productively
- **Bite-Sized Instruction**
- **Channel Energy**
- **Classbuilders**
- **Curriculum Shift**
- **Instruction Shift**
- **Multiple Intelligence: Bodily/Kinesthetic Instruction**
- **Sponge**

Energetic

teacher will have them draw or write, or he/she may read a story or poem to them. Have students sing a slow song, or draw or describe a tranquil place.

■ **Music at 60.** If an individual student or students in general are becoming restless, music written at 60 beats a minute, played softly in the background, calms them down.

■ **Progressive Relaxation.** Students become remarkably calmer if they do a few minutes of progressive relax-ation. They tighten up one muscle group to the slow count of five. Then they feel that group relax. After doing a series of muscle groups (feet, thighs, stomach, biceps, fists, and face), each in turn, they are ready to return to studies with more focused concentration and without excess energy. Students can learn to self-monitor their energy levels, and when levels climb, then they can do a few rounds of progres-sive relaxation on their own.

■ **Relaxation Breathing.** Have students practice relaxation breathing. They breath in through their noses for a quick count of four as fully as they can. They hold the breath for a slow count of seven and then release the air through their mouth to a slow count of eight, releasing the air as fully as possible. Abdominal breathing is encouraged. Once all students have learned this technique, you can ask an individual student to do a few rounds of relaxation breathing as necessary in the moment-of-disruption. The goal, of course, is that students dis-cover the power of this technique and begin to use it as neces-sary when they feel too anxious or restless.

■ **Remove Distractions.** All of us are energized by external stim-uli. Students labeled ADHD are distracted by external stimuli and find it hard to concentrate when there are competing stim-uli. One solution: remove distractions. This can be done for indi-vidual students by seating them in the front row (so they don't have to attend to all the other students) or for the class as a whole by having them clear their desks of everything but the one paper on which they are focusing. See the ADD Checklist, page 17.14.

■ **Visualization.** Visualizations work in two ways to calm students. First, they are done with eyes closed, reduc-ing the excitement of external stimuli. Second, they can take students to a calmer place or time. Just have stu-dents close their eyes and visualize a tranquil place. It can be a real place they have visited or one they have created mentally. Often a tranquil lake or some other scene with water will have the most calm-ing effect. Have them look around and enjoy the calm view. In their mind's eye, have them

Energetic

listen to the sound of nature, perhaps the sound of birds chirping. Having students listen to music with nature sounds enhances the effect.

Guided Imagery. Guided imagery differs from visualization in one critical way: the teacher is the guide. In visualization, the teacher sets the scene, telling students what to look and listen for, and then allows the students to explore in their mind's eye. In guided imagery, the teacher provides the script, guiding the students as they see and hear things with their eyes closed. The teacher can guide the students to see academic content, such as what is was like to work in a factory during the early industrial revolution, or he/she can guide them toward a calm place to set the stage for more focused work on any content. See the Guided Imagery Script on the following page.

Mental Retreats. A brief retreat from external stimuli has a calming effect. Have students take a brief one or two minute mental retreat: have them close their eyes and attend to the sound of their breath as they inhale and exhale. As simple as this would appear, mental retreats can be profoundly relaxing, allowing students to become far more focused.

Channeling Energy Productively

Bite-Sized Instructions. When students are getting off task because of excess energy or inability to concentrate for a prolonged time, one solution is to break the learning task into smaller chunks. Give a chunk of instructions that even the most distractible student can follow. Once those instructions are carried out, give the next chunk. Using bite-sized instructions is a good management technique in general, but is particularly useful in the moment-of-disruption if the disruption springs from high energy levels and distractibility.

Channel Energy. If a student is disruptive because of excess movement or talking, we can channel that energy into learning. Use a cooperative learning structure like Timed Pair Share and have the student talk about the academic content. Use Logic Line-Ups, Formations, Kinesthetic Symbols, or Agree-Disagree Line-Ups and have the student move to learn the content. All cooperative learning structures involve talking; many involve movement. For a comprehensive description of approximately 100 cooperative learning structures that can be used as part of any lesson, see *Cooperative Learning*.[9]

Classbuilders. Classbuilding structures all involve movement and are an excellent way to channel the movement of students into learning. For a comprehensive description of classbuilding structures like Find Someone Who and Inside-Outside Circle, see *Classbuilding*.[10]

Energetic

Guided Imagery Script: A Calm Place

Students, we are all going to visit a calm, beautiful place. But we are going to visit this place in our mind's eye.

First, I want you to sit comfortably, with your back straight in your chair, your feet flat on the floor, and your hands resting comfortably in your lap, palms up.

Now, take a few deep breaths and let them out slowly. Breathe in through your nose as deeply as you can and then slowly let the air out through your mouth. Breathe in quickly and breathe out slowly. Be sure to get the last bit of air out when you breathe out. Don't hold any stale air. Focus on the sound and feel of the air as you let it out slowly through your mouth. That's it. Get calm and relaxed.

Now, everyone please close your eyes. In your mind's eye I want you to see a beautiful calm lake. You are standing by the shore. There is white sand under your feet. The sand feels warm. You wiggle your toes in the sand and enjoy the feeling of the warmth. **[Pause]**

Now, look to the left. There are some green ferns and a palm tree. You walk over. You touch the fern and feel its fuzzy leaf. You let the leaf run slowly over your hand, enjoying the touch. **[Pause]**

Now, look up at the leaves of the palm tree. It is a coconut palm and has three coconuts in a cluster. You notice how pretty they are. You are enjoying the peacefulness of this place. **[Pause]**

Not far away you hear the sound of a bird chirping. You listen carefully. You can hear some crickets. And occasionally there is a frog croaking. Listen with all your attention. Enjoy it. You hear the sound of the water gently lapping on the shore. **[Pause]**

You turn and walk toward the water. It's so very blue. It stretches out in front of you flat and calm. You dip your warm feet into the cool water and enjoy the refreshing feeling. This seems like such a perfect place. Take a few moments to enjoy it and look around. **[Pause]**

Now, please don't open your eyes quite yet. I want you to focus on the calm, safe feeling you have. Notice how you are breathing easily. You feel perfectly comfortable. In a moment I will ask you to open your eyes. When I do, don't jump out of the calm feeling. Let it stay with you.

Now, slowly open your eyes. Don't say anything yet. Just look around and feel very calm, relaxed, and very alert. What do you see or hear?

13.42

Win-Win Discipline. Kagan Publishing • 1 (800) 933-2667 • www.KaganOnline.com

■ **Curriculum Shift.** A student may be bouncing off the wall and unable to focus when faced with one learning task and quite able to focus on another. If we follow a very energetic middle school student around from class to class, we find that he/she stays focused in some classes, but not in others, or with some curriculum and not others. Students have all the intelligences, but have them differentially developed. Knowing this, we have a powerful tool. We observe our high-energy students, determine which kinds of curriculum they focus on well, and shift to that kind of curriculum if they are becoming too energetic to concentrate.

■ **Instruction Shift.** Students may concentrate well when taught with one instructional strategy, but begin bouncing off the walls when taught with another. When the student just "isn't getting it," energy builds up and seeks release. Knowing this, we can observe students and note the instructional strategies they resonate to. We can shift to that kind of instruction when the student becomes too restless to concentrate. For example, some students do very well learning shapes with paper and pencil. Others concentrate more and grasp the content more thoroughly using geoboards. Knowing this, if a student is becoming disruptive during the paper and pencil task, we might try a shift to the geoboards.

■ **Multiple Intelligences: Bodily/Kinesthetic Instruction.** There are many bodily/kinesthetic instructional techniques that can be used with any content as part of any lesson. Students can symbolize the content with their hands (kinesthetic symbols); with their whole bodies (formations); act it out (pantomime, team charades); and express their agreement-disagreement by where they stand (agreement circles, agree-disagree line-ups). In the moment-of-disruption, if students are disruptive because they want to move, the Win-Win teacher lets them move, going with rather than against their position. But the movement is allowed without losing instructional time using one of these bodily/kinesthetic instructional structures. For details on the rationale for teaching with bodily/kinesthetic structures and specifics on how to use them, see *Multiple Intelligences*.[11]

■ **Sponge.** If a student finishes a task before others and is just waiting for them to finish, he/she is likely to become disruptive if there is not a good sponge activity in place. Sponge activities can include extension questions about the content, challenge problems, or simply expressing the content through another intelligence such as drawing. If, in the moment-of-disruption you see the disruption is occurring while a student is waiting for others to finish, provide a sponge activity to soak up the extra time productively.

Energetic

Moment-of-Disruption Structures for
Energetic

Recommended Structures

- Cues: Verbal and Non-verbal
- I-Messages Plus
- Make a Better Choice
- Picture It Right!
- Redirect
- Restart
- Right Now Validation
- Schedule Follow-Up

Also Useful

- Consequences
- Coupons
- Expectation Reminder
- Grandma's Rule
- Language of Choice
- Model It!
- Restructure Task
- Target, Stop, Do

For details of these structures, see Chapter 14. Moment-of-Disruption Structures.

Structures for When Students Are Energetic:

Cues: Verbal And Non-verbal

The teacher uses pre-established verbal or non-verbal cues to elicit appropriate behavior. Class cues are established; specific cues may be established for individual students. Verbal: *"Class, please take a moment now and look over the class rules chart."* Non-verbal: Teacher walks to and looks intently at the class rules chart.

I-Messages Plus

Calmly informing students of your own feelings is an I-Message, designed to make students aware of their stimulus value (effect on others). An I-Message Plus adds encouragement to adopt non-disruptive alternatives. *"I feel X when you do Y, and your classmates feel Z. Can you think of a better choice?"*

Make a Better Choice

Through Make a Better Choice, the teacher calls for reflection rather than obedience, leaving it to the student to create a more responsible alternative. *"I want you to think of a better choice to make right now."*

Picture It Right!

The class or an individual takes responsibility for imagining responsible alternatives as they pause, close their eyes, and picture it right. *"If we were at our very best right now, how would it look?"*

Energetic

■ **Redirect**

Redirect diverts attention and behavior away from a disruptive episode and toward a responsible learning activity. *"Have you done problem four yet?"*

■ **Restart**

When the class is out of control, like a computer that has crashed, it is time to Restart. We stop talking, stop doing, pause, see a positive and negative model by the teacher, see a positive model by a classmate, and then restart. *"Stop! Look! Listen!"*

■ **Right Now Validation**

The teacher acknowledges and validates the student or class position and then directs the student to more responsible behavior. *"Right now you are feeling _____. That's OK, but what you need to do is _____."*

■ **Schedule Follow-Up**

In order not to disrupt the class while implementing the three pillars, a follow-up meeting with the student is scheduled. *"We need to talk this through. Let's meet after...."*

Bored

Boredom is a physiological state. It involves low stimulation in two areas of the brain: attention and motivation. The opposite of boredom is intense concentration and high motivation.

Recent research has shown that the increased attention and motivation most people feel as a result of a cup of coffee is due to increased dopamine in the brain. Dopamine stimulates the brain's attention and motivation centers. Ritalin prompts hyperactive students to concentrate and finish tasks in the same way, stimulating the attention and motivation centers, but with much higher doses. Some hyperactive, inattentive students become attentive and motivated when Ritalin takes effect.

In this set of findings is a partial answer to the question of what to do in the moment-of-disruption when a student is disruptive due to boredom. A student is daydreaming, doodling, or looking around at everything but the task at hand. When asked, the student says the task is dumb. When we delve a bit deeper, we find that the student is not interested in the task and has no motivation to complete it. The student is in the position of boredom.

Is life not a thousand times too short for us to bore ourselves?
—Friedrich Wilhelm Nietzsche

Bored

What can we do in the moment-of-disruption when a student is disruptive due to boredom, disengaged, and/or distracting others? The Win-Win first response is not to buy the student a cup of coffee or to dose him/her with Ritalin. Our first response is to examine our curriculum, instruction, and management techniques in the moment-of-disruption to attempt to make them more motivating and interesting. This is not to say that Ritalin is always inappropriate; it is to say that a great deal of inattentiveness springs from curriculum and instruction which is not interesting and/or motivating for students. The first place we look, therefore, if we are seeking a Win-Win solution to deal with boredom, is making our teaching more engaging.

We have dealt extensively already with ways to make curriculum, instruction, and management more engaging. In **Chapter 6. Preventative Procedures: ABCD Disruptions**, we explored procedures to prevent disengagement. In **Chapter 8. Preventative Procedures: The Seven Positions**, we examined ways to prevent boredom. The focus in this section is not on general preventative procedures but, rather, on what to do in the moment-of-disruption when a student is bored. It turns out, of course, that often the best thing to do is implement the procedures described in those prior chapters. We will review them here, but we will also present some additional moment-of-disruption strategies as well as a motivating structure.

The long-range goal is to have students be self-motivated and self-engaging. The place to start, though, is by supporting motivation and engagement.

> **Everyone is a bore to someone. That is unimportant. The thing to avoid is being a bore to oneself.**
> —*Gerald Brenan*

Strategies for When Students Are Bored:

Cooperative Learning. At any moment in any lesson, a teacher can end boredom by using one of the many cooperative learning structures. The brain is more engaged when in interaction, explaining things to another person, than at any other time.[12] A simple RallyRobin will do the trick. The teacher says, *"Turn to the person next to you and take turns naming and explaining the five points we just covered."* A RallyCoach works wonders to breathe life into an otherwise boring worksheet — students alternate doing a problem while their partner observes, checks, coaches if necessary, and praises. The details of nearly 100 cooperative learning structures are described in *Cooperative Learning.*[13]

Curriculum Shift. Distributed practice creates greater learning than does mass practice. Shifting from one curriculum content to another also alleviates boredom. If math and reading normally require one hour each, and the teacher instead spends two half-hour blocks on each, separated in time, the students will not only retain more, but fewer will be disruptive due to boredom. At the moment-of-disruption stemming from boredom, it may be time for a curriculum shift.

Bored

Strategies for Responding When Students Are Bored

- **Cooperative Learning**
- **Curriculum Shift**
- **Developmentally Appropriate Curriculum**
- **Dramatic Reopeners**
- **Energizers**
- **Instruction Shift**
- **Intelligence Shift**
- **Interest Links**
- **Name Dropping**
- **Relevance**
- **Simultaneous Response Modes**

13.46

Win-Win Discipline. Kagan Publishing • 1 (800) 933-2667 • www.KaganOnline.com

■ **Developmentally Appropriate Curriculum.** Students will be bored if the curriculum is too easy. And when bored, they are more likely to disrupt. Assessing difficulty and providing developmentally appropriate curriculum is another way to prevent boredom. A disruption due to boredom may mean it is time to reevaluate the curriculum to determine if it is developmentally appropriate.

■ **Dramatic Reopeners.** Escalante introduced his calculus class to a math concept by loudly driving a machete through a watermelon! Anyone in the room during that dramatic opener was as far removed from bored as one can get. There are many dramatic devices, such as:

- Puzzling experiments that pique the curiosity
- Statements contrary to common belief
- A dramatic line from a story
- A suspenseful moment from history
- A claim to be able to make an unlikely math proof

In the moment of a disruption spurred by boredom, it may be time for a dramatic *reopener*. Drama does not have to occur only at the beginning of a lesson. And why not let the bored student be part of the team that creates the reopener for the rest of the class?

■ **Energizers.** We have already covered energizers. In the moment of a disruption springing from boredom, an energizer almost always ends the problem.

■ **Instruction Shift.** Each time we teach with a different instructional strategy, attention is alerted. Novelty engages the brain. When we sense attention and motivation is fading for a student or for the class as a whole, it is time to teach the same content in a different way.

■ **Intelligence Shift.** Modern brain science has given us a window into the brain. With active brain imaging techniques, we can see which parts of the brain are more active than usual while we engage in different tasks. When we look at visual material, the occipital lobes are more active than usual; when we shift to listening to auditory input, the temporal lobes are more active than usual. Each time there is an intelligence shift, different parts of the brain become more engaged. One implication: when we want to alleviate boredom, we can do frequent intelligence shifts. If a student is disruptive due to boredom, the probability is that you will end the disruption if you shift your instruction to a different intelligence. In *Multiple Intelligences*,[14] instructional strategies are provided for each of the following eight intelligences, which Howard Gardner identified as the most important eight:

Bored

- Verbal/Linguistic
- Logical/Mathematical
- Visual/Spatial
- Musical/Rhythmic
- Bodily/Kinesthetic
- Naturalist
- Interpersonal/Social
- Intrapersonal/Introspective

Because different students have the various intelligences differentially developed, it can pay to know the intelligences of your students. That way, in the moment-of-disruption, we can shift to the preferred intelligence of the disruptive student or have a solo task ready for that student that engages his/her preferred intelligence. In general, though, there is no need to individualize. Any shift from one intelligence to another is a shift to greater engagement.

Interest Links. If we know the interests of students, we can make the lesson more interesting by linking it to their interests. If we know the particular interests of individual students, in the moment-of-disruption we can make a link between the lesson and the interest of the disruptive student. An interest survey can be administered early in the school year to help with that process. It has the advantage of communicating to students that you want to get to know them better as people. A student may have a special interest we otherwise might not find out about, one that he/she could share with the class. See the Interest Survey form on the following page.

Name Dropping. To spark a student's interest if he/she slips into daydreaming, or to signal the student that he/she needs to focus on the lesson, you can simply slip a disruptive student's name in while continuing to teach.

"Supply and Demand is a very important economic concept, Patti, and one which we can apply to understand everyday events, even those in our own classroom...."

It gets that student's attention and refocuses him/her with little intrusion into the lesson.

Relevance. I will not be interested in a math worksheet and will not be motivated to finish it if I see no relevance to my life. Every lesson should include relevance — students need to see how they will use the information or skill acquired or how it will benefit them. Getting a good grade is not motivating for many students and does not make the content more interesting. There are many ways to increase the relevance of a lesson, including:

Bored

Interest Survey

Directions: Fill out this survey to help your teacher get to know you better.

Favorites

Hobbies _____

Food _____

Fast Food Restaurant _____

TV Program _____

Actor _____

Music Group _____

School Subject _____

After-School Activity _____

Goals

Dream profession _____

Realistic profession _____

Do you want to get married? _____

Have children? _____

If so, how many? _____

Dream place to live _____

Describe dream house _____

Pet Peeves

What bugs you most? _____

Least favorite school subject _____

Pets

Do you have a pet? _____

If so, describe it... _____

Is there a pet you would like to have? _____

What is the best pet you have had? _____

Getting to Know You

If someone were to get to know you better, what would be important for him/her to know? ____

_____

_____

_____

_____

Bored

- Showing real-life applications of skill or content, especially how the students can use the skill now in their daily lives
- Having students interview and report on those who use the content or skill
- Highlighting similarities between the lives of those studied and the life of the student
- Linking the content to classroom dynamics
- Explaining how past events affect our lives today
- Demonstrating how the new understanding will explain puzzling phenomena

In the moment-of-disruption, if we have put these methods in place, we can give a "relevance reminder" to boost interest and motivation. If we have not put them in place, we can stop and do so. A student's lack of interest is a clue that we need to provide more relevance.

Simultaneous Response Modes. Whenever you call on just one student at a time, it creates boredom opportunities for the rest of the class. To eliminate that possibility, use simultaneous response modes. During review, one teacher asks, *"Who can tell me the answer to 36 divided by 6?"* Hands go up, the teacher calls on one, and the other students tune out. A teacher using a simultaneous response mode says, *"Take out your AnswerBoard and solve the problem 36 divided by 6. Show your work."* Every student is engaged. There are many structures for simultaneous responses, including:

- Blackboard Share
- Card Responses
- Finger Responses
- Kinesthetic Responses
- Pantomime

For details on simultaneous response modes and other ways to implement the simultaneity principle, see *Cooperative Learning.*[15]

Structures for When Students Are Bored:

Grandma's Rule

The teacher uses a "When... then..." statement to indicate the responsible behavior and the incentive that will follow. The origin of Grandma's Rule is "When you eat your dinner, then you may have dessert." "When you finish your math practice sheet, you can go to the choice tables to pick a favorite learning game."

Make a Better Choice

Through Make a Better Choice, the teacher calls for reflection rather than obedience, leaving it to the student to create a more responsible alternative. "I want you to think of a better choice to make right now."

Moment-of-Disruption Structures for
Bored

BORED

Recommended Structures

- **Grandma's Rule**
- **Make a Better Choice**
- **Restart**

- **Right Now Validation**
- **Schedule Follow-Up**
- **To You... To Me**

Also Useful

- **Cues: Verbal and Non-verbal**
- **I-Messages Plus**
- **Language of Choice**
- **Model It!**

- **Redirect**
- **Restructure Task**
- **Target, Stop, Do**

For details of these structures, see Chapter 14. Moment-of-Disruption Structures.

■ **Restart**

When the class is out of control, like a computer that has crashed, it is time to Restart. We stop talking, stop doing, pause, see a positive and negative model by the teacher, see a positive model by a classmate, and then restart. "Stop! Look! Listen!"

■ **Right Now Validation**

The teacher acknowledges and validates the student or class position and then directs the student to more responsible behavior. "Right now you are feeling _____. That's OK, but what you need to do is _____."

■ **Schedule Follow-Up**

In order not to disrupt the class while implementing the three pillars, a follow-up meeting with the student is scheduled. "We need to talk this through. Let's meet after...."

■ **To You... To Me**

To You... To Me acknowledges the student's perspective and informs him/her of the teacher's perspective. In this way the teacher communicates understanding and facilitates a perspective shift in the student. "To you, this lesson may be boring; to me, it is important because...."

Bored

Uninformed

In some ways, the student in the uninformed position is the easiest of all to deal with; in other ways, the uninformed student is the most difficult.

It is easy because the disruption is not motivated by a strongly held emotion. When a student is very angry or passionately seeking control, he/she is highly motivated to express that anger or demonstrate control. So to end the disruption, we are opposing a great deal of drive. In contrast, when a student simply does not know, it is a cognitive deficit — a lack of information, skill, or habit. There is no human drive to be uninformed and thus no resistance to overcome. In fact, we have drive on our side — there is a human drive to know and understand.

The uninformed position, though, can be the most difficult and frustrating of all. The class has agreed on a rule. We have made the rule clear, given the rationale for the rule, demonstrated the rule, practiced the rule, had students make up ways to remember the rule — in short done all it seems possible to do. And then a student once again breaks the rule. At that point our initial impulse is to give up.

In the moment-of-disruption, we need to be sure the student is truly uninformed. The student's reaction to intervention is usually our best clue. A student walks into the room chewing gum. When we do a rule reminder, the student says, *"Oh! I forgot."* But how does the student say it? What is the tone? What is the body language of the student as his/her hand goes to the mouth, extricates the offending gum, and throws it in the wastebasket? Is it a toss? Is it an angry throw? Does the student act surprised by our rule reminder, or is the student angry — as if caught at something he/she was trying to get away with? Does the student give a sly smile indicating he/she knew the teacher would see, revealing the disruption is a bid for attention? We will not be able to tell for sure, but we gather all the clues we can. Is this really an uninformed position?

It does not matter how much we have taught and re-taught a rule. The student is uninformed in the moment-of-disruption if he/she truly does not remember the rule or cannot adhere to it. Ultimately, the uninformed position is an innocent position. It is a lack of learning. And our tools are the same as when a student doesn't grasp our academic content. We re-motivate the learning, we teach it again, in a different way, and we work with the student to discover what works for him/her to produce learning.

As frustrating as the uninformed position can be, if we can discover a way for the student to become informed, we have probably discovered a path to greater learning in the academic areas as well. The ultimate goal in working with the uninformed student is fostering the ability to learn how to learn.

Strategies for When Students Are Uninformed:

■ **Classroom Buddies.** Having classroom buddies is another way for students coming from an uninformed position to learn from positive role models. It is important to meet with the student who doesn't know and let him/her know what the behavior is that needs to be learned and actively involve him/her in the process. Buddies can support each other in making responsible behavior choices.

■ **Cooperative Learning.** Partner and teamwork is very helpful for students in an uninformed position because peers act as positive role models. It is helpful if the teacher meets with and enlists peers to support the uninformed student. Peers can look for uninformed behaviors, helping the student become informed.

Within the cooperative learning framework, there are a number of elements that help the uninformed student become informed:

- Team Questions (Three Before Me)
- Honoring Questions
- Offering Help
- Role of Checker
- Role of Coach
- Structures
- Gambits

These elements have been presented in **Chapter 8. Preventative Procedures: The Seven Positions.** In the moment-of-disruption, it can be a Win-Win solution to merely remind students of these elements. For example, a reminder about the Three Before Me rule might be all it takes to move a student from an uninformed to an informed position. Or the teacher may implement one of these elements. For example, if one or more students are uninformed, the teacher might assign a role of Checker, whose job it is to see that everyone on the team knows the rules or procedures.

Many structures can be used in the moment-of-disruption to ensure that uniformed students know the rules and procedures. For example, if a student is off-task, the teacher might say, *"I want everyone to turn to a partner and do a RallyRobin review of the steps of this procedure."* Or, *"In your teams, do a RoundTable, each person in turn recording the next step."*

Strategies for Responding When Students Are Uninformed

- **Classroom Buddies**
- **Cooperative Learning**
- **Draw Attention to a Positive Model**
- **Reflection Time; Improvement Plan**
- **Proximity**
- **Rule Reminder**

Uninformed

Win-Win Discipline. Kagan Publishing • 1 (800) 933-2667 • www.KaganOnline.com

13.53

Gambits are powerful tools for getting students to become self-informed. In the moment-of-disruption, if the teacher sees that one or more students are uninformed about the rules, he/she can have students practice gambits for asking for information or for offering information when they see that someone is uninformed.

■ **Draw Attention to a Positive Model.** In the moment-of-disruption with an uninformed student or students, often the best strategy is to ignore those students and draw attention to a positive model. I am reminded of the time I worked in a very off-task, disruptive middle school classroom. I ignored all the off-task behavior and disruptions and kept complimenting groups who were on task, quietly working. Within one hour every team was quietly working on task. That which we hold up as a model gets emulated.

■ **Reflection Time; Improvement Plan.** In the moment-of-disruption, we can pause and simply have students reflect on how well they are working, making an improvement plan. Reflection time and creating an improvement plan can be done as an individual activity or in pairs or groups. If it is done as an individual activity, it is helpful to have students share their improvement plan with at least one other person afterwards. Without a word from the teacher about how to improve or which rules or procedures students need to be following, students can inform themselves and their peers — often better than we could. See Improvement Plan on the following page.

■ **Proximity.** Proximity can be a non-verbal reminder. By standing close to a student who is not thinking of the rules, you bring the rules to mind. The student moves from an uninformed position to an informed position without a word having been spoken.

■ **Rule Reminder.** The most frequent response to a student disruption coming from an uninformed position is a rule reminder. The teacher reminds the student of the rule. This can be done verbally, stating the rule, or non-verbally, pointing to the rule on the rule chart. Rule Reminders might work in the moment, but they leave the responsibility for remembering the rule with the teacher. Asking responsible thinking questions and reflection and planning time are preferable when possible because they shift the responsibility to the student.

Uninformed

13.54

Win-Win Discipline. Kagan Publishing • 1 (800) 933-2667 • www.KaganOnline.com

Improvement Plan

■ **What has been going well as you work?**

_____

_____

_____

■ **What has not gone well?**

_____

_____

_____

■ **Have those around you been respectful and helpful?**

_____

_____

_____

■ **Have you been respectful and helpful to those around you?**

_____

_____

_____

■ **How could you improve your work and be more helpful to others?**

_____

_____

_____

Uninformed

■ **Teacher Gambits: When a Student Plays Dumb**

Examples of Students Playing Dumb:
- *"I don't know."*
- Student says nothing.
- *"You're the teacher, why don't you tell me what to do?"*

Possible Teacher Gambits:
- *"That's a difficult question. I'm not sure if I could answer it."*
- *"This really takes some deep thinking on your part."*
- *"Let me give you some more time."*
- *"Would more time help?"*
- *"Let's reverse the roles."*
- *"Let's keep thinking."*
- *"This takes courage."*
- *"If you did know, what would you say?"*
- *"What might you say to your parent(s)?"*
- *"Don't worry about the consequence right now."*
- *"Let's brainstorm."*
- *"Would it help to write it down?"*

Structures for When Students Are Uninformed:

■ **Expectation Reminder**
Prior to a possible disruption or at the outset of a disruption, students are reminded of pre-established expectations, procedures, or rules. When a number of students are violating the rules, the teacher may stop the lesson to re-teach the rules. *"Remember the expectations (rules, procedures) we agreed on. Let's take some time now to review how we want out class to be."*

■ **Restart**
When the class is out of control, like a computer that has crashed, it is time to Restart. We stop talking, stop doing, pause, see a positive and negative model by the teacher, see a positive model by a classmate, and then restart. *"Stop! Look! Listen!"*

■ **Right Now Validation**
The teacher acknowledges and validates the student or class position and then directs the student to more responsible behavior. *"Right now you are feeling _____. That's OK, but what you need to do is _____."*

■ **Schedule Follow-Up**
In order not to disrupt the class while implementing the three pillars, a follow-up meeting with the student is scheduled. *"We need to talk this through. Let's meet after...."*

Moment-of-Disruption Structures for
Uninformed

Recommended Structures

- Expectation Reminder
- Restart
- Right Now Validation
- Schedule Follow-Up

Also Useful

- Cues: Verbal and Non-verbal
- Grandma's Rule
- I-Messages Plus
- Language of Choice
- Model It!
- Restructure Task
- Target, Stop, Do

For details of these structures, see Chapter 14. Moment-of-Disruption Structures.

Moment-of-Disruption Responses: Tools We Are Glad to Have, But with Experience Seldom Have to Use

Ironically, we have spent more time on how to respond in the moment-of-disruption than on any other single topic, but the successful Win-Win teacher spends the least amount of time responding to disruptions! The successful Win-Win teacher prevents disruptions. Dedication to the moment-of-disruption response, however, is justified. It is how we respond in the moment-of-disruption that determines if a disruption is converted into a learning opportunity or simply squelched, generating resentment, lurking only to emerge later in another form.

Win-Win Discipline. Kagan Publishing • 1 (800) 933-2667 • www.KaganOnline.com

Uninformed

13.57

In the moment-of-disruption, the Win-Win teacher responds by considering both the type of disruption and the position of the disruptive student. The response in the moment-of-disruption puts to the ultimate test the skill of the Win-Win teacher. In a moment the teacher attempts to:

- Identify the type of disruption and the position of the disruptive student
- Respond appropriately to the type of disruption
- Validate the position of the student
- Communicate that disruptive behavior is not acceptable
- Communicate that the teacher is on the student's side, ready to help him/her create responsible alternatives
- Keep the interaction as succinct as possible to minimize downtime for the class

A tall order. A very tall order.

It is such a tall order that we know going in that often we will not be successful in achieving some or most of these components. It is highly unlikely that we will realize all of these objectives in the moment-of-disruption, especially when we are first learning the Win-Win approach. That is one of the reasons we need follow-ups. Follow-ups are our lifesaver in reserve. With time and practice, though, if we maintain a same-side orientation, increasingly we prevent disruptions and obtain Win-Win solutions in the moment-of-disruption, making follow-ups less often necessary.

If it is such a tall order, why travel the Win-Win path? In truth, the informed teacher does not have a viable alternative. Let's look at the alternatives to seeking Win-Win solutions:

Alternative 1: Forced Compliance. We could simply force compliance. But if we did, the student would not learn responsible behaviors. Forcing compliance teaches compliance, not responsibility. And forcing compliance breeds resentment and alienation. To take a win-lose approach is to have the disruption come back to bite us in another (usually more painful) place later.

Alternative 2: Wink. We could wink at the disruption and go on as if it did not occur. But to take a lose-win approach is a prescription for a different type of disaster. When the teacher abdicates control, students become more and more disruptive in their search for limits.

■ **Alternative 3: One-Size-Fits-All.** We could adopt one of the various simple one-size-fits-all discipline programs, ignoring disruption type and student position. That, however, is a prescription for a hit-and-miss success rate. Because not all students are in the same position, the same discipline response will work well for some but poorly or not at all for others. While one student needs to be reminded of the rules, it is the last thing another wants or needs, and it will actually increase the frequency of disruptions for a third student. While one student's needs are met by providing choices, choices only feed avoidance of failure in another.

■ **Win-Win: No Better Alternative.** No, there is no free lunch. We cannot be successful by ignoring our needs or the needs of the student. We cannot be consistently successful by ignoring either the type of disruption or the position of the student. Win-Win is the only option we have if we want to formulate consistently successful discipline responses.

While there are far too many possible discipline responses for any teacher to master in even a year or two, the good news is that we do not have to master or even be aware of them all. In this chapter and in the next we present many options. Think of them as a rich smorgasbord. You will select those items that appeal to you. Later you will come back for more. This book is not bedside reading — it is a use-again resource. Think of becoming a Win-Win teacher as a long-term goal. Remember: Every small advance you make in learning a new structure or in recognizing student positions takes you that much closer to your goal. With each step, you become a more effective teacher.

In the heat of the moment-of-disruption, it is very useful to have in the ready well-prepared, step-by-step responses. In the next chapter, we provide moment-of-disruption structures — those step-by-step responses to use with the range of disruption types and student positions. We present the structures as resources; you will turn to them repeatedly as you hone your discipline responses.

Quiz Yourself – Respond to the Disruption!

Below are vignettes of students needing discipline. We express our appreciation to Liz Warner, the talented Kagan Win-Win Trainer who wrote these vignettes and granted us permission to reproduce them here.

Your job:

- Identify the behavior, ABCD.
- Identify the position or positions from which the behavior springs.
- Tell how you would validate the position.
- Tell how you would communicate that the behavior is unacceptable and that you are on the same-side with the student, open to seek responsible alternatives.

Note: To make the vignettes realistic, some contain more than one type of behavior and/or more than one type of position. You are to identify the dominant position and behavior and respond to each.

Reminders:
1. Three Before B — Only use Breaking the Rules if the behavior does not fit Aggression, Confrontation, or Disengagement.
2. Aggression toward a teacher is classified as Confrontation.

Disruption Scenario Cards

1. Dixie

Dixie hits everyone on the way to the cafeteria. Once in line, she pushes and shoves her classmates and intentionally bumps into the first graders. When the lunch lady tries to serve her vegetables, she pushes the spoon away and knocks it out of her hand. She then stomps off to her table and shoves everyone down so that she can sit on the end of the bench. When the duty teacher approaches and asks her if there is a problem, Dixie says, *"It is none of your business; leave me alone."*

Type of Disruption, ABCD _____

Dominant Position _____

How would you validate the position? _____
_____
_____

How would you communicate that the behavior is unacceptable, but that you are there to seek Win-Win alternatives?
_____
_____
_____

2. Doug

Doug sits aimlessly in his seat. When it is time to start writing his spelling words, he never starts. The teacher approaches to encourage him to try, but Doug sits there and does not pick up his pencil. Even when the teacher reassures him that he will help him, Doug just looks away and does not pick up the pencil. The teacher asks him to try and Doug looks down at his desktop and starts scratching at a glob on the desk. Doug asks if he can be excused to go to the bathroom and stays there until the bell for recess rings.

Type of Disruption, ABCD _____

Dominant Position _____

How would you validate the position? _____
_____
_____

How would you communicate that the behavior is unacceptable, but that you are there to seek Win-Win alternatives?
_____
_____
_____

For Answers, See Part VII, Resources D.3.

Win-Win Discipline. Kagan Publishing • 1 (800) 933-2667 • www.KaganOnline.com

13.61

Disruption Scenario Cards (Continued)

3. Bob

Bob walks into the classroom, looking sullen and with lower jaw set and eyebrows in a frown. He slams his books down and slumps into the seat, looking disgusted. Someone taps him on the shoulder to alert him that papers are being passed, and he crumples the papers as he grabs them from Sue. The teacher asks him why he is being so disruptive and Bob replies in a grumpy tone, "Because I have to come to THIS stinking class and put up with YOU!"

Type of Disruption, ABCD _____

Dominant Position _____

How would you validate the position? _____
_____
_____

How would you communicate that the behavior is unacceptable, but that you are there to seek Win-Win alternatives?
_____
_____
_____

4. Sue

Sue is late yet again. She comes in quietly and sits down without making a sound. She sits down and quietly leans on her hand until she falls asleep. Soon her head is on the desk. She shows no interest in the language arts lesson. Each time the teacher wakes her by asking a question, she says, "I don't know." The teacher feels this is a case of not trying instead of not knowing the answers. When it is time to get started with the practice phase of the lesson, writing declarative sentences, Sue yawns and again puts her head on her desk.

Type of Disruption, ABCD _____

Dominant Position _____

How would you validate the position? _____
_____
_____

How would you communicate that the behavior is unacceptable, but that you are there to seek Win-Win alternatives?
_____
_____
_____

For Answers, See Part VII, Resources D.3.

13.62

Win-Win Discipline. Kagan Publishing · 1 (800) 933-2667 · www.KaganOnline.com

Disruption Scenario Cards (Continued)

5. Kathy

Kathy will not stay in her seat and even when she does, she fidgets and seems to be very busy. The noise of rustling papers and her desktop closing and opening fills the room, distracting the teacher and students. When answering questions, Kathy raises her hand, wildly waving it in the air. She seems to be bouncing out of her seat.

Type of Disruption, ABCD _____

Dominant Position _____

How would you validate the position? _____
_____
_____

How would you communicate that the behavior is unacceptable, but that you are there to seek Win-Win alternatives?
_____
_____
_____

6. Liz

Liz is running in the hall again for the fifth time this week. When the teacher stops her and reminds her of the rule about running, Liz replies, "What a stupid rule! You expect us to be at class on time and we don't have time to get there between classes. When am I supposed to see my boyfriend? I will get here when I GET here." Liz sits and immediately takes out her make-up case and begins putting on lipstick. When the teacher reminds her of the rules, Liz says, "YOU put on your makeup in class. Well, so can I, and you can't do a thing about it!" When the teacher asks her again to get out her books and begin reading, Liz replies, "Make me!"

Type of Disruption, ABCD _____

Dominant Position _____

How would you validate the position? _____
_____
_____

How would you communicate that the behavior is unacceptable, but that you are there to seek Win-Win alternatives?
_____
_____
_____

For Answers, See Part VII, Resources D.3.

Win-Win Discipline. Kagan Publishing • 1 (800) 933-2667 • www.KaganOnline.com

13.63

Disruption Scenario Cards (Continued)

7. Jody

Jody seems to be listening for a while in class, but every time the teacher mentions an assignment, Jody mutters under her breath, "OH MAN!" and rolls her eyes. There are a lot of sighing noises coming from Jody, and she frequently stops work on her lesson to look out the window. The pictures that cover the side of her note taking page are incredibly detailed. To get Jody to do anything is like pulling teeth. She seems to have no energy, and even though she doesn't often sleep in class, she is "not there" and seems to do lots of things to stimulate herself, like getting out other books or reading a magazine in class.

Type of Disruption, ABCD _____

Dominant Position _____

How would you validate the position? _____
_____

How would you communicate that the behavior is unacceptable, but that you are there to seek Win-Win alternatives?
_____
_____
_____

8. Alice

The teacher gives directions and then looks toward Alice because he knows she will now ask a question about directions he just gave. "So, you mean that the test won't count and we can do it again?" Alice always has questions, even when the assignment is very clearly explained. When the teacher asks for return of the permission slips for the field trip, Alice seems surprised that she needed one. The teacher thinks of her as an airhead and not very "with-it." Alice always comes to the teacher's desk with her paper and asks, "Is this right?" She will come up with questions for each of the problems if the teacher allows it. The teacher wishes Alice would become more attentive and feels like rolling his eyes in response to her questions.

Type of Disruption, ABCD _____

Dominant Position _____

How would you validate the position? _____
_____

How would you communicate that the behavior is unacceptable, but that you are there to seek Win-Win alternatives?
_____
_____
_____

For Answers, See Part VII, Resources D.3.

13.64

Win-Win Discipline. Kagan Publishing • 1 (800) 933-2667 • www.KaganOnline.com

Disruption Scenario Cards (Continued)

9. Carol

Carol comes into class today wearing blue hair, a too-short miniskirt with thigh-high boots and her nose ring in place. She makes a late entry just so that everyone will make comments about her dress, even though she realizes it is inappropriate for school. She asks loudly, "When is that paper due, again, Mrs. Kennedy?" She laughs when Mrs. Kennedy looks in disgust at her dress today. Carol moves quietly from desk to desk showing her new nose ring piercing to all her friends, even though it was disrupting the class. When Mrs. Kennedy asks her to quietly sit down, Carol sits, but not too quietly!

Type of Disruption, ABCD _____

Dominant Position _____

How would you validate the position? _____
_____
_____

How would you communicate that the behavior is unacceptable, but that you are there to seek Win-Win alternatives?
_____
_____
_____

For Answers, See Part VII, Resources D.3.

References

[1] Madsen, C. H., Jr., Becker, W. C., Thomas, D. R., Koser, L., & Plager, E. *An Analysis of the Reinforcing Function of "Sit Down" Commands.* In R. K. Parker (Ed.), *Readings in Educational Psychology.* Boston, MA: Allyn and Bacon, 1968 pp. 265–278.

[2] Buzan, T. *Use Both Sides of Your Brain, (3rd Ed.)* New York, NY: Penguin Publishing Group, 1991.

[3] Campbell, L., Campbell, B., & Dickinson, D. *Teaching and Learning through Multiple Intelligences.* Needham Heights, MA: Allyn & Bacon, 1996.

[4] Kagan S., & Kagan, M. *Multiple Intelligences: The Complete MI Book.* San Clemente, CA: Kagan Publishing, 1998.

[5] Canfield, J., Hansen, M.V., McCarty, H., & McCarty, M. (Eds). *A Fourth Course of Chicken Soup for the Soul.* Deerfield Beach, FL: Health Communications, Inc., 1997, pp. 154–156.

[6] Seligman, M. *Learned Optimism.* New York, NY: Alfred A. Knopf, 1991.

[7] Seligman, M. *Helplessness: On Depression, Development, and Death.* San Francisco, CA: W.H. Freeman and Company, 1975.

[8] Kagan, S. *Silly Sports and Goofy Games.* San Clemente, CA: Kagan Publishing, 2000.

[9] Kagan, S. *Cooperative Learning.* San Clemente, CA: Kagan Publishing, 1994.

[10] Kagan, S., Kagan, L., & Kagan, M. *Classbuilding.* San Clemente, CA: Kagan Publishing, 1995.

[11] Kagan S., & Kagan, M. *Multiple Intelligences: The Complete MI Book.* San Clemente, CA: Kagan Publishing, 1998.

[12] Carter, R. *Mapping the Mind.* Berkeley, CA: University of California Press, 1998.

[13] Kagan, S. *Cooperative Learning.* San Clemente, CA: Kagan Publishing, 1994.

[14] Kagan S., & Kagan, M. *Multiple Intelligences: The Complete MI Book.* San Clemente, CA: Kagan Publishing, 1998.

[15] Kagan, S. *Cooperative Learning.* San Clemente, CA: Kagan Publishing, 1994.

Chapter 14

Moment-of-Disruption Structures

This chapter provides detailed step-by-step descriptions of structures for the moment-of-disruption. The structures are organized alphabetically for easy access. Four tables are offered to help you find the structure or activity most appropriate to a particular disruption:

Moment-of-Disruption Structures. This table gives a thumbnail sketch of Win-Win structures recommended for the moment-of-disruption. Although many structures are recommended for many disruptions, we have coded the structures ● and ●. ● indicates what we feel are the most useful functions of the structure; ● indicates other types of disruptions for which the structure is also recommended.

Structures for ABCD Disruptions. This table is designed as a quick reference guide targeting those structures with proven success for each of the four types of disruptions. Note, although structures are listed only once, most can be used to respond to a range of types of disruptions.

Structures for the 7 Positions. This table is designed as a quick reference guide targeting those structures with proven success for each of the seven student positions. Note, with this table also, although structures are listed only once, most can be used to respond to a range of student positions.

Start and Stop Structures. When we are dealing with a student who is aggressive, breaking the rules, confrontational, angry, attention-seeking, control-seeking, or energetic, most often we need a structure to get the student to stop disruptive behavior. In contrast, when we are dealing with a student who is disengaged, avoiding failure, or bored, we most often need a structure to motivate the student. Some structures are designed to end disruptive behaviors; some are designed to get students to engage in desired behavior; some do both.

In this fourth table, moment-of-disruption structures are categorized as "Start" or "Stop" structures depending on whether they are most often used to get students to start desired behavior, to stop unacceptable behavior, or to do both. Further, the type of learning they foster is listed.

Some structures are intended for both the "Stop" and the "Start" functions, that is, to stop disruptive behavior and to motivate desired behavior. For example, Redirect orients students from disruptive toward responsible behavior. Similarly, Target, Stop, Do informs students of what they are doing and what they need to be doing instead.

Win-Win Solutions vs. Stopgap Solutions

Not all structures provided in this chapter have the three pillars of Win-Win "built in." For example, Target, Stop, Do may quickly end a disruption, but it usually fails all three tests of Win-Win — the three pillars: (1) There is nothing in the structure that creates a same-side orientation; (2) Students do not collaborate in creating the discipline solution; and (3) When a teacher uses Target, Stop, Do, students often do not learn more responsible behavior. Target, Stop, Do is not a Win-Win solution; it is merely a stopgap solution — something to quickly end a disruption in the moment.

We are not opposed to quickly ending disruptions in the moment they occur, but as Win-Win teachers, our efforts do not stop at ending disruptions. We keep our eye on the goal: converting disruptions into learning opportunities. In order to achieve learned responsibility, we put the three pillars of Win-Win in place. Thus, although a Win-Win teacher may use stopgap solutions like Target, Stop, Do, if, over time, the teacher discovers the three pillars of Win-Win are not in place, the teacher considers a follow-up. **Follow-ups are to be considered whenever a disruptive student is not making progress toward learned responsibility.** If the student is on track, learning responsibility at his/her pace, no follow-up is necessary. If, however, no progress is being made toward learned responsibility — if we are not on the right path — then a follow-up is in order. Follow-ups can be useful after any type of disruption or series of disruptions stemming from any position.

Structures Can't Be Labeled Win-Win

It is not possible to label structures as Win-Win structures or not. A structure may lead to a Win-Win solution for one student and not for another. A given structure may lead one student to feel on the same-side and to learn more responsible behavior, whereas that same structure used with another student may not put the pillars in place. There is no magic formula for obtaining Win-Win solutions — we must understand and work with our students.

To determine if a Win-Win orientation is being established with a student, the teacher focuses on the student, not on the structure. Whenever the three pillars are not in place with a given student, the Win-Win teacher knows a Win-Win solution has not yet been achieved and considers alternative moments-of-disruption and/or follow-up structures.

Pre-establishing Structure Procedures

Before using some structures in the moment-of-disruption, we must pre-establish procedures and generate buy-in. The structures that require pre-established procedures are easy to remember; they are the 5C's:

The 5C's: Structures that Require Pre-established Procedures

Cool Down

Consequences

Contracts

Coupons

Cues: Verbal & Non-verbal

For example, before we can use verbal or non-verbal cues in the moment-of-disruption, we must establish buy-in with the students for using the cues, what the cues will be, and how they will be used. Some procedures can be established with the whole class. Others need to be established in private with an individual student prior to a disruption. For example, with an individual student we might establish a Coupon Approach or Contract to which the rest of the class is not privy. In the tables, structures that need to be pre-established are marked with asterisks, and the step-by-step procedures for pre-establishing those structures are presented along with the structures. Pre-establishing procedures, of course, often occurs as a follow-up to a disruption in preparation for a similar disruption in the future.

Moment-of-Disruption Structures

Structure	Page	Disruption Type				Position							Thumbnail Sketch
		A	B	C	D	Attention-Seeking	Avoiding Failure	Angry	Control-Seeking	Energetic	Bored	Uninformed	
Acknowledge Student Power	12			●					●				The teacher calmly acknowledges the student's power, *"I can't make you."* The teacher then clarifies the consequences of alternatives from which the student can choose. This structure is designed to help students obtain a sense of control and take responsibility for their choices. Individual
Consequences* • Establishing Consequences • Consequences Reminder • Implementing Consequences	14	●	●	●	●	◐		●	●	◐			Prior to disruptions the teacher establishes just consequences. To avoid an impending disruption the teacher may remind students of the consequences. If the disruption continues the teacher implements the consequences. Thus there are three phases of Consequences: 1. Establishing Consequences; 2. Consequences Reminder; and 3. Implementing Consequences. *"Remember the consequences we agreed on." "We need to implement the consequences we agreed on now."* Individual; Class
Cool Down* • Establish Cool Down • Cool Down Reminder • Implement Cool Down	27	●		◐				●					Prior to the moment-of-disruption the teacher establishes cool down procedures. When emotions begin to escalate, the teacher gives a cool down reminder. *"Are we getting close to needing cool down?"* If emotions continue to escalate, the teacher implements pre-established cool down procedures. Implementing pre-established cool down procedures allows everyone to regain composure, minimizes loss of instructional time, and helps students internalize self-monitoring and self-control. *"Please take some time in the cool down area now."* Thus there are three phases of cool down: 1. Establish Cool Down; 2. Cool Down Reminder; and 3. Implement Cool Down. *"Are we getting close to needing cool down?"* *"Please take some time in the cool down area now."* Individual

* = These structures need pre-established procedures.

● = Most Useful

◐ = Also Recommended

Moment-of-Disruption Structures (Continued)

Structure	Page	Disruption Type				Position							Thumbnail Sketch
		A	B	C	D	Attention-Seeking	Avoiding Failure	Angry	Control-Seeking	Energetic	Bored	Uninformed	
Coupons* • Establish Coupons • Implement Coupons	35		●			●				●			Students are reminded to trade one of their limited supply of coupons for "too frequent" behavior. The coupon approach helps the student monitor and limit disruptive behavior, fostering self-control. *"Thank you for using your coupon wisely."* Individual
Cues: Verbal & Non-verbal*	39	●	●	●	●	●		●		●		●	The teacher uses pre-established verbal or non-verbal cues to elicit appropriate behavior. Class cues are established; specific cues may be established for individual students. Verbal: "Class, please take a moment now and look over the class rules chart." Non-verbal: Teacher walks to and looks intently at the class rules chart. Individual; Class
Expectation Reminder*	42	●	●	●	●	●		●		●		●	Prior to a possible disruption or at the outset of a disruption, students are reminded of pre-established expectations, procedures, or rules. When a number of students are violating the rules, the teacher may stop the lesson to re-teach the rules. *"Remember the expectations (rules, procedures) we agreed on. Let's take some time now to review how we want out class to be."* Individual; Class
Grandma's Rule	45			●	●	●	●		●	●	●	●	The teacher uses a "When... then..." statement to indicate the responsible behavior and the incentive that will follow. The origin of grandma's rule is "When you eat your dinner, then you may have dessert." "When you finish your math practice sheet, you can go to the choice tables to pick a favorite learning game." Individual; Class
I-Messages Plus	47	●	●	●	●	●		●	●	●	●	●	Calmly informing students of your own feelings is an I-Message, designed to make students aware of their stimulus value (effect on others). An I-Message Plus adds encouragement to adopt non-disruptive alternatives. "I feel X when you do Y, and your classmates feel Z. Can you think of a better choice?" Individual; Class

Moment-of-Disruption Structures (Continued)

Structure	Page	Disruption Type A	B	C	D	Position Attention-Seeking	Avoiding Failure	Angry	Control-Seeking	Energetic	Bored	Uninformed	Thumbnail Sketch
Language of Choice	50	●	●	◐	◐	◐		●	●	◐	◐	◐	Language of Choice provides immediate consequences, allowing the disruptive student to make a more responsible choice. *"You need to _____ or _____."* Individual; Class
Make a Better Choice	53	●	◐		◐	●	●	◐	●	●	●		Through Make a Better Choice, the teacher calls for reflection rather than obedience, leaving it to the student to create a more responsible alternative. *"I want you to think of a better choice to make right now."* Individual; Class
Model It!	56	◐	●	◐	◐	●		◐		◐		●	Modeling and disclosing one's own responsible behavior (self-control, persistence in the face of difficulty, politeness) helps students identify with the teacher and acquire responsible behaviors. *"Right now, I feel stuck. But I know if I keep tying, I will figure it out."* Individual; Class
Picture It Right!	59	●	◐		◐	●	◐	●	●	●			The class or an individual takes responsibility for imagining responsible alternatives as they pause, close their eyes, and picture it right. *"If we were at our very best right now, how would it look?"* Individual; Class
Redirect	61		●		●	●		◐		●	◐		Redirect diverts attention and behavior away from a disruptive episode and toward a responsible learning activity. *"Have you done problem four yet?"* Individual; Class
Restart	63	●	◐		◐	●		●	◐	●			When the class is out of control, like a computer that has crashed, it is time to Restart. We stop talking, stop doing, pause, see a positive and negative model by the teacher, see a positive model by a classmate, and then restart. *"Stop! Look! Listen!"* Class
Restructure the Task	66		●		●	●		◐		●	◐		The teacher restructures the learning task to stimulate greater engagement. *"Let's take this part a step at a time."* Individual; Class

* = These structures need pre-established procedures.
● = Most Useful
◐ = Also Recommended

Moment-of-Disruption Structures (Continued)

Structure	Page	A	B	C	D	Attention-Seeking	Avoiding Failure	Angry	Control-Seeking	Energetic	Bored	Uninformed	Thumbnail Sketch
Right Now Validation	68	●	●	●	●	●	●	●	●	●	●	●	The teacher acknowledges and validates the student or class position and then directs the student to more responsible behavior. "Right now you are feeling _____. That's OK, but what you need to do is _____." *Individual; Class*
Schedule Follow-up	71	●	●	●	●	●	●	●	●	●	●	●	In order not to disrupt the class while implementing the three pillars, a follow-up meeting with the student is scheduled. "We need to talk this through. Let's meet after...." *Individual*
Table the Matter	74	◐		●				●	●				The teacher uses Table the Matter to acknowledge the need to meet and discuss while allowing time for emotions to settle down and for student and teacher reflection before meeting. "Let's give this a rest for now. We can talk about it later when we are both calm." *Individual; Class*
Target, Stop, Do	77	●	●	◐		◐	◐	●		◐	◐	◐	Target, Stop, Do is a very brief, focused, forceful sequence, designed to get the disruptive student's attention, inform the student what he/she needs to stop doing, and redirect the student to what he/she needs to do. "Susie, Right now you are doing _____. You need to be doing _____." *Individual; Class*
To You... To Me	79			●					●		●		To You... To Me acknowledges the student's perspective and informs him/her of the teacher's perspective. In this way the teacher communicates understanding and facilitates a perspective shift in the student. "To you, this lesson may be boring; to me, it is important because...." *Individual*

* = These structures need pre-established procedures.
● = Most Useful
◐ = Also Recommended

Structures for ABCD Disruptions

Disruption Type	Recommended Structures[1,2]	Page
Aggression	Cool Down*	27
	Language of Choice	50
	Make a Better Choice	53
	Picture It Right!	59
	Target, Stop, Do	77
Breaking Rules	Consequences*	14
	Coupons*	35
	Cues: Verbal & Non-verbal*	39
	Expectation Reminder	42
	I-Messages Plus	47
Confrontation	Acknowledge Student Power	12
	Model It!	56
	Table the Matter	74
	To You... To Me	79
Disengagement	Grandma's Rule	45
	Redirect	61
	Right Now Validation	68
	Restart	63
	Restructure Task	66

* = These structures need pre-established procedures.

[1]This table is provided as a guide to some of the most useful structures for each of the ABCD disruptions. It is not a comprehensive list of all the structures or strategies that can be useful for each disruption type.

[2]Schedule a Follow-Up is not included. A follow-up should be scheduled any time a disruption has occurred and there has not been progress toward realizing the three Pillars: Same-Side, Shared Responsibility, and Learned Responsibility.

Structures for the 7 Positions

Position	Recommended Structures[3,4]	Page
Attention-Seeking	Coupons*	35
	I-Messages Plus	47
	Picture It Right!	59
Avoiding Failure	Restructure Task	66
Angry	Consequences*	14
	Cool Down*	27
	Language of Choice	50
	Model It!	56
	Table the Matter	74
	Target, Stop, Do	77
Control-Seeking	Acknowledge Student Power	12
	To You... To Me	79
Energetic	Cues: Verbal & Non-verbal*	39
	Make a Better Choice	53
	Redirect	61
Bored	Grandma's Rule	45
	Right Now Validation	68
Uninformed	Expectation Reminder	42
	Restart	63

* = These structures need pre-established procedures.

[3]This table is provided as a guide to some of the most useful structures for each of the student positions. It is not a comprehensive list of all the structures or strategies that can be useful for each disruption type.

[4]Schedule a Follow-Up is not included. A follow-up may be scheduled any time a disruption ordisruptions have occurred and over time there has not been progress toward realizing the three Pillars: Same Side, Shared Responsibility, and Learned Responsibility.

14.10

Win-Win Discipline. Kagan Publishing • 1 (800) 933-2667 • www.KaganOnline.com

Start and Stop Structures

	Page	Start	Stop	Learning Fostered
Acknowledge Student Power	12		●	Internal Sense of Power
Consequences	14		●	Planning; Self-Control; Consequences
Cool Down Reminder: Cool Down	27		●	Anger Management
Coupon Approach	35	●	●	Self-Control; Self-Motivation
Cues: Verbal and Non-verbal	39	●	●	Self-Control
Expectation Reminder	42		●	Consequences; Self-Control
Grandma's Rule	45	●		Self-Motivation
I-Messages Plus	47		●	Impact on Others
Language of Choice	50		●	Self-Control
Make a Better Choice	53	●	●	Problem Solving; Autonomy
Model It!	56	●		Self-Control
Picture It Right!	59	●		Creative Thinking; Responsibility
Redirect	61	●	●	Self-Control
Restart	63		●	Self-Control; Responsible Alternatives
Restructure Task	66	●		Self-Motivation
Right Now Validation	68		●	Self-Awareness
Schedule a Follow-Up	71		●	Consequences
Table the Matter	74		●	Self-Control
Target, Stop, Do	77	●	●	Self-Awareness
To You... To Me	79		●	Impact on Others

This table charts the stop-start functions of moment-of-disruption structures. Some structures are most often used to motivate responsible behavior, to stop disruptive behavior, or to do both. All foster learning, although some do so more directly than others.

Win-Win Discipline. Kagan Publishing • 1 (800) 933-2667 • www.KaganOnline.com

14.11

Acknowledge Student Power

The teacher calmly acknowledges the student's power,[1] *"I can't make you."* The teacher then clarifies the consequences of alternatives from which the student can choose. This approach is designed to help students obtain a sense of control and to take responsibility for their choices.

Ideal Outcomes

- By publicly acknowledging students' power, they experience a sense of control in the moment, decreasing their need to be disruptive.

- Over time students internalize a sense of control.

- Students realize that choosing responsible behavior actually benefits them.

- Students take responsibility for their choices.

- Students feel less need to challenge the teacher (no longer needing to refuse in order to show they have control).

- The teacher controls consequences without falling into the trap of trying to control student choices.

Recommended for...

Disruption
Confrontation

Position
Control-Seeking

Individual or Class
Individual

STEPS

1 Acknowledge Student Power

The teacher tells the student that he/she cannot make the student do anything. *"You are right! I can't make you sit down and do your journal entry."*

2 State Responsible Behavior

The teacher emphasizes the responsible thing to do. *"The responsible thing for you to do is to sit in your seat and begin your journal entry, Mary."*

3 State Choices and Consequences

The teacher reminds the student of his/her alternatives and the consequences of choosing. *"You can choose to do your journal entry in class now or you can choose to come back and complete it during your lunch period. Let me know what you decide to do, Mary. I know you will make a good choice."*

4 Allow the Choice

After the teacher states the alternatives and consequences, the teacher leaves the area to emphasize the choice is up to the student.

Cautions & Hints

- **Accept the Need.** Students who confront teachers are often seeking to establish a sense of control ("No one tells me what to do." "I am in charge of me."). One way to help these students meet their need for control is to Acknowledge Student Power.
- **Calm Voice.** Maintain a calm voice.
- **Believe It!** Teacher must feel that the choice is really up to the student.
- **No Manipulation.** Teacher does not try to manipulate the student.
- **Provide Space.** Allow the student time and space to make his/her choice.
- **Realistic Consequences.** The consequences must be something within the teacher's control. No hollow threats.
- **Time Frame.** Students need to know there is a fixed time in which they can make their choice.

Discussion and Journaling Topics

One-on-One Discussion Topics

Through a follow-up discussion, help the student realize that he/she can experience a sense of control through owning his/her choices — being aware of when and how they are choosing — and by choosing responsible behavior. "We are meeting to talk about the choices you made today. I saw that you chose X. Did you think about it as you made that choice? Did it feel good to be able to choose? How did you feel about your choice — does it feel like a wise choice to you, or would you choose differently if you had it to do over?"

Class Journaling or Discussion Topics

We all make many choices every hour. When we experience ourselves choosing, we feel free. What are choices you make that make you feel in control of yourself?

Consequences

Prior to disruptions the teacher establishes just consequences. To avoid an impending disruption the teacher may remind students of the consequences. If the disruption continues the teacher implements the consequences. Thus there are three phases of Consequences: 1. Establishing Consequences; 2. Consequences Reminder; and 3. Implementing Consequences. *"Remember the consequences we agreed on." "We need to implement the consequences we agreed on now."*

1. Establishing Consequences

Prior to the Moment-of-Disruption, consequences for disruptive behaviors are established with the whole class and/or an individual disruptive student, applying the three pillars of Win-Win, the three principles of just consequences, and the four types of consequences.

Ideal Outcomes

- Students see and identify with the need for consequences.

- Consequences are agreed upon prior to disruptions.

- Consequences are appropriate to the disruption.

- Students perceive the consequences as fair and appropriate.

- Students know which behaviors result in consequences.

- Students establish the consequences, working with the teacher.

- Students understand that once consequences are agreed upon, they are no longer negotiable.

- Eventually, students become responsible and are motivated to act responsibly out of feelings of pride and integrity.

- Students see the benefits of responsible behavior and make more responsible choices.

- Students feel a sense of control — that their choices always bring consequences and that at any moment they can make different choices.

- Loss of instructional time is minimized.

Recommended for...

Disruption
Aggression, Breaking the Rules, Confrontation, Disengaged

Position
Attention-Seeking, **Angry, Control-Seeking,** Energetic

Individual or Class
Both

STEPS

1 Set a Meeting Time

For the Class: The teacher schedules a time for the class to establish consequences for disruptive behaviors, often during a class meeting. *"Class, if we are to be successful in our mission of maximizing learning, we need to minimize disruptions. One way of doing that is to establish consequences for disruptive behaviors. During our next class meeting, we will schedule time to work together to establish consequences for disruptive behavior."*

For an Individual: The teacher tells the student that he/she would like to meet with the student to talk about behavior and establish consequences for disruptive behavior. *"We need to meet so that we can talk about your disruptive behavior. I want us to work together to solve the problem and we need a private time for us to do that. Let's meet this afternoon."*

2 Establish Need

During the meeting, the teacher uses analogies to establish the need for consequences. *"What would happen if there were no consequences for breaking laws, like the speeding law, or the law against stealing? Why are consequences necessary in the country? Why might they be necessary in our classroom? How can consequences help us? How do they help the teacher? How do they help students who might otherwise be disruptive? How do they help students who might otherwise disrupt others?"*

3 Establish Principles of Just, Win-Win Consequences

The teacher creates buy-in for principles of just consequences: 1) Appropriate to the Disruption; 2) Clear Conditions; 3) Pre-established. See Box: Just Consequences and Win-Win

Consequences, 14.18. *"As we think of possible consequences we need to keep in mind tests of just consequences. What makes consequences fair or unfair? I can think of three good tests:*

1. ***Appropriate.*** *First, consequences must be appropriate to the disruption. It would not be fair to fail a student just because of sharpening his/her pencil too often.*
2. ***Understandable.*** *Second, they must be clear. If we set up consequences for 'being disruptive,' we might disagree on what that is. If we set up consequences for 'making noises that distract others,' that might be clearer.*
3. ***Pre-established.*** *Third, to be just, consequences must be pre-established. It would feel unfair for me to make up consequences any time I feel like it. If ahead of time, we agree which kinds of consequences, then it will feel fair."*

4 Generate Possibilities

The teacher has the student(s) focus on a disruptive behavior and allows them to generate possible consequences, using a brainstorming structure like Jot Thoughts or 4S Brainstorming. In the case of an individual student, the teacher enters the brainstorming process so there is shared responsibility for generating possible consequences. See Box: Four Types of Consequences. *"In your teams you each have 5 slips of paper. As quickly as you can, write down as many possible consequences as you can, one per slip of paper. As you write them, announce them to your teammates so there will not be any duplicates. It is fine to list silly consequences as well as serious ones — we are just generating ideas. We can sort through them and choose later."*

Establishing Consequences

STEPS (Continued)

5 Select Consequences

The class in consultation with the teacher selects their best alternative using a decision-making structure like Sum the Ranks. In the case of an individual student, the teacher and student together select their best consequence. *"Let's rank these alternatives. Each team will rank the alternatives and then will post its rankings so we can sum the ranks."*

6 Establish Agreement, Commitment

The teacher and students work through the process of establishing agreement on the consequence and commitment to the responsible behavior. *"As a class, we agree that the best consequence for X is Y. Now, can we all promise that whenever X occurs we will Y?"*

Individual Student: *"We both agree that X is a fair consequence for Y. Can you commit to implementing that without delay or protest anytime you choose to X?"*

Cautions & Hints

• **Three Principles of Just Consequences.** Care should be taken to respect the three principles of just consequences: Appropriate, Clear, and Pre-established. See Just Consequences, page 14.18.

• **Three Pillars of Win-Win.** In establishing consequences, care should be taken to respect the three pillars of Win-Win: Same-Side, Shared Responsibility, Learned Responsibility. See Win-Win Consequences, page 14.19.

• **Four Keys to Successful Consequences.** The most important concepts leading to successful consequences are:

Keys to Successful Consequences

| Delivered with Heart | Instructive | Appropiate | Timely |

• **Types of Consequences.** In considering what types of consequences to establish, there are many options to consider. See Four Types of Consequences, page 14.20. Options include:

Responsible Thinking
Apology
Restitution
Delayed or Lost Activity, Access, or Interaction

Cautions & Hints (Continued)

- **Progressive Consequences.** In cases of likely repeated disruptions, student(s) and teacher may agree on some form of progressive consequences such as:

> First Offense → **Responsible Thinking + Apology**
> Second Offense → **Responsible Thinking + Apology + Restitution**
> Third Offense → **Responsible Thinking + Apology + Restitution + Visit with Principal**

- **No Posting of Negative Behaviors.** Posting negative behaviors that lead to consequences can be a trap. First, confronting students with visual reminders of negative behaviors actually increases the probability that they will manifest that behavior. A consequence poster that reads "Hitting → Trip to Principal's Office" keeps the idea of hitting in the student's minds.

Second, consequences appropriate for one student may not be appropriate for another. One student may be in a position of seeking control, whereas another may be uninformed or even unable to anticipate consequences. Posting class consequences focuses on behavior; in Win-Win we focus on the student — the student's position.

- **Consequences Are Pre-established.** Consequences Reminders and Implementing Consequences can be used only if consequences have been pre-established with the class or with an individual student. We pre-establish the behaviors that will result in consequences, but not exactly what the consequences will be. The consequences will be tailored to the disruption.

- **Examples Rather than Specifics.** It is not possible to pre-establish specific consequences for every type of disruptive behavior. Poking someone lightly in the shoulder with a finger should have a different consequence than smashing them hard in the face with a fist. Therefore, a general consequence for hitting will likely be too severe in some cases and too mild in others. A solution is to pre-establish that there will be consequences for disruptive behaviors and that the consequences will be appropriate to the disruption.

"Here are some examples of possible consequences:
- *A conference with me*
- *A visit with the principal*
- *A visit with your parents*

I won't limit myself to those options. We will find a consequence appropriate to the disruption!"

- **Anger.** With students coming from a position of anger, it is important to give everyone time to cool down before implementing or co-creating consequences.

- **Control-Seeking.** With students seeking control, it is important to emphasize shared responsibility: *"The consequences we agree on have to be those which we both think are fair and that we can both stick to. You will have a say and so will I. We need to resolve this together."*

Discussion and Journaling Topics

Class Journaling or Discussion Topic

Every time we make a choice, it has consequences. And we make choices every moment. So our choices determine our fate. Do you agree or disagree with this set of propositions? What are some of the choices you have made that have had good or bad consequences for you? Are there some choices you are making now in your life that will have consequences later? Could you be making some different choices than you are now making?

Just Consequences

• Principle 1: Appropriate and Linked

To the extent possible, consequences should be appropiate and linked to the type of disruption and commensurate with the size of the disruption. By linking the consequences, students are more likely to feel that the consequences are the results of their behavior and are more likely to think of them before becoming disruptive. By making consequences commensurate, students are more likely to perceive them as fair.

Disruption: A student spills paint.

Appropriate and Linked: The student cleans up the spilled paint.
Unlinked: The student does extra math problems for homework.
Incommensurate: The student cleans up the whole school.

Disruption: A student tears up a book.

Appropriate and Linked: The student replaces the book.
Unlinked: The student misses P.E.
Incommensurate: The student pays a $100 fine.

• Principle 2: Clear

To the extent possible, consequences should be clear. Vague phrases lead students to test and feel that consequences are being applied arbitrarily.

Clear: Students who fail to turn in their homework will do their homework during choice time.
Vague: Students who fail to turn in their homework will experience serious consequences.

Clear: Shoving in line will result in moving to the end of the line.
Vague: Being bad will mean five extra homework problems.

• Principle 3: Pre-established

That there will be consequences for certain kinds of disruptive behavior must be pre-established if consequences are to lead to more responsible behavior. When consequences are pre-established and non-negotiable, students are more likely to feel that they have brought about the consequences themselves and take more responsibility for having done so. If consequences are not pre-established, or if students believe they can talk their way out of the consequences, then students are more likely to feel that it is the teacher's arbitrary choice as to whether or what kind of consequences they experience. They do not take responsibility for having brought about the consequences.

We need to be willing to follow through on whatever consequence is established. If not, students will feel that consequences are arbitrary, the link between their behavior and the consequence will be weakened, and there will be less learned responsibility.

Because we cannot establish specific consequences for every possible disruption ahead of time, we can pre-establish that certain types of behavior will have consequences, but exactly what those consequences will be has to be determined when all factors surrounding the disruption are considered.

There is no way that we can have a readily prepared consequence for every eventuality, so there is a structure that allows for a consequence to be established, known, and avoided in the moment-of-disruption: the Language of Choice structure. To use that structure, the teacher says, *"Spencer, stop poking Bob and place your hands in your lap, or you will need to discuss this with Mrs. Scott."* If the student continues with the disruptive behavior and experiences the stated consequence, the student knows he/she brought about that consequence. The Language of Choice structure allows students to see the consequences as a result of their choices, rather than seeing them as arbitrarily imposed, leading to greater learned responsibility.

Win-Win Consequences

1. Same-Side

The teacher and student(s) experience themselves as being on the same-side, working as allies toward just consequences that they can both endorse. By modeling respectful interaction, the teacher ensures that students think about their own behavior choices. When a teacher is authoritarian or disrespectful, students shift their focus to teacher behavior rather than on their own behavior. By maintaining a same-side orientation, the teacher keeps the focus on the student behavior and creates a relationship more likely to result in a Win-Win solution.

2. Collaborative Solutions

Teacher and students jointly develop and implement consequences in a respectful manner. Students are far less likely to resist consequences they helped formulate. In the process of co-creating the consequences, students better understand the rationale for consequences, more fully identify with the justness of the consequences, and so are less likely to engage in the disruptive behavior that results in consequences. When you put the students in charge, they will often make sure their consequences are effective, because they want to make their idea work.

3. Learned Responsibility

Consequences are but a stop-gap discipline approach if they do not lead to learned responsibility. In effect, if consequences serve their purpose, they eliminate the need for consequences — students internalize and identify with the importance of responsible behavior. To that end, in the process of formulating the consequences, the focus should be on the necessity of consequences, the negative impact of disruptive behavior on others, the pride in acting responsibly, and the need for apology and restitution. The focus should not be on punishment or prevention — we approach learned responsibility far more directly using a carrot rather than a stick, focusing on the benefits of responsible behavior rather than the punishments associated with disruptive behavior.

Win-Win Discipline. Kagan Publishing • 1 (800) 933-2667 • www.KaganOnline.com

14.19

Four Types of Consequences

1. Responsible Thinking

When a student has been disruptive, as often as possible we want the student to engage in responsible thinking. In this way, responsible thinking becomes habitual. Following disruptive behavior, having the student(s) stop, think, and engage in responsible thinking in many cases is sufficient. Three W's symbolize the responsible thinking questions:

1. **W**hat if everyone acted that way? (How would our class be if everyone acted that way?)
2. **W**hich way would I like to be treated? (Did I treat others the way I would like to be treated?)
3. **W**hat would be a Win-Win solution? (What would meet everyone's needs?)

For details, see the Responsible Thinking Stucture, pages 16.22–25.

Students can express their responsible thinking in many ways, including verbally, in an essay, as a poster or drawing, in a skit, or role-play.

If the disruptive behavior has disrupted or harmed others, responsible thinking is not enough; the student needs to apologize and/or make restitution.

2. Apology

Apologies are social cushions — they soften the impact of hurtful behavior. It is amazing how far a sincere apology can go in cleaning the slate — but only if it is sincere. When we are hurt or bothered by someone, we want to know that the person knows how they have hurt us, to feel our pain. The instinct to hurt back is partially motivated by the desire to "show him how it feels." When we know someone feels the hurt he/she had caused, we are more prepared to let bygones be bygones.

Mistakes are inevitable. Learning to apologize is a basic relationship skill as well as an employability skill.

An apology has three components, each of which can be practiced and learned.[2]

1. **Statement of regret or remorse:** *"I feel bad that…" " I regret that…" "I wish I hadn't…"*
2. **Statement of appropriate future behavior:** *"Next time I will be sure to…" "I won't do that again; I will…"*
3. **Request for acceptance:** *"I hope you will accept my apology." "I hope you can forgive me."*

Sentences and sentence starters help students acquire the art of apology:

"When I did _____, it must have made you feel _____. I'm sorry."

"I really hurt you when I _____. I know how that feels. Next time I will _____. Please accept my apology."

"I'm sorry. What I did was wrong because it hurt you. I won't do that again."

"Class, my behavior stole time from your learning. It took away from our mission. I'm sorry. I will not make disruptive noises again."

It is inevitable that students will cause each other physical or psychological hurt at times. We can have an agreement in the class that whenever that happens, the person causing the hurt will give a sincere apology to the class as a whole or to the individuals who have been hurt or disrupted.

3. Restitution

The essence of restitution is simple: the student who has broken something needs to repair or replace it. The student who has made

14.20

Win-Win Discipline. Kagan Publishing • 1 (800) 933-2667 • www.KaganOnline.com

Four Types of Consequences (Continued)

a mess needs to clean it up. The student who has stolen time from academics needs to compensate by putting in extra time. Restitution is a very concrete way of taking responsibility for one's actions, for dealing with the consequences of one's own choices.

In cases of great expense or in the case of a child too young to pay the cost, at least some money needs to come from the student or at least some amount of school community service in lieu of payment. It is critical that the student himself/herself is involved in making restitution.

- I tore someone's backpack; so I will have it repaired or replaced.
- I drew graffiti on the school walls, so I must paint over it.
- I spilled the paint, so I will make my best effort to clean it up.

Restitution can take the form of making up lost time in a content area. The student who has used class time unwisely may need to make up that time during what would otherwise be free time. Caution: Do not steal time from one content area to pay for lost time in another. A student who has been disruptive during math should not lose time from P.E. or music. Rather, he/she should make up the lost time from what would be his/her own free or choice time.

Following the restitution, the teacher and the victim(s) need to express gratitude to the student who has made his/her best effort at restitution.

Restitution has the power to "heal the violator." That is, after making restitution, I clear my conscience. Mistakes that harm others are inevitable. Learning to make restitution is a life skill that allows us to feel good about ourselves. We can live with ourselves when we have done what we can to right a wrong we have created.

4. Lost Activity, Access, or Interaction

Lost Activity: If a student has shown disruptive behavior during an activity, one possible consequence is delayed or lost ability to participate in that activity for some time.

> **Disruption:** The student has thrown balls at other students in an attempt to hurt them.
> **Consequence:** The student may not participate in the class sport for a period of time.

Lost Access: If a student has abused resources, he/she may lose access to the materials for some time.

> **Disruption:** The student has been poking pencils into the back of a computer.
> **Consequence:** The student may not use the computer for a specified time.

Lost Interaction: If a student has been abusive to others, he/she may lose ability to interact with others for a time.

> **Disruption:** The student hit another student.
> **Consequence:** The student must work in isolation for a specified time.

Linking: By linking the loss to the disruption, it is more likely that a student will feel he/she brought about the consequences and reflect before bringing them about again. Hopefully, the student will reason:

> *I did not follow safety rules in shop class yesterday, so I am denied access today. I was banging on the Bunsen burner in science lab, so I cannot use it tomorrow.*

Caution: If inability to participate is the consequence for disruptive behavior, a student who desires not to participate may be disruptive intentionally to escape an undesirable activity.

2. Consequence Reminder

CONSEQUENCES:

At signs of an impending disruption, the teacher reminds the class or individual of pre-established consequences.

Ideal Outcomes

■ Students outgrow the need to be reminded, becoming self-reminding: they think ahead about the possible consequences of their actions.

■ Students learn to control impulses.

■ Students are motivated to act responsibly to avoid consequences.

■ Students feel responsible for bringing about or avoiding consequences.

■ Disruptions are prevented.

Recommended for...

Disruption
Aggression, Breaking the Rules,
Confrontation, Disengaged

Position
Attention-Seeking, **Angry,**
Control-Seeking, Energetic

Individual or Class
Both

STEPS

1 Remind Student or Students of Pre-established Consequences

If an individual student or the class as a whole appears likely to become disruptive, the teacher may remind the student(s) of pre-established consequences.
"Betty, we are getting very close to putting consequences in place. I believe you can avoid that. Think about a better choice that would help you, the class, and me. Thank you."

"Class, off-task behavior is getting to the point that we will need to implement the consequences we agreed on yesterday. I would prefer we use self-control."

Or the teacher may simply want to remind student(s) of consequences, to keep them salient, or to praise responsible behavior.

"Betty [as she enters class], please remember what we agreed upon in our meeting. I hope we get through the whole day without having to put consequences in place."

"Betty [as she leaves class], great job today. I appreciate how you helped me and the class by _____."

Cautions & Hints

• **Voice and Manner.** Teacher is calm and respectful, reminding students of prior agreement.

Consequence Reminder

CONSEQUENCES:

3. Implementing Consequences

CONSEQUENCES FOR:

In the moment-of-disruption the teacher implements pre-established consequences.

Ideal Outcomes

■ Students take responsibility for the consequences of their behavior.

■ The teacher maintains a cool, rational orientation — even in the face of serious disruptions.

■ The class sees and internalizes a model of a rational response to disruptive behavior.

Recommended for...

Disruption
Aggression, Breaking the Rules, Confrontation, Disengaged

Position
Attention-Seeking, **Angry,**
Control-Seeking, Energetic

Individual or Class
Both

STEPS

1 Implement Consequences

In the moment-of-disruption, if consequences have been well established, implementation requires only a reminder. *"Class, yesterday we agreed that the consequences for too much off-task behavior would be ten minutes of extra class time instead of recess. Right now there is far too much off-task behavior, so we need to put that consequence in place. I would prefer we exercise more self-control."*

"Betty, remember what we agreed were to be the consequences if you had your hands on another student. It is time to put those in place. What do you need to do?"

2 Check for Learned Responsibility

After implementing consequences, the teacher checks with the student for learned responsibility. *"Now that you have had some time to think it over, what did you learn from your behavior and the resulting consequences?"*

Cautions & Hints

• **When Consequences Are Not Pre-established.** The Language of Choice structure (14.50–14.52) is a fall-back when consequences have not been pre-established; it establishes immediate consequences while giving the student a choice.

• **Sticking to Consequences.** If consequences have been established, we need to stick to them. Otherwise, establishing consequences loses its meaning, we open ourselves to negotiation in the face of future infractions, and we give the perception of being inconsistent and unfair when we do stick to the consequences at a later time.

• **Guide Thinking.** If a student says that all he/she has learned is to not engage again in the disruptive behavior, guide him/her toward responsible thinking with questions like, *"What do you think the effect of your behavior was on Sue?" "Do you think your behavior helped or hurt you in reaching your own goals?" "What would have been the payoff for you and others of responsible behavior like _____?"*

• **Responsible Thinking Follow-Up.** Ideally, rather than having to rely on consequences, we would like students to engage in responsible thinking, especially considering on their own the consequences of their actions for themselves and others. If you find yourself relying often on Consequence Reminders or Implementing Consequences, it may be time for a follow-up to promote responsible thinking.

Discussion and Journaling Topics

One-on-One Discussion Topic

Today we implemented the consequences we had established. Did that feel fair to you? Are there some choices you could make so we would not have to implement those consequences?

Implementing Consequences

Long Hill Elementary School in Cumberland County, North Carolina, is happy with a five step color-coded consequences system that is shared with parents and students:

Consequences

Blue	→	1. Warning
Yellow	→	2. Reflection Time
Orange	→	3. Personal Improvement Plan
Red	→	4. Telephone Call to Parent or Guardian
		(Please make sure that we are able to contact you during the day. Keep us updated with telephone changes.)
White	→	5. Principal's Office – Student will be sent home.

A fresh start awaits you each day...

*Students creating constant disruption in the school environment will automatically be sent to the principal's office for disciplinary action. This disciplinary action will require a suspension hearing.

Consequences Overview

- **Consequences Are Our Last Line of Defense**
  Try peashooters before dragging out the consequence cannon.
  Remember, our goal is internalized responsibility, not compliance.
  Use progressive consequences.

- **Consequences Are for Unacceptable Behavior**
  Don't use consequences as an enticement.
  Consequences are a stick, not a carrot.

- **Just Consequences**
  Appropriate
  Clear
  Pre-established

- **Win-Win Consequences**
  Same-Side: Established for the Student
  Collaborative Solutions: Established with the Student
  Learned Responsibility: Instructive

- **Types of Consequences**
  Responsible Thinking
  Apology
  Restitution
  Lost Activity, Access, Interaction

Cool Down

Prior to the moment-of-disruption the teacher establishes cool down[3] procedures. When emotions begin to escalate, the teacher gives a cool down reminder. *"Are we getting close to needing cool down?"* If emotions continue to escalate, the teacher implements pre-established cool down procedures. Implementing pre-established cool down procedures allows everyone to regain his/her composure, minimizes loss of instructional time, and helps students internalize self-monitoring and self-control. *"Please take some time in the cool down area now."* Thus there are three phases of cool down: 1. Establish Cool Down; 2. Cool Down Reminder; and 3. Implement Cool Down. *"Are we getting close to needing cool down?" "Please take some time in the cool down area now."*

1. Establishing Cool Down

Cool down procedures are pre-established with an individual or the whole class. Procedures include the place, duration, and activities for cool down.

Ideal Outcomes

- Student and teacher are allowed to cool down when emotions are running hot.

- Students learn self-control and self-management of emotions and behaviors.

- The impulse-action chain is broken, inserting cognition.

- A self-selected alternative is provided for students who otherwise might "blow."

- Students internalize self-monitoring.

- Responsible behavior is modeled for other students.

- Class downtime is minimized during upsets.

- Students are more apt to accept consequences following a cool down.

Recommended for...

Disruption
Aggression, Confrontation

Position
Angry, Control-Seeking

Individual or Class
Both

STEPS

1 Establish Rationale, Model

The teacher shares the rationale for cool down time. The teacher gives examples, discussion quotes, and/or models his/her own cool down procedures. *"We all get angry, but we don't accomplish much when we are out of control. I know that if I say or do things when I am angry, I am likely to regret it later. What I do for myself to cool down is _____."*

2 Cool Down Procedures, Signal

The teacher establishes with the student, or the class as a whole, procedures and a cool down signal. The signal indicates that there is a need to calm down. The signal might be a plastic ice cream cone placed on a student's desk or a simple non-verbal signal. The procedures include going to a pre-established cool down area for a specified amount of time and engaging in pre-established activities such as quite reading, drawing, journaling, and/or relaxation breathing. *"Can we agree that when either of us uses this signal, it will be an indication that a trip is needed to the cool down area to calm down?"*

Cool Down Quotes and Proverbs

While in cool down, students may be asked to read over the following quotes and/or proverbs, select one, and write an essay or draw a picture of what it means to them.

Proverbs

- Control your anger, or it will control you.

- Anger is just one letter short of danger.

- Hot words never resulted in cool judgment.

- A sharp tongue cuts its own throat.

- The greatest remedy for anger is delay.

- If you speak when you're angry, you'll make the best speech you'll ever regret.

- When angry, your mouth and fists work faster than your mind.

- Blowing your stack creates air pollution.

Quotes

"When angry, count to ten before you speak; when very angry, count to a hundred."
— Thomas Jefferson

"Holding anger is like grasping a hot coal with the intent of throwing it at someone else; you are the one who gets burned."
— Buddha

"How much more grievous are the consequences of anger than the causes of it."
— Marcus Aurelius

"Anger is a brief lunacy."
— Horace

"Anger dwells only in the bosom of fools."
— Albert Einstein

"Often, anger is a mask. Behind the mask lies fear, hurt, or desire."
— Spencer Kagan

14.28

Win-Win Discipline. Kagan Publishing • 1 (800) 933-2667 • www.KaganOnline.com

Cautions & Hints

- **Be Proactive.** At the beginning of the school year, set the stage for cool down time. Students learn the rationale and procedures ahead of time. Emphasize that it is a proactive time to allow everyone to calm down before moving into consequences or solutions.

- **Requested Cool Down.** Ideally, students learn to recognize mounting feelings and can request the cool down area when needed. If students are allowed to self-select cool down, a student may use cool down time irresponsibly, using it to get out of doing schoolwork. Thus you may want to establish a signal granting permission to use cool-down.

- **Cool Down Cues.** In collaboration with the students, decide on a verbal or non-verbal cool down signal.

- **Cool Down Location.** Cool Down is usually within the class, but in special circumstances you may partner with another teacher so each has a cool down area in the room of the other. Removing the student from class may be necessary if the student is agitated in response to classroom stimuli, as when students are in a physical fight and refuse to withdraw from each other. Schools may designate an area outside of class for students to cool down. In the school cool down area, students are under the watchful eye of a staff member or administrator. Removal from class is an option of last resort, to be used when other options are not successful or when danger is high. Each teacher needs to know his/her back-up and support options in case a student is creating a dangerous situation or is unable to calm down in the classroom.

- **Class Cool Down.** Immediately following an angry outburst or aggressive incident, let the whole class cool down.

- **Class Cool Down Activities.** Activities that minimize interaction and attention to external stimuli help students cool down. Helpful activities include solo drawing, journaling, and even worksheet work.

  - For a list of dozens of ways to Cool Down, see **Chapter 8. Preventative Procedures: The Seven Positions.**

- **Cool Down Music.** Music at 60 beats a minute during the solo activities calms the class. See Music for the Mind Series, **Part VII, Resources F.**

Discussion and Journaling Topics

Class Journaling or Discussion Topics

Students can write or discuss the statement: *None of us can control what or how strongly we feel, but all of us can control what we do.*

2. Cool Down Reminder

When emotions show signs of getting out of control, the teacher reminds students that it may lead to needing a cool down.

Ideal Outcomes

- Students learn self-control and self-management of emotions and behaviors.

- The impulse-action chain is broken, inserting cognition.

- Students internalize self-monitoring.

Recommended for...

Disruption
Aggression, Confrontation

Position
Angry, Control-Seeking

Individual or Class
Individual

STEPS

Cool Down Reminder

1 **Cool Down Reminder.**
.With the class as a whole or with an individual student, as emotions escalate, a reminder may be all that is necessary to calm emotions. *"Class, emotions are escalating. I believe we can calm down without having to use the cool down procedure."*
[In private via note, signal, or conversation] *"Bob, I think you can manage your emotions well enough right now so that you will not have to go to the cool down area. Please give it your best try."*

Cautions & Hints

- **Spot the Signs.** Students learn to recognize and respond to early warning signs to prevent emotional melt-downs.

- **Verbal/Non-verbal Cues.** Establish with students verbal or non-verbal cues:
    Signals from teacher: *1) You are approaching need for cool down; 2) Go to cool down now.*
    Signal from student to teacher: *May I go to cool down?*

Cool Down Reminder

3. Implementing Cool Down

Teacher instructs the students to implement the pre-established cool down procedures.

Ideal Outcomes

- Student and teacher are allowed to cool down when emotions are running hot.

- Responsible behavior is modeled for other students.

- Class downtime is minimized during upsets.

- Students are more apt to accept consequences following a cool down.

Recommended for...

Disruption
Aggression, Confrontation

Position
Angry, Control-Seeking

Individual or Class
Individual

STEPS

1 **Implement Cool Down.**
The teacher signals that an individual or the class is to implement pre-established cool down procedures. *"Class, we all need to use the three-minute cool down. Everyone shut your eyes while I put on our cool down music. Remember, I want you to visit that calm relaxed place we have set up." "Jake, please take at least five minutes in the cool down area. I'm sure you will be much more focused after that."*

2 **Complete Cool Down Form.**
While in Cool Down, students may be asked to fill out a Cool Down Form (14.34). For younger students the Cool Down Form can be administered orally. For older students it can be the topic for a discussion.

Cautions & Hints

• **Cool Down Is Not a Punishment.** Cool Down is a time to gain self-control and focus. Your tone should indicate that cool down is a positive action for the student to take in the face of excess energy or escalating emotions.

• **Cool Down vs. Time Out.** Time out may be a visit to the principal's office because the student has demonstrated inability to cool down and/or work with others. Cool down in contrast is a procedure students can "own." It is a positive procedure to help students gain control of their emotions and/or focus their energy.

• **Cool Down Is Not an Excuse for Missed Work.** Students are held responsible for the work in class while they were in the cool down area.

• **Cool Down Form.** If appropriate, while in cool down time students fill out a Cool Down Form (14.34). After a student fills out the form, meet with him/her to discuss responses and formulate future choices.

The Cool Down Form is designed to have students reflect on their disruptive behavior and plan solutions for future situations. The students think about what they wanted in the situation and what they could do next time to achieve what they want through responsible behavior. The form also has them think about what help they could use in choosing responsible behavior and in being ready to go back to class.

The Cool Down Form is especially effective with students seeking control, because it actively involves students in the discipline process and gives them some control in a positive way. It is helpful also for angry students because it gets them to focus on cognition rather than emotion. It is important for the teacher or another adult to process the form with the student afterwards and to give students support in making more responsible behavior choices. Calming down enough to fill out the form responsibly can be a student's ticket back to class.

Discussion and Journaling Topics

Class Discussion Topic
To get the whole class to take "the same-side" with the student after an emotional outburst, you might have the class discuss how we all have emotions and how sometimes they are so strong we feel we just have to act on them. They can discuss what to do when emotions run so strong that we feel we might do something we would regret.

Cool Down Form

Name _____

Date _____

Time _____

■ Did I ask for cool down time, or was I asked to go to cool down?
  ☐ I asked
  ☐ I was asked

■ What was going on **before** I began to "heat up?"

■ What was the **very first thing** that got to me?

■ What did I **feel like doing**?

■ What **did I do**?

■ What did I do to **control** my impulses?

■ What else **could I have done**?

■ What could the teacher have done to help me?

■ What would have been the very best outcome for me?

■ What is the best **Win-Win solution** I can think of — what solution would make everyone feel good?

■ What do I plan to do **next time** I begin to "heat up?"

■ What is the most helpful question on this form? Why?

Signature _____

Coupons

Students are reminded to trade one of their limited number of pre-established coupons for "too frequent" behavior. The coupon approach helps the student monitor and limit disruptive behavior, fostering self-control. *"Thank you for using your coupon wisely."*

1. Establishing Coupons

A limited supply of coupons is allocated for "too frequent" behaviors. Students are coached in the wise use of their coupons.

Ideal Outcomes

- Students buy-in to the use of coupons.

- Concrete symbols for specific behaviors help students become more self-aware.

- Students monitor and manage themselves more.

- Students internalize self-management and are weaned from coupons.

- There are fewer classroom disruptions.

Recommended for...

Disruption
Breaking the Rules

Position
Attention-Seeking,
Energetic

Individual or Class
Individual

Establishing Coupons

STEPS

1 Meet, Describe, Mirror Disruptive Behavior

In a private follow-up meeting the teacher describes the disruptive behavior and the reason it is a problem. The teacher helps the student to see himself/herself as others do, taking care that the student knows the teacher is on the same-side rather than attacking or criticizing him/her. *"I am on your side and I want to help you. You may not be aware you are sharpening your pencil so often that it is disturbing others. Let me show you."*

2 Agree on Number of Coupons

The teacher and the student agree coupons will be allocated for the behavior and agree on the number of coupons that the student will be able to use each day/period. The student needs to use a coupon in order to choose the behavior. When the coupons are gone, the student must wait until the next day/period for new coupons. *"What is a reasonable number of coupons we can agree upon?"*

3 Support Wise Decisions

The teacher and student discuss how the student can make wise decisions about using coupons. A plan is developed. *"I know you will make good decisions about when to use your coupons. Sounds like you have a good plan."*

4 Follow-Up

The teacher and the student agree on a follow-up meeting time to review success. The teacher encourages the student's progress. *"Let's meet on Friday to see how you are doing. OK?"* *"So, I noticed today you used only two of your coupons. How did that feel? How did that help our class?"*

Establishing Coupons

Cautions & Hints

• **Agreeing on Number of Coupons.** If the student picks an unreasonable number, then say, "Let's talk about what we both can agree is a reasonable number. Forty-seven just doesn't seem reasonable to me. I was thinking more like four."

• **Practice.** When establishing coupons, practice with students how and when to relinquish their coupons and what to do if coupons run out.

• **Structure for Reflection, Self-Regulation.** Make it clear to the student that the goal is to get him/her to self-regulate. For example, for the student who repeatedly asks questions as an attention-seeking gambit, the coupons are introduced as a way to help him/her stop to think about possible answers before asking a question.

2. Implementing Coupons

Students trade one of their limited supply of coupons in exchange for engaging in a "too frequent" behavior.

Ideal Outcomes

■ Students regulate frequency of "too often" behavior.

■ Students become more self-aware.

■ Students internalize self-monitoring and self-management processes.

■ There are fewer classroom disruptions.

Recommended for...

Disruption
Breaking the Rules

Position
Attention-Seeking, Energetic

Individual or Class
Individual

STEPS

1 Redeem a Coupon.

The student gives the teacher one coupon, or deposits it in a coupon box in exchange for the right to engage in a behavior governed by the use of coupons.

Cautions & Hints

• **Target Behaviors.** Coupons work well for limiting the number of times a student engages in behaviors that are acceptable but overused. It is the overuse of the behavior that is disruptive; the behavior itself would otherwise be acceptable. For example, we might wish for the student to regulate how often he/she asks questions, asks for help, sharpens pencils, visits the restroom, or visits the school counselor.

• **Coupon Reminders.** It may be helpful to remind a student that he/she is "on coupons." Some students will need reminders of when or how to use coupons.

"Alice [as she enters class], *please pick up your coupons for today. I know you will use them wisely."*

"Alice [as she gets up to sharpen pencil], *please deposit one of your coupons in the bank. Thank you."*

• **Wean the Student from Coupons.** From the start, indicate coupons are a temporary crutch — the goal is self-regulation. Work with the student to develop a time line to end his/her use of coupons.

Discussion and Journaling Topics

One-on-One Discussion Topics

How do you feel about using coupons? Are you developing some strategies to limit the number of times you need to use a coupon? Do the coupons help you become aware of how often you _______?

Journaling or Team Discussion Topic

In a way, coupons are like money. We trade money for something we want and we trade coupons for something we want. How are coupons similar to money, and how are they different?

Cues: Verbal And Non-verbal

The teacher uses pre-established verbal or non-verbal cues to elicit appropriate behavior. Class cues are established; specific cues may be established for individual students. **Verbal:** *"Class, please take a moment now and look over the class rules chart."* **Non-verbal:** Teacher walks to and looks intently at the class rules chart.

Ideal Outcomes

- Disruptions are ended with minimal downtime.

- Class tone is improved.

- Expectations are clarified.

- Responsible behaviors are labeled, and become more concrete.

- Responsible behaviors are more likely to be remembered.

Recommended for...

Disruption
Aggression, **Breaking the Rules**, Confrontation, Disengaged

Position
Attention-Seeking, Angry, **Energetic,** Bored, Uninformed

Individual or Class
Both

Win-Win Discipline. Kagan Publishing • 1 (800) 933-2667 • www.KaganOnline.com

14.39

Cues: Verbal And Non-verbal

STEPS

1 Pre-establish the Cue(s)

The teacher establishes a verbal or non-verbal cue with the whole class or with an individual student. The cue is a signal to engage in a certain kind of behavior.

"Class, I don't want to talk over your talk, so I will use a quiet signal. When I raise my hand like this, I want all of you to do the same — raise your hands. That will be our quiet signal. When the quiet signal is on, I want all eyes on me; no talking, no writing. I want full attention on me. If someone is not aware the quiet signal is on, I will just wait. It will be your job, not mine, to signal that person to let him/her know the quiet signal is on."

Note: A "Secret Signal" may be established with an individual student. See Replacement Reminder, page 16.18, Step 7. For example:

"James, now that we have agreed that you will use some deep slow breathing to calm down when you are feeling too full of energy, I want to set up a signal with you. It will be our signal that you need to calm down. How about if I look at you and then just put my head on my hand like this? [Teacher brings palm to side of face]. Would that work for you as a signal that it is time to stop, take a few deep slow breaths and calm down?"

"What would be a good cue or reminder next time you are rustling around in your desk? What if I walk over and stand beside you? Will that be enough of a reminder? Would it be OK for me to put my hand on top of your desk if you don't notice me standing there?"

2 Use the Cue

With little or no loss of instructional time, the teacher uses the cue to signal the student(s) to engage in the pre-established behavior.

3 Teacher Monitors

The teacher monitors for responsible behavior.

Cues: Verbal And Non-verbal

Cautions & Hints

- **Additional Signals.** For a description of the many signals used in a Win-Win classroom, see Chapter 18. Win-Win Management.

- **Management Signals.** Management signals include Quiet Signal and Rule Reminders.

- **Teaching Signals.** Think (no talking), Silent Write, Discuss with Your Shoulder Partner, Discuss with Your Face Partner....

- **Student Signals.** Non-verbal signals from students to the teacher can be established. Among the most helpful are "I'm confused," "Please slow down," "I need processing time...."

- **Team Signals.** One of the most helpful signals in the classroom is the team signal called Team Question or Three Before Me. When students are working in their teams, if they have exhausted all their resources and cannot solve a problem or cannot agree, all four students raise their hands to request help from the teacher. The agreement is that no individual student will raise his/her hand. If the student has a question, the student first tries to get it answered in his/her team. Only if the teammates cannot answer the question is the teacher consulted.

Discussion and Journaling Topics

Appreciations
Class, thank you for that quick response to the quiet signal. You are all helping our class run efficiently.

Expectation Reminder

Prior to a possible disruption or at the outset of a disruption, students are reminded of pre-established expectations, procedures, or rules. When a number of students are violating the rules, the teacher may stop the lesson to re-teach the rules. *"Remember the expectations (rules, procedures) we agreed on. Let's take some time now to review how we want out class to be."*

Ideal Outcomes

- Disruptions are prevented in the moment via a brief rule or expectation reminder.

- Future disruptions are prevented by cementing the procedures.

- Students refresh their memory of the expectations.

- Students deepen their understanding of when rules apply.

- Students deepen their understanding of the rationale for rules or expectations.

- Students renew their commitment to following the rules or procedures and to living up to expectations.

- Students think about the effect of their behavior on others.

Recommended for...

Disruption
Aggression, **Breaking the Rules,** Confrontation, Disengaged

Position
Attention-Seeking, Angry, Energetic, **Uninformed**

Individual or Class
Both

STEPS

1 Remind Student(s) of Pre-established Expectations

If an individual student or the class as a whole appears likely to become disruptive, the teacher may remind the student(s) of pre-established expectations (rules, procedures, routines, or contracts). For details on establishing procedures and routines, see Chapter 17. Win-Win Management. *"Carol, can you remember our expectation about promoting learning and not interfering with the learning of others?"*

"Pete, I want you to look at the rule chart. Is there a rule that seems relevant for what you are doing right now? Don't tell me what it is. Show me with your behavior that you understand."

"Susie, what are you doing right now? What would be the responsible thing to do?"

"Class, I want each of you to turn to your shoulder partner and do a RallyRobin, taking turns stating our class expectations. Once you have named all five, decide as a pair which expectation our class is coming close to violating."

Non-verbal Expectation Reminder:
Without saying a word, the teacher walks to the "The Way We Want Our Class to Be" chart and looks at it intently, taking time for students to get the message. *"Class, I am concerned about our behavior right now. Let's stop and think about the expectations we agreed on. Which expectation am I concerned about?"*

"Chris, the basic expectation in this class is that no one will interfere with the learning of anyone else. In what way are you violating that expectation right now?"

Cautions & Hints

If students are unclear about expectations, in a brief sequence the teacher may re-establish expectations using a three step sequence: 1) focus on purpose, 2) practice, and 3) recommit:

- **Focus on Purpose**
Remind students of the purpose of the rule or expectation.

"Class, all of our rules relate back to our mission as a class — to maximize your development, to prepare you to be successful in life. How does the rule, 'Respect the rights of others' help us be successful in our mission?"

"Class, several of you have been tossing paper wads. Let's ask the 'What if question. What if any student was allowed to toss paper wads at any time during a lesson? How would that interfere with our reaching our mission?"

- **Promote Thinking.** In the moment-of-disruption the uninformed student is not thinking about the responsible behavior. To motivate responsible behavior, often all we need to do is prompt the student to think about the responsible thing to do. By repeatedly prompting responsible thinking, we create a habit of mind so, ultimately, students will think about responsible behavior on their own.

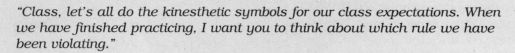

Cautions & Hints (Continued)

- **Practice Expectations**

Have the whole class practice one of the expectation reminders the class has developed.

"Class, let's all do the kinesthetic symbols for our class expectations. When we have finished practicing, I want you to think about which rule we have been violating."

- **Recommit**

Have students state in oral or written form why they commit to following the rules.

"Class, let's all take two or three minutes to put down in one or two sentences why we agree to establish this expectation for our class."

Expectations for "The Way We Want Our Class to Be" are established for the whole class initially when we teach the Win-Win philosophy. See **Chapter 9. Teaching the Win-Win Philosophy.** See also the Breaking the Rules section of **Chapter 6. Preventative Procedures: ABCD Disruptions** and the Uninformed section of **Chapter 8. Preventative Procedures: The Seven Positions.** If it is clear that an expectation reminder or the brief three-step sequence to re-establish expectations described here is not sufficient for an individual or class, the teacher may use a more elaborate follow-up structure to re-establish expectations. See Re-establish Expectations in **Chapter 16. Follow-Up Structures.**

Discussion and Journaling Topics

One-on-One Discussion Topic

Today I had to remind you of our rule about _____. How can we work together so that you remind yourself? How can you become more autonomously responsible?

Class Journaling or Discussion Topics

Rules are everywhere. We drive on the right side of the road. We stop at red lights. If we want to drive a car, we have to be of age and properly insured. We cannot serve alcohol to a minor. Certain drugs are outlawed. We can't take things from a store without paying for them. It is easy to see how rules limit our freedom — to see what they prevent us from doing. But rules also increase our freedom. How do those same rules make us freer? How do rules in the classroom make us freer to learn?

Expectation Reminder

Grandma's Rule

The teacher uses a *"When... then..."* statement to indicate the responsible behavior and the incentive that will follow. The origin of Grandma's Rule[4] is *"When you eat your dinner, then you may have dessert."* *"When you finish your math practice sheet, you can go to the choice table to pick a favorite learning game."*

Ideal Outcomes

■ Students are oriented to the task at hand.

■ Students are motivated to finish a task.

■ Students internalize a self-motivation technique.

■ Students increase impulse control.

Recommended for...

Disruption
Confrontation, **Disengaged**

Position
Attention-Seeking, Avoiding Failure, Angry, Control-Seeking, Energetic, **Bored,** Uninformed

Individual or Class
Both

Grandma's Rule

STEPS

1 State Responsible Behavior

The teacher indicates the responsible behavior. The statement starts with the word "when". *"When you are done with your math..."*

2 State Incentive (What Is in It for the Student?)

The teacher tells the student what the incentive is when the responsible behavior is completed. The statement starts with the word "then." The incentive can be created with the student. *"... then you may have free time on the computer."*

Cautions & Hints

• **Not a Collaborative Solution.** Often Grandma's Rule is merely a stopgap strategy to get students back on task and to motivate them. It does not involve shared responsibility. The "When... then" solution may come entirely from the teacher. Over time, however, use of Grandma's Rule can lead to learned responsibility because students may internalize the process of making fun the pay-off for work. Further, it conveys a same-side orientation: it communicates to students that you know what they would really like to be doing.

Discussion and Journaling Topics

One-on-One Discussion Topic:

After the moment-of-disruption, meet with the student and explain the rationale for Grandma's Rule. In my life, I finish my work before I can sit and read or go outside for a walk with my dog. That way, the fun things are more fun because I have completed my work beforehand. I use the fun things as a reward for doing my work and, that way, I do the work faster and with a better attitude, knowing there is a reward waiting.

Class Journaling or Discussion Topics:

What things are work and what things are fun? How can we make work more fun? Can we give ourselves rewards for finishing our work? Will that make the work more fun?

Grandma's Rule

I-Messages Plus

Calmly informing students of your own feelings is an "I-Message"[5] designed to make students aware of their stimulus value (effect on others). An I-Message Plus adds encouragement to adopt a non-disruptive alternative. *"I feel X when you do Y, and your classmates feel Z. Can you think of a better choice?"*

Ideal Outcomes

- The student becomes more aware of his/her "stimulus value" — the effect he/she is having on others.

- I-messages shift from authoritarian "right-wrong" to "person-to-person" relationships.

- I-messages shift from blame ("you did") to information ("When you do x, I feel y").

- Emphasis is placed on specific behaviors, paving way for change.

- The student can empathize with the teacher and others.

- The teacher maintains a calm, centered position.

- The I-message is a tight frame allowing quick, focused feedback to the disruptive student.

- The I-message avoids escalation of emotion. It helps prevent the disruptive student from feeling rejected.

Recommended for...

Disruption
Aggression, Breaking the Rules,
Disengaged

Position
Attention-Seeking, Avoiding Failure,
Angry, Control-Seeking, **Energetic,** Bored,
Uninformed

Individual or Class
Both

STEPS

1 ## Validate the Position

The teacher starts with a validation of the student. *"Sean, I understand you would like to share..."*

"Bob, this assignment is not the most interesting for you..."

2 ## State How the Disruption Makes You Feel

The teacher states the impact of the disruptive behavior with a "... but I feel _____ when you _____" statement. *"... but I feel annoyed when you talk while others are sharing."*

I-Messages Plus

3 ## Describe Effect of Disruptive Behavior on Classmates

The teacher states the effect the disruptive behavior has on others. *"If you talk while Trish is sharing, others cannot hear her. It is not polite to Trish. It is her turn. You would not want others to interrupt your turn."*

4 ## Redirect to Responsible Behavior to Meet Needs

The teacher helps the student commit to more responsible alternatives that would meet his/her needs without being disruptive. *"What are things you could choose that would allow you to share without interrupting others?"*

"Are there some ways you could make this task more interesting to yourself?"

Cautions & Hints

- **Private Please.** If possible, give I-messages in private.

- **Feedback, not Emotion.** The effective I-message does not give vent to irritation; it tells the student about the irritation. In a calm, non-irritated voice the teacher explains the impact of the student's behavior. By remaining calm while giving an I-message, we avoid the possible escalation of emotion and make it more likely the student can listen to the feedback.

- **Positive I-Messages.** Be sure to communicate the positive impact students are having on you with positive I-messages.

"When you keep trying even when the problems are difficult for you, it makes me feel proud to be a teacher. I know you value what we do in class."

"When all of you give me your full attention as you are doing right now, I feel proud to be a teacher. I know you value learning and what I am teaching you."

Discussion and Journaling Topics

One-on-One Discussion Topic

Today I told you I was irritated when you were talking while Trish was sharing. Have you thought about how that made Trish feel? Have you thought about what you can do apologize? What can you do to make sure that does not happen again?

Class Journaling or Discussion Topics

We all have a "stimulus value." That is, we all affect others. What we wear, how we talk, what we do, has an impact on others. What are some of the things you can do to have a positive impact on others?

Sometimes we say or do something that hurts others, but we do not even know that has happened. What can you do to determine the effect you are having on others?

Language of Choice

Language of choice[6] provides immediate consequences, allowing the disruptive student to make a more responsible choice. *"Your choice is _____ or _____."*

Ideal Outcomes

- The student is oriented toward responsible alternative.

- The student is prompted to reflect on consequences of his/her actions.

- Loss of instructional time is kept to a minimum.

- Expectations of responsible behavior are communicated to the student.

- The teacher is more easily able to control his/her reaction.

- The teacher is provided with a frame for a quick response in the face of disruptive behavior.

Recommended for...

Disruption
Aggression, Breaking the Rules,
Confrontation, Disengaged

Position
Attention-Seeking, **Angry, Control-Seeking,**
Energetic, Bored, Uninformed

Individual or Class
Both

Language of Choice

STEPS

1 Validate Student or Position
This step solidifies an empathetic understanding of the student. When the teacher lets a student know that they are on the Same-Side, positive results can follow. *"There is nothing wrong with getting upset when you make mistakes on the computer......"*

"If I haven't mentioned it lately, you are such a great asset to our class...."

2 State Responsible Behavior
("The responsible choice is _____.")
The teacher states the specific responsible behavior that the student needs to be exhibiting. *"The responsible choice is to use the computer keys appropriately and stop banging on them..."*

"The responsible choice is to stand in line with your hands to your side."

3 State Consequences *("or _____")*
The teacher then states what the consequence (cool down time, loss of privilege) will be if the student does not choose the responsible behavior. *"... or you can do the spreadsheet problems by hand."*

"... or you will need to go to the end of the line."

4 It's Your Choice
The teacher emphasizes that it is the student's option to choose the responsible behavior or the consequence. *"It is your choice: you can choose to use the computer or not."*

5 Encouragement
The teacher encourages the student to choose the responsible behavior. *"I'm sure you can make a responsible choice."*

6 If Non-Verbal, Non-Compliance
"It is evident by your actions and/or behavior that you have chosen to do the spreadsheet problems by hand. Is that correct?"

Cautions & Hints

• **Use Sparingly.** Language of Choice does not involve the student in creating the solution.

• **Attractive Choices.** By giving attractive choices, you make it easier for the student to choose a responsible alternative.

• **Private.** When possible, use Language of Choice without an audience. An audience can be an incentive to "not back down." It is easier to switch to responsible behavior if peers are not watching.

• **Stopgap.** Language of Choice is a quick intervention orienting the student to what he/she is doing and causing the student to take responsibility for the consequences of his/her actions. Nevertheless, it is not a Win-Win solution because it does not involve students proposing alternatives — shared responsibility for the solutions. If you find yourself using Language of Choice often with a student, it may be time for a Responsible Thinking Follow-up.

Cautions & Hints (Continued)

• **Counter-Indicated in Confrontation.** In the heat of a confrontation, Language of Choice can backfire, feeding a confrontation. During a "You can't make me" confrontation, Language of Choice will likely lead to an irresponsible choice because the student is bent on proving that the teacher can't get him/her to make the responsible choice. In the midst of a heated confrontation, the teacher is better off choosing Cool Down, Model It!, I-Messages, or a structure that does not force a choice.

• **Soft Tone.** If the disruption does not call for a forceful response, Language of Choice can be used with a soft tone: *"Please use the science equipment appropriately or you will lose the use of the equipment for today."*

• **Calm Voice.** Even if a student is being confrontational, only use Language of Choice if you think the student is likely to choose the responsible alternative. Take a moment to take a deep breath, pause, and consider carefully what you will say following the "or" of Language of Choice. Then use Language of Choice in a calm voice.

• **No False Threats.** To maintain credibility, when using Language of Choice, whatever comes after the "or" must be something you are willing to follow through with.

• **Avoiding Loss.** Language of Choice is a stop structure, whereas Grandma's Rule is a start structure. With Grandma's Rule we make salient the incentive for finishing a task; with Language of Choice we make salient the loss which will result from persisting in disruptive behavior.

• **Emphasize the Positive.** The emphasis should be on the positive side of the equation, not on the potential loss. OK: *"I'm sure you can return to your seat so we do not have to schedule a meeting with your parents to discuss this."* Not OK: *"If you don't return to your seat, I will be calling your parents to discuss this."*

Responsible Thinking and Responsible Behavior Follow-Ups: If you find yourself using Language of Choice with a student frequently, the student is not internalizing the process. It is time then for a follow-up focused on Responsible Thinking or Responsible Behavior.

Discussion and Journaling Topics

Class Journaling or Discussion Topic
We all make choices every day, and every choice we make has consequences. To some extent, then, we all determine our own fate. What are some choices that you have made recently that have had important consequences for you?

Make a Better Choice

Through Make a Better Choice, the teacher calls for reflection rather than obedience, leaving it to the student to create a more responsible alternative. *"I want you to think of a better choice you could make right now."*

Ideal Outcomes

- Students create solutions, and do not feel like pawns.

- There is greater shared responsibility for the solution.

- Students internalize the reflective process.

- Students make more autonomous responsible choices.

- Students engage in creative thinking.

- Pressure on the teacher is lessened.

Recommended for...

Disruption
Aggression, Breaking the Rules, Disengaged

Position
Attention-Seeking, Avoiding Failure, Angry, Control-Seeking, **Energetic, Bored**

Individual or Class
Both

Make a Better Choice

STEPS

1 Stop!

The teacher tells the student to stop disruptive behavior. *"Catherine, you need to stop throwing food."*

"Class, everyone stop what you are doing right now."

2 Think!

The teacher tells the student to think of better choices. *"Catherine, I want you to think of a better choice you could be making right now."*

"Class, I want each of you to think of a better choice you could be making right now."

3 Please Tell!

The teacher asks the student to verbalize his/her better choices. *"Catherine, please tell me. What is your better choice?"*

"Class, I want each of you to turn to your shoulder partner and share both ways. What is your better choice?"

4 Agree and Act or Disagree and Request Better Choices

The teacher paraphrases the "better choice" and expresses agreement or lack of agreement. *"Catherine, your better choice is to clean up the mess and not to throw food in the cafeteria again. [pause] I agree. Thank you. That is responsible thinking. Please make your better choice now."*

"Catherine, your better choice is to leave the cafeteria right now. [pause] I don't agree, because that would leave the mess for others to clean up. I think you can come up with a better choice yet. What is a better choice?"

"Class, I heard some great choices. Some of the things I heard were _____, _____, and _____. Thank you for your responsible thinking. Now let's align our actions with our thoughts."

Make a Better Choice

14.54

Win-Win Discipline. Kagan Publishing • 1 (800) 933-2667 • www.KaganOnline.com

Cautions & Hints

- **Make It Private.** Work with students in private if possible.

- **Think Time.** Allow students sufficient time to think of their "better choice." Ideally, you maintain patient waiting until they come up with the choice on their own.

- **Written Choice.** If a student needs more time, in some circumstances you may ask the student to sit and write or draw the better choice.

- **Compliment Students.** Appreciate students for their "Responsible Thinking."

Discussion and Journaling Topics

One-on-One Discussion Topic
At any moment we can make responsible choices or irresponsible choices. Why was your behavior in the cafeteria today irresponsible?

Class Journaling or Discussion Topic
What makes a choice responsible or irresponsible? Can you give some examples of each type of choice and tell why it is responsible or irresponsible?

Model It!

Modeling and disclosing one's own responsible behavior (self-control, persistence in the face of difficulty, politeness) helps students identify with the teacher and acquire responsible behaviors. *"Right now, I feel stuck. But I know if I keep tying, I will figure it out."*

Ideal Outcomes

- Helps students accept their own emotions, communicating that everyone at time has emotions one needs to manage.

- Fosters development of self-control, persistence, and other positive behaviors.

- Helps students identify with the teacher.

- Helps students see the effects of their behavior on others.

- Allows the teacher time to calm down.

- Allows students to see a positive model of responsible behaviors.

Recommended for...

Disruption
Aggression, Breaking the Rules, **Confrontation, Disengaged**

Position
Attention-Seeking, Avoiding Failure, **Angry, Control-Seeking,** Energetic, Bored, Uninformed

Individual or Class
Both

STEPS

Note:
In the example below, Model It! is described for controlling teacher anger. Remember, though, Model It! can be used to model a range of positive behaviors.

1 Model It!

In the moment-of-disruption when the teacher feels strong emotions or impulses, he/she places the class on hold for a moment and models using a self-control technique to regain composure and focus. *"Class, I don't want to respond right now. Everyone just wait a few moments. Let me take a few breaths and calm down. Then I can better respond to what just happened."*

2 Discuss Teacher Self-Control Technique

After the teacher and the students have calmed down, the teacher discusses the problem and its solution. The teacher reviews the process, drawing attention to how he/she controlled his/her reaction. *"I get angry (sad, upset, hurt) too. When my emotions are running strong, it helps me to take a moment before I react. When I calm down, I make better decisions. If I act out of my strong emotions, I might regret what I do. Did you notice how I calmed myself down when I was angry?"*

Model It!

Cautions & Hints

- **Modeling.** What a teacher does speaks much louder than what he/she says. Model It! provides a positive model for students to emulate.

- **Model It! for Persistence.** While demonstrating a complicated step in a math algorithm, for example, the teacher might say, *"Now this is the part that is difficult. Sometimes I feel like giving up. So I stop and remind myself of the steps...."* Or *"When I feel like giving up, what I say to myself is _____."*

- **Model It! for Anger Control.** A powerful way to manage anger is to use breathing to calm down. Take a very deep breath through your nose and then let the air out very slowly through your mouth, concentrating on the feeling and sound of the air releasing. Pay attention to your body relaxing as you slowly expel the air. Repeat several times. If taking a deep breath is not your preferred way of calming down, use an alternative approach — one you can share with the students and that they can also use. *"We all get angry sometimes. I am angry right now because aggression is not permitted in our classroom. Let me cool down before I decide what to do."*

- **Model It! for Any Process.** At any point in any lesson, a teacher can use Model It! For example, the teacher models counting to ten to control anger; the teacher models asking what the effect of his/her behavior will be on others; in making a decision regarding the responsible thing to do, the teacher models asking the question, *"What if everyone did that?"* *"When I feel like arguing but know that will not get me what I want, what I do is _____."* *"When I feel really down, one thing I do to cheer myself up is _____."*

The teacher can use Model It! for academic processes as well. *"The mnemonic I use to help myself remember that is _____."* *"Before I begin a letter, I always ask myself, How do I want the recipient to feel after reading this?"* *"After each paragraph that I read, I ask myself if I can summarize it in a sentence."* *"When I read about an historical event, I always think of what is going on in the world today that is similar to that."* *"When I read a new science finding, there are three questions I always ask: 1) What does this say about how things are?; 2) How could this be used?; and 3) What new questions does it raise? Let me model this process for you as I think out loud about this new finding...."*

Discussion and Journaling Topics

One-on-One Discussion Topic
Do you remember when I used deep breathing to calm down? Would you like to learn that technique? Let's try it together.

Class Journaling or Discussion Topics
When emotions run strong, we have the impulse to act. When we act out of anger or fear, we are likely to regret it. Have you ever acted out of strong emotion and regretted it later? What are ways you know to calm yourself down when emotions are strong?

Picture It Right!

The class or an individual takes responsibility for imagining responsible alternatives as they pause, close their eyes, and picture it right. *"If we were at our very best right now, how would it look?"*

Ideal Outcomes

- Students develop ability to envision the responsible alternative.

- Students feel proactively responsible.

- Students develop creative thinking skills.

- The "Shared Responsibility" pillar of Win-Win is reinforced.

- Compliance with the responsible alternative is dramatically increased.

- Meta-communication: You are responsible, capable, creative, independent.

- Pressure is taken off the teacher.

- The teacher is a facilitator rather than a disciplinarian.

Recommended for...

Disruption
Aggression, Breaking the Rules, Disengaged

Position
Attention-Seeking, Avoiding Failure, **Angry,** Control-Seeking, **Energetic**

Individual or Class
Both

Picture It Right!

STEPS

1 Stop!
The teacher announces things are not going right. *"Right now our class is not functioning at its best. I want everyone to stop. Put you hands on your desk. Take a breath. Close your eyes."*

2 Picture It Right!
The teacher gives students time to imagine a better alternative. *"If we were working at our best to maximize learning, how would our class look? What would you be doing? Take time to picture it right."*

3 Share
The teacher has the students share their vision with the teacher. *"Let me hear your vision. What is your picture of how we would be at our best?"*

4 Align
The teacher asks students to align their actions with their picture. *"Ok! Let's start again, but let's keep our vision in mind. Let's be the best we can be."*

Cautions & Hints

• **Quiet Stop.** In the first step, the teacher does not yell "Stop!"; rather, the teacher uses a pre-established quiet signal such as a raised hand or a verbal response such as *"If you can hear me, clap once... If you can hear me, clap twice..."*

• **Give Students Time.** Don't rush through the Picture It Right step. Give students time to establish a firm vision.

• **Guided Picture It Right!** For younger and uninformed students you may need to guide the picture while they have their eyes shut, using phrases like:
"Everyone is working well."
"No one is disturbing anyone else."
"Everyone has his/her hands to themselves."
"We are all having fun learning."

• **Correct or Provide a Picture.** If the student shares an inappropriate or inadequate picture, you may need to correct or supplement. *"That is not exactly what I had in mind. My picture is more like...."* Or *"Let's get serious for a moment...."*

• **Reinforce the Picture.** When students have turned to responsible behavior following Picture It Right!, reinforce their responsible behaviors with comments like *"I see your picture is working."* *"You really did picture it right!"*

Discussion and Journaling Topics

One-on-One Discussion Topics
Did it help you to get a picture of working at your best?" "Could you use Picture It Right on your own to help you? When?

Class Journaling or Discussion Topic
Athletes and dancers perform better when they take time to close their eyes and picture themselves doing their very best. Sometimes I ask you to Picture It Right. Why does it work?

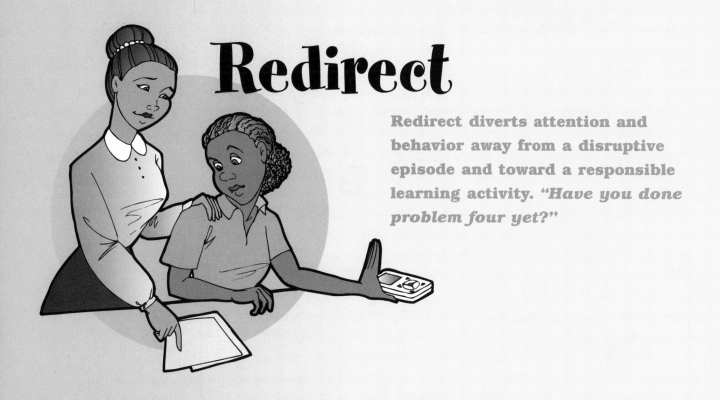

Redirect

Redirect diverts attention and behavior away from a disruptive episode and toward a responsible learning activity. *"Have you done problem four yet?"*

Ideal Outcomes

- Students turn from disruptive to responsible behavior.

- Students distinguish responsible from irresponsible behavior.

- Students learn to monitor their own off-task behavior.

- Off-task behavior is minimized.

Recommended for...

Disruption
Breaking the Rules, Disengaged

Position
Attention-Seeking, Angry,
Energetic, Bored

Individual or Class
Individual

Redirect

STEPS

1 Redirection

With a simple phrase the teacher redirects the off-task student to responsible behavior. *"What you need to be doing right now is _____."*

"The place you need to be right now is _____."

"We have not finished diagramming this sentence."

"We all need to focus on _____."

"Mary, remember our talk on replacement behavior. Now is a time you could be practicing replacement."

2 Monitor

The teacher monitors for responsible behavior.

Cautions & Hints

• **Tone.** The student will be more willing to redirect behavior if he/she feels that his/her position is truly validated — if he/she feels received. We can validate the position without validating the off-task behavior.

• **Be Brief.** Redirect usually takes but a few seconds. As a teacher walks through the class, she sees Robert doodling. Without even stopping she says, "Robert, what we are focusing on now is _____."

• **Replacement Reminder.** If you have had a follow-up with a student to develop replacement behavior for disruptive behavior, a redirect might be to simply remind him/her of the replacement behavior you and he/she have practiced. In some cases, a verbal or non-verbal cue may be established to make the Replacement Reminder quick and effective.

• **Responsible Thinking Reminders.** Redirect may take the form of reminding students of any of the pre-established Responsible Thinking Approaches. The three approaches most favored in Win-Win are: 1) Is your behavior leading to a Win-Win?; 2) What if everyone acted that way?; and 3) Would you like to be treated that way?

1) Robert, will what you are doing right now really get you and others what they want?
2) Stewart, what if everyone shouted out without raising his/her hand to be called on?
3) Tim, would you like to be treated that way?

• **Redirect vs. Right Now Validation.** Redirect is like Right Now Validation, without the validation of student position. It can be used when the student position is not clear or when a very brief intervention is necessary. Generally, though, we align our class with the Win-Win philosophy more if we take a moment to validate student position. Right Now Validation is generally preferable to a simple Redirect.

Discussion and Journaling Topics

Discussion or Journaling Topic
Sometimes we get off task and only later realize we have been off task. What are some of the things that lead you to get off task? How can you monitor yourself? What helps you stay on task? How does staying on task help you reach your goals?

Restart

When the class is out of control, like a computer that has crashed, it is time to Restart.[7] We stop talking, stop doing, pause, see a positive and negative model by the teacher, see a positive model by a classmate, and then restart. *"Stop! Look! Listen!"*

Ideal Outcomes

- Students see the need for more responsible behavior.

- Students see and understand a positive model.

- Negative behavior sequences are interrupted; positive sequences are substituted.

- The teacher regains control.

Recommended for...

Disruption
Aggression, **Breaking the Rules,** Confrontation, **Disengaged**

Position
Attention-Seeking, Angry, Control-Seeking, **Energetic, Bored,** Uninformed

Individual or Class
Class

Restart

STEPS

1 Stop! Look! Listen!

The teacher interrupts the ongoing behavior and waits to get full attention from every member of the class. *"Ok, I need everyone's eyes up here. Stop! Look! Listen!"* [Pause. Wait until all students pay full attention].

2 Direct Instruction: Desired Behavior

The teacher talks through the desired procedure or responsible behavior. *"Who is speaking right now? [The teacher points to himself/herself.] And when someone is talking, where should your eyes be? Attention to a speaker is a form of respect; ignoring someone is a form of disrespect. If we are to maximize learning in this classroom, we all need to show respect to one another."*

3 Positive Teacher Model

The teacher models the desired behavior. If the desired behavior involves interaction, the teacher selects a student and models the behavior in interaction with that student.

The teacher selects a student and asks him/her to start talking about what he/she did after school yesterday. The teacher models being a good listener by making eye contact, orienting toward the student, nodding, and showing understanding.

4 Negative Teacher Model

The teacher selects a student and asks him/her to start talking about what he/she did after school yesterday. The teacher models being an inattentive listener by looking away, not making eye contact, not orienting toward the student, not nodding, and showing no interest. *"Now watch me this time."* [The teacher models lack of listening.] *"How does it feel when someone is not listening to you? Is he/she showing respect or disrespect?"*

5 Positive Student Model

The teacher asks two students to stand up and for one to talk about his/her family. The teacher instructs the class to determine if the other student is a good listener. *"While Susie is talking, I want you to watch Jane to see if she is a good listener."* [The teacher whispers to Jane to be as good a listener as she can — to use eye contact and to pay full attention.]

6 Derive Rationale

The teacher has students derive the rationale for the responsible behavior. *"Class, I want you to do a RoundRobin in your teams, each in turn saying one reason good listening helps our class reach its goals."*

7 Restart

The teacher tells the students to start their activity again, practicing what has been modeled. *"Class, I think we are ready to restart. Let's practice being good listeners."*

Restart

Cautions & Hints

- **Modeling Is Key.** What we do imprints a positive model far more strongly than what we say.

- **Plus-Minus-Plus.** Effective modeling shows students what to do and what not to do. It has a plus, minus, plus sequence. First, the teacher models the responsible behavior. Then the teacher distinguishes that from the disruptive behavior by modeling the irresponsible behavior. Finally, the teacher or student(s) models the responsible behavior again.

Discussion and Journaling Topics

Class Discussion and Journaling Topic
Today we modeled good listening. What are some of the ways to show you are listening? How does it make the other person feel when he/she knows you are listening? How does it help you to be a good listener?

Restructure the Task

The teacher restructures the learning task to stimulate greater engagement. *"Let's take this part a step at a time."*

Ideal Outcomes

- Students have greater confidence in success.
- Students have greater joy in learning.
- Students have less rationalization of fear of failure.

- Students show less off-task behavior.
- Students show higher achievement.

Recommended for...

Disruption
Disengaged

Position
Avoiding Failure, Energetic, Bored, Uninformed

Individual or Class
Both

Restructure the Task

STEPS

1 Monitor Student Progress

While students are engaged in a learning task, the teacher monitors progress by walking around and observing and/or interacting with students. *"How is it going? What steps do you find easy? What steps do you find difficult?"*

2 Restructure the Task

The teacher restructures the task to ensure success, either for an individual student, a group of students, or for the whole class. Usually the restructuring is breaking a difficult part of the task into "bite-sized pieces." *"I see some of you are having trouble with this step. I can see why. I think we are trying to do too much at once. Let's take this part a step at a time."* [Teacher demonstrates.]

3 Re-engage the Students

The teacher reinitiates restructured task and monitors student performance.

Cautions & Hints

• **Watch for Rationalizations.** When students say, *"I won't do this,"* *"This is dumb,"* or *"This is boring,"* often they are rationalizing a fear of failure. It is more painful to admit *"I'm not sure I can do this"* than to say *"This is stupid."* When students fear failure, the first response of a Win-Win teacher is to restructure the task so all students see they can succeed.

• **Ways to Restructure.** There are a number of options in restructuring a task, so all students perceive they can be successful. Options include:
  • **Re-motivate,** emphasizing how the learning will empower the student(s).
  • **Re-teach,** emphasizing the procedures students are finding difficult.
  • Break the task into **Bite-Sized Pieces**.
  • **Distribute the Practice** (two 15 minute sessions add up to much more learning than one 30 minute session, and with fewer frustrations and discipline problems).
  • Teach to each of the different **Multiple Intelligences**.
  • Use any number of **Cooperative Learning Structures** that involve peer coaching, such as Team-Pair-Solo; Pairs Check; RallyCoach; Boss/Secretary; Telephone; See One-Do One-Teach One; Showdown; and Numbered Heads Together.[8]

Discussion and Journaling Topics

One-on-One Discussion Topic

Some of us like to learn by practicing alone, others like to learn with a partner, others yet in a team. How do you like to learn best?

Class Journaling or Discussion Topics

If I had to move 20 heavy boxes, I might give up. It would be too hard. But if I broke the task up, moving just two boxes a day for ten days, the task would be easy. When does it make sense to break a task into bite-sized pieces? Do you do that in your life? When? Is it easier to do all your homework at once, or half during study hall and half at home? When is it foolish to break a task up and not do it all at once?

Right Now Validation

The teacher acknowledges and validates the student or class position and then directs the student to more responsible behavior. *"Right now you are feeling _____. That's OK, but what you need to do is _____."*

Ideal Outcomes

- Students feel understood, validated — the same-side orientation is strengthened.

- Students gain greater acceptance of themselves.

- Students focus on responsible behaviors.

- Students learn a sequence of steps to follow when strong emotions or excess energy diverts them from the learning task: to autonomously check in with themselves, to acknowledge their feelings or energy, and then to refocus on the learning task.

Recommended for...

Disruption
Aggression, Breaking the Rules, Confrontation, Disengaged

Position
Attention-Seeking, Avoiding Failure, Angry, Control-Seeking, Energetic, Bored, Uninformed

Individual or Class
Both

STEPS

1 Validate the Student's Position

The teacher acknowledges and validates the student's position by saying something like:

"It seems that you are angry about this. That is understandable. We all feel angry at times...."

"Right now you are exploding with energy. That is great. I wish I had that much energy.... "

"I know this is not the most exciting assignment you have ever done...."

"I understand it would be fun for you to debate this with me now...."

"I know it might be more interesting to_____...."

2 Communicate that Disruptive Behavior Is Unacceptable

The teacher communicates that disruptive behavior violates rules or expectations for the class. *"Although I understand how angry you are, we have all agreed to maintain a safe class, so I cannot allow you to throw things."*

3 Request Responsible Behavior

The teacher redirects the student to the responsible behavior with a statement like:

"What you need to do is _____."

"Would you please _____."

4 Offer Support

The teacher offers support for the responsible behavior. *"Is there anything I can do to help you?"*

"Can I _____ to help you?"

Right Now Validation

Cautions & Hints

• **Genuine Validations.** Take a moment to place yourself in the student's shoes: remember a time you felt like the student is feeling.

• **Non-verbal Validation.** What we do speaks louder than what we say. Approximately 80 percent of communication is non-verbal. Saying you understand while your arms are crossed and your facial expression is fixed in a frown is not validation. Be congruent. Don't try to validate if you cannot put yourself in a same-side position.

• **Use Validation Gambits.**

"I can remember a time when I…"

"Sometimes I feel…"

"I can understand how you feel…"

"I've been there too…"

"Wow! You are really feeling… That is OK; we all feel that way sometimes."

"Everyone feels… sometimes."

• **Check for Understanding.** After requesting responsible behavior, check for understanding.

"Can you tell me in your own words what I asked you to do?"

Discussion and Journaling Topics

One-on-One Discussion Topics
Have you ever felt sad or angry, but knew you had a job to do and went ahead and completed the job without letting your feelings get in the way?

Have you ever had so much energy you just wanted to run and jump, but you knew what you needed to do was to sit down and focus on a task?

Class Journaling or Discussion Topic
Who is stronger: the person who is sad or angry and stops a task to focus on those feelings, or the person who keeps focused on the task? Why?

Schedule a Follow-Up

In order not to disrupt the class while implementing the three pillars, a follow-up meeting with the student is scheduled. *"We need to talk this through. Let's meet...."*

Ideal Outcomes

- Loss of instructional time is minimized.

- The student feels that his/her position is validated.

- Students understand the teacher takes their behavior seriously.

- The student learns that he/she can be heard, but without interrupting the learning process.

- A time and place is established so the three pillars can be implemented.

Recommended for...

Disruption
Aggression, Breaking the Rules, Confrontation, Disengaged

Position
Attention-Seeking, Avoiding Failure, Angry, Control-Seeking, Energetic, Bored, Uninformed

Individual or Class
Individual

Schedule a Follow-Up

STEPS

1 Validate Student's Position

Even if the student is attempting to start an argument with the teacher, the teacher validates the student's position, saying something like:
"I can tell you are upset and..."

"It seems that you feel this is really unfair and..."

2 Indicate Willingness to Discuss

The teacher indicates that he/she would like to discuss the matter with the student when the lesson is finished. *"... we can discuss this later."*

"... we need to talk this through."

3 Offer Choice of Follow-Up Time

The teacher suggests an appropriate time and place for a follow-up, giving a choice of time, if possible. *"I can meet with you at 9:00 or 11:00. Which do you prefer?"*

4 Conduct Follow-Up

The teacher and the student meet at the agreed time for the appropriate follow-up.

Cautions & Hints

- **Validation Takes the Wind Out.** A student will almost always calm down once he/she feels heard. Seek to understand before trying to be understood. For example, if a student who wants to argue about what he/she perceives as an unfair grade, don't first focus on why the grade is fair. Rather, first take a same-side position, *"I can see you feel strongly that the grade was unfair,"* and then request a follow-up. *"Let's schedule a follow-up to discuss this."* When the student feels understood, an argument or prolonged discussion is far less likely.

- **Choice Diffuses the Confrontation.** By giving the student a choice of times to meet, he/she is empowered and attention moves to the choice and away from the confrontation.

- **Diffusing the Dynamics.** Scheduling a follow-up avoids a power play in the moment and changes the dynamics in the classroom. When students are provoking power struggles, they are choosing the time, the place, the issue and the audience — and are doing all this when their feelings are running strong. Scheduling a follow-up gives you and the student an opportunity to defer the discussion to a time when the lesson is not being disrupted and the feelings have calmed down.

- **When a Student Refuses to Meet.** If a student refuses to meet for a follow-up, we make it clear that he/she cannot refuse without consequences. *"I would much rather meet with you alone than to have to schedule a meeting with you, your parents, and the principal."*

Discussion and Journaling Topics

One-on-One Discussion Topics
Does it feel different for us to meet when it is just the two of us in private rather than when the whole class is watching? Does this private meeting make it more likely we can reach a Win-Win solution?"

Class Journaling or Discussion Topics
Sometimes in class I will ask for an individual follow-up to meet with you privately after class or before. How does that make you feel? Do you look forward to a private chat, or is it something you dread? What could make the process easier for you? What are the advantages of a private meeting rather than discussion during class time?

Table the Matter

The teacher uses Table the Matter[9] to acknowledge the need to meet and discuss, while allowing time for emotions to settle down and for student and teacher reflection before meeting. *"Let's give this a rest for now. We can talk about it later when we are both calm."*

Ideal Outcomes

- Class disruption is minimized.

- The meeting occurs after emotions have cooled down.

- The teacher has a chance to think of options.

- The teacher maintains a same-side orientation, even during a confrontation.

- The student feels his/her issues will be taken seriously.

- Table the Matter models a positive process students can internalize: not making decisions in the heat of a confrontation.

- The student learns self-control.

Recommended for...

Disruption
Aggression, **Confrontation**

Position
Angry, Control-Seeking

Individual or Class
Both

STEPS

1 Acknowledge the Student's Feelings

The teacher acknowledges the student's feelings, using a validating tone and/or phrase. *"You are really angry about this."*

"I understand you feel the grade was unfair."

2 Indicate Need to Reschedule

The teacher makes a firm, but friendly statement indicating that this is not an appropriate time to discuss the problem. *"This is not an appropriate time to discuss this..."*

"I can't stop the lesson to discuss this now..."

3 Suggest Appropriate Time

The teacher makes a statement about when an appropriate time might be to discuss the matter. *"... but, I will be happy to discuss this with you after the lesson."*

"Let's meet right after school to talk this over. I'm sure we can find a solution."

"Your concerns are important. I look forward to working out a solution with you."

4 Meet with the Student

In a follow-up the teacher meets with the student to discuss and resolve the problem at a time that does not interrupt the learning process. Begin the follow-up by acknowledging how much better it is to talk after emotions have cooled down. Continue to validate the student's position, without necessarily accepting his/her point of view or request. *"I understand how hard you worked on the project and how disappointed you are that after all that work you received a poor grade. That must feel unfair. I wish I could give grades based on effort only. I really do appreciate your effort. But we have agreed to grade based on our rubric. Let's review the rubric we agreed on...."*

Table the Matter

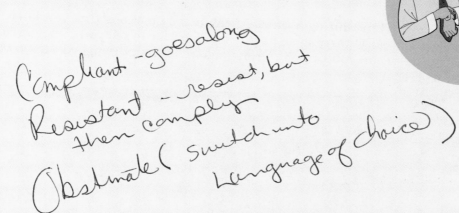

Compliant - goes along
Resistant - resist, but then comply
Obstinate (switch into
Language of choice)

Cautions & Hints

• **Voice.** The teacher uses a short, firm, but friendly tone, letting the student know that instructional time is not the appropriate time to discuss problems.

• **Jot It Down.** The teacher indicates in writing his/her commitment to dealing with the issue.

"This is very important. I want to be sure we deal with this later. Let me jot down a note to myself now, so we don't forget."

• **To You... To Me.** Often the "To You... To Me" structure (14.79) is useful in the follow-up, validating the student position, but communicating that other points of view are possible.

• **Self Disclosure.** Let the student know you are using Table the Matter to control your own reaction.

"I'm upset right now, so we will table this until later. That way, we will make a much wiser decision."

Discussion and Journaling Topics

One-on-One Discussion Topic
OK, let's try switching roles for a moment. I will first try to place my self in your situation and express your feelings and point of view. Then you can tell me if I have it right. Then you can try to place yourself in my position and see if you can say what I am thinking and feeling.

Class Journaling or Discussion Topics
Have you ever been really frustrated by a problem, try and try, but just not be able to solve it? Finally, you give up. Later you come back to the problem and it practically solves itself. Have you ever said to yourself, "Why didn't I see that in the first place?" Which kinds of problems are good to give up on and come back to later? When is it bad to give up on a problem, saying you will come back to it later?

Have you ever said or done something during a time of heightened emotions that you later regretted? What are some of the early warning signs you can look for to tell you to be careful when emotions are intense? How can you prevent strong emotions from driving you to do or say something you will later regret?

Target, Stop, Do

Target, Stop, Do[10] is a very brief, focused, forceful sequence, designed to get the disruptive student's attention, inform the student what he/she needs to stop doing, and redirect the student to what he/she needs to do. *"Susie, Right now you are doing _____, you need to be doing _____."*

Ideal Outcomes

■ Target, Stop, Do quickly focuses the student's attention.

■ The student receives immediate feedback for his/her unacceptable disruptive behavior, increasing self-awareness.

■ The student receives clear immediate input as to the responsible alternative.

■ The student learns to self-monitor and recognize his/her own off-task behavior.

■ The teacher and other students are free to focus on the learning task.

■ Nagging by the teacher is avoided.

■ Target, Stop, Do prevents inadvertently reinforcing disruptive behavior by not giving prolonged attention to the student in the moment-of-disruption.

■ Loss of instructional time is minimized.

Recommended for...

Disruption
Aggression, Breaking the Rules,
Disengaged

Position
Attention-Seeking, Avoiding Failure,
Angry, Control-Seeking, Energetic,
Bored, Uninformed

Individual or Class
Both

Target, Stop, Do

STEPS

1 Privately Target Student's Name

The teacher approaches the student and in private says the student's name.
(TARGET) *"Sally........."*

2 Stop Disruptive Behavior

The teacher asks student to stop the disruptive behavior, and names it specifically.
(STOP) *"Stop pulling Laurie's hair."*

3 State Responsible Behavior

The teacher states the responsible behavior on which the student needs to focus.
(DO) *"You need to work on your English assignment."*

4 Thank You!

The teacher watches for responsible behavior and thanks the student.
"Sally, I appreciate how you are helping us meet our goal of creating a safe classroom."

"Thank you, Laurie. You are helping me and the class by _____."

Cautions & Hints

• **Use Sparingly.** Target, Stop, Do is a powerful sequence that can change behavior quickly. It should not be used often for two reasons: 1) If used too often, it loses its power; 2) It is not a Win-Win solution because it does not communicate a Same-Side orientation and is not a Collaborative Solution. If you find yourself using Target, Stop, Do often with a student, it probably indicates need for a follow-up like Responsible Thinking or Same-Side Chat.

• **Private, Please.** Use Target, Stop, Do as privately as possible. Walk over to the student and use Target, Stop, Do in a stern, but private voice. As much as possible, we want to avoid public embarrassment.

• **Voice.** The teacher uses a loud, clear, firm, commanding voice. Target, Stop, Do will not be effective if the teacher has a pleading voice or if the tone sounds like a request. The voice, however, shifts to a soft accepting tone for the thank-you when the student adopts the responsible behavior.

Discussion and Journaling Topics

One-on-One Discussion Topics
What would happen if everyone _____? Why was your behavior not appropriate? How do you think _____ [others affected] felt when you _____?

Class Journaling or Discussion Topics
At any moment we can choose responsible or irresponsible behaviors. Fold a piece of paper in half and label the two columns responsible and irresponsible. Each team will pick a different setting like "in the store," "at a football game," "during math time," or "during dinner" and take turns adding items to the two columns. Be sure you have the same number of items in each of the two columns.

Win-Win Discipline. Kagan Publishing • 1 (800) 933-2667 • www.KaganOnline.com

14.78

To You...
To Me

To You... To Me[11] acknowledges the student's perspective and informs him/her of the teacher's perspective. In this way the teacher communicates understanding and facilitates a perspective shift in the student. *"To you, this lesson may be boring; to me, it is important because...."*

Ideal Outcomes

■ The student feels his/her point of view is accepted and dignified.

■ The disruptive student sees things from another's perspective.

■ Empathy is fostered.

■ It is a statement no one can argue with: a statement about your feelings.

■ The encounter sidesteps a debate, reorienting the encounter toward sharing points of view.

■ Argument is short-circuited.

■ Teacher and student reactions are controlled.

■ The student sees a model of honest expression of feelings.

■ The student experiences a model of agreeing to disagree, accepting diversity of opinions.

Recommended for...

Disruption
Confrontation

Position
Control-Seeking, Bored

Individual or Class
Individual

STEPS

To You... To Me

1 **To You...**
The teacher paraphrases his/her understanding of the student's perspective in the problem situation using a "To you..." statement. *"To you this lesson might seem dumb,..."*

2 **To Me...**
The teacher tells the student what the teacher's perspective is of the problem situation, using a "To me..." statement. *"... to me this is an important piece we need to learn before we can understand the next step."*

"... to me this assignment is an important step in learning a skill that will help you many times throughout your life."

To You... To Me

Cautions & Hints

• **Voice.** Your voice is firm. You convey with conviction your point of view without trying to change the point of view of the student.

• **Proactive, not Reactive.** You refuse to be drawn into a debate. You calmly accept the student's statement as his/her point of view, but then state your own. A statement of belief is not open to debate; it is merely a statement of your own point of view.

• **Refusing the Invitation.** A statement like "This class is boring," or "You really suck as a teacher" is an invitation to argue or debate. With a calm "To you _____; To me _____," you simply decline to accept the invitation, being proactive rather than reactive.

• **Same-Side Chat.** A same-side chat is the best follow-up to establish rapport and a shared perspective.

• **Disagreeing Politely.** When we have found it necessary to use To Me... To You, it is often because a student has not learned the skill of disagreeing politely.

Discussion and Journaling Topics

One-on-One Discussion Topics

Today you said this class was boring. I would really like for it to be interesting for you. Could we work together to find ways to make it work for you?

Today you said the assignment was stupid. I think I understand why you said that. I would like us to explore ways in which these skills may be of use to you in your life. Let's start by talking about what you would like to do when you get out of school....

Journaling or Team Discussion Topics

Everyone has different perspectives. Let's make a Placemat. Label the areas "One, Two, Three, and All." In your teams take turns making statements, and then poll each other to see where to write the statement. If two people believe it, write it in the Two section; if all four of you on the team believe it, then write it in the All section. Try to find statements that will go in each area of the Placemat.

Sample Consensus Placemat

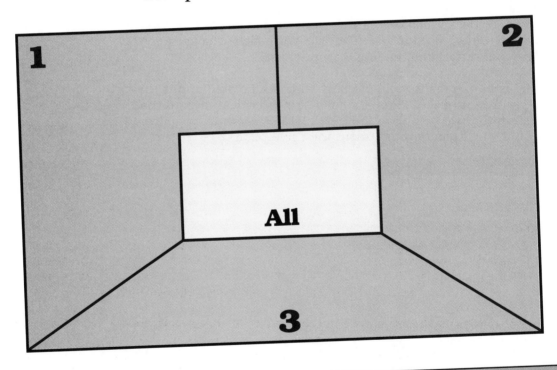

Moment-of-Disruption Structures: Step-by-Step Solutions

In the moment-of-disruption, we need proven strategies to quickly end the disruption. Ideally, we communicate an acceptance of the student's position while rejecting the disruptive behavior. In the heat of a disruption it is essential to have well-prepared responses. Thus the critical importance of structures, complete with their steps and their gambits.

For the Win-Win teacher, even the most efficient and graceful ending of a disruption is a beginning, not an end. The disruption is a clue. Disruptions indicate we need to re-examine our preventative procedures. No matter how quickly and efficiently we end a disruption, had the disruption been prevented, there would have been less down-time and a more positive class tone. Thus, while moment-of-disruption structures are necessary tools in every teacher's toolbox, they are tools experienced Win-Win teachers seldom need to use. The Win-Win teacher focuses on preventing rather than ending disruptions.

In the heat of a disruption, often we may not be able to put the three pillars in place. Thus, the follow-up is critical. It is to that question that we turn to in the next chapter: How do we follow-up after the disruption to cement the three pillars?

References

[1] Acknowledge Student Power is a strategy described by Albert, L. *Cooperative Discipline.* Circle Pines, MN: American Guidance Service, 1996.

[2] Black, D., Downs, J., Brown, L. & Wells, P. *Boys' Town.* Boys Town, NE: Father Flanagan's Boys' Home, 1984.

[3] A discussion of effective use of time-out may be found in Glasser, W. *The Quality School.* New York, NY: Harper Perennial, 1992.

[4] Grandma's Rule is a strategy described by Jones, J. T. & Jones, F. H. *Positive Classroom Discipline.* Santa Cruz, CA: Fredric H. Jones & Associates, Inc., 2000.

[5] I-Messages is a strategy described by: Gordon, T. *Teacher Effectiveness Training.* New York: David Mckay, 1987. & Curwin, R. & Mendler, A. N. *Discipline with Dignity.* Alexandria, VA: Association for Supervision and Curriculum Development, 1988.

[6] Language of Choice is a strategy described by Albert, L. *Cooperative Discipline.* Circle Pines, MN: American Guidance Service, 1996.

[7] Restart is a structure developed by Laurie Kagan to put an out-of-control class back on track. The steps below describe Restart to get students to pay attention to the teacher. The steps, however, can be used for a range of content when students have gotten off track doing problems, not lining up properly, not clearing their desks properly, not following the steps of a structure — not following any procedure properly.

[8] Kagan, S. *Cooperative Learning.* San Clemente, CA: Kagan Publishing, 1994.

[9] Table the Matter is a strategy described by Albert, L. *Cooperative Discipline.* Circle Pines, MN: American Guidance Service, 1996.

[10] Target, Stop, Do is a strategy described by Albert, L. *Cooperative Discipline.* Circle Pines, MN: American Guidance Service, 1996.

[11] To You… To Me is a strategy described by Albert, L. *Cooperative Discipline.* Circle Pines, MN: American Guidance Service, 1996.

Chapter 15

Following Up

There are many possible ways to follow up after a disruption. We can have meetings of different types with the disruptive students, with the class as a whole, with parents, administrators, counselors, or a school team. We can re-examine and/or change our curriculum, instruction, or management. We can use a range of follow-up structures. Or we could do nothing.

We respond differently depending on the type of disruption, the position of the student or students, and of course their history of disruptive behavior. In this chapter, we overview the range of possible follow-ups and when to use each. But before presenting how to follow up, we will ask if we should follow up, and why we have follow-ups.

When to Follow Up

Often following a disruption, no follow-up is necessary. The student has responded to our moment-of-disruption intervention, senses we are on the same-side, and is learning more responsible behavior. A follow-up is necessary only if, following the disruption, we feel we are not making progress toward putting the three pillars in place. Some form of follow-up is necessary if, following our response to a disruption, the disruptive student 1) does not experience us to be on the same-side, 2) does not accept the discipline response, and/or 3) is not learning more responsible behaviors. Thus to determine if a follow-up is necessary, we ask three questions related to the three pillars:

Pillar 1
Same-Side

1. **Same-Side:** Does the student feel I understand where he/she is coming from, I am on his/her side?
2. **Collaborative Solution:** Does the student accept the discipline solution, identify with it — feel it is a reasonable response to the disruption?
3. **Learned Responsibility:** Is the student learning to act responsibly; over time is the student becoming less disruptive?

Pillar 2
Collaborative Solutions

If in general the student senses we are on the same-side, accepts and identifies with the discipline solution, and is learning to be more responsible, there is no need to follow up.

Pillar 3
Learned Responsibility

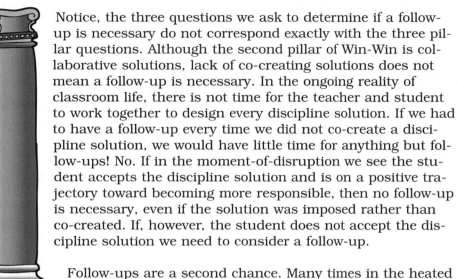

Follow-ups are a second chance to put the pillars in place.

Notice, the three questions we ask to determine if a follow-up is necessary do not correspond exactly with the three pillar questions. Although the second pillar of Win-Win is collaborative solutions, lack of co-creating solutions does not mean a follow-up is necessary. In the ongoing reality of classroom life, there is not time for the teacher and student to work together to design every discipline solution. If we had to have a follow-up every time we did not co-create a discipline solution, we would have little time for anything but follow-ups! No. If in the moment-of-disruption we see the student accepts the discipline solution and is on a positive trajectory toward becoming more responsible, then no follow-up is necessary, even if the solution was imposed rather than co-created. If, however, the student does not accept the discipline solution we need to consider a follow-up.

Follow-ups are a second chance. Many times in the heated moment of a disruption it is not possible to do more than reorient the disruptive student and his/her classmates to the learning task. There is not enough time or calm to implement the three pillars. For example, a quick strategy to reorient a disengaged, bored student might be to use his/her name in a teaching example and/or to use proximity, walking over and standing close to the student while continuing a presentation. While name dropping or proximity might work to solve the discipline problem in the moment, the teacher may not have communicated he/she is on the same-side as the student, the student did not participat in creating a discipline solution, and the student may not have learned more responsible behavior. In Win-Win we do not reject discipline strategies which quickly reoriented students to learning without implementing the three pillars. We see those strategies, though, as only short-term, stopgap patches, not long-term cures. The follow-up is a chance to go beyond stopgap measures – a second chance to put the pillars in place.

Why Follow Up?

The ultimate goal of Win-Win Discipline is learned responsibility. We want students leaving our classrooms to have learned responsible, non-disruptive ways to meet their needs. Positioning ourselves on the same-side with our students, validating their positions, co-creating discipline solutions, helping students accept the need to learn responsible behaviors are all but a means to that single goal — learned responsibility.

As indicated in the following table, what a student needs to learn differs depending on the student position.

Follow-Up Goal:
Autonomous Responsibility

Position	Autonomous Responsibility
Attention-Seeking	Self-Validation
Avoiding Embarrassment	Self-Confidence
Angry	Self-Control
Control-Seeking	Self-Determination
Energetic	Self-Directing
Bored	Self-Motivation
Uninformed	Self-Informing

The needs and drives of each position can be satisfied autonomously. That is what we call maturity. The mature person is responsible, filling his/her needs without being disruptive to others. The mature person takes responsibility for himself/herself. Much of what a parent does is to foster autonomous responsibility. Ultimately parents want their children to feed and dress themselves, and make wise decisions on their own. Similarly, much of what we do as Win-Win teachers is to foster autonomous responsibility, to get our students to act responsibly on their own. For example, if a student is repeatedly seeking attention, the student needs to learn to validate his/her own thoughts and accomplishments rather than to always seek external validation. If a student is repeatedly seeking control, the student needs to acquire an internal sense of control, a sense that he/she can make important choices to determine outcomes — a sense of self-determination.

As Win-Win teachers, given that our goal is helping students develop autonomous responsiblity, we are not satisfied with simply ending disruptions. For example, if we get an energetic student to sit quietly, we have eliminated some disruptive behavior. If, however, we get that energetic student to monitor his/her own restless behavior on an ongoing basis and to learn how to direct his/her energy productively and become self-directing, we have helped the student develop autonomous responsibility.

The Goal of Win-Win Discipline

The goal of Win-Win Discipline is not to end disruptions. It is to empower students with skills for a lifetime. We do not aim merely at getting students to behave responsibly, but rather to *become* responsible.

- *If we give a hungry man a fish, we help him for a day — if we teach a hungry man to fish, we empower him for a lifetime.*

- *If we end a disruption, we help for a moment. If we foster autonomous responsibility, we prevent future disruptions and empower our students for a lifetime.*

The ultimate goal of Win-Win: Autonomous Responsibility.

Follow-ups are designed to help students reach the ultimate goal of Win-Win Discipline: autonomous responsibility. Ultimately, we want students to act responsibly on their own so they do not need our assistance to behave responsibly. Autonomous responsibility, however, is not developed magically. To help students in the transition process, we intervene repeatedly, but all the while we keep in mind that the goal is not simply to get the student to behave responsibly, but rather, to get the student to become responsible.

How to Follow Up

Following a disruption, we have many options. At one end of the continuum, we may feel the disruption was handled well, the student is on the path toward acquiring a responsible orientation, and so there is no need to follow-up. At the other end of the continuum, we may feel we have exhausted our own resources and the student is still showing no progress toward learned responsibility. In that case we may turn to outside support such as an administrator, school counselor, or school support team. Usually, the situation falls somewhere between these two extremes.

Four Follow-Up Options

There are four primary follow-up options:

1. Establish new or re-establish old preventative procedures
2. Establish moment-of-disruption procedures for the next disruption
3. Implement follow-up structures. See **Chapter 16. Follow-Up Structures.**
4. Offer a life skill training. See **Chapter 20. Win-Win Life Skills.**

These four follow-up options are pictured in the Follow-Up Flow Chart.

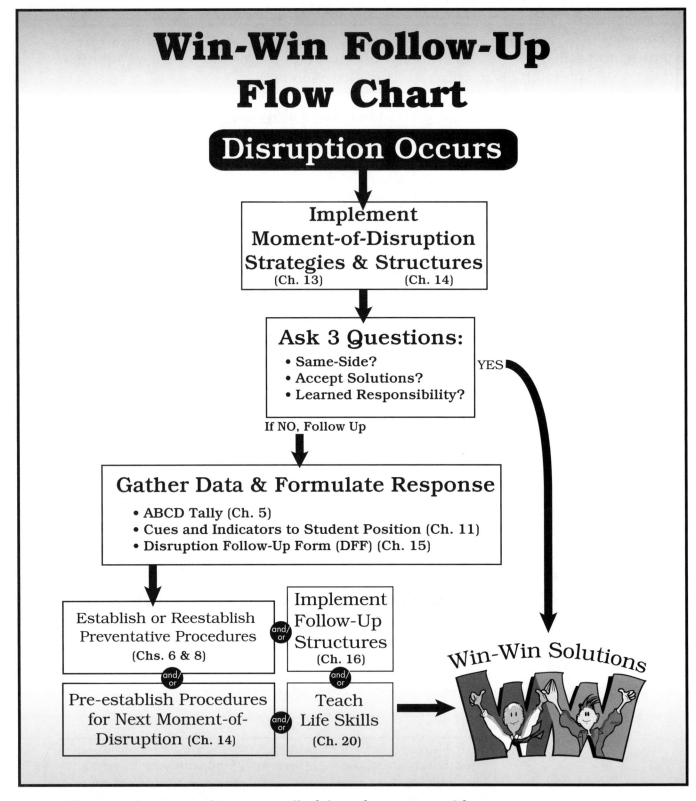

Win-Win Follow-Up Flow Chart

Disruption Occurs

Implement Moment-of-Disruption Strategies & Structures
(Ch. 13)   (Ch. 14)

Ask 3 Questions:
- Same-Side?
- Accept Solutions?
- Learned Responsibility?

YES

If NO, Follow Up

Gather Data & Formulate Response
- ABCD Tally (Ch. 5)
- Cues and Indicators to Student Position (Ch. 11)
- Disruption Follow-Up Form (DFF) (Ch. 15)

Establish or Reestablish Preventative Procedures (Chs. 6 & 8)

and/or

Implement Follow-Up Structures (Ch. 16)

and/or

Pre-establish Procedures for Next Moment-of-Disruption (Ch. 14)

and/or

Teach Life Skills (Ch. 20)

and/or

Win-Win Solutions

We may take any combination or all of these four options. Often in response to a repeated disruption, it is wise to implement several follow-up options. In order to know which option or options to take, we ask the questions outlined on the Disruption Follow-Up Form (DFF), page 15.7.

Disruption Follow-Up Form (DFF)

Student _____ Date of Disruption _____

Place of Disruption _____

Other Students Involved _____

Disruption

• Description of disruption:

• Frequency. How often does this type of disruption occur?

• Disruption Type, ABCD:

• Am I using an individual ABCD Tally?
• If so, it indicates:

Position

• Student position:

• Clues and indicators to position:

• Is more data needed to assess student position? Yes ___ No___
• If so, which kinds of clues or indicators?

Follow-Up Questions

• Same-Side: Yes ___ No___
Did the student feel I understand where he/she is coming from and that I am on his/her side?

• Acceptance of Solution: Yes ___ No___
Did the student accept the discipline solution, feel it is reasonable and fair?

• Collaborative Solution: Yes ___ No___
Has the student been involved in co-creating discipline solutions?

• Learned Responsibility: Yes ___ No___
Is the student learning to act responsibly; over time is the student becoming less disruptive?

(Continued)

Disruption Follow-Up Form (Continued)

Prevention

- Which relevant preventative procedures are in place?

- Which preventative procedures are to be instituted or reinforced?

Moment-of-Disruption

- Moment-of-disruption structure used:

- Response of student to structure used:

- Which alternative solution might I try in the next moment-of-disruption?

Pre-established Moment-of-Disruption Procedures

- Do new moment-of-disruption procedures need to be pre-established?
  Yes ___   No___
- If so, for which structure?

Follow-Up

- Is a follow-up structure recommended? Yes ___   No___
- If so, which?

Life Skill

- Is life skill training recommended? Yes ___   No___
- If so, which?

School Team and/or Parent Involvement

- Is a meeting, note, or phone call with parent indicated? Yes ___   No___
- Describe:

- Is a school team meeting indicated? Yes ___   No___

Notes

- Response of student to follow-up and/or life skill training:

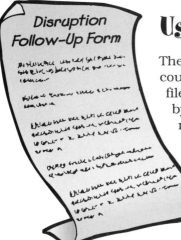

Disruption
Follow-Up Form

Using the Disruption Follow-Up Form

The Disruption Follow-Up Form is designed to help us chart a course of action after a disruption. Filed in individual student files by date, the DFF creates an ongoing record of disruptions by individual students so we can review prior disruptions and monitor progress over time. It is a powerful tool, helping us determine if a follow-up is necessary, the type of follow-up procedures to implement, if we need to change our approach to the disruptive student, and if the student is making progress over time. DFF forms are valuable to review with parents and/or school support teams and can be the basis of an informed individual plan.

Description of Disruption

The first step in using the DFF is to fill in the date, place, and brief description of the disruption. It is helpful to record the names of the other students involved. Over time this can reveal a pattern that may lead us to limit proximity or contact with certain students. Noting frequency helps us determine over time if learned responsibility is occurring.

In determining student position, we use all available data. If we have been keeping an ABCD Tally (See **Chapter 4. The Four Types of Disruptions: ABCD**) for the student, we check to determine the type of disruptive behavior the student is most frequently displaying. We also check the cues and indicators to best determine the most frequent position of the student. See **Chapter 11. Identifying Positions.** Knowing the behavior and position of the disruptive student(s) points us to the appropriate preventative procedures to establish or reinforce. The clues and indicators of student positions are reprinted in the box; they are detailed in **Chapter 11. Identifying Positions.**

Clues & Indicators for Student Positions

Clues in the Moment-of-Disruption
1. Your gut reaction
2. Your impulses
3. Disruptive student's reaction to intervention
4. Classmates' reactions to the disruption
5. Facial expressions and body language

Indicators following the Moment-of-Disruption
1. Disruptive student's reaction to different interventions
2. Interviews with disruptive student
3. Interviews with classmates
4. Interviews with prior teachers
5. Interviews with parents
6. Cumulative charts

Follow-Up Questions

Next, we ask ourselves the follow-up questions: Are we on the same-side? Does the student accept the solutions being offered? Did the student participate in creating the discipline solution? Is the student learning to become more responsible? If the answer to these questions is yes, we are on track to a Win-Win solution and no more need be done. If not, we probably need to choose one of the follow-up options.

If these critical questions reveal that the student perceives us to be "on his/her side," accepts the discipline solution, and is on a favorable learning curve toward responsibility, there is no need for a follow-up. A student may have simply forgotten a rule and gotten back on track with a simple rule reminder. A student may not have been paying attention and gotten refocused when we used his/her name in an example or when we used physical proximity. The nonverbal communications of the student — facial expression and body language — reveal if the student feels the rule is fair.

One student may feel grateful to go to a cool down area; another may resist. In one case the student identifies with the discipline solution; in the other case the student feels the solution has been imposed. Thus in one case no follow-up is necessary; in the other case a follow-up may be needed to co-create a Win-Win discipline solution and establish or re-establish a same-side orientation.

One of the most important determinants of whether we need to follow-up, of course, is the trajectory of learning. Are disruptions occurring more, or less frequently? After all, our ultimate goal is learned responsibility. If disruptions are occurring at a decreasing rate, we are on target and probably do not need a follow-up.

Prevention

After assessing the behavior and position of the student and asking the follow-up questions, we need to review the preventative procedures for the student's type of behavior and position (see **Chapter 6. Preventative Procedures: ABCD Disruptions** and **Chapter 8. Preventative Procedures: The Seven Positions**). Our first and best Win-Win response is always prevention, and there is always more that can be done to prevent disruptions.

Win-Win Discipline. Kagan Publishing • 1 (800) 933-2667 • www.KaganOnline.com

15.10

As pictured in the Follow-Up Flow Chart, our first option is prevention. If we understand the behavior and position of the student(s), we have a rich array of preventative procedures available. Even if we know that the preventative procedures will not eliminate all future disruptions, the more preventative procedures we put in place, the fewer disruptions we will have.

Moment-of-Disruption

One of the most important items on the DFF is the question that focuses on the response of the student to the discipline solution. A favorable response usually indicates we have correctly assessed and are responding appropriately to the student's position. An unfavorable response usually suggests we need to gather more data, re-evaluate the student position, and try an alternative strategy or structure. Finding the right discipline solution can be a hit and miss process. If one response does not work, we might try another, perhaps a response geared to a different position.

Pre-establishing Procedures for the Next Moment-of-Disruption

Knowing that future disruptions will occur, we want to be prepared. Some of our most powerful moment-of-disruption structures need to be pre-established, symbolized by 5Cs:

1. **Cool Down**
2. **Consequences**
3. **Contracts**
4. **Coupons**
5. **Cues: Verbal and Non-verbal**

In the moment-of-disruption we cannot use a cue or ask students for a coupon if we have not pre-established those procedures. So following a disruption, we may choose to pre-establish procedures — to have them in place for the next moment-of-disruption. We may pre-establish procedures for the whole class, as when we establish a verbal or non-verbal cue with the class, or we may pre-establish procedures with an individual student or a small group of students. Usually, pre-establishing procedures occurs in a private meeting with a student. The steps of establishing procedures for each of these moment-of-disruption structures are presented along with the structures in **Chapter 14. Moment-of-Disruption Structures.**

The type of procedure to pre-establish depends on the disruption type and position of the student. If students keep forgetting a rule or procedure, a cue may be established. For behavior that is acceptable, but must be limited, coupons may be implemented. For students who need time and space to regain control of strong emotions, we can establish cool down procedures. If we have tried less imposing solutions to no avail, we may need to establish a contract and/or consequences.

By pre-establishing with the disruptive student procedures for future disruptions, the Win-Win teacher accomplishes several things:

1. Downtime is minimized during future disruptions (the student knows where to go and for how long for cool down; the student returns to work following a pre-established non-verbal cue).
2. Some disruptions are prevented (e.g., the attention-seeking student knows he/she has only a certain number of coupons to spend on questions).
3. The student has an opportunity to reflect on the disruptive behavior and its consequences.
4. The teacher feels calmer in the moment-of-disruption. Knowing procedures are in place, the teacher does not have to invent a solution on the spot.

Once procedures have been established, they are used whenever a future disruption occurs. For example, the student and teacher may agree on a verbal or non-verbal cue the teacher may use to signal the student that his/her behavior is becoming disruptive and that he/she needs to behave more responsibly.

Follow-Up Structures

A structured student follow-up conference is a luxury. In the conference setting, we can calmly work with a student in a relaxed context. In contrast, in the moment-of-disruption we have to worry about keeping the rest of the class busy. In a structured follow-up we have undivided attention for the student.

The follow-up conference usually occurs later in the day of the disruption or the following day. It is scheduled at a time the teacher and student will not be interrupted, usually in the teacher's room during lunch, recess, planning time, or after school.

The form of the follow-up will be quite different depending on the type of disruption and the position of the student. The long-term goal, however, is always the same: to help the student find a path to learning autonomous, non-disruptive ways to meet his/her needs.

The follow-up structures are step-by-step sequences that lead to Win-Win solutions. They create willingness on the part of the student to consider and adopt alternative behaviors to replace the disruptive behaviors. As the Win-Win teacher experiments with and adapts the structures to his/her own style and needs of the students, he/she finds the most efficient follow-up structure for a given student. The structures are like tools in the teacher's toolbox, and as the teacher becomes more skilled in each tool, he/she is better able to craft successful, long-term Win-Win Discipline solutions.

Follow-up structures allow us to respond to the disruptive behaviors of the class or of an individual student. Generally, we use the least directive structures first, structuring so the student discovers or creates the discipline solution. The most important follow-up structure of all — by far — is the same-side chat. Through that structure we establish a same-side position with the student. Often that is all it takes for the student to commit to more responsible behavior. More directive follow-up structures are designed to have students practice responsible thinking, re-establish expectations, practice replacement behaviors, and establish contracts. As needed, we move from less to more controlling structures as follows:

1. **Same-Side Chat**
2. **Responsible Thinking**
3. **Re-establishing Expectations**
4. **Replacement Behavior**
5. **Establish Coupons**
6. **Write a Contract**
7. **Contact Parent and/or School Team**

The detailed steps of these follow-up structures are presented in **Chapter 16. Follow-Up Structures.**

Same-Side Chat

Remarkably, one of the best ways to prevent some disruptions is not to deal with the disruption at all! An informal "getting to know you better" chat can do wonders, especially for students who are confrontational and students who do not feel we are on their side. Many students "melt" when they know their teacher takes a special interest in them, cares about them as a person. An informal same-side chat may cover non-academic topics like the sports or hobbies the student enjoys, how many brothers and sisters the student has, what he/she enjoys doing after school, and so on. Taking time to get to know a student better communicates that you care. Once the student feels that you care, he/she is disposed to reciprocate. We can not get too far from the truth of the adage:

"A student does not care how much we know until they know how much we care."

"A really great teacher is someone who... **helps you sort things out if you need to talk.** *Samantha, 12, Perth Western Australia*[1]

Life Skill Trainings

Once we understand the position of a student, we can teach him/her responsible, non-disruptive ways to meet the needs associated with that position. Learning responsible ways to deal with anger or convert a boring task into an interesting task are life skills. Life skill trainings prepare students to meet their needs responsibly for a lifetime. There are many life skills we can teach, including how to:

> • Validate oneself instead of turning toward external sources for positive attention
> • Make attributions that lead to optimism rather than help-lessness
> • Spot the signs of mounting anger rather than acting out that anger
> • Define one's choices to obtain a sense of control
> • Re-direct one's energy in productive ways
> • Restructure tasks to convert boredom to engagement
> • Inform oneself when uncertain about rules or procedures

These and many other life skill are described in **Chapter 20. Win-Win Life Skills.** In that chapter you will find numerous resources to support life skill trainings.

The life skill trainings are designed to teach responsible ways of thinking and behaving so the student can meet the needs associated with his/her positions without becoming disruptive — a win for the teacher, the class, and the student.

The skill trainings are mini-teaching sessions. We teach students skills — life skills. For example, through one type of skill training, a student who does not know how to spot the signs of mounting anger learns to recognize the early warning signs of mounting anger. This reduces the probability he/she will act out anger in ways he/she (and others) will later regret. In another type of skill training, a student who gives up in the face of difficulty learns how to break a difficult task into small, less formidable pieces. In yet another skill training, a student who often seeks attention from teacher and peers learns how to provide self-validation. Skill trainings are geared to specific positions; they are designed to provide students with skills they can use to meet their unique needs without becoming disruptive.

Parental Involvement

Parental involvement can take a variety of forms including a note home, a signature system, a phone call, or a meeting. The form of parental involvement, if any, will depend on the type of disruption, the position of the student, and the frequency and intensity of the disruptions.

Parental involvement can be tailored to the behavior and position of the student as described in the "Parents as Partners" table.

A really great teacher is someone who... **can actually talk to the most disturbed student – the most closed student.** *Trinity, 12, Perth, Western Australia*[2]

A really great teacher is someone who... **stays after school to talk to you.** *Steve, 12, Cherry Hill, New Jersey*[3]

A really great teacher is someone who... **works with your parents to find solutions to your problems.** *Anthony, 10, Mishawaka, Indiana*[4]

Parents as Partners

Type of Disruption	Parental Involvement
Behavior	
Aggression	Inform parents of nature of aggression. Set up ongoing information system to reward non-aggression. Have parents work with students on importance of and types of non-violent alternatives. Seek information: Is student aggressive outside school? Establish consistent school/home response system.
Breaking the Rules	Inform parents of rules and rule infractions. Have parents review rules with student.
Confrontation	Is student confrontational with parents, other adults? Establish consistent school/home response system.
Disengagement	Elicit support from parents; establish importance of school work. Have parents reinforce engagement.
Position	
Attention-Seeking	Give student positive attention via phone call or note home.
Avoiding Failure	Establish home tutoring or support system for homework.
Anger	Have parents reinforce self-control procedures established at parent/student/teacher or counselor meeting.
Control-Seeking	Work with parents to establish areas of choice for student; to reinforce awareness of choices and consequences.
Energetic	Explore healthy outlets for energy. Establish consistent school/home self-control techniques.
Bored	Seek information: What is exciting for student? Seek ways to bring areas of interest into class work or homework.
Uninformed	Have parents help explain and reinforce rules and procedures.

Parent Conference

Parent conferences actively involve parents in creating the discipline solution. They allow input from the parents and an opportunity to align home and school discipline. When the student perceives the parents and teacher as allies, there is greater probability of a successful discipline solution. To set a positive tone at the beginning of the parent-teacher meeting, the teacher communicates he/she:

> 1. Has a same-side orientation with the student
> 2. Has a same-side orientation with the parents
> 3. Is aware of the positive qualities and behaviors of the student
> 4. Values the observations and suggestions of the parents

During the parent-teacher meeting, the teacher elicits help from the parents both in understanding the position of the student and in creating a discipline solution. The Win-Win teacher emphasizes that by teaming up, they can create a solution which will better

Win-Win Discipline. Kagan Publishing • 1 (800) 933-2667 • www.KaganOnline.com

15.15

meet everyone's needs — a Win-Win solution for everyone. The steps of a Parent Conference are detailed as a follow-up structure in Chapter 16.

Parent Alliances

There are many strategies to effectively create positive parent alliances in service of a Win-Win Discipline approach. In addition to conferences, there are a range of options to help us solicit and build parent input, support, follow-through, and back-up, including:

- Letters, Postcards; E-mail, Notes
- Phone calls; Conferences
- Home Visits
- Newsletters; Class Home Page
- Progress Reports; Project, Assignment Evaluations
- Portfolios; Exhibits of Student Work
- Parent/Teacher/Student Goal Setting
- Parent Volunteers; Parent Mentors
- PTA/PTO Presentations
- Parent Study Groups, Training Sessions
- Drop-in Centers
- PAL Workshops
- Performances for Parents
- Win-Win Homework
- Back to School Bar-B-Q
- Parties and Celebrations

Details of these and other ways to approach parents as partners are presented in **Chapter 18. Win-Win Management.**

School Support Team

With students who are frequently and seriously disruptive and who over time are not learning more responsible behaviors, we may need to turn to others for support. If our preventative and moment-of-disruption measures are not working and we have not been able to turn things around working with parents, a meeting with a school administrator, school counselor, and/or school support team is in order. When we turn to help from others, having filled in a DFF form for each disruption is a tremendously valuable tool. It provides a cumulative record of disruptions, attempted discipline solutions, and response of students to attempted solutions. It demonstrates we are responsible teachers.

Following Up: An Overview

Following a disruption, we have many options. Often no follow-up is necessary. If the disruptive student senses we are on the same-side, accepts the discipline solution, and over time is learning to be more responsible, there is no need to follow up. If, however, an antagonistic relationship has been created, the student protests or somehow displays resistance to the discipline solution, or he/she simply is not becoming more responsible over time, we probably want to follow up.

Our goal as a Win-Win teacher is always *learned responsibility*. We are not satisfied with just ending the disruption. If ending a disruption were our only aim, we would not need moment-of-disruption or follow-up strategies — we could simply purchase cheap handcuffs and leg irons! No. Our aim is to convert the disruption into a *learning opportunity* — so the student accepts his/her position and discovers and adopts non-disruptive, responsible ways to meet his/her needs. The follow-up offers a second chance to promote learned responsibility.

The type of follow-up we choose depends on the type of disruption, the severity of the disruption, the position of the student, the student's history of disruptive behavior, and the student's response to attempted discipline solutions. It depends also on our understanding of the position of the student. If we don't feel we have a good understanding of the student's position, we might engage in data gathering and/or a Same-Side Chat designed to help us better understand the student position.

Two forms help us in following up. The ABCD Tally helps us see classroom and individual patterns. When a clear classroom pattern emerges, we follow up by working with the whole class rather than following up only with the individual disruptive student. The ABCD Classroom Tally tells us if the disruption of the individual student is merely a symptom of the classroom pattern. For example, the classroom pattern may indicate we need to re-teach the rules, help the whole class meet the need for attention via teambuilding and classbuilding activities, or re-examine our curriculum, instruction, or management. The ABCD Individual Tally reveals the individual student pattern.

The second form that helps us in following up is the DFF. The Disruption Follow-Up Form helps us:

- Decide if we need to gather more data regarding the student position
- Decide if we need to change our approach to the disruptive student
- Decide which new preventative procedures to put in place or which old procedures to re-emphasize

- Decide if we need to pre-establish procedures for the next moment-of-disruption
- Decide if an individual follow-up meeting with the student is necessary, and if so, what the focus of that meeting should be
- Decide if a life skills training would be helpful
- Create an ongoing record of disruptions by individual students so we can review prior disruptions, monitor progress over time, and objectively share the discipline history with others, if necessary
- Record the reaction of the student to our follow-up meeting, if one is held

Our most important follow-up options include:

- An informal chat with the student designed to establish or re-establish a Win-Win, Same-Side Orientation. See Same-Side Chat, **Chapter 16. Follow-Up Structures.**
- Other follow-up structures, see **Chapter 16. Follow-Up Structures.**
- Parental involvement
- Eliciting help from another teacher, administrator, school counselor, or the school support team
- Life skills trainings to teach skills students need to convert unsuccessful, disruptive attempts to meet their needs into successful, responsible skills. See **Chapter 20. Win-Win Life Skills.**

Follow-ups are a rich array of tools designed to lead us to the ultimate goal of Win-Win: Autonomous Responsibility. In the next chapter we turn to the details of the most powerful follow-up tools: Follow-Up Structures.

References

[1, 2, 3, 4] Bluestein, J. (Ed.) *Mentors, Masters, and Mrs MacGregor: Stories of Teachers Making a Difference.* Deerfield Beach, FL: Health Communications, Inc., 1995, p. 117, 160, 72, 371.

Chapter 16

Follow-Up Structures

This chapter is a step-by-step presentation of follow-up structures, including the disruption types and positions for which they are best suited, as well as cautions and hints.

For easy reference, the follow-ups are summarized in Follow-Up Structures, on page 16.4. A glance at that table reveals that unlike the moment-of-disruption structures, follow-up structures are far more generic. That is, most of them can be used for the range of disruption types and positions.

How then do we select? Some follow-up structures are tailored to specific behavior. For example, Responsible Thinking works well for the impulsive student; it helps the student "look before you leap." Replacement Behavior works well to help a student break a disruptive habit. Thus one is more cognitive and the other more behavioral.

In general, the Win-Win teacher tries the "lightest" or least directive interventions first, giving the student as much responsibility as possible for generating the solution. If the lighter follow-ups fail, the teacher has more controlling approaches in reserve. We try honey before vinegar, a peashooter before dragging out the cannon. Keeping our eye on the ultimate goal of Win-Win, we would much rather have students behave responsibly based on responsible thinking rather than a contract or fear of punishment. Rather than imposing a rule, we would much rather re-establish a buy-in for "The Way We Want Our Class to Be," (See **Chapter 9. Teaching the Win-Win Philosophy**).

Following this, the follow-ups often take a sequence: we try Same-Side Chat first, establishing rapport and letting the student know we are there to help rather than punish or direct. Often that is all that is needed. It is remarkable how much students will do for us when they really know we are on their side. (But *telling* them we are on their side does little — we have to *be* on their side. That is the art of a true Same-Side Chat.)

If the student is still disruptive, we might try Responsible Thinking. If that does not work, we might focus on Re-establishing Expectations. If that fails, we would establish and practice Replacement Behavior. Only if that did not work would we resort to writing a Contract and/or calling for a Parent Conference.

Progressively More Controlling Follow-Ups

Same-Side Chat

⬇

Responsible Thinking

⬇

Re-establish Expectations

⬇

**Replacement Behavior,
Establishing Cool Down,
Establishing Coupons, or
Establishing Cues: Verbal & Non-verbal**

⬇

Establishing Consequences

⬇

Contract

⬇

Parent Conference

Note, one way to follow-up is to pre-establish a procedure for the moment of the next disruption. These procedures have been called the 5C's (see 14.4 and 15.11). These procedures are at the more intrusive end of the continuum, so we use them only after trying the less intrusive interventions first.

For easy reference, the follow-up structures are presented alphabetically in the following table. The table provides a thumbnail sketch of each follow-up structure, as well as the types of disruptions and positions for which they are most useful.

Follow-Up Structures

Structure	Page	Disruption Type				Position							Thumbnail Sketch
		A	B	C	D	Attention-Seeking	Avoiding Failure	Angry	Control-Seeking	Energetic	Bored	Uninformed	
Contracts	5	●	◐	●	◐	◐	◐	●	●	●	◐	◐	By creating a written contract, the teacher and student clarify the agreement and increase the probability the student will remember, identify with, and live up to it. *Individual*
Parent Conference	9	◐	◐	◐	◐	◐	◐	◐	◐	◐	◐	◐	Teacher and parent(s) meet to co-create discipline solutions. *Individual*
Re-establish Expectations	12	●	●	◐		◐	◐	●	◐	◐		●	Expectations, rules, procedures, and routines are re-established to reinforce knowledge, understanding, acceptance, application and adherence. *Individual; Class*
Replacement Behavior	17	●	◐	◐	◐	●	◐	●	◐	◐	◐	◐	The teacher guides the student(s) to generate, accept, and practice responsible behavior to replace disruptive behavior. *Individual; Class*
Responsible Thinking	22	◐	●	◐	◐	◐	◐	●	◐	◐	◐	◐	Students are guided toward responsible thinking via three questions that have them consider 1) their own needs as well as the needs of others; 2) if they have treated others as they would hope to be treated; and 3) if they have acted the way they would hope everyone would act. *Individual; Class*
Same-Side Chat	26	◐	◐	◐	◐	●	◐	◐	●	◐	◐	◐	When we don't understand a student's position and/or don't feel ourselves to be on the same-side with the student, we schedule a Same-Side Chat to get to know the student better and to develop empathy with the student — so we can honestly place ourselves on "the same-side." *Individual*

● = Most useful functions
◐ = Also Recommended

16.4

Win-Win Discipline. Kagan Publishing • 1 (800) 933-2667 • www.KaganOnline.com

Contracts

By creating a written contract, the teacher and student clarify the agreement and increase the probability the student will remember, identify with, and live up to it.

Ideal Outcomes

- Student and teacher are very clear on their roles and their agreement.

- Commitment by the student is strengthened.

- Student and teacher have a document to refer to later to check on fulfillment.

- Students learn to keep commitments and follow through on agreements and plans.

Recommended for...

Disruption
Aggression, Confrontation

Position
Angry, Control-Seeking, Energetic

Individual or Class
Individual

Contracts

STEPS

1 Express Caring

The teacher demonstrates that he/she cares for the student and wants to support him/her in choosing responsible behaviors. *"Anne, I care about you and want to help."*

2 Establish Need

The need for a contract is established. The teacher describes the specific disruptive behavior and "mirrors" the student's behavior. *"This is a serious concern. Let me show you what it looks like."*

3 Describe Problem in Writing

The teacher and the student give a written description of the specific problem. *"Let's start by describing the behaviors that are occurring that are causing disruptions to learning. Let's list together exactly what is going on at the time of disruptions. [List behaviors]. _____. Let's see if we can agree on what the problem is. [Discussion]. Do we agree that the problem is (written statement)?"*

4 Generate and Record Solution

The teacher and the student explore various solutions. The student and/or the teacher generate and record the agreement. *"What do you think are some solutions? Let's jot down our best ideas _____."*

"Once we agree on a solution — what we are both going to do to solve it — let's make an official agreement between the two of us, a contract!"

"So, which one of these do you think will work?"

"Now let's agree to and record a solution we both feel good about."

5 Create Incentive

The student and/or the teacher choose and record an incentive that will motivate the student to follow through on the plan. *"If you can do this, the pay-off for you is _____."*

6 Establish Consequences

The teacher and the student select and record a logical consequence if the disruptive behavior is repeated. *"But we both agree that if you choose to continue to _____, then the consequence will be _____."*

7 Commit to Contract, Establish Accountability

The teacher and the student solidify the contract agreements by signing the contract. Parent(s) also sign the contract, when appropriate. A time line is established for the contract and monitoring strategies. *"Now that we agree to this contract, let's both sign it and make it official. Let's decide when we will meet to review how it is going."*

STEPS (Continued)

8 Explore Position, Temptations, Commitment

When sufficient trust has been established, explore with the student his/her position. What are the needs met by the disruptive behavior? What are the temptations to break the contract? The teacher may share his/her perspective on the student's position, but the focus is on helping the student open up in a self-discovery process, not on telling the student.

Position

"It seems to me that you are pretty (angry, discouraged, bored). Am I off-base or pretty close?"

"No one likes to be told what to do. From what you are telling me, it sounds like homework assignments feel like that — being told what to do. Let's see if we can turn that around. One idea is to allow you some choice about what the assignment will be, or how you will present it...."

"We all like to be the center of attention sometimes. It is tempting to crack a joke. What could you tell yourself or do when you are tempted...?"

Temptations

"This contract means changing your behavior, and it is hard for all of us to break old habits. What part of the contract do you think will be difficult for you?"

"What might lead you to break the contract?"

Commitment

"In what ways are you going to remind yourself of our contract? What are you going to do to make sure you live up to it?"

"This may be difficult to stick to. What are you going to do when you are tempted to _____?"

Contracts

Cautions & Hints

- **Pace.** Don't rush the process; contracts are mutual, not imposed.

- **Be Sincere.** Don't say you care about the student if it is not honest that day. Students will know.

- **Positive, not Negative.** Emphasis is on alternative behaviors, not "stopping the disruptive behaviors." OK: Student agrees to keep hands to self. NOT OK: Student agrees not to touch other students. This point is very important. In the unconscious the negative is lost; therefore an agreement not to touch others calls up a mental picture of touching others, which becomes more likely. In contrast, an agreement to keep one's hands to oneself calls up the image of hands to oneself, which is more likely to be realized. *Negative agreements often actually increase the probability of the prohibited disruptive behavior.*

- **Same-Side Mirror.** Let students know you are not mocking them — that you are trying to help them see themselves as others see them.

- **Validate Input.** Validate student input and suggestions.

- **Multiple Disruptive Behaviors.** If there are several disruptive behaviors, the contract focuses on one or two that are good starting points.

- **Student Language.** Use student language in writing up the contract.

- **Concrete Language.** Describe the problem as specific, concrete, objective behaviors, not effects of behaviors. OK: Johnny taps his pencil on his desk, plays with Susie's hair, and makes strange noises. NOT OK: Johnny annoys others.

- **Student Input.** Imposed incentives and consequences won't work. Shared responsibility is the key to a collaborative solution.

- **Explore Temptations.** When the contract is established and signed, explore what might lead the student not to fulfill the contract and how the student can avoid temptations.

- **Congratulate.** Use non-verbal and verbal praise when you see the student acting in accord with the contract. Take a moment to congratulate the student.

Discussion and Journaling Topics

Discussion Topics

In a follow-up discussion, explore with the student how it feels to make and maintain a contract and/or failure to live up to the contract. "When I live up to an agreement, I feel proud of myself. It feels good to keep a commitment. How are you feeling about our contract and your living up to it?"

"Today you did not live up to your contract. We all slip sometimes. How did it feel to fall short? What can we do to help you live up to your contract in the future?"

Journaling or Team Discussion Topic

Contracts are important. One of the most important contracts in America is the Bill of Rights. Corporations make contracts. Individuals make contracts. What are some of the types of contracts you know of, and why are contracts important?

Parent Conference

Teacher and parent(s) meet to co-create discipline solutions.

Ideal Outcomes

- The parents feel that they are an important part of the discipline process.

- Parents support the teacher and the school in meeting the needs of their child.

- Parents provide valuable input; teacher develops or deepens understanding.

- Parents develop new understandings of their child.

- Parents learn new ways to relate to their child.

- Students understand the seriousness of their disruption.

- Students feel the teacher really cares.

- Students perceive teacher and parents as allies in supporting their growth.

Recommended for...

Disruption
All Disruptions

Position
All Positions

Individual or Class
Individual

Parent Conference

STEPS

1 Express Caring
Teacher tells the parents that he/she cares for the student and wants to support that student in choosing responsible behaviors.

2 Describe Disruptive and Responsible Behaviors
Teacher describes the responsible behaviors and strengths of the student. The teacher then focuses on the specific disruptive behavior without value judgments attached.

3 Explore Student Position
Teacher shares the student's position with the parent. The focus is on how it is possible for the student to meet these same needs through responsible behavior, indicating that is the long-range goal.

4 Discuss Solutions
Teacher and parent generate and develop possible solutions.

5 Plan for the Future
Teacher and parent discuss which solutions will be implemented and what each will do to help in the process. Plan a time to meet again to evaluate the effectiveness of the implemented solutions.

Parent Conference

When a Parent Is Angry

Parents sometimes come in with a hostile attitude, feeling their child has been unfairly treated. The best thing to do if a parent is angry is to utilize active listening skills. Even if you don't agree with the parent, make sure he/she feels listened to and heard. Use paraphrasing and encouragement. Parents will usually calm down when active listening is used. Do not attempt problem solving until a same-side orientation has been achieved. Sometimes parents are so angry they don't respond to the active listening. They might be abusive. Even though we have a professional obligation to continually invite parents to be allies, we don't have to take abuse. In the face of abuse we use the Language of Choice: *"You can choose to talk with me respectfully. or we can schedule a meeting later when we have calmed down."* It may be necessary to invite an administrator to attend the follow-up meeting.

Cautions & Hints

- **Warm Context.** Meet with the parent at a time and place where there will be no distractions. Give the parent full attention. Offer cookies and coffee. Play music softly at about 60 beats a minute. See Music in **Part VII, Resources F.**

- **Appreciate Parents, Student.** Take time to appreciate that parents made time in their busy schedule to meet. Begin conference by mentioning a number of positive qualities and accomplishments you have observed in their child. Compliment them on those qualities.

- **Listen More Than Talk.** Make the conference parent-centered. Show by your active listening that you value the parent input and respect the parent. Listen more than talk. State that you need their input, ideas — that you want to partner with them.

- **Value Parents as People.** Ask about their professions. Validate their accomplishments. Show interest in them as people.

- **Validate Parental Relationships.** Make it clear that the parent is the ultimate authority. *"You know your son better than I do." "You have had a lifetime with Johnny, can you tell me some things about him that might help me understand him better?"*

- **Recognize Parent Position.** If the conference is regarding disruptive behavior, the mention of that behavior is likely to elicit in parents some combination of the following feelings: guilt, inadequacy, anger, fear, defensiveness, as well as feelings of being overwhelmed and/or dependent. The extremely dependent parent might take the stance, "Just tell me what to do." The angry parent might direct his/her anger toward you, the school, and/or the student. The defensive parent is likely to make excuses or explanations for his/her child. Accept the parent position and look beyond it for the path to a Win-Win, Same-Side solution.

- **Solicit Parent Vision.** Ask about what they most want their child to learn this year. What is their dream profession for their child.

- **Offer Your Vision.** Share with parents what you feel their child can accomplish. *"If we work together, I think by the end of this school year, Jane will be able to..."*

- **Give Only Objective Input about Disruptive Behavior.** It is fine to say, *"Three or four times this week Billy answered out before he is called on."* It is not productive to say, *"Bill is often disruptive."*

- **Limit and Focus.** If a student is often disruptive in many ways, do not present parents with a catalog of misbehaviors. Rather, focus on one behavior that you would like to elicit help in changing, and cite only two or three examples.

- **Parents as Partners.** Review Parents as Partners (Section 6 of Chapter 18, Win-Win Management). In preparation for a parent meeting if you have on file a completed Parent Info Form (18.56), review it. If you do not have a completed form, you may want to have the parent(s) fill out and return one prior to the meeting. If appropriate, at the meeting have handy an extra copy of the Helpful Hints for Communicating with Your Child (18.60) to give the parent.

- **Follow Up.** Arrange at the conference that you will make contact with the parent(s) to follow up. Follow up via note, e-mail, and/or phone call.

Re-establish Expectations

Expectations, rules, procedures, and routines are re-established to reinforce knowledge, understanding, acceptance, application and adherence.

Ideal Outcomes

- Expectations are clarified and reinforced.

- Student memory for rules, routines, and procedures is strengthened.

- Students better understand the rationale for rules and procedures.

- Students are more committed to fulfilling class expectations.

- Same-Side orientation is strengthened.

- Fewer classroom disruptions occur.

Recommended for...

Disruption
Aggression, Breaking the Rules

Position
Angry, Uninformed

Individual or Class
Both

STEPS

1 Express Caring

The teacher demonstrates that he/she cares for the student and wants to support him/her in choosing responsible behaviors. *"Yvonne, I care about you and want to help."*

2 Establish Need

The need for a follow-up on rules is established. The teacher describes the specific disruptive behavior and/or "mirrors" the student's behavior. Let students know you are not mocking them — that you are trying to help them see themselves as others see them. *"Let me describe (or show you) what your behavior looks like."*

3 Check for Understanding

The student verbalizes his/her own understanding of the rule or procedure and why it was established. *"That kind of behavior breaks our class rules. Can you tell me which rule it breaks and why we have that rule?"*

"What would following the rule look like? How would that help you, me, and the rest of the class?"

"I know that not breaking the rule would keep you out of trouble. But are there any better reasons to keep the rule?"

4 Explain Rule and Its Impact

The teacher verbalizes his/her own understanding of the rule, benefits for all students, and how it is enacted. *"The way I understand this rule is _____."*

"The reason we have that rule is _____."

"The rule helps us because _____."

"What it looks like is _____."

5 Explore Obstacles

The teacher explores with the student why it might be difficult for the student to follow the rule. *"I know it is sometimes fun to stir up a bit of trouble. We all like excitement. It is really tempting to get something going. Am I on track?"*

"There are so many great things to do after school. I bet you find it hard to make time to do your homework. What are some things you could do to make sure your homework does not get put off until it is too late?"

"When you hit a hard problem, it is more fun to draw. And you are really good at drawing. Let's think about how you can have plenty of time to draw and still complete all of the problems."

6 Explore Incentives

The teacher makes salient the reasons to follow the rules, the pay-offs for the student. *"Well, can you think of any reason it would pay off for you to follow that rule? And I don't want to hear 'because that way I won't get punished.' "*

"What would you gain by having your homework done each day?"

"If you did not poke and put down any of your classmates, would there be a pay-off in terms of what they felt about you?"

"If you can do this, the pay-off for you is _____."

Re-establish Expectations

STEPS (Continued)

7 **Elicit Commitment**

The student commits to following the rule. *"Well, given what you said [paraphrase payoffs], would you be willing to make a fresh start and agree to follow the rule?"*

"What are some of the ways you are going to remind yourself about the rule? How are you going to keep yourself on track?"

8 **Offer Support**

The teacher offers support. *"I know it will be hard for you to change your behavior. Changing habits is always very difficult. That is why so many people promise to lose weight or quit smoking but never stick to their promise. It will be hard for you to change too, but I will do all I can to support you. I would like this to be a turn-around for you. How about if we meet back in a week and talk again? The other thing I can do is give you an occasional reminder if you would like, but just until you are able to manage this change on your own."*

Cautions & Hints

• **Avoid the Need.** You can avoid the need for individual follow-ups on rules by firmly implanting the need for and understanding of rules from the first day of class, by teaching the rules to the whole class in a variety of ways throughout the school year, and by using preventative procedures. See Chapters 6. Preventative Procedures: ABCD Disruptions; 8. Preventative Procedures: The Seven Positions; and 18. Win-Win Management.

• **Locate the Problem.** By asking a series of questions, the teacher can locate the problem and direct energy where it is needed:

  • Can the student state the rule?
  • Can the student state the rationale for the rule?
  • Does the student feel the rule is fair?
  • Does the student have a reason not to adhere to the rule?
  • Does the student want to remember and adhere to the rule?
  • What is the payoff to the student for not adhering to the rule?
  • What is the perceived pay-off for the student for adhering to the rule?

• **If It Is a Question of Buy-In.** Don't try to get commitment to rule adherence until you have taken the same-side with the student and understand how he/she perceives the rule. If the student perceives the rule as imposed, with no benefit to himself/herself, back up and work on fostering understanding of the rule, its rationale, and its fairness. See Responsible Thinking, 16.22.

• **If It Is a Question of Memory.** If the student buys in but slips because of lack of memory, then an individualized memory system can be created so the student can remind himself/herself of the rule. The most effective way is to identify the behavior that occurs right before the rule violation and get the student to do something or engage in self-talk at those moments to trigger memory.

Cautions & Hints (Continued)

• **If It Is a Question of Impulse Control.** If the student buys in but slips for lack of impulse control, suggest ways the student can control his/her impulses. The most effective way to control impulses is to focus on what to do, not on what not to do. That is, teach the student substitute behaviors for the moment of temptation. Avoid: "Don't draw in your book." Better: "Could you agree to take some notes with drawings? Let me show you how to have a column on your note taking page to symbolize the content, not with words but with drawings." See Replacement Behavior, 16.16.

• **Explore the Positive.** Review with the student the times when he/she was good at rule adherence. Praise those efforts. Explore what it was that the student did that enabled him/her to avoid temptation.

• **Catch 'em Being Good.** After the individual follow-up, reinforce rule adherence by a smile or comment when you see the student making the effort to follow the rules. You can use a secret signal to let the student know you appreciate his/her efforts.

• **Schedule a Check-Back.** Schedule a time to check back with the student, to give the student positive feedback on rule adherence.

• **Promote Thinking.** Rather than telling students the rule or expectation, when possible get them to remember it or think about it. *"What expectation are you violating right now?"* is usually better than, *"James, defacing school property is not allowed."* Or a responsible thinking question might be in order: *"If everyone were to dog-ear his/her text, what would happen for the next person who gets that text?"*

• **Multiple Intelligences.** Select one of the many ways to practice the rules based on the multiple intelligences:

1) Verbal/Linguistic:	Have students write a poem about the rule or expectation.
2) Logical/Mathematical:	Have students deduce reasons for the rule.
3) Visual/Spatial:	Have students make a poster to support the rule.
4) Musical/Rhythmic:	Have students write a rule rap, chant, or song.
5) Bodily/Kinesthetic:	Have students act out the rule or expectation.
6) Naturalist:	Have students create an analogy from nature.
7) Interpersonal:	Have students teach the rule or expectation to a partner.
8) Intrapersonal:	Have students chronicle their thoughts about the rule or expectation.

• **Voice and Manner.** Teacher is calm and respectful, reminding students of established expectations. Just as students will err in remembering and being able to apply the steps of long division, so too will they err in remembering and being able to apply the class expectations or rules. And so, we are in our element. We teach and re-teach the rules just as we would any academic content or procedure.

• **Expectations are Pre-established.** Re-establishing Expectations can be used only if expectations have been pre-established with the class and there is buy-in. See **Chapter 18. Win-Win Management.**

Cautions & Hints (Continued)

• **Generic Rules.** We cannot have a rule for every possible disruptive behavior. Thus it is crucial to establish generic rules like Come Prepared to Learn; Be Respectful of Others; Respect the Feelings and Property of Others; and Support the Class Mission: Learning.

• **Policing the Rules.** If we close our eyes to rule violations, soon the rules will be meaningless, or, at best, will be enforced only with great difficulty. If there is inconsistent application of the rules, then when we do enforce them we can expect comments like, *"But you didn't do anything when Sam did it,"* or, *"You are just picking on me; you never say anything when Susie doesn't complete her homework."* Thus we must continually "police the rules."

• **Responsible Thinking.** Ideally, rather than having to rely on rules, we would like students to engage in responsible thinking, on their own, considering the consequences of their actions for themselves and for others. If you find yourself relying often on Re-establishing Expectations, it probably indicates a need for more work on getting students to understand the impact of their own behavior on others and for more responsible thinking.

Win-Win Discipline. Kagan Publishing • 1 (800) 933-2667 • www.KaganOnline.com

Replacement Behavior

The teacher guides the student to generate, accept, and practice responsible behavior to replace disruptive behavior.

Ideal Outcomes

- Students find it easier to end disruptive behavior patterns by focusing on what to do rather than what not to do.

- Students understand how disruptive behavior is self-defeating.

- Students understand benefits of responsible behavior.

- Students learn a powerful self-management, self-control technique.

- Student self-esteem is increased.

- Same-Side and Shared Responsibility orientations are reinforced.

Recommended for...

Disruption
Aggression

Position
Attention-Seeking, Angry

Individual or Class
Both

Replacement Behavior

STEPS

1 Express Caring

The teacher demonstrates to the student that he/she cares for the student and wants to help the student. *"Jackie, I am concerned about your behavior and don't want to punish you. What I would really like is to team up with you and help you establish some behavior patterns that will help you, make you feel better about yourself, and be less disruptive to the class. Does that sound good to you?"*

2 Describe Disruptive Behavior

The teacher describes the disruptive behavior and how it is non-adaptive for the student and disruptive for the class. *"Jackie, let me tell you why I am concerned. You have great ideas to contribute, but often you do it in a way that does not get you what you want and makes it difficult for your team to function. Let me give you some concrete examples."*

"Today when Bobbie suggested your team could present its project with a skit, you said, 'No, I have a better idea.' Then you described the quiz show idea. Your quiz show idea was great, but Bobbie felt put down. Later he made fun of your quiz show idea."

"Yesterday when Jane did her presentation, you raised your hand and then corrected her. You were right, but Jane felt put down."

"What I want to work with you on is a way you can get your great ideas across, but without causing others to feel put down. What I would like for you is that others appreciate your ideas. How does that sound to you?"

3 Generate Buy-In for Replacement

The teacher works with the student to generate buy-in to the idea of change. *"Jackie, I know there are some ways you could get more of what you want. You want your ideas to be accepted and appreciated. You have great ideas. And you don't want others to resent you. Would you be willing to change what you do so you get your ideas across more and others feel appreciation rather than resentment? Do you like that idea?"* [Stay at this step until there is buy-in.]

4 Generate Replacement Behavior

The teacher works with the student to create replacement behavior. In the case of the uninformed student, the teacher simply informs the student of class and/or school norms and procedures, or works with the students to aquire the requisite skills. *"Jackie, let's work together to think of some things you could do or say that would let you get your great ideas across and have others feel appreciated rather than put down. What makes someone feel appreciated?"* [Teacher lets student talk about times he/she has felt appreciated. Role-play is used if necessary. They get to the point of agreeing that appreciation is being listened to, understood, and complimented. Appreciation gambits are generated.]

For the uninformed student: *"Jack, today when you wanted to get my attention, you shouted 'Hey, Teacher!' If all students did that, our class would be noisy and distracting. It is fine to want to get my attention, but I need to share with you a non-disruptive way."*

STEPS (Continued)

5 Teacher Models Replacement Behavior

The teacher models the replacement behavior. *"Jackie let's pretend Bobbie has just suggested the idea of a skit and you feel a quiz show would be better. You be Bobbie and I'll be you. Let me try some of the appreciation gambits we just generated, and you tell me how they feel to you."*

"Bobbie, I like your idea about the skit because _____."
"Bobbie, that is a super idea. Another way we could put on the skit would be _____."

6 Student Practices Replacement Behavior

The teacher and student role-play so the student can practice the replacement behavior. *"Jackie, now let's pretend I am Bobbie. I will suggest the idea of a skit and then you suggest the idea of a quiz show, but you use some appreciation gambits so I feel you have really listened to my idea and appreciated it. OK?"* [After the student has role-played the exact scenario the teacher has modeled, the teacher and student role-play additional scenarios so the student can generalize the replacement behavior to a range of situations.]

7 (Optional) Verbal/Non-verbal Cue Is Established

The teacher and student may agree on a verbal or non-verbal cue which will be a secret signal to the student to practice the replacement behavior. See Verbal and Non-verbal Cues, page 14.39. *"It will be difficult to always remember to _____ [replacement behavior]. What do you think about setting up a special signal to help you remember? Would that be helpful to you? [Establish buy-in.] As a signal I could catch your attention and then move the stress apple from one side of my desk to another. Would that work for you?"*

Win-Win Discipline. Kagan Publishing • 1 (800) 933-2667 • www.KaganOnline.com

16.19

Cautions & Hints

• **Replacement Reminders.** A brief verbal or non-verbal cue may be established as a Replacement Reminder. It is agreed that when the teacher gives the student a Replacement Reminder during class, the student will practice the replacement behavior that has been established. Examples of Replacement Reminders include using a special word, or using a verbal or non-verbal cue.

• **When Students Are Uninformed.** Some students simply do not know accepted school and classroom norms of behavior. To get someone's attention at home, they poke the person. So they do the same at school. At school, though, that violates basic norms of behavior. With these students the disruptive behavior is not motivated so much by a need, but rather by lack of understanding and knowledge of school and class norms. For students in the uninformed position, the replacement structure takes a slightly different form: The teacher informs the student of the appropriate behavior, models it, and then has the student practice it.

The student in an uninformed position in some ways presents us with the very challenge that drew us into teaching — the opportunity to teach. Many students today simply do not know responsible behaviors. A student pokes another instead of saying, *"Johnny, could you please..."* A student, when asked a question and not knowing the answer, looks down and is silent instead of making eye contact and saying, *"I'm not sure...."* A student uses inappropriate language without even realizing he/she has done something wrong. The list is long because many students today have not been socialized in the ways students of prior generations were socialized. When a student simply does not know the rules of the game, it is time to teach responsible replacement behaviors.

• **Buy-In.** You may need to spend some time before the student buys in to the idea of changing his/her behavior. But unless there is buy-in, you cannot proceed beyond step three. If the student does not want to change, end the session by telling the student "I want you to think about it." Then meet with the student again later.

• **Model Before Practice.** By modeling the replacement behavior before having the student practice it, you make it easy for the student to transition into the replacement behavior — all he/she has to do is copy your lead. Once that can be done successfully, you can graduate to generalization, trying on new scenarios.

• **Short-Term Perks — Long-Term Pit Falls.** It can be useful to students to understand that self-destructive habits and disruptive behaviors are often maintained because they are reinforcing in the short term while harmful in the long term — like that second piece of chocolate cake. Many disruptive behaviors are like the second piece of chocolate cake. The second piece of cake is rewarding in the moment, but the cumulative effect of often going for that second helping of dessert is to become overweight. Many disruptive behaviors are just like that — rewarding in the short term but punishing in the long run. The student who vents anger may feel better in the moment, but in the long run venting anger often means losing friends and becoming a discipline problem. Avoiding failure by saying "These problems are dumb" may be rewarding in the moment by getting the student out of facing a difficulty, but the long run of that strategy results in failing to learn, and ultimately becoming a failure. To seek attention and approval from others fulfills a need in the moment, but in the long run we are more rewarded by engaging in activities that are self-fulfilling. In the luxury of a follow-up, the teacher can direct the student to reflect on the short-term perks and the long-term pitfalls of disruptive behavior and explore the greater rewards of more responsible alternatives.

Possible Follow-Ups

Catch 'em Being Good

If you see the student using the replacement behavior, be sure to let him/her know you appreciate it, using verbal or non-verbal feedback to the student.

Discussion Topics

In a follow-up discussion explore with the student how it feels to use the replacement behavior. Is it getting him/her the pay-off the two of you hoped for? Does it feel comfortable? Share your appreciations.

Journaling or Team Discussion Topic

We all have habits. Some habits are harmful, like smoking, eating junk food, using drugs, staying up when we are tired, and putting others down. It is very hard to stop doing something once it has become a habit. One of the best ways to end a habit is to find a replacement for habit behavior. Some people begin chewing gum when they try to quit smoking. Some start eating carrots instead of junk food when they are attempting to lose weight. We call this replacement behavior. Have you every tried to change a habit? Have you ever used replacement behavior? Are there any habits you would like to change? Could you think of replacement behavior to do instead of the habit?

Win-Win Discipline. Kagan Publishing • 1 (800) 933-2667 • www.KaganOnline.com

16.21

Responsible Thinking

Students are guided toward responsible thinking via three questions: 1) Have they considered the needs of others as well as their own — sought a Win-Win solution; 2) Have they have treated others as they would hope to be treated; and 3) Have they have acted the way they would hope everyone would act.

Ideal Outcomes

- Students develop empathy and perspective-taking skills.

- Students develop impulse control and self-management skills.

- Students become more self-aware.

- Students learn to consider the impact of their behavior on others.

- Students learn to evaluate options by potential outcomes.

- Students learn to ask the 3W questions.

- Students become more responsible.

Recommended for...

Disruption
Breaking the Rules

Position
Angry

Individual or Class
Both

STEPS

1 Express Desire to Give Student Skills

The teacher lets the student know that he/she wants to share a critical thinking skill. *"Sam, I want to share with you a critical question that will help you make better decisions. The question will help you be successful in getting what you want and help you help others as well. Are you interested?"* [Note: Although there are three responsible thinking questions, each follow-up deals with only one.]

2 Obtain Buy-In

The teacher discusses advantages of responsible thinking until the student expresses interest. *"I find that in deciding what to do, there is a critical question to consider. If I take time to ask this question, I make better decisions for myself and for others. Would you like to learn about this question?"* [Stay at this step until student expresses desire to learn the question.]

3a Question 1: Win-Win?

The teacher engages the student(s) with a Responsible Thinking Question 1: What would be a Win-Win solution? What would meet the needs of everyone involved? *"Let's start with what we want. For example, let's say someone took my book. What do I want?* [Teacher works with student to list desired outcomes such as get the book back, have the person say he/she is sorry, be sure it won't happen again....] *Once I am very clear on the desired outcomes, it is a lot easier to decide how to act. Will hitting the person get me what I want? Will taking his/her book do it? What will get me what I really want?*

Now let's ask what the other person wants. Did he/she really want your book, or did he/she take it because they are angry at you? If he/she wants the book, is there a way you could share, or is there a way he/she could get his/her own? If the person is angry at you, is there a way you could work it through so he/she isn't angry? Can we find a Win-Win solution — a way the person could get what he/she needs and you could get what you need?"

3b Question 2: Which Way Would I Like...?

The teacher engages the student(s) with Responsible Thinking Question 2: *"How would you like to be treated? Have you treated others that way? If we treat others the way we would like to be treated, usually we will feel good about ourselves, they will feel fairly treated, and we will maintain good relations."*

3c Question 3: What Would Happen if Everyone...?

The teacher engages the student(s) with Responsible Thinking Question 3: "What would happen if everyone acted that way? *What would happen if everyone drove as fast as he/she wanted? What would happen if everyone just chose any side of the road to drive on? What if everyone hit others whenever they got angry? What kind of class would we have?"*

STEPS (Continued)

4 Practice

The teacher has the student(s) practice using the responsible thinking question that is the focus of the follow-up, applying the question to his/her own disruptive behavior. *"Let's try the responsible thinking question."* [The teacher has the student try applying the question first on some disruptive behavior the student has not done such as wandering around the room, not bringing in homework, hitting a classmate, carving on a desk, or making fun of a classmate. When the student shows ability to apply the responsible thinking question to the behavior of others,* the teacher has the student apply the question to his/her own disruptive behavior. If the student cannot apply the responsible thinking questions, the teacher models applying it.]

5 Elicit Willingness

The teacher works with the student to elicit willingness to apply the question on an ongoing basis. *"Are you willing to try it? I'm sure that if you did, you would be an excellent model for others and improve relations in our class."*

Cautions & Hints

- **One Approach at a Time.** Work on only one of the responsible thinking questions at a time. Make sure the student is applying that approach before working on a second one.

- **Sidestep Resistance.** If the student is resistant to applying the responsible thinking question to his/her own behavior, start with historical, literary, or imaginary examples. Only later move on to self-evaluation.

- **Private Talk.** Work in private with students as you try to foster responsible thinking.

- **Same-Side.** Communicate to students that you know what they are feeling. *"I have had things taken before and it really gets me angry."*

- **Foster Empathy.** Work with the student to feel what it is like to be the student he/she has yelled at or hit. *"Have you ever had someone yell at you and accuse you...?"*

Possible Follow-Ups

Discussion Topics
Is it easier to apply the responsible thinking question in the moment or afterwards? Why?

Journaling or Team Discussion Topic
When have you tried the responsible thinking question? What was the result?

Responsible Thinking Questions:
The 3W's

1. **W**hat would be a Win-Win solution?
(What would meet everyone's needs?)

2. **W**hich way would I like to be treated?
(Did I treat others the way I would like to be treated?)

3. **W**hat would happen if everyone acted that way?
(How would our class (or world) be if everyone acted that way?)

Same-Side Chat

When we don't understand a student's position and/or don't feel ourselves to be on the same-side with the student, we schedule a meeting to get to know the student better and to develop empathy with him/her — so we can honestly place ourselves on "the same-side" with the student.

Ideal Outcomes

- We better understand student position(s).

- We feel more empathetic toward the student — on the same-side.

- We establish rapport with the student.

- The student feels received and understood.

- The student is more open to share responsibility and to learn more responsible behaviors.

- Feeling more understood, that you are on his/her side, the student is less likely to be disruptive.

Recommended for...

Disruption
Confrontation

Position
Attention-Seeking, Control-Seeking

Individual or Class
Individual

STEPS

1 Schedule a Meeting

Set a time and place to meet so you and the student will not be interrupted. *"Johnny, I would like to get to know you better. Would you be willing to meet with me after class? I don't have any agenda other than to get to know you a little better."*

2 Meet

Indicate at the outset of the meeting that you have no other agenda than to get to know the student better. Let the student know you will not be talking about school. *"I would really like to know you a bit better. I would like to know what your life is like outside of school. Is that OK with you?"*

3 Stay in Student Comfort Zone

Do not probe. Let the student feel comfortable and talk about what he/she would like to share. Give the student choices as to what to talk about. *"Can you tell me a little bit about yourself, like some of the things you most like to do, or about your family or friends?"*

4 Positive Closure

After the meeting, let the student know you in fact have enjoyed getting to know him/her better, and invite future contact. *"I have enjoyed talking with you. I especially enjoyed learning that _____. If you would like to chat again sometime, please let me know and I will do the same. It helps me to get to know my students a bit better."*

Cautions & Hints

• **Follow the Lead of the Student.** Discuss what he/she would like, giving the student choices as to topics. Do not focus on his/her disruptive classroom behaviors. Stay within the comfort zone of the student. As the student is ready, explore family, friends, likes, dislikes, aspirations, and fears —but only as the student is ready.

• **Be Empathetic.** Maintain an empathetic, non-analytic, non-judgmental, non-manipulative manner. Don't try to change the student or figure him/her out. Assume a relaxed, casual posture and language.

• **Don't Play Analyst.** Don't worry about determining the student position — that will emerge when the student trusts you.

• **Same-Side.** Attempt as much as possible to feel what it is like to be the student and let the student know you know you are putting yourself in his/her place: *"I can see how you would feel _____ (sad, angry, happy, fearful, embarrassed...). That would have made me really angry."*

• **Use Reflection.** Use reflective, non-interpretative language. OK: *"You really like it when you are chosen for the team."* Not OK: *"Being chosen for the team makes you feel included."*

Possible Follow-Ups

Acknowledge the Bond

The next time you see the student, give him/her a warm greeting. Nod, smile, or comment: *"I really enjoyed our talk yesterday."* or *"How is your little brother Timmy doing?"* Let the student know you remember and have thought about the chat and that you care about him/her as a person.

Follow-Up Structures: Cementing the Pillars

Often in the moment-of-disruption we do not have time or presence of mind to co-create solutions. We may not even be able to validate the student's position in a way the student can feel validated. We may not be able to place ourselves in a Same-Side position. We may be glad just to be able to end the disruption and return to our mission of teaching. At the same time, the Win-Win teacher knows that when the pillars are not in place, the Win-Win structure begins to crumble. A follow-up is the solution. The follow-up is a second chance to put the pillars in place. In the calm of a scheduled follow-up, we build a Same-Side orientation and co-create, with the student, solutions so the student can learn long-term responsibility. The reason for the follow-up is to cement the three pillars.

Win-Win for Students with Special Needs

We all find ourselves in each of the seven positions at one time or another. Students identified as having special needs are no different: Regardless of any label that may have been placed on them, or any disorder or disability they may have, like all students, students with special needs may engage in any of the four disruptive behaviors and, at different times, may be in any of the seven positions. If we are to be Win-Win teachers, we must look beyond labels. We need to focus on and respond to the student's position at any one moment, not a label that someone has placed on him/her. If we formulate our discipline responses based on labels, our discipline program will be hit-and-miss; if we formulate our responses by seeing and relating to the position of the student, we will be successful.

Win-Win provides us with powerful tools that give us a great deal of leverage in teaching students identified as having special needs. Students with special needs, like all students, need to learn to meet their needs in responsible, non-disruptive ways. Win-Win also provides tools to help us align our classroom practices with the requirements of the laws that govern the treatment of students classified as having special needs.

Let's look in Part I at the intent and requirements of the law and how Win-Win is uniquely positioned to help us as we develop IEPs, FBAs, BIPs, and align classroom practice with what is called for in special education legislation. In Part II we explore the six risks associated with labels and how Win-Win solutions depend on getting beyond labels. In Part III we overview how three instructional programs create Win-Win solutions for students with special needs: Differentiated Instruction, Cooperative Learning, and Multiple Intelligences.

I. The Law, Inclusion, and Win-Win

Special Programs Are
Less Effective than Inclusion

Researchers have compared the effectiveness of special pull-out programs versus inclusive classrooms — the placement of students with disabilities in regular classrooms. Findings indicate that in general students with disabilities are better off being placed in regular classrooms than in special pull-out programs.[1] In a review of 50 studies comparing the academic achievement of students with disabilities in regular versus special programs, there was a **30-percentile difference** favoring inclusion in regular classroom over segregation.[2] More recent meta-analyses report students perform better academically and socially in inclusive general education classroom settings than in pull-out programs.[3] The Commission on Chapter I found pull-out remedial programs to be discriminatory and less effective than heterogeneous classrooms.[4] The vast majority of studies favor inclusion over pull-out and special education classrooms.[5]

As a result of these very favorable results, in the last two decades there has been a very dramatic shift toward inclusion. A study of 891 school districts in all 50 states found the number of schools moving to inclusive education is increasing, the range of disabilities being included in regular classrooms is increasing, and the results are positive for both general and special education students.[6] From 1990 to 1995 the number of students requiring special education services who were included at least 40% of the time in regular classrooms increased from 62% to 72%![7] Inclusion is increasing; it is essential if we are to provide equal educational opportunity and success both academically and socially for all students.

The Rationale for Inclusion

- Improve academic achievement for all
- Nurture the development of social skills
- Increase student and teacher expectations
- Eliminate prejudice, discrimination, stigmatization
- Foster warm and caring friendships
- Increase opportunity for positive peer models, observational learning
- Develop social skills and social cognition of students without disabilities
- Develop character virtues of helping and caring
- Provide equal opportunity for all students
- Equalize access to core curriculum
- Provide age-appropriate classroom settings
- Foster self-esteem among all students
- Encourage cooperation among teachers, professionals
- Enhance diversity skills

Inclusion Benefits Non-disabled Students

A growing number of studies document a range of gains for non-disabled students resulting from their interaction with special needs students in inclusive classrooms.[8] In our increasingly pluralistic society, the ability to get along with and work with others who look and act differently is an essential life skill. Through classroom interactions with differently-abled students, regular students develop social and emotional skills. The benefits of inclusion for students without disabilities include:

- Improved academic performance through tutoring
- Improved attitude toward students with disabilities
- Reduced fear of differences
- Increased ability to perform in heterogeneous situations
- Development of respect, tolerance, patience, caring, and cooperation
- Increased self-esteem
- Improved leadership skills
- Development of social skills

A Story of Inclusion[9]

Robert Jutras

Several years ago, I became familiar with a student named Jeb who was diagnosed as autistic. Jeb went to a school where he was in the Resource Room his entire day with other students with like diagnoses and disabilities. He was usually non-verbal, and his days were filled with non-responsive behaviors. In fourth grade, Jeb left that school and entered the elementary school where I was teaching fifth grade. He was to be in an inclusive fourth grade classroom. My good friend and colleague, Ann, was to be his teacher.

On the third day of school, a mother requested a quick after-school meeting. Ann obliged. The woman approached Ann and told how much her daughter, Erin, was enjoying Ann's class but, continuing, the mother's tone and message became different. "Erin is a high achieving student and will need plenty of support to make sure that she is challenged," stated the mother. "You have a very challenging task this year with the two new students, and I don't want Erin to lose out because of the time that those students are going to

require." Ann responded calmly, "I appreciate your concerns, and you are certainly right that, each year, I face unique challenges. But with support and experience, these challenges usually don't become any student's burden." Erin's mother replied, "I want my child removed from your class so she can get the attention that she will need to meet her potential."

Ann recommended that she and Erin's mother adjourn the meeting and reconvene when the principal was available. The parent insisted that now be the time.

The principal stood up from his desk, smiled and thanked the parent for addressing her concerns promptly and complimented her for putting her child's needs in the forefront. He went on to list the names of private schools in the area where she might have more of a say about the kind of classroom in which her daughter best learns. The mother's jaw dropped.

Erin remained in Ann's class. Erin was a sweet girl and had a great year, making

17.4

Win-Win Discipline. Kagan Publishing • 1 (800) 933-2667 • www.KaganOnline.com

A Story of Inclusion (Continued)

significant gains academically based on the state's standardized testing.

Her mother requested a meeting with Ann two days before the end of the school year: "I think we need to go to the principal to discuss Erin's placement for next year," said her mother. "I am allowed to make a request," she announced.

Erin's mother and Ann entered the principal's office. Before he could stand and greet them, Erin's mother started: "I am here in my daughter's best interest. I have the right under your policy to make a request to where Erin goes next year. I want her to go to Mr. Jutras' class. I already have a relationship with him because he taught my oldest son three years ago. In addition to this request, I want to make sure that Erin and Jeb are…" After a pause, she finished: "… in the same class next year." It was the principal and Ann's jaws that dropped this time.

Continuing, the mother spoke of how her very bright daughter not only gained aca-

demically throughout the year, but gained compassion and empathy. "Erin is a different girl because of Jeb. I never saw that side of her, frankly, I don't think it existed. I want to thank you both for a great year — a year that I am sure will always be a favorite of Erin's." Everyone in the room had a tear rolling down his/her cheek.

Erin and Jeb were in my class the following fall, and it was true. Erin introduced Jeb to new students in our class, and Jeb always responded by saying, "Erin is my best friend."

Jeb became more responsive throughout the year and once even assumed a position in Timeout for being too chatty! At appropriate times, Erin read to Jeb, and Jeb to her. Jeb was lucky. Erin was his friend.

That was five years ago, and Erin and Jeb went on to different middle schools and high schools. They are still friends. They exchange phone calls and holiday and birthday wishes still. I consider myself lucky because I, too, receive those pleasant wishes from these former students.

Inclusion Is Win-Win

Inclusion aligns with the philosophy of Win-Win. Students with special needs learn more and feel better about themselves. Regular education students learn an entirely new set of skills and feel better about themselves. Inclusion is a win also for our educational system: It aligns our educational system with the basic premise of education in a democracy—the philosophy of equal opportunity for all students.

Inclusion: To the Extent Appropriate

Based on the research, the law demands that, as much as possible, students with special needs be educated in regular rather than special classrooms; only in exceptional cases — only if regular education placements cannot be achieved satisfactorily — shall students with special needs be separated from regular education classrooms:

Letter of Inclusion Law

"...to the maximum extent appropriate, handicapped children, including those children in public and private institutions or other care facilities, are educated with children who are not handicapped, and that special classes, separate schooling, or other removal of handicapped children from the regular educational environment occurs only when the nature or severity of the handicap is such that education in regular classes with the use of supplementary aids and services cannot be achieved satisfactorily." — Public Law 101-476; Section 1412 [5][B]

The Education for All Handicapped Children Act of 1975 (PL 94-142)[10] called for placement of students with special needs in the least restrictive environment (LRE). Although some prominent educators have called for full inclusion of all students all of the time, most educators who deal with the full range of special needs conclude that full inclusion of all students with special needs is not in the interest of those students or their classmates. The principle of least restrictive environment demands we use inclusion as much as possible consistent with the needs of the student.

Heterogeneous Classrooms:
Another Form of Inclusion

There is a movement toward inclusion at various levels. Not only are students with disabilities being included in regular classrooms; increasingly students of all ability levels are being integrated in heterogeneous classrooms. A great deal of research indicates tracking and ability-grouped class assignment has a wide range of negative outcomes for most students.[11] Tracking has been criticized on ethical as well as empirical grounds.[12] The National Education Association resolved in 1992 that tracking as a practice is eliminated.[13] Arguments have been levied also against segregating gifted students.[14] In the words of Lorainne Monroe, *What's good for the best is good for the rest.*[15] Her work in raising an extraordinarily low achieving school to the level of an extraordinarily high achieving school by maintaining high expectations for all students is a testimony to the power of high expectations.

Inclusion Demands New Skills

With increasing inclusion comes a need for new skills for teachers. Presently educational institutions are not preparing teachers with the range of skills necessary for successful inclusion of many students. Three essential sets of skills for successful inclusion are cooperative learning, differentiated instruction, and multiple intelligence theory and methods.

Another part of the training necessary for successful inclusion is training in recognizing special needs, having the skills to meet those needs, and to teach students to meet those needs. Including students with special needs in regular classrooms means more potential for disruptions of every sort, and a need to institute programs proven to meet a greater range of student needs.

Finally, with the emphasis on inclusion comes new legal requirements for educators. Let's look at how Win-Win helps us meet those requirements.

Win-Win, IEPs, FBAs, & BIPs,

Win-Win Discipline provides support in creating Functional Behavior Assessments (FBAs) and Behavioral Intervention Plans (BIPs). A multi-disciplinary team (MDT) consisting of educators and parents determines the student's learning challenge and collaboratively develops an Individual Education Plan (IEP) or 504 Plan that details specific classroom accommodations.

IEP's, FBA's, BIP's

	What It Is	What It Does	Where Win-Win Fits In
IEP	Individual Education Plan	Sets goals for student: academic goals, career goals, life-skill goals, and placement goals. Determines least restrictive environment. Describes collaborative solution arrived at by parents and education teams.	Individual ABCD Tally indicates the specific responsible behaviors to include; determining position indicates life skills to be acquired.
FBA	Functional Behavior Assessment	Determines the function of behavior that impedes learning of the student or of others.	Position indicates function.
BIP	Behavioral Intervention Plan	States plan for teaching the student positive, responsible behaviors.	Includes Preventative Procedures; Moment-of-Disruption Structures and Strategies; Follow-up Structures and Strategies.

Individual Education Plans: IEPs. Win-Win Discipline provides specific recommendations to include in the development of the IEP or 504 Plan. The individual ABCD Tally indicates the responsible behaviors a student needs to learn. Analysis of student position indicates the life skills the student needs to acquire. Identifying each student's position leads the team to strategies that would most effectively meet the needs of the particular student, making the IEP process much richer. If cooperative learning is an instructional tool, then the IEP goals need to include types of behaviors that will allow the student to be successful in group interactions.

Functional Behavioral Assessment: FBA. If the behaviors of a student with special needs are impeding his/her learning or the learning of others, the reauthorization of IDEA (Individuals with Disabilities Education Act of 1997[16]) requires, as an integral part of the IEP process, for schools to conduct a Functional Behavioral Assessment (FBA). The emphasis in the law is on what purpose or function the problem behavior serves for the student with special needs. Win-Win provides an effective process for determining the function of behaviors: *Determining student position translates directly into understanding and being able to state the function of disruptive behavior.*

Identifying Student Positions. The function that disruptive behavior serves for a student with special needs is a function of the student's position, not necessarily his/her category of special need. We know more about the function of behavior, for example, if we know a student's position (avoiding failure, seeking control) than if we know the student's disability label (learning disorder, emotionally disturbed). For example, when we know the student is seeking attention, we better understand the function of his/her repeated clowning around in class and his/her breaking dress-code rules. Win-Win Discipline and its concept of student position is, therefore, an extremely valuable tool for determining the function of behavior.

By identifying student position, we have essential answers for the FBA:

- What do students gain, avoid, or escape through engaging in their disruptive behavior?
- Is the behavior allowing students to get the attention they are seeking?
- Is the disruption motivated by a fear of failure?
- Does the student need to vent energy or anger?
- Does the student simply not have knowledge or skill for behaving responsibly?

Identifying student position *is* identifying the function of disruptive behavior! See **Chapter 11. Identifying Positions.**

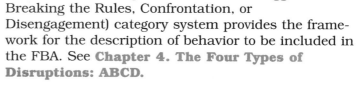

A Reminder:

Identifying Student Position

Clues in the Moment-of-Disruption
1) Your gut reaction
2) Your impulses
3) Disruptive student's reaction to intervention
4) Classmates' reactions to the disruption
5) Facial expressions and body language

Indicators Following the Moment-of-Disruption
1) Disruptive student's reaction to different interventions
2) Interviews with disruptive student
3) Interviews with classmates
4) Interviews with prior teachers
5) Interviews with parents
6) Cumulative charts

■ **Categorizing Disruptive Behavior: ABCD.** The FBA is to include a very specific description of the type of disruptive behaviors a student is choosing. Win-Win's ABCD (Aggression, Breaking the Rules, Confrontation, or Disengagement) category system provides the framework for the description of behavior to be included in the FBA. See **Chapter 4. The Four Types of Disruptions: ABCD.**

The ABCD Tally provides a very straightforward approach to categorizing disruptive behavior. See **Chapter 5. The ABCD Tally.** Additionally, in formulating the FBA, information can be gathered through observations and interviews of teachers, parents, peers, and the student regarding:

- When the behavior most likely occurs?
- When the behavior least likely occurs?
- What circumstances or individuals tend to trigger the behavior?
- What events follow the behavior?
- In what setting does the behavior occur?

■ **Behavior Intervention Plan: BIP.** The law also requires that we implement a positive behavior plan to teach the student with special needs proactive, responsible behaviors to replace disruptive behaviors. The law focuses on teaching responsible behaviors, and giving the student the knowledge, practice, and support in learning and implementing new alternative behaviors. The strategies in Win-Win Discipline that respond to the needs of the various students' positions provide practical tools to create effective Behavior Intervention Plans.

Win-Win Discipline. Kagan Publishing • 1 (800) 933-2667 • www.KaganOnline.com

17.9

The desired outcome in the law is perfectly aligned with the philosophy and methodology of Win-Win: The student with special needs and the teacher are on the same-side, working together to co-create positive solutions to discipline problems with the long-term goal of the student learning positive, responsible behaviors. Positive Behavior Support (PBS) strategies are created collaboratively based on the function or purpose the disruptive behavior serves for the student, or in other words, the student's position.

The emphasis in Win-Win on proactive interventions that respond to student position is exactly what the law demands when it requires positive interventions with supports for students with special needs to learn responsible replacement behaviors. Win-Win is invaluable in creating the required Behavior Intervention Plan, (BIP), with its Positive Behavior Supports, (PBS). Items in the BIP include:

- **Preventative Procedures**
- **Moment-of-Disruption Structures and Strategies**
- **Follow-Up Structures and Strategies**

Win-Win's concept of position helps formulate an effective Behavior Intervention Plan (BIP). We recognize there is not a one-to-one correspondence between the specific learning challenge of a student and the student's position. Understanding student position helps us determine the type of intervention needed. For an effective plan, we must look beyond a student's special needs to see the whole student. Determining a student's position is essential if we are to focus accurately on the student's true needs.

Win-Win aligns perfectly with the recommended process of creating a BIP: The BIP is created "with" the student and not "about" the student. We assume a *Same-Side orientation* and *co-create solutions*, two basic pillars of Win-Win. The student is an active participant in developing the Behavior Intervention Plan that comes out of the FBA.

Adapting Curriculum, Instruction, and Management. When developing a Behavior Intervention Plan, it is important to consider curriculum, instruction, and management strategies. Most students with special needs are capable of learning responsible alternatives to disruptive behavior. Their special needs, however, may make the process take longer, and may require more support, structure, and follow-through. The Win-Win teacher takes care to ensure curriculum has relevance for an individual student and is developmentally appropriate. Success can come by trying a range of instructional strategies, seeking a match with the unique needs of the student. Efficient management strategies prevent downtime, allowing less opportunity for disruptive behavior. One of the main purposes of developing Behavior Intervention Plans for special needs students is to increase their ability to get the most out of instruction. To this end, Win-Win approaches to instruction and management are very helpful. See **Chapter 18. Win-Win Management** and **Chapter 19. Win-Win Instruction.**

Parent Alliances. Creating alliances with parents is an essential part of the Functional Behavioral Assessments (FBA) and its Behavior Intervention Plan (BIP). The law requires parent participation, but if we are really going to meet the needs of all students, then involving students' parents as allies needs to go beyond just complying with the law. It needs to create an inviting atmosphere with parents as members of the team. The same "We" feeling rather than "You Versus Me" that is critical to Win-Win classrooms is an essential component of developing the Individual Education Plan, the Functional Behavior Assessment, and the Behavior Intervention Plan. See Parent Conference in **Chapter 15. Following Up.** Getting input and ideas from parents, truly listening to them, and eliciting their back-up, and support of the school plan at home are all elements that lead to Win-Win solutions for students with special needs. See Parents as Partners in **Chapter 18. Win-Win Management.**

II. Beyond Labels –
The Seven Risks of Labels

Win-Win is differentiated discipline. Instead of a one-size-fits-all approach, we identify, validate, and respond to the unique position of each student. A solution that fits well for a student seeking power will fail with a student avoiding failure. For consistently winning solutions, we must look beyond the disruptive behavior and see the student. Following that same approach, to create consistently winning solutions for students with special needs, we must look beyond any label they have been given and relate to their uniqueness.

Let's examine seven risks associated with labels and why Win-Win solutions depend on our ability to look beyond labels.

Risk 1: Changed Perceptions, Lowered Expectations. Once a student has a label, we begin to think about the student differently. Johnny is not just an energetic fellow; he is an ADHD student. Labels are likely to induce lowered expectations in the student and in those who view the student through the filter of the label. The student becomes likely to live up to (or, better put, live down to) those lowered expectations, and we become less likely to demand the student become all he/she can be.

Risk 2: Labels Undermine Individual Responsibility. Once a label has been applied, students may use it as an excuse for disruptive behavior. *(I can't help it; I am ADHD.)* Others may collaborate in this process. *(My son can't help it; he has ADHD.)* We may be tempted to tolerate disruptive behavior that we should not allow. Labels undermine individual responsibility.

Risk 3: Labels Involve Circular Reasoning. A very active student is labeled ADHD because he/she is very active. The label is then used to explain and excuse the high level of activity: *"Oh, he is hyperative because he has ADHD."*

Risk 4: Labels Are Arbitrary. The terminology used to describe special needs varies widely in the published literature, from state to state, and even among school districts. The same student is likely to receive one disability label from one professional, a different label from another, and no label at all from a third. The literature on disability is replete with arbitrarily different labels for the same symptoms. There is no established single common language for types of special needs; the only consensus seems to be convergence on words beginning with the letter "D!" The terms "Disorder," "Disturbance," "Disability," "Dysfunction," "Deficit," "Difference," "Difficulty," and even "Differently-abled" are used without meaningful distinctions. Too often, professionals use these D-words indiscriminately and interchangeably. Without meaningful distinctions, special needs in the area of learning are referred to variously as "Learning Disorders," Learning Dysfunctions," "Learning Deficits," "Learning Disabilities," and "Learning Difficulties." In the literature on special needs and among practitioners and professionals, these labels cover a wide spectrum of very different behaviors.

Risk 5: Labels Overlap. Labels for different types of disabilities and disorders fail to be informative in part because they are arbitrary, but also because they overlap. For example, "Mental Retardation" is both a symptom of other disabilities and a syndrome in and of itself.[17] Some, but not all, students with Cerebral Palsy are mentally retarded. Thus knowing someone has Cerebral Palsy does not inform us of his/her intellectual capability. Some, but not all ADHD students have Oppositional Defiant Disorder (ODD). Down syndrome has many forms: some students with Down syndrome function at quite high levels; others are severely mentally retarded. "Mental Retardation" always indicates a lower IQ, but it does not tell us if a student has Down syndrome, Cerebral Palsy, or any of the other two hundred known causes for mental retardation. Because labels overlap, they fail to inform us of the unique needs of an individual student. Because labels overlap and each student is unique, knowing the label of a student with a disability does not inform us of 1) her/his unique set of special needs; 2) his/her position; 3) the kind of disruption he/she might cause in class, if any, or 4) how best to teach the student. We cannot create winning solutions by relating to labels; we must relate to the student beyond the label.

> *Labels are likely to induce lowered expectations.*

> *The terms "Disorder," "Disturbance," "Disability," "Dysfunction," "Deficit," "Difference," "Difficulty," and even "Differently-abled" are used without meaningful distinctions.*

Win-Win Discipline. Kagan Publishing • 1 (800) 933-2667 • www.KaganOnline.com

17.12

Risk 6: Labels Are Behavior-Based. A cornerstone of Win-Win is that to create consistently winning solutions, we must look beyond behavior to see and relate to the position of the student. Disability and disorder labels usually are assigned based on a student's behavior. Thus they are often not helpful in formulating a discipline response. As we have seen, we must look beyond the behavior to view the student's position if we are to formulate a successful discipline program. In formulating a successful discipline response, knowing a student's label does not help us as much as knowing the student's position; we must see the student, not the label.

Risk 7: Labels Are Partially Social Constructs. In 1990 approximately 900,000 American students were diagnosed with ADD; ten years later the figure was 7 million![18] If ADD were simply a medical disease, we would have to conclude there is an incredibly devastating epidemic spreading across our land! In fact, no medical epidemic has occurred. ADD is not a disease; it is in part a social construct: Students once thought of as energetic, strong-willed, daydreamers, lazy, or obstinate are being labeled ADD.

To counter the notion that ADD is a disease, Thomas Armstrong wrote the book, *The Myth of the A.D.D. Child.*[19] ADD, though, is not merely a myth. Brain scans reveal predictable differences in some students labeled ADD,[20] and many (but not all) students labeled ADD benefit greatly from drugs like Ritalin, Adderal, or Dexedrine. Many students labeled ADD, however, can become quite successful and non-disruptive if we implement simple non-medical approaches. See The ADD Checklist.

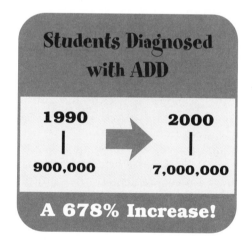

The ADD Checklist

Most of the strategies that are good for ADD and ADHD students are simply good strategies to use with all students. Nevertheless, it is helpful to review the strategies below when planning Win-Win solutions with students labeled ADD and ADHD.

Seating & Environment
- ❐ Seat students up front and/or near teacher's desk
- ❐ Surround students with good role models
- ❐ Do not seat near distractions: air conditioners, high traffic areas, heaters, doors, windows
- ❐ Monitor on field trips
- ❐ Create a stimuli-reduced study area as an option for students
- ❐ Have more than one seat for student; non-verbal cue to change seat

Instruction
- ❐ Frequent eye contact
- ❐ Frequent monitoring for on-task behavior
- ❐ Brief instructional bits
- ❐ Check for understanding
- ❐ Make help-seeking easy, acceptable
- ❐ Brief practice sessions
- ❐ Intelligence shifts
- ❐ Peer interaction, cooperative learning

Curriculum
- ❐ Stimulating, personally relevant content
- ❐ Student choice of projects
- ❐ Multi-modal access to curriculum

Satisfy Need for Movement
- ❐ Instructional strategies that include movement
- ❐ Frequent breaks
- ❐ Rotation learning centers
- ❐ Hands-on manipulatives
- ❐ Stress Apples
- ❐ Break up lectures with peer interaction

Use Calming Techniques
- ❐ Play music at 60 beats a minute
- ❐ Relaxation breathing
- ❐ Drawing
- ❐ Guided imagery to calm place
- ❐ Establish cool down cues
- ❐ Journaling

Assignments
- ❐ Have assignment book or assignment area of notebook
- ❐ Color-code or teach students to color-code assignments
- ❐ Assign small bite-sized chunks with feedback to follow each
- ❐ Give time for students to write assignments
- ❐ Have students record assignments in check-box form
- ❐ Monitor that assignments are recorded
- ❐ Include easy fun items at beginning and end of each assignment
- ❐ Provide choices of assignments

Assessment
- ❐ Alternative ways to demonstrate knowledge: Build It, Create a Model
- ❐ Break up testing sessions
- ❐ Schedule stretch breaks
- ❐ Test knowledge, not attention span
- ❐ Modify time requirement
- ❐ Pre-assess (ADD students may have missed prerequisite skills)

Encouragement & Praise
- ❐ Frequent feedback
- ❐ Give visual feedback (stickers)
- ❐ Frequent rewards
- ❐ Praise sustained effort
- ❐ Have peers praise sustained effort
- ❐ Have peers learn gambits to refocus student attention

Parental Support
- ❐ Have parents sign assignment book
- ❐ Call parents with "good news"
- ❐ Frequent, supportive communication

Organizational Skills Training
- ❐ Teach organization skills
- ❐ Use agendas, planners
- ❐ Check notebooks, desks, lockers

Self-Monitoring Skills Training
- ❐ Teach students to self-monitor and adjust

Opponents of drug approaches to ADD claim Ritalin is far too broadly used, is a very carefully controlled substance similar to amphetamines and cocaine, may lead to dependency, and leads students to internalize negative self-perceptions (*I'm bad, or I'm sick*). Opponents advocate alternative non-drug treatments such as neurofeedback[21] and a range of strategies such as diet, limiting television, positive self-talk, physical education, music, visualization, touch, focusing, peer tutoring, and consequences.[22]

To counter the notion that Learning Disabilities is a meaningful concept, Thomas Finlan wrote *Learning Disability: The Imaginary Disease*.[23] Learning Disabilities, though, like ADD are not simply social constructs. Approximately 85% of students labeled as having Learning Disabilities have dyslexia, and dyslexia is associated with predictable differences in brain functioning. Brain scans reveal dyslexics process language in a different part of the brain than students who are not dyslexic, and that training that cures certain forms of dyslexia causes the brain of the student who was dyslexic to function like the brain of students who are not *dyslexic*.[24] Dyslexia, like ADD, is not imaginary.

The problem is that some special needs labels like "ADD" and "Learning Disability" are *partially* social constructs, but *partially* describe real, treatable physical differences. If we treat the labels as purely social constructs we are driven to ignore hard science and important treatment options. If we treat labels as purely medical disease categories, we are driven to ignore the many wonderful and effective non-medical options that any teacher can institute. We simply must look beyond the label: Winning solutions depend on seeing and working with the individual student.

■ **Beyond Labels.** What conclusion can we draw? Each student is unique. To create consistently winning solutions for students with special needs we must respond to the unique needs of the student, not a label that has been given the student.

III. Meeting Special Needs: Three Win-Win Programs

Three programs are especially effective with students with special needs and each is aligned with the philosophy of Win-Win Discipline. The programs: 1. Differentiated Instruction; 2. Cooperative Learning; and 3. Multiple Intelligences.

1. Differentiated Instruction. Success with students with special needs is a function of our ability to understand their needs, their position, and our ability to adapt and modify our curriculum, instruction, management, and discipline approach accordingly. The special education literature and law use the terms "adaptations" and "modifications" to refer to differentiated instruction— responding differently to each student according to his/her needs, abilities, and learning styles.

2. Cooperative Learning. The research indicates cooperative learning is the single most effective educational approach for meeting the needs of all students in inclusive classrooms. Attempts at inclusion without cooperative learning often backfire, resulting in students with special needs feeling isolated and segregated. Further, cooperative learning without ample teambuilding, classbuilding, and social skill development can backfire resulting in negative stereotyping and exclusion of students with special needs. Thus, if we are to follow the law, if we are to create least restrictive learning environments, and if we are to integrate students with special needs into regular classrooms, it is mandatory that our instruction include frequent cooperative learning that includes teambuilding, classbuilding, and social skill development. Placing students in regular education classrooms is not inclusion; inclusion depends on effective cooperative learning.

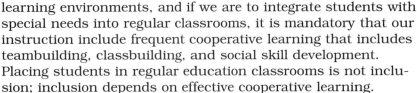

3. Multiple Intelligences. Miracles happen when multiple intelligences strategies are used to teach students with special needs. Simple instructional strategies called multiple intelligences structures fill the bill. By matching instruction with the way the student best learns, multiple intelligences structures allow students easy access to the curriculum. Dramatic accelerated achievement results for students with special needs.

1. Differentiated Instruction:
Adaptations and Modifications

When legislation was passed to require least restrictive environments (LRE) for students with special needs, that is, that students with special needs be mainstreamed into regular classrooms if at all possible, it was recognized that adjustments in instruction and curriculum would be necessary. To make inclusion possible, the law calls for "appropriate adaptations and modifications" for students with special needs.

• **Adaptations** involve changes to the environment, access changes, or a differentiated manner in which a student can demonstrate knowledge of a subject (e.g., while the team is discussing the First Amendment, a student on an adapted curriculum may draw a picture representing freedom of speech).

17.16

Win-Win Discipline. Kagan Publishing • 1 (800) 933-2667 • www.KaganOnline.com

• **Modifications** involve changes in the outcomes, expectations, and/or materials compared to those for the other students' in the classroom. The student may work on a parallel activity (e.g., student answers true-false questions while the class is answering short essay questions on a topic).

Adaptations vs. Modifications

Adaptations	Alternative Approaches to Acquiring and Demonstrating Learning
Modifications	Modified Learning Goals

For some students with special needs it is appropriate to maintain exactly the same expectations as for the other students in the class; we need only *adapt* the way we teach those students and/or the way we allow those students to demonstrate learning. For other students, it is appropriate to *modify* our learning goals. *It is extremely important that we attempt a range of adaptations before beginning to modify our expectations and goals.* Many times students blossom when a new instructional strategy is tried and the response of the teacher is to be astonished — finding the student was capable of far more than the teacher thought possible. See the care of Paula, 17.30. Some students who were not performing at all well in traditional classrooms flourish when cooperative learning or multiple intelligences instrction is used; the response of their teacher is to admit they did not realize the student was that smart. How smart a student is and how much the student can learn is a function, to a large degree, of the adaptations we institute. Not all students learn the same way, so any one approach to instruction or curriculum will fit for some but not all students. When we shift our approach, a new set of students benefit. Special need adaptations and modifications parallel those described in depth in the differentiated instruction literature.[25] See the Differentiated Instruction section of **Chapter 19. Win-Win Instruction.**

The seven most common adaptations and modifications are

> 1. **Adapt Time**
> 2. **Adapt Support**
> 3. **Adapt Teaching Strategies**
> 4. **Adapt Student Responses**
> 5. **Modify Workload**
> 6. **Modify Difficulty**
> 7. **Modify Participation**

Adaptations & Modifications for Inclusion

1. Adapt Time
Adapt the time allotted for completing a task or for learning materials. Students with disabilities may require different completion rates.

- Example: Special needs student is given more time to complete assignment.

2. Adapt Support
Provide increased support and materials. Personnel support may include: instructional aides, specialists, and/or parents. Support materials may include: books on tape, visuals, manipulatives, and Braille material.

- Example: An aide signs the teacher's speech for hearing disabled student.

3. Adapt Teaching Strategies
Adapt the teaching strategy. Use multimodal strategies to provide multiple modes of accessing the curriculum. Actively involve students with peers.

- Example: Use cooperative learning so special needs student interacts with classmates over content in a positive way.

4. Adapt Student Responses
Adapt the type of responses required from students. Students with certain disabilities will not be able to respond in the same way as other students. Some types of responses include: writing, speaking, reading, looking, pointing, moving manipulatives, drawing, painting, singing, dancing, or demonstrating. Select appropriate response modes for students with disabilities.

- Example: Allow special needs student to answer questions orally rather than in writing, or to select from pre-made response cards rather than writing answers.

5. Modify Workload
Modify the amount of work required. Individualize the task for students with disabilities.

- Example: Special needs student is required to list and define two rights and two responsibilities of citizens; other students are required to list more.

6. Modify Difficulty
Modify the skill level required. The difficulty of the task should be adjusted to the student's personal objective.

- Example: Special needs student may describe geographic features of one state; other students may be required to contrast the geographic features of two or more states.

7. Modify Participation
Modify the type of participation required.

- Example: Allow special needs student to fill a realistic role for the team project.

2. Cooperative Learning: True Inclusion

Cooperative learning is the royal road to successful inclusion. In the words of The National Center on Educational Restructuring and Inclusion (NCERI),

> The data indicate that instructional strategies and classroom practices that support inclusive education for the most part are the same ones that teachers believe are effective for students in general. They report that a precursor to inclusive programs is a belief in the benefits of heterogeneous classrooms. Of the districts reporting, cooperative learning is identified as the most important instructional strategy supporting inclusive education.[26]

When we mainstream students with disabilities into regular classrooms that do not use cooperative learning on a regular basis, they are often isolated and excluded. Often the other students reject them, belittle them, and make fun of them. It is instinctual for students to group with and become friends with those who are like them, those with whom they feel a connection. Only the very exceptional student will reach out to another student who appears different. Thus, with few exceptions, mainstreaming a student with special needs without special preparations fails to create inclusion — and often creates the opposite of an inclusive experience. With no special preparation for inclusion, students with special needs often become the brunt of jokes, put-downs, and social ostracization. As well intended as it may be, inclusion usually does not lead to an inclusive experience in traditional classrooms.

Cooperative learning is not a panacea. With no special preparation, students in a group will reject those who are different. Take for example, the following observation of student interaction in a Singapore classroom:

> Sandip, an Indian student, tried to move close to his group members so that he could participate in the group discussion. As he tried to move closer to the group, his groupmates moved further away. Frustrated, he walked around the group, looking for a space to move in. The teacher scolded Sandip for not being on task. Sandip tried once again to be part of the group. The group moved further away from him and huddled even closer together. It was clear to the observer that the group did not want Sandip to be part of the group.[27]

With no teambuilding or social skill development, students are likely to exclude and ostracize others in the class or team who are different than themselves racially, physically, emotionally, or cognitively. Students are not born with social skills; social skills are taught and learned, like any skills. In the same Singapore classrooms, when teambuilding and social skill training was instituted, students who otherwise would have been excluded were included far more often as seatmates, project partners, and best friends.[28]

Cooperative learning can have a life-transforming positive effect on students with special needs. The process, however, does not occur over night. Patience, faith, and teambuilding are required. With those in place, miracles can happen, as documented in the case of Haley, the girl who learned the meaning of I CAN!

I Can!

By Linda Pfleger[29]

… I had the privilege to teach Haley, a fourth grade student who was coded Special Ed and monitored through complete inclusion in my Language Arts classroom…. I had attended Dr. Kagan's Emotional Intelligence Workshop because I wanted affirmation that my teaching style and relationship-bound approach was effective and on target.

… Within the first week of school, it soon became apparent that Haley would be a challenge. Actively, we participated in team and class building to begin to set the tone for a risk free environment. Reluctantly, she participated, but barely. Easily, I could sense she was uncomfortable speaking aloud among her friends and definitely not in front of the entire class. She would hang her head, lower her eyes, and cower if I even appeared to glance her direction. In my six years of teaching, she had the lowest self-esteem of any student I have ever taught…. She struggled to retain and paraphrase what others said to her. Immediately, it became obvious that Haley had only learned in the traditional classroom, independently learning, and this style of teaching was foreign and completely out of her comfort zone.

… Patience became my silent motto. … Baby steps were vital! Often I implemented

Numbered Heads Together to introduce a topic, review concepts, share a variety of opinions, and promote higher-level thinking…. When Haley was chosen, I stood nearby. In the beginning, I would speak a word, she would add a word, and this process would continue until the entire thought was presented. Always, as a class we celebrated each small success she and all students experienced. Eventually, she was able to hold her head higher, make eye contact, and be more at ease with herself. Haley would tilt her head and ask, "I can???"

… Other Cooperative Learning Structures I regularly implemented to increase her skill and confidence were Pairs Check, Team-Pair-Solo, Mix-Pair-Share, Corners, RoundTable and RoundRobin, Timed Pair Share, Fan-N-Pick, and Showdown. One skill she eventually mastered was paraphrasing what others said or felt (that active listening part was a thorn in her side!), not only with her team, but also aloud in front of the class! Amazing!

In the state of Texas, fourth grade students are responsible for taking the Reading, Math, and Writing portion of the state mandated TAAS assessment test…. Under the umbrella of Special Ed, Haley had not taken these tests before. At the beginning of the

17.20

Win-Win Discipline. Kagan Publishing • 1 (800) 933-2667 • www.KaganOnline.com

year when she began writing, I was not sure I could teach her to untangle her thoughts to write a cohesive essay or story. Definitely, she had the imagination to succeed, but still, daily I reinforced that tilt of her head as she asked, "I can??" By February, she began to say, "I can." No elaboration or emotion, but no question in her voice either! PROGRESS had been made!

... One day in February, before the writing test, her classmates proudly jumped from their seats and gave Haley a standing ovation as she confidently shared her thoughts about a question and then boldly announced, "You know, I CAN!" Humbled by her classmates' response to her, I tearfully joined in the jubilant celebration of Haley and her obvious sense of confidence and success in herself.

... To say the least, she took the Writing and Reading Portion of the TAAS test. The constant class and team building made all

the difference for Haley. When the test scores arrived, I almost fell out of my chair! Not only did Haley pass, but she also earned a score of 3 (out of a possible 4) on the Writing part (quite subjective), which is proficient, and she earned a 97% on the Reading portion, which earned her ACADEMIC RECOGNITION! Truly, this was amazing and I attribute her success in attitude and academics to the Cooperative Learning environment that I learned from the Kagan workshops.

... Without a doubt, I believe passionately that all people and students need to be valued for the persons they are and given the opportunity to talk and truly listen to others' ideas and perspectives. This interactive approach to learning empowers students to believe in their abilities. Haley is a true example of a student who persevered daily to not only connect for learning, but to believe enough to confidently shout "I CAN!!"

When we mainstream students with special needs not into a classroom, but rather into a cohesive cooperative team and couple cooperative learning with teambuilding and social skill development, true inclusion occurs. Over 40 empirical studies show attitudes toward students with disabilities are far better in classrooms using cooperative learning.[30] Extensive reviews find cooperative learning more effective than individualistic and competitive learning for increasing academic performance and social acceptance of students with disabilities.[31] An annotated bibliography of studies involving students with moderate and severe disabilities reveals positive achievement in a wide range of subject areas.[32] When cooperative learning is in place, regular education students show greater tolerance, acceptance, liking, and caring for special education students mainstreamed into their classrooms and, in turn, students with special needs feel more acceptance, have a higher self-esteem, and perform better academically. Cooperative learning is the embodiment of the inclusive philosophy.

Mainstreaming without cooperative learning is not inclusion. There is a dramatic difference between being welcomed as a member of a team and being placed, isolated in a class of thirty students. Similarly, cooperative learning without teambuilding, classbuilding, and social skill development, often also fails to deliver on the promise of creating a supportive, inclusive experience for students with special needs. If teammates are focused only on the academic goal, having a teammate with special needs is like running a race with a handicap. Teambuilding, classbuilding, and social skill development broaden the curriculum. Teaching teamwork skills, diversity skills, and social skills will serve students in our interdependent, service-oriented economy. Teambuilding and classbuilding activities allow students to get to know and like each other, generate mutual support, and value individual differences.[33] Social skills programs teach students a range of skills such as how to encourage and praise others, patient waiting, understanding points of view different from one's own, and seeking consensus.[34]

Teambuilding, Classbuilding, Social Skills Development = Inclusion

Without Teambuilding
Johnny is the blind student.
After Teambuilding
Johnny is our teammate, who happens to be blind.
Without Classbuilding
Susie is the wheel chair student.
With Classbuilding
Susie is our classmate, who is sitting in a wheel chair.
Without Social Skills Development
Hurry up! You can't take all day!
With Social Skills Development
Take your time. We want you to do the best you can do.

When inclusion is coupled with comprehensive cooperative learning, inclusion is a win-win. Students with special needs win peer support and tutoring. Students without special needs win a more accepting, understanding, tolerant orientation. Of course the teacher wins also: The teacher wins a more harmonious classroom with higher academic achievement for all students.

Cooperative learning transforms the classroom orientation. The classroom becomes more caring, cooperative, and amenable to inclusion. Students in the cooperative learning classroom develop a more prosocial, inclusive orientation toward all students, not just those with disabilities. Race relations improve dramatically.[35] It is within this inclusive classroom context that the goals of inclusion become a reality. Students are transformed: The mainstreamed student becomes not the wheel chair student, but rather another student who happens to be in a wheel chair.

> " *Cooperative learning is one strategy that supports inclusion. Another is peer tutoring. Where they are being used, inclusion is successful.* "
> — *Franklin Northeast Supervisory Union, VT*[36]

Students focus not on the disabilities of others, but rather on their strengths. They relate to the student as a person, as an integral, important part of the team. Feeling this, students with special needs blossom.

Components of Cooperative Learning Supporting Inclusion

Successful cooperative learning does not occur by simply placing students on a team and telling them to work together and help each other. Kagan[37] has identified six keys to successful cooperative learning:

1. **Teams:** Careful assignment to heterogeneous, integrated teams
2. **Will:** Creating the will among students to work together (through classbuilding, teambuilding, and shared goals and rewards)
3. **Management:** Adopting specialized management techniques to maximize time-on-task in the cooperative classroom
4. **Social Skills:** Structuring so social skills are practiced and acquired
5. **PIES:** Implementing the four basic principles of cooperative learning:
   - Positive Interdependence
   - Individual Accountability
   - Equal Participation
   - Simultaneous Interaction
6. **Structures:** Using a range of cooperative learning structures as an integral part of daily instruction

Especially important for successful inclusion is ample use of teambuilding,[38] classbuilding,[39] communitybuilding,[40] and social skill development.[41] Regular class meetings are another important component of successful inclusion; see class meetings in **Chapter 18. Win-Win Management.** Win-Win sports and games also generate an inclusive climate both in the classroom and on the playground.[42] Through inclusive activities, students feel a sense of belonging on their teams and in their classroom. They create mutual support. And in this safe, inclusive environment, all students more fully reach their academic potential.

Cooperative learning structures can be used as part of any lesson. They are carefully designed to implement the basic principles of cooperative learning and as a consequence sharply reduce disruptive behaviors and increase achievement. The structures are effective with students with special needs, in all settings. See Box: Cooperative Learning: Gains for Learning Disabled.

Cooperative Learning: Gains for Learning Disabled

After taking Springfield's training in Cooperative Learning, each of our teachers is asked to do follow-up work. We recommend, but do not require, an action research project that allows the teachers to observe the gains in student performance when they utilize cooperative learning in the classroom. One of our new high school special education teachers, Mr. Charles Johnson, conducted his action research around the use of Find Someone Who in managing off-task behavior in his Learning Disabled class. His findings? I will quote from his report:

"A functional assessment using a single subject AB design was performed on the two most disruptive students. Baseline data indicated a significant decrease in off-task behavior. Occurrences dropped from 30–40% per 90-minute block to less than 10% per block. Student achievement was also measured by worksheets completed. Before the structure, completed percentages were at 30–35%. After the structure, completion percentages were at 80–90%."

Charles Johnson's work confirmed what we believe to be true: Structures are vehicles for success for all students, including special needs kids.

Pamela S. Hankins
Staff Development Specialist
Springfield Public Schools, Springfield, Missouri

Cooperative Learning Is an Adaptation

Cooperative learning can be one of the most powerful adaptations leading to success for the student with special needs. Many students with special needs have never received peer support and encouragement; some blossom with this new form of attention and reward. Many students will do for their peers what they will not do for their teacher. Some teachers are astonished at the gains of some special needs students when they have peer support and tutoring. The use of specific structures allows students to provide answers in formats other than the traditional paper and pencil method. It also allows the instructor to check for understanding in ways that do not isolate the special needs student as the only student participating in a nontraditional style.

Adapting Cooperative Learning for Special Needs

Cooperative learning can be adapted in many ways to better meet the needs of diverse learners. JoAnne Putnam[43] suggests the following:

1. Modify Manner of Student Response
2. Modify Presentation of Material
3. Reduce Workload
4. Lower Expectations
5. Personalize Objective
6. Modify Materials and Environment
7. Provide Tutorials, Study Skills, Individualized Support

Preparing Students for Inclusion

In a farsighted approach to preparing students for inclusion, Colleen Nichols coordinates PEERS (Partners Ensuring Equal Rights and Supports).[44] The program teaches general education students successful, caring ways to interact with classmates with disabilities. A member of PEERS, MacKenzie Bailey describes her second-grade experience with James, a non-ambulatory, non-verbal classmate: James is

> "... really fun. He understands what you say; you can see that in his eyes. He understands me. He laughs, and when his eyes go somewhere else, I just touch his hand to get him to look at me again."

James was invited to MacKenzie's birthday party at the roller rink.

> "He was a big help. We all hung onto his [wheel]chair, and he was our supporter."[45]

It is hard to imagine a more complete Win-Win. Both James' and MacKenzie's view of others and themselves were transformed in positive ways.

One of the most powerful ways in which cooperative learning can be successful with students with special needs is gambit development for students with special needs and for their teammates and classmates. Gambits are the functional phrases and actions that allow us to accomplish goals in social interaction situations. For example, some interruption gambits: *"Can you pardon me for a moment, please?"* and *"If you will excuse me, what I need to know is...."* Some praising gambits: *"What I really liked about what you just did is..."* and *"Great job!"*

"Can I help you with that?"

Gambit development is a two-way street: 1) Students with special needs need to acquire appropriate gambits *(Can you please read that to me slowly? Can you show me how to solve this problem?)*; 2) their teammates need to acquire appropriate gambits *(Can I help you with that? Would you like me to...?)*.

Students with special needs may not know what to do or say to fulfill their need. They benefit from gambit development. Teachers may work individually with students with special needs to help them acquire appropriate gambits. See boxes, Gambits for Students with Special Needs and Gambits for Teammates.

Gambits for Students with Special Needs

Empowering Students to Meet Their Needs

- **ADD**
  "My mind was wandering, let me refocus."

- **ADHD**
  "I feel antsy. Can I be the materials manager?"

- **Visually Impaired**
  "Would you please read that to me?"

- **Angry**
  "What I need to do is visit the cool down area."

Regular education students are also often unprepared with appropriate gambits to deal with special needs. They do not know what to do or say when they have a teammate who cannot write, who has emotional outbursts, whose attention is wandering, or who does not understand instructions. Teachers who take the time to teach gambits for dealing successfully with special needs reap two kinds of benefits: The student with special needs is surrounded by others who are willing to offer help and support; all students learn a caring, helping, and supportive orientation. Gambit development creates a win-win. The will to help is released through gambit development. In the absence of gambit development, the student with special needs is often ignored or even shunned. Putting down the student with special needs is a way of masking one's own inadequacy. Empowered with the appropriate gambits, students approach and deal successfully with others, a two-way win.

There are a number of approaches to gambit development. One of the most powerful approaches involves the students in the generation of gambits. For example, recognizing that students do not know what to do or say when a teammate is not paying attention, the teacher addresses the whole class and says something like this: *"Class, all of us have our attention wander sometimes. When that happens, we appreciate it if those around us can help us refocus on the task at hand without putting us down. What are some of the positive things others can say or do, if our attention wanders?"*

The class then generates a list of gambits to help the student with attention deficit to refocus on the task at hand, such as:

- *"Susie, we are trying to build X. Do you think we should put this piece here or over here?"*
- *"Johnnie, we are deciding how to do our team presentation. I would like to know your idea. Do you like the idea of a skit or a TV quiz show better?"*
- *"Frank, I would really like to hear your idea on that. Do you agree with X or with Y?"*

The class or teams can generate gambits to respond to any of the special needs.

Gambits for Teammates

What to Say to a Teammate Who Has...

- **ADD**
  "Let's all focus on..."
  "Pete, do you agree with that idea [bringing him back into the discussion]?"

- **ADHD**
  "We are getting antsy. Let's work hard — there is only ten minutes until break."
  "Johnny, would you like to be the recorder as we list our ideas?"

- **Anxiety**
  "Let's do some relaxation breathing."
  "Let's do a round of muscle relaxation."

- **Dyslexia**
  "Let's read that together."
  "Let's check that writing for reversals."

- **Blindness or Is Visually Impaired**
  "What it looks like to me is..."
  "Let me tell you what I see."

- **Deafness or Hearing Impaired**
  [Turning toward the student so lips are visible] *"Let me say that again."*
  [Sitting side-by-side and making his/her writing visible while talking]

Gambits for Teammates

What to Say to a Student with...

- ## Cognitive Needs
  "Let me try to explain that another way."
  "Let's build that together with manipulatives."
  "How about if I draw it?"

- ## Communicative/Linguistic Needs
  "May I read it to you?"
  "Let me check, do you mean...?"
  "Another way to say that would be...."

- ## Social/Emotional Needs
  ### Support
  *"Don't worry about making a mistake, we all make mistakes.
     That is how we learn."*
  "I'm glad to have you as a teammate."

  ### Encouragement
  "Take your time, we are in no rush."
  "Your answer will be just fine."

  ### Praise
  "Great job!"
  "I liked it when you...."

- ## Physical Needs
  "May I move the piece for you?"
  "Would you like me to write down your idea on that?"
  "Let me get that for you."

Special Needs Adaptations of Cooperative Learning Structures

Special adaptations and accommodations of cooperative learning structures especially designed for students with special needs are described in a four book, four video series.[46] Specific adaptations are provided for each of 28 cooperative learning structures for four categories of disabilities: A) Physical Disabilities, B) Cognitive Disabilities, and C) Behavioral or Emotional Disabilities. The book and video series provides ways to use the structures to allow all students to participate as fully as possible.

3. Multiple Intelligences:
Multiple Paths to Success

Multiple Intelligences theory, research, and classroom applications counter two deeply entrenched beliefs about intelligence: 1) that intelligence is relatively unitary, and 2) that intelligence is relatively fixed. There are different theories of Multiple Intelligences and different definitions of intelligence,[47] but common to Multiple Intelligences theory is breaking the equation between the IQ test scores and intelligence. There are ways to be smart not tapped by the IQ test and students who score low on an IQ test and who perform poorly with traditional instruction can be smart in other ways and can perform quite well when Multiple Intelligences instructional strategies are used.

Once we realize that there are many ways to be intelligent and that each of these intelligences can be developed, we begin to view and treat quite differently students with special needs. When a student fails to understand a concept or remember a fact, we look first at the possiblity that that student needs to learn in a different way. Instead of saying, *"That student is not smart,"* we say, *"That student must be smart in a different way than the way I am teaching."* There is an attribution shift. The problem is not the student; the problem is the way we are attempting to teach that student. Instead of lowering our expectations and modifying the curriculum, we maintain high expectations and look for adaptations — alternative ways to present the curriculum. Multiple Intelligences theory pushes us to explore alternative instructional strategies and alternative assessment strategies.

In this respect Muliple Intelligences and Differentiated Instruction go hand in hand. We attempt to provide access to the curriculum through alternative intelligences. We also provide alternative ways for students to demonstrate their learnings. When this happens, two very remarkable things happen: 1) Students master and demonstrate mastery of things we did not think possible; 2) Students develop their non-dominant intelligences — they become smarter. The Multiple Intelligences literature is replete with examples of students who blossom in remarkable ways when they are taught the way they are smart.

Entire schools show dramatic increases in academic, as well as extra curricular achievements when the Multiple Intelligences theory and methods are adopted.[48] The story, though, is perhaps best told through case studies of students with special needs:

Let's take a couple of examples. Bruce Campbell had in his classroom a girl who was not getting her multiplication facts. She practiced for hours with multiplication flash cards, but the facts did not stick. Noting that she was quite talented in drawing, one day Bruce suggested she simply draw a picture on each flashcard that she frequently missed. She readily went to work. When she had finished drawing a picture on the card, she simply knew the multiplication fact. She drew pictures on all the fact cards she was missing and learned them all easily. Tested several years later, she retained the information perfectly!

For our purposes here, *why* she learned the multiplication facts is not as important as *that* she learned them. The implication: A student, who is slow when taught one way, readily learns the content when taught another. Somehow by engaging her strongest intelligence the content was readily mastered.

For our next example, let's review the case of Paula.[49] Early in school, Paula was assessed as learning disabled. She was assigned to special education classes, developed a very low self-esteem, and a dislike for school. By fifth grade, she had fallen several grade levels behind her classmates. Paula attempted suicide in the summer before sixth grade. She was placed in a regular education class for sixth grade. Her sixth grade teacher noticed Paula moved with poise and dignity. Following her hunch that Paula would benefit from kinesthetic instruction, Paula's teacher asked her to create a "movement alphabet" — movements to form the letters of the alphabet. Paula responded. Not only did she create letters, she sequenced them into a dance. Paula went on to dance her name, the words on the blackboard, spelling words, and even entire sentences. She performed for her class. Paula's self-esteem and liking for school increased; by the end of sixth grade, Paula reached grade level in reading and writing. In seventh grade, she was mainstreamed in all classes and received above-average grades!

It is important to note that Paula not only performed better in the verbal/linguistic content, she actually developed her verbal/linguistic intelligence. Whereas at first she needed to engage her bodily/kinesthetic intelligence to master the content, after a time she could simply sit and learn the verbal/linguistic content. A transfer occurred: Initial access to the verbal/linguistic content was through the bodily/kinesthetic intelligence, but after a time the verbal/linguistic intelligence took over. Similar case studies show this tendency for a non-dominant intelligence to take over after initial experience with the content through a favored intelligence, as when students who need to draw the content later take notes, or students who need to build their math solutions later can write them.

Providing alternative ways to learn and express understanding can transform a student. Look at what happened to Tara.

Tara: The Power of Multiple Intelligences

By Dan Kuzma[50]

I had just returned from Reno, Nevada, after attending a Kagan Multiple Intelligences teachers' workshop concerning the application of Howard Gardner's Multiple Intelligences theory. Just before I left the workshop, Laurie Kagan, the trainer, pulled me aside and asked what I would be teaching when I arrived back at school. I told her that I would be teaching about the Declaration of Independence. She asked what I usually did, and suggested that for closure in my lesson on the 5 propositions in the second paragraph of the Declaration, I ask my students to select the idea in that paragraph that they thought had the greatest impact on our nation, and to express that idea on a single piece of unlined paper in pictures and symbols only.

I did just that! After giving instructions, I turned to pick up something on my desk. Out of the corner of my eye I saw Tara, who was sitting in the back of the room, put her pencil down. Tara was a girl who was failing this course. She was unhappy in school, and had turned in very few homework assignments. Her classmates didn't like her (Her car had been "keyed" several times!) and thought she was "dumb." During the course of the school year, I had failed to engage her in any meaningful way.

Out of anger and frustration, I turned and very forcefully said, "Tara, what are you doing?"

She replied, "Mr. Kuzma, I'm finished."

I blurted, "How can you be finished? You were supposed to select the idea that had the greatest impact on America and express it in pictures and symbols only."

Tara calmly stated, "I did!" and held up her paper.

I saw that her paper had a couple of lines on it and curtly asked, "What is that?"

She explained, "Mr. Kuzma, it is an equal sign, I think the idea that had the greatest impact was that all men are created equal."

Well, you could have heard a pin drop in that classroom. For what seemed like a very long time, there was silence. I looked at Tara. The students looked at Tara, and then turned to look at me. I was flabbergasted. Finally, I said, "Tara, that's great!" and she, and the whole class, could tell that I really meant it by the tone and volume of my voice, my body language, and the long silence that preceded the comment. Everyone in the class, myself included, instantaneously had a new and genuine respect for Tara and what she had done so quickly and so well. More importantly, you could easily see that Tara was very moved and pleased by the class's spontaneous and sincere reaction to her work.

It was then and there that I recognized the power of Multiple Intelligences theory in the classroom. The activity happened to match Tara's unique pattern of intelligences and Tara had been given "a window" into the curriculum. In addition, Tara, the class, and myself had been given the opportunity to celebrate Tara's logical and visual-spatial abilities.

From that point on, I frequently gave Tara and the class the opportunity and/or option to express themselves in pictures and symbols. The students in the class and myself began to look forward to what Tara and others would produce. Tara's self-esteem soared. She started doing her homework on a regular basis. She smiled much more and was involved in every class. She would say "Hello" to me in the halls (something she had never done before), and even stick her head into the doorway between classes to say "Hi!" Her relationships with other students in the class dramatically improved and she ended the year earning a "B" in that course.

... Tara taught this teacher a lesson that he will never forget.

Sometimes the dramatic blossoming of a student whose unique intelligence is honored seems to operate through enhanced self-esteem. For example, in one class a boy who was performing quite poorly improved dramatically after the teacher and class honored his ability to whistle any tune. Sometimes the blossoming of students with special needs occurs as a result of the teacher seeing the student with new eyes. Howard Gardner relates how a teacher, and subsequently her student, was transformed when the teacher discovered the boy was smart in a different way. Gardner describes the case of Donnie, who was having great trouble in first grade. After two months into that year, Donnie's teacher concluded he would have to be retained. When the teacher saw Donnie's exceptional abilities with mechanical content, the teacher's view of Donnie was profoundly transformed.

> "She had difficulty believing that this youngster, who experienced such trouble with school-related tasks, could do as well as many adults on this real-world endeavor. She told me afterwards that she could not sleep for three nights; she was distraught by her premature dismissal of Donnie and correspondingly eager to find ways to reach him. I am happy to report that Donnie subsequently improved in his school performance, possibly because he had seen that there were areas in which he could excel and that he possessed abilities that were esteemed by older people."[51]

There are three powerful visions that spring from Multiple Intelligences theory: Matching, Stretching, and Celebrating.[52] All three of these visions are realized when we teach with a range of instructional strategies designed to engage the range of intelligences. Simple Multiple Intelligences structures can be used as part of any lesson. Dozens of structures have been developed, tailored to each of the intelligences.[53] The more these structures are used, the more intelligences that are engaged, the more students are reached, and the more we develop the range of intelligences in each student.

17.32

Win-Win Discipline. Kagan Publishing • 1 (800) 933-2667 • www.KaganOnline.com

Three MI Visions
Matching, Stretching, and Celebrating

Matching. We match the way we teach with the way the student is smart. The case of Paula is a dramatic example of how matching provides alternative access to the curriculum. A student with special needs blossoms when taught in a way that matches his/her strengths.

Stretching. By engaging an intelligence, that intelligence becomes stronger. Paula's verbal/linguistic intelligence was given a stretch when it was engaged via the bodily/kinesthetic activities. In a few months, she made up years of deficit. The case studies in the Multiple Intelligences literature align well with evidence showing dramatic increases in IQ in humans as well as animals as a result of enriched experiences.[54] With practice, any of us can be smarter in any of the intelligences.

Celebrating. We view others and ourselves through new eyes when we realize there are many ways to be smart. The cases of Donnie and Tara are excellent examples; when the teacher appreciated he had other ways to be smart, both the teacher and Donnie saw Donnie with new eyes. The teacher and classmates saw Tara through new eyes. We come to celebrate our own uniqueness and that of others. Instead of asking of a student, *"How smart is he?"* we ask, *"How is he smart?"*

MI Structures

Dozens of structures, simple instructional strategies, have been designed to engage the range of intelligences as part of any lesson.[55] Below are a few sample structures.

Intelligence	Selected Structures
Verbal/Linguistic	**Telphone; Listen Right!**
Logical/Mathematical	**Find My Rule; Logic Line-Ups**
Visual/Spatial	**Team Mind-Mapping; Observe-Draw-RallyRobin**
Musical/Rhythmic	**Lyrical Lessons; Poems for Two Vocies**
Bodily/Kinesthetic	**Kinesthetic Symbols; Formations**
Naturalist	**Same-Different; Observe-Write-RoundRobin**
Interpersonal	**Paraphrase Passport; Three-Step Interview**
Intrapersonal	**Visualize Share; Timed Pair Share**

The promise of applied Multiple Intelligences theory for realizing the goals of full inclusion for students with special needs have been detailed.[56] When we teach with a range of instructional strategies designed to engage all of the intelligences, we allow all students in the classroom access to the entire curriculum through their strengths, creating an inclusive classroom. By engaging the full range of intelligences, we develop the full range of intelligences. And by broadening the ways we teach, we provide new opportunties to see the unique giftedness of each student.

Multiple Intelligences truly is a Win-Win. It is a win for teachers because teachers are more successful with their students. Teachers are able to reach students who otherwise would fall further and further behind. It is a win for students in many ways. They are more successful academically; they are accepted more fully by their teachers and peers; they develop more fully the range of their intellectual potential; they appreciate their own uniqueness. More fully engaged and having their needs met, they have no reason to become disegaged or disruptive.

Special Needs: Universal Needs

Students with special needs have the same needs we all have: The need for attention and support, to avoid failure, to express displeasure, to feel some control over outcomes, the need to express energy, the need for engaging stimulation, and the need to know the rules of the game. Often, though, because their needs are more intense, students with special needs make more salient our need to identify and validate positions and implement Win-Win preventative procedures, strategies for the moment of disruption, follow-ups, and engaging approaches to instruction.

References

[1] Meyer, L. H. & Putnam, J. W. *Social Integration.* In V. B. Van Hasselt, P. S. Strain, & M. Hersen (Eds.), *Handbook of Developmental and Physical Disabilities.* Elmsford, NY: Pergamon, 1988.

[2] Weiner, R. PL 94-142: *Impact on the Schools.* Washington, DC: Capitol Publications, 1985.

[3] Baker, E. T., M. C. Wang, & H. J. Walberg. *The Effects of Inclusion on Learning.* **Educational Leadership**, 15(4), 33–35, 1994/5.

References (Continued)

[4] Putnam, J. *The Movement Toward Teaching and Learning in Inclusive Classrooms.* In J. Putnam (Ed.), *Cooperative Learning and Strategies for Inclusion,* (2nd. Ed.). Baltimore, MD: Paul H. Brookes Publishing, 1998.

[5] D. K. Lipsky & A. Gartner (Eds.) *Beyond Separate Education: Quality Education for All.* Baltimore, MD: Paul H. Brookes Publishing Co., 1989.

[6] Lipsky, D. *National Study of Inclusive Education (2nd Ed.).* New York, NY: National Center on Educational Restructuring and Inclusion, City University of New York, 1995.

[7] U.S. Department of Education. *Seventeenth Annual Report to Congress on the Implementation of the Individuals with Disabilities Education Act.* Washington, DC: U.S. Government Printing Office, 1995, p. 14.

[8] Evans, I. M., Salisbury, C., Palombaro, M., & Goldberg, J. S. *Children's Perceptions of Fairness in Classroom and Interpersonal Situations Involving Peers with Severe Disabilities.* **Journal of the Association for Persons with Severe Handicaps,** 1994, **19,** 326–332.

Hunt, P., Staub, D., Alwell, M., & Goetez, L. Achievement by All Students Within the Context of Cooperative Learning Groups. **Journal of the Association for Persons with Severe Handicaps,** 1994, **19,** 290–301.

Staub, D. & Peck, C. A. *What Are the Outcomes for Nondisabled Students?* **Educational Leadership,** 1994/5, **52(4),** 36–40.

[9] Condensed from a longer article by Robert Jutras. **Kagan Online Magazine.** San Clemente, CA: Kagan Publishing, Winter 2004.

[10] Education for All Handicapped Children Act of 1975, PL 94–142, 20 U.S.C. §§ 1400 et seq.

[11] Oakes, J. & Lipton, M. *Detracking Schools: Early Lessons from the Field.* **Phi Delta Kappan,** 1992, **73(6),** 448–454.

[12] Gaoran, A. *Is Ability Grouping Equitable?* **Educational Leadership,** 1991, **50(2),** 11–17.

Wheelock, A. *Crossing the Tracks. How "Untracking" Can Save America's Schools.* New York, NY: The New Press, 1992.

[13] Oakes, J. & Lipton, M. *Detracking Schools: Early Lessons From the Field.* **Phi Delta Kappan,** 1992, **73(6),** 448–454.

[14] Knoll, J. & Meyer, L. H. *Integrated Schooling and Educational Quality: Principles and Effective Practices.* In M. Berres & P. Knoblock (Eds.), *Managerial Models of Mainstreaming.* Rockville, MD: Aspen Publishers, Inc. 1987, pp. 41–59.

[15] Monroe, L. *Nothing's Impossible: Leadership Lessons from Inside and Outside the Classroom.* New York, NY: PublicAffairs, 1999.

[16] U.S. Department of Education. *To Assure the Free Appropriate Public Education of All Children With Disabilities. Individuals with Disabilities Education Act (IDEA: P.L. 101-476).* Washington, DC: U.S. Department of Education, 1998.

References (Continued)

[17] F. J. Biasini, L. Grupe, L. Huffman, N. W. Bray, Ph.D. *Mental Retardation: A Symptom and a Syndrome.* In S. Netherton, D. Holmes, & C. E. Walker, (Eds.), *Comprehensive Textbook of Child and Adolescent Disorders.* New York, NY: Oxford University Press, in press.

[18] Jensen, E. *Different Brains, Different Learners: How to Reach the Hard to Reach.* San Diego, CA: The Brain Store, 2000.

[19] Armstrong, T. *The Myth of the A.D.D. Child.* New York, NY: Plume/Penguin-Putnam Group, 1997.

[20] Amen, D. *Healing ADD – The Breakthrough Program That Allows You to See and Heal the Six Types of ADD.* New York, NY: Penguin/Putnam Inc., 2001.

[21] Hill, R. W. & Castro, E. *Getting Rid of Ritalin: How Neurofeedback Can Successfully Treat Attention Deficit Disorder Without Drugs.* Charlottesville, VA: Hapton Roads Publising Company, 2002.

[22] Armstrong, T. *The Myth of the A.D.D. Child.* New York, NY: Plume/Penguin-Putnam Group, 1997.

[23] Finlan, T. G. *Learning Disability: The Imaginary Disease.* Westport, CT: Bergin & Garvey, 1994.

[24] Temple, E., Deutsch, G. K., Poldrack, R. A., Miller, S. L., Tallal, P., Merzenich, M. M. & Gabrieli, J. D. E. *Neural Deficits in Children with Dyslexia Ameliorated by Behavioral Remediation: Evidence From Functional MRI.* **Proceedings of the National Academy of Sciences Early Edition,** 2003, **100,** 2860–2865.

[25] Tomlinson, C. A. *The Differentiated Classroom: Responding to the Needs of All Learners.* Alexandria, VA: Association for Supervision and Curriculum Development, 1999, p. 2.

Chapman, C. and King, R. *Differentiated Instructional Strategies for Writing in the Content Areas.* Thousand Oaks, CA: Corwin Press, Inc., 2003

Gregory, G.H. *Differentiated Instructional Strategies. One Size Doesn't Fit All.* Thousand Oaks, CA: Corwin Press, Inc., 2002.

Tomlinson, C. A. *The Differentiated Classroom. Responding to the Needs of All Learners.* Alexandria, VA: Association for Supervision and Curriculum Development, 1999.

[26] National Center on Educational Restructuring and Inclusion (NCERI). *National Study of Inclusive Education. (2nd Ed.).* New York, NY: The Graduate School and University Center, 1995.

[27] Lee, Christine & Ng, Maureen. *A CASE STUDY: Cooperative Learning and Multi-ethnic Classrooms in Singapore.* **KaganOnline Magazine,** San Clemente, CA: Kagan Publishing, Fall, 1998.

[28] Lee, Christine & Ng, Maureen. *A CASE STUDY: Cooperative Learning and Multi-ethnic Classrooms in Singapore.* **KaganOnline Magazine,** San Clemente, CA: Kagan Publishing, Fall, 1998.

References (Continued)

[29] Condensed from a longer article by Pfleger, Linda. *I Can!* ***Kagan Online Magazine.*** San Clemente, CA: Kagan Publishing, Fall 2001.

[30] Johnson, D. W. & Johnson, R. *Cooperation and Competition: Theory and Research.* Edina, MN: Interaction Book Company, 1989.

Johnson, R. T., & Johnson, D. W. *Building Friendships Between Handicapped and Non-handicapped Students: Effects of Cooperative and Individualistic Instruction.* American Educational Research Journal, 1981, ***18(4),*** 415–423.

[31] Johnson, D. W., Maruyama, G., Johnson, R., Nelson, D. & Skon, L. *Effects of Cooperative, Competitive and Individualistic Goal Structures on Achievement: A Meta-analysis.* Psychological Bulletin, 1981, **89,** 47–62.

Johnson, D. W. & R. T. Johnson. *Cooperation and Competition: Theory and Research.* Edina, MN: Interaction Book Company, 1989.

Slavin, R. E. *Cooperative Learning: Theory, Research, and Practice.* Upper Saddle River, NJ: Prentice Hall, 1990.

Slavin, R. E. *Cooperative Learning: Theory, Research, and Practice (2nd Ed.).* Needham Heights, MA: Allyn & Bacon, 1995.

[32] Putnam, J. W. & Farnsworth-Lunt, J. *Cooperative Learning and the Integration of Students with Disabilities.* Missoula, MT: 1989.

[33] Kagan, S. *Cooperative Learning.* San Clemente, CA: Kagan Publishing, 1993.

Kagan, S. Kagan, L., & Kagan, M. *Cooperative Structures for Teambuilding.* San Clemente, CA: Kagan Publishing, 1997.

Kagan, M., Robertson, L. & Kagan, S. *Cooperative Structures for Classbuilding.* San Clemente, CA: Kagan Publishing, 1995.

[34] Kagan, S. *Cooperative Learning.* San Clemente, CA: Kagan Publishing, 1994.

[35] Kagan, S., Zahn, G. L., Widaman, K., Schwarzwald, J. & Tyrrell, G. *Classroom Structural Bias: Impact of Cooperative and Competitive Classroom Structures on Cooperative and Competitive Individuals and Groups.* In R. Slavin, S. Sharan, S. Kagan, R. Hertz-Lazarowitz, C. Webb & R. Schmuck (Eds.) *Learning to Cooperate, Cooperating to Learn.* New York, NY: Plenum, 1985.

[36] National Center on Educational Restructuring and Inclusion (NCERI). *National Study of Inclusive Education. (2nd Ed.).* New York, NY: The Graduate School and University Center, 1995.

[37] Kagan, S. *Cooperative Learning.* San Clemente, CA: Kagan Publishing, 1994.

[38] Kagan, S. Kagan, L., & Kagan, M. *Cooperative Structures for Teambuilding.* San Clemente, CA: Kagan Publishing, 1997.

[39] Kagan, M., Robertson, L. & Kagan, S. *Cooperative Structures for Classbuilding.* San Clemente, CA: Kagan Publishing, 1995.

References (Continued)

[40] Shaw, V. *Communitybuilding in the Classroom.* San Clemente, CA: Kagan Publishing, 1992.

[41] Kagan, S. *Cooperative Learning.* San Clemente, CA: Kagan Publishing, 1994.

[42] Kagan, S. *Silly Sports and Goofy Games.* San Clemente, CA: Kagan Publishing, 2000.

[43] Putnam, J. W. *Cooperative Learning in Diverse Classrooms.* Upper Saddle River, NJ: Prentice Hall, 1997.

J.W. Putnam (Ed.). *Cooperative Learning and Strategies for Inclusion; Celebrating Diversity in the Classroom.* Baltimore, MD: Paul H. Brookes Publishing, 1993.

[44] Jakupcak, A. *School Programs for Successful Inclusion of All Students. In J. W. Putnam (Ed.), Cooperative Learning and Strategies for Inclusion, (2nd Ed.).* Baltimore, MD: Paul H. Brookes Publishing, 1998.

[45] Jakupcak, A. *School Programs for Successful Inclusion of All Students. In J. W. Putnam (Ed.), Cooperative Learning and Strategies for Inclusion, (2nd Ed.).* Baltimore, MD: Paul H. Brookes Publishing, 1998, p. 208.

[46] Kagan, S., Kagan, M. & Kagan, L. *Reaching Mathematics Standards through Cooperative Learning: Providing for ALL Learners in General Education Classrooms.* San Clemente, CA: Kagan Publishing, 2000.

Kagan, S., Kagan, M. & Kagan, L. *Reaching English/Language Arts Standards through Cooperative Learning: Providing for ALL Learners in General Education Classrooms.* San Clemente, CA: Kagan Publishing, 2000.

Kagan, S., Kagan, M. & Kagan, L. *Reaching Social Studies Standards through Cooperative Learning: Providing for ALL Learners in General Education Classrooms.* San Clemente, CA: Kagan Publishing, 2000.

Kagan, S., Kagan, M. & Kagan, L. *Reaching Science Standards through Cooperative Learning: Providing for ALL Learners in General Education Classrooms.* San Clemente, CA: Kagan Publishing, 2000.

[47] Gardner, H. *Frames of Mind: The Theory of Multiple Intelligences.* New York, NY: Basic Books, 1993.

Sternberg, R. J. *Beyond IQ: A Triarchic Theory of Human Intelligence.* Cambridge, MA: Cambridge University Press, 1985.

Sternberg R. J. & Powell J. S. *Theories of Intelligence. In R. J. Sternberg (Ed.), Handbook of Human Intelligence.* Cambridge, MA: Cambridge University Press, 1982, pp. 975–1005.

[48] Campbell, L. & Campbell, B. *Multiple Intelligneces and Student Achievment: Success Stories from Six Schools.* Alexandria, VA: Association for Supervision and Curriculum Development, 1999.

[49] Campbell, L., Campbell, B., & Dickinson, D. *Teaching and Learning through Multiple Intelligences.* Stanwood, WA: Campbell & Associattes, Inc., 1992, pp. 7–8.

17.38

Win-Win Discipline. Kagan Publishing • 1 (800) 933-2667 • www.KaganOnline.com

References (Continued)

[50] Kuzma, D. F. *Tara: The Power of Multiple Intelligences.* **Kagan Online Magazine.** San Clemente, CA: Kagan Publishing, Winter 2002.

[51] Gardner, H. *Frames of Mind: The Theory of Multiple Intelligences.* New York, NY: Basic Books, 1993, p. 109.

[52] Kagan, S. & Kagan, M. *Multiple Intelligences: The Complete MI Book.* San Clemente, CA: Kagan Publishing, 1998.

[53] Kagan, S. & Kagan, M. *Multiple Intelligences: The Complete MI Book.* San Clemente, CA: Kagan Publishing, 1998.

[54] Diamond, M.C. *Enriching Heredity: The Impact of the Environment on the Anatomy of the Brain.* New York, NY: Free Press, 1988.

Feuerstein, R. *Instrumental Enrichment. An Intervention Program for Cognitive Modifiability.* Glenview, IL: Scott, Foresman and Co., 1980.

[55] Kagan, L. *Multiple Intelligences Structures and Activities.* San Clemente, CA: Kagan Publishing, 2000.

Kagan, S. & Kagan, M. *Multiple Intelligences: The Complete MI Book.* San Clemente, CA: Kagan Publishing, 1998.

[56] Kagan, S. *New Cooperative Learning, Multiple Intelligences, and Inclusion.* In J. W. Putnam (Ed.). *Cooperative Learning and Strategies for Inclusion. Celebrating Diversity in the Classroom (2nd Ed.).* Baltimore, MD: Paul H. Brookes Publishing, 1998.

Chapter 18

Win-Win
Management

When Alfie Kohn decided to see the discipline approach favored by the best teachers, he visited classrooms of especially gifted teachers. What did he find? To his surprise, they were not using a discipline approach. In fact, there was no need to discipline their students. Their students were busily engaged in learning; they were not disruptive.[1]

How did this happen? How is it that some teachers have so many discipline problems and others have almost none? How can we make discipline problems disappear? In this chapter we will examine one approach to making discipline problems disappear: Win-Win Management. The present chapter examines ways to align classroom management with the philosophy of Win-Win:

> 1. **Class Meetings**
> 2. **Signals**
> 3. **Role Assignment**
> 4. **Room Arrangement/Content**
> 5. **Procedures and Routines**
> 6. **Parents as Partners**

1. Class Meetings. The single most important management technique for a Win-Win classroom is the Class Meeting. The class meeting embodies the Win-Win philosophy: we all work together and make management decisions for the benefit of all.

2. Signals. If we are to respond to student positions, we need to allow students to tell us where they are. Communication in the Win-Win classroom is a two-way street. Thus, the Win-Win classroom is rich in communication devices, so on an ongoing basis students can communicate with the teacher and the teacher can communicate with individuals and with the class as a whole.

3. Role Assignments. If we are to create an "Our Class" orientation, a class oriented toward meeting the needs of everyone, then it is a participatory class. In the Win-Win classroom everyone is working toward the common good. As students fulfill important roles in the classroom, their needs for attention, control, and release of energy are met. As students assume responsibility for managing the class, the same-side and learned responsibility pillars are fortified.

4. Room Arrangement/Content. If a picture communicates a thousand words, the physical layout of the classroom communicates volumes. The content and arrangement of the Win-Win classroom meet the needs of the seven positions and communicate that we are here to work together for everyone's benefit — for Win-Win outcomes. Thus we address how furniture arrangement, bulletin boards, posters, music, and even plants and animals contribute to creating a Win-Win classroom.

5. Procedures and Routines. In the Win-Win classroom there is a social contract — an agreement about how we will behave and how we will treat each other. From this basic Win-Win contract flows expectations, procedures, and routines. We all need to avoid embarrassment associated with a public failure. We agree then to return graded papers in a private way. Procedures flow from an understanding and acceptance of positions.

When everyone has shared expectations and knows the procedures and routines, there is less testing of limits and less time off task. Fewer disruptive behaviors occur when it is clear exactly how to make up missed assignments; visit your locker; turn in papers; request a forgotten pencil; line up; store one's lunch box; and ask for a bathroom break. Weak teachers nag and discipline; Win-Win teachers manage through procedures and routines. Clear expectations, procedures, and routines make discipline problems disappear.

6. Parents as Partners. Win-Win teachers extend the Win-Win orientation to their relationship with parents. They assume a Same-Side orientation, teaming up with parents to provide a coherent and mutually complimentary approach to discipline. The Win-Win teacher and the parent have a common goal for the student — learned responsibility. As the teacher elicits support in this process from parents, they satisfy their need to be involved, to make a difference in the lives of their children. Assuming a Same-Side orientation with parents results in reduced defensiveness and added support from parents.

1. Class Meetings

"How can we possibly prepare our students for full participation in a democracy by structuring our classroom autocratically? It is an amazing feature of our democratic educational system that we have settled so universally on an autocratic social organization of our classrooms. The teacher is the Congress, (making the laws), the President, (carrying them out), as well as the Judge, the Jury, and too often, the Executioner. Is it any wonder that teachers feel tired at the end of the day?"
— Spencer Kagan[2]

Class meetings set the tone in the Win-Win classroom. The meta-communication: this is a place where we all come together to create an environment that will benefit everyone. In effect, by having class meetings the teacher is saying, "This is not my class; this is *our* class."

Class meetings are a time we all get on the same-side, share the responsibility for co-creating solutions, and learn more responsible behavior. It is hard to imagine any management approach more aligned with the philosophy of Win-Win.

Class meetings meet the position needs of students, especially those seeking attention, a sense of control, and engagement. They are a place also to deal with issues of anger, disengagement, and positive ways to release energy. Class meetings help students responsibly meet their needs. They are our time to seek Win-Win solutions, solutions that meet the needs of everyone in the class. The advantages of class meetings are many:

Advantages of Class Meetings

1. Students learn democratic decision-making processes.
2. Students obtain a sense of control.
3. Students acquire mutual respect, caring, and social awareness.
4. Students feel peer support.
5. Students take responsibility for their decisions.
6. Commitment to class decisions is increased.
7. Students learn consensus-seeking skills.
8. Students learn planning and evaluation skills.
9. Problems and issues are aired.
10. Students are more willing to cool off in the moment of disruption, knowing a problem will be addressed in the next class meeting.
11. Many heads are better than one for problem solving.
12. The class obtains a sense of identity.
13. The teacher receives support from the class.
14. The Same-Side and Collaborative Solutions Pillars are reinforced.

We recommend a regularly scheduled class meeting with a fixed agenda, along with occasional special meetings for specific purposes.

The Regular Class Meeting

Having a predetermined agenda for regular class meetings has several advantages. Students know how much time will pass until an issue is dealt with. Placing items on the class meeting agenda provides a cooling-off period. Often those items are resolved before the next meeting. The agenda takes the teacher off the spot of having to solve every problem in the moment of its occurrence. The teacher can add items to the agenda; students

*A really great teacher is someone who... **lets kids participate in everything.** Lily, 13, Rye, New York*[3]

Win-Win Discipline. Kagan Publishing • 1 (800) 933-2667 • www.KaganOnline.com

18.4

A really great teacher is someone who...

lets the children talk about what they had done during the holidays, weekend, or after school.

Chandra, 12, Lockridge, Western Australia[4]

can propose items. When problems are dealt with on a regular basis and are not allowed to build up, class meetings become a time to come together to share and appreciate, not just to problem solve.

Some elementary teachers have a brief daily end-of-the-day class meeting; others prefer a weekly or bi-weekly meeting. Secondary teachers gravitate to less frequent and shorter meetings, but still find advantages in a regular schedule.

Usually, a rule dictates that an item must be placed on the agenda prior to the meeting. Nothing is placed on the agenda unless the teacher feels comfortable with it, and no decision can be made unless the teacher agrees.

Agenda for Class Meetings

1. **Announcements**
2. **Appreciations/Inspirations**
3. **Suggestions/Problem Solving**
4. **Evaluating Progress**
5. **Planning**
6. **Mutual Support Activity**

■ **Announcements.** A student or pair of students read or present the announcements. Items for announcement may be submitted for teacher approval prior to the meeting. Announcements include upcoming assignments, tests, birthdays, school and class events.

■ **Appreciations/Inspirations.** On a rotating basis, different students read the contents of the appreciation box. The appreciation box (a decorated cardboard shoe box with a slot in the top) is available on an ongoing basis for students to submit appreciation slips at any time prior to the class meeting. Appreciation slips and a marker are kept by the box. An appreciation slip is a simple slip of paper with a sentence starter: "I appreciate _____ (name or names) _____ because _____." See the reproducible Appreciation Slips, page 18.6.

Students can deposit inspirational quotes or personal poetry to be read. Luci Bowers (Frank Jewett School, Bonny Eagle School District, W. Buxton, Maine) gift wrapped a shoe box. All week students deposit positive items. During the Friday class meetings, there is time to "Read the Box." Students praise one another and provide inspirational quotes such as:

> TEAM = *T*ogether *E*veryone *A*chieves *M*ore.
> "To have a friend is to be one."
> "We > I."
> "All of us are smarter than any one of us."
> "Persistence melts resistance."

Appreciation Slips

I appreciate _____
(name or names)

because_____

_____

_____

_____ Signature _____

I appreciate _____
(name or names)

because_____

_____

_____

_____ Signature _____

I appreciate _____
(name or names)

because_____

_____

_____

_____ Signature _____

I appreciate _____
(name or names)

because_____

_____

_____

_____ Signature _____

Students are encouraged to "catch each other being good" and give appreciations to the whole class, not just to individuals.

"One thing I really appreciate in our class is how Frank takes time to give compliments. Yesterday I heard him give Pete a great compliment. He said...."

"One of the best things about this class is how you know everyone is rooting for you to do your best."

■ **Appreciation Circles.** To form an appreciation circle, all students face inward so each can see all of the others. In random order they take turns giving appreciations to the class or to each other. Students can pass if they want. Students are encouraged to give appreciation for responsible behaviors. Students appreciate others for how they contribute to their team or class:

> *"Jack helped our team today by...."*
> *"Sally did a nice job decorating the bulletin board."*
> *"Mary gave Susie a nice compliment today; she said...."*

Back-handed compliments, such as *"Mary did not put anyone down today,"* are recognized as such and discouraged. Compliments about dress and looks, such as *"Jack has a nice shirt on today"* and *"Sally is cute,"* are also discouraged.

■ **Suggestions/Problem Solving.** On a rotating basis students read items from the suggestion box. Suggestions are signed. Teachers may exercise the right "to filter" the suggestions, discussing with the author how to modify inappropriate suggestions. The goal, though, is to foster sufficient autonomous responsibility among students so that no prior review is necessary. The suggestion box and suggestion slips are available to the students on an ongoing basis, so students can place items in the sug gestion box at any time. During the Suggestion/Problem Solving phase of the class meeting, by consensus, suggestion slips are placed in three piles:

1. To Be Solved Now
2. To Be Solved in a Later Class Meeting
3. To Be Solved by Individuals Involved

At first the facilitator of the meeting is the teacher. After the teacher has modeled that role often and the students are mature enough, students may rotate in the role of facilitator. To deal with problems, the facilitator reads a problem slip and asks, *"I see that Jack and Samantha had a problem this week. Is it still a problem?"* If the answer is no, the facilitator goes on to the next item. If the answer is yes, the facilitator gets a brief description of the problem and then seeks helpful suggestions from the class. Active involvement of all of the students in the solution process is desirable. A student recorder keeps track of adopted solutions so that positive progress can be checked later. An attempt is made to devote most energy to class problems rather than individual conflicts. Content includes items such as shoving while lining up, name-calling, put-downs, tardies, homework completion, increasing contributions to class charity, lack of supplies, and clean-up.

During the Suggestion/Problem Solving phase of the meeting, a variety of cooperative brainstorming, consensus-seeking, and decision-making structures may be used, including:

> • **Placemat Consensus**
> • **Dot-the-Wall**
> • **Fist to Five**
> • **Four S Brainstorming**
> • **Jot Thoughts**
> • **Proactive Prioritizing**
> • **Spend-a-Buck**
> • **Sum-the-Ranks**

Details of these structures are found in *Cooperative Meetings.*[5]

Unexpected, creative, student-generated solutions to problems can occur during class meetings because many heads are better than one, students are less tied to traditions, and students are closer to many of the problems for which they seek help. At one class meeting the students worked on how a blind boy could participate in kickball. When the students created a solution, it was used for the remaining years of that child's elementary education.

"The students like it because, through the class meetings, they feel listened to and respected."[8]

"This is different from what I might have done a few years ago because I would have told them what to do rather than asking them what we should do.... When they have input, their commitment is different."[9]

Suggestion Form

Problem: _____
_____
_____
_____

Suggestion: _____
_____
_____
_____
_____
_____
_____

By: _____ **Date:** _____

Suggestion Form

Problem: _____
_____
_____
_____

Suggestion: _____
_____
_____
_____
_____
_____
_____

By: _____ **Date:** _____

Win-Win Discipline. Kagan Publishing • 1 (800) 933-2667 • www.KaganOnline.com

18.9

■ **Evaluating Progress.** Time is taken to evaluate progress in implementing decisions made at prior class meetings. For example, if the students had resolved to increase homework submissions by a phone buddy system, as part of their report on how well the homework buddy system is working, the committee in charge of overseeing that plan might present a graph showing rate of homework submissions. If early in the year a class made a poster on "How we want our class to be," at several points during the school year that poster can be a topic for evaluation — how well we are living up to our plan and if there is need to modify the goals poster.

■ **Planning.** Students may break up into committees during the meeting. The charity committee can work together planning ways to make the class charity drive a success; the homework committee can plan ways to increase completion of homework; the class sunshine committee devises novel ways to celebrate successes; the class beautification committee improves the class environment. Committees report back to the class as a whole.

■ **Mutual Support Activity.** The class meeting ends on a positive note. Students may do a classbuilding activity such as Find Someone Who. For scores of mutual support classbuilding structures and activities, see *Classbuilding*.[6] Alternatively, the class meeting may end with a Silly Sport or Goofy Game. *Silly Sports and Goofy Games*[7] contains over 200 Silly Sport and Goofy Game energizers. See Silly Sports, **Part VII, Resources E.**

The Special Class Meeting

Special class meetings are called on a one-time basis to address specific issues or goals. Among the types of special class meetings are:

1. Problem Solving
2. Check-in Meetings
3. Planning and Decision-Making
4. Consciousness-Raising Meetings

Different types of class meetings are described in depth in a wonderful book, *Ways We Want Our Class to Be. Class Meetings that Build Commitment to Kindness and Learning.*[12] The book provides very concrete examples of each type of meeting. In that book you will find pointers for creating a comfortable atmosphere, establishing ground rules, physical set-up, setting time frames, questioning strategies, ways to encourage and manage participation, reaching consensus, and troubleshooting.

"During a class meeting we talked about how we would feel if we were a substitute. Kids came up with things like, 'nervous' and 'stupid because you don't know everybody's name.' ... we discussed what we could do to make the substitute feel comfortable.... That really worked well. The substitute that the class later had said she had never been with such an attentive group of children."[10]

18.10

Win-Win Discipline. Kagan Publishing • 1 (800) 933-2667 • www.KaganOnline.com

"... I don't any longer say things like 'I think you should go apologize.' I ask them to figure out what's right."[11]

Eight Building Blocks of Effective Class Meetings

Class meetings are central to Positive Discipline, an approach to discipline philosophically aligned with Win-Win Discipline.[13] Positive Discipline recognizes eight building blocks to effective class meetings:

1. Form a circle
2. Practice compliments and appreciations
3. Create an agenda
4. Develop communication skills
5. Learn about separate realities
6. Recognize reasons people do what they do (positions)
7. Practice role-playing and brainstorming
8. Focus on non-punitive solutions

To put these building blocks in place, Positive Discipline provides concrete activities. For example, to get students to create a Win-Win orientation, they are encouraged to tell how they feel, what they do, and what they learn when others try to control them. They are guided to realize that Win-Win solutions are based on mutual respect and the core belief that no one is more or less than anyone else. We are different, not better or worse, right or wrong.

2. Signals

Signals are Win-Win solutions. With the proper signals in place:

- The teacher can allow animated interaction, yet bring the class back to full, alert attention within a few seconds.

- Students can let a teacher know that he/she is lecturing too fast or that they just don't understand, without interrupting the teacher.

- Students can continue working on a worksheet while signaling the teacher that they need help.

- The teacher can signal the class that noise is escalating and that they need to use their inner voices — without saying a word.

- Students can ask permission and be granted permission for a bathroom break without saying a word and without interrupting the class.

- The teacher can signal an individual student that he/she needs to use a pre-established self-control technique to deal with escalating emotion.

• A team can signal the teacher after they have exhausted their resources and need to consult with him/her; without interrupting the class, the teacher can signal back that he/she has received their request and will attend to them soon.

In each case the otherwise disruptive students win (their needs are met), the teacher wins (little or no time is taken from teaching), and the rest of the class wins (time off learning is minimized).

The steps of establishing verbal and non-verbal cues are presented in **Chapter 14. Moment-of-Disruption Structures.** The following is a thumbnail sketch of the classroom signals that most contribute to a Win-Win class.

Management Signals

Quiet Signals. If students are interacting and in a normal voice you say, "May I have your attention please," they won't hear you. You will be forced to raise your voice and ask repeatedly for their attention, losing days of valuable class time (see box). The alternative is to adopt one or more quiet signals. Some favorites are:

• **Kagan Quiet Signal.** When the teacher raises his/her hand, the students are to 1) Raise their hands, 2) Focus fully on the teacher, and 3) Signal other students who have not seen the quiet signal. If it ever takes over five seconds for the whole class to come to full alert attention focused on the teacher, everything stops and students practice the quiet signal.[14] The teacher spends time so all students learn what each of three fingers of the quiet signal stand for, and may have a Quiet Signal Poster for the classroom.

Time Lost: 18 Days of Instruction!

If it takes about a minute each time you want to get the full attention of your class and you need to do that about 30 times a day, you lose a half hour of valuable instructional time in one day. Multiply that by the days in a week and you have lost two and a half hours during the school week. Multiply that by the weeks in a school year and the total is 18 days. Eighteen days lost in one school year — just managing attention! With a quiet signal, you can have complete attention of the entire class in under five seconds. Do the math. You save over 15 of the 18 days!

Quiet Signal

1. Raise Hand

2. Focus Fully on Teacher
(no talking, no working)

3. Signal Others

Win-Win Discipline. Kagan Publishing • 1 (800) 933-2667 • www.KaganOnline.com

18.13

There are many variations on the quiet signal:

- **Chime.** At the sound of a chime (or bell or train whistle) the students are to stop talking and give the teacher full attention.
- **Lights.** The teacher flips the lights off and back on to get attention.
- **Music.** A snippet of music can do the trick. We know a teacher who has the first few lines of "RESPECT" on an audiocassette that he plays to get students to focus on him. Not only do his students know that this is the signal and that it is whole group time, but it also delivers a nice message at the same time.
- **Clap a Rhythm.** The teacher claps a rhythm to which the students respond by clapping a response rhythm.
- **If You Hear Me, Clap Once.** The teacher says, "If you hear me, clap once." The teacher then claps once to model the requested response. Not all students hear the teacher but many do, so many clap back. The teacher then says, "If you hear me, clap twice." The teacher then claps twice. Most students clap back twice. By the third time the whole class is tuned in and the teacher has full attention.
- **Student Choice.** If a variety of quiet signals are introduced, students can choose the quiet signal for the day of the week.

Evaluation of Quiet Signals

Signals that include the following three features are most effective.

1. Signals that actively involve the students by having them raise their hands or clap are more powerful than passive signals because they interrupt ongoing sequences of talking or writing.
2. Signals that have students signal others are preferable because they spread more quickly as students help the teacher and they give students greater responsibility.
3. Signals that do not require equipment, such as a bell or light switch, are preferable because the teacher can use them wherever he/she is in the room. Literally, they are handy!

Team Voices. As students interact with one another in cooperative learning teams, noise escalates. As one team talks, the team next to them talks louder to hear themselves. This leads the first team to talk even louder. Noise escalates for a second reason: students in cooperative learning are very engaged as they plan, coach, praise, and problem solve together. Their voices become loud because they are excited. Engagement and excitement are positive, but we need to occasionally bring the escalating noise back down.

Knowing this, the teacher has had students practice a team voice — a voice that can be heard by teammates but not by other teams. Once the students have identified and practiced the team voice, the teacher and students develop a signal for the team voice. It can be an index finger to the lips or a hand to the ear. Whatever the signal, the teacher has students practice it so that without saying a word the teacher can give the signal to a team or the whole class to quickly, silently bring escalating noise under control.

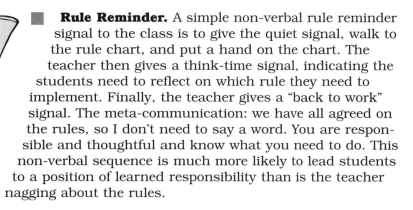

Rule Reminder. A simple non-verbal rule reminder signal to the class is to give the quiet signal, walk to the rule chart, and put a hand on the chart. The teacher then gives a think-time signal, indicating the students need to reflect on which rule they need to implement. Finally, the teacher gives a "back to work" signal. The meta-communication: we have all agreed on the rules, so I don't need to say a word. You are responsible and thoughtful and know what you need to do. This non-verbal sequence is much more likely to lead students to a position of learned responsibility than is the teacher nagging about the rules.

Secret Signals. The teacher may establish a secret signal with an individual student. For example, the signal reminding a student to keep his/her hands off others may be that the teacher crosses his/her arms after getting the attention of the disruptive student. The teacher works with individual students to establish an agreement to use secret verbal or non-verbal cues to refocus on work, return to seat, go to cool down area…. For the steps of establishing verbal and non-verbal cues, see **Chapter 14. Moment-of-Disruption Structures.**

Instructional Signals

Think Time. After asking a question, the teacher places an index finger to the side of his/her forehead. The signal has been pre-established so all students spend a moment of silent think time before the teacher signals for them to turn to their shoulder partner to RallyRobin their answers. To engage the kinesthetic intelligence and to have the student internalize the signals, the teacher may have the students put their finger to their foreheads during think time.

Turn to Your Shoulder Partner; Face Partner. On the whole, pair work is better than square work. When students interact in pairs in the same amount of time, each student has twice as much time to verbalize their answers compared to when they interact in groups of four. This means twice as much opportunity to get attention and validation and to be actively engaged. Students avoiding failure find it much easier to share their answers with one other student than with a team or the whole class. Thus the Win-Win teacher often has students RallyRobin (take turns sharing answers) with their shoulder partner (student next to them) or face partner (student across from them). Non-verbal signals cue students how to pair: Teacher taps his/her shoulder to cue shoulder partner interaction; teacher places palms together to cue face partner interaction. Thus the sequence goes like this:

> Teacher asks a question.
> Teacher signals think time.
> Teacher allows 3–5 seconds of silent think time.
> Teacher taps his/her shoulder to cue students to RallyRobin with shoulder partner.

By including signals, the teacher creates more focus and variety than if the teacher gives all directives verbally.

Think Trix. Frank Lyman has developed Think Trix.[15] Rather than signaling students to simply "think," the teacher signals students to engage in a specific type of thinking. For example, Find Similarities is signaled by thumb and forefinger on each hand forming a circle and having the two circles overlap, indicating the overlapping part of a Venn Diagram. Find Differences is signaled by the thumb and forefinger on each hand forming a circle but having the circles not overlap. Thus the teacher asks a question and then calls for a specific type of think time. Think Trix emphasizes 17 types of thinking including Cause/Effect, Recall, Example to Idea, Idea to Example, and Evaluation. These types of thinking are summarized in a Think-Pair-Share SmartCard.[16]

Student Signals

I Want to Speak. In the traditional classroom, when a student wants to speak, the student raises his/her hand, waiting to be called on by the teacher. Typically, the teacher asks a question, and about ten students raise their hands, hoping to be called on. Calling on one student is a Win-Lose structure. The student being called on gets the attention he/she is bidding for while the nine who were not called on lower their hands in disappointment. One winner and nine losers — it's not a good ratio.

The Win-Win teacher avoids this traditional Win-Lose call-on-one structure. Instead, the teacher asks a question and then has students all individually respond by writing an answer on a

Signal for, "Turn to your shoulder partner."

Signal for, "Face partner."

slate, signaling their answer with a thumb up or down (true/false), holding up a number of fingers, or using a pre-established kinesthetic response. All students receive attention, and the teacher has a much more authentic assessment of the class — a Win-Win solution.

One way of responding that meets the needs of energetic students is Take Off; Touch Down. The teacher makes a statement, and students who agree with that statement Take Off (Stand). If they agree with the next statement, they remain standing; otherwise they Touch Down (Sit).

■ **I Need Help.** While working on a worksheet, a student may use a signal to call for help. Signals teachers have established include:

• **Book Up.** High school students are comfortable with the following simple signal: If I would like the teacher to come over and consult with me, I simply place my textbook standing up. Otherwise, I keep it laying flat on the desk.
• **Table Tents.** Elementary school students enjoy a more colorful signal system: Students cover a table tent half red and half green. The tent stands on their desk. They place the red side up when they are stuck.

Table Tents

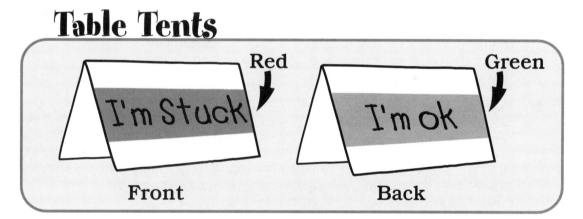

Front   Back

■ **Please Slow Down.** Have you ever been in a lecture and simply wished the presenter would just slow down? You do not have a specific question and don't want to raise your hand, but are getting lost because the teacher/presenter is going too fast. It is a Lose-Lose situation. The teacher loses because his/her teaching is ineffective; the student loses because content is not understood.

What do we need? A signal. Laurie Kagan designed a simple "Please Slow Down" signal: The student puts two hands together, palms touching and then slowly separates the hands. The teacher can respond by slowing down without wasting time to call on the student — a Win-Win solution.

■ **I Need Processing Time.** Working memory can only hold at most a dozen things, and the next new thing is held only by dropping out something else. To keep giving input when working memory is full is like pouring more water into a full glass. The content of working memory is cleared by interacting over the content. When students interact over the content, they tag the contents of working memory for longer-term memory. Thus frequent processing is the earmark of a brain-friendly classroom. Students need to signal the teacher when they need processing time. Rather than looking at you with glassy eyes, the usual sign that working memory is full, they can signal you.

Signal for,
"I need think time."

- **I Need Think Time.** To signal that they would like some think time, students can use the talking gesture facing themselves. That is, they open and close one hand as in a mouth talking (thumb below; fingers above, opening and closing). But to indicate the need for think time, the mouth faces their own face, as in, "I need to talk with myself."
- **I Need Interaction Time.** The signal that they would like to talk it over with a partner is to use the same talking gesture, but with both hands, with the hands facing each other.

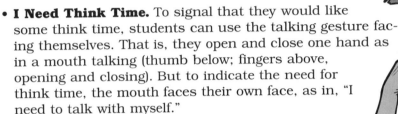

Signal for,
"I want to talk it over."

■ **Over My Head.** Have you ever been just lost in a lecture? And the lecturer does not know it, and, therefore, keeps rambling on? We do not want to keep presenting when students are lost. The solution: an "Over My Head" signal. Laurie Kagan designed a simple "Over My Head" signal: Students who are lost wave one hand above their head, palm down, indicating the content is "over my head."

■ **I'm Finished.** Many times we give students a task such as diagramming a sentence or completing a problem. We want the students to work alone and then check afterwards for mastery. Students finish at different rates. We want to pull the whole class back together when almost all the students are finished. How do we know when most of the students are finished? The answer: a Finished Signal. Some favorites are:

Signal for,
"Over my head."

- **Fist Down; Thumb Up.** Students can place their fist on the table with their thumb up to signal they are finished.
- **Hands Folded.** Other "I'm Finished" signals commonly used are hands folded in lap, hands flat on desk, or pencil in a pencil cup.
- **AnswerBoards Over.** If you use AnswerBoards, they are a different color on each side, so we simply tell the students to turn their AnswerBoards over when they are finished. The room literally changes color as the students finish, giving us a clear picture of what percent of our class is finished. See Answerboards, **Part VII, Resources F.**
- **Pencils Down.** The most common "I'm Finished" signal in high school is simply to have students put their pens or pencils down.

Signal for,
"I'm finished."

Win-Win Discipline. Kagan Publishing • 1 (800) 933-2667 • www.KaganOnline.com

18.18

Team Signals

■ **Team Question or "Three Before Me."** While students are interacting within teams, they may need help. A rule often used in cooperative learning classrooms is "Team Questions Only." Here is how it goes: If an individual student has a question, he/she is not to hold up a hand and interrupt the teacher. Rather, the student is to wait for student-student interaction time and then asks his/her shoulder partner. If the shoulder partner cannot answer the question, then the two students have a pair question and they are to ask their face partners. If all four students working together cannot answer the question, then they have a Team Question. They signal the teacher they have a team question by each holding up a hand. Four hands up is the signal to the teacher that the team has exhausted their resources.

The response of the teacher is to consult with the team. Allowing the other teams to continue their work, the teacher walks over to the team and **randomly** calls on one student in the group to state the question. This ensures that the team members have all wrestled with the question. Next, the teacher responds, sometimes simply answering the question, but more often telling the team where they could find the resources to answer the question or reframing the question in a way the students will discover an answer.

Team Questions – A Three-Way Win!

Team Questions have three advantages over the traditional approach to student questions. The traditional approach to student questions is a three-way lose: 1) Traditionally, any student at any time can derail any lesson by simply raising his/her hand. The question may be an "off the wall" question, but the traditional structure demands that the teacher stop teaching and respond to the question, even if it has no relevance for any of the other students in the class. The teacher is disempowered, giving up the power to control the class to the students. 2) The class loses too, as there is downtime as they listen to an irrelevant question. 3) Finally, the student asking the question loses, as he/she will get a cursory or irritated response because the teacher does not want the lesson to be derailed.

The Team Questions approach is a three-way win: 1) The teacher's lesson is not derailed, 2) there is no downtime for the class, and 3) the student gets a more detailed, responsive answer because the teacher is not attempting to answer the question while the rest of the class is spinning gears. Often in consulting with the student, the teacher discovers the question is different than what he/she would have answered in the rush of trying to answer and quickly get the rest of the class back on track. Through Team Questions, the teacher can take more time with the question and be more responsive, knowing the rest of the class is productively engaged.

Although the Team Questions procedure is established as the norm, it remains acceptable for a student to ask an individual question of the teacher.

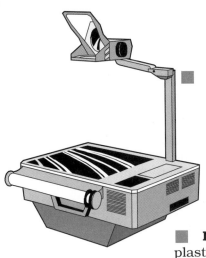

Overhead Projector Signals

■ **TeachTimer.** Another very helpful signal is provided by an overhead TeachTimer. The timer signals students to let them know how much time is left to complete a task and gives an audible warning as well as a blinking signal at preset warning and ending times.[17] It allows students to see at a glance how much time they have for a task and to self-manage.

■ **Projector Pals.** Colorful transparent plastic teaching tools called Projector Pals improve management. They project management, pointer, and structure messages, indicating who is to speak first, what structure students are to use, which points are to be emphasized, and highlight homework assignments and due dates.[18] See Projector Pals, Part **VII, Resources F.**

3. Role Assignment

The primary goal of Win-Win Discipline is for students to learn autonomous responsibility. Assigning students roles that they fulfill on their own is direct practice in autonomous responsibility. Thus Win-Win teachers use student role assignment extensively. Rather than walking around and handing each student a piece of paper, the Win-Win teacher says, *"Will the materials manager in each team please go to the resource supplies cabinet and get four pieces of paper, one for yourself and one for each of your teammates."* It is a win all around: students feel more responsible for managing the class, the papers are passed out more quickly, the teacher has less work to do, a quarter of the class burns off a bit of excess energy, and that same quarter of the class experiences, for a moment, a sense of special importance. The more often we use roles, the more often students meet the needs associated with their positions.

Assigning students roles and developing with students the gambits they need to fulfill their roles is one of the four primary approaches to developing social skills among students. We will limit our discussion here to a presentation of the 12 most frequently assigned roles, their function in the classroom, the positions/needs they fulfill, and ways to foster among students skillful role fulfillment and an internalization of the social skills associated with each role. For a fuller discussion of ways to develop the range of social skills among students, see *Cooperative Learning.*[19]

Roles and Their Gambits

The twelve most essential classroom roles identified by Kagan are reproduced below:[20]

1. Encourager. The Encourager "brings out" the reluctant student, and attempts to motivate the team if it gets bogged down. The Encourager goes to work before a student has spoken, with gambits such as, *"Let's listen to Pete."*

2. Praiser. In contrast to the Encourager, the Praiser goes to work after a student has spoken to show appreciation with such gambits as, *"Great idea."*

3. Cheerleader. The Cheerleader, unlike the Praiser, does not say things like, "Fantastic job." Rather, he/she gets the team to show appreciation for the accomplishments of one teammate or the team as a whole. The cheerleader literally leads the group in a cheer with gambits like, "Let's all give Pedro a pat on the back."

One of my favorite cheerleader gambits is to have students pick two positive adjectives or phrases and then chant the first phrase three times and the second one once. For example, students would chant, *"Great! Great! Great! Fantastic!"*

4. Gatekeeper. The Gatekeeper equalizes participation. If one student is talking too much and another very little, the Gatekeeper literally shuts the gate for one and opens it for another using gambits like, *"That is very interesting, Joe. Sally, what is your opinion?"* or *"Bill, do you agree with the point that Pat just made?"*

5. Coach. The Coach helps a student master academic content, but is very careful not to do the problems for the student. Coaches use gambits like, *"Remember Rule 2,"* and, *"Check over problem two again."*

6. Question Commander. The Question Commander occasionally checks to see if anyone in the group has any questions and, if so, makes sure they are asked and the group attempts to answer them. The rule is that the team attempts to answer all questions first. If the team cannot, then the team has a "Team Question," and the Question Commander uses a signal to let the teacher know that the team has exhausted its resources. My favorite signal for a team question is simply to have all four students on the team raise their hands. Alternatively, the Question Commander can have a red flag (slip of paper) to hold up.

7. Checker. The Checker makes sure everyone has mastered the material. The team knows that students are on their own during the quiz or exam, so the team must check to see that each person is prepared. The Checker leads the team in this with gambits like, *"Let's do one problem each while the team watches to make*

sure we all understand it." Sometimes the teacher assigns other job definitions to the checker, so the checker may be asked to check for understanding, check for agreement, check for completeness, or check to see if the team is following a specific rule.

8. Taskmaster. The Taskmaster keeps the group on task. It is important to distinguish positive and negative gambits for the taskmaster; they are to say things like, *"We have not done problem three yet,"* but not to say things like, *"Stop fooling around."*

9. Recorder. The Recorder writes down group decisions and answers. Sometimes the role of the Recorder may be modified so that he or she is simply responsible for making sure things get recorded.

10. Reflector. The Reflector leads the group in looking back. Group process is improved if the Reflector occasionally summarizes group process. Also, most importantly, the Reflector has the team reflect on how well it is using the Skill-of-the-Week, using gambits like, *"How well did we all stay on task?"*

11. Quiet Captain. The Quiet Captain makes sure the team does not talk loudly enough to be overheard by other teams. A teacher may wish to distinguish "loud voices," "twelve-inch voices," and "six-inch voices." It is the job of the Quiet Captain to make sure teammates huddle and whisper if the teacher has called for six-inch voices.

12. Materials Monitor. The Materials Monitor obtains and returns supplies and makes sure the team cleans up.

A colorful Pop-up Role Card Kit is available from Kagan Publishing.[21] See Role Card Kit, **Part VII, Resources F.**

When Not to Use Roles

Most Structures. Most simple cooperative learning structures, like Numbered Heads Together, Three-Step Interview, Roundtable, and Roundrobin, do not need roles. In fact, role assignment would detract from the effectiveness of these structures.

When to Use Roles

Team Projects. Whenever teams work on projects, roles are important. Roles allow more efficient management and improve social skills. For example, with no roles, given an interesting or challenging task, it is probable that the highest achieving students will "take over" and do the task for the team. It is the job of the Gatekeeper to make sure all participate. If each student has his/her role, such as Checker, Recorder, Taskmaster, or Cheerleader, there is a much greater probability that all will participate and each will feel he/she has made a unique contribution to the project.

Win-Win Discipline. Kagan Publishing • 1 (800) 933-2667 • www.KaganOnline.com

18.22

■ **Team Discussions:** Without roles team discussions often consist of one or two students talking most or all of the time. As a remedy, you might assign some of the following roles: Gatekeeper (who makes sure all participate), Taskmaster (who makes sure the team stays on the topic), Reflector (who makes sure the team occasionally reflects on its progress and on its use of any particular social skill which is the focus), and a Cheerleader (who makes sure the group stops and celebrates its accomplishments).

Roles Fill Needs

Role	Classroom Function	Attention-Seeking	Avoiding Failure	Angry	Control-Seeking	Energetic	Bored	Uninformed
		Position Needs Fulfilled						
Encourager	Encouraging and motivating	●	●	●				
Praiser	Praising others	●	●	●			●	●
Cheerleader	Getting others to celebrate accomplishments	●	●	●	●	●	●	
Gatekeeper	Equalizing participation	●			●			
Coach	Helping	●	●		●			●
Question Commander	Eliciting questions	●	●					●
Checker	Checking for understanding	●	●					●
Taskmaster	Keeping the group on task	●			●		●	●
Recorder	Recording ideas	●			●		●	●
Reflector	Getting group to reflect on group progress	●			●			●
Quiet Captain	Keeping the noise level down	●			●			
Materials Monitor	Efficiently distributing materials	●			●	●	●	

Win-Win Discipline. Kagan Publishing • 1 (800) 933-2667 • www.KaganOnline.com

18.23

Structures, however, eliminate the need to assign roles. For example, Talking Chips equalizes participation; Paraphrase Passport creates intense listening. For these and scores of other cooperative learning structures, see *Cooperative Learning*.[22]

Roles Fill Needs

Roles fill the needs of positions in various ways. First, roles allow direct fulfillment of needs, as when the Taskmaster fills the need for control by directing the group to stay on task, or the Cheerleader fills the need for attention by coming up with a novel way for the group to celebrate an accomplishment. Second, roles fill needs indirectly: as one student fills a role, that student helps another student meet his/her needs. For example, when the Checker or the Coach fill his/her role, students who are uninformed or those avoiding failure receive the help they need. Role assignment gives students a sense of importance, a place in the team and class, attention, a positive identity, and a boost in self-esteem!

Role Fulfillment

■ **Gambit Development.** Students are not born with the ability to gracefully fulfill the range of social roles. If we assign students the role of Taskmaster without teaching them what to say or do to fill that role well, we will hear things like *"Shut-up! Stop talking about that! We need to do problem three."* If, on the other hand, we have instructed students on graceful role-fulfillment, we might hear, *"That is very interesting. Let's be sure to talk about that later. Right now what we need to do is problem three."*

How do we promote skillful, responsible role-fulfillment? The most important tool is to teach gambits. Gambits are the phrases and actions that allow role-fulfillment. Gambits can be taught directly, modeled, reinforced, and practiced. Sample gambits for each of the twelve roles are found in the following chart:

Roles and their Gambits

Role	Verbal Gambits	Behavioral Gambits
Encourager	"You can do it!"	Patient waiting.
Praiser	"Great job!"	Thumbs up!
Cheerleader	"Let's all do a team handshake."	Leads team cheer.
Gatekeeper	"Susan, that is interesting; do you agree, Bob?"	Non-verbal, focusing the attention of group on the one who has not yet contributed.
Coach	"Let's start from the beginning and go slowly, step-by-step."	Models a method.
Question Commander	"Does anyone in the group have any questions?"	Stops the group to elicit questions.
Checker	"Let's make sure everyone on the team can solve it on his/her own."	May have each person perform on his/her own to check for understanding.
Taskmaster	"What we need to do is focus on the last two problems."	Re-focuses the group on task at hand by pointing or gesturing to the task.
Recorder	"Let me make sure I am getting this down right."	Records group ideas or answers.
Reflector	"So far we have agreed on..."	Has group pause to review progress.
Quiet Captain	"Let's use our team voices."	Gives team a pre-arranged quiet signal.
Materials Monitor	"Please hand me your papers, so I can turn them in for the group."	Brings materials to and from the team; checks to make sure the team tub is well-stocked.

■ **Role Cards.** One of the most efficient ways to have students learn the gambits associated with each role is to provide or have students make role cards. Role cards are a colored piece of card-stock folded to sit on the table like a table tent.

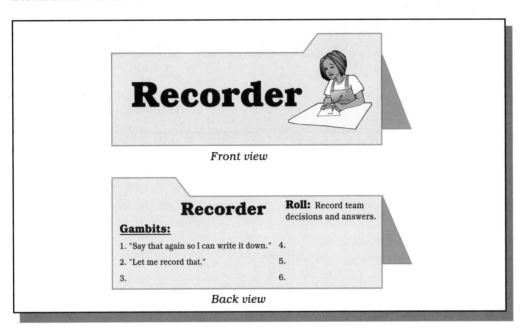

Front view

Recorder   **Roll:** Record team decisions and answers.

Gambits:

1. "Say that again so I can write it down."   4.
2. "Let me record that."   5.
3.   6.

Back view

On the front of the role card is the name of the role. On the back, facing the student whose role it is, are a few gambits — prompts to remind the student of responsible ways to fill the role. A colorful set of pop-up role cards with pre-written gambits is available inexpensively for the whole class.[23] See Role Card Kit, **Part VII, Resources F**. Students can create their own role cards and generate the appropriate gambits for each.

Hints on Roles

- Pace the introduction of new roles.
- Introduce roles by modeling poor and skillful role fulfillment.
- After modeling, have students derive the rationale for each role.
- Have students generate and practice gambits for each new role.
- Use structured role-plays to have students practice roles.
- Compliment students publicly and privately on skillful role fulfillment.
- Allow students to assimilate one role well before introducing the next role.
- Use rotating roles (have students pass the role cards one clockwise).
- Keep a set of role cards in each team's team tub.
- After a range of roles have been introduced, have teams decide which roles they will need for a given project.

■ **Introducing Roles: Modeling.** Actions speak louder than words. When introducing a new role, work with one team to have them model the use of a role, emphasizing associated gambits. Have other teams observe and record the gambits modeled.

■ **Deriving the Rationale.** Have one team model poor and skillful role fulfillment. Have the other teams derive the rationale for skillful role-fulfillment by asking questions like:

> • How did the other students feel when there was poor or skillful role fulfillment?
> • How would poor vs. skillful role fulfillment affect group productivity? Why?

■ **Supporting Role-Fulfillment: Catch 'em Being Good!** As you see good role fulfillment in the class, stop the class and have the student repeat the gambit he/she used. Appreciate good role-fulfillment both privately and publicly.

4. Room Arrangement/Content

Room arrangement/content refers to both the physical layout of the objects in the classroom (Does the teacher's desk go in front or back of the room?) and the areas and objects in the room (Is there a cool down area? Is there a conflict resolution poster?). Room arrangement/content communicates worlds to students. If students enter a classroom with uninteresting bulletin boards, little posted on the walls, no plants or animals, and nothing that "catches their interest," from moment one the class is screaming, "There will be nothing in here to meet your needs." In that drab environment students with a strong need for novelty and stimulation are likely to create some novelty — but not the kind the teacher most wants.

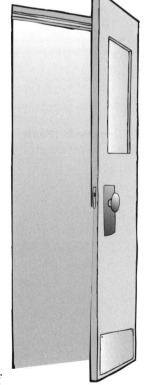

In contrast, a classroom with varied mini-environments within it, with novel and interesting things to see, hear, touch, smell, and interact with provides a different meta-communication: *"In this classroom your needs will be met. Learning in this class is going to be fun."*

Classroom layouts and contents are an extremely important component of designing a Win-Win class.

Classroom Environment for the Seven Positions

With no formal knowledge of student positions, good teachers have instinctively arranged and filled their classrooms to accommodate the needs of students, a major step toward preventing disruptions and creating a Win-Win classroom. Following are methods to meet student needs.

Attention-Seeking

Displaying Work. Being able to display one's work on a regular basis is one responsible way to meet the need for attention. Knowing one's work will be posted, the student seeking attention will put in extra effort. Each week each student selects a product to post.

Birthday Poster. Colorful dry-erase pens are used to write on a laminated Birthday of the Month poster. The poster displays the names and days of those students having a birthday each month. The teacher does not do the work. Rather, a rotating role is created: "Birthday Captain." The Birthday Captain is responsible for posting the names and days of students' birthdays as well as flipping the birthday chart in secondary classes.

Birthday Interview. On a student's birthday, the student is asked to go to the front of the class for a birthday interview. The class asks questions about things of interest to the student such as:

- Favorites things to do on a birthday
- Describe favorite birthday
- Favorite birthday present
- Family
- Favorite after-school activities
- Trips have taken or want to take

Special Events Bulletin Board. A bulletin board is dedicated to upcoming special events in the lives of students. The special events bulletin board is a springboard for generating student interest in the lives of their fellow students, fulfilling the need for attention. For many students, attention from peers is the most important attention they can receive. The Special Events Bulletin Board is a prompt for students to ask each other about upcoming trips or trips they have just taken; a new, expecting, or sick pet; and/or family parties or celebrations. Students are encouraged to post photos on the Special Events Bulletin Board with brief captions — just enough to spark the interest and questions from classmates.

Graffiti Board. Bathroom and freeway graffiti is a silent scream to be seen or heard, a bid for attention. Even if it is not signed, graffiti yells out, "Please listen to me," or "Please see my drawing." This bid for attention can be legitimized by a class Graffiti Board where students can doodle, draw, or write. Of course, in cooperation with the teacher, ground rules must be set as to when students can make entries on the Graffiti Board, how long entries will be posted, and, most importantly, what is acceptable and unacceptable to post. At first, in some classes, potential entries must first pass the "acceptability filter" – provided by the teacher or a committee of responsible students.

Avoiding Failure

Feedback Folders. Each student receives feedback privately. A part of the fear of failure is the fear of public embarrassment. This fear can be eliminated, if students know others will not see their grades. Students receive their graded work privately, using a feedback folder system. The folders allow materials monitors to pass out and collect papers while maintaining private feedback.

Feedback Board. On the Feedback Board students post non-evaluated work, such as poems, drawings, photographs, and essays, to receive feedback from their peers. Below each posting is a place to tack student feedback forms filled out and signed by other students. Feedback can be lengthy (*"Your poem reminded me of..."*) or brief (*"Great Job — Steve"*, *"I liked your bright colors — Sue."*). The only rule: positive feedback only. If you don't have anything positive to say, don't say anything. The teacher's positive feedback becomes a model. Structure so that every posting gets at least some positive feedback. Students may draw names and give feedback to each other on a rotating basis.

Peer Coaching Sign-up. In the Win-Win classroom you are likely to see a peer coaching sign-up sheet. This is a time for students to work together on content that is giving them difficulty. Students who are doing well with various content are qualified as peer coaches; others can sign up to circle around that coach for help during the free-choice peer coaching time. Coaches are instructed how to coach — not to tell answers, but to show how to arrive at answers.

Angry

Cool Down Area. The cool down area is a comfortable, secluded area of the room with limited stimuli. It might consist of a chair, facing away from the class so students can compose themselves without additional external stimuli. At secondary levels, a cool down area may be designated within the school rather than within classrooms.

Conflict Resolution Poster. On the wall in the Win-Win classroom is a poster to remind students of the modes of conflict resolution. See the Eight Modes of Conflict Resolution Poster, on page 6.4.

Control-Seeking

■ **Posted Work.** Students can choose which of their work is to be posted each week. They may fill out a brief statement to accompany the work they post: *"I choose to display this work because..."*

■ **Student-Created Bulletin Board.** Students have their own bulletin board and take charge of changing the content on a monthly basis. The content of the bulletin board is decided at the class meeting and the rule may be that it must be subject related. The monthly bulletin board team may be a rotating role or may be selected at random from volunteers for the month.

■ **Student Room Rearrangement.** Students can choose how to rearrange the room either Friday afternoons or once a month. The teacher may want to put limits on possibilities, requiring that certain things remain fixed and/or that only a certain number of pieces of furniture may be moved. Those in charge of implementing the change are in charge of returning the room to the usual arrangement unless the teacher is more comfortable in the new arrangement.

Energetic

■ **Movement Area.** When possible, furniture is arranged to allow whole-group movement, as when students do a classbuilding structure[24] or one of the many Silly Sports and Goofy Games.[25] See Silly Sports, **Part VII, Resources F.**

■ **Silly Sport Cards.** Pages from the Silly Sports and Goofy Games book are copied onto cardstock and laminated. They are placed in a box for students to check out to take to recess so they can experiment with new games.

■ **Stations.** The room may contain a station stocked with hands-on manipulatives. These manipulatives are content-related (math manipulatives; art manipulatives) and the station may be used as a sponge activity to soak up extra time productively for those who finish early: *"If you finish your work early, one of your options is to go to the manipulative station."*

Bored

■ **Sponge Area.** Anyone who finishes an assignment early can go to one of the sponge stations to work on content-related challenge tasks.

■ **Puzzle of the Day.** A brain teaser of the day is posted. Students who solve the brain teaser check their solution with the daily Puzzle Captain, who allows those who solve the puzzle to sign their name on the daily brain teaser log.

Uninformed

■ **Today's Agenda.** The daily schedule is posted and reviewed. Students may be asked to quiz each other on the schedule and devise ways to remind themselves of the schedule.

■ **Homework Assignments.** The homework assignment is posted in the same place in the room each day.

■ **Monthly Assignment Calendar.** The assignment calendar has assignments for the month posted, with due dates in red.

■ **Reminders.** Upcoming due dates are posted in the reminder section of the board.

Classroom Environment for the Multiple Intelligences

One way of aligning the classroom environment with student needs is to consider the eight intelligences. See *Multiple Intelligences.*[26]

■ **Verbal/Linguistic.** The class has the following:

> • Reading center
> • Class library
> • Quotes poster

One approach is to have a quote of the day or quote of the week. Quotes to foster reflection on character are one possibility. *Character Quotations*[27] provides ready-made bulletin board quotes on character virtues — one for every day of the school year.

■ **Logical/Mathematical.** Students appreciate having the daily schedule, or the class period schedule posted. This keeps the class as a whole informed and provides some students with the security of knowing exactly what to expect during a given lesson or during the course of the day. A posted brain teaser or puzzle of the day is another way to meet the needs of the student strong in the logical intelligence.

■ **Visual/Spatial.** A student strong in the visual/spatial intelligence feels immediately welcome in a classroom rich in posters, colorful bulletin boards, and other interesting things to see. The feast for the eyes communicates that the class will be a place that fills this student's needs. Consider including three-dimensional bulletin boards and mobiles. If fire-code permits, colorful signs on, or hanging from, the ceiling add an additional visual/spatial dimension. Laurie Kagan used the hall outside her room to post student art work, which the students changed weekly. Even before students entered her room, the message was "Inside this class, we will create and celebrate the visual/spatial."

Musical/Rhythmic. Music playing at 60 beats a minute increases relaxed alertness that enhances concentration and learning. To further satisfy the musical/rhythmic needs, a classroom can contain a music listening library, complete with earphones so as not to disturb others, musical instruments, and a tape recorder for students to record their content-related poetry, raps, and music. The teacher plays a variety of music, including music above 60 beats per minute to energize the class and music at a very slow rate to calm the class. See Music for the Mind, **Part VII, Resources F.**

Bodily/Kinesthetic. The student with plenty of energy has less need to be disruptive to meet his/her needs, if a classroom has curriculum-related manipulatives, stress apples, and activities in different centers in the room so movement occurs on a regular basis. Of course, if possible there is an open area for classbuilding activities[28] which can be used as part of any lesson and for Silly Sports and Goofy Games.[29] When movement is included as part of instruction, students burn off excess energy that otherwise might be used in the process of a creative disruption.

Naturalist. There are two ways to meet the needs of students strong in the naturalist intelligence: bring students out to nature, and bring nature in to the students. Field trips, a class garden, and exploration of nature in the school and neighborhood are examples of the first approach. Examples of the second approach include a class fish tank, amphibian tank, plants, and class pets. Students may raise butterflies from cocoons, have an ant colony to observe, and have ongoing experiments such as the effect of different soil types, watering patterns, and sunlight on the sprouting of seeds. The classroom designed to meet naturalist needs has plenty of natural sunlight and incandescent or full spectrum rather than florescent lights.

Interpersonal. In a survey of what leads students to have a "bad day at school," the most frequent response was not getting along with peers.[30] Belonging, being "in," peer acceptance, and approval are primary concerns for almost all students. Thus we want to arrange the room to tell students, "In this classroom, you will belong; you will have opportunity to interact with your peers; you will be doing fun things together." Students sit in teams, have team names prominently displayed, and the team has its own team tub. To meet the interpersonal needs of students, there are partner centers and partner and small group sponges. That is, a student who finishes individual work will sometimes have the option of moving to a challenging sponge activity center set up for pair or triad interaction over content.

Intrapersonal. A quiet zone in the classroom communicates respect for students' need to remove themselves from external stimuli and turn inward, to reflect. In the quiet zone, there may be a feeling poster to help students connect to their inner experience. Reflection may center on content themes, planning, evalu-

18.32

Win-Win Discipline. Kagan Publishing • 1 (800) 933-2667 • www.KaganOnline.com

ating progress toward self-defined goals, or connecting the academic content to personal experience. Students have the option of moving to a quiet zone for reflection. For example, the teacher may say, *"If you finish your team (or individual) work, one option is take out your journal for some journal reflections on today's quote of the day. Those of you choosing that option can move to the quiet zone."*

■ **Multiple Intelligences Centers.** The teacher many set up MI centers through which the students rotate. The content of the Grandma Moses Center, the Mozart Center, the Einstein Center, and so on, are each changed on a weekly basis.

Room Arrangement

Furniture layout determines how much proximity a teacher has to students which, in turn, is one of the most important factors in preventing disruptions. By simply moving the teacher's desk from the front to the back or side of the room, the teacher gains greater proximity to all students and significantly decreases disruptions. Care must be taken also that students have proximity and visual access to the teacher during cooperative learning; too much distance among teammates translates into less effective cooperative learning. An excellent discussion of the critical importance of room arrangement and the various options is presented in *Tools for Teaching*.[31] Arrangements for cooperative learning are presented in *Cooperative Learning*.[32] Some factors to consider are discussed below.

■ **Student Furniture Movers.** If the Win-Win classroom shares a room, students need to become efficient furniture movers. Students learn how to arrange and rearrange the furniture for various activities. Quickly and quietly they re-arrange their desks from a team arrangement for their cooperative activities to a solo arrangement for their tests and individual work. Each student learns exactly where to move his/her desk because the procedure has been practiced. In some rooms, tape on the floor is a visual reminder of where desks are to be placed for different types of activities. Tape or marks on the floor are important too because over time desks get scooted around, so students need to know where to put them when the teacher calls for a "desk check."

■ **Carpet Squares.** For the young students, a carpet with squares is used (or squares are marked off on the rug, or carpet patches are used) so each student knows her/his place for rug time.

■ **The Teacher in Motion.** "Management by working the crowd" allows teachers to monitor student activity on an ongoing basis. If the teacher is not moving about the room while the students work or interact with each other, the teacher cannot know if the students are on task and mastering the content. Student disruptive behavior decreases when students know the teacher is monitoring what they are doing. The proper place for the teacher when students are doing their seat work and when they are interacting in pairs or teams is to be out and about, monitoring and interacting with students.

Interior Loops. One way to allow frequent and easy access to all students is to arrange desks with an "interior loop," a path you can walk within the group of desks. If you only walk the perimeter, at every moment there are students far away. By more often walking the interior loop, more students are in proximity more of the time. Fred Jones describes the advantages of interior loops in his excellent book on classroom management.[33]

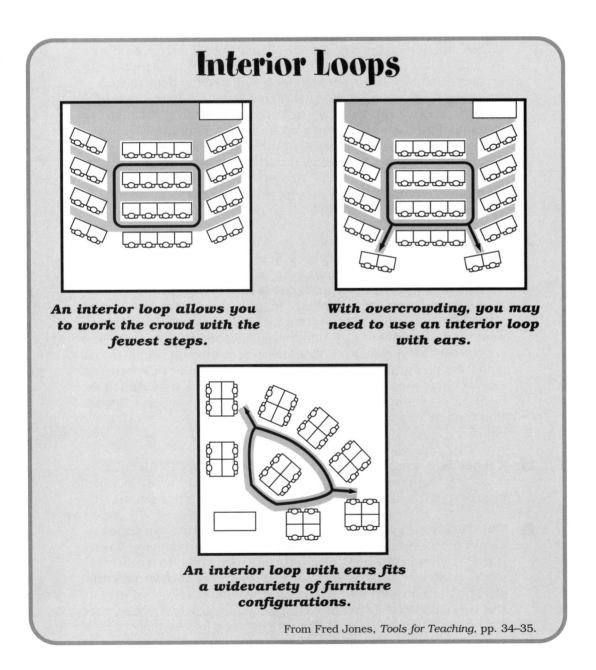

Interior Loops

An interior loop allows you to work the crowd with the fewest steps.

With overcrowding, you may need to use an interior loop with ears.

An interior loop with ears fits a widevariety of furniture configurations.

From Fred Jones, *Tools for Teaching*, pp. 34–35.

■ **Cooperative Learning.** When students are in cooperative learning teams, the rule is that each student should be equal distance from each teammate (it won't make for good teamwork if students are far from each other) and that they can all easily see the board or overhead screen (no one has his/her back to the front). Because drawing desks together for cooperative learning work frees up space, this arrangement allows more room to create other areas such as a movement area or a music area.

■ **Teacher's Desk.** The best location for the teacher's desk is in back of the class, or in classrooms with plenty of room to the side of the room. Why is the location of the teacher's desk of critical importance? The answer: proximity. Proximity is a crucial management tool. By keeping the teacher's desk in back or to the side rather than just in front of the class, student chairs can be pulled closer to the board so there is greater proximity between the teacher and every student in the classroom when the teacher is presenting.

5. Procedures and Routines

It is important to distinguish and address in different ways five related concepts: Agreements, Expectations, Procedures, Routines, and Rules. If we distinguish and implement each of these management tools appropriately, we dramatically reduce discipline problems. Let's start with some definitions and examples:

Agreements, Expectations, Procedures, Routines, and Rules

	Definition	Example
Agreement	Harmony of opinion; common understanding.	We will all work to make our class a safe place.
Expectation	Eager anticipation.	We expect every student to be engaged and to learn.
Procedure	A series of steps taken to accomplish an end.	As we enter class, we move our role card to show we are present.
Routine	A sequence of procedures.	Our morning routine is to enter the room (moving our role card and going quietly to our seats), do bell work, go over the day's agenda…
Rule	A prescribed regulation for conduct.	Students are to show respect for the property, person, and feelings of classmates.

■ **Agreements.** Agreements are at the heart of Win-Win. They are a concrete manifestation of the Same-Side Pillar. Agreements are our social contract. They express the way we want our class to be. We have presented ways to establish class agreements in depth in **Chapter 9. Teaching the Win-Win Philosophy.**

■ **Expectations.** Expectations are an attitude; they determine our orientation toward students. Research has demonstrated that expectations are a self-fulfilling prophecy: expectations teachers hold for students significantly determine their performance and even their IQ scores![34] The Win-Win teacher communicates positive expectations for academic performance and behavior. We communicate positive expectations not just by what we say, but also by what we do. With a look, glance, or smile, we communicate that we know a student can succeed academically and can behave responsibly. Positive expectations are especially important in meeting the needs of the student avoiding failure. Positive expectations are not something we can fake. We really need to believe in our students if we are to help them become responsible.

■ **Procedures.** Procedures are the practiced steps we take to accomplish a goal. In the Win-Win classroom there are well-rehearsed procedures for almost all repeated behaviors, including entering the room, lining up, asking for permission to sharpen a pencil, and moving furniture from teams to individual seating arrangement. Explaining, rehearsing, and reinforcing procedures eliminate more disruptions than any other single management tool.

■ **Routines.** Routines are ordered sets of procedures. Routines are time-ordered sequences: what follows what. By following routines, our classroom becomes predictable; expectations are established; students feel secure. Routines create an even flow of work, minimizing downtime between tasks. Routines eliminate the anxiety associated with an unpredictable environment. When procedures and routines are well-established, students are productively engaged most of the time, achievement is greater, and there is less opportunity and desire to be disruptive.

Procedures vs. Routines

• **Procedures.** How to take role efficiently. How to move desks for test taking. How to line up for dismissal.
• **Elementary Morning Routine.** Line up to enter class; greet teacher; store jacket and lunch pail; move clothespin to indicate present; check hot lunch sheet; go to seat; begin bell work.
• **Secondary Start of Period Routine.** Greet teacher at door; place homework in the homework bin; take seat quietly; begin bell work.

Procedure = Steps to efficiently do X.
Routine = First we complete procedure X, then Y, then Z.

■ **Rules.** Rules are prescriptions for behavior. Rules are often imposed and are often associated with consequences for disobedience. When agreements, expectations, procedures, and routines are firmly in place, there is little need to rely on rules. Because rules feel imposed, they are an invitation to test and to challenge. Because agreements feel like internal commitments, there is less impulse to challenge — after all, who feels a need to disagree with themselves? We have examined rules in depth in **Chapter 6. Preventative Procedures: ABCD Disruptions.**

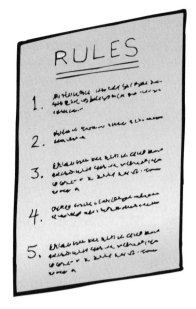

Because agreements, expectations, and rules have been covered in other chapters of this book, our focus here will be on procedures and routines.

Putting Procedures and Routines in Place

The teacher establishes some procedures; students design others, usually during class meetings. For instance, the teacher wants students to be able to interact with each other, but also to be able to get their attention back quickly and fully. So the quiet signal is one of the very first procedures to put in place and have students practice. Students may design the Visitor Procedure: during a class meeting raises with the students the question of how our class might best treat a visitor or a new student, leaving it to the students (with the teacher's questioning or guidance) to design a procedure. The procedure might include a rotating role of host and the design and creation of a guest book for visitors to sign.

Whether the teacher establishes the procedure or it is one instituted by the students, there are several steps in firmly establishing a procedure:

1. Derive Rationale
2. Teach Procedure
3. Check for Understanding
4. Practice
5. Reinforce
6. Re-teach

■ **Derive Rationale.** Students are presented with a problem, such as taking too long to pass out supplies, a slow or inadequate response to the quiet signal, or shoving and tripping over desks as students rush to line up. Students then state why the problem interferes with the way we want to be. Alternatively, with very young children, or with some teacher-established procedures, the teacher simply explains the rationale.

■ **Teach Procedure.** The most effective way to teach a procedure is to model it or have students model it. Other teaching techniques might include a procedure poster with step-by-step instructions.

■ **Check for Understanding.** The teacher checks for understanding of both the rationale and the steps. Students might be asked to verbalize the rationale to a partner and show understanding of the steps by carrying them out.

■ **Practice.** Distributed practice leads to greater retention, so the procedure is practiced on different days.

■ **Reinforce.** The teacher compliments students or the class on good implementation of the procedure. He/she catches them being good.

■ **Re-teach.** If students fail to follow the procedure, the teacher re-teaches, beginning with review of the rationale.

Common Procedures

What are the procedures we need for a well-managed classroom? There are myriad possible procedures. Among the most common procedures are:

Common Classroom Procedures

The Morning Routine
Entering the classroom
Role-taking
Absences
Tardies
Hot lunch count
Announcements
Bell work
Managing Materials
Missing materials
Passing out supplies
Storing materials
Managing Schoolwork
Asking for help
Asking questions
Homework
Learning centers
Signals to teacher
Missing homework
Passing in papers
Peer Tutoring
Recording homework assignments
Returning graded papers
Student questions
What to do when finished
Managing Noise
Quiet signal

Going Somewhere?
Bathroom use
Field trips
Hall passes
Hall traffic patterns
Lining up
Movement within the room
Moving desks
Permission slips
Someone New
New student
Visitors
Let's Eat!
Drinking fountain
Lunch seating
Lunch clean-up
Snacks
Water breaks
Emergencies
Earthquake
Fire drill
Natural disasters
Clean-ups
Cleaning the board
Cleaning desks
Let's Wrap It Up!
End of the day/period clean-up
Dismissal

Many of these procedures have been described in various places in this book. The remainder of this section will focus on the following categories:

- **Getting Started: Beginning of the Period, or The Morning Routine**
- **Managing Materials**
- **Managing Noise**
- **Going Somewhere?**
- **Let's Eat!**
- **Let's Wrap It Up!**

Getting Started: The Beginning of Period, or Morning Routine

■ **Entering Class.** The routine for entering class at elementary school may include any of the following: lining up until the teacher gives the signal to enter class, taking off snow boots to leave outside, greeting the teacher, moving a magnet to indicate presence, storing jacket and lunch, depositing homework in the homework bin, sharpening pencil, putting on nametag, and beginning bell work. Students are complimented on how quickly they follow the routine. At the secondary level, the beginning of the period routine is usually simpler, consisting of greeting the teacher at the door; placing homework in the homework file; moving the homework file to the present area; taking ones seat; beginning bell work.

■ **Greeting the Teacher.** Depending on the age of the students, it might be a high five, a handshake, or a hug. Some teachers give students a choice (*"Will it be a high five or a hug today?"*), satisfying the need for students to make choices and serving as a barometer of the student's position that day.

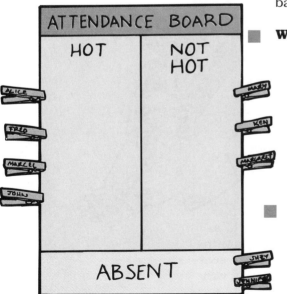

■ **Who's Here? The Clothespin Count.** Each student has a clothespin with his/her name on it. To indicate he/she is present, as the student enters class he/she moves the clothespin from the left side of the attendance board to the right. Any clothespins that are not moved indicate an absence, unless, of course, that student needs a procedure reminder! Cards in slots and magnetic dots or checks by names also work to quickly take role.

■ **Hot Lunch Count: Clothespins Revisited.** Rather than having to interrupt bell work for a hot lunch count, the hot lunch count can be incorporated into the attendance procedure. If students are going to order a hot lunch, they clip their clothespin to the "hot" area of the attendance board; if not, to the "not" area.

■ **Who's Here? File Folder System.** An alternative role-taking system is to have a file folder for each student with his/her name on it. Students take their file folder with them to their seats. Remaining file folders belong to the absent students for the day. The file folder system serves also to give private feedback to students on their work and return graded papers "for your eyes only" — an extremely important benefit when a student is in the avoiding failure position. Distribution of file folders can be speeded up if folders are filed by team, so the materials monitor can distribute and return them.

Adding Days of Instruction

Both the clothespin count and the file folder system add days of time to the instructional calendar without a moment more time in class. These role-taking approaches save at least five minutes a day compared to "calling role." Five minutes a day times the school week is almost half an hour a week. Multiply that by the number of weeks in a school year and you have added days of instructional time! Further you have reduced downtime that breeds discipline problems.

■ **Rotating Role: Attendance Messenger.** Delivering the attendance sheet and lunch count to the office is managed by a rotating role: The Attendance Sheet Messenger.

- **Nametags.** For the first weeks of school, students wear nametags (or have name placards on their desks) to help their peers and the teacher learn their names. Reusable nametags can be created in a number of ways: younger students can wear cardstock nametags with yarn around their necks; older students can pin them on.
- **Team Hats.** One creative teacher had team hats. She purchased inexpensive white paint hats from the local paint store and had each team decorate their hats with a team logo. On the front of each hat was the student's name.
- **Team Mobiles.** Another creative teacher had each team create a team mobile with team name and teammates' names that hung above the team desk.

■ **Make-up Work.** Absent students need to make up work they missed. A procedure for teammates to give them the assignments and to explain missed instruction is helpful.

■ **Bell Work.** Bell Work, Board Work, or Ready, Set, Go Work, as it is variously called, is a key component of the morning routine. Students silently begin the board work as soon as they are seated. To create interest, the bell work can vary to engage the various intelligences.

Multiple Intelligences Bell Work

- **Verbal/Linguistic.** Look up the definitions of three new vocabulary words. If you have more time, write a sentence or paragraph that includes all three words.
- **Logical/Mathematical.** Work on a brain teaser.
- **Visual/Spatial and Bodily/Kinesthetic.** Build as tall a tower as possible with four paper clips and a single sheet of paper.
- **Musical/Rhythmic and Logical/Mathematical.** Read a passage about a famous historical musician and, using a Venn Diagram, compare him/her to a contemporary musical artist of your choice.
- **Naturalist.** Make and defend a prediction about tomorrow's weather.
- **Interpersonal.** Talk quietly with a partner about which homework problem was most difficult for you and why.
- **Intrapersonal.** Make a journal entry about your dream profession.

■ **Announcements.** Announcements may be read by a student using a rotating role system. An announcement poster has the students' names on it and after reading the announcements, the Announcement Captain moves the marker one down to indicate who will fill that role the next day. The teacher reads announcements for young students. If a school radio station or television station broadcasts the announcements for the day, there is a procedure to produce attentive listening: on a fairly regular basis, students are quizzed on what was announced.

■ **Today's Schedule.** The morning/beginning of period routine ends with going over the schedule for the day that is posted on the board or a flip chart. The teacher does not spend much time on this. The teacher highlights transition points such as *"As soon as you finish x, you are to y."*

Managing Materials

Managing materials involves obtaining, storing, distributing, re-storing, and re-stocking student supplies, team supplies, and class supplies. How this is done can either contribute to a smooth running class or steal valuable time from instruction and open the door to disruptions and discipline problems. The more efficiently we manage materials, the more time will be spent on instruction and the fewer discipline problems will emerge.

■ **Student Supplies: What Do Students Need?** Some schools have a grade level list that goes home schoolwide. Other schools leave student supply lists to the individual teacher. Depending on the grade level, content, and resources of students, the list might include many or just a few of the supplies on the following page.

Student Supplies

- Three-ring binder
- Binder filler paper, lined and plain
- Pencil pouch for binder
- Pencils
- Pencil eraser
- Pen
- Box of colored markers
- Crayon box
- Pair of scissors
- Ruler
- Compass
- Small bottle of glue (will be refilled at school)
- Glue sticks (3)
- Sticky note pads (4)
- Boxes of tissues (2)
- Old sock to be used as slate board eraser
- Calculator
- Book covers

See the Materials Checklist Form on page 18.57.

Who Provides Supplies? Schools differ in their policies. Some schools require students to bring supplies; other schools do not. If asking for supplies is appropriate, parents prefer to get the supply list prior to school starting. They can beat the shopping rush the first week. If your school posts the class list the weekend before school starts, perhaps the supply list can also be posted. Remember to keep extra copies of the supply list to have on hand for new students entering during the school year.

Remind students and parents that the supply items do not need to be new. In a letter home, ask them to look around the house for the items before going out and purchasing new ones. You may want to include something like the following in your request: "If you have or are willing to obtain extra supplies for the class supply reserve, we would very much appreciate that. The class reserve will be used for students who cannot obtain the supplies or who unexpectedly run out of supplies."

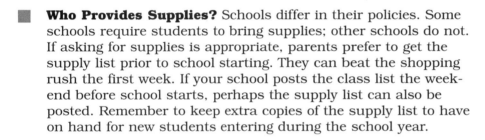

If it is inappropriate to request certain supplies from students, and the school cannot afford them, appeals to local stationary or businesses can fill the void. During the school year, students are encouraged to share supplies with others who run out, until they can be replenished — a win-win as students practice caring and downtime is minimized.

If a Student Forgets or Cannot Afford Supplies. Students will forget; some cannot afford the supplies. A Win-Win classroom is not a punitive classroom. Students can draw from the supply cabinet. In some cases, they may need to leave a promissory note, which is redeemed when they replenish the supplies they have borrowed.

Replenishing Supplies

■ **Stocking Stuffers.** As supplies run low, use your classroom newsletter to request that parents provide students with a new set of color markers, glue, etc. Suggest that these items make great stocking stuffers.

■ **Inventory Control.** An occasional supply check can keep things running smoothly. Students are given a copy of the supply list and asked to inventory their supplies. They are to check those things missing or about to run out so they can re-stock.

Where Are Supplies Kept?

Individual student supplies at the elementary level are kept in student desks and notebooks; at the secondary level, students are to bring their supplies to each class.

■ **Team Tubs.** Team Tubs can save a lot of time. For example, if students each need a pair of scissors for a project, it can take quite a lot of time to look through their desks to find them. If instead the teacher can say, *"Team materials monitors, reach into the team tub and take out a pair of scissors to give to each of your teammates and yourself,"* time is saved. Team tubs can be anything from a decorated shoebox to plastic tubs with covers. Team tubs might contain items the school or teacher provides, such as think pad paper, roll-up crayons, question spinners, and other frequently used manipulatives. They can contain items students are asked to bring from home, such as scissors, tape, and sticky note pads.

■ **Team Bins.** In addition to or instead of a team tub, some teachers prefer a team bin. Bins are stored in an area and are brought to the team during cooperative work. They can contain larger items than the typical team tub.

■ **Class Supply Cabinet.** The class supply cabinet contains clearly labeled consumables within reach of students, such as paper, cardstock, staplers, calculators, water colors, string, tape, pencils, paper, glue, and carbon paper. By having the materials accessible to the students, the teacher can ask the materials monitor from each team to go to the cabinet and bring back four unlined sheets of paper for their team, without having to distribute the materials one at a time.

Who Brings Supplies To and From Storage?

■ **Rationale for Roles.** Whereas one teacher passes out paper one at a time to students, another says, "Materials monitors from each team, go to the supply cabinet and get enough paper so each person on your team has a sheet." In the latter classroom, time is saved, there is less downtime to breed disruptions, and students feel more responsible and important. Students take greater ownership of the class if they fulfill important roles; if we want them to be responsible, we have to give them responsibilities.

■ **Rotating Roles.** To pass around the responsibility, some teachers choose a rotating role system. On Monday person one on each team is the materials monitor, on Tuesdays person two, and so on.

■ **Random Role Assignment.** To create interest and variety, some teachers use an overhead spinner and give it a spin to assign roles. The teacher might say, "Let's see who will get the paper for her/his team," and then give the student selector a spin. See **Part VII, Resources F.**

Storage of Student Possessions

■ **Backpacks.** Clear norms and expectations set a positive tone in the classroom. Unstated expectations are less likely to be fulfilled. Thus at the elementary level we set and reinforce norms and procedures for storage of items such as:

> Backpacks
> Coats
> Boots
> Gloves
> Books
> Lunch boxes and bags
> Materials brought from home to share

At the secondary level we set clear norms for lockers: what can and cannot be placed in lockers, when lockers can be accessed, when they must be cleaned out.

One norm some teachers use is to place backpacks and/or lunch boxes in a line as students line up in the morning. A placed backpack saves a student's place in line. Snow boots are neatly lined up against the wall in the hallway outside the classroom. To prevent misplaced lunch boxes, some teachers have a basket in the cafeteria for their class's lunch boxes, freeing students from bringing the boxes with them to after-lunch recess.

The Lunch Box Basket

"Due to the bee problems in the afternoons at our school, each teacher now has a basket that is left in the cafeteria. When students are dismissed to go outside, cold lunch students put their boxes in their classroom basket. Once students are back in the classroom after lunch, the teacher has the lunch box helpers retrieve the basket. This has saved many a 'lunch boxes on the roof' and parents calling, looking for lunch boxes."

— Sally Scott, School Principal

The exact nature of the routines and procedures are not as important as that they are clear to all students.

Managing Noise

■ **Quiet Cooperation.** Cooperative learning is a hallmark of the Win-Win classroom because mutually supportive peer interaction goes a long way toward meeting the needs associated with student positions. Without good management techniques, noise escalates during cooperative learning because there is excitement of the content, which leads a team to raise their voices. This in turn causes a nearby team to raise their own voices to be heard, which in turn causes the first team to raise their voices even louder. Only with strong management techniques is noise level kept to a minimum.

■ **Quiet Signal.** The quiet signal is not a way to manage noise. It is a great device for getting students to stop what they are doing and attend to the teacher, but it does not prevent noise escalation. Without additional management techniques, noise immediately escalates when students return to work following the quiet signal. A teacher who tries to manage noise with the quiet signal will end up looking like a puppet with someone jerking up their hand every few minutes! See Quiet Signal poster on page 18.13.

■ **Quiet Captain.** The rotating role of Quiet Captain is an excellent way to maintain quiet cooperation. It is the job of the quiet captain to monitor noise level in his/her group on an ongoing basis and return the team to quiet cooperation when noise escalates. See the Quiet Captain gambits in the Roles section of this chapter.

■ **Inside Voice.** The teacher can promote quiet cooperation by teaching students the "inside voice." The inside voice is a voice that can be heard within the team but not understood by another team. To establish the level of an inside voice, have a team talk at first loudly and then more and more softly while a neighboring team stays at their team table and attempts to understand what is being said. When the voice is soft enough that the neighboring team cannot understand the words, we have established the level of an inside voice. We then have the students practice that level until they get to a point they can return to that level at will when the teacher calls for inside voice.

■ **6-inch Voice or Partner Voice.** A 6-inch voice is at a volume that cannot be understood more than six inches away. A partner voice is at a level that can be understood by partners in a team but not by the other two teammates. These voice levels can be established in the same way as an inside voice. Some teachers prefer using the term "whisper voice."

■ **Star System.** Teachers put different colors of paper (Stars) on the board indicating what type of voice is appropriate:

Red = Independent work; No talking.
Orange = Pair work; Partner or 6-inch voices.
Green = Teamwork; Inside voices.

■ **Class Noise Monitor.** In addition to team Quiet Captains, during cooperative work you may choose to have a rotating role of Class Noise Monitor. It is the job of the class noise monitor to signal the class when noise level has escalated, bringing the class back to inside voices.

■ **The Yacker Tracker.** A commercial product, the Yacker Tracker, looks like a traffic signal with red, yellow, and green lights. It monitors sound decibels and signals the class with a warning sound and light when noise exceeds a teacher-determined level. The Yacker Tracker is essentially a mechanical Class Noise Monitor.[35]

Going Somewhere?

Having students know exactly where to line up inside and outside the class, how to move from their seats to the line, the order to line up in, and appropriate behavior while in line are all mini-procedures which, if well established and practiced, create an orderly and efficient class, minimizing disruptive behaviors and discipline problems. The line-up order and procedures are among the very first to be taught: students need to go outside with the teacher to practice them before the first recess! Even at the high school level, students must learn procedures to enter and leave class in an orderly way.

When clear procedures are established and reinforced, students have a sense of security, knowing how things are to be done. Clear procedures and norms for behavior put us all on the same-side. Just as the rules of the road create security and efficiency as we drive our cars, so too, do the rules and procedures for movement within, to and from, and outside the class. Traffic patterns and procedures minimize disruptions as students come and go to class, library, cafeteria, recess, lunch, lockers, clinic, principal, and home. Each time students move, it can be an opportunity to practice responsible mutual respect or an opportunity for disruptive behavior. Thus we need procedures for:

• Hallway traffic patterns
• Hall passes
• Lining up
• Where and when running is permitted
• Playground rules (e.g., no running after the bell)
• Areas where students are and are not permitted
• Fire drills
• Earthquake drills
• Terrorist drills
• Permission to leave class (to visit bathroom, clinic, library)

To treat each of these movement patterns in detail is beyond the scope of this book. We will concentrate on only two examples: hall passes and lining up. The same attention to detail, however, when establishing procedures for the other types of movement is equally important if we are to maximize responsible behavior and minimize disruptions.

■ **Hall Passes.** Hall passes are a signal to others that students have permission to be out of the classroom. Thus they should be large and colorful. Procedures are established for requesting a pass and returning a pass and how long a pass permits a student to be out. Students may log out and in, to keep a written record of time out and to allow a teacher to know where all students are at any time. A mechanical hall pass timer is available; it begins timing when taken from its stand and ends timing when replaced in its stand.[36]

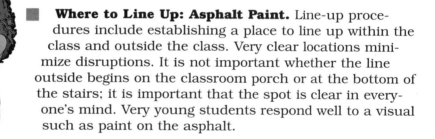

■ **Hallway Behavior.** During passing periods, hallways are busy, and rules of the road are essential if, literally, we are to be on the same-side and minimize disruptions. Walking on the right side, maintaining quiet voices, and no running are common rules. Like all procedures, if the rationale for these rules is firmly established, students are far less likely to test the limits.

■ **Where to Line Up: Asphalt Paint.** Line-up procedures include establishing a place to line up within the class and outside the class. Very clear locations minimize disruptions. It is not important whether the line outside begins on the classroom porch or at the bottom of the stairs; it is important that the spot is clear in everyone's mind. Very young students respond well to a visual such as paint on the asphalt.

■ **How to Enter Line: Ice Cream Sticks vs. Chaos.** In one classroom the teacher calls for students to line up and there is a mad scramble, students tripping over chairs, elbowing each other for a place in line. Next door the teacher says, *"When I call your team's number, you will stand up, put your chairs under your desks, and wait. Then when I say go, your team will walk over and take your place in line. Ready?* [The teacher draws an ice cream stick from a cup. Each stick has on it a team number.] *Team Three.* [Pause until all team three members are standing calmly behind their pushed in chairs.] *Go. Next team? Team seven..."*

In the first classroom it is everyone for himself/herself — survival of the fittest. The meta-communication: This is a Win-Lose classroom. Some students will win in the race to be first; others will lose. In the second classroom the meta-communication is different: This is a fair classroom. Sometimes our number is early, other times it is not. But we all are in the draw together. There is no fight, we calmly line up.

■ **Line-up Order: Beyond Ice Cream Sticks.** There are many possible line-up orders. To create variety, one day the teacher might draw ice cream sticks; another day the teacher might have students line up in reverse alphabetical order by second letter of their last name; another time it could be by characteristics, (number of times they have moved homes). The line-up order can involve problem solving: number of letters in first name multiplied by two added to the number of letters in middle and last names. Student teams can devise and submit creative line-up formulas to be drawn at random.

Characteristics Line-Ups

"If you have no brothers, stand; push your chairs in; walk to the line. Next, stand please, those of you who have just one sister and who are not yet in the line. Next, stand if you rode your bicycle to school today. Those of you seated, if your last name ends in a letter that comes before M in the alphabet, please stand. Now, everyone who is still seated, please stand."

■ **Line-up Behavior: Hands, Feet, Mouths.** Establishing appropriate behavior while in line can be as simple as having students know exactly what their hands, feet, and mouths should be doing while they are in line. Students can be reminded by questions. The rule: If your hands are not to yourself, your feet planted, and your mouth closed, then you walk to the end of the line. *"Jane, what were your hands doing just now? What do they need to be doing? What do you need to do?"* When the procedure has been established, Jane responds: *"Touching Sue; keeping to myself; walking to the end of the line."*

■ **Outside Line-ups: Rock-Paper-Scissors.** For outside line-ups before school and when returning from recess, very clear procedures must be established because students are less often supervised. We establish conflict resolution procedures. For example, if there is a disagreement among students concerning who entered the line first, they are to resolve the problem with a Rock-Paper-Scissors. Can students save a place in line for a friend? Perhaps a class vote is in order. All of these questions need to be addressed before the first recess on the first day. During the first week of school, teachers should make it a point to monitor students during recess so appropriate behavior is reinforced.

Let's Eat, Drink, and Be Brain-Friendly!

Win-Win is based on a fulfillment philosophy. That is, we are less disruptive if there are responsible ways to meet our needs. Hunger and thirst, of course, are basic drives. When the body is hungry or thirsty, attention is diverted from thinking and learning. A Win-Win solution is to fill rather than ignore basic needs. How then do we manage nutrition and hydration?

Nutrition Breaks. The type of food we eat has a dramatic impact on our ability to concentrate and our motivation. We have all at one time or another been lethargic and unable to concentrate after a big meal followed by a big dessert. We have all felt refreshed and alert after drinking a glass of water, not even having realized beforehand that dehydration was interfering with our attention and motivation.

Why is a piece of cheesecake more brain-friendly than a piece of chocolate cake? Sugars give a quick burst of energy followed by a let down. A balance of proteins and carbohydrates provides a more sustained release of energy. It is this sustained release of energy, not ups and downs, that we want in our classrooms. What our students eat will determine to some extent how much they find themselves with too much or too little energy to maximize learning. Are the students bouncing off the wall? Are they bored and uninterested? Nutrition is playing a role.

For some students a healthy morning snack is a bit of extra brain fuel; for others it is the first nutrition of the day. An ideal Win-Win solution is to make sure all students have brain-friendly nutrition. Students win, their classmates win, and we are better able to teach. Making sure that all brains have proper nutrition will take a different form in different schools. The extent to which the school and/or teacher need to be involved differs dramatically. In some schools a hot breakfast is served because the school has determined it will be the only possibility of good morning nutrition. In others, snacks are provided. In yet others, snacks are allowed. In most cases this means allowing a morning snack.

Snack policy may be schoolwide or up to the individual teacher. If snacks are permitted, clear procedures are needed regarding storage, when they can be consumed (at any time vs. at designated snack breaks), what kinds of snacks are encouraged, and what kinds are discouraged or prohibited. If snacks are provided or allowed, ideally they would provide sustained energy release, not a peak of energy followed by a valley of boredom. A slice of cheese and apple, nuts and raisins, or a power bar are suitable alternatives to sugary snacks. Prohibit donuts, candy bars, and junk food!

If snacks are permitted but not provided, we may need to supplement because, unfortunately, those students who most need a morning snack are least likely to bring one — often due to no fault of their own. Procedures can be instituted to equalize opportunity. Your school can turn to the PTA, local businesses, concerned parent groups, and/or entitlement monies to fill the void.

Water: Pass the Bottle. Thirst actually releases stress hormones that interfere with learning. Students who are dehydrated show stronger stress reactions, are inattentive, and show lower levels of cognitive performance. Within five minutes of consuming water, there is a marked decline in the stress hormones (corticoids and ACTH) and attention and retention increases.[37] Proper hydration also helps maintain optimal neuronal firing. For these reasons a water bottle on each student's desk has become a hallmark of brain-based instruction. Students need 4 to 6 ten-ounce glasses of water a day. Juice, soft drinks, coffee, and tea do not provide the benefits of pure water because they are not Ph neutral; it actually takes 16 ounces of juice to get the same hydration benefits as obtained in 8 ounces of water. The decision to allow students to drink at their desk, however, comes at the cost of needing to manage filling and storing water bottles as well as more frequent bathroom breaks. Some teachers simply schedule more frequent bathroom breaks. Water bottles should be seen as a privilege that can be lost temporarily if abused. Yes, student water bottles create more trips to the rest rooms and the need to institute other procedures, but the benefits outweigh the disadvantages.

An alternative to water bottles at desks is to schedule more frequent hydration via hydration breaks, or establishing a rotating role of hydration monitor. Small paper cups or student cups can be used and the hydration monitor can be assigned the task of bringing water to the team.

Drinking Fountains: Five Second Whisper Counts. The drinking fountain is a source of conflict if clear procedures are not established. Although drinking fountains are the norm inside schools throughout the country, outside fountains are usually found only in states where the climate is mild; they are not maintained in states where freezing occurs during the winter months. If an outside fountain is available, a drink of water and a bathroom break are encouraged before returning to class.

Routines must be established and maintained for outside, hallway, and classroom fountains. To manage time at the fountain, you might try a five second whisper count. The student behind the one drinking does a slow count to five. When the count is over, the drink is over. If the student is still thirsty, he/she can go to the end of the line and take a second drink. The procedure reduces complaints and equalizes access.

Lunch Area: Litter-Free Days. To keep the lunch area clean, we can have a rotating role of Lunch Monitor. The job of the lunch monitor is not to clean the mess left by others, but to be sure they attend to cleaning up after themselves. To put it on a positive basis, litter-free days can be tallied, and the class can celebrate each week they go the entire week litter-free. Procedures for rainy day lunches include seating and clean-up. If students are allowed to rearrange desks and chairs for rainy day lunch, procedures are established for quickly returning the furniture to its original place.

■ **Nourish the Brain: Fresh Cool Air.** Water and food nourish the brain. There is another kind of nourishment, the importance of which is often underestimated: fresh air. The brain runs on oxygen. Movement such as classbuilders and silly sports make students more alert in part by increasing heart and breathing rates and volume, which pumps more oxygen to the brain. We can nourish more on an ongoing basis if there is a good supply of fresh air in the room. If that is not possible, more frequent "brain breaks" — movement activities — can compensate.

Another underestimated important variable is room temperature. As the room temperature increases from around 70–72 degrees Fahrenheit, alertness decreases. Again, if maintaining a cool room temperature is not possible, we can compensate by more frequent brain breaks.

After lunch, classes are lethargic. Why? The blood is in the belly, helping digest food. There is less available for the brain. So, if we are to schedule brain breaks, right after lunch is optimal as it will compensate for the after-lunch lull.

It's a Wrap!

When students learn wrap-up procedures, they learn important organizational life skills. We approach our next new task with more energy if we have closure on our last task. Wrap-up procedures are a win-win all around:

Students gain an important organizational life skill, feel greater responsibility for their class, and obtain a sense of completion.

Teachers feel support from students, have a more organized class, and reduce stress.

Custodians feel less irritation and can dedicate their energy to tasks only they can do.

■ **Project Clean-up: Clothespins Again!** Give your students a clothespin with their name or student number on it. At the end of work on ongoing projects, students use the clothespin to clip the pieces of their project together to store in the team bin. For some projects a file folder or a shoebox are the organizer of choice.

■ **End of the Day/Period Clean-up: Wrap-up Tasks.** On a rotating basis, each team is assigned wrap-up tasks: cleaning the white board or chalkboard, cleaning the erasers, and sharpening pencils so they are ready for the next day. Other wrap-up tasks are the responsibility of each team each day: stacking their chairs and picking up paper and trash in their area.

If teams are not the norm, the tasks can be assigned to individuals on a rotating basis. Each student stacks his/her own chair, cleans up under his/her own desk, and then becomes a "quiet vacuum cleaner" to pick up papers and items off the floor. A cleanup crew (selected on a rotating basis) helps with the other jobs.

Making Clean-up a Game

A typical elementary school clean-up: *"Today everyone needs to pick up a certain number of things off the floor. The number of things you need to pick up is the number of syllables in this word: 'communication.' Show me with your fingers how many things you need to pick up.* [Students respond]. *After you have picked up five items, stand by your desk to show me you are ready to go home."*

When the clean-up is finished, in preparation for the end of the day/period dismissal, students stand by their desk with all their items. If it is a primary classroom, they may be instructed to sit on the floor.

■ **Homework Check.** Before dismissal, a ritual in elementary school is to make sure everyone has written down his/her homework assignment. At the secondary level it may be appropriate to give time and method for recording homework and to assign "homework buddies" so students can call if they have difficulties with the assignment.

■ **Custodian Confirmation.** To create a Win-Win orientation with the custodian, on a regular basis check to see what he/she thinks of the condition of your classroom at the end of the day. Is there anything my students or I can do to make your job more efficient? Have the custodian visit your class and share appreciations and/or requests.

6. Parents as Partners

The Win-Win philosophy extends to parent-teacher relations. The Win-Win teacher sees the parent as a partner in the discipline process. Most parents with disruptive students are seeking help and are grateful to learn the Win-Win approach. Rather than hearing from the teacher that there is something wrong with their child or that child student has been "misbehaving," they hear that he/she has perfectly normal universal needs and that the teacher wants to team up with them to help their child learn adaptive, non-disruptive ways to meet his/her needs — learn skills that will help him/her for a lifetime. Rather than being told they should be doing something different, parents are asked to be partners, to work together to seek solutions.

Win-Win Discipline. Kagan Publishing • 1 (800) 933-2667 • www.KaganOnline.com

18.52

> *A really great teacher is someone who...* **calls your parents and tells them how you are doing, for good and bad.** Sierra, 12, Portland, Oregon.[38]

The most important element in creating a Win-Win parent-teacher partnership is communication. It is the job of the Win-Win teacher to communicate the Win-Win philosophy to parents early and repeatedly and to help each parent establish a Win-Win Discipline orientation with his/her child. When parents and teachers communicate the same discipline message, they each make the job of the other easier. And the message is simple: we always accept positions and their associated needs; we never accept disruptive behaviors; we are here to help you discover non-disruptive, satisfying ways to meet your needs. It is an easy message to sell because it puts parents, teachers, and students all on the same side.

Communicate Early

The Win-Win teacher is proactive, establishing a positive relationship with parents — communicating the Win-Win philosophy before any disruptions occur. If the Win-Win philosophy is communicated to parents before students have been disruptive, the message falls on more responsive ears. Once a student has been disruptive, parents are likely to be on the defensive, making open communication more difficult.

■ **Welcome Letter.** As soon as you get your class list in August, compose and send a letter to parents. The letter can include some of the following:

- **Welcome.** *"I am so pleased to have Billy in my class this coming year. I look forward to working with him to..."*
- **Goals.** *"This year our emphasis will be on...."* Include a very brief description of important topics and explain why they are important.
- **Invitation.** *"Prior to the first day of school, we will have a get-acquainted social gathering for parents and students at Holmbsby Park on..."*
- **Description of Win-Win.** *"I have a Win-Win philosophy. The basis of this philosophy is that each student has his/her unique abilities and needs, and part of the job of the teacher is to teach students how to maximize their potential and satisfy their needs while acting in harmony with the potential and needs of others. Win-Win is a democratic, positive, empowering philosophy for life, and I look forward to sharing this approach with you and your child."*
- **Getting to Know You Form.** *"In order to get to know you and your child a bit better, I would appreciate it if you would fill out and return the enclosed Getting to Know You form."* See the Parent Info Form on page 18.56.
- **Parent Helper Form.** *If there are some ways you would be willing to help out at school this year, please let me know. For you convenience, I have enclosed a Parent Helper checklist."* See the *Are You Willing to Help Out?* Form, page 18.58.
- **Student Strength Checklist.** *"In order to get to know your student better, I have enclosed the Student Strengths Checklist. Please fill it out and return. By the way, it can be*

a great conversation topic if you fill it out with your student. Your responses will give me a better idea of your student's strengths." See the Student Strengths Checklist Form, page 18.59.

- **Materials Checklist.** "*In order to maximize learning and minimize downtime, it would be very helpful if each student could bring his/her school supplies to class the very first day. Enclosed you will find a checklist of supplies. Do not feel the supplies all have to be new; used pencils or scotch tape roles are fine. We will be replenishing supplies as the year progresses. If you have any difficulty in obtaining the supplies, please contact me before school starts so I can help make arrangements.*" See the Materials Checklist Form, page 18.57.

- **Mark Your Calendar.** "*Please mark your calendar with the following important dates:*

  - Before-School Get-Acquainted Picnic:
  - Open House:
  - Class Bar-B-Q:
  - Class Fall Performance for Parents:
  - First PTA Meeting:

  Include a one-sentence description of why attending each of these events is important.

- **Class Procedures.** "There are a few class procedures I would like you to be aware of, so please find included a summary of our Class Procedures. I would appreciate it if you would go over these procedures with your child and both sign and return the slip that states you have read and agree to the procedures. Again, if you or your child have any questions or concerns about our procedures, please do not hesitate to call." On a separate sheet or sheets, include a brief summary of procedures, rules, and philosophy:

  - Homework
  - Grading
  - Absences
  - Make-up work
  - Dress code
  - Win-Win Discipline

- **Suggested Reading.** Suggest a book for end-of-summer reading.

- **Helpful Communication Hints.** "*The key to creating Win-Win solutions is open, two-way communication. You may find it useful to look over an enclosed form, Helpful Hints for Communicating with Your Child. They are hints I find useful in the classroom and you may find them of use as well.*" See the Helpful Hints for Communicating with Your Child form, page 18.60.

- **Invitation to Call.** End with an invitation for the parents to call so you can discuss or answer questions and concerns.

Win-Win
Welcome Letter

Dear Parent,

I want to thank you for the opportunity to have <u>Patricia</u> in my class this year. I want to take this opportunity to share with you a bit about the Win-Win philosophy that will guide us.

Along with maximizing academic success, I am dedicated to maximizing the individual development of each student. Each student brings to class unique ways of learning, interacting, and unique needs. My goal will be to understand your student's needs and to help your student learn responsible ways to realize <u>her</u> potential.

My goal is to maximize both academic success and the acquisition of positive character virtues for each student. To learn to work well with others, students will often work together in teams, have class meetings, and collaboratively solve problems. I want every student to learn to seek Win-Win solutions — to find ways to interact with others so everyone's needs are met.

Each student is unique. I attempt to understand that uniqueness to best fashion successful learning opportunities. As a teacher, I am committed to providing developmentally appropriate curriculum and using a range of engaging instructional strategies. If students are not being successful, I will work with them to find ways to make the curriculum or instruction more appropriate and engaging — my goal is for every student to be as successful as possible and to express and develop <u>her</u> unique talents. In our class, if there is ever a problem, we look at how to restructure so every student can meet <u>her</u> unique needs.

Communication is the key to Win-Win. If you ever become aware of the class not meeting the needs of your student — if you feel <u>she</u> is not realizing her full potential — please contact me right away so we can collaboratively seek a solution. If there is any way you feel our class can better meet <u>Patricia's</u> needs, I want to hear about it. You know your student better than I; please help me make this year as successful as possible. I look forward to working with <u>Patricia</u> this year. I thank you for the privilege of having <u>her</u> in my class, and look forward to meeting you.

Sincerely,

_____
Teacher Name

Parent Info Form

Dear Parents,

In order to better serve the needs of your student, please fill out and return this form.

Contact Info
Name_____ Occupation_____
Home Phone_____ Work Phone _____

Name_____ Occupation_____
Home Phone_____ Work Phone _____

• When would be the best times to schedule meetings?_____

Family Info
• Acivities or hobbies parents enjoys _____
_____

• Things the family likes to do together_____
_____

• Activities your student enjoys_____
_____

• Strengths or positive qualities of your student_____
_____

• Is there anything you can tell me about your student or your family that might assist me in addressing his/her educational, emotional, or special needs or abilities? _____
_____
_____
_____

Classroom Help
• Are you available to chaperone field trips?   Yes   No

• Are you available to work with students in the classroom?   Yes   No

• Are you willing to volunteer your time or services in the classroom (computers, art work, music, making snacks, etc.)?   Yes   No   If yes, describe how_____

• Would you like to be a guest speaker or do you have a skill you are willing to demonstrate?   Yes   No
If yes, describe_____

Other comments?_____
_____

Thank you for your help. We are looking forward to a great year!

Materials Checklist

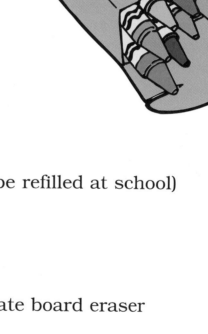

- ❑ Three-ring binder
- ❑ Binder filler paper, lined and plain
- ❑ Pencil pouch for binder
- ❑ Pencils
- ❑ Pencil eraser
- ❑ Pen
- ❑ Box of colored markers
- ❑ Crayon box
- ❑ Pair of scissors
- ❑ Ruler
- ❑ Compass
- ❑ Protractor
- ❑ Small bottle of glue (will be refilled at school)
- ❑ Glue sticks (3)
- ❑ Sticky note pads (4)
- ❑ Boxes of tissues (2)
- ❑ Old sock to be used as slate board eraser
- ❑ Calculator
- ❑ Book covers

Are You Willing to Help Out?

Are there some ways you would be willing to help out at school this year? Please check below.

❑ Help build resources and equipment
  (bird houses, collecting nets, shelves, learning centers).

❑ Act as monitor for cafeteria, hall, or playground.

❑ Prepare and bring food items.

❑ Assist with special tutoring.

❑ Make a presentation or performance.

❑ Read to students.

❑ Job sharing.

❑ Help make classroom decorations and design learning walls, etc.

❑ File, sort, hole punch, copy, etc. Help with secretarial chores.

❑ Make learning games.

❑ Contact and/or organize other parents.

❑ Chaperone a field trip (even if it is just to the grove of trees at the end of the campus).

❑ Help prepare materials for labs and projects.

❑ Donate materials.

❑ Help with special classroom or school events and projects.

❑ Assist with pet or plant care.

❑ Contact businesses about possible donations or sponsorships.

❑ Help with class newsletter.

❑ Help with web site.

❑ Help students with computers and other technological aids.

❑ Other:

_____

_____

_____

Student Name_____

Parent Name_____

Parent Signature_____

Date_____

Adapted from: Silver, D. & Selby, M. *He Said/She Said: The Home-School Connection.* National Middle School Association (NMSA) 29th Annual Conference: Building Bridges to the Future. Portland, Oregon. November, 2002.

Student Strengths Checklist

Directions: Check as many boxes in each column as are true. Feel free to write in and check additional positive characteristics by the boxes at the bottom of each column.

Student Name

Character Virtues	Mental	Emotional	Artistic	Social	Personality	Physical
☐ Citizenship	☐ Clever, Wise	☐ Caring	☐ Acting	☐ Appreciative	☐ Cheerful	☐ Active
☐ Courage	☐ Exact	☐ Empathic	☐ Arranging	☐ Cooperative	☐ Determined	☐ Athletic
☐ Fairness	☐ Imaginative	☐ Enthusiastic	☐ Crafting	☐ Forgiving	☐ Flexible	☐ Coordinated
☐ Honesty	☐ Informed	☐ Expressive	☐ Designing	☐ Friendly	☐ Humorous	☐ Dexterous
☐ Integrity	☐ Inquisitive	☐ Happy	☐ Drawing	☐ Kind	☐ Motivated	☐ Energetic
☐ Loyalty	☐ Mathematical	☐ Insightful	☐ Fashionable	☐ Leadership	☐ Organized	☐ Flexible
☐ Pride in One's Work	☐ Observant	☐ Motivated	☐ Painting	☐ Socially Skilled	☐ Positive	☐ Graceful
☐ Respectfulness	☐ Open-Minded	☐ Resilient	☐ Photographing	☐ Supportive	☐ Serene	☐ Poised
☐ Responsibility	☐ Plans	☐ Self-Controlled	☐ Poetic	☐ Tolerant	☐	☐ Quick
☐ Self-Discipline	☐ Verbal	☐	☐ Sculpting	☐ Understanding	☐	☐ Strong
☐	☐ Witty	☐	☐ Singing	☐	☐	☐ Tireless
☐	☐	☐	☐	☐	☐	☐
☐	☐	☐	☐	☐	☐	☐

Helpful Hints for Communicating with Your Child

1. Listen with your FULL attention. A good way to ensure his/her full attention is put them in the front seat of your car and drive them around as you talk with them. (Unless they want to hurl themselves from a moving vehicle, they've got no place to run.)

2. Be aware of body language, both yours and theirs.

3. Use silence to understand your child's meanings and feelings.

4. Use open responses to keep the child talking. *"I see." "Tell me more about that part."*

5. Accept and respect your child's feelings. Feelings don't have to be justified, they just ARE.

6. Don't interrupt.

7. Check out your child's feelings by reflecting what he/she says. *"I think I heard you say that you were really angry with Susan." "So you were feeling helpless? Like you wanted to hide?"*

8. Be calm. Speak in a quiet voice. Use economy of words (don't talk too much).

9. Stick to the subject.

10. Don't assume that you are making yourself clear. Check for understanding periodically. *"Can you tell me in your own words what you think I'm telling you?"*

11. Problem solve by discussing a variety of solutions. Emphasize your child's choice in selecting a plan of action.

12. Give your point of view as just that. It's not the law or the only good solution.

13. Don't be a dictator. Remember that children also learn by failing. Allow the child to learn successful problem solving from failing once in a while

14. Avoid nagging, threatening, criticizing, lecturing, or probing.

15. NO Name Calling!!! Attack the problem, not the person.

16. Whenever possible, use humor.

Reprinted with permission from: Silver, D. *Drumming to the Beat of a Different Marcher: Finding the Rhythm for Teaching a Differentiated Classroom*, Nashville, TN: Incentive Publications, 2003.

■ **Letter, Postcard for Secondary Students.** At the secondary level, the welcome letter or postcard is addressed to the student and may be just a few sentences (see sample), but it sets a positive tone.

Dear Juan:

I look forward to having you in my third period Geometry class this year. Geometry will change the way you view the world!

On the first day of class, please be sure to bring a three-ring binder, blank and lined paper, a ruler, compass, and sharpened pencil so we can get to work right away.

Sincerely,

Mr. Jones

Juan Martinez
1234 Maple Dr.
Lost City, CA 92344

■ **Welcome Phone Call.** Some teachers follow up the welcome letter with a welcome phone call. Whereas thirty phone calls is a considerable investment of time, it has a dramatic payoff in establishing a Same-Side orientation. Once a problem does occur, parents come to that first conference with a whole different attitude if they know you care and if initial rapport has been established. If the welcome phone call occurs during the first few weeks of school, you will have an opportunity to share some positive observations you have regarding the strengths of the student.

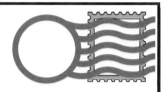

The welcome phone call may include the following:

- **Introduce Yourself.** Express your enthusiasm for content, why you think it is important, and your enthusiasm for teaching.
- **Describe Highlights of Curriculum.** *"This year one of our most important topics will be individual state reports…"*
- **Share Strengths.** Share with the parent positive observations you have made of the child. Consider academic areas of strength, social skills, character virtues, humor, and energy.
- **Check for Special Needs.** *"One thing I like to ask parents is if their child has any special medical needs or in any other way may need some special attention. Are there any medical or emotional needs it would help me to know about?"*

- **Emphasize Your Need for Help, Communication.** *"In order to be the best teacher I can for your child this year, I really need your help. You will be more aware than I of things that are going on. If you see Joan particularly frustrated with a type of homework, or if there is something impacting her emotionally, I would appreciate you giving me a phone call or sending me a note. I would like to keep our lines of communication open.... With some class events I will be asking for help from parents. If you are willing to contribute with cooking, organizing, or clean-up, we could really use the help. Also, this year we will have some parents come in to share information about their professions and hobbies. Do you have any special interests or hobbies you think the students might enjoy learning about?"*
- **Procedures and Philosophy.** If the phone call is a follow-up to the welcome letter, it is an opportunity to discuss classroom procedures and the Win-Win philosophy.
- **Invitation.** *"Please do mark your calendar. Our first parent night will be..."*

Communicate Frequently

Frequent Phone Calls. Phone calls to parents or guardians are the single most under-utilized and misused ways to build Win-Win school-home relations.[39] Most parents dread phone calls from schools because most calls either report their child being hurt or their child being a discipline problem. When teachers and administrators turn this around and make most calls to report positive behaviors and/or simply open avenues of communication, remarkable things happen. Parents see teachers as allies: Win-Win relations develop.

A very effective way to institutionalize regular positive phone calls is to make a commitment to make three calls a week and for each call to begin with some positive aspect of the student's behavior. An open-ended phone call that begins with *"Hi, this is Mr. Jones, Sally's teacher at Wallback Elementary. I'm making regular phone calls to touch base with you. I would like to know if you have any questions, or if there is anything you would like to talk about."* The first call is generally the most difficult because parents have become accustomed to receiving only negative news. When parents realize the teacher is truly interested in listening, they generally open up and provide very valuable information.[40] The teacher may learn about a death in the family, extra-curricular activities that are interfering with homework, or any number of things to help them more fully assume a Same-Side orientation with their student. Naturally, phone calls are a time to inform parents of upcoming events and to invite their participation, increasing participation.

Most importantly, regular positive phone calls home have had a dramatic impact on discipline. They increase compliance with requirements, such as homework, and reduce the incidence of discipline problems.[41] One first-year middle school teacher achieved a remarkable 100% completion rate on homework assignments and had no classroom management problems and no discipline problems. When asked how she accomplished this remarkable record she replied, *"I've talked to all my kids' parents, and they're helping me."* The teacher made an average of three phone calls each night![42]

Cell Phone Magic

Ms. Johnson, principal of an elementary school, wears her cell phone prominently in a holster as she walks the school. She has the daytime phone number of the parent or guardian of every child programmed into her cell phone. As often as she can, when she "catches a child being good," she dials the number and on the spot gives the parent the good news. She then hands the phone to the child to chat for a few minutes with the parent or guardian. As a result of the parent calls, parent attendance at open house jumped from 20% to 80% over a six-year period.[43]

- **Hat Trick Phone Calls.** To strengthen the parent-teacher alliance, some teachers pull two names from a hat each week and call those parents. By making proactive calls rather than only calling when there is a problem, communication can remain more positive. Even if you are calling regarding disruptive behavior, be sure to begin and end by commenting on positive qualities or behaviors of the student. Give the parent many things to glow on, only one to grow on.

- **Student Progress Letters.** Have students write progress letters home to keep their parents informed. See Sample Progress Letter on page 18.64.

- **Student "Dear Parent" Letters.** Students can take time in class to compose letters to their parents to describe classroom and school events, such as assemblies, project presentations, field trips, experiments, and what they learned upon completion of a chapter.

Communicate in Many Ways

- **Two-Way Communication.** If parents are to be partners, there is frequent two-way communication. Not only is there a flow of information from school to home, there is also a flow of information from home to school.

- **Notes, E-mail.** E-mail increasingly opens easier avenues of communication. If e-mail is not possible, the traditional note will suffice, but to increase two-way communication, notes should often include invitations to respond. Notes and e-mails are not the communication avenue of choice for discussing misbehavior. Phone calls or meetings are more appropriate.

Sample Progress Letter

Dear _____,

My grade is a _____ so far in _____.

Mr. Jones thought you might want to know about this before progress reports/report cards came out. Averages for the different sections of the grade are:

___ in _____

___ in _____

___ in _____

My strongest area is _____. I think I am strong in this area because _____.

My weakest area is _____. Mr. Jones advised me to:

Please sign and date this to show that you have discussed this with me.

_____	_____
You	Date
_____	_____
Me	Date
_____	_____
Mr. Jones	Date

Win-Win Discipline. Kagan Publishing • 1 (800) 933-2667 • www.KaganOnline.com

18.64

Types of Notes and E-mails

• **I Am Proud of...** Catch students being good and share it with parents.

• **Coming Attractions.** *"What we will be studying next is..."*

• **Reminders.** *"Upcoming events for this month are..."*

• **What We Have Learned.** Parents will be better partners and appreciate the school and you more if on an ongoing basis they understand what has been accomplished.

• **Help Needed.** The note may take the form of a slip sent home: *"For the following project we will need..."*

• **Thursday Folders.** Each Thursday student work is sent home in a folder. It is stamped "graded" or "non-graded." If it is corrected or graded for only a specific performance, that is indicated. For example, writing might be corrected for punctuation, but not spelling, if that is the focus. Naturally, it is important to indicate that to parents the basis of the grading and/or corrections. A stamp or stamps can make the teacher's job easier in that regard. The Thursday folder has a comment sheet to be returned, signed by a parent.

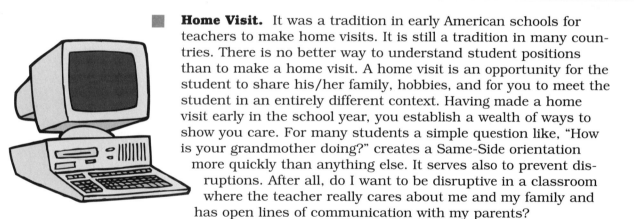

Home Visit. It was a tradition in early American schools for teachers to make home visits. It is still a tradition in many countries. There is no better way to understand student positions than to make a home visit. A home visit is an opportunity for the student to share his/her family, hobbies, and for you to meet the student in an entirely different context. Having made a home visit early in the school year, you establish a wealth of ways to show you care. For many students a simple question like, "How is your grandmother doing?" creates a Same-Side orientation more quickly than anything else. It serves also to prevent disruptions. After all, do I want to be disruptive in a classroom where the teacher really cares about me and my family and has open lines of communication with my parents?

Class Home Page. The world-wide web has opened up new avenues of communication. Increasingly, teachers are taking advantage of this opportunity and classrooms have their own web page. For an example of a award-winning class home page, go to Candler Kids On the Web, http://home.att.net/~candlers/. Laura Candler's fifth grade class home page includes:

- All About Us
- Holiday Happenings
- A Guest Book
- Classroom News
- Spelling Lists
- Vocabulary Words
- A Hangman Vocabulary Game
- Assignment Due Dates

- Web Site Links
- Favorite Books
- Literature Circle Books
- Photos of Classroom Activities
- Student Photos and Self-Descriptions
- Samples of Creative Products
- Parent Resources

In addition to the ample list of resources, at the time of this writing, Laura's site also contains a photo album of her summer trip to Belize.

Newsletter. A weekly or bi-weekly class newsletter can include many of the same items as the class home page. Elementary students can contribute to the class newsletter; secondary students can create it.

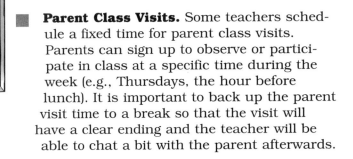

Parent Class Visits. Some teachers schedule a fixed time for parent class visits. Parents can sign up to observe or participate in class at a specific time during the week (e.g., Thursdays, the hour before lunch). It is important to back up the parent visit time to a break so that the visit will have a clear ending and the teacher will be able to chat a bit with the parent afterwards.

Progress Reports. Weekly or monthly progress reports can take many forms. The report may resemble the report card, include a checklist, or may take the form of a few paragraphs the teacher writes to the parent indicating areas of strength and areas on which to focus. Beginning each progress report with an appreciation (*"One thing I especially like about having Ben in class is…"*) sets a positive tone, lowers parental defenses, and makes it more likely that the parent and student will see the teacher on their side. The progress report can offer specific suggestions for parent-child practice and should have a place for both parent and child to enter comments to the teacher and to sign.

Project, Assignment Evaluations. The Win-Win teacher does not focus on how well a student stacks up against the other students in the class, but rather how well the student is living up to her/his potential. The same performance by two students may represent a great improvement on the part of one and a lax performance by the other. Accordingly, evaluations focus primarily not on how well a student compares to class or other norms, but rather on student improvement and how fully a student is living up to her/his own potential. A grade without an explanation communicates little or nothing and will not motivate and direct improvement nearly as clearly as comments and/or an objective scoring rubric. If the teacher clearly shares expectations with students and parents before the student begins the project (via a rubric or objective scoring criteria), students are far more likely

Win-Win Discipline. Kagan Publishing • 1 (800) 933-2667 • www.KaganOnline.com

to perform well. Examples of excellence are another way of communicating expectations. If the Internet is available for all families, the class home page can be an easy way to post prior successful projects as examples. When teachers make criteria for evaluation explicit and objective at the outset, parents can help students focus on and meet learning objectives. In the Win-Win classroom, evaluation is designed to foster learning, not ranking.

Portfolios, Exhibits. Portfolios and exhibits are wonderful Win-Win tools for many reasons. They meet student needs for attention and control, and foster pride and a sense of accomplishment. We all have the need to show off our best work and be appreciated for it. Students have input as to which work they will display and have the opportunity to evaluate their own work, fostering responsibility. Portfolios also can mitigate fear of failure: Students are allowed to choose which accomplishments to display and over time see their own progress and development. Portfolios communicate the progress of the student far more than does a report card; they give students a sense of accomplishment that students cannot obtain via a teacher's mark on a paper or a report card from the teacher. Increasingly teachers are including videos of student interviews and performances as part of student portfolios to allow students a fuller range of ways of expressing what they have learned and their own reflections on their learning. This allows parents yet another way to understand and appreciate their child's development.

Conferences. Parent conferences are among the most powerful tools we have to create positive parent-teacher alliances. The steps for parent conferences along with many cautions and hints are described in **Chapter 16. Follow-Up Structures.**

Tracking Parent Communication
In order to keep track of communication with parents, it is useful to keep a communication record.[44] The Communication Record has students listed alphabetically by last name in the left-hand column and then columns to date newsletters, telephone conversations, notes sent, notes received, conferences, and unscheduled talks. See sample.

Parent Communication Log

Surname	Note Sent	Note Received	Newsletter	Telephone	Conference	Unscheduled Talk

Win-Win Discipline. Kagan Publishing • 1 (800) 933-2667 • www.KaganOnline.com

18.67

Parent Involvement

▪ **Open House.** Nearly 90% of parents consider open house to be the most effective communication device for gathering information about the school and their child's teacher.[45] Open house is an opportunity to *show* rather than *talk about* what is happening and to get direct input from parents. If cooperative learning structures are being used with students, open house is an opportunity for parents to experience those structures firsthand. Resistance melts when parents discover the power of simple structures like RallyRobin and Timed Pair Share and learn that the structures are to promote learning, but that all grades will be based on individual work. By having parents experience what students do in school we create greater parent engagement and understanding. The two greatest concerns among parents are to know their child's teacher is competent and that their child's teacher cares about their student.[46] Demonstrating competence in instructional strategies speaks much louder than talking about strategies. Comments to each parent demonstrating a concern and care for the unique abilities and needs of their child allows the parent to trust their child to the care of the teacher. Communicating competence and care set the stage for establishing a Win-Win relationship in which the parent will support the teacher's efforts.

▪ **Parent/Teacher/Student Goal Setting.** A great Win-Win strategy is to conduct Parent/Teacher/Student Goal Setting Conferences. It is very empowering to have all working together. The student needs to be in charge of this process as much as possible. The teacher would guide the process, but true collaboration would be the main goal.

▪ **Parent Mentors, Tutors.** Parents can be very valuable as mentors or tutors. There is never enough of the teacher to go around and this maximizes learning time. It is important that parents get concrete direction and training so the tutoring maximizes positive impact. Using parents as mentors creates Win-Win situations. It benefits the students being mentored and helps the parents to connect with the school and the classroom.

▪ **Parent Volunteers.** Allow parents to volunteer to help in various ways in the class and school. When parents feel welcome and feel that they can contribute to the school, it creates positive connections and facilitates their being allies in the discipline process. Create a volunteer handbook so parents know what to do. Involve volunteers in the planning process. Profiling parent volunteers in the school newsletter creates positive feelings and encourages volunteering. Feature volunteers on the school web site. Have VIP buttons for volunteers.

When parents know their child's teacher as a person and that the teacher is teaching responsibility, not just academics, parent response is more apt to be collaborative. Parents can be involved in co-creating the discipline solution.

"Here is a possible plan. Can you help me develop the plan? Can you give me some input to the plan? I would really appreciate any suggestions you can make. Are there any ways you can back up, support, and follow through with this plan at home?"

Invite parents to be allies in the discipline process and really listen to what they have to contribute.

PTA/PTO Presentations. Presentations at PTA/PTO meetings can include mini presentations on how to help students meet the needs of each position. One month the focus is on Attention, the next month on Avoiding Failure, and so on. If parents learn to recognize student positions and to coach students in filling their needs, students will be less likely to be disruptive in class.

Study Groups, Training Sessions. Parents can sign up for Win-Win study groups or training sessions. Sections from the Win-Win book can be the focus. As parents learn to recognize and validate student positions, students receive a consistent message from school and home: your position, your needs are always acceptable; your job is to find non-disruptive, fulfilling ways to meet those needs.

Drop-in Center. Some schools have a parent drop-in center. A coffee pot is usually brewing. It is a place where parents can meet with each other and with teachers to discuss school, discipline, and other concerns.

PAL Workshops. PAL Workshops stand for Parents Aiding Learning. On a given day each month, parents come to the classroom to help prepare learning materials such as letters to be cut, patterns to be traced, and centers to be prepared. Parents, many bringing their small children, join in to help create the learning activities for the month.[47]

Performances for Parents. Other ways for parents to participate in, learn about, and support the classroom include profession days (parents come in and share their work with students); breakfasts for parents (students prepare a before-school breakfast for parents); Grandparents Day (students bring their grandparents or pictures of their grandparents to share with the class); and class Bar-B-Q's (parents cook hot dogs for students and may join in for some Silly Sports and Goofy Games during an extended recess).

Win-Win Homework. Homework is more often dreaded by students if it consists mostly or exclusively of problems to solve that have a right-wrong answer and if it is confined to verbal/linguistic and logical/mathematical response modes. It is a win for students strong in those intelligences but often a loss for students weak in those intelligences. Win-Win homework respects the diversity of strengths among students and allows students to express themselves in a variety of ways. To further meet student needs, the teacher may assign homework designed as a cooperative learning experience, so parents and students work together to share and learn.

■ **Multiple Intelligences Homework.** For variety and to respect and foster diversity of cognitive skills, homework assignments may include drawing, interviewing, investigating, mind-mapping, observing, performing, and journaling. For a wide range of multiple intelligences structures and activities, see *Multiple Intelligences: The Complete MI Book.*[48]

■ **Cooperative Homework.** Today's youth crave more attention from and interaction with their parents. Cooperative parent-child homework is designed to foster positive student-child interaction and to fill student needs. Cooperative homework is not designed for the parent to teach the student or for the student to teach the parent. Rather, the teacher structures cooperative homework so the parent and student work collaboratively to seek solutions or to create a product. For a model of simple cooperative send-home science projects for students to conduct with their parents, see *Science Buddies: Cooperative Science Activities.*[49]

Celebrate Together

■ **Back-to-School Bar-B-Q.** What better way to get to know parents and establish positive relations than a back-to-school Bar-B-Q or picnic? The event can be held prior to the first day of school or on a weekend following one of the first weeks of school. You can ask for volunteers in August when you make your welcome phone calls or write your letters. The event can feature non-competitive sports and games. For dozens of suggestions, see *Silly Sports and Goofy Games.*[50] The silly sports and goofy games do not require special equipment beyond balloons, and the Silly Sports can be copied onto cards, so teams of parents or students can facilitate them.

■ **Parties, Celebrations.** Inviting parents to classroom parties and celebrations is a win for everyone. Parents feel included, students feel appreciated not only by the teacher and classmates, but by parents as well, and the teacher gains allies. Presentations by teams or displays or reports by students take on an extra importance if parents are invited. Students anticipate with more excitement the completion of a class unit if they are to display or perform for parents: The larger the audience, the greater potential to meet needs for attention and validation, and so students work with more eagerness and effort.

Win-Win Management: Preventative Discipline

With regard to discipline, sometimes the shortest distance between two points is not a straight line. One of the best examples is what happened to secondary schools when they switched to block scheduling. Unexpectedly, in many schools the incidence of discipline problems was reduced — sometimes by as much as half! What had happened? Most serious discipline problems occur in the halls during passing periods when students have less supervision. By moving to block scheduling, without intending to cut down discipline referrals, schools had cut the number of passing periods in half so students had far fewer opportunities for serious discipline problems.

So it is with management. It is a longer path to have students generate rules in a class meeting, but that detour into self-governance not only imparts democratic values — it generates "buy-in" to rules and procedures which in the long run means far fewer disruptions. Who wants to break a rule he/she has had a hand in creating? When students can signal the teacher they need help, they get the help they need and are able to quickly return to work. When they cannot signal for help, they drift off task, and sometimes the drift is into a disruption. When the teacher creates more teacher-student proximity, disruptions are less likely. When there are efficient procedures and routines, students are on task more of the time and less likely to engage in disruptive behaviors. Having parents involved, informed, engaged, and supportive creates many helpers supporting the discipline program and school success. When students know their parents will know right away if they have gotten off track, they think twice before becoming disruptive. More importantly, if students know their parents will hear about it right away when they have been helpful or successful, students are more likely to be helpful and successful. Good management is good teaching, resulting in more time on task and greater academic success. Good management is also preventative discipline. Successful and productively occupied students are not disruptive students.

References

[1] Kohn, A. *Beyond Discipline: From Compliance to Community.* Alexandria, Virginia: Association for Supervision and Curriculum Development, 1996.

[2] Class Meetings is a strategy described by Dreikurs, R., Grunwald, B. B., & Pepper, F. C. *Maintaining Sanity in the Classroom: Classroom Management Techniques.* New York, NY: Harper & Row, 1990.; Glasser, W. *Schools Without Failure.* New York: Harper & Row, 1969.; Nelsen, J., Lott, L., Glenn, S. H. *Positive Discipline in the Classroom.* Rocklin, CA: Prima Publishing, 1993.; Kohn, A. *Beyond Discipline: From Compliance to Community.* Alexandria, VA: Association for Supervision and Curriculum Development, 1996.

[3, 4] Bluestein, J. (Ed.) *Mentors, Masters, and Mrs MacGregor: Stories of Teachers Making a Difference.* Deerfield Beach, FL: Health Communications, Inc., 1995, p. 160, 216.

[5] Kagan, S., Kettle, K., McClean, D., & Ward, C. *Cooperative Meetings: Charting the Voyage Toward a Community of Leaders and Learners.* San Clemente, CA: Kagan Publishing, In Press, Available Fall 2003.

[6] Kagan, S., Kagan, L., & Kagan, M. *Classbuilding.* San Clemente, CA: Kagan Publishing, 1995.

[7] Kagan, S. *Silly Sports and Goofy Games.* San Clemente, CA: Kagan Publishing, 2000.

[8] Developmental Studies Center. *Ways We Want Our Class to Be.* Oakland, CA: Developmental Studies Center, 1996, p. 26.

[9] Developmental Studies Center. *Ways We Want Our Class to Be.* Oakland, CA: Developmental Studies Center, 1996, p. 41.

[10] Developmental Studies Center. *Ways We Want Our Class to Be.* Oakland, CA: Developmental Studies Center, 1996, p. 72.

[11] Developmental Studies Center. *Ways We Want Our Class to Be.* Oakland, CA: Developmental Studies Center, 1996, p. 106.

[12] Developmental Studies Center. *Ways We Want Our Class to Be.* Oakland, CA: Developmental Studies Center, 1996.

[13] Nelsen, J., Lott, L., & Glenn, H.S. *Positive Discipline in the Classroom.* Westminster, MD: Random House/Pantheon Books, 2000.

[14] Adapted from Kagan, S. *Cooperative Learning.* San Clemente, CA: Kagan Publishing, 1994.

[15] Lyman, F. The Think-Trix: "A Classroom Tool for Thinking in Response to Reading." In *Reading Issues and Practices. Yearbook of the State of Maryland International Reading Association Council, Volume 4.* Westminster, MD: State of Maryland international reading Association Council, 1987, pp. 15–18.

[16] Lyman, F. Think-Pair-Share Smartcard. San Clemente, CA: Kagan Publishing, 2003.

[17] The TeachTimer is distributed by Kagan Publishing, San Clemente, CA.

References (Continued)

[18] Projector Pals are manufactured and distributed by Kagan Publishing, San Clemente, CA.

[19] Kagan, S. *Cooperative Learning.* San Clemente, CA: Kagan Publishing, 1994.

[20] Kagan, S. *Cooperative Learning.* San Clemente, CA: Kagan Publishing, 1994.

[21] Kagan, S. Pop-up Social Role Card Kit. San Clemente, CA: Kagan Publishing, 1999.

[22] Kagan, S. *Cooperative Learning.* San Clemente, CA: Kagan Publishing, 1994.

[23] Kagan, S. Pop-up Social Role Card Kit. San Clemente, CA: Kagan Publishing, 1999.

[24] Kagan, S., Kagan, L., & Kagan, M. *Classbuilding.* San Clemente, CA: Kagan Publishing, 1995.

[25] Kagan, S. *Silly Sports and Goofy Games.* San Clemente, CA: Kagan Publishing, 2000.

[26] Kagan S., & Kagan, M. *Multiple Intelligences: The Complete MI Book.* San Clemente, CA: Kagan Publishing, 1998.

[27] Likona, T. & Davidson, M. *Character Quotations.* San Clemente, CA: Kagan Publishing, 2003.

[28] Kagan, S., Kagan, L., & Kagan, M. *Classbuilding.* San Clemente, CA: Kagan Publishing, 1995.

[29] Kagan, S. *Silly Sports and Goofy Games.* San Clemente, CA: Kagan Publishing, 2000.

[30] Harris Interactive Poll, USA Today, February 10, 2003.

[31] Jones, T. T*ools for Teaching.* Santa Cruz, CA: Fred H. Jones and Associates, Inc., 2000.

[32] Kagan, S. *Cooperative Learning.* San Clemente, CA: Kagan Publishing, 1994.

[33] Jones, T. *Tools for Teaching.* Santa Cruz, CA: Fred H. Jones and Associates, Inc., 2000.

[34] Rosenthal, R. *Pygmalian Effects: Existence, Magnitude, and Social Importance.* **Educational Researcher**, 1987, **16(9)**, 37–41; Rosenthal, R. & Ruben, D. B. *Interpersonal Expectancy Effects: The First 345 Studies.* **Behavioral and Brain Sciences,** 1978, **3,** 377–451; Rosenthal, R., Baratz, S. S. & Hall, C. M. *Teacher Behavior, Teacher Expectations, and Gains in Pupils' Rated Creativity.* **Journal of Genetic Psychology,** 1974, **124,** 115–121).

[35] The Yacker Tracker is distributed by Kagan Publishing, San Clemente, CA.

[36] The Hall Pass Timer is distributed by Kagan Publishing, San Clemente, CA.

[37] Jensen, E. *Optimal Hydration.* **Kagan Online Magazine,** 2001, **1(13).**

[38] Bluestein, J. (Ed.) *Mentors, Masters, and Mrs MacGregor: Stories of Teachers Making a Difference.* Deerfield Beach, FL: Health Communications, Inc., 1995.

References (Continued)

[39, 40] Guskey, T. R. & Bailey, J. M. *Developing Grading Systems and Reporting Systems for Student Learning.* Thousand Oaks, CA: Corwin Press, Inc., 2001.

Gustafson, C. *Phone Home.* Educational Leadership, 1998, 56(2), 31–32.

[41] Guskey, T. R. *Evaluating Professional Development.* Presentation: New Orleans, National Staff Development Council, December 6, 2003.

[42] Guskey, T. R. & Bailey, J. M. *Developing Grading Systems and Reporting Systems for Student Learning.* Thousand Oaks, CA: Corwin Press, Inc., 2001.

[43] Guskey, T. R. *Evaluating Professional Development.* Presentation: New Orleans, National Staff Development Council, December 6, 2003.

[44] This idea is proposed by Senter, G. W. & Charles, C. M. *Elementary Classroom Management, 3rd Edition.* Boston, MA: Allyn and Bacon, 2002.

[45] Langdow, C. A. *The Fifth Phi Delta Kappen Poll of Parents' Attitudes Toward the Public Schools.* Phi Delta Kappen, 1999, 80(8), 611–618.

[46] Guskey, T. R. & Bailey, J. M. *Developing Grading Systems and Reporting Systems for Student Learning.* Thousand Oaks, CA: Corwin Press, Inc., 2001.

[47] Offered by Louise Burman, Burlington, Iowa. Described in Shepardson, R. D. *Elementary Teacher's Discipline Desk Book.* West Nyack, New York: Parker Publishing Company, Inc., 1980, p. 118.

[48] Kagan, S. & Kagan, M. *Multiple Intelligences: The Complete MI Book.* San Clemente, CA: Kagan Publishing, 1998.

[49] Candler, L. *Science Buddies: Cooperative Science Activities.* San Clemente, CA: Kagan Publishing, 2000.

[50] Kagan, S. *Silly Sports and Goofy Games.* San Clemente, CA: Kagan Publishing, 2000.

Chapter 19

Win-Win Instruction

There is a paradox: how we teach, the instructional strategies we adopt, can do more to reduce the incidence of discipline problems than most discipline programs! There is a simple explanation: we can teach with strategies that meet students' needs so they do not need to be disruptive to meet their needs, or we can teach with strategies that frustrate students' needs so they become disruptive in attempts to meet their needs.

A simple example tells the story. We can use instructional strategies like classbuilding structures that involve talking and moving or we can choose an approach to instruction that requires students to sit still and not talk. If we choose this latter option, some students will talk and/or move anyway. Those students are considered discipline problems. In contrast, the same students placed in a class in which movement and talking is integral to the approach to instruction discharges their energy and need for social contact in acceptable ways and no discipline problem is created.

In the Win-Win classroom, therefore, we align instruction with the needs associated with the seven positions. That is, we teach in ways that meet basic needs.

Many of the teaching strategies associated with the seven positions have been presented in **Chapter 8. Preventative Procedures: The Seven Positions.** In this chapter we will briefly overview four powerful approaches to instruction that align well with Win-Win Discipline:

> - **Cooperative Learning**
> - **Multiple Intelligences**
> - **Differentiated Instruction**
> - **Brain-Based Instruction**

In the second part of the chapter we examine how a Win-Win approach to instruction reduces the incidents of discipline problems — why student-centered instruction leads to disappearing discipline.

A really great teacher is someone who... **teaches from your needs, not hers.** *Maria, 13, Kahului, Maui, Hawaii*[1]

A really great teacher is someone who... **knows how to present his subject in an original manner so that it is a pleasure to attend his lessons.** *Jeroen, 20, Utrecht, Holland*[2]

A really great teacher is someone who... **doesn't just try to get through the book without teaching the kids.** *Tamica, 16, Medora, Indiana*[3]

I. Win-Win, Learner-Friendly Instructional Programs

Instruction based on the needs of students is Win-Win instruction: students' needs are fulfilled, and the needs of the teacher and class to teach and learn are met. We will overview four differentiated approaches to instruction; each in a different way responds to the needs of individual students.

Cooperative Learning

The most frequent causes of discipline problems are students socializing rather than attending to the teacher or their work and students interacting inappropriately, as when they get into a conflict. Cooperative learning approaches address these sources of discipline problems directly by 1) allowing social interaction while mastering academic content, so the need for socialization is fulfilled in the process of teaching; 2) creating more harmonious relations among students by including teambuilding and classbuilding; 3) indirectly and directly teaching social skills, so interpersonal conflicts arise less often and are more often approached with a Win-Win orientation when they do arise; and 4) creating a much higher rate of academic engagement and success, which reduces the incidence of discipline problems.

Frequent Social Interaction. Common to all cooperative learning approaches is frequent social interaction. Frequency of social interaction is accomplished by application of the simultaneity principle — many people are talking at any one moment.

In the traditional classroom, talk is limited to one person at a time, either a teacher talking to the class or an individual student being called on, responding to the teacher. This approach necessarily frustrates the biggest need among students — to receive attention. In a classroom of thirty, calling on the students one at a time, it would take a full hour to give each student two minutes of attention, if the teacher did not say a word! But, of course, during the hour the teacher must lecture, ask questions, respond to students, talking more than all the students combined. Thus on the average in the traditional classroom, each hour each student gets less than a minute of attention. At any one moment, one student is getting attention while all the others are waiting — a prescription for frustration, off-task behaviors, and discipline problems.

In the cooperative learning classroom the teacher often has students turn to a partner or their teammates to discuss academic content. If a teacher has students working in pairs and does a Timed Pair Share for two minutes (students share their ideas with their partner for a minute each), each student has received full undivided attention for a full minute. Because the students in the classroom are all interacting simultaneously, in only two minutes each student in the class has received a minute of attention. In terms of filling the need for attention, in two minutes the teacher using a cooperative learning approach to instruction has accomplished what it would take the traditional teacher a full hour to accomplish!

■ **Harmonious Relations.** Because students on cooperative teams have a common goal, the gain of one becomes the gain of another. In technical terms, they are in a situation of *positive interdependence*. Naturally, then, the students experience themselves as being "on the same-side," just as does an athletic team. Teammates begin to celebrate each other's success and tutor and encourage each other. This, of course, creates a generalized positive orientation toward each other that eliminates many of the social relations problems that create discipline problems.

Harmonious relations are created also by teambuilding and classbuilding activities designed to allow students to know each other better, form a strong positive team and class identity, celebrate diversity, and provide each other mutual support. Hundreds of teambuilding activities are provided in a book entitled *Teambuilding*[8] and hundreds of additional activities are provided in a book entitled *Classbuilding*.[9]

■ **Social Skills.** Research reveals that students placed in cooperative learning teams develop social skills, even in the absence of an explicit social skills instructional component.[10] Most cooperative learning approaches, however, include explicit social skills instruction that enhances social skill acquisition even more. Development of social skills, such as empathy, praising, keeping a group on task, and peacemaking skills, reduces dramatically the incidence of conflicts, disruptions, and classroom discipline problems. Kagan identifies four tools that can be used to promote any social skill[11] — this four-tool approach to social skills is spelled out in more detail in the second section of this chapter.

■ **Academic Success.** Students who are more successful are less often disruptive. They find schoolwork more rewarding than disruptive behavior and do not become disruptive in the process of avoiding failure. Hundreds of research studies demonstrate that cooperative learning increases academic success, especially for low-achieving students who otherwise would be the most likely to create discipline problems.[12]

A really great teacher is someone who... **inspires you to work rather than forcing you to learn.** *Jennifer, 18, Mays Landing, New Jersey*[5]

A really great teacher is someone who... **is able to use different methods of teaching.** *Rachel, 17, Mays Landing, New Jersey*[13]

A really great teacher is someone who... **figures out when you're not learning by one method, and finds different ways and uses different things to help you learn.** *Maria, 13, Kahului, Maui, Hawaii*[14]

Multiple Intelligences

Engaged students are not discipline problems. Students who are more successful with the curriculum also create fewer discipline problems. Multiple intelligences instruction creates engagement and success by using a range of strategies to match, stretch, and celebrate each of the intelligences.[16]

Engagement. Engagement is far greater with multiple intelligences instruction compared to traditional instruction because students receive instruction via their favored intelligence and there is a greater variety of instructional strategies that produces interest. Kagan and Kagan in their book, *Multiple Intelligences*, provide a wide range of instructional strategies to engage each of the intelligences.[17] The MI structures can be used as part of any lesson at any grade to deliver any academic content.

Academic Success. Case studies demonstrate extraordinary academic and extracurricular gains in schools adopting multiple intelligences approaches to instruction.[18] These gains were found at the elementary, middle, and high school levels and were dramatic — schools performing at the bottom in their district rose to the top of their district academically.

Differentiated Instruction

The philosophy of differentiated instruction and Win-Win Discipline are remarkably parallel:

> In differentiated classrooms, teachers begin where students are, not the front of a curriculum guide. They accept and build upon the premise that learners differ in important ways. Thus, they also accept and act on the premise that teachers must be ready to engage students in instruction through different learning modalities, by appealing to differing interests, and by using varied rates of instruction along with varied degrees of complexity.[22]

Differentiated instruction does for instruction what Win-Win Discipline does for discipline. Many of the basic principles of differentiated instruction sound like the basic principles of Win-Win, except they are applied to instruction. See table, Differentiated Instruction and Win-Win Discipline on page 19.6.

Differentiated Instruction and Win-Win Discipline

Differentiated Instruction	Win-Win Discipline
The Teacher Attends to Student Differences	The Teacher Attends to Student Positions
The Teacher Modifies Content, Process, and Products	The Teacher Selects Strategies and Structures Appropriate for Different Individuals
All Students Participate in Respectful Work	The Teacher Accepts and Validates Student Positions
The Teacher and Students Collaborate in Learning	The Teacher and Students Create Collaborative Solutions
The Teacher and Students Work Together Flexibly	The Teacher and Students have a Same-Side Orientation

The emphasis in differentiated instruction is responding to the student's needs just as the emphasis in Win-Win Discipline is responding to the student's positions. In order to respond to student needs, differentiated instruction is guided by principles such as creating respectful tasks, flexible grouping, ongoing assessment, and adjustment. The teacher can differentiate the content, the process, or the product according to students' readiness, interests, and learning profile.

Differentiated instruction borrows from many instructional approaches in order to realize these goals. The many approaches advocated by proponents of differentiated instruction include:[23]

- 4MAT
- Anchor Activities
- Choice Boards
- Compacting
- Cooperative Learning
- Cubing
- Flexible Grouping
- Graphic Organizers
- Independent Study
- Individualized Problem-based Learning
- Interest Centers
- Interest Groups
- Learning Contracts
- Learning Styles
- Literature Circles
- Metaphors
- Multi-age Grouping
- Multiple Intelligences

- Orbitals
- Portfolios
- Stations
- Taped Material
- Thinking Styles
- Tiered Centers
- Tiered Lessons
- Tiered Products
- Varied Homework
- Varied Journal Prompts
- Varied Questioning Strategies
- Varied Supplementary Materials
- Varied Texts
- Varied Organizers

A really great teacher is someone who... **instinctively knows each student's individual needs.**
La Kisha, 18, Mays Landing, New Jersey[21]

Win-Win Discipline. Kagan Publishing • 1 (800) 933-2667 • www.KaganOnline.com

19.6

Brain-Based Instruction

Brain science reveals that students perform well in classrooms in which five conditions are met: 1) there is physical, psychological, and social safety; 2) the brain is well nourished; 3) there is ample opportunity for social interaction; 4) there is emotion linked to the academic content; and 5) the content presentation style aligns with how the brain best processes information.[25] Each of these five principles aligns well with fulfilling the needs associated with the seven positions.

Safety. Brain chemistry changes in a number of ways favorable to learning when students feel safe. This principle links most strongly to the needs of students avoiding failure. Students who are unsafe, afraid to show what they do not know, avoid failure by pretending that they know when they don't or by not completing assignments or tests. By creating a psychologically safe classroom (e.g., test feedback is given in private), the need to avoid public embarrassment associated with failure is eliminated. The result: fewer disruptions and more learning.

Nourishment. Brains attend, retain, recall, and problem solve better when they are well nourished. The two principal fuels for the brain are oxygen and glucose, and the most efficient way to increase nourishment to the brain is frequent physical activity such as classbuilding activities,[26] as well as energizers and brain breaks.[27] This principle aligns most strongly with the energetic position. Students with a great deal of energy have their needs filled when instruction includes frequent movement.

Social Interaction. The royal road to brain engagement is social interaction. (See the pet scans, page 6.22). When teachers use cooperative learning strategies, they are aligning instruction with this third principle of brain-based instruction. Social interaction creates a Win-Win classroom also by meeting the needs of students in the position of seeking attention.

> *A really great teacher is someone who...*
> **uses games to teach things like capitals or math.**
> *Allison, 10, Pittsburgh, Pennsylvania*[24]

Five Principles of Brain-Based Instruction

1. Safety
2. Nourishment
3. Social Interaction
4. Emotion
5. Information Processing

■ **Emotion.** When the student experiences emotion, brain neurons actually fire at an increased rate, tagging the content as worth remembering. We are biologically prepared to store and recall content associated with emotion because emotional content has survival value. Content that elicits emotion, of course, also meets the needs of students who otherwise would be disruptive due to boredom.

■ **Information Processing.** There are many principles regarding how the brain best processes information. For example, there are five distinct memory systems (Semantic, Procedural, Episodic, Working, and Spatial).[28] To maximize memory of content, we need to address each memory system with different instructional strategies. When we do this, we create firm memories, addressing the need of the otherwise uninformed student. When we say, *"I have told him a hundred times and he still does not know,"* we well might be saying, *"I have attempted to create a procedural memory by using an instructional strategy that addresses the semantic memory system!"* Respecting the principles of information processing creates a Win-Win classroom in a variety of ways: it involves a variety of instructional strategies, reducing boredom; it generates greater success, which meets the needs of those avoiding failure; it gives students a greater sense of control; and it reduces frustration that would otherwise be a precursor to anger.

Brain-based instruction, like differentiated instruction, does not provide an instructional methodology of its own, but rather borrows from and supports many instructional approaches. Among the techniques advocated on the basis of brain function are:[29]

- Aerobic Exercise
- Air Quality
- Artistic Expression
- Attention Management
- Breathing Exercises
- Challenge Problems
- Change Environments
- Choice
- Community
- Cooperative Learning
- Developmentally Opportune Teaching
- Distributed Practice
- Emotion-Content Links
- Engaging, Challenging Curriculum
- Energizers
- Engaging Multiple Memory Systems
- Enrichment of Environment
- Field Trips
- Frequent Feedback
- Full-Spectrum Lighting
- Goal Setting
- Humor
- Hydration
- Integrated Instruction
- Intrinsic Motivation
- Journaling
- Manipulatives
- Meaningful Content
- Mind-Mapping
- Mnemonics
- Model Making
- Movement
- Multi-sensory Input
- Music
- Novelty and Routines
- Peer Tutoring
- Play
- Relaxation
- Relevant Content
- Safety
- Simulations
- Storytelling
- Stress Reduction
- Temperature Control
- Visualization

As we overview the instructional strategies advocated in Cooperative Learning, Multiple Intelligences, Differentiated Instruction, and Brain-Based Instruction, we find many commonalities. Advocates of differentiated instruction and brain-based learning call for the use of cooperative learning and multiple intelligences instructional strategies. The four approaches suggest many common practices; they are complementary because they all spring from the same place: focusing first on the needs of the learner. It is the same place from which springs Win-Win Discipline. Win-Win Discipline and the four approaches reviewed here are all Learner-Friendly Approaches to Education.

II: Disappearing Discipline Problems

Any instructional strategy or program that recognizes and responds to the needs of individual students shares the philosophy of Win-Win and reduces the incidence of discipline problems. When student needs are met by the way we teach, students less often need to be disruptive to meet their needs. In fact, many non-discipline programs do more to eliminate discipline problems than do discipline programs!

This phenomena, disappearing discipline, is well illustrated by the history of my own development of cooperative learning. It is a story that can be told as a journey in four stages. It was not until the second half of that journey that I realized where Win-Win fit into the bigger picture of educational reform. Let's turn now to that story. Note, however, a similar story could be told about any of the learner-friendly approaches to education.

Discipline Disappears in Four Stages

Stage 1: Three Discoveries
Stage 2: Four Tools for Social Skills
Stage 3: Proactive Preventative Procedures
Stage 4: Reactive Responses: Structures for the Moment-of-Disruption and After

Cooperative Learning and Disappearing Discipline Problems

Stage 1: Three Discoveries

In 1980 Dr. I introducing cooperative learning to classrooms that had used traditional instruction almost exclusively. I had not expected to impact on discipline; I was concerned primarily with boosting academic achievement and improving social skills and social and race relations. But I got a big surprise: when successful cooperative learning was introduced into classrooms, it had a major impact on discipline. Teachers and administrators consistently reported dramatically reduced incidence of discipline referrals.

The introduction of cooperative learning had three unexpected results: 1) the frequency of disruptive behavior declined; 2) different students were discipline problems — many students who were discipline problems were no longer problems, but some students who had not been discipline problems became problems; and 3) the type of discipline problems shifted. These three discoveries are illustrated in: Discipline Problems Eliminated by Cooperative Learning, on page 19.11.

Notice, as illustrated figure on page 19.11, when we shift from the traditional to the cooperative classroom, the set of students who are discipline problems shrinks (represented by the smaller circle to the right). Further, some students who are not disruptive in the traditional classroom become disruptive in the cooperative classroom (the small circle is not all within the larger circle; it includes students who were not disruptive in the traditional classroom). Some students, as we might expect, cause disruptions in both classrooms (represented by the intersection of the two circles). Most important for the story of disappearing discipline: many students who were discipline problems in the traditional classroom are not problems in the cooperative classroom (the small circle does not include most of the students in the large circle).

Win-Win Discipline. Kagan Publishing • 1 (800) 933-2667 • www.KaganOnline.com

19.10

Discipline Problems Eliminated by Cooperative Learning.

Discipline Problems in:

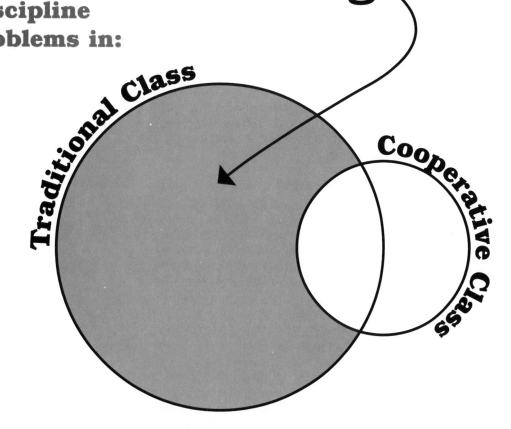

Traditional Class

Cooperative Class

1. **Many Discipline Problems Eliminated**
2. **Different Types of Discipline Problems Emerged**
3. **Different Students Became Disruptive**

■ **Discovery 1: Dramatic Overall Decrease.** When cooperative learning was instituted, many teachers and administrators reported that the number of discipline problems decreased dramatically. I vividly remember administrators asking me what new discipline program had been introduced along with the cooperative learning. With surprise, I answered, *"None."* They persisted, *"There must be a new discipline program. We are getting far fewer referrals for discipline problems."*

In puzzling over why cooperative learning had caused a decrease in discipline problems, an explanation emerged. Our empirical tests and informal interviews indicated that almost all students were much happier working in carefully structured groups. When asked why, students responded with comments like:

- We get to talk.
- We get to move.
- We get to work together.
- We get to help each other.

Younger students, of course, were less articulate. Their most common response: *"Its funner."* Overall, the vast majority of students were reporting cooperative learning was letting them do what they wanted to do.

This turned on the light; we had an explanation. There was a dramatic reduction in the number of discipline problems when we introduced cooperative learning because we were going **"with"** rather than **"against"** the students' basic needs. In traditional classrooms, from the very first day of kindergarten we begin a fight with students. They want to walk around, and we tell them to sit down. They want to squirm in their chairs, and we tell them to sit quietly. They want to talk to their neighbors, and we tell them to be quiet. They want to grab and hold and manipulate things and others, and we tell them to keep their hands to themselves. We are going against their basic needs.

In many ways, these young people were right and we were wrong! Recent findings from brain science reveal it is not optimal for learning to sit for prolonged times. When we sit for extended time periods, heart rate and breathing rate decrease and blood pools in our bodies, resulting in less blood flow to the brain. Blood carries oxygen and glucose, the two primary nutrients that allow optimal brain functioning. The students were telling us with their bodies what they needed — they needed movement. We were attempting to restrict the very thing that would allow optimal brain functioning. Those students in whom the need to move was strongest resisted us the most forcibly. Those students persisted in trying to fill their biological need to move in spite of our attempts to prohibit them from moving and were labeled "discipline problems."

The same argument can be made for students who wanted to manipulate things, talk to their peers, and interact. Now we know that the best way to learn is to manipulate things and interact over the subject matter. We actually defined as discipline problems those students who most strongly tried to fill healthy needs!

What does this have to do with the reduction of discipline problems observed when we switch from traditional to cooperative learning? When we switch from traditional to cooperative learning, we encourage movement, hands-on learning, and, most importantly, social interaction. We are going "with" rather than "against" the students. We are encouraging them to express and fulfill their basic needs. Having their needs filled, they do not need to become discipline problems to fill their needs.

Discovery 2: Different Discipline Problems. When we shift from traditional instruction to cooperative learning, a second remarkable thing happens. Disruptions occur, but they are different types of disruptions, occurring for different reasons. Moving and talking are allowed, so that is not the problem. In cooperative learning classrooms, most disruptions occur because students do not know how to get along with each other. When we shift to cooperative learning, we are asking students to work with each other, but they are lacking a host of cooperative skills. Sitting in rows in a traditional classroom, students never acquire teamwork skills. Among the many cooperative skills they have not yet acquired when we first begin cooperative learning are:

- How to make group decisions
- How to resolve conflicts
- What to do if the group cannot agree
- How to disagree politely
- How to fairly share tasks and resources
- How to include the ideas of everyone
- How to share the task of presenting the group product
- How to keep a group on task
- What to do if the group gets off task
- What to do if someone refuses to participate
- What to do if a group gets too noisy
- How to really listen

The list is long, and for each skill the students lack, there is a potential disruption. We found instruction in social skills was one of the six keys to successful cooperative learning — an essential element. When students lack social skills, there are many disruptions that are mistaken for "discipline problems." When a good social skills program is present, the need for a discipline program to treat those kinds of disruptions disappears. (Parenthetically, as described below, we found that the most efficient way to foster social skill instruction was not direct instruction on social skills but, rather, structuring interaction so skills are acquired as students work on their regular academic tasks and projects.)

■ **Discovery 3: Different Students.** The third discovery we made was that when we shifted from traditional to cooperative learning, a group of students who had caused no problems in the traditional classroom were causing problems in the cooperative classroom.

> *Susan was the perfect student in the traditional classroom. She sat quietly and did her assignments very well and on time. She never gave her teacher a problem. Then her teacher introduced cooperative learning. Susan was assigned to a team with three other students. The teacher was using heterogeneous teams; so on each team there was a high-achieving student, two middle-achieving students, and one low-achieving student. Susan was the highest achieving student in her team.*

> *The teacher observed the first difficulty when he/she first formed teams. Susan said she did not want to work with Patti. When the team did their first project, another problem emerged. Most teams ran smoothly, but Susan's team had difficulties. Susan assumed the role of "boss," telling her teammates what to do and how to do it. Resentments built up. Before long, other students asked the teacher if they could be reassigned. They did not want to be in a group with Susan! They did not like being bossed around.*

Susan was not a problem in the traditional classroom, but became disruptive in the cooperative classroom. Susan and others like her are represented on the right side of the smaller circle in the Venn Diagram on page 19.11. Cooperative learning had eliminated far more discipline problems than it had created, but it had created some new problems to solve!

Stage 2: Four Tools for Social Skills

What was the problem? Why were a few good students who performed well in the traditional classroom having and creating difficulties in the cooperative classroom? It turns out that performing well in the traditional classroom takes a different set of skills than does performing well in the cooperative classroom.

In the traditional classroom, students need to know how to focus only on their own work. When we introduce cooperative learning, we introduce the need to work with others. Some students who work quite well on their own lack the ability to work well with others. Inability to work well with others can take many forms, including (but not limited to):

- Bossiness, unwillingness to share power or control
- Disrespectfulness: intolerance of different cognitive styles, cognitive pace
- Failure or inability to disagree politely
- Getting off task, not knowing how to set and maintain an agenda
- Inability to admit when wrong or when one does not know
- Inadequate listening skills
- Intolerance for diversity of opinion
- Lack of conflict resolution skills
- Not knowing how to compromise
- Refusing to work with others
- Shyness
- Being too loud
- Being too social
- Using put-downs

When first attempting to implement cooperative learning, some teachers observe all the social problems associated with cooperative learning and conclude that it creates discipline problems. I am reminded of the teacher who actually said, *"I wish I could do cooperative learning, but my students aren't cooperative enough."*

Cooperative learning does not create the lack of social skills among students; it *reveals* the lack of social skills. Students who have never worked with others do not acquire social skills magically. Social skills are learned. There is a hole in the traditional curriculum: social skills. If we never ask students to work together, we never discover they are missing social skills. It is only when we turn the chairs around and ask students to cooperate that we discover that they do not know how.

Those of us committed to making cooperative learning work well quickly discovered that we needed to include in our cooperative learning training an approach to social skills. Over time we discovered the most powerful approach to social skills was not to teach separate lessons on social skills, but rather to use four tools to foster social skills acquisition as part of any lesson.

4 Tools for Social Skills

1. **Roles and Gambits**
2. **Modeling, Reinforcement and Practice**
3. **Reflection and Planning**
4. **Structures**

The program describing the use of these four tools is presented in detail in *Cooperative Learning*.[30] The tools can be used at any time to develop any social skill. In brief, the four tools are:

1. **Roles and Gambits.** Students acquire social skills by being assigned roles and learning the associated verbal and non-verbal gambits,[31] what to do and say to fill that role. For example, students learn what to say and do to praise a teammate. When praising becomes the norm, put-downs drop away. Kagan distinguishes twelve essential roles for successful cooperative learning.[32] See Social Roles, pages 18.20–27.

2. **Modeling, Reinforcement and Practice.** When the teacher sees positive use of social skills, the teacher gives positive attention to that behavior, holds it up as a model, and has all students practice the behavior. For example, when the student sees another student offering help to a teammate, the teacher might say, *"Class I want you all to see what is going on in this group. Johnny, can you please repeat what you just said to Susan?"* After Johnny says, *"Susan, can I help you with that,"* the teacher says, *"Class, everyone turn to your shoulder partner and say to each other, 'Can I help you with that?'"*

3. **Reflection and Planning.** On a regular basis, the teacher has students reflect on how well they are using a social skill and plan how they could develop that skill even more. For example, the teacher might say, *"We are about a third of the way through our time for these projects. Take a moment and ask yourselves in your teams how well you have been staying on task."* After that the teacher would say, *"Now, take another moment to make a plan. How could your team stay on task even more?"*

4. **Structures.** There are specific social skill structures. For example, Paraphrase Passport improves listening skills. When the students use Paraphrase Passport, their right to speak is to accurately paraphrase the opinion of the person who spoke just before them. There are many social skills structures[33] that build specific social skills:

Social Skills Structures

Skill	Structures
Listening	Paraphrase Passport, Three-Step Interview, RoundRobin
Turn-Taking	Talking Chips, Team Interview, Turn Toss
Helping	RallyCoach, Numbered Heads Together
Praising	Affirmation Chips, Pairs Check

By fostering social skill development we prepare students with life skills. Over 70% of companies in the United States today have their employees work at least part of the time in teams.[34] And the percent is increasing each year as companies discover the power of teams in the workplace. Teamwork skills are at or near the top of all major national surveys of employer-determined employability skills. Where will students get teamwork skills if not in schools?

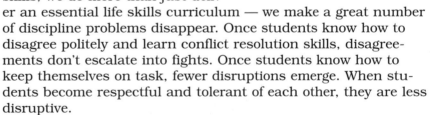

By using the four tools for social skills, we do more than just deliver an essential life skills curriculum — we make a great number of discipline problems disappear. Once students know how to disagree politely and learn conflict resolution skills, disagreements don't escalate into fights. Once students know how to keep themselves on task, fewer disruptions emerge. When students become respectful and tolerant of each other, they are less disruptive.

The first stage in making discipline problems disappear was to institute cooperative learning. That eliminated the bulk of discipline problems (See Discipline Problems Eliminated by Cooperative Learning, page 19.11). The social skills program was the second act, eliminating another large group of discipline problems (See Discipline Problems Eliminated by Kagan Social Skills Program, page 19.18). At this point we had eliminated most of the left and right sides of the Venn. What remained was the intersection.

Discipline Problems Eliminated by Kagan Social Skills Program

Discipline Problems in:

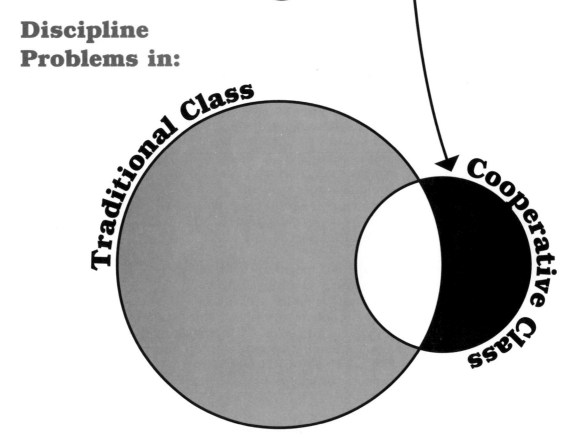

Stage 3: Proactive Preventative Procedures

Unfortunately, simply instituting cooperative learning with a social skills program does not eliminate all discipline problems. If so, there would be no need for this book. This book, in effect, deals with "the rest of the story."

At the end of a traditional math lesson, the teacher says, *"Your math homework tonight is the problems on pages 25 and 26 of your math book."* Alex stands up and shouts at the teacher, *"No way. You can't make me do that!"*

We institute cooperative learning. Students are happier. There are fewer discipline problems. At the end of the math lesson the teacher says, *"Your math homework tonight is the problems on pages 25 and 26 of your math book."* Alex stands up and shouts at the teacher. *"No way. You can't make me do that!"*

Cooperative learning is not a panacea. Even with a social skills component, cooperative learning does not make all discipline problems disappear. Alex may be:

- Seeking attention or approval from peers
- Seeking to avoid failure by not doing the problems
- Trying to establish a sense of control (*No one tells me what to do!*)
- Angry at the teacher
- Coming from some other position

The fact that we have put cooperative learning in place did not change Alex's position. The discipline problems eliminated by putting cooperative learning and social skills in place are those created by the traditional classroom. The traditional classroom ignores and fails to fill basic needs for interaction, movement, and choice. Cooperative learning takes care of those needs. But it does not fill all the needs associated with student positions. Discipline problems that remain after we put cooperative learning and social skills in place are problems students bring to the classroom. Their disruptive behavior springs from their needs, where they are, their position. Discipline problems that persist when we shift the classroom structure are not a result of the classroom structure; they are a result of something the students bring to the classroom, their position. To eliminate position-based disruptions, we must understand and relate to student positions.

Discipline Problems Eliminated by Win-Win Preventative Procedures.

Discipline Problems in:

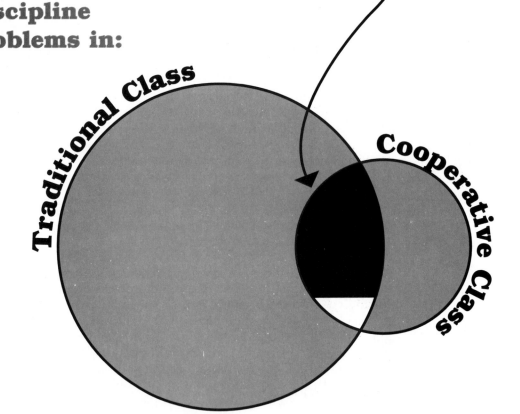

19.20

Win-Win Discipline. Kagan Publishing • 1 (800) 933-2667 • www.KaganOnline.com

There are two approaches to eliminating position-based disruptions: proactive and reactive. Proactive approaches are preventative; they are the procedures we put in place before discipline problems ever occur. Because, for example, students need attention, we can prevent disruptions aimed at fulfilling that need by meeting that need proactively, or teaching students to fulfill their need responsibly. We can greet each student at the door, use student names in examples, comment when they perform well on an assignment or they give good effort, or even when they wear a new outfit or change their hairstyle. We can teach students myriad responsible ways to get positive attention. These are a few of the many proactive preventative procedures of Win-Win Discipline. There are preventative procedures for each of the student positions. Because students need to avoid failure, we structure carefully so they know how to do their homework assignments before sending them home to do them. Because students need to establish control, we build choices into our lesson plans. When student needs are met on an ongoing basis through daily Win-Win procedures, they have less need to become disruptive to meet their needs. If Alex does not fear failure and does not need to establish a sense of control, he will be less likely to need to stand up and shout, *"No way. You can't make me do that!"* The preventative procedures of Win-Win Discipline eliminate most of the problems in the center segment of the Venn Diagram. See, Discipline Problems Eliminated by Win-Win Preventative Procedures, page 19.22.

- The preventative procedures for each position are presented in **Chapter 8. Preventative Procedures: The Seven Positions.**

Stage 4: Reactive Responses: Structures for the Moment-of-Disruption and After

Win-Win proactive preventative procedures eliminate almost all the remaining discipline problems. But disruptions still occur on an occasional basis and we need to know what to do when one erupts. We need reactive responses. Win-Win reactive responses are for the moment-of-disruption and afterwards.

Win-Win structures are carefully tailored to respond in the moment-of-disruption to the needs associated with each of the seven student positions. Identifying and responding to student position is critical because a strategy that works well with one position does not work at all with another. Offering a student choices responds to the need for control but does not respond to the need to avoid failure. When Alex shouts, *"No way. You can't make me do that!"* to be effective we need to know Alex's position. Is he trying to establish control, or is he avoiding failure? If

Discipline Problems Addressed by Win-Win Structures & Follow-Ups.

Discipline Problems in:

Traditional Class

Cooperative Class

we do not know, our response to his disruption will have a hit-or-miss outcome. If we know, we can choose a response that works well for his position.

Thus, as pictured in the figure Discipline Problems Addressed by Win-Win Structures and Follow-ups on page 19.22, structures and follow-ups respond to the last segment of disruptions — those occasional disruptions that occur after the cooperative learning, social skills, and preventative measures are all in place.

After a disruption, we may choose to use a Win-Win follow-up structure. Carefully crafted Win-Win follow-ups go a long way toward eliminating future disruptions. After responding to a disruption in the moment, we ask if the student feels on the same-side, accepts the discipline solution, and if the student is learning responsible alternative behaviors. If not, we use a follow-up to put those pillars in place. Our goal, after all, is not just ending disruptions; it is having students learn responsible life skills so they will not need to be disruptive in the future.

- Win-Win Structures for the Moment-of-Disruption are presented in Chapter 14. Moment-of-Disruption Structures.
- Win-Win Follow-Up Structures are presented in Chapter 16. Follow-Up Structures.

A summary of Disappearing Discipline in four stages is pictured in the figure, Disappearing Discipline Problems, page 19.24. In sum, many discipline problems were eliminated by the transition from the traditional classroom structure to cooperative learning, but cooperative learning failed to eliminate some problems and even brought about some new challenges. The new problems were addressed by implementation of a social skills program.

What remained at that point was addressing those students who were discipline problems in both the traditional and cooperative learning classrooms, the center of the Venn Diagram. Those students were not reacting to the classroom structure. Rather, they were in the same position regardless of classroom structures. They brought these needs to both types of classrooms. The challenges they created, therefore, were best addressed by responding to their needs. That is where Win-Win preventative procedures and structures for the moment-of-disruption fit into the picture.

But the story of cooperative learning and disappearing discipline problems is not unique. Whenever more engaging curriculum or instruction is implemented, there is a corresponding decrease in discipline problems. Engaged students are not disruptive. And students become more engaged via developmentally appropriate, challenging curriculum and instructional strategies that meet basic needs. Thus many

Disappearing Discipline Problems

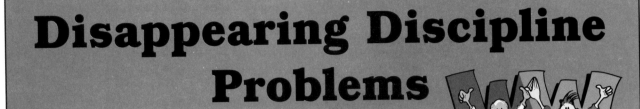

**Eliminated by
Kagan Structures**

**Eliminated by
Kagan Social Skills
Programs**

**Eliminated by
Win-Win
Preventative Procedures**

**Addressed by
Win-Win
Moment-of-Disruption
Strategies & Structures,
and Follow-Ups**

PROACTIVE

REACTIVE

learner-friendly educational programs can boast of decreasing discipline problems. Each, however, reduces discipline in different ways.

- When cooperative learning is implemented, students get to do what they most want to do — talk with peers, make decisions, and move.
- When a multiple intelligences program is instituted, students who were not engaged are suddenly very involved because they are able to learn and express their learning through their own preferred intelligence.
- When developmentally appropriate practices are implemented via differentiated instruction, students who were frustrated and disruptive are suddenly actively engaged with the curriculum, and so discipline problems disappear.
- Cooperative Learning, Multiple Intelligences, and Differentiated Instruction all align classroom practices with how the brain best learns. They provide a safe, brain-nourishing, challenging, meaningful, emotionally relevant, learning environment.

Win-Win Instruction:
Teaching with the Learner in Mind

When we teach in a way that meets student needs, students do not need to be disruptive to meet their needs. There are many learner-friendly approaches to instruction, including Cooperative Learning, Multiple Intelligences, Differentiated Instruction, and Brain-Based Instruction. These approaches to instruction share with Win-Win Discipline the premise that the starting point in designing a successful classroom must be the needs of the learner. They go *with* rather than *against* basic needs accepting the obvious: Each student has his/her unique abilities, intelligences, style, and brain so a one-size-fits-all approach will necessarily be hit or miss.

Cooperative Learning transforms the teacher. The teacher becomes the "guide on the side" rather than the "sage on the stage." In cooperative learning, students have input, deciding team names, team projects, team presentations, how to help their teammates learn, and sometimes even what to learn and how to learn it. Why give students so much responsibility? Because students who have no say feel like puppets. When we treat students like puppets, we force ourselves to forever be pulling strings to get students to move. When we treat students as independent, thoughtful, curious, resourceful learners — when we give students a voice — we discover their true potential. If we give students no voice, we force them to become disruptive to be heard. If student input is valued, students do not need to be disruptive to meet their needs. The philosophy is the same in Win-Win Discipline: When students co-create discipline solutions — when we give students a voice — they have less need to subvert the discipline process. It is then that we discover their potential for learned responsibility. If we want students to be responsible, we must give them responsibilities.

Multiple Intelligences, Differentiated Instruction, and Brain-Based Learning share the premise: Each learner has unique needs, styles, and abilities; solid instruction must respond to each learner's uniqueness. An approach that fosters great learning in one student is boring and almost useless to another. It is the same with Win-Win Discipline: A discipline solution perfect for one student is a disaster for another. The bottom line: When we teach with the learner in mind, we are traveling the path of preventing discipline problems. Successful learners and learners whose basic needs are met are not disruptive.

References

[1, 2, 3, 4, 5, 6, 7, 13, 14, 15, 19, 20, 21, 24] Bluestein, J. (Ed.). *Mentors, Masters, and Mrs. MacGregor: Stories of Teachers Making a Difference.* Deerfield Beach, FL: Health Communications, Inc., 1995, p. 74, 75, 216, 36, 272, 38, 163, 162, 74, 73, 314, 163, 272, 72.

[8] Kagan, S., Kagan, L., & Kagan, M. *Teambuilding.* San Clemente, CA: Kagan Publishing, 1997.

[9] Kagan, S., Kagan, L., & Kagan, M. *Classbuilding.* San Clemente, CA: Kagan Publishing, 1995.

[10] Kagan, S. Zahn, G. L., Widaman, K., Schwarzwald, J. & Tyrrell, G. *Classroom Structural Bias: Impact of Cooperative and Competitive Classroom Structures on Cooperative and Competitive Individuals and Groups,* in R. Slavin, S. Sharan, S. Kagan, R. Hertz-Lazarowitz, C. Webb & R. Schmuck (Eds.) *Learning to Cooperate, Cooperating to Learn.* New York: Plenum, 1985.

[11] Kagan, S. *Cooperative Learning.* San Clemente, CA: Kagan Publishing, 1994.

[12] Johnson, D. W., Maruyama, G., Johnson, R. Nelson, D. & Skon, L. *Effects of Cooperative, Competitive and Individualistic Goal Structures on Achievement: A Meta-analysis.* **Psychological Bulletin,** 1981, **89,** 47–62.

19.26

Win-Win Discipline. Kagan Publishing • 1 (800) 933-2667 • www.KaganOnline.com

References (Continued)

[16] Kagan, S., & Kagan, M. *Multiple Intelligences: The Complete MI Book.* San Clemente, CA: Kagan Publishing, 1998.

[17] Kagan, S., & Kagan, M. *Multiple Intelligences: The Complete MI Book.* San Clemente, CA: Kagan Publishing, 1998.

[18] Cambell, L. & Cambell, B. *Multiple Intelligences and Student Achievement: Success Stories from Six Schools.* Alexandria, VA: Association for Supervision and Curriculum Development, 1999.

[22] Tomlinson, C. A. *The Differentiated Classroom: Responding to the Needs of All Learners.* Alexandria, VA: Association for Supervision and Curriculum Development, 1999, p. 2.

[23] Chapman, C. and King, R. *Differentiated Instructional Strategies for Writing in the Content Areas.* Thousand Oaks, CA: Corwin Press, Inc., 2003.

Gregory, G. H. *Differentiated Instructional Strategies. One Size Doesn't Fit All.* Thousand Oaks, CA: Corwin Press, Inc., 2002.

Silver, D. *Drumming to the Beat of a Different Marcher: Finding the Rhythm for Teaching a Differentiated Classroom.* Nashville, TN: Incentive Publications, 2003.

Tomlinson, C. A. *The Differentiated Classroom. Responding to the Needs of All Learners.* Alexandria, VA.: Association for Supervision and Curriculum Development, 1999.

[25] Kagan, S. *Staff Development and the Structural Approach to Cooperative Learning, in C. M. Brody, N. Davidson & C. Cooper,* **Professional Development for Cooperative Learning: Issues and Approaches.** Teachers College Press, New York, 1998.

[26] Kagan, S., Kagan, L., & Kagan, M. *Classbuilding.* San Clemente, CA: Kagan Publishing, 1995.

[27] Kagan, S. *Silly Sports and Goofy Games.* San Clemente, CA: Kagan Publishing, 2000.

[28] Memory Systems SmartCard. San Clemente, CA: Kagan Publishing, 2003.

[29] Erlauer, L. *The Brain-Compatible Classroom. Using What We Know About Learning to Improve Teaching.* Alexandria, VA: Association for Supervision and Curriculum Development, 2003.

Kaufeldt, M. *Begin With the Brain: Orchestrating the Learning-Centered Classroom.* Tucson, AZ: Zephyr Press, 1999.

Jensen, A. *Teaching With the Brain in Mind.* Alexandria, VA: Association for Supervision and Curriculum Development, 1998.

Sylwester, R. *A Biological Brain in a Cultural Classroom: Applying Biological Research to Classroom Management.* Thousand Oaks, CA: Corwin Press, Inc. 2000.

Wolfe, P. *Brain Matters: Translating Research into Classroom Practice.* Alexandria, VA: Association for Supervision and Curriculum Development, 2001.

References (Continued)

[30] Kagan, S. *Cooperative Learning.* San Clemente, CA: Kagan Publishing, 1994.

[31] Kagan, S. Communication Boosters SmartCard. San Clemente, CA: Kagan Publishing, 2002.

[32] Kagan, S. Pop-up Social Role Card Kit. San Clemente, CA: Kagan Publishing, 1999.

[33] Kagan, S. *Cooperative Learning.* San Clemente, CA: Kagan Publishing, 1994.

[34] Filipczak, B. Industry Report. *Training Magazine*, 1994, **31**(10), 59–65.

Chapter 20

Win-Win
Life Skills

A comprehensive discipline program includes life skills. As students acquire life skills, they are less disruptive.

A student puts down another student. Having been publicly belittled, the recipient of the put-down has the impulse to retaliate to give back a put-down or even initiate a fight. To the extent the student has acquired the life skills of **self-control, anger management,** and/or **good judgment,** a discipline problem is averted.

A student is finding an assignment difficult. He/She is tempted to avoid failure by saying to himself/herself and others, "This assignment is stupid." To the extent the student has acquired **self-motivation, pride in his/her work,** and **perseverance,** *a discipline problem is averted.*

A student is placed on a team with another student he/she does not like. The student is tempted to call out, "Yuck! Look who we are stuck with!" To the extent the student has acquired **relationship skills, cooperativeness, empathy,** and **kindness,** a *discipline problem is averted.*

We could multiply these examples endlessly. Life skills realize the aim of an effective discipline program: to make discipline problems disappear by fostering responsibility.

As students learn life skills such as anger management, perseverance, and pride in one's work, the incidence of discipline problems in the classroom decreases. Life skill trainings, however, are not our first option if our goal is immediate reduction of discipline problems. First come the preventative procedures — they have the biggest immediate effect. Next come moment-of-disruption and follow-up structures. Only when those procedures and structures are in place have we established the proper context for life skill trainings.

While life skills are the last component of Win-Win in the adoption sequence, they are the most important. In preparing a student for a successful and rewarding life, acquiring a life skill like listening or empathy is far more important than learning one more math algorithm or history fact. Learning to set goals and monitor goal attainment will have a more profound positive impact on a student for a lifetime than mastering additional spelling words.

The ultimate goal of Win-Win Discipline is not ending disruptions, but preparing students with lifetime abilities to

> "*A really great teacher is someone who...* **not only teaches lessons on the course work, but life lessons as well.**"
> **Colleen, 17, Mays Landing, New Jersey**[1]

Win-Win Discipline. Kagan Publishing • 1 (800) 933-2667 • www.KaganOnline.com

20.2

meet their needs in responsible ways — to acquire discipline. By modeling and teaching with a Win-Win orientation, we transform students — they adopt the Win-Win philosophy. The result is a profound impact on a range of life skills including empathy, impulse control, communication skills, anger management, self-esteem, motivation, teamwork skills, social orientation, and the development of a range of character virtues.

We foster these positive life skills indirectly by who we are, how we treat our students, and the approach we take to curriculum, management, instruction, and discipline. In addition, we can nourish the various life skills directly by adopting or creating life skill programs.

The emphasis in this final chapter is overviewing some of the most important life skill frameworks aligned with the philosophy of Win-Win and providing references to existing life skills programs as points of departure for those who would explore further. Before providing that overview, however, let's review why life skills training is arguably the most important thing we can teach.

Life Skills:
Not Important, Imperative

Any teacher who has been in the profession for a couple of decades can tell you that students today are radically different from students a generation ago. Students of past generations came to class with basic virtues and life skills such as honesty, courtesy, and perseverance. If we fast-forward from that time to today, we find the norm has become dishonesty, rudeness, and impulsiveness. Students were sensitive to the feelings of others; today's students too often treat others as objects. An alarming percentage of students have lost the fundamental values of respect, honesty, kindness, and lawfulness.

In short, today's students do not come to school with basic life skills. Compared to students of a generation ago, students today lack basic **social skills:** they are rude, uncooperative. They lack emotional skills: they do not control their impulses when it would be adaptive to do so; they act out their feelings without awareness of the feelings. They lack **personal organizational and planning skills.** And they lack basic **citizenship skills:** with shocking frequency they lie, cheat, and steal.

The decline of character and emotional intelligence is not just an impression among those of us who have been educators for a number of years; shocking statistics substantiate the radical transformation of the nation's youth.

The Youth of Today

- **160,000 students skip school each day because they fear bullies.[3]**

- **More than 1 in 3 students report they do not feel safe at school.[4]**

- **83% of girls and 60% of boys have been sexually harassed at school — touched, pinched, or grabbed in a sexual way.[5]**

- **54% of middle school and 70% of high school students cheated on a test in the last year.[6]**

- **47% of high school students report they stole from a store in the past 12 months.[7]**

- **In 1950, among youth of 14–17 years of age, less than half of one percent were arrested; by 1990 the figure had climbed to over 13%.[8]**

Why Is Supply Down?

Supply is down. Unlike prior generations, students today do not come to school with an extensive repertoire of positive life skills. Why?

There are many factors contributing to the erosion of character and the lack of life skills among today's youth:

- Economics have shifted, making a two-parent income a necessity with the consequences that parents are less available to socialize their children. In 1950, 11% of mothers with children under six worked; by 1990 the percentage had climbed to 58.2%; by 2000 the figure was 64.6%![9]

- Far more families are divorced or never married. In 1940, 3.8% of babies were born to unwed mothers; today the figure is over 32%![10] In 1960, only 9% of the nation's youth lived in single-parent homes; by 2000 the percentage had reached 27%.[11] Of children born today, over half will be reared part-time in a single-parent family before they reach 18 years.

- Today's families are mobile. Families move on the average of two to three times during a child's school age years.[12] Because of increased mobility, neighbors do not know the children that play on their street, so students are no longer under the watchful eye of others who care for them. Grandparents are no longer a living presence in the home, and communication between grandparent and grandchild has been reduced, in most cases, to a phone call. Thus neighbors, grandparents, and community members are no longer an important force in transmitting positive values and life skills.

- Families are smaller.[13] As a result, younger children do not have older children as positive models and caregivers, and the older children do not learn to care for others — an orientation once integral to family life.

Thus in the last half century many forces have converged to create the *abandoned generation* — students who are not receiving life skills training outside of school and who, to a frightening extent, are rearing themselves, struggling on their own to formulate values and learn life skills.

Children of the abandoned generation have turned to television and video games in an attempt to fill the socialization void, to formulate their values. Children today spend 1180 minutes a week watching television;[14] they spend 38.5 minutes a week in meaningful conversation with a parent.[15] The average American child sees 200,000 violent acts on TV by age 18.[16] Ninety-two percent of children and adolescents play video games, and 90% of the top selling games contain violence.[17] Half of the top-selling video games today contain serious violence.[18] In most violent video games, violence is portrayed as justified and goes unpunished.[19] Violent TV and video games are hardly the model needed to fill the socialization void.

Along with the media, peer influence has become the primary socializer of today's youth. It is revealing that the gang leader is most often called "father." Today's youth gangs are a substitute family, merely an attempt to fill the socialization void for the abandoned generation. For the first time, lacking adult supervision, students have created a peer-based value system. Students are creating their own "rights" and "wrongs." Today, what a teacher or parent says is right or wrong is not nearly as important as what a peer says. Because peers are deriving their values from television and media, they contribute to, rather than fill, the values void for the abandoned generation.

Life Skills: Demand Is Up

At the same time supply of positive life skills is down, demand is increasing dramatically. The work world has changed so that social skills are at a premium. Over 70% of jobs today involve membership in a team, and the number is increasing.[20] Increased technology in the workplace is associated with interdependence — no one person working alone can design a computer. Teams cooperate with other teams. In today's world teamwork skills are employability skills.

Large national surveys from a number of countries reveal that employers state that the most important employability skills are ability to work well with others, communication skills, and teamwork skills. For example, the National Training Organizations of England found skills shortages in ability to work with customers, teamwork skills, and communication skills were greater than shortages in numeracy and literacy.[21] The Conference Board of Canada states that the skills most needed to "participate and progress in today's dynamic world of work" are of three types: fundamental skills, personal management skills, and teamwork skills.[22] In the United States, the two largest studies of employability skills, one by the American Society of Training and Development[23] and one by the Secretary's Commission on Achieving Necessary Skills (SCANS),[24] both emphasize the importance of group effectiveness skills (teamwork skills, interpersonal skills); developmental skills (self-esteem, motivation and goal-setting, career planning); and communication skills. For example, the SCANS report concluded the following: "The emphasis on teamwork in more and more workplaces means that instructional approaches must also emphasize learning collaboratively not just individually. For all types and levels of schooling and training, the fields emerging research findings challenge what we teach and how we teach it."[25]

To cope with the increasing pace and the accelerated change rate that characterizes modern life, our students also need new life skills such as the ability to deal with stress and frustration. Today's students will have many new jobs over the course of their lives, with associated frustration and need for flexibility. As medical science advances, it will place additional demands on future generations: more than previous generations they will be called to care for older adults with special needs. Kindness, compassion, and care giving skills will be in demand. As mobility increases, society will include greater and greater diversity, so tolerance and diversity skills also will be at a premium.

In short, demand for a wide range of life skills is up.

Addressing the Life Skills Crisis

Thus at the very moment when the supply of life skills is down, the need is up. How are we in the educational community going to respond to this crisis? Narrow curricula that focus exclusively on academic achievement and ignore the traditional social skills and virtues will contribute to the crisis. We need to broaden our curricula to include life skills. The alternative can spell disaster for our students and our society. In short, there is no question about the need to educate for life skills. There also is no lack of resources to educate for life skills. All that is lacking is the courage among educators to act on what they know to be true: the greatest need in education today is the need to educate for life skills.

Given the importance of life skills for both the quality of life of our students and the health of our society, we in the educational community need to re-evaluate our priorities. We need to educate for life skills. One question remains: How is this best achieved? A comprehensive answer to that question is beyond the scope of this book, but what is provided in the remainder of the book is an overview of ways to conceptualize life skills (life skills frameworks), plans for teaching life skills (life skills curricula), and an integrated approach to life skills along with key references and resources.

Life Skills Frameworks and Curricula

A number of frameworks exist for categorizing life skills, but none is completely comprehensive or satisfying. Kagan has presented the relationships among various life skills frameworks and life skills curricula.[26] He demonstrates that the frameworks overlap in various ways, but that each has its own focus, including some skills to the exclusion of others. Among the most important ways to categorize life skills are the following four distinct but overlapping broad frameworks:

Life Skills Frameworks
I.   **Emotional Intelligence**
II. **Character Education**
III. **Habits for Success**
IV. **Multiple Intelligences**

In addition to the broad life skills frameworks, there are specific life skills curricula and numerous teacher-friendly books on how to teach specific life skills such as friendship skills, conflict resolution skills, and communication skills. A complete overview of all life skills resources is beyond the scope of this book, but we will briefly examine two life skills curricula:

Life Skills Curricula
I.   **The Prepare Curriculum**
II. **Skillstreaming**

Life Skills Frameworks and Their Links
I. Emotional Intelligence

The emotional intelligence framework as presented by Daniel Goleman distinguishes five broad sets of skills:

1. **Self-Knowledge**
2. **Self-Control**
3. **Self-Motivation**
4. **Empathy**
5. **Social Skills**

In his formative book, *Emotional Intelligence*, Goleman provides the rationale for emotional intelligence, showing in many ways that it is more important than IQ in predicting job and life success.[27]

Books on emotional intelligence provide classroom activities to help students obtain emotional literacy.[28] Although the emotional intelligence framework is broad enough to encompass most of the important life skills, it is so broad that it provides little guidance for educators beyond establishing the importance of life skills. For example, it identifies the importance of social skills, but it does not identify or categorize the myriad social skills that need be taught and does not provide detailed guidance in how to teach them.

> *Self-reverence, self-knowledge, self-control: These three alone lead life to sovereign power.*
> —*Alfred Tennyson (1809–1892)*

II. Character Education

Character Education focuses on the acquisition of traditional virtues such as honesty, respect, and responsibility. Wisdom, considered by the ancient Greeks to be the master virtue, includes the study of moral principles and the development of moral reasoning.[29] Thomas Lickona provides the rationale for character education in his classic book, *Educating for Character*.[30] Lickona documents the lack in today's youth of the character virtues fundamental to a civilized society. Lying, cheating, and abusing others have become so much the norm that they produce in today's students no remorse.

Popular character education programs emphasize different virtues, as seen in the table, Virtues In Character Education Programs.

Virtues in Character Education Programs

Character Counts[SM]	Integrated Thematic Instruction	WiseSkills™	Character Matters
	Active Listening*		
Caring	Caring	Caring	Love
Citizenship		Citizenship	
	Common Sense		
		Conflict Resolution	
	Cooperation		
		Courage	
	Curiosity		
	Effort	Diligence	Hard Work
Fairness		Fairness	Justice
	Flexibility		
	Friendship		
			Gratitude
Honesty	Truthfulness*	Honesty	
			Humility
	Initiative		
	Integrity	Integrity	Integrity
	No Put-Downs*		
	Organization		
	Patience		
	Perseverance		Fortitude
	Personal Best*		
		Personal Goals	
		Positive Attitude	Positive Attitude
	Problem-Solving		
		Relationships	
Respect		Respect	
Responsiblity	Responsiblity	Responsiblity	
		Self-Discipline	Self-Control
	Sense of Humor		
	Trustworthiness*	Trustworthiness	
			Wisdom

* In the ITI model Trustworthiness, Truthfulness, Active Listening, No Put-Downs, and Personal Best are "Lifelong Guidelines," which are a combination of traditional virtues and modern social skills.

Categorizing, Promoting the Virtues

Character Counts[31] advocates six core virtues. Integrated Thematic Instruction[32] offers fifteen virtues called "Lifeskills" and five additional virtues and social skills called "Lifelong Guidelines." The WiseSkills Program[33] includes fifteen virtues, but not all virtues at all grade levels. Thomas Lickona in his book, *Character Matters*,[34] supports the importance of ten essential virtues. Longer lists are available. Kagan provides a comprehensive list of virtues from A to Z.[35]

Virtues from A to Z

• Ambition	• Generosity	• Patriotism
• Appreciation	• Gentleness	• Peacefulness
• Assertiveness	• Genuineness	• Perseverance
• Attentiveness	• Gratitude	• Politeness
• Bravery	• Happiness	• Pride
• Caring	• Harmony	• Priority
• Charisma	• Helpfulness	• Purpose
• Charity	• Honesty	• Reliability
• Citizenship	• Honor	• Resilience
• Cleanliness	• Humility	• Resolution
• Commitment	• Humor	• Respect
• Compassion	• Idealism	• Responsibility
• Concern	• Identity	• Restraint
• Confidence	• Imagination	• Reverence
• Conscience	• Industriousness	• Righteousness
• Constancy	• Ingenuity	• Self-Awareness
• Contentedness	• Inspiration	• Self-Control
• Cooperation	• Integrity	• Self-Esteem
• Courage	• Inventiveness	• Self-Reliance
• Courtesy	• Joyfulness	• Selflessness
• Creativity	• Justice	• Sensitivity
• Deference	• Kindness	• Sharing
• Dependability	• Leadership	• Sincerity
• Devotion	• Leniency	• Steadfastness
• Direction	• Love	• Temperance
• Empathy	• Loyalty	• Thankfulness
• Endurance	• Mercy	• Thriftiness
• Enthusiasm	• Moderation	• Tolerance
• Equality	• Morality	• Tranquility
• Excellence	• Neatness	• Vision
• Fairness	• Optimism	• Wisdom
• Faithfulness	• Order	• Zeal
• Forgiveness	• Patience	

There is a great deal of overlap among different character education programs. Interestingly, among the programs reviewed, only caring/love was common to all four. A number of virtues are common to three of the four programs: effort/diligence/hard work; fairness/justice; honesty; integrity; and responsibility.

Also of interest: Some programs are unique in their emphasis on specific virtues. Character Matters emphasizes traditional virtues and is the only one to include gratitude, humility, and wisdom. The ITI Model is unique in emphasis on the following school-related virtues and Lifelong Guidance: active listening, curiosity, initiative, no put-downs, organization, problem-solving, and personal best. WiseSkills™, unlike the others, includes conflict resolution, courage, personal goals, and relationships.

The LifeSkills program is a differentiated program for four grade level groups, consisting of eight monthly character themes with 32 weekly skills and hundreds of projects, discussion ideas, group activities, journals, and logs. It is used ten to fifteen minutes during each school day. The program includes conflict resolution materials and parent involvement and has four versions, one for each of the grade levels K–2, 3–5, 6–8, and 9–12. The high school version focuses on a somewhat different set of virtues than do the pre-high school programs.

Numerous books are available for teachers wishing to implement character education programs.[36] Character programs foster virtue acquisition via a range of methods:

Ten Approaches to Virtue Acquisition

1. Recognizing, acknowledging, celebrating successful use of virtues in self and others
2. Recognizing, discussing virtues in contemporary, historical, and literary figures
3. Deriving and discussing the moral of stories (don't kill the goose that lays the golden egg; don't cry wolf)
4. Teacher modeling virtues
5. Student planning use of virtues
6. Student debriefing use of virtues
7. Activities to foster the virtues, including analysis of moral dilemmas
8. Studying, discussing wise quotes, sage advice, and moral precepts
9. Instituting Virtue-of-the-Week or Virtue-of-the-Month programs which include the points above
10. Instituting school-wide character education programs

Throughout the ages philosophers have offered moral precepts which are excellent discussion starters.

Moral Precepts

What is hurtful to you, do not do to any other person.
— **Moses (15th–13th Century B.C.)**

What you do not want done to yourself, do not do to others.
— **Confucius (551–479 B.C.)**

It is not how much we give, but how much love we put in the giving.
— **Mother Teresa (1910–1997)**

The worst sin toward our fellow-creatures is not to hate them but to be indifferent to them; that's the essence of inhumanity.
— **George Bernard Shaw (1856–1950)**

We make a living by what we get. We make a life by what we give.
— **Winston Churchill (1874–1965)**

The way to heaven is to benefit others.
— **Lao Tzu (604–531 B.C.)**

Happiness is not having what you want, but wanting what you have.
— **Hyman Judah Schuctel**

If you want others to be happy, practice compassion. If you want to be happy, practice compassion.
— **Dalai Lama**

Studying moral precepts and developing one's own moral principles are important components of becoming a person of character.

Structures for Virtues

In my own approach to categorizing virtues and fostering virtue acquisition,[37] I categorize virtues in three domains (Personal, Relationship, and Community) with five core virtues or sets of related virtues in each domain:

Kagan's Three Types of Virtues[38]

Personal Virtues
- **Courage**
- **Good Judgment/Wisdom**
- **Self-Discipline/Impulse Control/Perseverance**
- **Integrity/Pride in One's Work**
- **Self-Motivation/Positive Attitude**

Relationship Virtues
- **Respect/Courtesy**
- **Caring/Kindness**
- **Cooperativeness/Helpfulness**
- **Honesty**
- **Understanding**

Community Virtues
- **Citizenship**
- **Fairness**
- **Leadership**
- **Responsibility**
- **Loyalty/Trustworthiness**

The Kagan approach advocates fostering virtues based on instructional strategies called structures. Rather than (or in addition to) teaching lessons on virtues and instituting the ten approaches to fostering virtue acquisition, the teacher chooses instructional strategies that include virtues as an embedded curriculum. For example, as students do a simple RallyRobin (taking turns sharing ideas), they are acquiring the academic content but also are learning to take turns. As they do a three-step interview on any content, students acquire listening skills. Kagan offers structures to promote acquisition of each of the fifteen virtues in his model.

Structures for Virtue Acquisition

Kagan Structure	Embedded Virtues
Circle-the-Sage	Leadership, Helpfulness
Estimate and Probability Line-Ups	Good Judgment
Expert Group Jigsaw	Cooperation, Helpfulness, Leadership
Folded Agree-Disagree Line-Ups	Courage, Respect, Understanding
Draw-a-Chip	Courtesy
Paraphrase Passport	Caring, Impulse Control, Respect, Understanding
Pass-N-Praise	Kindness
Spend-a-Buck	Fairness
Talking Chips	Impulse Control
Team-Pair-Solo	Cooperation, Helpfulness, Leadership, Self-Motivation, Pride in One's Work
Team Statements	Citizenship, Cooperation, Integrity, Respect
Three-Step Interview	Understanding, Responsibility

An advantage of the structural approach to virtue acquisition is that no time is taken from academic content; the virtues are acquired as the teacher delivers regular academic content. With lessons on virtues, students learn about a virtue; with structures, students acquire the virtues. The structures create distributed practice because the virtues are practiced all school year.

Links: Emotional Intelligence and Character Development

Development of emotional intelligence and development of character virtues are very closely linked:

> **"There is an old-fashioned word for the body of skills that emotional intelligence represents: Character."**
> **—Daniel Goleman**[39]

The life skills advocated in Emotional Intelligence and Character Development are remarkably aligned:

Links: Emotional Intelligence and Character Education

Emotional Intelligence	Character Education
Self-Knowledge	Wisdom, Integrity, Honesty (with self)
Self-Control	Good Judgment, Common Sense, Self-Discipline
Self-Motivation	Perseverance, Diligence, Personal Best, Personal Goals, Initiative
Empathy	Understanding, Respect
Relationship Skills	Cooperativeness, Caring, Kindness, Fairness, Trustworthiness, Patience, Friendship, Cooperation, Respect, Honesty (with others)

An advantage for educators of the character education approach over the emotional intelligence approach to life skills is that the character virtues are concrete and specific and more easily translate into teachable, learnable curricula. It is hard for most teachers to translate "relationship skills" into classroom lessons and activities, whereas it is much easier to deal with "caring," "cooperation," or "fairness" as discrete, teachable virtues. An additional advantage of the character education framework over the emotional intelligence framework is that it is more comprehensive. Virtues such as citizenship, common sense, and curiosity are generally accepted as important life skills but do not fit neatly into the EQ framework. Wisdom is based in part on self-knowledge (we cannot make wise choices if we do not know what we want), but it is far more encompassing, including ability to predict short- and long-term consequences of actions, understanding and living in accord with moral principles, and ability to engage in sophisticated moral reasoning.

III. Habits of Success

In reviewing the "literature of success" published in the United States since 1776, Steven Covey uncovered a remarkable trend.[40] For the first 150 years or so since the founding of our country, success was deemed a function of character. The road to success and happiness was to acquire virtues such as humility, fidelity, temperance, courage, justice, patience, industry, and simplicity. Following World War I the success literature shifted; the focus moved from character to personality and skills. The literature emphasized having a positive mental attitude, impressing others, communication skills, being liked, and playing the power game. Covey argues for a paradigm shift to a principle-centered approach and identifies seven habits of highly effective people:

> ### Covey's Seven Habits
>
> 1. **Be Proactive**
> 2. **Begin with the End in Mind**
> 3. **Put First Things First**
> 4. **Think Win/Win**
> 5. **Seek First to Understand... Then to Be Understood**
> 6. **Synergize**
> 7. **Sharpen the Saw**

Covey provides wonderful examples, quotes, and personal anecdotes to support each of these habits. The seven habits are a powerful life skills curriculum.

The seven habits align well with emotional intelligence and character education:

Links: Seven Habits, Character Virtues, & Emotional Intelligence

Seven Habits	Character Virtue	Emotional Intelligence
1. Proactive	Initiative	Self-Motivation
2. End in Mind	Integrity	Self-Knowledge
3. First Things First	Good Judgment	Self-Control
4. Win/Win	Fairness	Relationship Skill
5. Understand First	Understanding	Empathy
6. Synergize	Cooperation	Relationship Skill
7. Sharpen the Saw	Pride in One's Self	Self-Knowledge

Win-Win Discipline. Kagan Publishing • 1 (800) 933-2667 • www.KaganOnline.com

20.15

Having students study the seven habits can be a powerful component of a comprehensive life skills program. In *Seven Habits of Highly Effective Teens*, Covey's son, Sean Covey, explains the seven habits in the context of teen life.[41]

IV. Multiple Intelligences

*Emotional Intelligence is an **affective** approach.*
*Character Education is a **moral** approach.*
*Seven Habits is a **principle-based** approach.*
*Multiple Intelligences is a **cognitive** approach.*

No life skills program is complete if it does not foster the development of the various ways to be smart. Howard Gardner's theory of multiple intelligences[42] identifies eight intelligences:

Gardner's Eight Intelligences

1. Verbal/Linguistic
2. Logical/Mathematical
3. Visual/Spatial
4. Musical/Rhythmic
5. Bodily/Kinesthetic
6. Naturalist
7. Interpersonal
8. Intrapersonal

In contrast to traditional IQ-style thinking, MI theory makes the case that each of these intelligences is not fixed for life but, rather, can be developed. This provides the rationale for including them in a comprehensive approach to life skills. A number of comprehensive resources provide lessons and activities to engage and develop the intelligences.[43]

MI Links to Other Approaches

Like each of the life skills formulations, MI has important unique elements and important links to the other approaches. The five dimensions of Emotional Intelligence are all part of what Howard Gardner originally called the Personal Intelligences: the first three EQ skills are forms of Intrapersonal Intelligence; the last two are forms of the Interpersonal Intelligence.

Links: Emotional Intelligences & Multiple Intelligences

Emotional Intelligence	Multiple Intelligences
Self-Knowledge Self-Control Self-Motivation	*Intra*personal Intelligence
Empathy Relationship Skills	*Inter*personal Intelligence

Although the two theories overlap, there are distinct differences: MI theory emphasizes cognitive abilities (knowing what another is feeling) whereas EQ places more emphasis on emotion (feeling what another is feeling). MI emphasizes "social smarts": Who is friends with whom in this classroom? EQ emphasizes "social sensitivity": What is Johnny feeling right now?

Links exist between the multiple intelligences, the character virtues, and the seven habits. For example, good judgment and doing first things first are both dependent on the logical intelligence.

Although in many cases the various life skills frameworks are alternative languages to discuss and promote the same life skills, each framework provides a unique contribution.

Life Skill Curricula

I. The Prepare Curriculum

The Prepare Curriculum[44] is a very comprehensive program with theory and research supporting the need to teach ten life skills:

1. Problem Solving
2. Interpersonal Skills
3. Situation Perception
4. Anger Control
5. Moral Reasoning
6. Stress Management
7. Empathy
8. Recruiting Supportive Models
9. Cooperation
10. Understanding and Using Groups

The Prepare Curriculum combines in-depth theory and research along with detailed lesson plans to develop each of the ten life skills. Each life skill is presented in depth. For example, interpersonal skills training provides role-plays for 50 interpersonal skills divided into six categories:

1. **Beginning Social Skills**
   Listening, Asking a Question, Giving a Compliment...
2. **Advanced Social Skills**
   Giving Instructions, Apologizing, Convincing Others...
3. **Dealing with Feelings**
   Knowing Your Feelings, Dealing with Someone Else's Anger, Expressing Affection...
4. **Alternatives to Aggression**
   Negotiating, Using Self Control, Responding to Teasing...
5. **Dealing with Stress**
   Dealing with Embarrassment, Responding to a Failure, Dealing with Group Pressure...

6. **Planning**
   Setting a Goal, Arranging Problems by Importance, Making a Decision...

II. Skillstreaming

Skillsteaming[45] is a comprehensive curriculum to develop pro-social skills. The skills are divided into five groups, with ten to twenty-five distinct skills in each group:

1. **Classroom Survival Skills**
   Listening, Completing Assignments, Making Corrections...
2. **Friendship-Making Skills**
   Introducing Yourself, Joining In, Apologizing...
3. **Dealing with Feelings**
   Knowing Your Feelings, Understanding Another's Feelings, Dealing with Fear...
4. **Alternatives to Aggression**
   Using Self-Control, Staying Out of Fights, Negotiating...
5. **Dealing with Stress**
   Dealing with Boredom, Answering a Complaint, Dealing with Group Pressure...

The life skills curricula, like the life skills frameworks, emphasize overlapping sets of skills, each with its own unique skills and focus. The life skills curricula may be seen as ways to implement the life skills frameworks. For example, knowing the feelings of others is common to both curricula and central to Emotional Intelligence (Empathy), Character Education (Understanding), Seven Habits (Understand First), and Multiple Intelligences (Interpersonal Intelligence).

Outline of Essential Life Skills

The life skills frameworks (EQ, CD, 7 Habits, MI) and the life skills curricula each provide a powerful rationale for the inclusion of life skills and each provides unique ways to organize and conceptualize life skills. The life skills frameworks and life skills curricula have areas of overlap among and between them, but each makes a unique contribution toward a comprehensive life skills program. Each has areas of concentration and areas of neglect. Numerous popular classroom activity books provide ready-to-use activities, but focus on one or a limited number of skills. Many volumes have been written on specific skills, such as anger management and leadership, and very different approaches to fostering each skill can be taken. A complete list of life skills, along with references to implementation resources, has not been assembled. The reminder of this chapter is a very tentative first step toward compiling that resource.

While the broad stroke life skills frameworks help us categorize life skills, they do not detail the myriad specific skills in each category or how to teach them. What follows is a categorization of some of the most important life skills to include in a comprehensive life skills program, along with some key references for educators.

The life skills are organized via six categories:*

Six Categories of Life Skills

1. Personal Skills
2. Affective Skills
3. Motivational Skills
4. Cognitive Skills
5. Social Skills
6. Physical Skills

*Although some of the skills fall rather neatly into one category (anger management is clearly an affective skill), others do not. For example, while learned optimism training is a cognitive skill (students learn to make new cognitive attributions), the consequences of learned optimism, however, are not limited to the cognitive domain. There is a shift in self-image, self-esteem, motivation, and social relations.

Even anger management that seems to fit neatly into the category of affective skills, upon reflection, crosses domains. Anger management (an affective skill — one component of emotional self-control) can be approached with cognitive techniques (visualize yourself in a tranquil setting), physiological techniques (slow breathing, progressive relaxation), moral reflection (treat others as you would like to be treated), and behavioral techniques (count to ten), among others.

Even though many of the life skills encompass interrelated skills in the cognitive, emotional, motivational, social, character, and physical domains, a category system by domain is more useful than a simple alphabetical list.

The attempt in the list that follows was to make a "best-fit" placement of the skills.

1. Personal Skills

Personal skills are rooted in self-knowledge — including, but not limited to, self-knowledge of one's own feelings as described in the theory of emotional intelligence. Personal skills are based on self-knowledge in the broader sense, including knowledge of one's own strengths and weaknesses, values and beliefs, social roles, and social responsibilities. It includes the formation of one's identity, including one's role in the family and society. Personal skills provide grounding. They give us the basis for setting goals, prioritizing our actions, and organizing our life. With the development of personal skills comes a sense of who we are and where we want to go. Only when we know our own beliefs can we develop integrity, which includes the ability to align our actions with our beliefs. When we know ourselves, and align our actions with our beliefs, we walk with dignity, feel proud of who we are; we like ourselves. Only with the development of self-knowledge in the broadest sense can we obtain wisdom. After all, part of wisdom is the ability to make decisions that will actualize one's values, and without the development of clear values there can be no alignment. Self-knowledge in the broad sense allows us to be proactive, to act on the world, not just be acted upon. It is then that we gain a sense of our own purpose and power. Without personal skills we are adrift, navigating the open sea without a clear destination and without compass or map. The personal skills allow us to be an effective person.

Personal Skills Across Frameworks

Framework	Personal Skills
Emotional Intelligence	Self-Knowledge
Character Development	Integrity, Pride
Seven Habits	Be Proactive, Sharpen the Saw
Multiple Intelligences	Intrapersonal Intelligence

Personal Life Skills

- Assertiveness, Being Proactive
- Goal Setting and Clarifying Values
  - Prioritizing Objectives
  - Re-evaluating Priorities
- Independence Skills
- Integrity, Identity Formation

- Personal Organizational Skills
- Pride, Personal Power
- Self-Knowledge
- Self-Reward, Self-Love

For resources on personal life skills, see Life Skill Resources section at the end of this chapter.

2. Affective Skills

Either we learn to manage our emotions or we are managed by our emotions. Daniel Goleman eloquently makes the case for the importance of affective skills.[46] Affective skills include knowing and dealing effectively with one's feelings. We may not be able to choose whether we are angry or not, but we can choose what we do about our anger. Without affective skills we "act out" our feelings rather than "act from" our feelings. The extreme example of lack of affective skills is the student who initiates a fight, but does not have a clue that he/she is angry. The student only discovers he/she was angry *afterwards*, while talking with a counselor or the principal. Affective skills involve more than anger management; they involve coping effectively with the whole range of feelings and their associated impulses, including fear, embarrassment, and anxiety. As change rates accelerate in society, increasingly the ability to manage stress is another prerequisite for effective functioning. Impulse control determines if we finish our homework or go out to play, finish school or drop out. Ability to control one's impulses allows one to stay on task in the face of distractions and difficulties — it is among the most important determinants of life success.

Affective Skills Across Frameworks

Framework	Affective Skills
Emotional Intelligence	Self-Knowledge, Self-Control
Character Development	Caring, Positive Attitude, Self-Control, Self-Discipline
Seven Habits	Seek First to Understand… Then to Be Understood, Sharpen the Saw
Multiple Intelligences	Interpersonal Intelligence

Affective Life Skills

- Anger Management
  - Preventing, Avoiding, Ending Fights
- Coping With, Expressing Feelings
  - Anxiety, Fear, Embarrassment
- Identifying and Monitoring Feelings
  - Distinguishing Feelings, Sensations, Emotions, Moods

- Impulse Control, Delay of Gratification, Self-Control
- Self Confidence; Self-Acceptance; Self-Esteem
- Stress Management, Relaxation Response

For resources on affective life skills, see Life Skill Resources section at the end of this chapter.

3. Motivational Skills

Can we pick ourselves up after we get knocked down? Resiliency becomes more important as the change rate accelerates. Students of past generations could prepare for one job for a lifetime; children of future generations will have many jobs. Just as the buggy-whip manufacturer had to look for a new job when cars replaced horse-drawn carriages, students of today many times will have to look for new jobs or redefine their positions in companies in response to increasingly rapid transformations of the workplace. As future generations telecommute, working from home, often for many companies, ability to motivate oneself without external perks or supervision becomes essential. High technology means complexity, steep learning curves, and failures. Our increasingly mobile society brings with it not just job changes but long-distance moves which also steal sense of security. Ability to adapt to change, flexibility, perseverance in the face of failure, and ability to respond with resiliency to change, difficulties, and loss are increasingly important life skills.

Motivational Skills Across Frameworks

Framework	Motivational Skills
Emotional Intelligence	Self-Motivation
Character Development	Courage, Perseverance, Optimism, Positive Attitude, Self-Motivation, Self-Discipline
Seven Habits	First Things First
Multiple Intelligences	Intrapersonal Intelligence

Motivational Life Skills

- Flow Training
- Intrinsic Motivation, Self-Motivation
  - Coping with Boredom, Courage/Bravery in the Face of Fear
- Learned Optimism, Positive Attitude, Perseverance
  - Resiliency Following Failure, Resistance to and Coping with Depression

- Self-Discipline
  - Staying on Task, Even in the Face of Difficulty
- Self-Talk; Inner Dialogue

For resources on motivational life skills, see Life Skill Resources section at the end of this chapter.

20.22

Win-Win Discipline. Kagan Publishing • 1 (800) 933-2667 • www.KaganOnline.com

4. Cognitive Skills

Traditionally, schooling has emphasized content over process. We are in transition toward an emphasis of process over content. Knowing facts is no longer as important as being able to analyze, synthesize, prioritize, categorize, and evaluate information. Why is this transformation occurring?[47] In this information age information is generated at an increasingly rapid rate — so fast that much of the content we teach today will be of little use to students compared to their ability to deal effectively with new content. Multiple intelligences theory points out that intelligence is not fixed and not one-dimensional. The more we engage each intelligence, the stronger it becomes. Life skills in the information age include ability to process many types of information in many ways. To prepare students for success, we need to provide them with a rich array of types of information and allow them to process the information verbally, visually, logically, intuitively, socially, and kinesthetically. By having students gather, organize, question, prioritize, and evaluate information, we prepare them with essential life skills. Only by processing a wide range of internal and external information in a wide range of ways can students obtain the ultimate virtue: Wisdom.

Cognitive Skills Across Frameworks

Framework	Cognitive Skills
Emotional Intelligence	Self-Control, Empathy
Character Development	Good Judgment, Wisdom
Seven Habits	Begin with the End in Mind, Put First Things First, Synergize
Multiple Intelligences	All Eight Intelligences

Cognitive Life Skills

- Creativity
- Decision-Making, Good Judgment, Wisdom
  - Anticipating Consequences of Potential Decisions (for self and others)
  - Prioritizing Objectives
- Gathering, Organizing Information
- Memory Development
- Moral Reasoning

- Planning, Prioritizing
  - Anticipating Intended and Unintended Consequences
  - Designing and Implementing Preventative Measures
  - Sequencing Steps of a Process Toward a Goal
- Problem Solving
- Questioning Skills
- Re-attribution Training

For resources on cognitive life skills, see Life Skill Resources section at the end of this chapter

5. Social Skills

As complexity increases, so does interdependence. No one person builds a computer or an airplane. High technology means teams working to coordinate their efforts with other teams. Teamwork skills are life skills. More students lose their first job for lack of ability to get along with others than for lack of technical skills. Social skills are core to all the life skills frameworks. The most fundamental social skill is empathy. Once empathy is obtained, the other social skills follow. Morality springs from empathy because with empathy, it hurts us to hurt another. Understanding, communication, friendship, caring, diversity skills, leadership skills, and teamwork skills all hinge on the ability to feel what it is like to be the other person. How can we resolve a conflict with a Win-Win solution if we do not know what the other person would consider a win? Without empathy, caring is not possible. In the family, the workplace, and society, the ability to understand and work with others spells success. Social skills are fundamental life skills.

Social Skills Across Frameworks

Framework	Social Skills
Emotional Intelligence	Empathy, Social Skills
Character Development	Caring, Kindness, Cooperation, Honesty, Understanding, Respect, Courtesy
Seven Habits	Think Win/Win, Seek First to Understand... Then to Be Understood, Synergize
Multiple Intelligences	Interpersonal Intelligence

Social Life Skills

- Avoiding Conflicts
  - Disagreeing Politely
- Citizenship Skills, Community Virtues, Communitybuilding
- Communication Skills: Self-Disclosure
  - Asking Questions (Expressing Confusion or Lack of Knowledge)
  - Expressing a Compliment
  - Expressing Appreciation (Saying Thank-You)
  - Expressing Feelings Appropriately (Affection, Anger...)
  - Stating Point of View, Offering Ideas
- Communication Skills: Conversation Skills
  - Asking Questions (Getting to Know Others)
  - Beginning and Ending Conversations
  - Checking for Understanding
  - Following the Lead of Others
  - Listening Skills
  - Non-verbal Communication: Encoding and Decoding Body Language
  - Offering Clarification

- Putting Others at Ease
- Responding Proactively
- Showing Interest
- Understanding Another's Point of View
- Conflict Resolution Skills
- Diversity Skills
- Empathy
- Friendship Skills
- Good Sportsmanship
- Leadership Skills
- Resisting Peer Pressure
  - Responding to Put-Downs, Teasing, Bullying, Being Ostracized
- Responding to Criticism
  - Seeking Constructive Criticism
- Social Skills, Relationship Skills
- Apologizing
  - Asking for Clarification
  - Asking for Help

For resources on social life skills, see Life Skill Resources section at the end of this chapter.

6. Physical Skills

Educators and brain scientists are increasingly aware of the impossibility of separating mind and body.[48] The hungry student cannot concentrate, The student who sits too long has less oxygen and glucose — less fuel — for the brain. The anxious student has more ACTH and cortisol in the brain, interfering with learning and memory, The student who exercises regularly actually builds new capillaries to increase ongoing nourishment in the brain. The student who creates a kinesthetic symbol for the content remembers it better because there is "memory in the muscles." It is not possible to separate mental health from physical health. Given our new knowledge of mind-body connections and the importance of nutrition, exercise, and neurokinesiology, we must re-elevate the importance of physical skills: physical skills are life skills.

Physical Skills Across Frameworks

Framework	Physical Skills
Emotional Intelligence	Not a Primary Focus
Character Development	Courage
Seven Habits	Not a Primary Focus
Multiple Intelligences	Bodily/Kinesthetic Intelligence

Physical Life Skills

- Aerobic and Anaerobic Exercise
- Brain Exercises
- Nutrition
- Personal Hygiene

- Physical Skills
- Play Skills
- Teamwork Skills

For resources on physical life skills, see Life Skill Resources section at the end of this chapter

Win-Win Discipline. Kagan Publishing • 1 (800) 933-2667 • www.KaganOnline.com

20.25

Life Skills: Walking Upstream

In conclusion, let me share a parable I have shared before:[49]

Two women are standing on a bank of a swift river. In the strong current, flailing about, desperately struggling to stay afloat, a man is carried downstream toward them. The women both jump in, pulling the man to safety. While the brave rescuers are tending the victim, the current carries toward them a second man, also desperate and screaming for help. Again, the women jump into the river to the rescue. As they are pulling out this second victim, they spot a third man, desperate, carried downstream. One woman quickly jumps in to save the latest victim. As she does, she turns to see the other woman resolutely walking upstream. "Why aren't you helping?" she cries. "I am!" states the other. "I am going to see who is pushing them in!"

The parable expresses the Win-Win philosophy. In dealing with discipline problems, we have a choice: We can be reactive and respond to each discipline problem as it erupts, or we can be proactive and see the place from which the discipline problem springs. We can continually treat symptoms or we can cure the disease. When we jump into the stream each time a discipline problem occurs, we may win the battle, but we will lose the war. Only by walking upstream — seeing the position of the disruptive student and teaching the student more responsible ways to meet his/her needs — only then can we achieve the goal of a good discipline program: To prevent future discipline problems by empowering students for a lifetime with skills to responsibly meet their needs.

Life Skill Resources

1. Personal Skills

Assertiveness, Being Proactive
- Bolton, R. Ph.D. *People Skills.* New York, NY: Simon & Schuster, Inc., 1979.
- Johnson, S. & Blanchard, K. *Who Moved My Cheese?* New York, NY: Penguin/Putnam Publishing Group, 1998.

Goal Setting, Clarifying Values
- Blanchard, K. T*he One Minute Manager.* New York NY: William Morrow & Co., Inc. 1982.
- Covey, S. *The Seven Habits of Highly Effective Teens.* New York, NY: Fireside Division, Simon and Shuster, Inc., 1998.
- Gust, J. *Developing Character-Building Values. A Whole Language Approach.* Morristown, NJ: Good Apple, 1995.
- McElherne, L. *Jump Starters: Quick Classroom Activities That Develop Self-Esteem, Creativity, and Cooperation.* Minneapolis, MN: Free Spirit Publishing, 1999.
- McGuire, J. V. & Heuss, B. *Bridges: A Self-Esteem Activity Book for Students in Grades 4–6.* Needham Heights, MA: Allyn and Bacon, 1995.
- Raths, L., Harmin, M., & Simon, S. *Values and Teaching: Working with Values in the Classroom, Second Edition.* Columbus, OH: Charles E. Merrill Publishing Company, 1978.
- Schwartz, L. *Teaching Values—Reaching Kids.* Santa Barbara, CA: The Learning Works, Inc., 1997.
- Wilson, D. & Wilson, R. *Promoting Positive Values for School and Everyday Life.* Greensboro, NC: Carson-Dellosa Publishing Company, Inc., 1997.

Independence Skills
- McKisson, M. Chrysalis. N*urturing Creative and Independent Thought in Children, Grades 4–12.* Tucson, AZ: Zephyr Press, 1981.

Integrity, Identity Formation
- Erikson, E. *Childhood and Society.* New York, NY: W. W. Norton, 1963.
- Erikson, E. *Identity: Youth and Crisis.* New York, NY: W. W. Norton, 1968.
- Schwartz, L. *Marvelous Me – A Learning Works Skill Builder, Ages 5–8.* Huntington Beach, CA: Creative Teaching Press, 1978.

Personal Organizational Skills
- Covey, S. *Principle Centered Leadership.* New York, NY: Simon & Schuster, Inc., 1990.
- McElherne, L. *Jump Starters: Quick Classroom Activities That Develop Self-Esteem, Creativity, and Cooperation.* Minneapolis, MN: Free Spirit Publishing, 1999.

Pride, Personal Power
- Garnett, P. *Investigating Morals and Values in Today's Society.* Torrance, CA: Good Apple Publishing, 1988.
- Huggins, P. & Moen, L. *Building Self-Esteem in the Classroom: Intermediate Version (The Assist Program, Affective Social Skills: Instructional Strategies & Techniques Series).* Logmont, CO: Sopris West Educational Services, 1994.
- Huggins, P. & Moen, L. *Building Self-Esteem in the Classroom: Primary Version (The Assist Program, Affective Social Skills: Instructional Strategies & Techniques Series).* Logmont, CO: Sopris West Educational Services, 1995.
- Kaufman, G., Raphael, L., Espeland, P. *Stick Up for Yourself! Every Kid's Guide to Personal Power and Positive Self-Esteem, Revised Edition.* Minneapolis, MN: Free Spirit Publishing Inc., 1999.

- Kaufman, G., Raphael, L., Espeland, P. *A Teacher's Guide To Stick Up for Yourself! Every Kid's Guide to Personal Power and Positive Self-Esteem.* Minneapolis, MN: Free Spirit Publishing Inc., 2000.
- Shackelford, K. & Wilson, M. *Glad to Be Me.* Dallas, TX: Lasting Lessons, 1992.

Self-Knowledge

- Canfield, J, Wells, H. *100 Ways to Enhance Self-Concept in the Classroom: A Handbook for Teachers and Parents.* Englewood Cliffs, NJ: Prentice-Hall, Inc., 1976.
- Delisle, D. & Delisle, J. *Growing Good Kids: 28 Activities to Enhance Self-Awareness, Compassion, and Leadership.* Minneapolis, MN: Free Spirit Publishing, 1996.
- McElherne, L. *Jump Starters: Quick Classroom Activities That Develop Self-Esteem, Creativity, and Cooperation.* Minneapolis, MN: Free Spirit Publishing, 1999.
- Schmidt, J. *Making and Keeping Friends: Ready-to-Use Lessons, Stories, and Activities for Building Relationships.* West Nyack, NY: Center for Applied Research in Education, 1997.
- Schwartz, L. *The Month-To-Month Me.* Huntington Beach, CA: Creative Teaching Press, 1976.

Self-Reward, Self-Love

- Canfield, J, Wells, H. *100 Ways to Enhance Self-Concept in the Classroom: A Handbook for Teachers and Parents.* Englewood Cliffs, NJ: Prentice-Hall, Inc., 1976.

2. Affective Skills

Anger Management

- Dolan, M. R. *School Violence... Calming the Storm.* Marietta, Georgia: Rising Sun Publications, 1998.
- Eggert, L. L. *Anger Management for Youth: Stemming Aggression and Violence.* Bloomington, Indiana, 1994.
- Huggins, P. & Huggins, D. *Helping Kids Handle Anger: A Validated Washington State Innovative Education Program, Third Edition.* Logmont, CO: Sopris West Educational Services, 1993.
- Huggins, P. *Helping Kids Handle Anger.* Logmont, CO: Sopris West Educational Services, 1991.

Coping with and Expressing Feelings

- Aiken, D. *Taming Butterflies: Activities for Emotional and Social Growth.* San Luis Obispo, CA: Dandy Lion Publications, 1983.
- Gordon, S. Ph.D. *When Living Hurts.* New York, NY: Dell Publishing, 1985.
- Gajewski, N., Hirn, P., & Mayo, P. *Social Skill Strategies, Book B.* Eau Claire, WI: Thinking Publications, 1989.
- McGuire, J. V. & Heuss, B. *Bridges: A Self-Esteem Activity Book for Students in Grades 4–6.* Needham Heights, MA: Allyn and Bacon, 1995.
- Mosatache, H. & Unger, K. *Too Old for This, Too Young for That! Your Survival Guide for the Middle-School Years.* Minneapolis, MN: Free Spirit Publishing, 2000.

Identifying and Monitoring Feelings

- Lewkowicz, A.D. *Teaching Emotional Intelligence: Making Informed Choices.* Arlington Heights, IL: Skylight Professional Development, 1999.

Impulse Control, Delay of Gratification, Self-Control

- Mapes, K. *Stop! Think! Choose! Building Emotional Intelligence in Young People.* Tucson, Arizona: Zephyr Press, 2000.

Self-Confidence, Self-Acceptance, Self-Esteem

- Borba, M. *Esteem Builders: A K–8 Self-Esteem Curriculum of Improving Student Achievement, Behavior, and School Climate.* Torrance, CA: Jalmar Press, 1989.

- Canfield, J, Wells, H. *100 Ways to Enhance Self-Concept in the Classroom: A Handbook for Teachers and Parents.* Englewood Cliffs, NJ: Prentice-Hall, Inc., 1976.
- Glenn, H. S. & Brock, M. *Seven Strategies for Developing Capable Students.* Rockland, CA: Prima Publishing, 1998.
- Kaufman, G., Raphael, L., & Espeland, P. *Stick Up for Yourself: Every Kid's Guide to Personal Power and Positive Self-Esteem.* Minneapolis, MN: Free Spirit Publishing, 1999.
- McDaniel, S. & Bielen, P. *Project Self-Esteem.* Rolling Hills Estates, CA: Jalmar Press, 1990.
- McGuire, J. V. & Heuss, B. *Bridges: A Self-Esteem Activity Book for Students in Grades 4–6.* Needham Heights, MA: Allyn and Bacon, 1995.
- Mosatache, H. & Unger, K. *Too Old for This, Too Young for That! Your Survival Guide for the Middle-School Years.* Minneapolis, MN: Free Spirit Publishing, 2000.

Stress Management, Relaxation Response

- Benson, H. *The Relaxation Response.* New York, NY: William Morrow & Co., 1975.
- Hipp, E. *Fighting Invisible Tigers: A Stress Management Guide for Teens.* Minneapolis, MN: Free Spirit Publishing, 1995.
- Orlick, T. *Free to Feel Great: Teaching Children to Excel at Living.* Carp, Ont., Canada: Creative Bound Inc., 1993.

3. Motivational Skills

Flow Training

- Csikszentmihalyi, M. *Flow. The Psychology of Optimal Experience.* New York, NY: Harper, 1990.

Intrinsic Motivation, Self-Motivation

- Chandler, S. *100 Ways to Motivate Yourself – Change Your Life Forever.* Franklin Lakes, NJ: Career Press, 1996.
- Deci, E. L. *Intrinsic Motivation.* New York, NY: Plenum Press, 1975.
- Kohn, A. *Punished by Rewards.* Boston, MA: Houghton Mifflin Company, 1993.

Learned Optimism, Positive Attitude, Perseverance

- Seligman, M. E. P. *Learned Optimism.* New York, NY: Alfred A. Knopf, 1991.

Self-Discipline

- Chandler, S. *One Hundred Ways to Motivate Yourself.* Franklin Lakes, NJ: Career Press, 1996.
- Seligman, M. E. P. *Learned Optimism.* New York, NY: Alfred A. Knopf, 1991.

Self-Talk, Inner Dialogue

- Bloch, D. & Merritt, J. *Positive Self-Talk for Children.* New York, NY: Bantam, 1993.
- Isaacs, S. & Richey, W. *I Think I Can, I Know I Can: Using Self-Talk to Help Raise Confident, Secure Kids.* New York, NY: St. Martin's, 1991.

4. Cognitive Skills

Creativity

- DeBono, E. *Lateral Thinking: Creativity Step by Step.* New York, NY: Harper and Row Publishers, 1973.
- McKisson, M. *Chrysalis: Nuturing Creative and Independent Thought in Children, Grades 4–12.* Tucson, AZ: Zephyr Press, 1981.

Decision-Making, Good Judgment, Wisdom
- Glenn, H. S. & Brock, M. *Seven Strategies for Developing Capable Students*. Rockland, CA: Prima Publishing, 1998.
- Johnson, D. W. & Johnson, F. P. *Joining Together. Group Theory and Group Skills*. Boston: Allyn & Bacon, 1994.
- Wilson, D. & Wilson, R. *Promoting Positive Values for School and Everyday Life*. Greensboro, NC: Carson-Dellosa Publishing Company, Inc., 1997.

Gathering, Organizing Information
- Buzan, T. & Buzan, B. *The Mind Map Book: How to Use Radiant Thinking to Maximize Your Brain's Untapped Potential*. New York, NY: Plume Publishing, 1996.
- Buzan, T. *How to Mind Map: Make the Most of Your Mind and Learn to Create, Organize, and Plan*. New York, NY: Thorsons Publishing, 2003.
- Bromley, K., Irwin-DeVitis, L., Modlo, M. *Graphic Organizers*. New York, NY: Scholastic, Inc., 1995.
- Marguiles, N. *Mapping Inner Space*. Tucson, AZ: Zephyr Press, 1991.

Memory Development
- Buzan, T. *Use Your Perfect Memory, Third Edition*. New York, NY: Penguin Group, 1991.

Moral Reasoning
- Fox, R. *Moral Reasoning: A Philosophical Approach to Applied Ethics*. Belmont, CA: Wadsworth Publishing, 2000.
- Schwartz, L. *What Do You Think? A Kid's Guide to Dealing with Daily Dilemmas*. Santa Barbara, CA: Learning Works, 1993.

Planning, Prioritizing
- Covey, S. *The Seven Habits of Highly Effective Teens*. New York, NY: Fireside Division, Simon and Shuster, Inc., 1998.
- Covey, S. *First Things First*. New York, NY: Fireside Publishing, 1994.
- Glenn, H. S. & Brock, M. *Seven Strategies for Developing Capable Students*. Rockland, CA: Prima Publishing, 1998.

Problem Solving
- Schwartz, L. *What Do You Think? A Kid's Guide to Dealing with Daily Dilemmas*. Santa Barbara, CA: Learning Works, 1993.
- Torp, L. and Sage, S. *Problems as Possibilities*. Alexandria, VA: ASCD 1998.

Questioning Skills
- Wiederhold, C. *Cooperative Learning and Higher-Level Thinking*. San Clemente, CA: Kagan Publishing, 1998.

Re-attribution Training
- Seligman, M. *Learned Optimism*. New York, NY: Alfred A. Knopf, 1991.

5. Social Skills

Avoiding Conflicts
- Johnson, D. W. & Johnson, F. P. *Joining Together. Group Theory and Group Skills*. Boston: Allyn & Bacon, 1994.
- Keller, E. & Warner, S. T. *GAMBITS: Responders, Closers & Inventory: The Third of Three Modules*. Ottowa, Canada: Minister of Supply and Services Canada, 1979.

Citizenship Skills, Community Virtues, Communitybuilding
- Drew, N. *Learning the Skills of Peacemaking*. Rolling Hills, CA: Jalmar, 1987.

Win-Win Discipline. Kagan Publishing • 1 (800) 933-2667 • www.KaganOnline.com

20.30

- Forni, P. M. *Choosing Civility – The Twenty-five Rules of Considerate Conduct.* New York, NY: St. Martin's Press, 2002.
- Gibbs, J. *Tribes: A New Way of Learning and Being Together.* V ndsor, CA: CenterSource Systems, LLC., 2001.
- Johnson, S. & Blanchard, K. *Who Moved My Cheese?* New York, NY: Penguin/Putnam Publishing Group, 1998.
- Lewis, B. *The Kids Guide to Service Projects: Over 500 Service Ideas for Young People Who Want to Make a Difference.* Minneapolis, MN: Free Spirit Publishing, 1995.
- Kagan, M., Kagan, L., Kagan, S. *Cooperative Learning Structures for Classbuilding.* San Clemente, CA: Kagan Publishing, 1995.
- Shaw, V. C*ommunitybuilding in the Classroom.* San Clemente, CA: Kagan Publishing, 1992.

Communication Skills: Self-Disclosure

- Bocchino, R. *Emotional Literacy.* Thousand Oaks, CA: Corwin Press, 1999.
- Cihak, M. & Heron, B. *Games Children Should Play: Sequential Lessons for Teaching Communication Skills in Grades K–6.* Glenview, IL: Scott, Foresman and Co., 1980.
- Waldo, P. *Scripting: Social Communication for Adolescents.* Eau Claire, WI: Thinking Publications, 1994.
- Gajewski, N., Hirn, P., & Mayo, P. *Social Star. General Interaction Skills.* Eau Claire, WI: Thinking Publications, 1996.
- Koenig, T. *Caring Kids: Social Skills and Character Education Lessons for Grades 1–3.* Eau Claire, WI: Thinking Publications, 1999.
- Keller, E. & Warner, S. T. *GAMBITS: Openers: The First of Three Modules.* Ottowa, Canada: Minister of Supply and Services Canada, 1976.
- Keller, E. & Warner, S. T. *GAMBITS: Links: The Second of Three Modules.* Ottowa, Canada: Minister of Supply and Services Canada, 1979.

Communication Skills: Conversation Skills

- Keller, E. & Warner, S. T. *GAMBITS: Openers: The First of Three Modules.* Ottowa, Canada: Minister of Supply and Services Canada, 1976.
- Keller, E. & Warner, S. T. *GAMBITS: Links: The Second of Three Modules.* Ottowa, Canada: Minister of Supply and Services Canada, 1979.
- Keller, E. & Warner, S. T. *GAMBITS: Responders, Closers & Inventory: The Third of Three Modules.* Ottowa, Canada: Minister of Supply and Services Canada, 1979.
- Johnson, D. W. *Reaching Out. Interpersonal Effectiveness and Self-Actualization.* Boston, MA: Allyn and Bacon, 1993.
- Fast, J. *Body Language.* New York, NY: MJF Books, 1970.
- Ekman, P. & Friesen, W. V. *Unmasking the Face.* Englewood Cliffs, NJ: Prentice-Hall, Inc., 1975.
- Schwatz, L. *Taking Steps Towards Tolerance and Compassion.* Santa Barbara, CA: The Learning Works, Inc., 2001.
- Gajewski, N., Hirn, P., & Mayo, P. *Social Skill Strategies, Book A.* Eau Claire, WI: Thinking Publications, 1989.

Conflict Resolution Skills

- Freeman, S. & McLaughlin, J. *Developing Group Skills, Fifth Ed.* Waconia, MN: F.I.G.Publications, 1995.
- Gajewski, N., Hirn, P., & Mayo, P. *Social Star. Conflict Resolution and Community Interaction Skills.* Eau Claire, WI: Thinking Publications, 1996.
- Johnson, D. W. & Johnson, R. T. *Teaching Students to be Peacemakers.* Edina, MN: Interaction Book Co., 1991.
- Kreidler, W. J. *Creative Conflict Resolution.* Glenview, IL: Scott, Foresman and Co., 1984.
- Kreidler, W. J. *Teaching Concepts of Peace and Conflict.* Cambridge, MA: Educators for Social Responsibility, 1990.
- Kreidler, W. J. & Furlong, L. *Adventures in Peacemaking.* Cambridge, MA: Educators for Social Responsibility, 1995.
- Huggins, P. & Shakarian, L. *Helping Kids Handle Conflicts: Primary Version (The Assist Program, Affective Social Skills: Instructional Strategies & Techniques Series)* Logmont, CO: Sopris West Educational Services, 1999.
- Teolis, B. *Ready-to-Use Conflict-Resolution Activities for Elementary Students.* West Nyack, NY: The Center for Applied Resaearch in Education, 1998.

Diversity Skills

- Kagan, M., Kagan, L., Kagan, S. *Cooperative Learning Structures for Classbuilding.* San Clemente, CA: Kagan Publishing, 1995.
- Kagan, L., Kagan, M., Kagan, S. *Cooperative Learning Structures for Teambuilding.* San Clemente, CA: Kagan Publishing, 1997.

Empathy

- Delisle, D. & Delisle, J. *Growing Good Kids: 28 Activities to Enhance Self-Awareness, Compassion, and Leadership.* Minneapolis, MN: Free Spirit Publishing, 1996.
- Kaufman, G., Raphael, L., & Espeland, P. *Stick Up for Yourself: Every Kid's Guide to Personal Power and Positive Self-Esteem.* Minneapolis, MN: Free Spirit Publishing, 1999.
- Feshbach, N., Feshbach, S., Fauvre, M. & Ballard-Campbell, M. *Learning to Care: Classroom Activities for Social and Affective Development.* Glenview, IL: Scott, Foresman and Company, 1983.

Friendship Skills

- Huggins, P. & Moen, L. *Teaching Friendship Skills: Primary Version (The Assist Program, Affective Social Skills: Instructional Strategies & Techniques Series)* Logmont, CO: Sopris West Educational Services, 1995.
- Huggins, P. & Moen, L. *Teaching Friendship Skills: Intermediate Version (The Assist Program, Affective Social Skills: Instructional Strategies & Techniques Series)* Logmont, CO: Sopris West Educational Services, 1993.
- Schmidt, J. *Making and Keeping Friends: Ready-to-Use Lessons, Stories, and Activities for Building Relationships.* West Nyack, NY: Center for Applied Research in Education, 1997.

Good Sportsmanship

- Fluegelman, A. *More New Games.* Tiburan, CA: Headlands Press, Inc 1981.
- Selleck, G. *Raising a Good Sport in an In-Your-Face World: Seven Steps to Building Character, On the Field – and Off.* New York, NY: McGraw Hill/Contemporary Books, 2002.
- Sheehy, H. *Raising a Team Player: Teaching Kids Lasting Values on the Field, on the Court and on the Bench.* North Adams, MA: Storey Books, 2002.

Leadership Skills

- Delisle, D. & Delisle, J. *Growing Good Kids: 28 Activities to Enhance Self-Awareness, Compassion, and Leadership.* Minneapolis, MN: Free Spirit Publishing, 1996.
- Garnett, P. *Investigating Morals and Values in Today's Society.* Torrance, CA: Good Apple Publishing, 1988.
- Johnson, D. W. & Johnson, F. P. *Joining Together. Group Theory and Group Skills.* Boston: Allyn & Bacon, 1994.

Resisting Peer Pressure

- Kaufman, G., Raphael, L., & Espeland, P. *Stick Up for Yourself: Every Kid's Guide to Personal Power and Positive Self-Esteem.* Minneapolis, MN: Free Spirit Publishing, 1999.
- Huggins, P. *Helping Kids Handle Put-Downs: A Validated Washington State Innovative Education Program.* Logmont, CO: Sopris West Educational Services, 1998.

Responding to Criticism

- Gajewski, N., Hirn, P., & Mayo, P. *Social Skill Strategies, Book B.* Eau Claire, WI: Thinking Publications, 1989.

Social Skills, Relationship Skills

- Aiken, D. *Taming Butterflies: Activities for Emotional and Social Growth.* San Luis Obispo, CA: Dandy Lion Publications, 1983.
- Bolton, R. *Social Style/Management Style.* New York NY: American Management Association, 1984.

Win-Win Discipline. Kagan Publishing • 1 (800) 933-2667 • www.KaganOnline.com

20.32

- Covey, S. *The Seven Habits of Highly Effective Teens.* New York, NY: Fireside Division, Simon and Shuster, Inc., 1998.
- Cummings, C. *Sharing Is Caring.* Edmonds, WA: Teaching, Inc., 1992.
- Forni, P. M. *Choosing Civility – The Twenty-five Rules of Considerate Conduct.* New York, NY: St. Martin's Press, 2002.

Teamwork and Group Skills

- Cain, J. & Jolliff, B. *Teamwork and Teamplay.* Dubuque, Iowa: Kendall/Hunt Publishing Co, 1998.
- Freeman, S. & McLaughlin, J. *Developing Group Skills, Fifth Ed.* Waconia, MN: F.I.G.Publications. 1995.
- Gajewski, N., Hirn, P., & Mayo, P. *Social Star. Peer Interaction Skills.* Eau Claire, WI: Thinking Publications, 1996.
- Garnett, P. *Investigating Morals and Values in Today's Society.* Torrance, CA: Good Apple Publishing, 1988.
- Gibbs, J. *Tribes. A New Way of Learning and Being Together.* Saulsalito, CA: Center Sources Systems, 1995.
- Johnson, D. W. & Johnson, F. P. *Joining Together. Group Theory and Group Skills.* Boston: Allyn & Bacon, 1994.
- Kagan, S. *Cooperative Learning.* San Clemente, CA: Kagan Publishing, 1994.
- Pirtle, S. *Linking Up!* Cambridge, MA: Educators for Social Responsibility, 1998.

Understanding Social Cues and Social Norms

- Gajewski, N., Hirn, P., & Mayo, P. *Social Skill Strategies, Book A.* Eau Claire, WI: Thinking Publications, 1989.
- Lipson, G. *Manners, Please! Poems and Activities That Teach Responsible Behavior.* Carthage, IL: Teaching & Learning Company, 1995.

6. Physical Skills

Aerobic and Anaerobic Exercise

- Anderson, B., Pearl, B., Burke, E., Anderson, J. *Getting in Shape: 32 Workout Programs for Lifelong Fitness, Second Edition.* Bolinas, CA: Shelter Publications, 2002.
- Cooper, K. *Aerobics Program for Total Well-Being: Exercise, Diet, and Emotional Balance.* New York, NY: Bantam Books, 1985.
- Johnson, Jill R. *Oxycise!* Littleton, CO: Oxycise! Internation, Inc., 1997.
- Nitti, J., Nitti, K., Lewis, C. *The Interval Training Workout: Build Muscle and Burn Fat with Anaerobic Exercise.* Alameda, CA: Hunter House, 2001.

Brain Exercises

- Ayres, J. *Sensory Integration and the Child.* Los Angeles, CA: WPS Publishers, 1995.
- Belknap, M. *Mind Body Magic.* Duluth, MN: Whole Person Associates, 1997.
- Blaydes, Jean. *Thinking on Your Feet. 100+ Activities That Make Learning a Moving Experience.* Richardson, TX: Action Based Learning, 2000. www.Actionbasedlearning.com
- Dennison, P. E. & Dennison, G. E. *Brain Gym.* Ventura, CA: Edu-Kinesthetics, Inc., 1986.
- Hannaford, C. *Smart Moves: Why Learning is Not All in Your Head.* Arlington, VA: Great Ocean Publishers, 1995.
- Hannaford, C. *The Dominance Factor.* Arlington, VA: Great Ocean Publishers, 1997.
- Jensen, E. *Learning with the Body in Mind.* San Diego, CA: The Brain Store, 2000.
- Kline, P. *The Everyday Genius.* Arlington, VA: Great Ocean Publishers, 1988.
- Promislow, S. *Making the Brain Body Connection.* Toronto, Ont, Canada: Hushion House, 1998.

Win-Win Discipline. Kagan Publishing • 1 (800) 933-2667 • www.KaganOnline.com

20.33

Nutrition

- Conners, K. *Feeding the Brain.* New York, NY: Plenum Press, 1989.
- McKisson, M. *Chrysalis: Nurturing Creative and Independent Thought in Children, Grades 4–12.* Tucson, AZ: Zephyr Press, 1981.
- Wurtman, J. *Managing Your Mind and Mood Through Food.* New York, NY: Harper & Row, 1986.

Personal Hygiene

- Gajewski, N., Hirn, P., & Mayo, P. *Social Star. General Interaction Skills.* Eau Claire, WI: Thinking Publications, 1996.
- Llewellyn, C. & Gordon, M. *Why Wash? Learning About Person Hygiene (Me and My Body).* London, England: Hodder & Stoughton Children's Division, 1999.
- Schaefer, V. & Bendell, N. *The Care and Keeping of You: The Body Book for Girls.* Middleton, WI: Pleasant Company Publications, 1998.
- Sommers, M. *Everything You Need to Know About Looking and Feeling Your Best: A Guide for Guys.* New York, NY: Powerkids Press, 1999.

Physical Skills

- Finnigan, D. *The Zen of Juggling.* Edmonds, WA: Jugglebug, 1993.
- Henton, M. *Adventure in the Classroom: Using Adventure to Strengthen Learning and Build a Community of Life-Long Learners.* Dubuque, Iowa: Kendall/Hunt Publishing Co, 1996.
- Stewart, M. & Phillips, K. *Yoga for Children.* New York, NY: Fireside Press, 1990.
- Summerford, C. *PE-4-ME: Teaching Lifelong Health and Fitness.* Champaign, IL: Human Kinetics, 2000.

Play Skills

- Bruner, J., Jolly, A., Sylva, K. (Eds.) *Play: Its Role in Development and Evolution.* New York, NY:Basic Books, Inc., Publishers, 1976.
- Jensen, E. *Learning with the Body in Mind.* San Diego, CA: The Brain Store, 2000.
- Kagan, S. *Cooperative Learning.* San Clemente, CA: Kagan Publishing, 1994.
- Kagan, S. *Silly Sports and Goofy Games.* San Clemente, CA: Kagan Publishing, 2000.
- Orlick, T. *The Cooperative Sports & Games Book.* New York, NY: Pantheon Books, 1978.
- Orlick, T. *The Second Cooperative Sports & Games Book.* New York, NY: Pantheon Books, 1982.
- Summerford, C. *PE-4-Me. Teaching Lifelong Health and Fitness.* Champaign, IL: Human Kinetics, 2000.

Teamwork Skills

- Cain, J. & Jolliff, B. *Teamwork and Teamplay.* Dubuque, Iowa: Kendall/Hunt Publishing Co, 1998.
- Kagan, S. *Cooperative Learning.* San Clemente, CA: Kagan Publishing, 1994.
- Kagan, L., Kagan, M., Kagan, S. *Cooperative Learning Structures for Teambuilding.* San Clemente, CA: Kagan Publishing, 1997.

References

[1,2] Bluestein, J. (Ed.). *Mentors, Masters, and Mrs. MacGregor: Stories of Teachers Making a Difference.* Deerfield Beach, FL: Health Communications, Inc., 1995, pp. 273, 315.

[3] National Association of School Psychologists, USA Today, April 10, 2001.

[4] Josephson Institute of Ethics. *2001 Report Card on the Ethics of American Youth.* Los Angeles, CA: Josephson Institute of Ethics, 2001. http://www.josephsoninstitute.org/

[5] American Educational Research Association Journal, 1996.

[6] Josephson Institute of Ethics. *1998 Report Card on the Ethics of American Youth.* Los Angeles, CA: Josephson Institute of Ethics, 1998. http://www.josephsoninstitute.org/

[7] Josephson Institute of Ethics. *1998 Report Card on the Ethics of American Youth.* Los Angeles, CA: Josephson Institute of Ethics, 1998. http://www.josephsoninstitute.org/

[8] U.S. Department of Education, Office of Educational Research and Improvement. *Youth Indicators 1993: Trends in Well Being of American Youth.* 1993.

[9] U.S. Department of Labor, Bureau of Labor Statistics. Various Years. http://stats.bls.gov

[10] Federal Interagency Forum on Child and Family Statistics. *America's Children: Key National Indicators of Well Being Annual Report.* 2002. Table POP6.B http://www.Childstats.gov

[11] U.S. Bureau of the Census. Table CH-1. *Living Arrangement of Children Under 18 Years Old: 1960 to Present.* 6/12/03.

[12] Hansen, K. U.S. Bureau of the Census. *Geographical Mobility.* 2001. http://www.census.gov/population/www/pop-profile/geomob.html

[13] U.S. Bureau of the Census. *America's Families and Living Arrangements: Population Characteristics.* Washington, DC: U.S. Census Bureau, 2001. www.census.gov/prod/2001pubs/p20-537.pdf

[14] A. C. Nielson and Company. *Nielson Media Research,* 2000.

[15] American Family Research Council. *Parents Fight "Time Famine" as Economic Pressures Increase.* 1990.

[16] Senate Judiciary Committee Staff Report. *Children, Violence, and the Media.* 1999.

[17] Smith, S. L., Lachlan, K. A., Tamborini, R. Popular Video Games: Quantifying the Presentation of Violence and its Context. *Journal of Broadcasting and Electronic Media,* 47 (1), 2003.

[18] Children Now. *Play Fair: Violence, Gender, and Race in Video Games.* Oakland, CA: Children Now, 2001.

[19] Smith, S. L., Lachlan, K. A., Tamborini, R. Popular Video Games: Quantifying the Presentation of Violence and its Context. *Journal of Broadcasting and Electronic Media,* 47 (1), 2003.

[20] Filipczak, B. Industry Report. *Training Magazine,* 1994, 31(10), 59–65.

References (Continued)

[21] NTO National Council, NTO National Council Skills Survey, 1999.

[22] Conference Board of Canada. Employability Skills 2000+. Ottawa, Ontario: Conference Board of Canada, 2000. http://www.conferenceboard.ca/education/learning-tools/employability-skills.htm

[23] Carnevale, A. P., Gainer, L. J., & Meltzer, A. S. *Workplace Basics: The Essential Skills Employers Want.* San Francisco: Jossey-Bass, 1990.

[24] Secretary's Commission on Achieving Necessary Skills. *What Work Requires of Schools: A SCANS Report for America 2000.* Washington, DC: U.S. Department of Labor, 1991.

[25] Secretary's Commission on Achieving Necessary Skills. *What Work Requires of Schools: A SCANS Report for America 2000.* Washington, DC: U.S. Department of Labor, 1991, p. 6.

[26] Kagan, Spencer. *Addressing the Life Skills Crisis.* **Kagan Online Magazine, Summer 2003.** San Clemente, CA: Kagan Publishing, 2003.

[27] Goleman, D. *Emotional Intelligence.* New York, NY: Bantam Books, 1995.

[28] Neuman, S. B. & Panoff, R. P. *Exploring Feelings.* Atlanta, Georgia: Humaics Limited, 1994.

Bocchino, R. *Emotional Literacy.* Thousand Oaks, CA: Corwin Press, 1999.

Waldo, P. *Scripting: Social Communication for Adolescents.* Eau Claire, WI: Thinking Publications, 1994.

[29] I am indebted to Thomas Likona for guiding me to this way of conceptualizing the relation of moral reasoning, moral principles, and virtues.

[30] Likona, T. *Educating for Character.* New York, NY: Bantam, 1992.

[31] Character Counts: www.charactercounts.org

[32] Kovalik, S. *ITI: The Model. Integrated Thematic Instruction, 3rd Ed.* Kent, WA: Books for Educators, 1994.

[33] WiseSkills Resources. *WiseWords. Wisdom for Making Good Choices. A Comprehensive Character-Building Program.* Santa Cruz, CA: WiseSkills Resources, 1998.

[34] Lickona, T. *Character Matters: How to Help our Children Develop Good Judgment, Integrity, and Other Essential Virtues.* Riverside, NJ: Simon & Schuster, 2004, In Press.

[35] Kagan, M. & Kagan, S. Character Education Smart Card. San Clemente, CA: Kagan Publishing, 1999.

[36] Borba, M. *Character Builders: Responsibility & Trustworthiness, a K–6 Character Education Program.* Torrance, CA: Jalmar Press. 2000.

Carroll, J., Gladhart, M., & Peterson, D. *Character Building: Literature-Based Theme Units.* Carthage, IL: Teaching & Learning Company, 1997.

Halter, M., Lang, B. *Making Choices: Life Skills for Adolescents Workbook.* Santa Barbara, CA: Advocacy Press, 1994.

Win-Win Discipline. Kagan Publishing • 1 (800) 933-2667 • www.KaganOnline.com

20.36

References (Continued)

Heidel, J., Lyman-Mersereau, M. *Character Education: Grades K–6, Year 2.* Nashville, TN: Incentive Publications, Inc., 1999.

Lewis, B. *What Do You Stand For? A Kids Guide to Building Character.* Minneapolis, MN: Free Spirit Publishing, Inc., 1998.

McAdam, C., McAdam, R., Bange, D. *Portraits of Character: One.* San Clemente, CA: Kagan Publishing, 2001.

McAdam, C., McAdam, R., Bange, D. *Portraits of Character: Two.* San Clemente, CA: Kagan Publishing, 2001.

Ryan, K., Bohlin, K. *Building Character in School: Practical Ways to Bring Moral Instruction to Life.* San Francisco, CA: Jossey-Bass Publishers, 1999.

Wiley, L. *Comprehensive Character-Building Classroom: Handbook for Teachers.* DeBary, FL: Longwood Communications, 1998.

[37] Kagan, S. *The Structural Approach to Character Education.* San Clemente, CA. Kagan Online Magazine. January, 2000. http://www.KaganOnline.com/Newsletter/

[38] The Kagan Model is not perfect because some virtues fit in more than one category. For example, honesty fits in two categories because a person can be honest with others and honest with him/herself. The community virtues can be displayed with others in relationships as well as in the broader community.

[39] Goleman, D. *Emotional Intelligence.* New York: Bantam Books, 1995, p. 285.

[40] Covey, S. R. *The Seven Habits of Highly Effective People. Powerful Lessons in Personal Change.* New York, NY: Fireside Division, Simon and Shuster, Inc., 1989.

[41] Covey, S. *The Seven Habits of Highly Effective Teens.* New York, NY: Fireside Division, Simon and Shuster, Inc., 1998.

[42] Gardner, H. *Frames of Mind. The Theory of Multiple Intelligences.* New York, NY: BasicBooks, 1983.

Gardner, H. *Intelligence Reframed: Multiple Intelligences for the 21st Century.* New York, NY: Basic Books. 1999.

[43] Armstrong, T. *Multiple Intelligences in the Classroom.* Alexandria, VA: Association for Supervision and Curriculum Development, 1994.

Campbell, B. *The Multiple Intelligences Handbook.* Stanwood, WA: Campbell & Assoc., Inc., 1994.

Campbell, L., Campbell, B., & Dickinson, D. *Teaching and Learning Through Multiple Intelligences.* Needham Heights, MA: Allyn & Bacon, 1996.

Huggins, P. *Multiple Intelligences: Helping Kids Discover the Many Ways to Be Smart: A Validated Washington State Improvement Program.* Logmont, CO: Sopris West Educational Services, 1997.

Kagan S. & Kagan, M. *Multiple Intelligences: The Complete MI Book.* San Clemente, CA: Kagan Publishing, 1998.

Lazear, D. *Eight Ways of Knowing: Teaching for Multiple Intelligences, Third Edition.* Arlington Heights, IL: SkyLight Training and Publishing, 1991.

Vialle, W. & Perry, J. *Nurturing Multiple Intelligences in the Australian Classroom.* Victoria, Australia: Hawker Brownlow Education, 1995.

References (Continued)

[44] Goldstein, A. P. *The Prepare Curriculum. Teaching Prosocial Competencies.* Champaign, IL: Research Press, 1988.

[45] Mcginnis, E. & Goldstein, A. P. *Skillstreaming the Elementary School Child, Revised Edition.* Champaign, Ill.: Research Press, 1997.

[46] Goleman, D. *Emotional Intelligence.* New York: Bantam Books, 1995.

[47] Kagan, S. "Kagan Structures for Thinking Skills." **Kagan Online magazine. October, 2003.** http://www.KaganOnline.com/Newsletter/

[48] Pert, C. B. *Molecules of Emotion.* New York, NY: Scribner, 1997.

[49] Kagan, S. "Teaching for Character and Community." Educational Leadership, 2001, 59(2), 50–55.

Resources

Author Index

Subject Index

Subject Index (Continued)

Win-Win Discipline. Kagan Publishing • 1 (800) 933-2667 • www.KaganOnline.com

Subject Index (Continued)

Win-Win Discipline. Kagan Publishing • 1 (800) 933-2667 • www.KaganOnline.com

B.3

Subject Index (Continued)

Win-Win Discipline. Kagan Publishing • 1 (800) 933-2667 • www.KaganOnline.com

Subject Index (Continued)

Subject Index (Continued)

Win-Win Discipline. Kagan Publishing • 1 (800) 933-2667 • www.KaganOnline.com

B.6

Index of Tables and Forms

Index of Tables and Forms (Continued)

Index of Tables and Forms (Continued)

Win-Win Discipline. Kagan Publishing • 1 (800) 933-2667 • www.KaganOnline.com

C.3

Answers to Self-Quizzes

Chapter 4

Page 4.10
Self Quiz: Identify that Disruption: ABCD

Disruption	A	B	C	D
Banging on desk	●			
Cheating		●		
Doodling				●
Eating in class		●		
Making fun of others	●			
Lying to the teacher			●	
Ignoring directions			●	
Late or missing homework		●		
Insolent facial expressions		●		
Not doing the work				●
Stealing	●			
Singing out		●		
Swearing at the teacher			●	
Skipping class				●
Sleeping				●
Displaying weapons	●			

Chapter 7

Page 7.19-20

	Position
1. Stephanie	Control-Seeking
2. Steve	Angry
3. Todd	Bored
4. Karen	Avoiding Failure
5. Alice	Attention Seeking
6. Austin	Energetic
7. Frank	Uninformed

Answers to Self-Quizzes (Continued)

Chapter 11

Page 11.26

1. Attention Seeking	E
2. Avoiding Failure	C
3. Angry	A
4. Control-Seeking	F
5. Bored	G
6. Energetic	B
7. Uninformed	D

Page 11.27

1. Energetic
2. Control-Seeking
3. Uninformed
4. Bored
5. Angry
6. Attention Seeking
7. Avoiding Failure

Page 11.28

1. Angry
2. Avoiding Failure
3. Energetic
4. Control-Seeking
5. Attention Seeking
6. Uninformed
7. Bored

Page 11.29

1. Angry
2. Uninformed
3. Energetic
4. Control-Seeking
5. Attention Seeking
6. Avoiding Failure
7. Bored

Chapter 12

Page 12.13–15

	Disruption	Position
1. Fran	Breaking Rules	Uninformed
2. Allison	Aggression	Anger
3. Anthony	Disengaged	Avoiding-Failure
4. Enrique	Aggression	Energetic
5. Charlie	Confrontation	Control-Seeking
6. Betty	Disengaged	Bored
7. Abe	Breaking Rules	Attention-Seeking

Win-Win Discipline. Kagan Publishing • 1 (800) 933-2667 • www.KaganOnline.com

D.2

Answers to Self-Quizzes (Continued)

Chapter 13

Page 13.61-65	Disruption	Position
1. Dixie	Aggression	Angry
2. Doug	Disengagement	Avoiding-Failure
3. Bob	Confrontation	Angry
4. Sue	Disengaged	Bored
5. Kathy	Breaking Rules	Energetic
6. Liz	Confrontation	Control-Seeking
7. Jody	Disengaged	Bored
8. Alice	Disengaged	Uninformed
9. Carol	Breaking Rules	Attention-Seeking

D.3

Win-Win Discipline. Kagan Publishing • 1 (800) 933-2667 • www.KaganOnline.com

Silly Sports & Goofy Games

Silly Sports & Goofy Games is referenced in various places in *Win-Win Discipline*. In this section, you will find three example games taken from the book: 1. Ten Count, 2. Everyone's It!, 3. Maze Walker.

Game 1

ten count

Can your group count to ten? It is harder than it sounds!

1 Players Form Groups
Players form groups of about a dozen.

2 The Count Begins
Any player in the group starts off the count, saying "One." Any player can say "two" at any time. The goal is for the group to count to 10.

3 Tie? Try Again
Any time two players call out a number at the same time, the group must start over. Although this game sounds easy and does not sound like much fun, players are surprised, both by how difficult it is and how much fun it is. Interesting strategies and group dynamics evolve.

crazy challenges

Source: Kagan, S. *Silly Sports & Goofy Games*. San Clemente, CA: Kagan Publishing, 2000.

Win-Win Discipline. Kagan Publishing • 1 (800) 933-2667 • www.KaganOnline.com

E.1

Game 2

everyone's it!

With a few rounds of Everyone's It all the players are energized and laughing.

1 Players Spread Out
Boundaries of the playing field are defined and players spread out within the boundaries.

2 Everyone Is It
The leader tells players everyone is It. If you are tagged by an It, you must freeze in whatever position you are in at the moment of the tag. The leader reminds the players that there is a difference between tagging someone and being tagged. If you tag someone, he/she is frozen, but you are not.

3 "Go!"
The leader shouts, "Go!"

4 Everyone Is Frozen – Save One
When everyone is frozen save the last person, that person yells, "Everyone's It!" and the players begin another round of Everyone's It.

Source: Kagan, S. *Silly Sports & Goofy Games*. San Clemente, CA: Kagan Publishing, 2000.

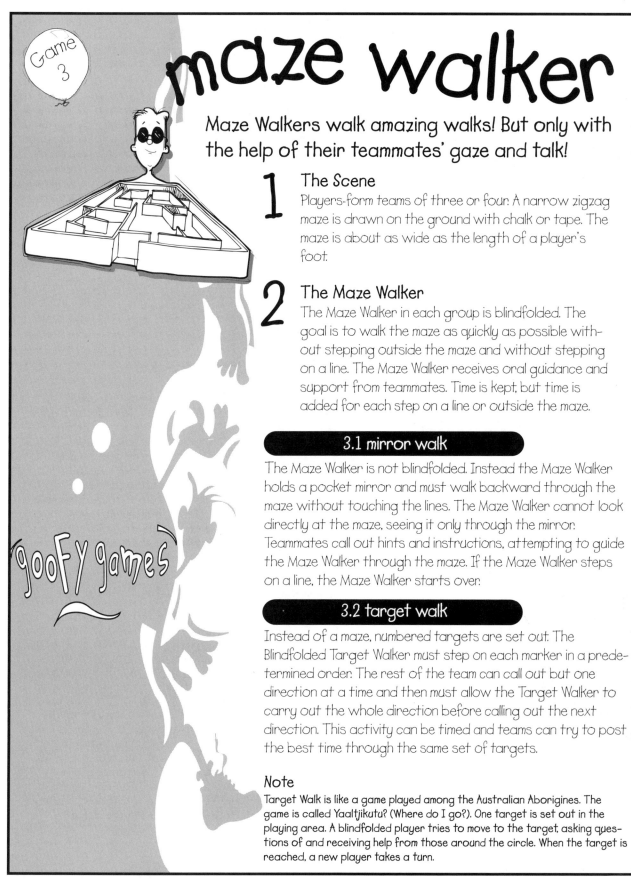

maze walker

Maze Walkers walk amazing walks! But only with the help of their teammates' gaze and talk!

Game 3

1 The Scene

Players-form teams of three or four. A narrow zigzag maze is drawn on the ground with chalk or tape. The maze is about as wide as the length of a player's foot.

2 The Maze Walker

The Maze Walker in each group is blindfolded. The goal is to walk the maze as quickly as possible without stepping outside the maze and without stepping on a line. The Maze Walker receives oral guidance and support from teammates. Time is kept, but time is added for each step on a line or outside the maze.

3.1 mirror walk

The Maze Walker is not blindfolded. Instead the Maze Walker holds a pocket mirror and must walk backward through the maze without touching the lines. The Maze Walker cannot look directly at the maze, seeing it only through the mirror. Teammates call out hints and instructions, attempting to guide the Maze Walker through the maze. If the Maze Walker steps on a line, the Maze Walker starts over.

3.2 target walk

Instead of a maze, numbered targets are set out. The Blindfolded Target Walker must step on each marker in a predetermined order. The rest of the team can call out but one direction at a time and then must allow the Target Walker to carry out the whole direction before calling out the next direction. This activity can be timed and teams can try to post the best time through the same set of targets.

Note

Target Walk is like a game played among the Australian Aborigines. The game is called Yaaltjikutu? (Where do I go?). One target is set out in the playing area. A blindfolded player tries to move to the target, asking questions of and receiving help from those around the circle. When the target is reached, a new player takes a turn.

Source: Kagan, S. *Silly Sports & Goofy Games*. San Clemente, CA: Kagan Publishing, 2000.

Win-Win Discipline. Kagan Publishing • 1 (800) 933-2667 • www.KaganOnline.com

E.3

Selected Resources

Below are illustrations and descriptions of selected resources cited in Win-Win Discipline.

Stress Apples & Squish Balls

Students release excess energy and stress as they squeeze these relaxable foam apples and balls. Give individual students one to squeeze, give one to each team, or place them in the cool down area. **See page 8.24**

Social Role Card Kit

Assigning students roles creates Win-Win solutions: The student seeking control can control in acceptable ways; the uninformed student learns appropriate gambits; the energetic student may become the Encourager or Materials Manager — learning acceptable ways to express energy. And, of course, having students fill roles is a win for the teacher: students not only learn a range of responsible behaviors, they help the class run efficiently. **See page 18.22**

Hand Candy

Hand Candy, a colorful putty, also reduces stress and releases energy as students squish and mold it. The advantage of this playful putty is that it may be used in a range of creative projects. **See page 8.24**

Yacker Tracker

Rather than the teacher being "the noise police," students are given the responsibility of monitoring their noise level. Designed like a stoplight, the Yacker Tracker offers students a visual signal of when they're being too loud. Green means OK; yellow means it is getting too loud; and red means stop, the noise is out of control. Adjustable controls allow the teacher to set the level at which students will receive a warning. **See page 18.46**

Teach Timer

Teachers report this versatile overhead projector tool transforms their classrooms. Instead of looking at their watches, teachers can focus on their students during timed tasks, confident that the timer will give an audible and visible signal when time is up. Students become more responsible as they learn to monitor their own time — a win for the teacher and students alike. Variable warning times can be set, and the timer makes an excellent clock, chronographer, and has count up and count down functions. **See page 18.20**

Student Selector Spinner

Students learn to manage themselves when each team has a Student Selector Spinner. Teams spin the spinner to decide who goes first in the team, which student will represent the team when the team is called on, and which students will perform different roles. As students let the spinner decide, arguments over role-assignments are avoided and the class runs more smoothly. The meta-communication: "Students, you can manage yourselves!" **See page 18.44**

Selected Resources (Continued)

AnswerBoards

These dry-erase boards create a win-win by allowing all students to respond at once. Rather than being called on one time out of thirty, students are called on every time, meeting students' need for attention and to be actively engaged. It is a win for the teacher too — The teacher gets authentic assessment, hearing from all students, not just the high achievers who raise their hands. AnswerBoards are double-sided — one sided is lined and the other has a grid. **See page 18.18**

Projector Pals

Without saying a word, the teacher can place these colorful transparent plastic pointers and messages on the overhead projector to congratulate the class, emphasize a point on a transparency, set up bell work, and/or call for a cooperative learning structure. Projector Pals respond to the needs of the students who are bored, and uninformed, and promote greater compliance with directions. **See page 18.20**

Gary Lamb Music

Gary Lamb is the master of music at 60 beats per minute — the perfect tempo to create relaxed alertness. Gary Lamb's music soothes the angry student but energizes the bored student. With music at a higher tempo, students become more alert — but at the expense of calmness. At a lower tempo, students become more relaxed — but at the expense of alertness. Relaxed alertness is the optimal state for learning, and Gary's music is the optimal 60 bpm music! **See page 18.32**

Music for the Mind

Use this classroom music to reduce stress and focus students on learning. Match the right music to your learning objective and watch your students turn the volume down on disruptions and tune out distractions. CDs in this series:
• Relaxed Alertness
• Producive Flow
• Problem Solving
• Reading & Writing
• In the Zone
• Projects
See page 18.32

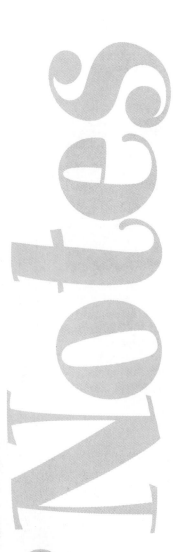

Win-Win Discipline. Kagan Publishing • 1 (800) 933-2667 • www.KaganOnline.com

Notes